ETHICS
AND SOCIAL
CONCERN

ETHICS
AND SOCIAL
CONCERN

EDITED BY
ANTHONY SERAFINI

PARAGON HOUSE

New York

First edition, 1989
Published in the United States by

Paragon House Publishers
90 Fifth Avenue
New York, NY 10011

Philosophy Editor: Don Fehr
Production Editor: Edward Paige
Copy Editor: Alex Grant

Library of Congress Cataloging-in-Publication Data

Ethics and social concern / edited by Anthony Serafini.—1st ed.
    p.   cm.
  Bibliography: p.
  ISBN 1-55778-062-5
  1. Social ethics.   I. Serafini, Anthony.
HM216.E768   1989   89-3334
303.3'72—dc20   CIP

Manufactured in the United States of America

The paper used in this publication meets the minimum requirements of American
National Standard for Information Sciences—Permanence of Paper for Printed
Library Materials, ANSI Z39.48-1984.

TABLE OF CONTENTS

PART III. BUSINESS ETHICS

PART IV. JOURNALISTIC ETHICS

ACKNOWLEDGMENTS

"Moral Judgments: Subjective Yet Universal" by Paul Allen III, Ph.D. Reprinted by permission of the author.

"The Limits of Confidentiality" by Sissela Bok. Reprinted by permission of the author and The Hastings Center.

"Euthanasia For Incompetent Patients, A Proposed Model" by Joram Graf Haber. Originally published, 3 *Pace Law Review* 351 (1983). Reprinted by permission of the Editor-in-Chief and the author.

"Sperm and Ova as Property" by Robert Jansen from *Journal of Medical Ethics*. Reprinted by permission of the *Journal of Medical Ethics*.

"Teaching Ethics on Rounds: The Ethicist as Teacher, Consultant, and Decision-Maker" by Glover, Thomasma, and Ozar. Reprinted by permission of the authors.

"Teaching Medical Ethics in Other Countries" by Gordon Wolstenholme from *Journal of Medical Ethics*. Reprinted by permission of the author and the *Journal of Medical Ethics*.

"The Unruly Rise of Medical Capitalism" by James A. Morone. Reproduced by permission of the author and The Hastings Center. © The Hastings Center.

"Kindness and Duties in the Abortion Issue" by Michael J. Matthis from *The New Scholasticism*, Autumn, 1983. Reprinted by permission of the author and *The New Scholasticism*.

"Medical Ethics in the Clinical Setting: Challenging the M.D. Monopoly" by Janet Fleetwood from *International Journal of Applied*

Philosophy Fall, 1987. Reprinted by permission of the author and Editor.

"Should AIDS Victims Be Quarantined?" by William B. Irvine. Used by permission of the author.

"Abortion Decisions: Personal Morality" by Daniel Callahan. Used by permission of the author.

"Feminist Ethics and In Vitro Fertilization" by Susan Sherwin. Used by permission of the author and CJP (Canadian Journal of Philosophy).

"Active and Passive Euthanasia" by James Rachels. *New England Journal of Medicine* Vol. 292, pp. 78–80. Copyright © 1975 Massachusetts Medical Society. Reprinted by permission of Massachusetts Medical Society and the author.

"Euthanasia and the Care of the Dying" by Sissela Bok. Reprinted by permission of *Bioscience*.

"Medicine and the Concept of a Person" by H. Tristram Engelhardt, Jr. Reprinted by permission of author.

"Ethics, Advertising and the Definition of a Profession" by Allen Dyer from *Journal of Medical Ethics* 1985, II, 72–78. Reprinted by permission of author and the *Journal of Medical Ethics*.

"Business Ethics: Ideology or Utopia?" by Jeffrey Burkhardt, originally published in *Metaphilosophy*, 16:2/3, 1985, pp. 118–129. Copyright © The Metaphilosophy Foundation and Basil Blackwell, Inc. Reprinted by permission of the author, Basil Blackwell, and *Metaphilosophy*.

"Toward an Integrated Approach to Business Ethics" by Kenneth E. Goodpaster from *Thought*, Vol. 60, 237, June, 1985. Reprinted by permission of the author.

"Publicity and the Control of Corporate Conduct: Hester Prynne's New Image," Chapter 14 of *Corporate and Collective Responsibility* by Peter A. French. Copyright © 1984 Columbia University Press. Used by permission of Columbia University Press.

"French on Corporate Punishment: Some Problems" by J. Angelo Corlett. Used by permission of the author.

"Five Moral Rules for Multinationals Operating Overseas" by Richard T. De George. Published originally in *Ethikos*, January/February 1988. Reprinted by permission of the Editor and Publisher.

"An Ethical Analysis of Deception in Advertising" by Thomas L. Carson, Richard E. Wokutch, James E. Cox, Jr. from *Journal of Business Ethics*, Vol. 4, No. 2, 1985. Reprinted by permission of D. Reidel Publishing Company and the author.

"Business Ethics, Interdisciplinarity and Higher Education" by Peter Madsen. Reprinted by permission of the author and *Listening/Journal of Religion and Culture*.

"The Profit Motive in Medicine" by Dan W. Brock and Allen E. Buchanan. Used by permission of the authors.

"The Nature of the State" by John Hospers. Originally published in THE PERSONALIST. Reprinted by permission of the author.

"Should Sponsors Screen for Moral Values?" by Kenneth E. Goodpaster. Copyright © The Hastings Center. Reprinted by permission of the author and The Hastings Center.

"The Strange Tilted World of TV Network News" by Edward Jay Epstein. Reprinted with permission from the February 1974 Reader's Digest. Copyright © 1974 by The Reader's Digest Assn., Inc.

"Contemporary Approaches to Journalistic Ethics" by John P. Ferré, *Communication Quarterly*. Reprinted by permission of Eastern Communication Association and the author.

"How to Avoid Resting Journalistic Ethics on a Mistake" by Anita Silvers, *Journal of Social Philosophy*, Fall, 1985, pp. 20–35. Reprinted by permission of the Editor and the author.

"Liberty and its Limits" by Michael Levin. Used by permission of the author.

"Speech, Expression and the Constitution" by Frank Morrow from *Ethics* 85 (1975). Copyright © 1975 University of Chicago Press.

"Whistle-blowing: The Reporter's Role" by Frederick A. Elliston. Reprinted from the "Symposium on Journalism" in THE INTERNATIONAL JOURNAL OF APPLIED PHILOSOPHY, Vol.3, No.

2, Fall 1986 by permission of the Editor. This paper was originally presented at the 16th Annual California State University Fullerton (CSUF) Philosophy Symposium entitled "Philosophical Issues in Journalism and the Media," March 12–14, 1986.

"Blackmail: A Preliminary Inquiry" by Jeffrie G. Murphy. Reprinted by permission of the author and the editor of *the monist*.

"The Press, the Government, and the Ethics Vacuum" by John C. Merrill. Reprinted by permission of the author.

"Foundations and Limits of Freedom of the Press" by Judith Lichtenberg from *Philosophy & Public Affairs* Vol. 16, no.4 (Fall, 1987). Copyright © 1987 by Princeton University Press. Reprinted with permission of Princeton University Press.

"Is Objectivity Possible" by Donald McDonald from *The Center Magazine*, Vol IV, #5, Sept/Oct 1971. Reprinted by permission of Center for the Study of Democratic Institutions.

"On Integrity in Journalism" by James A. Michener. Originally appeared as an editorial in *U.S. News and World Report* on May 4, 1981. Used by permission of *U.S. News and World Report* and the author.

"Privacy and the Right to Privacy" by H.J. McCloskey. Copyright H.J. McCloskey. Used by permission of the author and Cambridge University Press.

"Myron Farber's Confidential Sources—Christians" by Rotzoll and Fackler. Reprinted by permission of the authors and Longman, Inc.

"Reflections on the Ethics of Televangelism" by Robert C. Good. Reprinted by permission of the author.

"Media Ethic: Cases and Moral Reasoning, Second Edition, by Clifford G. Christians, Kim B. Rotzoll, and Mark Fackler. Copyright © 1987 by Longman, Inc. Reprinted by permission.

INTRODUCTION

For centuries, philosophers interested in ethics were concerned primarily in what has been called metaethics. The latter preoccupies itself with such things as the analysis of moral concepts and moral arguments as well as the construction of general theories about the meaning of basic moral ideas.

Yet in recent years, all this has changed. The public, students (with their demands for "relevance" in the 1960s and 1970s), and philosophers themselves have grown increasingly dissatisfied with a purely metaethical approach. It is true, after all, that morals touch everyone. That is why ethics courses are almost always required by colleges and universities. With such dramatic incidents as the "Baby M" case, ethical problems generated by the new reproductive technologies, controversy over abortion and corruption in the business and journalistic worlds, universities and the philosophers in them have realized that they can no longer afford to focus on metaethical issues to the exclusion of practical ethical problems of everyday life.

Students too, welcome this shift, and not because the approach is "relevant." In teaching over the past 20 years, I have found an ever-increasing interest on the part of students in the application of practical ethical analysis to professional issues.

In capitalizing on this, philosophy teachers tend to rely on a number of different approaches. One choice emphasizes metaethics. Another tends to focus on practical problems as mentioned above, and these seem to interest students the most. Still other teachers blend these approaches: In some cases they may spend a few weeks teaching the "classical" ethical theories of Mill, Kant, etc. and then begin to apply them to contemporary issues. Alternatively, they may launch right into the contemporary issues, pointing out relevant metaethical considerations as they go along.

Not surprisingly, the available texts follow these patterns. Some concentrate on the great meta-ethical readings, while more contemporary ones center only on the burning practical problems of the day, such as abortion, capital punishment, etc. There is yet another category of texts which, like the present one, combine both historical/meta-ethical and "applied" approaches. The problem with most in the latter category, however, is that they tend to include far too few articles on any given area of contemporary concern: the reader may see one or two articles on medical ethics, business ethics, or the ethics of the family and *none* on mass media ethics.

Ethics and Social Concern uses a unique approach and it differs from all current anthologies in at least *four* distinct ways. First, like others, it includes ethical theory and contemporary applications within the covers of a single text but—it is restricted to only *three* important categories of ethical problems. Thus it provides instructors and students with a wide range of articles covering the history of ethical theory and analysis of contemporary moral issues. Yet because it restricts itself to three main categories—business, medical and mass media ethics—there is ample material to offer a comprehensive, though of course not exhaustive, coverage of each of these three areas. Instead of only two or three articles on, e.g., medical ethics, there are *fourteen*. This offers tremendous flexibility for the instructor: considerable time can be spent on abortion, or AIDS or euthanasia, or several other topics. Much the same applies to business and mass media ethics. Hence this book could be used for a course in medical ethics alone, or just a business ethics or journalistic ethics course.

The second unique feature of this work is that the introductions to the various sections ferret out the affinities and connections between one article and another. So, where one philosopher touches on a theme already dealt with by another, it is pointed out. This is done even "across" fields: that is an issue dealt with in, say, medical ethics, has a counterpart in, for example, journalistic ethics which the introductions will note. Often the pieces in and of themselves incorporate this "interdisciplinary" or "holistic" dimension. (Morone's piece on medical capitalism, e.g., which obviously touches on both medical and business ethics, for instance.) This factor was considered when selecting pieces for inclusion. Students and instructors will, doubtless, find many other connections overlooked by the editor.

The third unique feature of this text is the space and attention given to mass media/journalistic ethics. Surprisingly, despite the importance and amount of contemporary controversy over mass media ethics, most such textbooks by philosophers either ignore it completely or give it only the scantiest coverage. To the extent that it *is* covered, the editors tend to cover mainly press freedom and censorship. Of course the latter are of vast importance; yet there are other problems, such as reporter-source relationships, blackmail, objectivity and special problems of *television* journalism (as opposed to print) which have been almost completely ignored by professional philosophers and ethics texts. It is hoped that this book will not only fill in that gap to some extent, but stimulate philosophers to further work on such problems.

Finally, unlike any other such text, material relevant to the *teaching* of these contemporary moral problems is included, a feature which will be invaluable, particularly to those philosophers working in hospital ethics/humanities programs, at business schools, etc.

The reader will also note the relative paucity of legal opinions and decisions by Supreme Court jurists and other such persons. Although it has become fashionable to include these in other contemporary texts (*Human Values in Health Care* being a notable exception), this has been resisted. The reason is that such decisions are always made by individual persons who, no matter how much they may have thought about the particular case at hand, are almost always unaware of the very large amount of scholarly thinking that has gone into the larger questions surrounding this or that particular case.

Also, of course, law and ethics are quite distinct fields: In using other texts which do include legal precedents and opinions it was noticed that students are often led to believe that what is legal is, *ipso facto*, ethical which, of course, is not the case.

The book is divided into four parts. Part I includes selections from the work of Plato through that of contemporary moral theorists. These selections are chronologically ordered. Part II covers a number of topics of current moral relevance in medical practice, including euthanasia, abortion, feminism, in vitro fertilization, AIDS, the business side of medicine and the teaching of medical ethics.

Part III deals with issues in business ethics such as corporate punishment, the ethics of businesses operating in foreign cultures, the ethics of advertising, profit and medical practice, corporations as moral "persons" and so forth.

Part IV deals with issues in journalistic ethics such as privacy, freedom of the press, obscenity, "televangelism," objectivity in journalism, blackmail, moral problems in using television as an educational aid and so forth.

Analysis is offered only so far as it may shed light on interpreting and understanding the readings. I have also noted interrelations between theory and social applications wherever this can be done without wandering too far afield.

The bibliographies are offered to provide some guidance for further reading and research.

Suggestions for discussion have also been added. These questions are not intended merely as study guides. Their aim is to encourage student reflection on the connections between theory and application as well and how the conclusions or issues raised in one essay may bear importantly on issues raised in another; even in an essay in another section of the book, as discussed above. It is hoped that such questions will also generate conversations among students, both formally and informally.

PART I

Some Classical/ Contemporary Ethical Theories

Thomas Jefferson once said, in defense of freedom of thought: "It does me no injury for my neighbor to say there are twenty gods or no God. It neither picks my pocket nor breaks my leg." (Jefferson: *Notes on Virginia*, quoted in *Dissent* and prepared by The Institute for Contemporary Curriculum Development, New York and Cambridge, 1972, p. 18.)

Some of the most crucial elements in contemporary moral controversy are embedded in this acute remark: The question of free speech, the morality of lying and the suggestion that one ought to evaluate actions by their effects. Still, the moral philosopher does not usually call for deliberate action to reform society (though Professor Burkhardt's piece in this volume is a notable exception). Instead he or she will explain what makes an act right or a person virtuous, or what the criteria are for determining morality. The moral philosopher also tries to solve definitional problems: what do we mean when we say an action or person is "moral?"

Yet, in recent years, moral philosophy has grown even more complex than this. To mention just one example: Since the times of ancient Greece, moral concepts and moral responsibilities were thought to apply only to persons or organized groups of persons, such as governments—the chief intention being to make it clear that they did not apply to, e.g., animals and plants. Until recently, that view has been accepted. However, this view has altered in recent years. For, as philosophers like French have pointed out,

1

other larger entities such as corporations are now necessary sub-jects of moral analysis: "If ascriptions of moral responsibility ap-peared to be about groups, organizations or corporate bodies, they were either nonsensical or they were reducible to statements about individual human beings. . . ." and further, "Corporations are far from being social fictions. A moral theory that must treat them as such is sadly impoverished."

It is true, of course, that many people—a nurse, or a well-intentioned plastics engineer—might discourse on these sorts of questions. But that kind of "philosophizing" tends to be inefficient, often wandering down well-trodden blind alleys, since such per-sons do not have the necessary philosophical background. More-over, such ad hoc philosophizing may either keep the discussion too morally neutral, or degenerate into cracker-barrell hystrionics.

The philosopher, by contrast, will attempt guarded, careful steps into new moral territory while retaining a firm foothold in the history of her discipline.

In this part of the work, some selections from the great classical philosophers are offered. While the reasons for this may be ob-vious to many, perhaps a word or two is in order for the student who may find this work to be his or her first introduction to the great problems of philosophical ethics.

To most, ethics will be a familiar enough term: one hears it everyday in the news media, offhand conversation, from parents, counselors, evangelists, etc. The odds are, however, that the sense in which one hears this term in daily life is not the sense in which philosophers have traditionally used it. Where, in everyday life, ethics usually denotes the rights and wrongs of this or that par-ticular action, in philosophy it means something different, albeit related to the everyday sense of the term.

Historically, the meaning of "ethics" has paralleled the meaning of the term "philosophy" itself; both refer to a study of founda-tional queries. "Philosophy of religion," for instance, refers to a study of the most fundamental and basic questions underlying religious faith—the existence of God, the difficulty of reconciling evil with a benevolent, all-powerful God and so forth, queries that are very real and of daily concern to many. And in ethics histor-ically, philosophers have devoted considerable time to queries about the nature of goodness, the definition of justice and so forth. It is true, of course, that in recent years, philosophers have given more and more time to study of daily, practical questions about abortion, capital punishment and so forth.

Nevertheless, just as metaethical considerations are vacuous without regard to normative issues, we also do not believe that discussions of real-life queries of ethics can ever be entirely divorced from a study of the classical, metaethical issues. Hence this historical section. In it, an attempt has been made to select classic discussions of the great foundational questions. Additionally, in other sections, there are selections which, to the extent possible, deal with the pressing practical questions in business ethics, medical ethics and journalistic ethics—the three major areas covered in this volume. Although some of the classical sections themselves touch on more "modern" issues.

In the selection from Plato's *Apology* for instance, Socrates discusses the issue of life and death—clearly a critical question for medical ethics.

While many today would object to Socrates' suggestion that death may be viewed as a long sleep, or a voyage of the soul from one place to another, certainly the issues raised are critical, especially the question of whether a life should ever be sacrificed for any reason, or whether death is an absolute evil that cannot be overriden by any other consideration.

Aristotle's piece, taken from his *Nichomachaen Ethics* also tries to analyze the nature of a fundamental metaethical question. In this case, it is the nature of *virtue*. This essay is particularly important inasmuch as several of the authors make specific reference to Aristotle's views in developing their own position. Professor Haldane is a case in point. There are, of course, traditional and well-known objections to Aristotle's view. Certainly one can quarrel with Aristotle's idea that virtue is a matter of *habit*, or with the utility of his famous notion of the "golden mean." Many would suggest also that the problem with the latter is that so many of the great ethical problems of the day are not a matter of finding such a mean. The controversy over the ethical "rights" of embryos or the right to a free press and free expression do not, on the face of it, seem to be helped by this idea, since in both cases the rights and wrongs may be an "either-or" situation, where the idea of a mean is simply inapplicable.

On the other hand, some may find value in Aristotle's suggestions when it comes to such questions as the obligations of big business to the environment, where the idea of finding some happy medium or "mean" between economic growth and a healthy environment may be workable.

Thus Aristotle's work represents, at least from a modern point of view, something of an advance over the Socratic/Platonic conception of virtue presented in the first selection, in that Aristotle's approach to ethics is *empirical*, an approach to philosophy taken much later on by the utilitarians, Mill and Bentham, and later by T.H. Huxley as well. Adaptions and modifications of Mill's views have received much attention in recent years by numerous contemporary philosophers, including J.O. Urmson, Robert Nozick and many others. As the reader will see, a number of the authors included rest their claims on utilitarian principles.

Kant, also is one of the great philosophers of history, whose main ideas are stated in three major critiques—the *Critique of Pure Reason*, the *Critique of Practical Reason* and the *Critique of Judgment*. He lived in Konigsberg in East Prussia and taught at the university there.

His *Critique of Pure Reason* deals with epistemology and metaphysics, the *Critique of Practical Reason* with ethics, and the *Critique of Judgment* with aesthetics. He further developed his ethical theory in the foundations of the *Metaphysics of Morals*, from which this selection is taken.

Specifically Kant holds that ethical principles are universal— they hold for all persons in all situations. In his view, also, ethics is a matter of *categorical imperatives*. An imperative is simply a command, and a categorical imperative is a command to act out of consideration for duty that allows no possible exceptions. Kant further distinguishes these from "hypothetical" imperatives, or what might be called imperatives of skill. These merely urge one to act in a certain way if one wishes to accomplish some goal. (If you wish to stabilize the table, put a book under one leg.) In his view, these types of imperatives are unrelated to morality.

In Kant's ethics, motives and intentions also have a place. To act morally, is to do something solely because it is right and not, for instance, because it may bring wealth, fame, etc.

As with Mill, a number of the authors represented in this volume also adopt Kantian positions in handling contemporary problems. Paul Allen analyzes the idea of moral judgments in a manner reminiscent of Kant. And to be sure, Kant's idea has some intuitive plausibility: it is difficult to regard an action as moral if we cannot at the same time imagine everybody doing it also. Still, that kind of approach to ethics has fallen on hard times in recent years, in that theoreticians are conspicuously suspicious of any "absolutist" moral judgments, as these seem too dogmatic and inflexible to many.

On the other hand, I have tried to include authors with Kantian perspectives for this reason: It is tediously common for authors without background in formal ethics and philosophy to drone on about the ethical issues in their field from a simplistic kind of ethical relativism (pompously called, in some quarters, "situation ethics"). Journalists, for instance, have produced reams of such worthless "theorizing" over the years, precisely in the manner and for the reasons just given. (With many notable exceptions of course, including Professor John Merrill.)

The reader should be aware that there are numerous problems with Kant, my comments above notwithstanding. While Kant's ethics purports to be à priori, he tacitly smuggles in appeals to the consequences of a person's actions, as a measure of their moral worth. He does this when he suggests, e.g., that the making of lying promises is wrong because on his criterion it would be disruptive to society.

The selection from Mill is taken from his classic work. *On Liberty*. Born in 1806, John Stuart Mill was one of England's most important philosophers and social reformers. Very early in life, he learned mathematics, logic, science and Greek. Later on, he contributed important work to mathematics, philosophy of science, political philosophy and ethics. He is also known to have composed one of the most important early defenses of the rights of women, in his essay "The Subjection of Women." Other important works include his *System of Logic, Principles of Political Economy, Utilitarianism* and *On Liberty*.

In the latter work, Mill tries to map out those areas of human action which, he believes, should be totally free from governmental interference. Mill's utilitarian sympathies also emerge in this essay, believing as he does that individual conduct and governmental actions should be praised or blamed according to whether or not they produce the greatest happiness for the greatest number of people. The great vitality of the principle is shown in that several of the authors here make reference to it.

Conversely, Mill himself refers to some of the great normative issues raised by many contemporary ethicists. His discussion of liberty and freedom of expression is taken up again in the section on press ethics by several authors.

Yet, despite the great attention given to utilitarianism these days, great problems remain. Certainly one fundamental defect in the principle as a criterion of morality is the fact that it seems to be vulnerable to certain kinds of counterexamples—counterexamples that reflect the fact that the principle does not sufficiently consider the question of what Ross and others have called *prima facie* rights. No one would suggest, for example, that it is moral for a certain society to persecute a small minority within that society even if doing so increased the total amount of happiness within that society. To do so would ignore the legitimate rights of that minority.

In Professor Paul Allen's piece, "Moral Judgments: Subjective Yet Universal." Professor Allen puts forth a striking and highly original metaethical position; he argues that no one is ever willing to give up the freedom to act in the way he is now choosing to act. Because this unwillingness to give up one's "immediate freedom" is inevitable, all agents, including the dramatic example of Hare's fanatics, are required *not* to decide to undercut the freedom of others. Thus, according to Professor Allen, all persons have to arrive at moral judgments to the effect that they ought to respect the freedom of others.

Building on some ideas from Professor R.M. Hare, Allen goes on to argue that such judgments depend on each person's willingness to give up his own immediate freedom. In this sense, such judgments are "subjective." Yet, according to Allen, because *all* persons are bound by logic to arrive at such judgments, we should consider them to be universal as well.

Allen's thesis is ingenious, and the influence of Kant and Hare will not escape students of philosophy. Interesting issues arise at the point where Allen suggests that decisions are "logically required." Perhaps a question here is whether the concept of logical necessity is really applicable to mental actions. (Though it may be that all Allen means is that anyone who does not arrive, or refuses to arrive at such judgments, is simply being inconsistent or irrational.)

Nevertheless, Allen offers a provocative and challenging view.

From the point of view of both student and professional philosopher, this essay should be kept in mind in reading the other works in this volume. The reason is that many of the other readings take the more usual view, treating moral judgments as subjective and nonuniversal. The Serafini piece is a case in point and the essay by Thomasma *et al*. Also, Allen's purely theoretical discussion of the nature of freedom provides a helpful metaethical backdrop for the various discussions of free speech and expression, such as those of Professor Judith Lichtenberg and Professor Good, both of whom are well-known for their incisive analyses of freedom of thought and expression.

On Being Sentenced to Death

Socrates

For the sake of no long space of time, O Athenians! you will incure the character and reproach at the hands of those who wish to defame the city, of having put that wise man, Socrates, to death. For those who wish to defame you will assert that I am wise, though I am not. If, then, you had waited for a short time, this would have happened of its own accord; for observe my age, that it is far advanced in life, and near death.

But I say this not to you all, but to those only who have condemned me to die. And I say this, too, to the same persons. Perhaps you think, O Athenians! that I have been convicted through the want of arguments, by which I might have persuaded you, had I thought it right to do and say anything, so that I might escape punishment. Far otherwise: I have been convicted through want indeed, yet not of arguments, but of audacity and impudence, and of the inclination to say such things to you as would have been most agreeable for you to hear, had I lamented and bewailed and done and said many other things unworthy of me, as I affirm, but such as you are accustomed to hear from others. But neither did I then think that I ought, for the sake of avoiding danger, to do anything unworthy of a freeman, nor do I now repent of having so defended myself; but I should much rather choose to die, having so defended myself, than to live in that way.

For neither in a trial nor in battle is it right that I or anyone else should employ every possible means whereby he may avoid death; for in battle it is frequently evident that a man might escape death by laying down his arms, and throwing himself on the mercy of his pursuers. And there are many other devices in every danger, by which to avoid death, if a man dares to do and say everything. But this is not difficult, O Athenians! to escape death; but it is much more difficult to avoid depravity, for it runs swifter than death.

And now I, being slow and aged, am overtaken by the slower of the two, but my accusers, being strong and active, have been overtaken by the swifter, wickedness. And now I depart, condemned by you to death; but they condemned by truth, as guilty of iniquity and injustice: and I abide my sentence, and so do they. These things, perhaps, ought so to be, and I think that they are for the best.

In the next place, I desire to predict to you who have condemned me what will be your fate; for I am now in that condition in which men most frequently prophesy—namely, when they are about to die. I say, then, to you, O Athenians! who have condemned me to death, that immediately after my death a punishment will overtake you, far more severe, by Zeus! than that which you have inflicted on me. For you have done this, thinking you would be freed from the necessity of giving an account of your lives. The very contrary, however, as I affirm, will happen to you. Your accusers will be more numerous, whom I have now restrained, though you did not perceive it; and they will be more severe, inasmuch as they are younger, and you will be more indignant. For, if you think that by putting men to death you will restrain anyone from upbraiding you because you do not live well, you are much mistaken; for this method of escape is neither possible nor honorable; but that other is most honorable and most easy, not to put a check upon others, but for a man to take heed to himself how he may be most perfect. Having predicted thus much to those of you who have condemned me, I take my leave of you.

But with you who have voted for my acquittal, I would gladly hold converse on what has now taken place, while the magistrates are busy, and I am not yet carried to the place where I must die. Stay with me, then, so long, O Athenians! for nothing hinders our conversing with each other while we are permitted to do so, for I wish to make known to you, as being my friends, the meaning of that which has just now befallen me.

To me, then, O my judges!—and in calling you judges I call you rightly—a strange thing has happened. For the wonted prophetic voice of my guardian deity on every former occasion, even in the most trifling affairs, opposed me if I was about to do anything wrong; but now that has befallen me which ye yourselves behold, and which anyone would think, and which is supposed to be the extremity of evil; yet neither when I departed from home in the morning did the warning of the god oppose me, not when I came up here to the place of trial, nor in my address when I was about to say anything; yet on other occasions it has frequently restrained me in the midst of speaking. But now it has never, throughout this proceeding, opposed me, either in what I did or said. What, then, do I suppose to be the cause of this? I will tell you: what has befallen me appears to be a blessing; and it is impossible that we think rightly who suppose that death is an evil. A great proof of this to me is the fact that it is impossible but that the accustomed signal should have opposed me, unless I had been about to meet with some good.

Moreover, we may hence conclude that there is great hope that death is a blessing. For to die is one of two things: for either the dead may be annihilated, and have no sensation of anything whatever; or, as it is said, there are a certain change and passage of the soul from one place to another. And if it is a privation of all sensation, as it were a sleep in which the sleeper has no dream, death would be a wonderful gain. For I think that if anyone, having selected a night in which he slept so soundly as not to have had a dream, and having compared this night with all the other nights and days of his life, should be required, on consideration, to say how many days and nights he had passed better and more pleasantly than this night throughout his life, I think that, not only a private person, but even the great king himself, would find them easy to number, in comparison with other days and nights.

If, therefore, death is a thing of this kind, I say it is a gain; for thus all futurity appears to be nothing more than one night. But if, on the other hand, death is a removal from hence to another place, and what is said be true, that all the dead are there, what greater blessing can there be than this, my judges? For if, on arriving at Hades, released from these who pretend to be judges, one shall find those who are true judges, and who are said to judge there, Minos and Rhadamanthus, Æacus and Triptolemus, and such others of the demigods as were just during their own lives, would this be a sad removal? At what price would you not estimate a conference with Orpheus and Musæus, Hesiod and Homer?

I, indeed, should be willing to die often, if this be true. For to me the sojourn there would be admirable, when I should meet with Palamedes, and Ajax, son of Telamon, and any other of the ancients who have died by an unjust sentence. The comparing my sufferings with theirs would, I think, be no unpleasing occupation. But the greatest pleasure would be to spend my time in questioning and examining the people there as I have done those here, and discovering who among them is wise, and who fancies himself to be so but is not. At what price, my judges, would not anyone estimate the opportunity of questioning him who led that mighty army against Troy, or Ulysses, or Sisyphus, or ten thousand others whom one might mention, both men and women—with whom to converse and associate, and to question them, would be an inconceivable happiness? Surely for that the judges there do not condemn to death; for in other respects those who live there are more happy than those who are here, and are henceforth immortal, if, at least, what is said be true.

You, therefore, O my judges! ought to entertain good hopes with respect to death, and to meditate on this one truth, that to a good man nothing is evil, neither while living nor when dead, nor are his concerns neglected by the gods. And what has befallen me is not the effect of chance; but this is clear to me, that now to die and be freed from my cares is better for me. On this account the warning in no way turned me aside; and I bear no resentment toward those who condemned me, or against my accusers, although they did not condemn and accuse me with this intention, but thinking to injure me: in this they deserve to be blamed.

Thus much, however, I beg of them. Punish my sons when they grow up, O judges! paining them, as I have pained you, if they appear to you to care for riches or anything else before virtue; and if they think themselves to be something when they are nothing, reproach them as I have done you, for not attending to what they ought, and for conceiving themselves to be something when they are worth nothing. If ye do this, both I and my sons shall have met with just treatment at your hands.

But it is now time to depart—for me to die, for you to live. But which of us is going to a better state is unknown to everyone but God.

Study Questions

1. Do you agree with Socrates' view that death is really like a pleasant sleep? If not, what *do* you believe death is and how does it affect your moral decisions.
2. What do you think of Socrates' view that death really should not be of concern to those who have acted morally in life? Need such a view depend on belief in an afterlife?

Virtue

Aristotle

Virtue, . . . being of two kinds, intellectual and moral, intellectual virtue in the main owes both its birth and its growth to teaching (for which reason it requires experience and time), while moral virtue comes about as a result of habit, whence also its name *ethike* is one that is formed by a slight variation from the word *ethos* (habit). From this it is also plain that none of the moral virtues arises in us by nature; for nothing that exists by nature can form a habit contrary to its nature. For instance the stone which by nature moves downwards cannot be habituated to move upwards, not even if one tries to train it by throwing it up ten thousand times; nor can fire be habituated to move downwards, nor can anything else that by nature behaves in one way be trained to behave in another. Neither by nature, then, nor contrary to nature do the virtues arise in us; rather we are adapted by nature to receive them, and are made perfect by habit.

Again, of all the things that come to us by nature we first acquire the potentiality and later exhibit the activity (this is plain in the case of the senses; for it was not by often seeing or often hearing that we got these senses, but on the contrary we had them before we used them, and did not come to have them by using them); but the virtues we get by first exercising them, as also happens in the case of the arts as well. For the things we have to learn

From *Nicomachean Ethics*.

before we can do them, we learn by doing them, e.g., men become builders by building and lyre-players by playing the lyre; so too we become just by doing just acts, temperate by doing temperate acts, brave by doing brave acts.

This is confirmed by what happens in states; for legislators make the citizens good by forming habits in them, and this is the wish of every legislator, and those who do not effect it miss their mark, and it is this that a good constitution differs from a bad one.

Again, it is from the same causes and by the same means that every virtue is both produced and destroyed, and similarly every art; for it is from playing the lyre that both good and bad lyre-players are produced. And the corresponding statement is true of builders and of all the rest; men will be good or bad builders as a result of building well or badly. For if this were not so, there would have been no need of a teacher, but all men would have been born good or bad at their craft. This, then, is the case with the virtues also; by doing the acts that we do in our transactions with other men we become just or unjust, and by doing the acts that we do in the presence of danger, and being habituated to feel fear or confidence, we become brave or cowardly. The same is true of appetites and feelings of anger; some men become temperate and good-tempered, others self-indulgent and irascible, by behaving in one way or the other in the appropriate circumstances. Thus, in one word, states of character arise out of like activities. This is why the activities we exhibit must be of a certain kind; it is because the states of character correspond to the differences between these. It makes no small difference, then, whether we form habits of one kind or of another from our very youth; it makes a very great difference, or rather *all* the difference.

Since, then, the present inquiry does not aim at theoretical knowledge like the others (for we are inquiring not in order to know what virtue is, but in order to become good, since otherwise our inquiry would have been of no use), we must examine the nature of actions, namely how we ought to do them; for these determine also the nature of the states of character that are produced, . . . Now, that we must act according to the right rule is a common principle and must be assumed . . . i.e., both what the right rule is, and how it is related to the other virtues. But this must be agreed upon beforehand, that the whole account of matters of conduct must be given in outline and not precisely; . . . matters concerned with conduct and questions of what is good for us to have no fixity, any more than matters of health. The general account being of this nature, the account of particular cases is yet more lacking in exactness; for they do not fall under any art or precept but the agents themselves must in each case consider what is appropriate to the occasion, as happens also in the art of medicine or of navigation.

But though our present account is of this nature we must give what help we can. First, then, let us consider this, that it is the nature of such things to be destroyed by defect and excess, as we see in the case of strength and of health (for to gain light on things imperceptible we must use the evidence of sensible things); both excessive and defective exercise destroys the strength, and similarly drink or food which is above or below a certain amount destroys the health, while that which is proportionate both produces and increases and preserves it. So too is it, then, in the case of temperance and courage and the other virtues. For the man who flies from and fears everything and does not stand his ground against anything becomes a coward, and the man who fears nothing at all but goes to meet every danger becomes rash; and similarly the man who indulges in every pleasure and abstains from none becomes self-indulgent, while the man who shuns every pleasure, as boors do, becomes in a way insensible; temperance and courage, then, are destroyed by excess and defect, and preserved by the mean.

But not only are the sources and causes of their origination and growth the same as those of their destruction, but also the sphere of their actualization will be the same; for this is also true of the things which are more evident to sense, e.g., of strength; it is produced by taking much food and undergoing much exertion, and it is the strong man that will be most able to do these things. So too is it with the virtues; by abstaining from pleasures we become temperate, and it is when we have become so that we are most able to abstain from them; and similarly too in the case of courage; for by being habituated to despise things that are terrible and to stand our ground against them we become brave, and it is when we have become so that we shall be most able to stand our ground against them.

We must take as a sign of states of character the pleasure or pain that ensues on acts; for the man who abstains from bodily pleasures and delights in this very fact is temperate, while the man who is annoyed at it is self-indulgent, and he who stands his ground against things that are terrible and delights in this or at least is not pained is brave, while the man who is pained is a coward. For moral excellence is concerned with pleasures and pains; it is on account of the pleasure that we do bad things, and on account of the pain that we abstain from noble ones. Hence we ought to have been brought up in a particular way from our very youth, as Plato says, so as both to delight in and to be pained by the things that we ought; for this is the right education.

Again, if the virtues are concerned with actions and passions, and every passion and every action is accompanied by pleasure and pain, for this reason also virtue will be concerned with pleasures and pains. This is indicated also by the fact that punishment is inflicted by these means; for it is a kind of cure, and it is the nature of cures to be effected by contraries.

Again, . . . every state of soul has a nature relative to and concerned with the kind of things by which it tends to be made worse or better; but it is by reason of pleasures and pains that men become bad, by pursuing and avoiding these—either the pleasures and pains they ought not or when they ought not or as they ought not, or by going wrong in one of the other similar ways that may be distinguished. Hence men even define the virtues as certain states of impassivity and rest; not well, however, because they speak absolutely, and do not say 'as one ought' and 'as one ought not' and 'when one ought or ought not', and the other things may be added. We assume, then, that this kind of excellence tends to do what is best with regard to pleasures and pains, and vice does the contrary.

The following facts also may show us that virtue and vice are concerned with these same things. There being three objects of choice and three of avoidance, the noble, the advantageous, the pleasant, and their contraries, the base, the injurious, the painful, about all of these the good man tends to go right and the bad man to go wrong, and especially about pleasure; for this is common to the animals, and also it accompanies all objects of choice; for even the noble and the advantageous appear pleasant.

Again, it has grown up with us all from our infancy; this is why it is difficult to rub off this passion, engrained as it is in our life. And we measure even our actions, some of us more and others less, by the rule of pleasure and pain. For this reason, then, our whole inquiry must be about these; for to feel delight and pain rightly or wrongly has no small effect on our actions.

Again, it is harder to fight with pleasure than with anger, to use Heraclitus' phrase, but both art and virtue are always concerned with what is harder; for even the good is better when it is harder. Therefore for this reason also the whole concern both of virtue and of political science is with pleasures and pains; for the man who uses these well will be good, he who uses them badly bad.

That virtue, then, is concerned with pleasures and pains, and that by the acts from which it arises it is both increased and, if they are done differently, destroyed, and that the acts from which it arose are those in which it actualizes itself—let this be taken as said.

The question might be asked, what we mean by saying that we must become just by doing just acts, and temperate by doing temperate acts; for if men do just and temperate acts, they are already just and temperate, exactly as, if they do what is in accordance with the laws of grammar and of music, they are grammarians and musicians.

Or is this not true even of the arts? It is possible to do something that is in accordance with the laws of grammar, either by chance or at the suggestion of another. A man will be a grammarian, then, only when he has both done something grammatical and done it grammatically; and this means doing it in accordance with the grammatical knowledge in himself.

Again, the case of the arts and that of the virtues are not similar; for the products of the arts have their goodness in themselves, so that it is enough that they should have a certain character, but if the acts that are in accordance with the virtues have themselves a certain character it does not follow that they are done justly or temperately. The agent also must be in a certain condition when he does them; in the first place he must have knowledge, secondly he must choose the acts, and choose them for their own sakes, and thirdly his action must proceed from a firm and unchangeable character. These are not reckoned in as conditions of the possession of the arts, except the bare knowledge; but as a condition of the possession of the virtues knowledge has little or no weight, while the other conditions count not for a little but for everything, i.e., the very conditions which result from often doing just and temperate acts.

Actions, then, are called just and temperate when they are such as the just or the temperate man would do; but it is not the man who does these that is just and temperate, but the man who does them *as* just and temperate men do them. It is well said, then, that it is by doing just acts that the just man is produced, and by doing temperate acts the temperate man; without doing these no one would have even a prospect of becoming good.

But most people do not do these, but take refuge in theory and think they are being philosophers and will become good in this way, behaving somewhat like patients who listen attentively to their doctors, but do none of the things they are ordered to do. As the latter will not be made well in body by such a course of treatment, the former will not be made well in soul by such a course of philosophy.

Next we must consider what virtue is. Since things that are found in the soul are of three kinds—passions, faculties, states of character, virtue must be one of these. By passions I mean appetite, anger, fear, confidence, envy, joy, friendly feeling, hatred, longing, emulation, pity, and in general the feelings that are accompanied by pleasure or pain; by faculties the things in virtue of which we are said to be capable of feeling these, e.g., of becoming angry or being pained or feeling pity; by states of character the things in virtue of which we stand well or badly with reference to the passions, e.g., with reference to anger we stand badly if we feel it violently or too weakly, and well if we feel it moderately; and similarly with reference to the other passions.

Now neither the virtues nor the vices are *passions*, because we are not called good or bad on the ground of our passions, but are so called on the ground of our virtues and our vices, and because we are neither praised nor blamed for our passions (for the man who feels fear or anger is not praised, nor is the man who simply feels anger blamed, but the man who feels it in a certain way), but for our virtues and our vices we *are* praised or blamed.

Again, we feel anger and fear without choice, but the virtues are modes of choice or involve choice. Further, in respect of the passions we are said to be moved, but in respect of the virtues and the vices we are said not to be moved but to be disposed in a particular way.

For these reasons also they are not *faculties*; for we are neither called good nor bad, nor praised nor blamed, for the simple capacity of feeling the passions; again, we have the faculties by nature, but we are not made good or bad by nature . . . .

If, then, the virtues are neither passions nor faculties, all that remains is that they should be *states of character*.

Thus we have stated what virtue is in respect of its genus.

We must, however, not only describe virtue as a state of character, but also say what sort of state it is. We may remark, then, that every virtue or excellence both brings into good condition the thing of which it is the excellence and makes the work of that thing be done well; e.g., the excellence of the eye makes both the eye and its work good; for it is by the excellence of the eye that we see well. Similarly the excellence of the horse makes a horse both good in itself and good at running and at carrying its rider and at awaiting the attack of the enemy. Therefore, if this is true in every case, the virtue of man also will be the state of character which makes a man good and which makes him do his own work well.

. . . In everything that is continuous and divisible it is possible to take more, less, or an equal amount, and that either in terms of the thing itself or relatively to us; and the equal is an intermediate between excess and defect. By the intermediate in the object I mean that which is equidistant from each of the extremes, which is one and the same for all men; by the intermediate relatively to us that which is neither too much nor too little—and this is not one, nor the same for all. For instance, if ten is many and two is few, six is the intermediate, taken in terms of the object; for it exceeds and is exceeded by an equal amount; this is intermediate according to arithmetical proportion. But the intermediate relatively to us is not to be taken so; if ten pounds are too much for a particular person to eat and two too little, it does not follow that the trainer will order six pounds; for this also is perhaps too much for the person who is to take it, or too little— too little for Milo, too much for the beginner in athletic exercises. The same is true of running and wrestling. Thus a master of any art avoids excess and defect, but seeks the intermediate and chooses this—the intermediate not in the object but relatively to us.

If it is thus, then, that every art does its work well—by looking to the intermediate and judging its works by this standard (so that we often say of good works of art that it is not possible either to take away or to add anything, implying that excess and defect destroy the goodness of works of art, while the mean preserves it; and good artists, as we say, look to this in their work), and if, further, virtue is more exact and better than any art, as nature also is, then virtue must have the quality of aiming at the intermediate. I mean moral virtue; for it is this that is concerned with passions and actions, and in these there is excess, defect, and the intermediate. For instance, both fear and confidence and appetite and anger and pity and in general pleasure and pain may be felt both too much and too little, and in both cases not well; but to feel them at the right times, with reference to the right objects, towards the right people, with the right motive, and in the right way, is what is both intermediate and best, and this is characteristic of virtue. Similarly with regard to actions also there is excess, defect, and the intermediate. Now virtue is concerned with passions and actions, in which excess is a form of failure, and so is defect, while the intermediate is praised and is a form of success; and being praised and being successful are both characteristics of virtue. Therefore virtue is a kind of mean, since, as we have seen, it aims at what is intermediate.

Again, it is possible to fail in many ways (for evil belongs to the class of the unlimited, as the Pythagoreans conjectured, and good to that of the limited), while to succeed is possible only in one way (for which reason also one is easy and the other difficult—to miss the mark easy, to hit it difficult); for these reasons also, then, excess and defect are characteristic of vice, and the mean of virtue;

For men are good in but one way, but bad in many.

Virtue, then, is a state of character concerned with choice, lying in a mean, i.e., the mean relative to us, this being determined by a rational principle, and by that principle by which the man of practical wisdom would determine it. Now it is a mean between two vices, that which depends on excess and that which depends on defect; and again it is a mean because the vices respectively fall short of or exceed what is right in both passions and actions, while virtue both finds and chooses that which is intermediate. Hence in respect of its substance and the definition which states its essence virtue is a mean, with regard to what is best and right an extreme.

But not every action nor every passion admits of a mean; for some have names that already imply badness, e.g., spite, shamelessness, envy, and in the case of actions adultery, theft, murder; for all of these and suchlike things imply by their names that they are themselves bad, and not the excesses or deficiencies of them. It is not possible, then, ever to be right with regard to them; one must always be wrong. Nor does goodness or badness with regard to such things depend on committing adultery with the right woman, at the right time, and in the right way, but simply to do any of them is to go wrong. It would be equally absurd, then, to expect that in unjust, cowardly, and voluptuous action there should be a mean, an excess, and a deficiency; for at that rate there would be a mean of excess and of deficiency, an excess of excess, and a deficiency of deficiency. But as there is no excess and deficiency of temperance and courage because what is intermediate is in a sense an extreme, so too of the actions we have mentioned there is no mean nor any excess and deficiency, but however they are done they are wrong; for in general there is neither a mean of excess and deficiency, nor excess and deficiency of a mean.

We must, however, not only make this general statement, but also apply it to the individual facts. For among statements about conduct those which are general apply more widely, but those which are particular are more genuine, since conduct has to do with individual cases, and our statements must harmonize with the facts in these cases. We may take these cases from our table. With regard to feelings of fear and confidence courage is the mean; of the people who exceed, he who exceeds in fearlessness has no name (many of the states have no name), while the man who exceeds in confidence is rash, and he who exceeds in fear and falls short in confidence is a coward. With regard to pleasures and pains—not all of them, and not so much with regard to the pains— the mean is temperance, the excess self-indulgence. Persons deficient with regard to the pleasures are not often found; hence such persons also have received no name. But let us call them "insensible."

With regard to giving and taking of money the mean is liberality, the excess and the defect prodigality and meanness. In these actions people exceed and fall short in contrary ways; the prodigal exceeds in spending and falls short in taking, while the mean man exceeds in taking and falls short in spending. . . . With regard to money there are also other dispositions—a mean, magnificence (for the magnificent man differs from the liberal man; the former deals with large sums, the latter with small ones), and excess, tastelessness and vulgarity, and a deficiency, niggardliness; these differ from the states opposed to liberality. . . .

With regard to honor and dishonor the mean is proper pride, the excess is known as a sort of "empty vanity," and the deficiency is undue humility; . . . liberality [is] related to magnificence, differing from it by dealing with small sums, so there is a state similarly related to proper pride, being concerned with small honors while that is concerned with great. For it is possible to desire honor as one ought, and more than one ought, and less, and the man who exceeds in his desires is called ambitious, the man who falls short unambitious, while the intermediate person has no name. The dispositions also are nameless, except that that of the ambitious man is called ambition. Hence the people who are at the extremes lay claim to the middle place; and we ourselves sometimes call the intermediate person ambitious and sometimes unambitious, and sometimes praise the ambitious man and sometimes the unambitious. . . . now let us speak of the remaining states according to the method which has been indicated.

With regard to anger also there is an excess, a deficiency, and a mean. Although they can scarcely be said to have names, yet since we call the intermediate person good-tempered let us call the mean good temper; of the persons at the extremes let the one who exceeds be called irascible, and his vice irascibility, and the man who falls short an inirascible sort of person, and the deficiency inirascibility.

There are also three other means, which have a certain likeness to one another, but differ from one another: for they are all concerned with intercourse in words and actions, but differ in that one is concerned with truth in this sphere, the other two with

pleasantness; and of this one kind is exhibited in giving amusement, the other in all the circumstances of life. We must therefore
speak of these too, that we may the better see that in all things
the mean is praiseworthy, and the extremes neither praiseworthy
nor right, but worthy of blame. Now most of these states also
have no names, but we must try, as in the other cases, to invent
names ourselves so that we may be clear and easy to follow. With
regard to truth, then, the intermediate is a truthful sort of person
and the mean may be called truthfulness, while the pretence which
exaggerates is boastfulness and the person characterized by it a
boaster, and that which understates is mock modesty and the
person characterized by it mock-modest. With regard to pleasantness in the giving of amusement the intermediate person is
ready-witted and the disposition ready wit, the excess is buffoon-
ery and the person characterized by it a buffoon, while the man
who falls short is a sort of boor and his state is boorishness. With
regard to the remaining kind of pleasantness, that which is exhibited in life in general, the man who is pleasant in the right
way is friendly and the mean is friendliness, while the man who
exceeds is an obsequious person if he has no end in view, a
flatterer if he is aiming at his own advantage, and the man who
falls short and is unpleasant in all circumstances is a quarrelsome
and surly sort of person.

There are also means in the passions and concerned with the
passions; since shame is not a virtue, and yet praise is extended
to the modest man. For even in these matters one man is said to
be intermediate, and another to exceed, as for instance the bashful
man who is ashamed of everything; while he who falls short or
is not ashamed of anything at all is shameless, and the intermediate person is modest. Righteous indignation is a mean between
envy and spite, and these states are concerned with the pain and
pleasures that are felt at the fortunes of our neighbors; the man
who is characterized by righteous indignation is pained at un-
deserved good fortune, the envious man, going beyond him, is
pained at all good fortune, and the spiteful man falls so far short
of being pained that he even rejoices. . . .

There are three kinds of disposition, then, two of them vices,
involving excess and deficiency respectively, and one a virtue,
viz., the mean, and all are in a sense opposed to all; for the extreme

states are contrary both to the intermediate state and to each other, and the intermediate to the extremes; as the equal is greater relatively to the less, less relatively to the greater, so the middle states are excessive relatively to the deficiencies, deficient relatively to the excesses, both in passions and in actions. For the brave man appears rash relatively to the coward, and cowardly relatively to the rash man; and similarly the temperate man appears self-indulgent relatively to the insensible man, insensible relatively to the self-indulgent, and the liberal man prodigal relatively to the mean man, mean relatively to the prodigal. Hence also the people at the extremes push the intermediate man each over to the other, and the brave man is called rash by the coward, cowardly by the rash man, and correspondingly in the other cases.

These states being thus opposed to one another, the greatest contrariety is that of the extremes to each other, rather than to the intermediate; for these are further from each other than from the intermediate, as the great is further from the small and the small from the great than both are from the equal. Again, to the intermediate some extremes show a certain likeness, as that of rashness to courage and that of prodigality to liberality; but the extremes show the greatest unlikeness to each other; now contraries are defined as the things that are furthest from each other, so that things that are further apart are more contrary.

To the mean in some cases the deficiency, in some of the excess is more opposed; e.g., it is not rashness, which is an excess, but cowardice, which is a deficiency, that is more opposed to courage, and not insensibility, which is a deficiency, but self-indulgence, which is an excess, that is more opposed to temperance. This happens from two reasons, one being drawn from the thing itself; for because one extreme is nearer and liker to the intermediate, we oppose not this but rather its contrary to the intermediate. E.g., since rashness is thought liker and nearer to courage, and cowardice more unlike, we oppose rather the latter to courage; for things that are further from the intermediate are thought more contrary to it. This, then, is one cause, drawn from the thing itself; another is drawn from ourselves; for the things to which we ourselves more naturally tend seem more contrary to the intermediate. For instance, we ourselves tend more naturally to pleasures, and hence are more easily carried away towards self-indulgence than towards propriety. We describe as contrary to the mean, then, rather the directions in which we more often go to great lengths; and therefore self-indulgence, which is an excess, is the more contrary to temperance.

That moral virtue is a mean, then, and in what sense it is so, and that it is a mean between two vices, the one involving excess, the other deficiency, and that it is such because its character is to aim at what is intermediate in passions and in actions, has been sufficiently stated. Hence also it is no easy task to be good. For in everything it is no easy task to find the middle, e.g., to find the middle of a circle is not for everyone but for him who knows; so too, any one can get angry—that is easy—or give or spend money; but to do this to the right person, to the right extent, at the right time, with the right motive, and in the right way, *that* is not for every one, nor is it easy; wherefore goodness is both rare and laudable and noble.

Hence he who aims at the intermediate must first depart from what is the more contrary to it, as Calypso advises—

> Hold the ship out beyond that surf and spray.

For of the extremes one is more erroneous, one less so; therefore, since to hit the mean is hard in the extreme, we must as a second best, as people say, take the least of the evils; and this will be done best in the way we describe.

But we must consider the things towards which we ourselves also are easily carried away; for some of us tend to one thing, some to another; and this will be recognizable from the pleasure and the pain we feel. We must drag ourselves away to the contrary extreme; for we shall get into the intermediate state by drawing well away from error, as people do in straightening sticks that are bent.

Now in everything the pleasant or pleasure is most to be guarded against; for we do not judge it impartially. We ought, then, to feel towards pleasure as the elders of the people felt towards Helen, and in all circumstances repeat their saying; for if we dismiss pleasure thus we are less likely to go astray. It is by doing this, then (to sum the matter up) that we shall best be able to hit the mean.

But this is no doubt difficult, and especially in individual cases;

for it is not easy to determine both how and with whom and on what provocation and how long one should be angry; for we too sometimes praise those who fall short and call them good-tempered, but sometimes we praise those who get angry and call them manly. The man, however, who deviates little from goodness is not blamed, whether he do so in the direction of the more or of the less, but only the man who deviates more widely; for he does not fail to be noticed. But up to what point and to what extent a man must deviate before he becomes blameworthy it is not easy to determine by reasoning, any more than anything else that is perceived by the senses; such things depend on particular facts, and the decision rests with perception. So much, then, is plain, that the intermediate state is in all things to be praised, but that we must incline sometimes towards the excess, sometimes towards the deficiency; for so shall we most easily hit the mean and what is right.

Study Questions

1. What role does *reason* play in Aristotle's moral theory?
2. Could Aristotle's doctrine of the "golden mean" benefit those concerned with contemporary ethical problems, such as international expansion of business or embryo experimentation? Can it be argued that his principle is too general to cover the awesome complexities of contemporary moral problems?
3. Do you agree with Aristotle's contention that being virtuous is a matter of "practice?" Why or why not?

Good Will, Duty, and the Categorical Imperative

Immanuel Kant

Nothing can possibly be conceived in the world, or even out of it, which can be called good, without qualification, except a Good Will. Intelligence, wit, judgment, and the other *talents* of the mind, however they may be named, or courage, resolution, perseverance, as qualities of temperament, are undoubtedly good and desirable in many respects; but these gifts of nature may also become extremely bad and mischievous if the will which is to make use of them, and which, therefore, constitutes what is called *character*, is not good. It is the same with the *gifts of fortune*. Power, riches, honor, even health, and the general well-being and contentment with one's condition which is called *happiness*, inspire pride, and often presumption, if there is not a good will to correct the influence of these on the mind, and with this also to rectify the whole principle of acting, and adapt it to its end. The sight of a being who is not adorned with a single feature of a pure and good will, enjoying unbroken prosperity, can never give pleasure to an impartial rational spectator. Thus a good will appears to constitute the indispensable condition even of being worthy of happiness.

There are even some qualities which are of service to this good will itself, and may facilitate its action, yet which have no intrinsic unconditional value, but always presuppose a good will, and this qualifies the esteem that we justly have for them, and does not permit us to regard them as absolutely good. Moderation in the affections and passions, self-control, and calm deliberation are not only good in many respects, but even seem to constitute part of the intrinsic worth of the person; but they are far from deserving to be called good without qualification, although they have been so unconditionally praised by the ancients. For without the principles of a good will, they may become extremely bad; and the coolness of a villain not only makes him far more dangerous, but also directly makes him more abominable in our eyes than he would have been without it.

A good will is good not because of what it performs or effects, not by it aptness for the attainment of some proposed end, but simply by virtue of the volition, that is, it is good in itself, and considered by itself is to be esteemed much higher than all that can be brought about by it in favor of any inclination, nay, even of the sum-total of all inclinations. Even if it should happen that, owing to special disfavor of fortune, or the niggardly provision of a step-motherly nature, this will should wholly lack power to accomplish its purpose, if with its greatest efforts it should yet achieve nothing, and there should remain only the good will (not, to be sure, a mere wish, but the summoning of all means in our power), then, like a jewel, it would still shine by its own light, as a thing which has its whole value in itself. Its usefulness or fruitlessness can neither add to nor take away anything from this value.

Thus the moral worth of an action does not lie in the effect expected from it, nor in any principle of action which requires to borrow its motive from this expected effect. For all these effects—agreeableness of one's condition, and even the promotion of the happiness of others—could have been also brought about by other causes, so that for this there would have been no need of the will of a rational being; whereas it is in this alone that the supreme and unconditional good can be found. The pre-eminent good which we call moral can therefore consist in nothing else than *the conception of law* in itself, *which certainly is only possible in a rational being*, in so far as this conception, and not the expected effect, determines the will. This is a good which is already present in the person who acts accordingly, and we have not to wait for it to appear first in the result.

But what sort of law can that be, the conception of which must determine the will, even without paying any regard to the effect expected from it, in order that this will may be called good absolutely and without qualification? As I have deprived the will of every impulse which could arise to it from obedience to any law, there remains nothing but the universal conformity of its actions to law in general, which alone is to serve the will as a principle, *i.e.* I am never to act otherwise than *so that I could also will that my maxim should become a universal law.* Here, now, it is the simple conformity to law in general, without assuming any particular law applicable to certain actions, that serves the will as its principle, and must so serve it, if duty is not to be a vain delusion and a chimeric vision. The common reason of men in its practical judgments correctly coincides with this and always has in view the principle here suggested. Let the question be, for example: May I when in distress make a promise with the intention not to keep it? I readily distinguish here between the two significations which the question may have: Whether it is prudent, or whether it is right, to make a false promise? The former may undoubtedly often be the case. I see clearly indeed that it is not enough to extricate myself from a present difficulty by means of this subterfuge, but it must be well considered whether there may not hereafter spring from this lie much greater inconvenience than that from which I now free myself, and as, with all my supposed *cunning*, the consequences cannot be so easily foreseen but that credit once lost may be much more injurious to me than any mischief which I seek to avoid at present, it should be considered whether it would not be more *prudent* to act herein according to a universal maxim, and to make it a habit to promise nothing except with the intention of keeping it. But it is soon clear to me that such a maxim will still only be based on the fear of consequences. Now it is a wholly different thing to be truthful from duty, and to be so from apprehension of injurious consequences. In the first case, the very notion of the action already implies a law for me; in the second case, I must first look about elsewhere to see what results may be combined with it which would affect myself. For to deviate from the principle of duty is beyond all doubt wicked; but to be unfaithful to my maxim of prudence may often be very advantageous to me, although to abide by it is certainly safer. The shortest way, however, and an unerring one, to discover the answer to this question whether a lying promise is consistent with duty, is to ask myself, Should I be content that my maxim (to extricate myself from difficulty by a false promise) should hold good as a universal law, for myself as well as for others? and should I be able to say to myself, "Every one may make a deceitful promise when he finds himself in a difficulty from which he cannot otherwise extricate himself"? Then I presently become aware that while I can will the lie, I can by no means will that lying should be a universal law. For with such a law there would be no promises at all, since it would be in vain to allege my intention in regard to my future actions to those who would not believe this allegation, or if they over-hastily did so, would pay me back in my own coin. Hence my maxim, as soon as it should be made a universal law, would necessarily destroy itself.

I do not, therefore, need any far-reaching penetration to discern what I have to do in order that my will be morally good. Inexperienced in the course of the world, incapable of being prepared for all its contingencies, I only ask myself: Canst thou also will that thy maxim should be a universal law? If not, then it must be rejected, and that not because of a disadvantage accruing from it to myself or even to others, but because it cannot enter as a principle into a possible universal legislation, and reason extorts from me immediate respect for such legislation. I do not indeed as yet *discern* on what this respect is based (this the philosopher may inquire), but at least I understand this, that it is an estimation of the worth which far outweighs all worth of what is recommended by inclination, and that the necessity of acting from *pure* respect for the practical law is what constitutes duty, to which every other motive must give place, because it is the condition of a will being good *in itself*, and the worth of such a will is above everything. . . .

. . . Everything in nature works according to laws. Rational beings alone have the faculty of acting according *to the conception* of laws, that is according to principles, *i.e.*, have a *will*. Since the deduction of actions from principles requires *reason*, the will is nothing but practical reason. If reason infallibly determines the will, then the actions of such a being which are recognized as objectively necessary are subjectively necessary also, *i.e.*, the will is a faculty to choose *that only* which reason independent on inclination recognizes as practically necessary, *i.e.*, as good. But if reason of itself does not sufficiently determine the will, if the latter is subject also to subjective conditions (particular impulses) which do not always coincide with the objective conditions; in a word, if the will does not *in itself* completely accord with reason (which is actually the case with men), then the actions which objectively are recognized as necessary are subjectively contingent, and the determination of such a will according to objective laws is *obligation*, that is to say, the relation of the objective laws to a will that is not thoroughly good is conceived as the determination of the will of a rational being by principles of reason, but which the will from its nature does not of necessity follow.

The conception of an objective principle, in so far as it is obligatory for a will, is called a command (of reason), and the formula of the command is called an Imperative. . . .

Now all *imperatives* command either *hypothetically* or *categorically*. The former represent the practical necessity of a possible action as means to something else that is willed (or at least which one might possibly will). The categorical imperative would be that which represented an action as necessary of itself without reference to another end, *i.e.*, as objectively necessary.

Since every practical law represents a possible action as good, and on this account, for a subject who is practically determinable by reason, necessary, all imperatives are formulae determining an action which is necessary according to the principle of a will good in some respects. If now the action is good only as a means *to something else*, then the imperative is *hypothetical*; if it is conceived as good *in itself* and consequently as being necessarily the principle of a will which of itself conforms to reason, then it is *categorical*. . . .

When I conceive a hypothetical imperative, in general I do not know beforehand what it will contain until I am given the condition. But when I conceive a categorical imperative, I know at once what it contains. For as the imperative contains besides the law only the necessity that the maxims shall conform to this law, while the law contains no conditions restricting it, there remains nothing but the general statement that the maxim of the action should conform to a universal law, and it is this conformity alone that the imperative properly represents as necessary.

There is . . . but one categorical imperative, namely, this: *Act only on that maxim whereby thou canst at the same time will that it should become a universal law.*

Now if all imperatives of duty can be deduced from this one

imperative as from their principle, then, although it should remain undecided whether what is called duty is not merely a vain notion, yet at least we shall be able to show what we understand by it and what this notion means.

Since the universality of the law according to which effects are produced constitutes what is properly called *nature* in the most general sense (as to form), that is the existence of things so far as it is determined by general laws, the imperative of duty may be expressed thus: *Act as if the maxim of thy action were to become by thy will a universal law of nature.*

We will now enumerate a few duties, adopting the usual division of them into duties to ourselves and to others, and into perfect and imperfect duties.

1. A man reduced to despair by a series of misfortunes feels wearied of life, but is still so far in possession of his reason that he can ask himself whether it would not be contrary to his duty to himself to take his own life. Now he inquires whether the maxim of his action could become a universal law of nature. His maxim is: From self-love I adopt it as a principle to shorten my life when its longer duration is likely to bring more evil than satisfaction. It is asked then simply whether this principle founded on self-love can become a universal law of nature. Now we see at once that a system of nature of which it should be a law to destroy life by means of the very feeling whose special nature it is to impel to the improvement of life would contradict itself, and therefore could not exist as a system of nature; hence that maxim cannot possibly exist as a universal law of nature, and consequently would be wholly inconsistent with the supreme principle of all duty.

2. Another finds himself forced by necessity to borrow money. He knows that he will not be able to repay it, but sees also that nothing will be lent to him, unless he promises stoutly to repay it in a definite time. He desires to make this promise, but he has still so much conscience as to ask himself: Is it not unlawful and inconsistent with duty to get out of a difficulty in this way? Suppose, however, that he resolves to do so, then the maxim of his action would be expressed thus: When I think myself in want of money, I will borrow money and promise to repay it, although I know that I never can do so. Now this principle of self-love or of one's own advantage may perhaps be consistent with my whole future welfare; but the question now is, Is it right? I change then

the suggestion of self-love into a universal law, and state the question thus: How would it be if my maxim were a universal law? Then I see at once that it could never hold as a universal law of nature, but would necessarily contradict itself. For supposing it to be a universal law that everyone when he thinks himself in a difficulty should be able to promise whatever he pleases, with the purpose of not keeping his promise, the promise itself would become impossible, as well as the end that one might have in view in it, since no one would consider that anything was promised to him, but would ridicule all such statements as vain pretences.

3. A third finds in himself a talent which with the help of some culture might make him a useful man in many respects. But he finds himself in comfortable circumstances, and prefers to indulge in pleasure rather than to take pains in enlarging and improving his happy natural capacities. He asks, however, whether his maxim of neglect of his natural gifts, besides agreeing with his inclination to indulgence, agrees also with what is called duty. He sees then that a system of nature could indeed subsist with such a universal law although men (like the South Sea islanders) should let their talents rest, and resolve to devote their lives merely to idleness, amusement, and propagation of their species—in a word, to enjoyment; but he cannot possibly *will* that this should be a universal law of nature, or be implanted in us as such by a natural instinct. For, as a rational being, he necessarily wills that his faculties be developed, since they serve him, and have been given him, for all sorts of possible purposes.

4. A fourth, who is in prosperity, while he sees that others have to contend with great wretchedness and that he could help them, thinks: What concern is it of mine? Let everyone be as happy as Heaven pleases, or as he can make himself; I will take nothing from him nor even envy him, only I do not wish to contribute anything to his welfare or to his assistance in distress! Now no doubt if such a mode of thinking were a universal law, the human race might very well subsist, and doubtless even better than in a state in which everyone talks of sympathy and good-will, or even takes care occasionally to put it into practice, but, on the other side, also cheats when he can, betrays the rights of men, or otherwise violates them. But although it is possible that a universal law of nature might exist in accordance with that

maxim, it is impossible to *will* that such a principle should have the universal validity of a law of nature. For a will which resolved this would contradict itself, inasmuch as many cases might occur in which one would have need of the love and sympathy of others, and in which, by such a law of nature, sprung from his own will, he would deprive himself of all hope of the aid he desires. . . .

We have thus established at least this much, that if duty is a conception which is to have any import and real legislative authority for our actions, it can only be expressed in categorical, and not at all in hypothetical imperatives. We have also, which is of great importance, exhibited clearly and definitely for every practical application the content of the categorical imperative, which must contain the principle of all duty if there is such a thing at all. We have not yet, however, advanced so far as to prove *à priori* that there actually is such an imperative, that there is a practical law which commands absolutely of itself, and without any other impulse, and that the following of this law is duty. . . .

Now I say: man and generally any rational being *exists* as an end in himself, *not merely as a means* to be arbitrarily used by this or that will, but in all his actions, whether they concern himself or other rational beings, must be always regarded at the same time as an end. All objects of the inclinations have only a conditional worth; for if the inclinations and the wants founded on them did not exist, then their object would be without value. But the inclinations themselves being sources of want are so far from having an absolute worth for which they should be desired, that, on the contrary, it must be the universal wish of every rational being to be wholly free from them. Thus the worth of any object which is *to be acquired* by our action is always conditional. Beings whose existence depends not on our will but on nature's, have nevertheless, if they are rational beings, only a relative value as means, and are therefore called *things*; rational beings, on the contrary, are called *persons*, because their very nature points them out as ends in themselves, that is as something which must not be used merely as means, and so far therefore restricts freedom of action (and is an object of respect). These, therefore, are not merely subjective ends whose existence has a worth *for us* as an effort of our action, but *objective ends*, that is things whose existence is an end in itself: an end moreover for which no other can be substituted, which they should subserve *merely* as means, for otherwise nothing whatever would possess *absolute worth*; but if all worth were conditioned and therefore contingent, then there would be no supreme practical principle of reason whatever.

If then there is a supreme practical principle or, in respect of the human will, a categorical imperative, it must be one which, being drawn from the conception of that which is necessarily an end for everyone because it is an *an end in itself*, constitutes an *objective* principle of will, and can therefore serve as a universal practical law. The foundation of this principle is: *rational nature exists as an end in itself*. Man necessarily conceives his own existence as being so: so far then this is a *subjective* principle of human actions. But every other rational being regards its existence similarly, just on the same rational principle, that holds for me: so that it is at the same time an objective principle, from which as a supreme practical law all laws of the will must be capable of being deduced. Accordingly the practical imperative will be as follows: *So act as to treat humanity, whether in thine own person or in that of any other, in every case as an end withal, never as means only. . . .*

Study Questions

1. Compare Kant's categorical imperative ("My maxim should hold good as a universal law, for myself as well as for others.") with the "golden rule." ("Do unto others as you would have them do unto you.") How far do the two overlap? Is there any situation that would be covered by one but not the other?

2. In his fourth item of "a few duties" Kant appears to show some doubt of his principle, admitting that if the innocent but indifferent rich man's "mode of thinking were a universal law, the human race might very well subsist, and doubtless even better than in a state in which everyone [talks and sometimes acts altruistically but] also cheats when he can, betrays the rights of men, or otherwise violates them." Does Kant reject this way of acting on universal grounds or for some other reason? What is the reason.

From On Liberty

John Stuart Mill

Introductory

The object of this essay is to assert one very simple principle, as entitled to govern absolutely the dealings of society with the individual in the way of compulsion and control, whether the means used be physical force in the form of legal penalties or the moral coercion of public opinion. That principle is that the sole end for which mankind are warranted, individually or collectively, in interfering with the liberty of action of any of their number is self-protection. That the only purpose for which power can be rightfully exercised over any member of a civilized community, against his will, is to prevent harm to others. His own good, either physical or moral, is not a sufficient warrant. He cannot rightfully be compelled to do or forbear because it will be better for him to do so, because it will make him happier, because, in the opinions of others, to do so would be wise or even right. These are good reasons for remonstrating with him, or reasoning with him, or persuading him, or entreating him, but not for compelling him or visiting him with any evil in case he do otherwise. To justify that, the conduct from which it is desired to deter him must be calculated to produce evil to someone else. The only part of the conduct of anyone for which he is amenable to society is that which concerns others. In the part which merely concerns himself, his independence is, of right, absolute. Over himself, over his own body and mind, the individual is sovereign.

It is, perhaps, hardly necessary to say that this doctrine is meant to apply only to human beings in the maturity of their faculties. We are not speaking of children or of young persons below the age which the law may fix as that of manhood or womanhood. Those who are still in a state to require being taken care of by others must be protected against their own actions as well as against external injury. For the same reason we may leave out of consideration those backward states of society in which the race itself may be considered as in its nonage. The early difficulties in the way of spontaneous progress are so great that there is seldom any choice of means for overcoming them; and a ruler full of the spirit of improvement is warranted in the use of any expedients that will attain an end perhaps otherwise unattainable. Despotism is a legitimate mode of government in dealing with barbarians, provided the end be their improvement and the means justified by actually effecting that end. Liberty, as a principle, has no application to any state of things anterior to the time when mankind have become capable of being improved by free and equal discussion. Until then, there is nothing for them but implicit obedience to an Akbar or a Charlemagne,[1] if they are so fortunate as to find one. But as soon as mankind have attained the capacity of being guided to their own improvement by convictions or persuasion (a period long since reached in all nations with whom we need here concern ourselves), compulsion, either in the direct form or in that of pains and penalties for noncompliance, is no longer admissible as a means to their own good, and justifiable only for the security of others. . . .

There is a sphere of action in which society, as distinguished from the individual, has, if any, only an indirect interest: comprehending all that portion of a person's life and conduct which affects only himself or, if it also affects others, only with their free, voluntary, and undeceived consent and participation. When I say only himself, I mean directly and in the first instance; for whatever affects himself may affect others through himself; and the objection which may be grounded on this contingency will receive consideration in the sequel. This, then, is the appropriate region of human liberty. It comprises, first, the inward domain of consciousness, demanding liberty of conscience in the most comprehensive sense, liberty of thought and feeling, absolute freedom of opinion and sentiment on all subjects, practical or speculative, scientific, moral, or theological. The liberty of expressing and publishing opinions may seem to fall under a different principle, since it belongs to that part of the conduct of an individual which concerns other people, but, being almost of as much importance as the liberty of thought itself and resting in great part on the same reasons, is practically inseparable from it. Secondly, the principle requires liberty of tastes and pursuits, of framing the plan of our life to suit our own character, of doing as we like, subject to such consequences as may follow, without impediment from our fellow creatures, so long as what we do does not harm them, even though they should think our conduct foolish, perverse, or wrong. Thirdly, from this liberty of each individual follows the liberty, within the same limits, of combination among individuals; freedom to unite for any purpose not involving harm to others: the persons combining being supposed to be of full age and not forced or deceived.

No society in which these liberties are not, on the whole, respected is free, whatever may be its form of government; and none is completely free in which they do not exist absolute and unqualified. The only freedom which deserves the name is that of pursuing our own good in our own way, so long as we do not attempt to deprive others of theirs or impede their efforts to obtain it. Each is the proper guardian of his own health, whether bodily or mental and spiritual. Mankind are greater gainers by suffering each other to live as seems good to themselves than by compelling each to live as seems good to the rest. . . .

Of the Liberty of Thought and Discussion

The time, it is to be hoped, is gone by when any defense would be necessary of the "liberty of the press" as one of the securities against corrupt or tyrannical government. No argument, we may suppose, can now be needed against permitting a legislature or an executive, not identified in interest with the people, to prescribe opinions to them and determine what doctrines or what arguments they shall be allowed to hear. This aspect of the question, besides, has been so often and so triumphantly enforced by preceding writers that it need not be specially insisted on in this place. Though the law of England, on the subject of the press, is as servile to this day as it was in the time of the Tudors,[2] there is little danger of its being actually put in force against political discussion except during some temporary panic when fear of insurrection drives ministers and judges from their propriety; and, speaking generally, it is not, in constitutional countries, to be apprehended that the government, whether completely responsible to the people or not, will often attempt to control the expression of opinion, except when in doing so it makes itself the organ of the general intolerance of the public. Let us suppose, therefore, that the government is entirely at one with the people, and never thinks of exerting any power of coercion unless in agreement with what it conceives to be their voice. But I deny the right of the people to exercise such coercion, either by themselves or by their government. The power itself is illegitimate. The best government has no more title to it than the worst. It is as noxious, or more noxious, when exerted in accordance with public opinion than when in opposition to it. If all mankind minus one were of one opinion, mankind would be no more justified in silencing that one person than he, if he had the power, would be justified in silencing mankind. Were an opinion a personal possession of no value except to the owner, if to be obstructed in the enjoyment of it were simply a private injury, it would make some difference whether the injury was inflicted only on a few persons or on many. But the peculiar evil of silencing the expression of an opinion is that it is robbing the human race, posterity as well as the existing generations—those who dissent from the opinion, still more than those who hold it. If the opinion is right, they are deprived of the opportunity of exchanging error for truth; if wrong, they lose, what is almost as great a benefit, the clearer perception and livelier impression of truth produced by its collision with error. . . .

We have now recognized the necessity to the mental well-being of mankind (on which all their other well-being depends) of freedom of opinion, and freedom of the expression of opinion, on four distant grounds, which we will now briefly recapitulate:

First, if any opinion is compelled to silence, that opinion may, for aught we can certainly know, be true. To deny this is to assume our own infallibility.

Secondly, though the silenced opinion be an error, it may, and very commonly does, contain a portion of truth; and since the general or prevailing opinion on any subject is rarely or never the whole truth, it is only by the collision of adverse opinions that the remainder of the truth has any chance of being supplied.

Thirdly, even if the received opinion be not only true, but the whole truth; unless it is suffered to be, and actually is, vigorously and earnestly contested, it will, by most of those who receive it, be held in the manner of a prejudice, with little comprehension or feeling of its rational grounds. And not only this, but, fourthly, the meaning of the doctrine itself will be in danger of being lost or enfeebled, and deprived of its vital effect on the character and conduct: the dogma becoming a mere formal profession, inefficacious for good, but cumbering the ground and preventing the growth of any real and heartfelt conviction from reason or personal experience.

Before quitting the subject of freedom of opinion, it is fit to take some notice of those who say that the free expression of all opinions should be permitted on condition that the manner be temperate, and do not pass the bounds of fair discussion. Much might be said on the impossibility of fixing where these supposed bounds are to be placed; for if the test be offense to those whose opinions are attacked, I think experience testifies that this offense is given whenever the attack is telling and powerful, and that every opponent who pushes them hard, and whom they find it difficult to answer, appears to them, if he shows any strong feeling on the subject, an intemperate opponent. But this, though an important consideration in a practical point of view, merges in a more fundamental objection. Undoubtedly, the manner of asserting an opinion, even though it be a true one, may be very objectionable and may justly incur severe censure. But the principal offenses of the kind are such as it is mostly impossible, unless by accidental self-betrayal, to bring home to conviction. The gravest of them is, to argue sophistically, to suppress facts or arguments, to misstate the elements of the case, or misrepresent the opposite opinion. But all this, even to the most aggravated degree, is so continually done in perfect good faith by persons who are not considered, and in many other respects may not deserve to be considered, ignorant or incompetent, that it is rarely possible, on adequate grounds, conscientiously to stamp the misrepresentation as morally culpable, and still less could law presume to interfere with this kind of controversial misconduct. With regard to what is commonly meant by intemperate discussion, namely invective, sarcasm, personality, and the like, the denunciation of these weapons would deserve more sympathy if it were ever proposed to interdict them equally to both sides; but it is only desired to restrain the employment of them against the prevailing opinion; against the unprevailing they may not only be used without general disapproval, but will be likely to obtain for him who uses them the praise of honest zeal and righteous indignation. Yet whatever mischief arises from their use is greatest when they are employed against the comparatively defenseless; and whatever unfair advantage can be derived by any opinion from this mode of asserting it accrues almost exclusively to received opinions. The worst offense of this kind which can be committed by a polemic is to stigmatize those who hold the contrary opinion as bad and immoral men. To calumny of this sort, those who hold any unpopular opinion are peculiarly exposed, because they are in general few and uninfluential, and nobody but themselves feels much interested in seeing justice done them; but this weapon is, from the nature of the case, denied to those who attack a prevailing opinion: they can neither use it with safety to themselves, nor, if they could, would it do anything but recoil on their own cause. In general, opinions contrary to those commonly received can only obtain a hearing by studied moderation of language and the most cautious avoidance of unnecessary offense, from which they hardly ever deviate even in a slight degree without losing ground, while unmeasured vituperation employed on the side of the prevailing opinion really does deter people from professing contrary opinions and from listening to those who profess them. For the interest, therefore, of truth and justice it is far more important to restrain this employment of vituperative language than the other; and, for example, if it were necessary to choose, there would be much more need to discourage offensive attacks on infidelity than on religion. It is, however, obvious that law and authority have no business with restraining either, while opinion ought, in every instance, to determine its verdict by the circumstances of the individual case—condemning everyone, on whichever side of the argument he places himself, in whose mode of advocacy either want of candor, or malignity, bigotry, or intolerance of feeling manifest themselves; but not inferring these vices from the side which a person takes, though it be the contrary side of the question to our own; and giving merited honor to everyone, whatever opinion he may hold, who has calmness to see and honesty to state what his opponents and their opinions really are, exaggerating nothing to their discredit, keeping nothing back which tells, or can be supposed to tell, in their favor. This is the real morality of public discussion; and if often violated, I am happy to think that there are many controversialists who to a great extent observe it, and a still greater number who conscientiously strive toward it.

Of the Limits to the Authority of Society over the Individual

What, then, is the rightful limit to the sovereignty of the individual over himself? Where does the authority of society begin? How much of human life should be assigned to individuality, and how much to society?

Each will receive its proper share if each has that which more particularly concerns it. To individuality should belong the part of life in which it is chiefly the individual that is interested; to society, the part which chiefly interests society.

Though society is not founded on a contract, and though no good purpose is answered by inventing a contract in order to deduce social obligations from it, everyone who receives the protection of society owes a return for the benefit, and the fact of living in society renders it indispensable that each should be bound to observe a certain line of conduct toward the rest. This conduct consists, first, in not injuring the interests of one another, or rather certain interests which, either by express legal provision or by tacit understanding, ought to be considered as rights; and secondly, in each person's bearing his share (to be fixed on some equitable principle) of the labors and sacrifices incurred for defending the society or its members from injury and molestation. These conditions society is justified in enforcing at all costs to those who endeavor to withhold fulfillment. Nor is this all that society may do. The acts of an individual may be hurtful to others or wanting in due consideration for their welfare, without going to the length of violating any of their constituted rights. The offender may then be justly punished by opinion, though not by law. As soon as any part of a person's conduct affects prejudicially the interests of others, society has jurisdiction over it, and the question whether the general welfare will or will not be promoted by interfering with it becomes open to discussion. But there is no room for entertaining any such question when a person's conduct affects the interests of no persons besides himself, or needs not affect them unless they like (all the persons concerned being of full age and the ordinary amount of understanding). In all such cases, there should be perfect freedom, legal and social, to do the action and stand the consequences. . . .

The distinction here pointed out between the part of a person's life which concerns only himself and that which concerns others, many persons will refuse to admit. How (it may be asked) can any part of the conduct of a member of society be a matter of indifference to the other members? No person is an entirely isolated being; it is impossible for a person to do anything seriously or permanently hurtful to himself without mischief reaching at least to his near connections, and often far beyond them. If he injures his property, he does harm to those who directly or indirectly derived support from it, and usually diminishes, by a greater or less amount, the general resources of the community. If he deteriorates his bodily or mental faculties, he not only brings evil upon all who depended on him for any portion of their happiness, but disqualifies himself for rendering the services which he owes to his fellow creatures generally, perhaps becomes a burden on their affection or benevolence; and if such conduct were very frequent hardly any offense that is committed would detract more from the general sum of good. Finally, if by his vices or follies a person does no direct harm to others, he is nevertheless (it may be said) injurious by his example, and ought to be compelled to control himself for the sake of those whom the sight or knowledge of his conduct might corrupt or mislead.

And even (it will be added) if the consequences of misconduct could be confined to the vicious or thoughtless individual, ought society to abandon to their own guidance those who are manifestly unfit for it? If protection against themselves is confessedly due to children and persons under age, is not society equally bound to afford it to persons of mature years who are equally incapable of self-government? If gambling, or drunkenness, or incontinence, or idleness, or uncleanliness are as injurious to happiness, and as great a hindrance to improvement, as many or most of the acts prohibited by law, why (it may be asked) should not law, so far as is consistent with practicability and social convenience, endeavor to repress these also? And as a supplement to the unavoidable imperfections of law, ought not opinion at least to organize a powerful police against these vices and visit rigidly with social penalties those who are known to practice them? There is no question here (it may be said) about restricting individuality, or impeding the trial of new and original experiments in living. The only things it is sought to prevent are things which have been tried and condemned from the beginning of the world until now—things which experience has shown not to be useful or suitable to any person's individuality. There must be some length of time and amount of experience after which a moral or prudential truth may be regarded as established; and it is merely desired to prevent generation after generation from falling over the same precipice which has been fatal to their predecessors.

I fully admit that the mischief which a person does to himself may seriously affect, both through their sympathies and their interests, those nearly connected with him and, in a minor degree, society at large. When, by conduct of this sort, a person is led to violate a distinct and assignable obligation to any other person or persons, the case is taken out of the self-regarding class and becomes amenable to moral disapprobation in the proper sense of the term. If, for example, a man, through intemperance or extravagance, becomes unable to pay his debts, or, having undertaken the moral responsibility of a family, becomes from the same cause incapable of supporting or educating them, he is deservedly reprobated and might be justly punished; but it is for the breach of duty to his family or creditors, not for the extravagance. If the resources which ought to have been devoted to them had been diverted from them for the most prudent investment, the moral culpability would have been the same. George Barnwell[3] murdered his uncle to get money for his mistress, but if he had done it to set himself up in business, he would equally have been hanged. Again, in the frequent case of a man who causes grief to his family by addiction to bad habits, he deserves reproach for his unkindness or ingratitude; but so he may for cultivating habits not in themselves vicious, if they are painful to those with whom he passes his life, or who from personal ties are dependent on him for their comfort. Whoever fails in the consideration generally due to the interests and feelings of others, not being compelled by some more imperative duty, or justified by allowable self-preference, is a subject of moral disapprobation for that failure, but not for the cause of it, nor for the errors, merely personal to himself, which may have remotely led to it. In like manner, when a person disables himself, by conduct purely self-regarding, from the performance of some definite duty incumbent on him to the public, he is guilty of a social offense. No person ought to be punished simply for being drunk; but a soldier or a policeman should be punished for being drunk on duty. Whenever, in short, there is a definite damage, or a definite risk of damage, either to an individual or to the public, the case is taken out of the province of liberty and placed in that of morality or law. . . .

But the strongest of all the arguments against the interference of the public with purely personal conduct is that, when it does interfere, the odds are that it interferes wrongly and in the wrong place. On questions of social morality, of duty to others, the opinion of the public, that is, of an overruling majority, though often wrong, is likely to be still oftener right, because on such questions they are only required to judge of their own interests, of the manner in which some mode of conduct, if allowed to be practiced, would affect themselves. But the opinion of a similar majority, imposed as a law on the minority, on questions of self-regarding conduct is quite as likely to be wrong as right, for in these cases public opinion means, at the best, some people's opinion of what is good or bad for other people, while very often it does not even mean that—the public, with the most perfect indifference, passing over the pleasure or convenience of those whose conduct they censure and considering only their own preference. There are many who consider as an injury to themselves any conduct which they have a distaste for, and resent it as an outrage to their feelings; as a religious bigot, when charged with disregarding the religious feelings of others, has been known to retort that they disregard his feelings by persisting in their abominable worship or creed. But there is no parity between the feeling of a person for his own opinion and the feeling of another who is offended at his holding it, no more than between the desire of a thief to take a purse and the desire of the right owner to keep it. And a person's taste is as much his own peculiar concern as his opinion or his purse. It is easy for anyone to imagine an ideal public which leaves the freedom and choice of individuals in all uncertain matters undisturbed and only requires them to abstain from modes of conduct which universal experience has condemned. But where has there been seen a public which set any such limit to its censorship? Or when does the public trouble itself about universal experience? In its interferences with personal conduct it is seldom thinking of anything but the enormity of acting or feeling differently from itself; and this standard of judgment, thinly disguised, is held up to mankind as the dictate of religion and philosophy by nine-tenths of all moralists and speculative writers. These teach that things are right because they are right; because we feel them to be so. They tell us to search in our own minds and hearts for laws of conduct binding on ourselves and on all others. What can the poor public do but apply these instructions and make their own personal feelings of good and evil, if they are tolerably unanimous in them, obligatory on all the world?

The evil here pointed out is not one which exists only in theory; and it may perhaps be expected that I should specify the instances in which the public of this age and country improperly invests its own preferences with the character of moral laws. I am not writing an essay on the aberrations of existing moral feeling. That is too weighty a subject to be discussed parenthetically, and by way of illustration. Yet examples are necessary to show that the principle I maintain is of serious and practical moment, and that I am not endeavoring to erect a barrier against imaginary evils. And it is not difficult to show, by abundant instances, that to extend the bounds of what may be called moral police until it encroaches on the most unquestionably legitimate liberty of the individual is one of the most universal of all human propensities. . . .

Without dwelling upon supposititious cases,[4] there are, in our own day, gross usurpations upon the liberty of private life actually practiced, and still greater ones threatened with some expectation of success, and opinions propounded which assert an unlimited right in the public not only to prohibit by law everything which it thinks wrong, but, in order to get at what it thinks wrong, to prohibit a number of things which it admits to be innocent.

Under the name of preventing intemperance, the people of one English colony, and of nearly half the United States, have been interdicted by law[5] from making any use whatever of fermented drinks, except for medical purposes, for prohibition of their sale is in fact, as it is intended to be, prohibition of their use. And though the impracticability of executing the law has caused its repeal in several of the States which had adopted it, including the one from which it derives its name, an attempt has notwithstanding been commenced, and is prosecuted with considerable zeal by many of the professed philanthropists, to agitate for a similar law in this country. The association, or "Alliance," as it terms itself, which has been formed for this purpose, has acquired some notoriety through the publicity given to a correspondence between its secretary and one of the very few English public men who hold that a politician's opinions ought to be founded on principles. Lord Stanley's share in this correspondence is calculated to strengthen the hopes already built on him by those who know how rare such qualities as are manifested in some of his public appearances unhappily are among those who figure in political life. The organ of the Alliance, who would "deeply deplore the recognition of any principle which could be wrested to justify bigotry and persecution," undertakes to point out the "broad and impassable barrier" which divides such principles from those of the association. "All matters relating to thought, opinion, conscience, appear to me," he says, "to be without the sphere of legislation, all pertaining to social act, habit, relation, subject only to a discretionary power vested in the State itself, and not in the individual, to be within it." No mention is made of a third class, different from either of these, viz., acts and habits which are not social, but individual; although it is to this class, surely, that the act of drinking fermented liquors belongs. Selling fermented liquors, however, is trading, and trading is a social act. But the infringement complained of is not on the liberty of the seller, but on that of the buyer and consumer; since the State might just as well forbid him to drink wine as purposely make it impossible for him to obtain it. The secretary, however, says, "I claim, as a citizen, a right to legislate whenever my social rights are invaded by the social act of another." And now for the definition of these "social rights:" "If anything invades my social rights, certainly the traffic in strong drink does. It destroys my primary right of security by constantly creating and stimulating social disorder. It invades my right of equality by deriving a profit from the creation of a misery I am taxed to support. It impedes my right to free moral and intellectual development by surrounding my path with dangers and by weakening and demoralizing society, from which I have a right to claim mutual aid and intercourse." A theory of "social rights" the like of which probably never before found its way into distinct language: being nothing short of this—that it is the absolute social right of every individual that every other individual shall act in every respect exactly as he ought; that whosoever fails thereof in the smallest particular violates my social right and entitles me to demand from the legislature the removal of the grievance. So monstrous a principle is far more dangerous than any single interference with liberty; there is no violation of liberty which it would not justify; it acknowledges no right to any freedom whatever, except perhaps to that of holding opinions in secret, without ever disclosing them; for the moment an opinion which I consider noxious passes anyone's lips, it invades all the "social rights" attributed to me by the Alliance. The doctrine ascribes to all mankind a vested interest in each other's moral, intellectual, and even physical perfection, to be defined by each claimant according to his own standard. . . .

NOTES

1. **Akbar . . . Charlemagne**—Akbar (1542–1605), Mogul Emperor of India; Charlemagne (742–815), King of the Franks, and later Emperor of the West (all notes are the editors').
2. **the time of the Tudors**—the period in England from the reign of Henry VII through the reign of Queen Elizabeth I; i.e., 1485–1603.
3. **George Barnwell**—an apprentice in a popular ballad and in George Lillo's play, *The London Merchant* (1731).
4. **supposititious cases**—cases depending on a supposition; hypothetical cases.
5. **law**—the Maine Liquor Law (1851) prohibited the manufacture, sale, and use of intoxicating drinks, with some exceptions.

Study Questions

1. Do you agree with Mill's defense of freedom of the press? Would you modify his views in light of alleged press abuses of their freedom in recent years?

2. Do you agree with Mill that *governments* really have no right to exercise any restraint on free expression?
3. Do you agree with Mill that the only circumstances under which a government can restrain free exercise of expression is to prevent harm to others? Is this admission by Mill totally consistent with other things he says about freedom of expression?

Moral Judgments: Subjective Yet Universal

Paul Allen, III

An "Overriding Inclination" May Help Us Censure Hare's Fanatic

Most of us are unwilling to be killed or jailed, or to be treated in any other violent or injurious manner. It follows from this, according to R.M. Hare, that we are required by logic not to decide to treat others in such a manner either. For example, if I try to send someone to jail for failing to pay a debt under a given set of conditions but am unwilling to have myself jailed for failing to pay a debt under those same conditions, then, Hare argues, I would be prescribing for the other person something I was not prescribing for myself. I would be thinking, "What's good for the goose is *not* good for the gander," and therefore would be contradicting myself. Thus, according to Hare's thesis of universalizability, logic requires us to decide to do to others only what we are willing to have done to ourselves—under relevantly similar circumstances.[1]

Hare bases his conclusion solely on the logic of moral reasoning—by showing that the agent would contradict himself by prescribing for others what he would not prescribe for himself. In this way, Hare does not have to hinge his system on any prior assumptions about certain purposes being good, such as happiness or human fulfillment. That is, he thereby avoids any form of the "naturalistic fallacy."

Furthermore, he does not start from a factual premise such as

"Everyone desires pleasure" or "Lying disrupts society" and try to infer a value or moral judgment, e.g., "Pleasure is good" or "Lying is wrong." To do so would be fallacious, Hare and many others insist, because factual sentences are fundamentally different from value or moral ones. Facts cannot entail values. You cannot derive an "ought" sentence from an "is" sentence. Thus, by having his system focus only on the logic of moral reasoning, Hare avoids the naturalistic fallacy and any attempt to derive "ought" from "is."[2]

However, Hare's theory does have a serious weakness, which has become rather notorious. As indicated above, the logical requirement for an agent to decide against murdering, assaulting, etc., stems from his own willingness to be murdered or assaulted. It follows that if someone *is* willing to suffer such treatment, it is logically permissible for him to decide to treat others that way. Indeed, there may be certain rare individuals, "true fanatics" Hare calls them, who are so wedded to an ideal that they can assent to any sort of suffering or death for the sake of the ideal. There may be Nazis who, if they found out they were Jewish, would assent to being killed in order to further their ideal of a pure Aryan race. Since such a true Nazi fanatic could assent to having himself killed for his ideal, he would, according to Hare, be perfectly consistent in prescribing the killing of others for that ideal.[3]

Thus, fanatics can "get away with murder" under Hare's system. And many critics believe that this inability to censure the fanatic is a fatal weakness in Hare's theory. "Surely a moral theory should be able to tell anyone who is committing murder that he is wrong," say these critics. And consider the recent rise in hijacking, bombing, and other terrorist activities being performed in the name of political and religious ideals: indeed it is now more important than ever that we have grounds for declaring such behavior morally wrong.

On the other hand, let's imagine for a moment that there were no *true* fanatics in the world. Suppose that no human being could ever willingly sacrifice his life for the sake of an ideal such as Nazism. Imagine that all of us, including all Nazis and other so-called fanatics, have some overriding inclination which makes us unwilling to suffer death, torture, imprisonment, and so on, for the sake of any ideal. If this were so, if would seem that every human being—fanatics and the rest—would be required by logic always to decide against inflicting such harm on others. And Hare's fanatic problem would be eliminated.

Although Hare does not think there is any such overriding inclination, writings of a few other philosophers, especially Alan Gewirth, suggest that there may be.[4] Making use of this insight, in the next two sections I shall develop a thesis which is partially based on Gewirth's analysis and which provides a solution to Hare's fanatic problem. Then in the last two sections we will investigate whether this solution to the fanatic problem provides an objective grounding for morality. My conclusion will be that the moral judgments it leads to can be thought of as subjective but that they are universal as well.

One Thing No One Will Ever Give Up is "Immediate Freedom"

In instances where a person does an act involuntarily or unthinkingly, it is likely that he does not want to do the act, or that he feels neutral about it. However, if a person voluntarily performs an act, he must have a "pro-attitude" toward it. For, if the agent acts freely and purposively, he necessarily favors his doing of the act or else he would not bother to do it. Using Hare's terminology, if an agent chooses to do an act, he must at that moment be *prescribing* that he do it.

It is also clear that if an agent prescribes his doing of an act at a given moment, he must at that moment be against having anything prevent him from doing it. That is to say, he must be prescribing that he be able to do the act, i.e., that he be free to do it. For example, even if a Nazi chose to give up his life for his ideal, he would not be giving up his freedom to do the thing he was immediately deciding to do, namely, to die to for Nazism. Rather, in choosing Nazism over his own life, he would be exercising and appreciating his freedom to carry out what he was choosing to do. He would be expecting and prescribing for himself the opportunity to have the fate he was selecting, viz., death for the sake of Nazism.

I will use the term "immediate freedom" for this freedom to do what one is now choosing to do. It must be contrasted with what may be called one's "future prerogatives." People sometimes do voluntarily give up their future prerogatives. The Nazi fanatic who finds out he is Jewish might very well turn himself over to the authorities so that they can make all future decisions about what he is to do. But in voluntarily giving himself up in such a way, the Nazi fanatic would be expecting and prescribing that he be free to do the very thing he is now choosing to do, namely, to turn himself over to the authorities. If a friend (or "deprogrammer") found him on his way to the Nazi headquarters and kidnapped him to prevent him from throwing away his future, the Nazi fanatic would feel frustrated and angry (assuming, of course, that he was sincerely committed to turning himself over to the authorities).

In general then, every agent, including Hare's fanatic, necessarily values and prescribes his own immediate freedom in an overriding way. Even though one may value some ideal more than his own life or pleasure, he will never value the ideal more than his own freedom to do what he is presently choosing to do. For choosing to promote an ideal presupposes exercising, appreciating, and thus prescribing the freedom to promote it.

Logic Requires Us to Prescribe Others' Freedom As Well As Our Own

It may be inappropriate to classify this prescribing of immediate freedom as an inclination, but it functions as we suggested an overriding inclination might function. Since no one will give up his immediate freedom for an ideal or anything else, no one will assent to having others take away that freedom. That is, all of us inevitably prescribe our own immediate freedom; but in doing so, we are at the same time prescribing that nothing undermine that freedom, including other people.

Now we can apply Hare's thesis of universalizability and make the following observation: Since every agent inevitably is unwilling to have anyone thwart his immediate freedom, every agent is required by logic not to decide to thwart the immediate freedom of others.

Of course, in this and any other application of the thesis of universalizability, Hare would want us to keep in mind the question of relevant similarity. Logic requires the agent not to decide to thwart the other person's freedom only if the agent and the other person are similar in all relevant respects. A "relevant respect" is any feature of the parties or situation which the agent uses as a basis for his decision. If the Nazi fanatic claims that Jewishness is grounds for killing a Jew and is willing to be killed if he himself turned out to be Jewish, then he is consistently using Jewishness as a basis for his decision. And Jewishness is therefore a relevant criterion as he makes his decision whether to kill the Jew.[5]

However, no agent can consistently claim that race or anything else is a relevant feature when it comes to deciding whether to undermine someone else's freedom. To do so, the agent would have to assent to his own freedom of the present moment being denied if he turned out to have the other person's race (or whatever the quality might be). But the agent will not assent to this freedom being denied; for, as we have seen, in making his decision about whether to interfere with the other person's freedom, the agent would be exercising and appreciating his own immediate freedom and thereby prescribing that it *not* be denied.[6]

To return to the main point, every agent is logically required to prescribe other people's freedom just as he prescribes his own. This requirement is a result of logic plus his inevitable valuing of his own freedom. In short, because every agent prescribes that he be free to act as he sees fit, he is logically required to prescribe that others have similar freedom.

To summarize briefly, we seem to have found a way out of Hare's fanatic problem. Thanks to insights of certain other philosophers, especially Gewirth, we have found something which functions as if it were an overriding inclination: no one, not even the fanatic, can assent to the loss of his immediate freedom to do what he is choosing to do. Therefore, even the fanatic is required by logic to conclude that he ought to avoid acts (e.g., murder or hijacking) which would undermine others' immediate freedom.

Have We Discovered An Objective Grounding For Morality?

It may seem as if we have also arrived at a derivation of "ought" from "is," or some other sort of objective grounding for morality.

For example, Gewirth claims to have inferred an "ought" from an "is" by means of a derivation which is somewhat like the one I have presented. And other writers, while not stating that they have derived "ought" from "is," have claimed that somewhat similar derivations provide an objective basis for morality.[7]

For reasons I must not go into here (but have given elsewhere[8]) I believe that derivations such as that sketched above cannot yield an "ought" from an "is." But what I do want to show now is that this sort of derivation yields moral judgments which, though they must be thought of as subjective, can be thought of as universal none the less. (Incidentally, in order to avoid the clumsy expression "undermining the freedom of others," I will often speak of "coercing others.")

To see why the moral judgment "I ought not to undermine the freedom of others" (or "I ought not to coerce others") should be called subjective, we must postpone for a moment our discussion of freedom and review more of Hare's analysis of universalizability.

Let's imagine that Mr. Smith, an employer, wants to fire a clerk for coming to work late under conditions x, y, and z. Imagine also, however, that Mr. Smith cannot assent to being fired if he himself were late under those conditions.[9]

Now, Mr. Smith would be contradicting himself if we went ahead and decided to fire the clerk anyway. That is, he would be contradicting himself if he reasoned, "I prescribed that I not be fired if late under conditions x, y, and z; and I prescribe that the clerk, who is relevantly similar to me, *be* fired if late under conditions x, y, and z." He would be contradicting himself because he would be prescribing that one person (the clerk) be fired and that another person (himself) not be fired in the very same circumstances, even though both persons were identical in all relevant respects. Accordingly, as long as Mr. Smith is unwilling to be fired if he were late under conditions x, y, and z, he must (if he is to be consistent) admit that he ought not to fire the clerk.

Although Mr. Smith's unwillingness to be fired makes it logically necessary for him to conclude that he shouldn't fire the clerk, Mr. Smith's unwillingness does not make it necessary for *another* person, e.g., his colleague Mrs. Green, to conclude that the clerk shouldn't be fired. As we just saw, Mr. Smith would be contradicting himself if he said, "I prescribe that I not be fired if late under conditions x, y, and z; and I prescribe that the clerk, who is relevantly similar to me be fired if late under those conditions." Nevertheless, Mrs. Green would not be contradicting herself in saying, "Mr. Smith prescribes that he himself not be fired if late under conditions x, y, and z; but *I* do recommend that the clerk be fired if late under conditions x, y, and z." Her sentence would be perfectly consistent because she is not making two conflicting prescriptions. Although she is making a presciption of her own, she is only *reporting* Mr. Smith's prescription.

We can see from this example that each agent's logical requirement to arrive at a certain "ought" conclusion stems from his *own* unwillingness to be treated a certain way, not from anyone else's unwillingness. Accordingly, Hare's analysis shows that an agent's inclinations can make it necessary for the agent himself to infer a particular "ought" conclusion, but not for anyone else to do so.

To take this insight from Hare and apply it to the question of freedom, we can see that the logical relationships just described pertain not only to the sort of inclinations Hare had in mind (the desire to keep a job, etc.) but also to our "overriding inclination"— one's inevitable unwillingness to be coerced. Just as Mr. Smith's unwillingness to be fired makes him—but not Mrs. Green—logically bound to avoid prescribing the firing of the clerk, so Mr. Smith's unwillingness to give up his freedom makes him—but not Mrs. Green—logically bound to conclude, "I ought not to coerce others." But of course, Mrs. Green's *own* unwillingness to be coerced makes her logically bound to reach that moral conclusion for herself.

In general, *my* unwillingness to lose my freedom makes it logically necessary for *me* not to prescribe the coercing of others; *your* unwillingness makes it necessary for *you* not to prescribe the coercing of others; and so on for each agent. Thus, *my* unwillingness to lose my freedom does not make *another* person logically bound to avoid prescribing the coercing of others. And from other agents' unwillingness to be coerced you and I cannot infer, "They ought not to coerce others."

In short, each agent's logical requirement to avoid prescribing the coercing of others is a function of his *own* unwillingness to be coerced. And a particular agent's unwillingness to be coerced makes only him—not others—logically required to avoid prescribing the coercing of others.

If we apply the term "subjective" to moral judgments which are dependent on, or a function of, the individual agent's own inclinations or preferences, then the judgments under discussion should be called subjective. That is, although every logically consistent agent arrives at the same judgment ("I ought not to coerce others"), this judgment can be called subjective because it is a function of the individual agent's own unwillingness to give up his immediate freedom and because no one but the agent making the judgment is bound by the entailment being expressed.

Therefore, philosophers and other moralists cannot start with the observation that no one is willing to lose his immediate freedom and infer an "objective moral truth" binding upon all people such as "No one ought to interfere with the freedom of others." Instead, the philosopher or moralist must settle for "subjective" moral judgments which stem from his own unwillingness to be coerced and which express a logical requirement that is binding upon himself alone ("I ought not to coerce others," "I ought not to attack him," etc.).

Though Subjective, These Judgments Are Also Universal

Although the maxim "I ought not to undermine the freedom of others" and the more specific injunctions which can be derived from it (e.g., "I ought not to attack him") are subjective in the sense just explained, no one, not even Hare's fanatic, can willingly assent to the loss of his immediate freedom. This "overriding inclination," when coupled with the logic of universalizability, makes it logically necessary for all of us to avoid prescribing the coercing of others. Therefore, the maxim "I ought not to coerce others" and the more specific maxims which flow from it are inevitably arrived at by *all* agents insofar as they are thinking logically. And in this sense we can call these judgments universal.

Putting it another way, Hare's thesis is essentially that we are logically required not to decide to do anything we are unwilling to have others do to us. We have joined onto this another thesis; that *everyone* is unwilling to have his immediate freedom taken away and that everyone is therefore logically required not to prescribe the undermining of others' immediate freedom. From this it follows that *all* of us are logically bound to subscribe to the maxim "I ought not to undermine the immediate freedom of others." Since this maxim is logically binding upon all of us, we can call it universal.

Still, let's remember *why* the maxim is binding on all of us: only because of each agent's own individual unwillingness to give up his immediate freedom. And remember that each agent's unwillingness produces a logical entailment that pertains only to that particular agent. In this sense, the resulting maxim ("I ought not to coerce others") is personal, logically individualistic, or "subjective." No one can make it into an "objective moral truth" binding upon others, such as "Everyone ought to avoid coercing others."

To conclude, the moral judgment "I ought not to coerce others" is subjective in that it is logically a function of each agent's own unwillingness to be coerced; yet it is universal because all agents turn out to be logically required to make this judgment, since all of them are unwilling to be coerced.

NOTES

1. R.M. Hare, *Freedom and Reason*, Oxford University Press, Oxford, 1963, pp. 86–111. *Moral Thinking*, Oxford University Press, Oxford, 1981, pp. 80 ff.
2. Hare, *Freedom and Reason*, pp. 186–202.
3. Hare, *Freedom and Reason*, p. 172.
4. Alan Gewirth, *Reason and Morality*, The University of Chicago Press, Chicago, 1978, pp. 48 ff; "Categorial Consistency in Ethics," *The Philosophical Quarterly* 17 (1967), 289–299; "Must One Play the Moral Language Game?" *American Philosophical Quarterly* 7, no. 2 (April 1970), 107–118; "The Justification of Egalitarian Justice," *American Philosophical Quarterly* 8, no. 4 (October 1971). The others I have in mind are Lansing Pollock and John Wilson. See Lansing Pollock, "Freedom and Universalizability," *Mind* (1973), 234–48; "The Freedom Principle," *Ethics* 86, no. 4 (July 1976), 332–42; and John Wilson, "Why Should Other People Be Treated As Equals?" *Revue Internationale de Philosophie* 97 (1971), 272–86.
5. Cf. Hare, *Freedom and Reason*, pp. 139 f.
6. Gewirth expresses essentially the same insight in various places. See Gewirth, *Reason and Morality*, pp. 104 f.; "Categorial Consistency in Ethics," p. 290; and "The Justification of Egalitarian Justice," pp. 338 f.

7. Alan Gewirth, *Reason and Morality*, p. 149; "The Normative Structure of Action," *The Review of Metaphysics* 25 (1971), p. 259; and "The 'Is-Ought' Problem Resolved," Presidential Address to the American Philosophical Association, *Proceedings and Addresses of the American Philosophical Association* 47 (1974), p. 57. Pollock, "Freedom and Universalizability," pp. 242 f; and "The Freedom Principle," pp. 341 f. Wilson, "Why Should Other People Be Treated As Equals?" pp. 280–83.
8. Paul Allen III, "A Critique of Gewirth's 'Is-Ought' Derivation," *Ethics* 92, no. 2 (January 1982), 211–226; " 'Ought' from 'Is'? What Hare and Gewirth Should Have Said," *American Journal of Theology and Philosophy* 3, no. 3 (September 1982), 90–97.
9. This is an adaptation of one of Hare's examples. R.M. Hare, *The Language of Morals*, Oxford University Press, Oxford, 1952, p. 56.

Study Questions

1. Much of Allen's case seems to depend on a somewhat unusual conception of "freedom." Do you agree with this conception?
2. Do you agree with Allen's final conclusion that the judgments he discusses are "subjective," yet universal? Is he using the term "subjective" in a straightforward, ordinary way, or is he perhaps redefining it to some extent?

PART II

Medical Ethics

Medical ethics have been around a long time. Certainly the practice of medicine in ancient civilizations necessitated moral judgments, even if there were no formal philosophical systems on which to base them. Even in the twentieth century, the systematic study and teaching of medical ethics has only recently begun to emerge as an established, accepted branch of human inquiry. As early as 1969, interest in medical ethics surfaced due to Elisabeth Kubler-Ross's book, ON DEATH AND DYING.

Very soon after that, many organizations, symposia, conferences, etc. began to appear to study the ethical problems in medicine. Perhaps best known of these is the reknowned Hastings Center, a group of scholars from various disciplines, including law, theology, philosophy, psychology, etc. Through meetings, publications such as *The Hastings Center Report* and *The Hastings Center Studies*, scholars such as Sissela Bok, Robert Veatch, Daniel Callahan, Paul Ramsey continually share their discoveries with the public. Results have been rapid and significant.

By 1970 the Kansas legislature had already enacted a new statutory definition of death.

Additional impetus for the growing interest in medical/biological questions came with the 1972 International Conference on Population Education held at Harvard University. It was during that conference that some participants began to grapple with ethical issues in biology and medicine, the present author included.

All the proceedings were later published in book form under the title, ISSUES IN POPULATION EDUCATION, by Lexington Books/D. C. Heath.

In the last half of the 1970s, suitable textbooks in medical ethics became available for classroom use, confirming a new importance accorded medical ethics in colleges and universities all over the world. Public interest in ethical questions in medicine increased still further in 1975 with the New Jersey Superior Court's decision concerning the maintenance or withdrawal of life-preserving treatments of Karen Ann Quinlan.

This section includes some of the best recent work in medical ethics, including excellent pieces on AIDS and articles reflecting the feminist perspective on medical ethics. At the same time (except when unavoidable) good pieces that have been reprinted countless times have been omitted. Nor does the list of articles include only writings by philosophers. In some sympathy with the widely held view that progress will best come in this field with many disciplines participating, authors with varied backgrounds are represented.

As before, the list is not intended to be comprehensive. Instead, the hope is that these readings will stimulate further research on the issues. Some of the articles deal with ethical issues that are comparatively new in medicine—often born from developments in the new reproductive technologies. Various articles deal with euthanasia, embryo research, childbearing contracts and the teaching of medical ethics. Also, in keeping with the desire to display the affinities between the various branches of applied ethics whenever possible, there are some pieces on the business side of medicine.

In "Euthanasia For Incompetent Patients, A Proposed Model," Professor Haber raises the question of whether a surrogate decision to discontinue life-sustaining medical treatment can be made on behalf of a terminally ill patient. It is possible that the spirit of Haber's paper is closest to Jansen's. Jansen deals, directly or indirectly, with the question of when human life begins. The question of when meaningful human life *ends* is really the mirror image of that question.

Haber's piece was also included because it relates strongly to Professor Murphy's article in the journalistic ethics section. As the reader will see, both pieces involve complex questions relating to privacy. Using two landmark court cases as a basis, Haber argues that a decision to end life may be made provided certain conditions are met designed to protect the patient against possible abuses. He then proceeds to list these conditions and argues that they withstand the traditional objections against surrogate euthanasia decisions.

Perhaps the only problem I have with Haber's analysis is with his answer to a serious problem with euthanasia. This objection, in Haber's words, is that ". . . physicians often misdiagnose maladies or that new treatments are frequently discovered." He answers by urging that "The model . . . assures the court, beyond a reasonable doubt, that the patient has no reasonable chance of recovery and that a miraculous treatment is not foreseeable."

While this may sidestep the legal force of the objection, it does not appear to satisfy the objection when the objection is intended solely as a description of reality—of what might, in fact, happen or not happen. That is, it seems to be true, plainly and simply, that physicians do misdiagnose and that in any given case of a "terminal" illness, there is a chance, no matter how remote, that something will be discovered. Is being sure "beyond a reasonable doubt" good enough?

"Sperm and Ova as Property" asks the question: To whom do sperm and ova belong? Few tissues are produced by the human body with more waste than the sperm cells. Yet dominion over the sperm cells, and over the early embryo that results from their union in vitro is behind much of the emotion that modern reproductive intervention can engender. The sperm cells differ from other human tissues that can be donated or transplanted because they carry readily utilizable genetic information. Eventual expression of the germ cells' genetic potential is the legitimate concern and responsibility of their donors, although in the right circumstances the responsibility can by agreement be entrusted to institutions administering gamete or embryo donor programs; these institutions, in turn, may need to assume responsibility for decisions if, in the case of embryo storage, the wishes of the two donors conflict. The fact of sperm and ovum ownership (and the genetic potential that goes with it) before individuals part with these tissues is beyond dispute. Some contentious issues may be clarified if this area of human dominion, namely control over genetic expression among offspring, is acknowledged to be the legitimate persisting concern of those who have produced sperm and ova after storage begins. Given all this, Jansen's paper bears some relationship to Brown's insofar as both deal with the general issue of treating human or at least potential human tissue as "commodities."

The strongest part of Jansen's paper seems to be the attack on the Warnock Committee report, which he accuses of putting forth "inflexible recommendations." In his view, it is not unreasonable to suppose that sperm, ova and even embryos can become the "property" of the donors. As Jansen himself points out, the Warnock Committee's recommendations to the contrary may have been motivated by fear of and desire to forestall trade in human embryos. Certainly this is a legitimate fear, especially given the importance of the issue of experimentation on embryos. It may be that some more subtle distinctions will have to be made. A possible clue lies in Jansen's remark that "This potential should always remain the responsibility, the provenance, the dominion, perhaps the property, of the donor." It is possible that "property" is too strong, and that "dominion" may be the right word. It seems reasonable, for example, to say that one may be entrusted with children and have dominion over them, but not own them. In any case these issues need further exploration. Dr. Bok discusses similar issues in her paper.

Professor Dyer's paper was selected not only for its excellence, but for its obvious connection with business and journalistic ethics, in that it focuses on advertising in medicine. In it, he discusses the growing question of whether the medical profession has been and continues to be in restraint of trade because physicians are not allowed to advertise.

Recently the FTC has attemped to define medicine as a trade precisely to overcome this problem. As Professor Dyer sees it, the concept of a profession, both legally, historically, sociologically and philosophically, involves an ethic of service just as much as technical skills. (That being the case, it is worth comparing his analysis with Professor Silvers', who also discusses the concept of a profession.) He suggests that the medical profession should "pay more attention to its service ideal at this time when doctors are widely perceived to be technically preoccupied.

According to the piece, "Teaching Ethics on Rounds: The Ethicist as Teacher, Consultant, and Decision-Maker," there is—or ought to be a close relationship between consulting and discussion in clinical medical ethics. Given the emphasis on teaching, this paper clearly relates to Sir Wolstenholme's paper on teaching medical ethics. However, I believe it would be useful to compare Thomasma's paper and Serafini's as well as Professor Madsen's piece on education and business ethics, since part of the point of this anthology is to draw out the affinities between the various branches of professional ethics.

The authors present two possible models of the ethics consultant, arguing that one of the prime functions of the consultant is making decision-making easier and more efficient. In their concluding section they point to some of the challenges in clinical ethics teaching.

One interesting point is that Thomasma *et al.*, appear to endorse the concept of ethical guidelines or codes. Given the experience of journalists with these codes, one has to look carefully at the recommendations for such codes in other areas of professional ethics.

Sir Wolstenholme, in his article "Teaching Medical Ethics in Other Countries," points out that in the past 20 years there has been enormous growth in the teaching of medical ethics around the world. As mentioned above, it should be noted that Thomasma's paper deals with the same general issue. It appears that this teaching is bound to have its greatest effect not at the undergraduate period, but in graduate and postgraduate work. The work in this field is best justified if it leads to better international cooperation among physicians, according to Sir Wolstenholme.

Again, criticism is mostly off the point with a paper such as this. Perhaps the only point to be made is that it would surely be good if either Sir Wolstenholme or another would extend this sort of research to cover more Third World countries.

"The Unruly Rise of Medical Capitalism" is Professor James Morone's excellent contribution to this book. Dealing, as it does, with the business side of medicine, it unquestionably must be studied along with Professor Dyer's piece on advertising in medicine; for if the trend Morone discusses continues, one could reasonably expect to see more advertising by physicians, or by the corporations controlling them.

The piece itself is a description of corporate capitalism's increasing involvement with the practice of medicine over the years.

He points out that companies that did not even exist 20 years ago now own nursing homes, hospital supply companies, etc. He explains on a philosophical basis—that the United States, unlike most industrial nations—has tended to reject the idea of health care as a fundamental human right which ought to be provided by the state. That, coupled with powerful lobbying efforts by physicians to remain autonomous, has effectively stymied any meaningful state action.

One problem I have with this is that it does not seem to me that Morone has actually *proven* some of his theses. He argues, for example, that business-owned medicine will inevitably turn away from the patients' best interests, since the point of a corporation is to make a profit, rather than provide quality care. ("The threat to medical judgment can be traced not simply to *ad hoc* accounts of pressured physicians . . . but to the logic of the organizational form itself.")

While this may be true, it also appears true that, in general, and, admittedly with many exceptions, history has shown that any business has to ultimately satisfy the consumer. Indeed, as Morone himself seems to admit, business intervention has been able to ". . . increase the intensity of care, attract physicians with the latest technology and private bathrooms and color television."

While Morone seems skeptical of the latter, are they not important? Surely some sense of dignity and even some luxuries are not too much to ask for anyone suffering in a hospital. His real point, though he doesn't elaborate on it, is that corporations increased the quality of care for the *relatively well-to-do*. That, of course, is true. But the question is where to look for the root cause of the plight of the poor. Is it the corporations, or something more fundamental about the American way of life?

In "Kindnesses and Duties in the Abortion Issue," Professor Michael Matthis takes yet one more look at Professor Thomson's classic and widely discussed article, "A Defense of Abortion." As this piece deals with the general question of rights over human tissue, Professor Matthis' piece should be studied in conjunction with the articles by Davies and Jansen, especially the latter.

As Matthis interprets her analysis, her primary position is that no one has any right to demand another's help unless that person has explicitly authorized it through a prior agreement.

He then identifies the central problem in Thomson's argument as her unexamined faith in the notion that "unkind" or indecent actions are conceptually the opposite of kind and decent acts. He then tries to show, via some ingenious argumentation, that the assumption is false. To this end, he argues that if failure to be kind is to be unkind, then a "kind" act can never be "morally neutral," as Thomson claims. His last step is to assert that if it indeed is false, then it does not follow that such acts are "morally neutral," as Thomson claims. But if that thesis collapses, then Thomson's entire position caves in.

Perhaps the stickiest point in Matthis' claim is his suggestion that "Assuredly, unkindness *means* the opposite of kindness, but the exact conceptual opposite of kindness, that is, the act that signifies a *failure* to be kind, is something else." He buttresses the point by suggesting (tentatively) that "indifference" or "obliviousness" may instead be the conceptual opposite of kindness. Yet it seems the case that, under appropriate circumstances, the latter terms could also *mean* the opposite of "kindness." If that is so, then what becomes of his claim that "conceptually opposite" and "difference in meaning" are two different things?

"Medical Ethics in the Clinical Setting: Challenging the MD Monopoly," is Dr. Janet Fleetwood's contribution to the same issue as dealt with by Sir Wolstenholme and Thomasma *et al*. While she appears to be in general agreement with Thomasma's position, she focuses more on what kinds of specific changes should be made in medicine to incorporate the role of the ethicist. Interestingly, she argues that " . . . ethicists in a clinical setting should limit themselves to suggesting morally appropriate alternatives, encouraging open discussion and facilitating clear conceptual analysis."

In her piece, Dr. Fleetwood reviews the role of the medical ethicist in a clinical setting, focusing on two major areas—educational activities and institutional projects. She argues that challenging the MD monopoly in medical ethics requires a strong philosophic background, a familiarity with modern medicine, and a willingness to interact and collaborate with health care professionals at all levels. She further points out that this relatively new collaboration between doctors and medical ethicists reflects the recognition of the need for change, as well as the strong desire on both sides to make those changes in a reasoned and systematic way.

The relatively limited role Dr. Fleetwood assigns to the medical ethicist in a clinical setting, however, undercuts the possibility for influence. If it is indeed true that, as she puts it, "Medical ethicists, unlike neurosurgeons, . . . are not certified specialists with greater moral expertise . . . ," then it is indeed difficult to see why medical personnel should pay heed to their advice. However, it is hard not to believe that, in fact, trained ethicists *do* possess greater moral expertise. (This does not mean, of course, that ethicists are *themselves* more moral. These two very different positions are often confused with one another.) Surely, for example, Professor Thomson's abilities to conceptually analyze ethical problems in medicine must be greater than that of the average nurse or GP?

In re Storar: Euthanasia for Incompetent Patients, A Proposed Model

Joram Graf Haber

I. Introduction

Euthanasia,[1] or mercy killing, is a subject of increasing judicial concern.[2] The New York Court of Appeals recently addressed this concern when it decided *In re Storar*[3] and its companion case, *Eichner v. Dillon.*[4] Both *Storar* and *Eichner* presented the question of whether a surrogate decision to discontinue life-sustaining medical treatment can be made on behalf of an incompetent patient, diagnosed as fatally ill, with no reasonable chance of recovery.[5]

Part II of this note details the facts of *Storar* and *Eichner*. Part III explores the legal principles governing these cases, including the doctrines of informed consent and the right of privacy. Part IV examines how the court of appeals applied these principles and Part V analyzes the court's decisions. After concluding that neither informed consent nor the right of privacy are adequate doctrines with which to decide euthanasia cases, Part VI proposes a model which provides constructive guidance to those upon whom the burden of making a surrogate decision is placed.

---

* Professor Haber teaches philosophy at the C.W. Post campus of Long Island University and also has taught at Hunter College. He holds an M.A. in Philosophy from Columbia University and has a J.D. from the Pace School of Law.

II. Facts[6]

Eichner concerned Brother Joseph Fox, an 83-year-old member of a Catholic religious order, whose life was being maintained on a respirator in a permanent vegetative state.[7] He entered this state following a hernia operation during which he suffered cardiac arrest, with resulting loss of oxygen to the brain and substantial brain damage.[8] Before the operation rendered him incompetent, Brother Fox had indicated that he would not wish to be placed on a respirator if he ever entered a vegetative state. He had first expressed his desire in 1976, when his religious order, the Society of Mary, discussed the implications of the *Quinlan* case; and later, after the Pope had announced that Catholicism permitted the termination of extraordinary life-support systems.[9]

Father Phillip Eichner, the director of the Society, asked the hospital to remove the respirator on the ground that continuing it was against the patient's wishes expressed prior to becoming incompetent. He made this request after consulting physicians regarding the hopelessness of Brother Fox's condition.[10] The hospital refused to discontinue the respirator without a court order.[11]

In re Storar concerned John Storar, a profoundly retarded 52-year-old man with terminal cancer of the bladder.[12] He had been a member of a state facility, the Newark Development Center, since he was five, and had the mental age of about eighteen months.[13] In 1979, physicians at the Center noticed blood in his urine and, after diagnostic tests, determined that he had cancer of the bladder.[14] After a period of remission, physicians again noticed blood in his urine and concluded that the cancer was terminal.[15] In an effort to compensate for the loss of blood, the physicians recommended that he undergo blood transfusions which, while painful, were needed to sustain the patient's life.[16]

John Storar's mother was his legal guardian and closest relative.[17] She resided near the facility and had visited him daily from the time he was institutionalized.[18] Upon learning of the need for transfusions, she consented but later withdrew her consent believing that it would only prolong his discomfort and be against his wishes were he able to express them.[19] A state official then brought a proceeding, pursuant to section 33.03 of the Mental Hygiene Law,[20] seeking permission to continue transfusions.[21]

In each case, the trial courts and appellate divisions held that treatment should be discontinued.[22] The orders of the lower courts were stayed, however, and treatment continued pending appeal. In the interim, both patients died. The court of appeals reviewed the cases despite the mootness of their issues, reversing *Storar* and modifying *Eichner*.[23]

In *Eichner*, the court of appeals held that the removal of Brother Fox's respirator was supported by the common law right of a competent adult to refuse medical treatment, even if necessary to sustain life.[24] The court reasoned that since, prior to becoming incompetent, Brother Fox had manifestly refused to be placed on a respirator, removal was authorized at Father Eichner's request.[25] In *Storar*, by contrast, the court declined to apply this common law theory since at no time in his life had John Storar been competent. Instead, the court ruled that John Storar was functionally an infant, and held that while the parent of an infant has the right to consent to medical treatment on an infant's behalf, he may not deprive the infant of lifesaving treatment.[26] The court also invoked the principle of *parens patriae,* reasoning that the state's interest in protecting the welfare of the child outweighs a parent's interest in refusing medical treatment.[27]

III. Governing Principles

A. Common Law Principles

The law treats mercy killing no differently than other cases involving the taking of human life.[28] What distinguishes euthanasia from homicide or suicide is not so much the law as it is written, but rather the law as it is applied.[29] For example, those who take life out of mercy are frequently not indicted. If the killer is indicted, he is often acquitted or convicted of a lesser offense.[30] These disparities in the application of the law have alerted the judiciary to the need for a consistent doctrine with which to decide euthanasia cases.[31]

One doctrine which the courts have frequently employed is that of informed consent.[32] Originally articulated by Judge Cardozo in *Schloendorff v. Society of New York Hospital,*[33] and more recently affirmed in *Natanson v. Kline,*[34] the crux of the doctrine provides that "every human being of adult years and sound mind has a right to determine what shall be done to his own body."[35] From this, the courts have deduced that if a patient has control over any decision affecting medical treatment, his right to consent implies his right to refuse as well.[36]

The doctrine of informed consent stems from a premise of Anglo-American law that each individual has the inalienable right to self-determination.[37] According to this premise, there are certain decisions an individual must be permitted to make even if he decides them irrationally or incorrectly.[38] As Justice Burger wrote, sitting as a district judge, in a dissenting opinion to *In re President and Directors of Georgetown College, Inc.,*[39] "some matters of essentially private concern and others of enormous public concern . . . are beyond the reach of judges."[40]

The doctrine of informed consent also furthers one of the objectives of tort law. To the extent that tort law seeks to achieve an efficient allocation of resources, it aspires to place the responsibility for particular decisions upon those best able to avoid the costs arising from those decisions.[41] Thus, while the physician can best determine a patient's medical needs, the patient can best determine his nonmedical needs. The cost to the physician of discovering the patient's psychological, social and business needs is simply too great. Only the patient sufficiently knows his own value preferences so as to determine the desirability of a particular course of treatment.

B. Constitutional Considerations

Another doctrine the courts have employed in an effort to decide euthanasia cases involves the constitutionally protected right of privacy. Originally articulated by Justice Douglas in *Griswold v. Connecticut,*[42] and later expanded in *Roe v. Wade,*[43] the right of privacy protects certain decisions which are so private that they are beyond the reach of the state. In *Griswold,* for example, the Supreme Court invalidated a Connecticut statute proscribing the use of contraceptives by married couples.[44] And in *Roe,* the Supreme Court held that a woman has, within certain limits, the right to decide whether or not to have an abortion.[45]

The right of privacy as applied to medical treatment appears to have been inspired by Justice Brandeis in a dissenting opinion to *Olmstead v. United States.*[46] There, he spoke of a "right to be let alone."[47] Relying upon this rationale, Justice Burger later averred that "such privacy includes the right to refuse medical treatment."[48] Utilizing this rationale, a Pennsylvania district court in *In re Yetter*[49] later held that the constitutional right of privacy includes the right of a mature competent adult to refuse medical treatment that may prolong his life.[50] And it was this theory which the New Jersey Supreme Court principally employed in deciding the celebrated case of *In re Quinlan*.[51]

IV. The Court of Appeals' Decisions in *In re Storar*

Although *Eichner*[52] and *Storar*[53] are facially similar in that both give rise to the surrogate issue, each was decided upon different principles. In *Eichner*, the court of appeals invoked the doctrine of informed consent in holding that approval for the discontinuance of Brother Fox's respirator was supported by the common law right of a competent adult to refuse medical treatment.[54] The court reasoned that since, prior to becoming incompetent, Brother Fox manifestly refused to be placed on a respirator,[55] removal was authorized at Father Eichner's request.[56] The court declined to reach the constitutional issue since common law principles supported its decision.[57]

In *Storar*, the court of appeals refused to invoke the doctrine of informed consent since at no time in his life had John Storar been competent.[58] The court reasoned that it would be futile to speculate whether he would want such treatment since he was never able to make reasoned decisions.[59] Accordingly, the court ruled that the patient was functionally an infant and subject to the state's interest as *parens patriae*.[60] Since New York Public Health Law section 2504(2)[61] permits a parent to consent to medical treatment on an infant's behalf, but not to deprive him of lifesaving treatment, the mother's request was denied.[62]

V. Analysis of the Court's Reasoning

A. Failing To Decide the Surrogate Issue

In both *Storar* and *Eichner*, the court of appeals was asked to decide whether a surrogate decision to discontinue life-sustaining medical treatment could be made on behalf of a dying incompetent patient. In neither case, did the court comply. In *Eichner*, the court sidestepped the issue by relying upon the patient's prior informed consent rather than the surrogate's motives and desires. In *Storar*, the court evaded the issue by declaring the patient functionally an infant and then invoking public health laws and the doctrine of *parens patriae*.[63]

It is easy to see why the court was evasive. The surrogate issue, if answered affirmatively, may conflict with existing state laws against homicide and suicide. As previously mentioned, the law treats mercy killing no differently than other cases involving the taking of human life.[64] It is at least arguable that if a court were to sanction the termination of one's life at another's request, then the court as well as the requesting party would be a partner to the "crime."[65] On the other hand, if the surrogate issue were answered negatively, then the court would be faced with the moral dilemma of prolonging the agony of one who is presently incurable, suffering, and beyond the aid of potential respite.[66] It is for these reasons that courts resort to the doctrine of informed consent or, alternatively, to the constitutional right of privacy. Both doctrines shift the burden of making the life-death decision away from the court and on to the patient.

Despite the appeal of these two doctrines, each is highly problematic. The doctrine of informed consent is inapposite when applied to situations where a patient is irrevocably unconscious, and a surrogate decision is requested on his behalf. In this situation, either the patient is unconscious and informed consent cannot be obtained, or, the patient has failed to manifest his consent prior to becoming incompetent.[67] Unlike Brother Fox, many people, for psychological reasons, refuse to address the issue of euthanasia when they are healthy and competent.[68] And for those who do address the issue at a time when they are healthy and competent, it is arguable that their decisions would differ when faced with an actual life-death situation.

The right of privacy is similarly of questionable utility.[69] First, it is by no means settled that the right of privacy encompasses the right to die. *Quinlan*[70] notwithstanding, the Supreme Court has repeatedly declined to consider whether the right to die is an incident of the right of privacy.[71] Second, even if there is a constitutionally protected right to die, it may not be exercisable by third parties since the law generally grants standing only to those parties whose own constitutional rights have been violated.[72]

By a careful ellipsis, the court of appeals refused to address the problems raised by these two doctrines. Of course, one could argue that for this very reason its decision is sound, since directly deciding the surrogate issue might raise greater problems than it would ostensibly solve. Opponents of third-party decisions frequently fear that allowing surrogate decisions in some cases, for example, where a patient is terminally ill, suffering, and has no reasonable chance of recovery, opens the door to allowing third-party decisions in other cases, such as where a person has outgrown his usefulness to society, or where a person is prone to criminal activity and is "beyond rehabilitation."[73] Having entertained the surrogate issue however, the court of appeals should have addressed these subsidiary issues directly. As Judge Jones argued in dissent, the majority's decision fails to provide constructive guidance to the person on whom the burden of making a surrogate decision falls.[74]

B. Departing From the Doctrine of Mootness

The court's evasiveness is further compounded by the fact that it decided moot issues. As a general rule, courts may not decide moot questions, only actual cases or controversies.[75] An exception to this rule permits courts to review moot questions if there is a showing of: (1) significant questions not previously passed on; (2) a likelihood of repetition; and (3) phenomena typically evading review.[76]

The exception to the doctrine of mootness makes sense only on the assumption that a court's decision will provide constructive guidance in gray areas of law. Otherwise, the task is best reserved for the legislature. Thus, in those cases where the doctrine has been applied, courts have consistently held that only in exceptional cases, where the urgency of establishing a rule of future conduct is imperative and manifest, will a departure from mootness be justified.[77] Since In re Storar failed to decide the surrogate issue, but rather relied upon a set of uncontroversial doctrines,[78] the court's decision to decide moot questions was unjustified. Little is gained by throwing red herrings at academic questions.

VI. Constructive Guidance for Resolving the Surrogate Issue: A Proposed Model

A. The Model of Substituted Judgment

The court of appeals' decision in *In re Storar*[79] underscores the need for a model providing constructive guidance for deciding the surrogate issue.[80] Such a model should contain a body of operating principles which provide a defensible rationale for making life-death decisions, and should also be simple enough to be readily applicable. The following model strives to satisfy the foregoing criteria.

A vicarious decision to terminate life-sustaining medical treatment on behalf of a terminally ill incompetent patient should be authorized where, under the totality of the circumstances, the patient is a proper candidate for euthanasia, and the party requesting termination of treatment is sufficiently related to the patient so he can speak on the patient's behalf with respect to the patient's interests, desires, and beliefs.[81]

To satisfy the first requirement that the patient is a proper candidate for euthanasia, the surrogate would prove, *beyond a reasonable doubt*,[82] that the patient is terminally ill with no reasonable chance of recovery and that either (1) the patient is irreversibly comatose, or (2) the patient is suffering and sustaining his life would only prolong his suffering.[83] Having demonstrated this, he would next convince the court, by *clear and convincing* evidence,[84] that he is competent to speak on the patient's behalf. Criteria to consider in determining the competency of the surrogate would include the following:

(1) The surrogate's relationship to the patient, including the quality of the relationship;
(2) The surrogate's past and present associations with the patient, including the quality of the associations;
(3) The extent to which the surrogate is acquainted with the patient's past moral and religious convictions (if any), including awareness of their strength and fortitude;
(4) The surrogate's ability to comprehend and appreciate the solemnity of the decision;
(5) The reasons and motives for the surrogate's request; and
(6) Any other factor(s) which would tend to establish the surrogate's competency to speak on behalf of the dying patient.[85]

This model, which might be labeled the model of substituted judgment, withstands the canonical arguments usually advanced against the legalization of euthanasia.[86] Those opposed to euthanasia often claim that human life is inviolable and that it ought not to be taken under any circumstances.[87] The model answers this argument by requiring a threshold inquiry into whether a patient is a proper candidate for euthanasia, which assures the court that no reasonable man would choose to live under such circumstances. This threshold determination is met by requiring the surrogate to prove, beyond a reasonable doubt, that the patient is terminally ill with no reasonable chance of recovery and is either irreversibly comatose, or suffering and that sustaining his life would only prolong his suffering. In such states, dying persons see or would see themselves as stripped of their dignity and character.[88]

A second argument against euthanasia is that physicians often misdiagnose maladies or that new treatments are frequently discovered.[89] The model's initial inquiry, however, assures the court, beyond a reasonable doubt, that the patient has no reasonable chance of recovery and that a miraculous treatment is not foreseeable. This reply is similar to the rebuttal frequently made to opponents of capital punishment. The fact that capital punishment is irreversible is not, by itself, a compelling reason against its employment. As in all criminal cases, the defendant must be proved guilty beyond a reasonable doubt—the same burden suggested here.

A third argument is that giving wide discretion to interested parties, such as doctors and family members, concerning the conditions under which euthanasia is appropriate, creates a risk of abuse so serious that it far outweighs the benefits of terminating life. The model, however, provides adequate safeguards in applying the criteria under which a court will authorize a surrogate decision.

Criterion (1) requires the court to examine the relationship between the surrogate and the patient. The court would determine whether the surrogate is a relative, and if so, how closely related he is to the patient.[90] If, for example, the surrogate is the dying patient's spouse, and not estranged from the patient, this would weigh in favor of authorizing a surrogate decision.[91] If, on the other hand, the surrogate is a friend or distant relative who just recently expressed an interest in the patient's welfare, this would weigh against authorizing a surrogate decision. In any event, the court should look beyond facial sufficiency to determine the possibility of collusion.[92]

Criterion (2) requires the court to examine the surrogate's past and present associations with the patient. The court would determine to what extent the surrogate knew the patient so as to be able to make a substituted judgment on his behalf. Frequency of association and depth of association would weigh heavily in favor of the surrogate's authorization. Conversely, if the surrogate and the patient were only casually acquainted, this would weight against his authorization.

Criterion (3) requires the court to examine the extent to which the surrogate is acquainted with the patient's past moral and religious convictions (if any), and his awareness of their strength and fortitude. The court would determine whether and to what extent the patient has previously manifested his views on euthanasia and the conditions under which they were revealed.[93] The possibilities here are endless. If, for example, the patient was an avid anti-euthanasianist prior to becoming incompetent, this would weigh heavily against authorizing euthanasia. If he was silent on the issue, and the surrogate proves that the patient was fanatical about his religion, which included as one of its tenets the approval of euthanasia, this would weigh in favor of court authorization. And if the patient had indicated his approval of euthanasia, but did so casually and on just one occasion, this, without more, would weigh against authorization.

Criterion (4) requires the court to examine the surrogate's ability to comprehend and appreciate the seriousness of the decision. The surrogate must persuade the court by clear and convincing evidence, that he is of sufficient age and intelligence to make a decision on the patient's behalf. He must prove that he fully appreciates the patient's condition, the medical procedures that are presently available, and the solemnity of the occasion.

Criterion (5) requires the court to examine the reasons and motives for the surrogate's request. A surrogate may request euthanasia for a variety of reasons. The usual situation is where the surrogate observes the patient's suffering and pain and is motivated out of compassion to end that suffering.[94] It is conceivable, however, that the surrogate may be motivated by malice, personal profit, or the financial burden of providing health care that delays death through the use of expensive mechanical devices. The court would determine to what extent any of these motives are sufficiently meritorious so as to effect authorization. It should again look beyond facial sufficiency.[95]

Criterion (6) is a catch-all provision which enables the court to examine any additional factors which would tend to establish or negate the surrogate's competency to speak on behalf of the dying patient. The model and its six criteria provide a totality of the circumstances test which gives the court wide latitude in examining the surrogate.

A final argument opposing euthanasia is that any euthanasia proposals which permit the taking of human life, will erode other structures against the taking of human life.[96] The model with its above criteria, however, adequately safeguards the sanctity of human life. Not only must the surrogate prove, beyond a reasonable doubt, that the patient is a proper candidate for euthanasia, but he must also prove, by clear and convincing evidence, that he himself is competent to make a substitute judgment. Both standards are difficult to meet and adequately assure a just determination.[97]

The proposed model must also withstand application of the existing laws concerning homicide and suicide. The model assumes that there is a morally relevant distinction between "causing death" and "allowing a person to die" which should be incorporated into our legal system. There are many who argue that there is an important difference between standing aside and letting someone die and actively pushing that person toward death.[98] When a person is allowed to die it is his disease or condition that causes death; but if an individual administers a toxic drug, then that individual actively causes the patient's death. In the one case death seems to be natural, while in the other case it is artificially induced. Because of this distinction, the law should distinguish euthanasia and except it from the laws concerning homicide and suicide.[99] In this way, neither the surrogate nor the court would be parties to a "crime."[100]

The proposed model is also preferable to existing doctrines which have been used to decide euthanasia cases. It is preferable to the right of privacy at least to the extent the Supreme Court maintains its silence on whether the right of privacy includes the right to die, and whether the right of privacy may be vicariously asserted. It is preferable to informed consent since it is not restricted to those cases in which a patient has manifestly demonstrated his consent prior to becoming incompetent. Although as previously indicated it is questionable to what extent an individual can ever make a reasoned decision concerning his own death, the proposed model makes prior consent one of several factors in determining surrogate competency. To this extent, it mitigates the argument so damaging to informed consent theory; that informed consent, an arguable fiction when applied to decisions to discontinue life-sustaining treatment, should not be the sole determinative factor.[101]

B. The Model of Substituted Judgment as Applied to In re Storar and Eichner v. Dillon

In *Eichner*,[102] the proposed model of substituted judgment could have been applied as follows. Father Eichner, having been refused his request that the hospital remove Brother Fox's respirator, would apply for a court order authorizing removal.[103] To prevail, he would have to establish, beyond a reasonable doubt, that Brother Fox was terminally ill with no reasonable chance of recovery, and that he was (1) irreversibly comatose, or (2) suffering and that sustaining his life would only prolong his suffering.

Father Eichner would arguably have met this burden since there was uncontroverted evidence that there was no reasonable chance of recovery, and that Brother Fox would never emerge from his vegetative coma or regain his cognitive ability.[104] The court would then determine whether Father Eichner was competent to substitute his judgment for that of Brother Fox by applying the six criteria. First, it would inquire into the relationship between Father Eichner and Brother Fox. Father Eichner was the director of a religious order of which Brother Fox was a member.[105] The fact that he, and not a family member, requested removal might be a factor which would weigh against court authorization, especially since the record was silent as to how long Father Eichner knew Brother Fox and whether or not he knew him well. While it is true that Father Eichner's request was supported by Brother Fox's ten nieces and nephews,[106] the court would be cognizant that these are distant relatives and weigh this accordingly.

The second inquiry the court would make concerns Father Eichner's associations with Brother Fox. Again, the record was silent as to what extent Father Eichner knew Brother Fox so as to enable him to make a substituted judgment on his behalf. The director of a religious order may or may not have frequent and substantial contact with members under its auspices. Father Eichner would be required to demonstrate the extent to which he knew Brother Fox.

The third inquiry the court would make concerns the extent to which Father Eichner was familiar with Brother Fox's moral and religious convictions. Since Brother Fox clearly manifested that he would not desire to be placed on a respirator, and that he expressed this desire after having given thoughtful consideration to the gravity of his decision,[107] this would weigh heavily in favor of court authorization.

The fourth inquiry the court would make is whether Father Eichner himself is sufficiently able to appreciate the solemnity of his decision. Presumably, Father Eichner is an intelligent and thoughtful person who fully understands the gravity of the situation. He had consulted two neurosurgeons who confirmed the diagnosis and fully appreciated the religious implications of his decision. The fact that both he and Brother Fox apparently shared the same religious beliefs would further weigh in favor of authorization.

The court would finally inquire into the motives and reasons for Father Eichner's request. Although once again the record was silent, Father Eichner apparently desired a merciful end to Brother Fox's existence. Furthermore, since the director of a religious order is likely to be free of moral turpitude, his own reputation would be hard to impeach.

Assuming the absence of any other factors which might influence this decision, the court would weigh and balance the relevant factors in arriving at its decision. It is submitted that, on balance, the court would authorize Father Eichner's request although a contrary decision could justifiably be reached. The decision would turn, arguably, on the weight assigned to Brother Fox's past convictions against the apparant absence of a substantial nexus between Father Eichner and Brother Fox.

Storar[108] presents other difficulties. It is highly questionable whether Mrs. Storar could prove that her son is a proper candidate for euthanasia. Although John Storar was terminally ill with no reasonable chance of recovery, he was neither irreversibly comatose nor was it beyond a reasonable doubt that he was suffering to the extent that blood transfusions would only prolong his suffering.

It was conceded that John Storar found the blood transfusions to be disagreeable.[109] His physicians observed, however, that after the transfusions, he had more energy and was able to resume most of his usual activities.[110] While his physicians did recognize that it was possible that the transfusions would eventually be ineffective, at the time of the hearing they were highly efficacious.[111] There thus appears to be a reasonable doubt as to whether sustaining John Storar's life would only serve to prolong his agony.

Assuming arguendo that Mrs. Storar could meet her burden, the court would conduct its second line of inquiry. Mrs. Storar was obviously the patient's mother and had an honorable mother-son relationship. From the time her son was institutionalized, Mrs. Storar had visited him daily and had taken up residence near the facility.[112] These considerations would adequately satisfy the first two of the proposed criteria.

The third criterion would present some difficulties since any convictions John Storar might have had would have been tempered by the fact that he had the mental capacity of an eighteen-month-old child.[113] The fourth criterion would present even further difficulties since it is by no means clear that Mrs. Storar fully comprehended the ramifications of her decision. Apparently, Mrs. Storar desired the termination of treatment because she wanted her son to be comfortable, and admitted that no one had explained to her the implications of administering blood transfusions.[114] She was also hesitant about whether she truly desired to terminate treatment.[115]

With respect to the fifth criterion, Mrs. Storar's motives were seemingly meritorious since she desired only to alleviate her son's suffering. The reasons for her request were less than sufficient, however, since she did not fully understand the implications of her decision.[116]

Finally, Mrs. Storar admitted that she was not quite certain whether John Storar truly desired to die.[117] In view of this fact, as well as the above considerations, it is submitted that a court would decide, under the totality of the circumstances, that Mrs.

Storar was unable to speak on behalf of her son with respect to his interests, desires, and beliefs.[118] For this reason, authorization would be denied.

VII. Conclusion

Euthanasia is an extraordinarily complex issue. It involves such legal disciplines as criminal law, tort law, and contract law, as well as nonlegal disciplines such as philosophy, theology, and psychology. By relying on two doctrines of only marginal utility, the New York Court of Appeals in *In re Storar* failed to squarely address the surrogate issue, thus providing little guidance to those who are faced with resolving life-death decisions on behalf of others.

The inconsistency of the New York courts in their treatment of euthanasia cases underscores the need for a rationally defensible and easily applicable model for making life-death decisions. Furthermore, with future cases likely to increase as medical technology becomes more advanced, it is imperative that the judiciary provide clear and controlling legal principles. This note proposes such a model, which perhaps will aid future courts in their determination of cases such as *In re Storar*, and which, if adopted, will provide guidance to those upon whom the burden of making a surrogate decision is placed.

NOTES

1. The term "euthanasia," derived from the Greek meaning "painless death" (*eu* means painless, *thanatos* means death), is a broad term meaning mercy killing of all types. Euthanasia can refer to the positive action taken to end the life of an incurable patient (active euthanasia) or it can refer to the failure to take positive action to prolong the life of an incurable patient (passive euthanasia). Euthanasia may be performed with the patient's consent (voluntary euthanasia) or it can be performed without the patient's consent (nonvoluntary euthanasia). These distinctions are more than semantic. They underscore the difference between legally permissible action and murder in the first degree. *See* Note, *The Right to Die*, 7 Hous. L. Rev. 654, 659 (1970) [hereinafter cited as Note, *The Right to Die*]. *See infra* note 28 and accompanying text. As used in this

note, "euthanasia" means nonvoluntary passive euthanasia. Kurner, *Euthanasia: Due Process for Death with Dignity: The Living Will*, 54 IND. L.J. 201 (1979) [hereinafter cited as Kutner].

2. *See, e.g.,* the celebrated case of *In re* Quinlan, 137 N.J. Super. 227 (1975), *rev'd*, 70 N.J. 10, 335 A.2d 647, *cert. denied sub nom.* Garger v. New Jersey, 429 U.S. 922 (1976) (parents of 19-year-old girl requested that hospital authorities remove a respirator after the girl had entered a vegetative coma).

3. 52 N.Y.2d 363, 420 N.E.2nd 64, 438 N.Y.S.2d 266 (1981).

4. *Id.*

5. Throughout this paper, this question is referred to as the "surrogate issue." The courts are divided on how to decide the surrogate issue. *See* Ufford, *Brain Death/Termination of Heroic Efforts to Save Life-Who Decides?*, 19 WASHBURN L.J. 225, 255 (1980). *In re* Quinlan, 70 N.J. 10, 54, 335 A.2d 647, 671, *cert. denied sub nom.* Garger v. New Jersey, 429 U.S. 922 (1976), held that a surrogate decision to terminate life-sustaining treatment can be made without court approval if it is agreed to by a hospital ethics committee, a guardian *ad litem*, parents, and an attending physician, Superintendent of Belchertown State School v. Saikewicz, 373 Mass. 728, 756, 370 N.E.2d 417, 433 (1977), however, held that a probate court had to determine the choice of treatment for an incompetent 67-year-old man with an I.Q. of ten. In both *Quinlan* and *Saikewicz*, the court relied upon the constitutionally protected right of privacy which, they said, protects individuals from an unwarranted infringement of bodily integrity. *In re* Quinlan, 70 N.J. 10, 41, 335 A.2d 647, 664, *cert. denied sub nom.* Garger v. New Jersey, 429 U.S. 922 (1976); Superintendent of Belchertown State School v. Saikewicz, 373 Mass. at 738-39, 370 N.E.2d at 424.

   See infra text accompanying notes 42–51. *See also In re* Dinnerstein, 6 Mass. App. Ct. 466, 380 N.E.2d 134 (1978), which further limits Saikewicz.

6. The facts presented are from the two consolidated cases which are cited together as *In re* Storar, 52 N.Y.2d 363, 420 N.E.2d 64, 438 N.Y.S.2d 266 (1981).

7. *Id.* at 371, 420 N.E.2d at 67, 438 N.Y.S.2d at 269.

8. *Id.*

9. *Id.* at 371–72, 420 N.E.2d at 68, 438 N.Y.S.2d at 270. Brother Fox's desires were expressed during formal discussions prompted by the concern of his religious order to teach and promulgate Catholic moral principles.

10. *Id.* at 371, 420 N.E.2d at 67, 438 N.Y.S.2d at 269–70. Father Eichner consulted two neurosurgeons who confirmed the attending physicians' diagnosis that Brother Fox had lost the ability to breathe spontaneously and would require a respirator to maintain him in a permanent vegetative state.

11. *Id.* at 371, 420 N.E.2d at 67, 438 N.Y.S.2d at 269.

12. *Id.* at 373, 420 N.E.2d at 68, 438 N.Y.S.2d at 270–71.

13. *Id.* at 373, 420 N.E.2d at 68, 438 N.Y.S.2d at 270.

14. *Id.* at 373, 420 N.E.2d at 68–69, 438 N.Y.S.2d at 270–71.
15. *Id.*
16. *Id.* at 373–74, 420 N.E.2d at 69, 438 N.Y.S.2d at 271.
17. *Id.* at 373, 420 N.E.2d at 68, 438 N.Y.S.2d at 270.
18. *Id.*
19. *Id.* at 375, 420 N.E.2d at 69–70, 438 N.Y.S.2d at 272.
20. *See* N.Y. MENTAL HYG. LAW § 33.03 (McKinney 1978).
21. *In re* Storar, 52 N.Y.2d at 373–74, 420 N.E.2d at 69, 438 N.Y.S.2d at 271.
22. *Id.* at 369, 420 N.E.2d at 66, 438 N.Y.S.2d at 268. In *In re* Eichner, 73 A.D.2d 431, 460–61, 426 N.Y.S.2d 517, 536 (1980), the trial court based its decision on the common law right of bodily self-determination and the constitutionally protected right of privacy. In *In re* Storar, 106 Misc. 2d 880, 433 N.Y.S.2d 388 (Sup. Ct. Monroe County 1980), the trial court based its decision on an individual's right to decide what will be done to his own body and held that when a patient is incompetent, this right can be exercised by another on his behalf.
23. *In re* Storar, 52 N.Y.2d at 370, 420 N.E.2d at 67, 438 N.Y.S.2d at 269.
24. *Id.* at 376, 420 N.E.2d at 70, 438 N.Y.S.2d at 272. *See* Kutner, *supra* note 1, at 207: "Every man has the right . . . to forego treatment or even a cure if it involves what, to *him,* seem intolerable consequences or risks."
25. The court of appeals found the evidence on this point to be clear and convincing. They agreed that this was the appropriate burden and that it had been met. *In re* Storar, 52 N.Y.2d at 379–80, 420 N.E.2d at 72, 438 N.Y.S.2d at 274. *See* Addington v. Texas, 441 U.S. 418, 424 (1979) (Where particularly important personal interests are at stake, clear and convincing evidence should be required.).
26. *In re* Storar, 52 N.Y.2d at 380–81, 420 N.E.2d at 72–73, 438 N.Y.S.2d at 274–75. The court relied upon N.Y. PUB. HEALTH LAW § 2504(2) (McKinney 1977), which provides: "Any person who has been married or who has borne a child may give effective consent for medical, dental, health and hospital services for his or her child."
27. The state's interest, as *parens patriae,* is to protect the health and welfare of the child. Jehovah's Witnesses v. King County Hosp. Unit No. 1, 390 U.S. 598 (1968), *aff'd,* 278 F. Supp. 488, 504 (N.D. Wash. 1967); People *ex rel.* Wallace v. Labrenz, 411 Ill. 618, 623–24, 104 N.E.2d 769, 773, *cert. denied,* 344 U.S. 824 (1952); Annot. 30 A.L.R.2d 1138 (1953). *See also* Note, *The Right to Die, supra* note 1, at 664:

> The state's power to protect children and incompetent adults under the doctrine of *parens patriae* has been invoked on numerous occasions to require medical treatment for children over the objections of their parents. Such intervention by the courts has been justified on the premise that the lives of "youth, who constitute the hope of racial survival and progress, [are] of vital concern to the very life of the nation."

Id. (citing Morrison v. State, 252 S.W.2d 97, 103 (Mo. Ct. App. 1952));
cf. Prince v. Massachusetts, 321 U.S. 158, 166 (1944).

28. *See* Kamisar, *Some Non-Religious Views Against Proposed "Mercy-Kill-ing" Legislation,* 42 MINN. L. REV. 969, 970 n.9 (1958) [hereinafter cited as Kamisar]: "In Anglo-American jurisprudence a 'mercy-kill-ing' is murder. In theory, neither good motive nor consent of the victim is relevant." *See id.* at 970–71 n.9 (citing PERKINS, CRIMINAL LAW 721 (1957); 1 WHARTON, CRIMINAL LAW AND PROCEDURE § 194 (Anderson 1957); Orth, *Legal Aspects Relating to Euthanasia,* 2 MD. MED. J. 120 (1953) (symposium on euthanasia)). *See also* 2 W. BURDICK, LAW OF CRIME §§ 422, 447 (1946); J. MILLER, CRIMINAL LAW 55, 172 (1934); 48 MICH. L. REV. 1199 (1950); Annot., 25 A.L.R. 1007 (1923).

29. 13 RULING CASE LAW *Homicide* § 36 (1916).

30. *See, e.g.,* Repouille v. United States, 165 F.2d 152 (2d Cir. 1947); *cf.* Kutner, *supra* note 1, at 209 n.53 (citing People v. Werner, Crm. No. 58-3636 (Cook Co. Ct., Ill. 1958), where a 69-year-old defendant had suffocated his wife, a hopeless cripple bedridden by arthritis. "In arraignment proceedings, the state waived the murder charge and permitted the defendant to enter a guilty plea to the charge of manslaughter. The court then found the defendant guilty of this charge on his stipulated admission of killing. After hearing testimony of the defendant's . . ." care and devotion for his wife, the court allowed the defendant to withdraw his plea and entertained a plea of not guilty). *Id. But see* People v. Roberts, 211 Mich. 187, 178 N.W. 690 (1920), which represents one of the few cases where a mercy killer has been convicted for murder. In *Roberts,* the defendant-husband gave his dying wife poison at her request. The husband was found guilty of murder in the first degree because he had assisted his wife, who wished to die, by providing a means for her to commit suicide.

31. Legal commentary has also struggled to provide a viable rationale with which to decide euthanasia cases. *See, e.g.,* Sharpe & Hargest, *Lifesaving Treatment for Unwilling Patients,* 36 FORDHAM L. REV. 695 (1968); Note, *Unauthorized Rendition of Lifesaving Medical Treatment,* 53 CALIF. L. REV. 860 (1965); Note, *The Right to Die,* 7 HOUS. L. REV. 654 (1970); Note, *Compulsory Medical Treatment and the Free Exercise of Religion,* 42 IND. L.J. 386 (1967); Note, *The Dying Patient: A Qualified Right to Refuse Medical Treatment,* 7 J. FAM. L. 644 (1968); Note, *Compulsory Medical Treatment: The State's Interest Re-evaluated,* 51 MINN. L. REV. 293 (1966).

32. The doctrine of informed consent emerged out of medical malpractice suits as courts heard cases involving doctors treating patients without their consent. *See* Pratt v. Davis, 118 Ill. App. 161, 168 (1950), *aff'd,* 224 Ill. 300, 79 N.E. 562 (1906).

33. 211 N.Y. 125, 105 N.E. 92 (1914).

34. 186 Kan. 393, 350 P.2d 1093, *reh'g denied,* 187 Kan. 186, 354 P.2d 670 (1960).

35. Schloendorff v. Soc'y of N.Y. Hosp., 211 N.Y. 125, 129, 105 N.E. 92, 93 (1914).
36. *See* Erickson v. Dilgard, 44 Misc. 2d 27, 252 N.Y.S.2d 705 (Sup. Ct. 1962) (which held that an adult has the right to refuse medical treatment); Kutner, *supra* note 1, at 207. *But cf. In re* Collins, 44 Misc. 2d 622, 254 N.Y.S.2d 666 (Sup. Ct. 1964) (where the patient was compelled to accept treatment).
37. The underpinnings of the doctrine of informed consent can be traced to John Stuart Mill. *See* Mill, *On Liberty*, in THE PHILOSOPHY OF JOHN STUART MILL 185 (M. Cohen ed. 1961).
38. *See* 2 F. HARPER & F. JAMES, THE LAW OF TORTS 61 (Supp. 1968).
39. 331 F.2d 1010, 1015 (D.C. Cir. 1964) (Burger, J., dissenting), *cert. denied sub nom.* Jones v. President and Directors of Georgetown College, Inc., 377 U.S. 978 (1964).
40. *Id.* at 1018.
41. *See* Note, *Informed Consent and the Dying Patient*, 83 YALE L.J. 1632, 1645–46 (1974) (citing G. CALABRESI, THE COSTS OF ACCIDENTS (1969)).
42. 381 U.S. 479 (1965).
43. 410 U.S. 113 (1973).
44. Griswold v. Connecticut, 381 U.S. 479 (1965). Justice Douglas, writing for the Court, viewed several amendments of the Bill of Rights as creating "zones of privacy." *Id.* at 485. Justice Goldberg, concurring, found the right of privacy in the ninth amendment and therefore required the states to demonstrate a compelling interest for restriction of the right. *Id.* at 486–87. Justices White and Harlan, while not referring to "privacy" *per se* in their concurrences, considered the Connecticut statute unconstitutional under the fourteenth amendment. *Id.* at 500, 502. In recognizing the right of privacy, the Court did not articulate a definition, but rather left it to be developed on a case by case basis. *See* Eisenstadt v. Baird, 405 U.S. 438, 453 (1972) (Court recognized the "right of the *individual*, married or single, to be free from unwarranted governmental intrusion into matters so fundamentally affecting a person as the decision whether to bear or beget a child"); Stanley v. Georgia, 394 U.S. 557, 565 (1969) (individual has "the right to read or observe what he pleases" within his home).
45. Roe v. Wade, 410 U.S. 113 (1973). Justice Blackmun, writing for the majority, found only compelling state interests can justify governmental interference with this choice. *Id.* at 155. This decision rested on fourteenth amendment grounds. *But see* Doe v. Bolton, 410 U.S. 179 (1973) (Court relied on the right of privacy to invalidate a Georgia antiabortion statute without commenting on its origin).
46. 277 U.S. 438, 469 (1928) (Brandeis, J., dissenting).
47. *Id.* at 478.
48. *In re* President and Directors of Georgetown College, Inc., 331 F.2d 1010, 1015 (D.C. Cir.) (Burger, J., dissenting), *cert. denied sub nom.*

Jones v. President and Directors of Georgetown College, Inc., 377 U.S. 978 (1964).

49. Annot. 93 A.L.R.3d 67, 74 (1979) (citing *In re* Yetter, 62 Pa. D. & C.2d 619 (1973)).

50. *Id.* at 4. The lower court in *Yetter* said:

In our opinion the constitutional right of privacy includes the right of a mature competent adult to refuse to accept medical recommendations that may prolong one's life and which, to a third person at least, appear to be in his best interests, in short, that the right of privacy includes the right to die with which the state should not interfere.

51. 70 N.J. 10, 355 A.2d 647 (1976), *cert. denied sub nom.* Garger v. New Jersey, 429 U.S. 922 (1976).

52. *In re* Storar, 52 N.Y.2d 363, 420 N.E.2d 64, 438 N.Y.S.2d 266 (1981).

53. *Id.*

54. *In re* Storar, 52 N.Y.2d at 376, 420 N.E.2d at 70, 438 N.Y.S.2d at 272.

55. *See supra* note 9 and accompanying text.

56. *In re* Storar, 52 N.Y.2d at 371–72, 420 N.E.2d at 68, 438 N.Y.S.2d at 270. The District Attorney urged that a patient's right to refuse medical treatment conflicts with the state's interest in prohibiting one person from causing the death of another. *Id.* at 377, 420 N.E.2d at 71, 438 N.Y.S.2d at 273. According to the court of appeals, however, "a state which imposes civil liability on a doctor if he violates the patient's right cannot also hold him criminally responsibile if he respects that right." *Id.*

Unless "cannot" means "should not" in the court's statement, this reasoning is not entirely correct. It is true that existing statutory law supports the right of a competent adult to make his own decision by imposing civil liability on those who perform medical treatment without consent. It is not true that the state will not impose criminal liability if the doctor respects that right. Indeed, under New York law, this arguably constitutes aiding and abetting suicide which is manslaughter in the second degree. N.Y. PENAL LAW § 125.25(3) (McKinney 1975). *See* Note, *The Right to Die, supra* note 1, at 654–57; Note, *Informed Consent and the Dying Patient.* 83 YALE L.J. 1632, 1635 (1974).

57. *In re* Storar, 52 N.Y.2d at 376–77, 420 N.E.2d at 70, 438 N.Y.S.2d at 272–73. "Neither do we reach that question in this case because the relief granted to the petition, Eichner, is adequately supported by common-law principles." *Id.* at 377, 420 N.E.2d at 70, 438 N.Y.S.2d at 273. *See also* Byrn, *Compulsory Lifesaving Treatment for the Competent Adult,* 44 FORDHAM L. REV. 1, 15 n.64 (1975) [hereinafter cited as Byrn].

58. *See supra* notes 12–13 and accompanying text.

59. *In re* Storar, 52 N.Y.2d at 380, 420 N.E.2d at 72–73, 438 N.Y.S.2d at 274–75.

60. *Id.* at 380–81, 420 N.E.2d at 73, 438 N.Y.S.2d at 275.
61. N.Y. Pub. Health Law § 2504(2) (McKinney 1977). *See supra* note 26.
62. *In re* Storar, 52 N.Y.2d at 381–82, 420 N.E.2d at 73–74, 438 N.Y.S.2d at 276.
63. *See supra* notes 26–27.
64. *See supra* notes 28–29 and accompanying text.
65. This reasoning would also apply to physicians and hospital authorities involved in the decision.
66. A very strong case for this moral dilemma is presented in Kamisar, *supra* note 28, at 975.
67. Despite this difficulty, the doctrine of informed consent is widely used to decide euthanasia cases. *See, e.g.*, Natanson v. Kline, 186 Kan. 393, 350 P.2d 1093, *reh'g denied*, 187 Kan. 186, 354 P.2d 670 (1960); Mohr v. Williams, 95 Minn. 261, 268–69, 104 N.W. 12, 14–15 (1905); Schloendorff v. Soc'y of N.Y. Hosp., 211 N.Y. 125, 105 N.E. 92 (1914); Note, *Suicide and the Compulsion of Life Saving Medical Procedures: An Analysis of the Refusal of Treatment Cases*, 44 Brooklyn L. Rev. 285, 293 (1978) (citing Palm Springs Gen. Hosp. v. Martinez, Civ. No. 71–12,687 (Dade County Cir. Ct., filed July 2, 1971)); Byrn, *supra* note 49, at 13 n.58 (citing Palm Springs Gen. Hosp. v. Martinez, Civ. No. 71–12,687 (Dade County Cir. Ct., filed July 2, 1971)).
68. *See Preface* to E. Becker, The Denial of Death at ix (1973):

[T]he idea of death, the fear of it, haunts the human animal like nothing else; it is a mainspring of human activity—activity designed largely to avoid the fatality of death, to overcome it by denying in some way that it is the final destiny of man.

Id.

Becker's thesis raises the possibility that under no conditions can a person make a rational decision about his own death, but rather he is always *in extremis* hence *non compos mentis* concerning his ultimate destiny. *See generally Hearings to Explore the Problems of Treating Terminally Ill Patients Before the Special Senate Committee on Aging*, 92d Cong., 2d Sess. 68–70 (1972) (statement of W. Reich, Sr. Research Scholar, Georgetown U.); N. Brown, Life Against Death: The Psychoanalytical Meaning of History (1959); R. Dumont & D. Foss, The American View of Death: Acceptance or Denial? (1972); S. Grof & J. Halifax, The Human Encounter With Death (1977); M. Heidegger, Being and Time (1962); R. Kastenbaum & R. Aisenberg, The Psychology of Death (1972); S. Kierkegaard, The Sickness Unto Death (1954); E. Kubler-Ross, On Death and Dying (1969); J. Meyer, Death and Neurosis (1975); A. Weisman, On Dying and Denying (1972); Note, *Informed Consent and the Dying Patient*, 83 Yale L.J. 1632 (1974). This list is not exhaustive. *See also* Kamisar, *supra* note 28, at 989 n.56 (citing J. Walsh, *Life is Sacred*, 94

THE FORUM, 333, 333–34), which recalls the following Aesop's fable that illustrates Becker's thesis:

> It was a bitter-cold day in the wintertime, and an old man was gathering branches in the forest to make a fire at home. The branches were covered with ice, many of them were frozen and had to be pulled apart, and his discomfort was intense. Finally the poor old fellow became so thoroughly wrought up by his suffering that he called loudly upon death to come. To his surprise, Death came at once and asked what he wanted. Very hastily the old man replied, "Oh, nothing; nothing except to help me carry this bundle of sticks home so that I may make a fire."

> *Id.*

69. For an interesting discussion concerning the relative merits of informed consent and the right of privacy, *see In Re Storar: The Right to Die and Incompetent Patients*, 43 U. PITT. L. REV. 1087, 1097–98 (1982).
70. *In re* Quinlan, 70 N.J. 10, 355 A.2d 647, *cert. denied sub nom.* Garger v. New Jersey, 429 U.S. 922 (1976).
71. *In re* Storar, 52 N.Y.2d at 376, 420 N.E.2d at 70, 438 N.Y.S.2d at 272–73. Based on recent decisions, however, it would appear that if and when the Supreme Court does finally decide the issue, it will rule in favor of a patient's right to refuse ordinary medical treatment based on the right of privacy. The Court's decisive 7–2 margin in Roe v. Wade, 410 U.S. 113 (1972), is the clearest indicator. For legal commentary concerning this issue, *see* Brant, *The Right to Die in Peace: Substituted Consent and the Mentally Incompetent*, 11 SUFFOLK U. L. REV. 959 (1977); Cantor, *Quinlan, Privacy, and the Handling of Incompetent Dying Patients*, 30 RUTGERS L. REV. 243 (1977); Delgado, *Euthanasia Reconsidered—The Choice of Death as an Aspect of the Right of Privacy*, 17 ARIZ. L. REV. 474 (1975).
72. *See* Collester, *Death, Dying and the Law: A Prosecutorial View of the Quinlan Case*, 30 RUTGERS L. REV. 304 (1977) [hereinafter cited as Collester].
73. *See infra* note 95 and accompanying text.
74. *In re* Storar, 52 N.Y.2d 363, 383, 420 N.E.2d 64, 74, 438 N.Y.S.2d 266, 276 (1981) (Jones, J., dissenting). Judge Fuchsberg argued that the majority went too far after incanting the need for judicial restraint. *Id.* at 391–92, 420 N.W.2d at 79, 438 N.Y.S.2d at 281.

At least one commentator has argued that since mercy killers are rarely indicted, the surrogate problem is more illusory than real. *See* Kamisar, *supra* note 28, at 971. Others have argued that public confidence in the administration of law requires consistency of judgment and guidance as to moral conduct, neither of which are provided by reliance upon prosecutorial discretion or jury nullification. *See* Collester, *supra* note 72, at 313 (citing Silving, *Euthanasia: A Study in*

Comparative Criminal Law, 103 U. PA. L. REV. 350, 354 (1954)). This note sympathizes with the latter position.

75. *See in re* Hearst Corp., 50 N.Y.2d 707, 707–08, 409 N.E.2d 876, 877–78, 431 N.Y.S.2d 400, 402 (1980); *In re* Westchester Rockland Newspapers, Inc., 48 N.Y.2d 430, 436–37, 399 N.E.2d 518, 521, 423 N.Y.S.2d 630, 633–34 (1979); People v. Smith, 44 N.Y.2d 613, 617, 378 N.E.2d 1032, 1033–34, 407 N.Y.S.2d 462, 464 (1978); Gannett v. De Pasquale, 43 N.Y.2d 370, 376, 372 N.E.2d 544, 547, 401 N.Y.S.2d 756, 759 (1977); *In re* Oliver, 30 N.Y.2d 171, 177–78, 282 N.E.2d 306, 308, 331 N.Y.S.2d 407, 411 (1972). *See generally* H. COHEN & A. KARGER, POWERS OF THE NEW YORK COURT OF APPEALS 420–421 (1952).

76. Although the appeal has become moot and academic, we refrain from dismissing it because of the importance of the issue presented. Affecting as it does the administration of the emergency housing legislation in the City of New York, the question is one of major importance and, because it will arise again and again, one that invites immediate decision.

In re Rosenbluth, 300 N.Y. 402, 404, 91 N.E.2d 581, 581 (1950).

77. *See In re* Glenram Wine & Liquor Corp., 295 N.Y. 336, 340, 67 N.E.2d 570, 571 (1946). The appeal in this case involved a determination of the State Liquor Authority revoking a liquor license. The appeal was entertained even though the licensing period had expired, on the grounds that "the questions presented on this appeal are of importance in the administration of the Alcoholic Beverage Control Law and in the future conduct of the business of respondent and other licensees under said law." *Id.*

78. *In re* Storar, 52 N.Y.2d 363, 383, 420 N.E.2d 64, 74, 438 N.Y.S.2d 266, 276 (1981). Judge Jones said in partial concurrence, "Judge Wachtler's opinion constitutes an accurate and clear statement of the highest common factors on which all members of the court are in agreement." *Id.*

79. 52 N.Y.2d 363, 420 N.E.2d 64, 438 N.Y.S.2d 266 (1981).

80. *See* Clark, *When Doctors Play God*, NEWSWEEK, Aug. 31, 1981, at 52, col. 2; "New York's high court [in *In re* Storar] did little to clarify the issue of terminating treatment."

81. The surrogate issue is directly addressed by focusing on the nexus between the surrogate and the patient. Where the nexus is strong, the surrogate can justifiably assert that he has a legitimate interest in speaking on the patient's behalf, thus satisfying the requirement of standing. *See supra* note 72 and accompanying text.

82. *See infra* text following note 88.

83. In determining whether the surrogate has met his burden, the court would make, *sua sponte,* a motion to dismiss, and then determine whether the surrogate has presented enough evidence to withstand this motion.

84. In light of the court of appeals' discussion concerning the quantum

of evidence in *In re* Storar, 52 N.Y.2d at 379, 420 N.E.2d at 71–72, 438 N.Y.S.2d at 274, this would appear to be the appropriate burden. *See supra* note 25. More than this may well be impossible to meet, thus defeating the model's utility. Less than this may not afford adequate safeguards which the model is designed to provide.

85. There are two problems which are immediately apparent in determining the utility of this model. The first concerns the type of evidence the surrogate would bring in proving the relevant nexus. Presumably, the surrogate would summon live witnesses to testify to his relationship with the patient. This occurred in *Eichner* where Father Eichner demonstrated that Brother Fox's ten nieces and nephews concurred with his decision. *In re* Storar, 52 N.Y.2d at 371, 420 N.E.2d at 67, 438 N.Y.S.2d at 269–70. Documentary evidence may be brought in as well.

   At right angles to this problem is the court's obvious interest in whether there .re other parties who oppose the surrogate's decision. This can be handled in one of two ways. Either the court can appoint, *ad litem*, an attorney who would technically oppose the surrogate, or the court could presume that anyone opposing the surrogate's decision has constructive knowledge of the proceedings. The first alternative is frequently employed in family law actions to determine the best interests of a child who is the subject of a custody proceeding. Due to the delicate nature of euthanasia cases and due to the injustice to the patient which would result if the proceedings were unduly lengthy, the second alternative is preferred. It is submitted that anyone aware of a surrogate's interest in terminating the life of a particular patient has constructive knowledge of any proceeding that may be brought before a tribunal. If that person opposes the action, he will no doubt challenge the surrogate's request. In *In re* Quinlan, 70 N.J. 10, 355 A.2d 647, *cert. denied sub nom.* Garger v. New Jersey, 429 U.S. 922 (1976), all of Karen's immediate family members concurred in the decision to remove her from the respirator. The result may have been different if either parent had objected.

   The second problem concerns the surrogate's necessity for relying upon hearsay evidence in proving his relationship with the patient. This problem could be met by invoking something akin to FED. R. EVID. 804(b)(6). This rule provides, as an exception to the general rule excluding hearsay evidence, that a statement which is otherwise hearsay may be admitted into evidence if "(C) the general purposes of these rules and the interests of justice will best be served by admission of the statement into evidence." *Id.*

86. For a summary of these arguments, *see generally* T. BEAUCHAMP & T. PINKARD, ETHICS AND PUBLIC POLICY 256–58 (1983) [hereinafter cited as BEAUCHAMP & PINKARD].

87. *Id.* at 257.

88. One could argue that entering such states should be a sufficient condition for authorizing euthanasia. While this might be true from

a moral point of view, it is not sufficient in the eyes of the law, since even in such states, a third party cannot terminate the patient's life. *See supra* note 28 and accompanying text. According to the model, however, entering such states constitutes an initial condition for third party action, with the subsequent condition that the surrogate has demonstrated that he is competent to speak on the patient's behalf.

89. *See supra* note 86.
90. Ordinarily, the Anglo-American legal system gives priority to family members over distant relatives and friends. For example, property is inherited by immediate family regardless of how close the heir is to the decedent. With respect to this criterion, the court may presumptively conclude that the patient's immediate family members have a prima facie claim to surrogate competency. This presumption, however, must be rebuttable.
91. The fact that the surrogate is a spouse or even a parent should not, in and of itself, establish surrogate competency since it is possible that a spouse or parent is incompetent to speak on behalf of a patient's interests, beliefs, and desires. Such a relationship, however, might entitle the potential surrogate to a rebuttable presumption. *See* discussion *supra* note 90.
92. The court must be particularly sensitive to the possibility of collusion where, for example, an estranged wife has appealed to the court for termination of treatment. The court must scrutinize the quality of the relationship which existed between the surrogate and the patient.
93. If, for example, the patient had executed a living will, this would weigh heavily in favor of court authorization.
94. *See* Kutner, *supra* note 1, at 201–02.
95. *See supra* note 92.
96. Nonvoluntary euthanasia proposals are said to be the "thin edge of a wedge" leading to euthanasia against one's consent, infanticide, etc. *See* BEAUCHAMP & PINKARD, *supra* note 86, at 258. Euthanasia proposals must always be resisted, it is argued, or society will ultimately be unable to draw the line ending practices that take human life. *Id.*
97. *See supra* notes 82 and 84 and accompanying text. *See also supra* note 88.
98. This is the so-called "doctrine of double effect." Beauchamp, *Introduction* to Ch. 6, ETHICS AND PUBLIC POLICY 306 (T. Beauchamp ed. 1975). For an interesting discussion concerning the merits of this doctrine *see* Beauchamp, *A Reply to Rachels on Active and Passive Euthanasia, id.* at 318; Rachels, *Active and Passive Euthanasia*, in ETHICS AND PUBLIC POLICY 312 (T. Beauchamp & T. Pinkard eds. 1983). *See also supra* note 1 for the distinction between active and passive euthanasia. For an interesting discussion arising in a slightly different context see Bennett, *Whatever the Consequences*, in ETHICS AND PUBLIC POLICY 328 (T. Beauchamp ed. 1975).
99. Because of this distinction, it is seriously questionable whether the

actus reus requirement for homicide is met when an individual stands aside while letting nature take its course.

100. *See supra* note 65 and accompanying text.
101. *See supra* notes 67–68 and accompanying text.
102. *In re* Storar, 52 N.Y.2d 363, 420 N.E.2d 64, 438 N.Y.S.2d 266 (1981).
103. Presumably, a surrogate court would be the proper court of jurisdiction.
104. *In re* Storar, 52 N.Y.2d at 371, 420 N.E.2d at 67, 438 N.Y.S.2d at 269.
105. *Id.*
106. *Id.* at 371, 420 N.E.2d at 67, 438 N.Y.S.2d at 269–70.
107. *Id.* at 371–72, 420 N.E.2d at 68, 438 N.Y.S.2d at 270. *See supra* note 9 and accompanying text.
108. *In re* Storar, 52 N.Y.2d 363, 420 N.E.2d 64, 438 N.Y.S.2d 266 (1981).
109. *Id.* at 375, 420 N.E.2d at 69, 438 N.Y.S.2d at 271.
110. *Id.* at 374, 420 N.E.2d at 69, 438 N.Y.S.2d at 271.
111. *Id.* at 374, n.4, 420 N.E.2d at 69 n.4, 438 N.Y.S.2d at 271 n.4.
112. *Id.* at 373, 420 N.E.2d at 68, 438 N.Y.S.2d at 270.
113. *Id.*
114. *Id.* at 375, 420 N.E.2d at 70, 438 N.Y.S.2d at 272.
115. Mrs. Storar had on two occasions consented to treatment only to revoke her consent. In 1979, when John Storar's physicians first noticed blood in his urine and asked Mrs. Storar for permission to conduct diagnostic tests, she initially refused and gave her consent only after discussions with the institution's staff. In 1980, when blood again was observed in John Storar's urine, Mrs. Storar initially refused permission allowing physicians to administer blood transfusions, but withdrew her refusal the following day. *Id.* at 373, 420 N.E.2d at 68–69, 438 N.Y.S.2d at 270–71.
116. *Id.* at 375, 420 N.E.2d at 70, 438 N.Y.S.2d at 272.
117. *Id.*
118. *But cf.* the dissent's opinion that Mrs. Storar "had come to know and sense his wants and needs and was acutely sensitive to his best interests; that she had provided more love, personal care, and affection for John than any other person or institution, and was closer to feeling what John was feeling than anyone else. . . ." *Id.* at 391, 420 N.E.2d at 78–79, 438 N.Y.S.2d at 280–81 (Jones, J., dissenting).

Study Questions

1. Haber maintains that the New York Court of Appeals failed to decide "the surrogate decision" raised by *In re Storar* and *Eichner v. Dillon*. Do you agree? Why or why not?
2. Do you agree with Haber that his model of substituted judgment is rationally defensible? Is it "simple enough to be readily applicable" as he maintains?
3. Do you agree with Haber that John Storar should *not* have been authorized to receive blood transfusions?

Sperm and Ova as Property

Robert P.S. Jansen*

Who cares about what happens to our sperm or about what happens to our ova? Does anyone care about the fate of the sperm produced from a man's seminiferous tubules or the eggs produced from a woman's ovaries? Should one care? Is one allowed to care? These questions and their answers are important quantitatively and qualitatively.

First, *quantitatively*. We can look at the numbers of eggs (the term "eggs" includes oocytes and ova) for which a woman might assume responsibility. All the oocytes that a woman will ever produce are formed during fetal life—by four months from the time she herself was conceived[1]. So, five months before birth the human female has all the eggs she will ever have: about 7 million. Oocyte loss begins before she is born. By the time of birth 1 or 2 million eggs remain. Even before birth the process of atresia, in which oocytes start their development only to degenerate and be lost, has almost decimated the oocyte population. By puberty, at which time oocytes become candidates for ovulation and, perhaps, fertilization, only about 300,000 are left. Then if one of these 300,000 eggs ovulates each month for the twenty-five years, say, that constitute the reproductive years, it is clear that only about 300 eggs have any chance at all of ending up as babies. Indeed,

---

* Dr. Jansen is a physician interested in the clinical and theoretical aspects of medical ethics at the Royal Prince Alfred Hospital, in Sydney, Australia.

because of opportunities lost during pregnancy there is not the time for more than about 15 or 20 of the eggs (69 if multiple ovulations are included)[2] to become babies. The other 299,000 or more are destined for oblivion.

The attrition of gametes is even more spectacular among men. If a man with an average sperm count ejaculates, say, 6000 times in his lifetime, he will have let loose upon the world, or its drain-pipes, no fewer than one thousand thousand million potential fertilisers-of-an-egg. Of these spermatozoa, perhaps 2 or 3 or 200, at most an infinitesimal fraction, are likely to find successful expression by fertilizing an egg that will ultimately become another individual.

Does anyone care that all these sperm and ova are wasted? Not likely. Not only would it be futile for even the most dedicated of us to have more than a marginal impact on the number of sperm and ova lost, but it would, in a well–populated world, be arrogant and irresponsible. This notion of responsibility, which stops most people taking part in all-out promiscuous procreation, is one side of the *qualitative* considerations we bring to bear on the destiny we will allow even one sperm or one ovum.

Why the dichotomy? Why could we not care less about the millions of sperm washed out of the linen or about the thousands of eggs that might, with a stroke of the scalpel, accompany a surgically removed ovary into the formalin bottle, when the fate of one ovum, of one frozen straw of spermatozoa, let alone the fate of an early embryo[3], fills so many people with emotion. What is it about them that makes sperm and ova different from arms and legs or a pint of blood?

Notwithstanding some modern American challenges[4], the courts of common-law countries such as Australia and the United Kingdom have held that once organs or tissues are separated from a person that person (if alive, or that person's estate if dead) has little or no right of ownership or legally-enforceable control over the separated parts. Human body parts in law appear simply to be incapable of being owned[5]. Nevertheless in medical practice an agreement is often implied whereby the use of which separated tissues might be put is limited. For example, kidney transplants from living donors, who are put at considerable risk through the fact of the donation, are carried out with the clear understanding that the recipient will be the individual identified by the donor.

Similarly, if a person's limb is severed in an accident and accompanies him to the hospital, the surgeon attempting to sew it back on is presumably under some sort of obligation not to graft it to someone else. But if the kidney transplant fails, or if the limb is unsuitable for use, the law does not recognize the person who provided it as having any particular provenance over it: the tissue, for example, cannot automatically be taken home or sold to a museum.

Perhaps, in the absence of specific laws to the contrary, this lack of firm dominion over body parts or tissues could also apply to sperm kept frozen in a sperm bank for donation (a common practice) and to spare ova that may be fertilized and donated (so far an uncommon practice)[6]. Yet it is unthinkable for a woman, having been put at some risk and discomfort, to lose claim to an ovum recovered for the purpose of *in vitro* fertilization, and for the embryologist at whim to use the ovum for another purpose. It is also unattractive to imagine that sperm, stored for a man embarking on a course of cytotoxic drugs that might jeopardize his fertility, could be used for any purpose other than the express one for which the semen is being stored—namely to impregnate that man's wife. Ignoring the directions of the donors of sperm or ova would not be contemplated in responsible institutions and an agreement, implicit or explicit, exists between the donor and the storing institution or agency.

So far in my argument I have not yet developed any real difference (other than the obvious difference in purpose) between the agreements that govern deposition of gametes for storage and, say, live-donor kidney transplantation. The fact the gametes can be stored for many years is not very important. It could be argued that all that cryostorage does is to allow the special purpose's realization to be postponed; that, given appropriate techniques, kidneys could be stored for just as long. A more basic difference between the two types of donation is that sperm donations do not put the donor at risk; when the technology for harvesting immature oocytes develops, ovum donations, too, will presumably be incidental to a surgical operation performed for another reason and so carry no added physical risk; embryo donations are usually made after the event of fertilization, when there is also no added risk or physical discomfort for the donor. Another difference is that the providers of the isolated tissue, whether sperm, ovum or embryo, do not always have the same immediate objective of relieving suffering for a relative (as would the live donor of a kidney) or for themselves (in the case of a severed limb); in this sense gamete donations are often more like donations of blood or even like agreements to donate kidneys, a liver or a heart in the event of death—donations made without a specific recipient in mind. But blood for transfusions or promises of posthumous kidney donations are unlikely to carry for the donors much more mental impact than a moderate sense of altruism, whereas dispossession of gametes or embryos is capable of causing a great deal more concern. Indeed, the contrast is striking.

With a gamete donations or an embryo donation there is a donation of genetic information. This is a special attribute that the reproductive tissues, the germ cells, do not share with other tissues. Even though these other tissues contain millions of living cells, each carrying all the genetic information needed to code for the synthesis of a person, the specific difference is that the genetic information carried by sperm and ova is *usable*. It is this single fact that makes the gametes so special. When our sperm or ova go down the drain we generally could not care less (unless for some reason there are no more sperm or ova to take their place). The reason we do not care is that once down the drain the information they contain, in practical terms, is not usable: it will never find genetic expression: it will never mix with another germ cell's information to produce a new individual: we can forget about it.

Interestingly, the law is coming to grips with the sanctity of information-content in several spheres. For example, copyright laws exist to cover not just verbal prose and illustrations but are also being considered to cover the steps and strategies involved in computer programs[7]. The United States Supreme Court has ruled that the cloned genetic material of bacteria used to manufacture the human proteins insulin and growth hormone through recombinant DNA technology is protected: this genetic material, this biological stuff that contains information, can be patented[8,9]. There is therefore some precedent for distinguishing the usable genetic information contained in sperm and ova from the much less readily usable genetic information contained in the cells of a donated kidney or an amputated leg.

The uniqueness of sperm and ova may be brought out further with another analogy. Manufacturers of silicon chips, used in computers, have apparently had problems keeping the design of their integrated circuits protected from those who want to copy them for easy commercial gain—from those who simply buy one of these complicated but cheap bits of silicon and etch them away slowly, layer by layer, to decipher the information they contain, copy the chip's circuitry, and so cheat the original chip maker from the fruits of building up the information from nothing. It's reported that chip makers can discourage these tactics by incorporating confusing elements, dummy circuits, which look like working parts but which, when copied, make the copy inoperable (7). What the chip makers are protecting is not the chip itself—chips's extrinsic value is only a few pounds—but the usable information coded into the chip's structure.

In the same way, each ejaculate for each ovulation hardly constitutes a major drain on an individual's resources. One simply does not care if ejaculates or ova are lost—provided that they are *actually* lost and that their information content, their genetic potential, is not going to be realized in a way one's not happy with. It is this substantial *potential* that ova and sperm have, through the usable information they contain, that compels their use in donor programs to be quite unlike that of other parts of the body. This potential should always remain the responsibility, the provenance, the dominion, perhaps the property, of the donor.

The Warnock Committee expressed the hope that a couple party to *in vitro* fertilization would recognize their responsibility to make firm decisions on use and disposal of any embryos kept in storage (10). But the Warnock report also recommends "that legislation be enacted to ensure there is no right of ownership in a human embryo." One presumes this suggestion is intended to stop commercial trade in embryos, in which case less indignation among owning couples might follow a more simple recommendation to make such trade illegal, together with formalizing the rights of institutions or storage authorities (or their ethics committees) to make decisions in difficult situations. Making recommendations similar to those advocated in 1982 by the National Health and Medical Research Council (NH and MRC) in Australia (11), the Warnock report advises that when one of a couple dies the right to use or dispose of any embryo stored by that couple should pass to the survivor; in the event of 1) the absence of a survivor, 2) a dispute among the couple, or 3) the elapse of the time of normal reproductive need of the couple (generally of the order of 10 years) the storage institution (11) or authority (10) should have the power to make decisions, which in the NH and MRC's research guidelines, but not in the Warnock report, are taken to mean a decision to dispose of rather than to use the embryo. Despite this apparent difference in managing situations when no instructions exist, everyone agrees that donors' wishes on use or disposal should, as far as possible, be explicit well before the need to make such decisions arises.

The Warnock report may underestimate the stake donors or providers might have in the fate of their sperm, ova or embryos. The Warnock inquiry expressed "grave misgivings" about Artificial Insemination with semen from a Husband (AIH) who has died but who has left semen in a sperm bank, the misgivings apparently being based on possible psychological problems for the child and the mother[10]. Moreover, any child born by AIH not *in utero* at the date of the death of its father shall, according to Warnock's recommendations[11], be disregarded for the purposes of succession to and inheritance from the father (although not, presumably, from rights of inheritance from the mother). My conclusions on sperm and ovum provenance or dominion based on their genetic potential may put these inflexible recommendations in a different light.

A woman chooses not just a companion when she marries but also a father to her children, someone to complement her genetically and help endow her children with traits she considers desirable. This, in my view, gives her substantial justification, if her husband's semen has been stored, to continue to have access to it after his death, he not having disagreed and her medical attendant being willing to help. It would be quite unfair of society to insist that she think again (and so marry again) in her quest for children. Moreover men often store semen when they learn they have a life-threatening disease. On the face of it the motive may seem to be that they are to receive cancer-killing drugs which are likely, as a side-effect, to destroy the sperm-forming tissues in the testes. But from my contact with these men I am aware they often have another motive: to preserve their genetic potential in the event that they die as a result of their disease. Many dying patients take comfort in the fact that they have children, that it is not the end of the road genetically. On the other hand among the causes of anguish adolescents have in facing death is unfulfillment of their procreative instincts. This does not give society an obligation to use reproductive technolgy to fulfill these desires, but, because the implied motive in leaving stored semen behind after death is the wish for it to be used to secure offspring, an explicit or testamentary wish for passage of inheritance rights during the reproductive life of the wife should, if she wants it that way, be allowed. Similarly the death through noninheritable cause of a gamete donor should not necessarily mean withdrawal of his or her gametes from a donor program.

It may soon become possible for the genetic potential of non-germ (somatic) cells to be realized. One technique that has already been successfully carried out in frogs, at least to the stage of producing tadpoles[12], consists of transferring an adult somatic cell's nucleus to recently fertilized or activated ovum whose own nucleus has been removed. A mature ovum has the chemical machinery to strip off the basic proteins that normally mask much somatic cell deoxyribonucleic acid (DNA) (it does the same to the tightly packed DNA from the sperm nucleus after fertilization) and the ovum may then read that DNA, as cell devision gets underway, in exactly the manner in which, a generation before, the same DNA started the life of the individual from whom the somatic cell was obtained. The second individual will be a precise genetic replica of the first.

Development of this cloning technology, ethically and socially aborrhent though it might be, would confer on somatic cells the same property, usable genetic information, that today distinguishes the germ cells. It is entirely plausible that the somatic cells most suitable or closest at hand for such experiments would come from aborted fetuses or from more or less standarized human cell lines kept in tissue culture for various purposes. Ms. Henrietta Lacks, in 1951 a 31-year-old black woman but now long dead from cancer of the cervix, has endowed the world's tissue-culture laboratories with "HeLa" cancer cells for viral cultures[13]. The distribution of HeLa cells has become so widespread and the reported reseach based on HeLa cells has become so voluminous that *Index Medicus* has immortalized her with her own category. True, her DNA has probably been changed beyond recognition both by the cancer's original neoplasia and by subsequent transformation in culture, but that is not the point. The possibility remains that the witting or unwitting donor of any tissue could quite soon be put in the position of having himself or herself genetically replicated.

Society's intention to exert ethical control over human reproductive research is evident in many Western democracies today and it is unlikely that any scientist carrying out human cloning experiments, let alone using DNA from unsuspecting donors, would do so without alarming his or her peers and scandalizing the community. But the technical possibility of such cloning experiments needs to be taken into account. The NH and MRC in Australia, in its guidelines on ethics in medical research involving the fetus and human fetal tissue[14], advises that specific consent be sought from at least the genetic mother for the use of fetal tissues in any research that involves live-cell storage, propagation in tissue culture, or transplantation into a recipient human being. It should be clear that maintaining cells alive for research is no longer the same as preserving dead cells in formalin.

Whereas cloning, if at all, is for the future, ownership of the genetic information contained in sperm and ova is with us now. The fact of this ownership, at least before one parts with sperm or ova in any way that allows this information to be used, lies behind much of the concern that accompanies gamete donation and the development of human embryos *in vitro*. Some of the debated issues would be clarified by acknowledging that this area of human dominion, namely control over genetic expression among offspring, is still important after sperm, ova or embryos are parted with.

I thank Russell Scott LL B for our discussions.

Acknowledgement

This paper is based on an address delivered at the centenary celebrations of Royal Prince Alfred Hospital in Sydney.

NOTES

1. Baker T G. Oogenesis and ovarian development. In: Balin H. Glasser S., eds. *Reproductive biology*. Amsterdam: Excerpta Medica, 1972; 398–437.

2. Anonymous. Reproductivity; motherhood; most children; world. In: McWhirter N., ed. *Guinness book of records*. (29th ed) Enfield, Middlesex: Guinness Superlatives, 1983: 17.
3. Holden C. Two fertilized eggs stir global furor. *Science* 1984; 225: 35.
4. Anonymous. Patient sues for title of own cells. *Nature* 1984; 311: 198.
5. Scott R. *The body as property*. London: Allen Lane, 1981: 6–7, 186–197.
6. Trounson A., Leeton J., Besanko M., Wood C., Conti A. Pregnancy established in an infertile patient after transfer of a donated embryo fertilized *in vitro*. *British medical journal*; 286: 835–838.
7. *The economist* 1982 May 19: 93.
8. *The economist* 1982 Jan 16: 84.
9. Beardsley T. Cohen-Boyer patent finally confirmed. *Nature* 1984; 311: 3.
10. Warnock M. (Chairman): *Report of the committee of inquiry into human fertilization and embryology*. London: Her Majesty's Stationery Office, 1984: 18, 55–57.
11. National Health and Medical Research Council. *Ethics in medical research*. Canberra: Australian Government Publishing Service, 1983: 26–28.
12. McLaren A. Methods and success of nuclear transplantation in mammals. *Nature* 1984; 309: 671–672.
13. Jones H. W. Jr, McKusick V. A., Harper P. S., Wuu K. D., George Otto Gey (1899–1970). The HeLa cell and a reappraisal of its origin. *Obstetrics and gynaecology* 1971; 38: 945–949.
14. National Health and Medical Research Council. *Ethics in medical research involving the human fetus and human fetal tissues*. Canberra: Australian Government Publishing Service, 1983: 17–19.

Study Questions

1. Much of Jansen's argument seems to depend on the "uniqueness" of sperm and ova—that, e.g., the genetic information in the sperm and ova are usable for reproduction where the genetic information in other tissues is not. Would you agree that this feature supports Jansen's general conclusion?
2. The Warnock Commission report argued that any child born by AIH not *in utero* at the time of the father's death should be disregarded for purposes of inheritance from the father. Jansen feels this may be incorrect, on the basis of his agruments. Do you agree with Jansen or the Commission?

Teaching Ethics on Rounds: The Ethicist as Teacher, Consultant, and Decision-Maker

Jacqueline J. Glover,
David T. Ozar and
David C. Thomasma

1. Introduction

One of the basic assumptions among individuals teaching ethics to medical students is that the topic must be integrated into the clinical setting. This view has been supported by a wide range of medical ethics professionals, including many who attended the 1983 conference "Basic curricular goals in medical ethics." (Culver *et al.* 1985) The conference report discusses ethics consultations as an important way of linking ethics teaching with the clinical setting. The authors of the report write, "Ethical consultation should be prominent in hospitals that train medical students or residents, so that physicians become aware of the availability, method, and importance of such consultation during their training years." (Culver *et al.* 1985) One member dissented, however, indicating "there were still too few data about the process and outcome of ethical

104

consultations to recommend their widespread adoption." (Culver *et al.* 1985)

Our aim in this paper is to analyze the relationship between teaching and consultation in the clinical setting, and to examine the relationship of each to clinical decision-making. It is our thesis that the ethicist's role of teacher and consultant are distinct, but complementary, and that an understanding of the ethicist's contribution to clinical decisions in each of these roles depends in part on a conception of the physician's own role in clinical decision-making.

We will begin with an account of the goals of teaching in a clinical setting and introduce the problem of the relationship between teaching and consulting. In the second section we will describe some of our own experiences as teachers during clinical rounds and as consultants. Then we will examine the relationship between teaching and consulting, as each of them affect decisions being made regarding patient care. The final section will examine some of the challenges of such teaching and consulting.

2. Goals of Teaching on Clinical Rounds

The goal of teaching medical ethics in a clinical setting, stated generally, is to integrate more effectively concern for values into the education of medical students and eventually into their practice as physicians. More specifically, what we hope to accomplish is: (1) to assist the students in articulating explicitly various ethical issues involved in their clinical experience; (2) to familiarize students with processes of reasoning concerning ethical issues in order to enable them to be more effective in discussing and coming to an acceptable resolution of these issues; (3) to do the same for clinical faculty and staff, including house staff and nurses, and to facilitate and demonstrate the value of dialogue between all these groups, including patients and their families, (and others, such as chaplains and social workers) in the resolution of ethical issues; and (4) to indicate to all parties additional resources for research and reflection to promote sustained analysis of ethical issues among health care professionals.

One way of trying to accomplish these goals, and the one we have adopted at the Loyola University Medical Center, is for medical humanities faculty to accompany the attending physician, residents, and medical students during their clinical rounds. Students spend their third and fourth years working in the hospital, where instruction takes place only in occasional lectures. Most of the teaching takes place in discussions of the service's patients with attending physicians during the systematic review of patients known as rounds. Most often this occurs as physicians and students actually visit each patient, but it also may occur more informally around a conference table. In either setting, the students report on their patients, and the attending physician asks them relevant questions, discusses treatment options with them and the residents, and together they develop plans for patient care. The attending physician thereby models appropriate patient care through actual contact with the patient and through discussion and implementation of appropriate diagnostic and therapeutic measures. In a similar manner the ethics teacher on rounds also asks relevant questions and models thoughtful ethical reflection for the students by discussing ethical issues raised by the case at hand, and by working with the students and the rest of the rounding group through a process of ethical reasoning about these issues.

One of the major difficulties in fulfilling our goals in the clinical setting has been the proper balance between the more traditional models of teaching in the Humanities and the teaching model just described. Medical school relies heavily on a mentor system of teaching in which advanced students learn chiefly by hands-on experience and practice, in imitation of and under the supervision of more experienced clinicians. Students literally learn by doing, as their teachers teach by doing.

But this is an unusual role for an ethics teacher, whose more traditional role is to stimulate thinking concerning an issue rather than action. When teaching on rounds, is the ethics teacher's role now that of actually making ethical decisions about the cases discussed? Are ethics teachers to function as clinical consultants, who bring to the clinical encounter a special expertise and set of problem-solving skills which they then excercise on the problems at hand, so the students can learn by observing and then imitating their "doing?" Do they recommend a specific course of action to the attending physician? Or is the teaching of the ethicist in the clinical setting somehow different from the teaching of the clinical faculty? Is their teaching role separate from any consulting role which they might have? These are the questions we wish to address in this paper. In order to respond to these questions, each of the authors has formulated a brief description of the role of the teaching ethicist on rounds and in consultations and has developed a concrete example of this role from his or her clinical experience.

3. Roles of The Ethicist

In our clinical experience, we have identified three distinct roles that the ethicist fills at different times. The first can be described as that of the teacher/consultant. This role is most suited to clinical rounds where the primary aim is to educate students and staff about ethical issues through a practical modeling approach. Here the ethicist's primary aim is to *instruct* students and staff on a process of moral reasoning by facilitating and exemplifying it. Another product of this kind of instruction is an indication of what course of action is most justified, given the particular circumstances.

A second role can be described as that of the consultant/teacher. This role is most suited to those situations in which the ethicist is called by an attending physician outside of the formal teaching structure to give advice about the ethical dimension of a particular patient's care. The ethicist brings knowledge of a process of moral reasoning and relevant literature which he or she is now asked to use to analyze a case and to recommend an appropriate course of action. The ethicist cannot accomplish this in isolation, and a discussion usually occurs between the ethicist and the caregivers, such as residents, nurses, and social workers, as well as the attending physician and the patient and/or patients' family, to gather the appropriate information about the case and move towards its resolution. In guiding the discussion and thereby instructing those involved concerning the values of the case and the justification of various courses of action, the ethicist's primary aim is to help in the *choice* of a best course of action. Another product of the process, however, is the instruction of staff who are involved.

Both of these distinguish between the activities of the teacher and the consultant and yet claim their complementary character in that neither activity can be accomplished without the other. A third role of the ethicist, however, maintains a separation between the two activities. As a teacher in the clinical setting, the ethicist also has the role of identifying and clarifying broader issues, beyond the case at hand, that require further study and reflection. In this role, the ethicist functions as a more traditional Humanities professional, citing relevant ideas from associated disciplines. This activity is independent of any attempt to provide guidance regarding the resolution of specific issues in cases at hand.

In the paragraphs that follow, we will illustrate these three roles through examples from our clinical experiences. In the following section we will discuss the implications these roles have for the ethicist's participation in decision-making regarding patient care.

4. Experiences

Teacher/Consultant

The role of the ethicist as teacher/consultant is well exemplified in this experience which took place not long ago. I was rounding in the Neurology service, accompanying on that occasion one attending, one resident, and three students. We had visited several other patients when we came to the room of Mr. S, who had suffered for many years from Parkinson's disease and had been admitted on this occasion because his medications were proving less and less effective in preserving his stability. He was a fairly well educated man in his late sixties who was still working as a structural engineer on a consulting basis.

Outside of Mr. S's room, the resident explained the case to the team and told us that over that last week a variety of dosages of medications had been tried in order to reduce Mr. S's dizziness and unsteadiness when he walked. Unfortunately the dosage needed to control his neurological symptoms had the side-effect of confusing Mr. S and weakening his memory. "What we have to determine," said the attending, "is whether we should trade stability for clear-headedness or the other way around."

I asked, "Why don't you ask him?" My point was not to accuse anyone of having failed to do something they should have. In fact, I could hardly do that, since I did not know if Mr. S was even able to give a coherent answer to the question. My point was simply to say: Here is a part of the process of resolving this matter which you have perhaps not thought of.

"Well it's obvious," said the resident, "that he would choose in favor of stability on his feet, so he can walk around and interact effectively with his environment."

"Oh, no," said the attending. "Obviously he would prefer to be clearheaded."

Both doctors looked at me. This conversation was the first time they had realized that they differed on this matter, in spite of several months of work side-by-side. This brief conversation had made it clear that neither of them could set the priority for Mr. S because there is no universally valid ranking of these two values which can decide a case like this for everyone. The team decided to ask Mr. S.

Mr. S was sitting up in his chair next to the bed. The attending sat on the bed facing him and began to chat. It was clear that Mr. S was having a good day and was very lucid. Before long, the attending was discussing Mr. S's situation with him, explaining the problems which they had uncovered in trying to find a dosage level which would preserve his stability without confusing him. Mr. S understood the matter and responded thoughtfully, first with a few questions to complete his undertanding, and then with a clear choice. Outside Mr. S's room, we discussed the available courses of action if Mr. S had not been so clear-headed. Mr. S had never been married, but a life-long friend visited often and was known to the team. It was decided that seeking information from him would have been the next best alternative and the team decided to explain Mr. S's choice to the friend to support the conviction that this was Mr. S's sincere choice and to be better prepared for future episodes of confusion and memory loss.

In this case, the ethicist did not tell the team what they should do. Rather the ethicist was able to help them carry out a clearer, more fully articulated, more inclusive process of ethical reflection than they were likely to have done otherwise. The ethicist provided a model for ethical reflection by asking a few questions that no one had yet asked, and helped in the resolution of an important issue in the patient's care. The discussion was not an abstract one of patient autonomy, competence, or informed consent. Rather

the ethicist participated in the process of decision-making by helping to clarify important ways of looking at the clinical question.
The students took home a model for resolving conflicts concerning
alternative therapies, and the patient took home a course of therapy more suited to his individual preferences.

Consultant/Teacher

A second role for the ethicist is that of the consultant/teacher.
Here is a case where the ethicist is called by an attending physician
to help in the resolution of an ethical issue.

In this instance, a faculty member was called by a physician in
Obstetrics and Gynecology to discuss the case of a woman with
sickle cell anemia who was about 26 weeks pregnant. She had
had several crisis episodes and the question of blood transfusions
was raised. She was a devout Jehovah's Witness and refused
transfusion. The question was raised whether she should be transfused for the benefit of her unborn child. After discussion with
the attending physician, primary nurse, and social worker, it was
decided that she should be transfused when, in the physician's
judgment, the child was in danger. It was further recommended
that a discussion take place with her concerning the need for
transfusion in the delivery of the child since a cesarean section
seemed likely.

The patient was very adamant about not receiving blood, and
the attending physician in the case believed he did not have adequate evidence to suggest that the baby was being threatened.
All tests indicated there was no fetal distress. The hospital attorney
was called, however, in the event a court order should be necessary. Later the mother went into a crisis and delivery was seen
as necessary. The mother was still adamant about not receiving
blood during a cesarean section. The anesthesiology staff was not
aware of the previous discussion and was similarly unclear about
whether they should transfuse her for the sake of the baby. A
second ethics consult was called and a meeting was held with the
anesthesiology staff, some OB residents, the hospital lawyer, a
representative from the hospital's office of risk management and
a representative of the state Attorney General's office. While this
meeting was in progress, the patient's condition became very
serious and an immediate decision was necessary regarding trans-

fusion. A judge was contacted immediately and custody was granted. The ethicist recommended that if the baby were in danger, a transfusion be performed. But transfusion should not be initiated once the baby had been delivered (although, once started, it should not be stopped when the baby had been delivered).

In this case the ethicist was more directly involved in the decision about appropriate patient care. His advice was solicited because of a special set of skills he brought to the discussion, including knowledge of medical ethics, as well as legal precidents, and analytic tools for applying general principles of ethics to the case at hand. But note that the ethicist did not act independently. Rather he functioned as a resource of information and procedures for reaching a decision, and as a kind of facilitator of the meeting, guiding the discussion, helping to gather important information, and helping the group reach a consensus among individuals representing varied interests. Although a product of the discussion was the instruction of the other persons involved in the decision process, and a discussion session with the entire anesthesiology staff on the subject was later offered, the ethicists' primary responsibility in this case was in helping to decide upon a best course of action.

Teacher of Broader Issues and Principles

A third role of the ethicist is that of teacher independent of the consultant role. In this role, the ethicist does not provide guidance regarding the resolution of specific problems, but rather indicates broader issues that require further reflection. Because this role of the ethicist is different from the medical model that associates teaching with pragmatic consulting, it is the most difficult to integrate into the clinical setting. But we believe it is essential nonetheless, as the example described below illustrates. For medicine is not practiced in a vacuum and it is sometimes the role of the ethicist to indicate links between ethical issues in medicine and ethical issues in other settings, and between values and principles prominent in health care and other important human values and principles of ethical reflection.

One of the greatest difficulties with this aspect of teaching during clinical rounds is finding the best time and format for discussion. Because clinical rounds are working sessions where the

attending and residents need to get basic patient care issues resolved, there is usually not adequate time to raise broader concerns. For example, rounding in Pediatrics begins with a morning
report session where the new admissions from the previous night
are discussed. Everyone is anxious to hear basic information about
the case and to begin a diagnostic and treatment plan. Only very
brief and specific remarks about the individual cases are useful.
For example, one morning we discussed the case of the near-
drowning of a 5 months old child. It had taken emergency personnel almost 45 minutes to restore a heartbeat and it was not
known how long the child had been in the water. A question was
raised about how long such a resuscitation attempt should proceed
and about the appropriate action of the emergency room staff. It
was decided, after discussion, that even though it was debatable
whether she should have been resuscitated when she arrived at
the emergency room, it was not the role of the E.R. staff to try to
make this determination. Their obligation was to resuscitate if
possible, and then a more thoughtful decision could be made later,
based on more information, although exceptions where futility
was obvious were cited. Although this discussion had no direct
bearing on the immediate diagnostic and treatment plan, it did
point to such broader issues as the definition of death, and the
need for clear social and institutional policy on decisions not to
resuscitate. It also alerted the team to the possibility of a future
decision not to treat.

During the actual patient-care rounds that follow morning report, the concern for timing and format is also apparent. This
instructor has found it useful to use the rounding sessions to learn
about specific cases and then to plan more extensive discussions
with the students and residents later. For example, during a recent
rounding session, we heard an update on the case of a child who
was involved in an auto accident some years ago and was now
completely paralyzed and respirator-dependent. The child was
restored to the present level of functioning after considerable time
in the hospital and great expense. The child was currently hospitalized, as on numerous previous occasions, for care of bedsores.
The social situation was a source of constant concern for the attending physician, and abuse of public funding was an important
issue for many caregivers in the case. The topic of cost/benefit
analysis came up in the discussion. Was the initial cost to save

the child too much? Is the cost over the child's lifetime too much? How are cost factors considered in clinical decisions? Such questions could be raised in the brief time available on rounds, but it was obvious that a more extensive discussion was necessary. So plans were made to discuss the case during an hour-long conference with the students and residents the following week.

In this role, the ethicist is a teacher according to the traditional Humanities model rather than the medical model. The ethicist's input is not focused on the care of a specific patient, but rather on raising issues that are of concern for medical care and society generally. It is important that those who are in clinical practice be aware of such broader issues and be involved in discussions concerning them. This model of teaching, though more removed from direct patient care, still will affect patient care indirectly and over the long run by making a difference in physician's thinking and participation in larger social issues as they are resolved. It also provides the students with a broader, more inclusive base on which to build their own habits of ethical reflection and action.

5. Clinical Decision-Making

Two of the roles just described have an obvious relationship to decisions made concerning patient care. Is the ethicist then invading the turf of the physician who is responsible for patient care? What is the relationship between the ethics teacher and consultant and the primary physician?

To begin, we will defend our position that ethicists must often be involved in decisions about appropriate actions. They cannot always function only as teachers according to the more traditional Humanities model, although they should at times. In fact, if they are to be as effective as possible in the clinical setting, the majority of their medical school teaching must involve a more pragmatic medical-model approach. This is true for several reasons.

First of all, it is the very nature of values in medicine that they are essentially bound up with clinical decision-making. For the ethicist to be true to the nature of values in medicine, this association cannot be severed. Those teaching values in medicine must recognize this and act accordingly. The best way to show how values are involved in clinical decision-making is through actual involvement in the decision-making process. Teaching *about* the clinical decision-making process, without being involved, has its place and can be very valuable. Our point is that it necessarily falls short of addressing values in the way in which they arise in medical practice. This is why it is so widely accepted that ethics teaching must be integrated into the clinical setting.

But not just any interaction between ethicists and health care professionals is helpful. The goals of clinical teaching will not somehow magically be reached by the mere presence of ethicists in the clinical setting. For values, and values-teachers, to be integrated in the clinical setting, they must be associated in an essential way with the clincial enterprise, namely, decision-making concerning the health and well-being of particular patients.

Secondly, teaching by doing is a more effective way to reach the general goal of changing the behavior of future physicians. The teaching of medical ethics is not supposed to be merely an intellectual exercise for medical students, but it is meant to be an essential part of their learning to be physicians. By "doing" ethics with and for the students, the students are more likely to "do" ethics on their own. Application breeds application. This is the premise behind the entire mentor approach in medical school. Students are learning to do something, and the more they see what they are supposed to do being done, and the more they practice themselves, the more likely they are to eventually do it well themselves. So effective pedagogy argues for ethicists to take on all the roles we have described.

There is a third reason why ethicists must be involved in the decision-making process in the ways we have described. This is simply the way things are done in medical school. Teaching is accomplished by doing and the credibility of the teacher as teacher is linked to his or her ability to *do* as well. Medical schools are unlike many other parts of the university in that intellectual activity is not so much valued for itself as for its relevance to practice. This feature can, and perhaps should, be challenged to some extent, although its essential validity seems obvious. Nevertheless humanists must also accommodate themselves to the patterns of the institution in which they teach.

Even granted that ethicists should be involved in decision-making, however, we can still ask what form this involvement should take. What is the proper relationship between the ethics teacher and consultant and the primary physician? There seem to be two basic models of the relationship between the ethicist as pragmatic consultant and the primary physician. One is the model of the "individual expert" and the other is the model of the "decision facilitator." We will argue that the roles of the ethicist in the clinical setting are better understood in terms of the second model than the first.

Individual Expert

There is an established model for consulting that is an important part of medical practice and is, perhaps, the prime motivator behind ethics consulting in the first place. When a physician has questions or needs advice concerning a particular aspect of his or her patient's care, the physician calls a specialist in that area to provide an expert judgment. For example, an internist whose patient has lapsed into a coma will call a neurologist to answer questions and give advice concerning diagnosis, prognosis, and therapy.

One characteristic of this model is that the primary physician maintains sole responsibility for decisions regarding patient care. But the information the consultant gives is useful in making those decisions. The consultant does not take responsibility for the patient in the sense that he or she takes action to ensure that the appropriate decision in the consultant's view is made. The special authority of the consultant comes from his or her special knowledge of a particular field. So although the consultant does not make the final decision, his or her advice cannot merely be ignored since it is based on principles of scientific proof and sound medical judgment, the same basis for the authority of the primary physician.

A further characteristic of this model is that the participants in it seem to function as relatively isolated individuals. One neurologist is called rather than the entire neurology service. One individual is regarded as an expert, in the sense that he or she has special knowledge of a particular field that can help another individual make an appropriate decision. The neurologist has special knowledge of the anatomy, physiology, and pathology of the neurological system, and the primary physician has special knowledge of the particular patient.

It is easy to see how this model might apply to the contributions of the ethicist. The primary physician has a question or needs advice concerning the ethical dimension of a patient's care. The physician calls an ethics "expert," an individual with special knowledge of the field of medical ethics. The ethicist, like the neurologist, answers questions and gives advice. He or she has special knowledge of the ethical literature, legal precedents, and processes of moral reasoning.

As in the case of the neurologist, the ethicist does not take any action to insure that an appropriate decision is made. The sole responsibility for the decision is with the primary physician. But by what authority does the ethicist claim his or her advice ought to be taken? According to this model, it would have to be a shared acceptance of the basic values involved in the case, a consensus in the literature, and the physician's acceptance of the adequacy of the training of a different professional. As there is a shared understanding of medical science and of the principles of sound medical judgment between the primary physician and the neurologist or other medical consultant, so there must be a shared understanding of the value component of medical judgments between physician and ethicist. In addition, as in the case of the clinical consultant, there must be a component of trust or acceptance on the physician's part of the adequacy of the ethicists' training in processes of moral reasoning concerning the inherent values. In fact this seems even more important here than in a clinical consult since a physician does have knowledge of the standards of medical judgment that the other physician must meet. He or she accepts that the other professional has been adequately trained, but he or she also has a certain amount of knowledge to judge that this is the case. The risk of relying on an "individual expert" is somewhat reduced. It can be assessed whether the individual adequately represents the field as a whole.

But what about the ethicist? The physician does not have the same kind of knowledge to assess the adequacy of the advice against some kind of standard. What is the standard for ethical decision-making? This is where the model of the "individual expert" breaks down. There seems to be a greater risk of making less appropriate decisions by relying on individual ethicists to independently render ethical decisions in the same way one relies on an individual clinical consultant. This risk is not mainly associated with the adequacy of training, although it could be; it has to do primarily with the nature of ethical decision-making itself. Ethical decision-making is far more a community enterprise than the clinical diagnostic judgment. Consequently the relationship between ethicist and primary physician should not simply follow the "independent expert" model. It should not follow the same pattern as we observe in clinical consults.

Decision Facilitator

A second model for the ethicist/consultant portrays the ethicist as necessarily involved with others in the resolution of ethical issues. Rather than acting independently to give expert advice on ethical issues, the ethicist works with others involved in the case to reach a decision. The ethicist acts as a facilitator in that he or she helps gather the individuals involved, sort out the essential information, and lead the discussion about the application of ethical principles in the particular case.

This kind of involvement of others is essential because ethical wisdom and sound decision-making are at their best when they can draw on the perspectives and insights of a community of persons rather than a single individual. In the absence of a set of values acceptable to all, decisions must be made that take account of as many values as possible. Where there is conflict, rational debate among those representing varied interests is the best way to a thoughtful resolution. Unless we rely on someone authoritative, and perhaps dogmatic source of advice, our actions must bear the test of open debate. This is important on a societal level, but also on an institutional level where individual standards of care are developed and implemented by a variety of individuals and professionals working together. The practice of medicine necessarily involves a shared understanding of what it means to benefit a patient, and this shared understanding includes ethical standards as well.

The persons involved in this process would depend not only on the specifics of the case, but also on the setting, whether it is during clinical rounds or on a consultation. Those involved might include not only the primary physician, residents, medical students, patient, and/or patients' family, but also nurses, social workers, and chaplains. On clinical rounds where such additional personnel are not usually present, the ethicist can point to the value of their involvement at some later time.

There are other, and perhaps more pragmatic, reasons for the involvement of a community of reflective persons in the decision-making process. First of all, involving various persons who represent different interests makes it more likely that a greater range of values and interests will be considered. Values and concerns important to the case are less likely to be overlooked if all those affected by the decision are involved.

Secondly, many ethical issues involve breaches, or potential breaches, in communication. For example, there may be some misunderstanding about the wishes of the patient, as when conflicting information has been given to the residents and to nurses. Involving all the principals in a case increases communication and helps insure that all the relevant information is available and accurate.

Finally, a shared decision-making process is more likely to result in effective action. If those who are to be involved in implementing the chosen course of action are involved in the decision, there is less likelihood of misunderstanding. And if the reasoning behind the action is understood by all, actions that deviate from the intended outcome are more likely to be identified and altered.

We have identified the ethicist's role in clinical decision-making, the remaining and more difficult issue is the physician's own role. One can see how the logic of our argument leads us to at least question the model of the physician's role as "individual expert." We claim that ethical and clinical decisions are essentially bound up together; ethical decisions are best made through a community process; therefore, it seems that the physician cannot be isolated from participation as one member among many in this process. But there is an obvious tension here with the more traditional concept of the physician/patient relationship which places the primary obligation for care on the physician. There is also a tension with the legal framework associated with the physician as responsible decider.

The whole question of the proper role of the physician in decision-making is a very complicated one that we cannot address properly in this paper. Our intent is to analyze the role of the ethics teacher and consultant. We have found in this process that there are necessary implications for the role of the physician as well. How one views the ethicist in the decision process depends on how one views the physician. If one uses an "individual expert" model for the physician, then the ethicist is likely to be viewed in the same way. Even if a "decision facilitator" model is accepted for the ethicist, the physician will be outside the community process, choosing to use or ignore the advice as given. We cannot here propose a complete argument to challenge the model of the physician as sole decision-maker, but we would like to offer the following ideas for further discussion.

As with the ethicist, the physician does not work as an isolated individual. He or she relies on information from others to help make the best decision possible. The physician is obligated to act in the best interest of the patient, but he or she relies on others to help determine what that best interest may be. Also, the physician is not the only moral agent responsible for acting in the best interest of the patient. Patients are moral agents whose wishes must be respected. Other health professionals are also affected by the decision and must be true to their own moral standards.

In some ways, even the model of the physician as an individual decider is a straw person and many, if not most, physicians do not actually function this way. Although in certain critical care areas the individual decider model may be accurate, in other areas, especially chronic and primary care, for example, physicians function more as members of a health care team where the decision-making process is an expanded one.[1]

It should be clear from our discussion of the model of the ethics consultant as decision facilitator that we think ethics consultants are different from clinical consultants and should be. The model of the consultant as individual expert is not appropriate for the ethics consultant. It is a model that dangerously distorts the nature of ethical decision-making, which is essentially community based. Moreover, the ethicist's role as consultant is always linked with a teaching function. This might be claimed of clinical consultants as well, but perhaps not in the same way. The ethicist models awareness of important values and a process of ethical reasoning and decision-making. He or she does not come with pieces of discreet information and research citations to back it up. Rather, the ethicist points out what values are important to consider in a case, and indicates important ways they are to be considered. Of course in practice, especially in times of urgent decision-making, the ethicist alone may be asked to assist the primary physician. While not the ideal, even in this situation the ethicist can still represent the considered judgments of the communities with whom he or she is regularly in dialogue.[2]

Additionally, the ethicist's teaching role expands his or her area of concern. Unlike the clinical consultant who is only interested in the decision that needs to be made at the particular bedside, the ethicist must also look to broader concerns. Not all decisions that affect medicine are made at the bedside, and physicians and others need to be aware of these other decisions and involved in discussing them nonetheless. The ethicist is responsible for showing the links between medicine and other values and institutions in society. Societal choices can have a radical effect on medical practice.

This points to perhaps the most important difference between ethics and clinical consultants. Ethics consultants do not share completely the same value structure as the primary physician whom they assist. Clinical personnel are concerned primarily, and perhaps exclusively, with promoting the values of medicine. Ethics consultants must consider all values, both those inside and outside of medicine. The ethicist functions as a kind of bridge that links medical values with other values. He or she can never function properly from a position completely within medicine. (Churchill 1978)

We have argued that ethics consultants *should* not function according to the model of the clinical consultant, but perhaps there is a strong sense in which they even *could* not. Ethicists, educated in the Humanities, are not trained to be the executors of decisions. The ambience in which their skills developed is very different from that of the clinician. It is a world of slow deliberation, isolated from the immediacy of decisions that so directly affect the lives of others. Some would caution that this is why ethicists perhaps should not be involved in the clinic, but rather ethics teaching should be done by physicians. (Siegler 1979) But one could also argue that this is exactly why ethicists *should* be involved in the clinic working in partnership with physicians and others. Medicine is not an isolated activity. Rather through its deep commitment to caring for human needs, it is intricately bound to the entire range of human values. And the pull of the clinic with the immediacy of meeting medical needs makes the consideration of other human values outside of health extremely difficult. An individual who *can* only come part way into medicine is perhaps the best bridge between medicine and other human values. But this "partialness" also leads to many problems in integrating the ethicist in the clinical setting. In the following section we will briefly point out some of the challenges we have encountered, in hopes of stimulating discussion about their possible resolution.

6. Challenges for Clinical Teaching

The first major challenge is the obvious one of balancing the multiple roles we have described for the ethics teacher, as teacher/consultant, consultant/teacher, or simply teacher. The ethicist must be very sensitive as to what is required in each particular case. Is the managing physician looking for help in making a decision or is he or she more interested in educating the students? When is it useful to raise broader issues or when is this a hindrance for the patient care occuring in the same session? Who are the persons that should be involved in the decision-making process and how open is the physician to such a discussion? There must be a balance between teaching and consulting so that health care professionals are not frustrated with a more theoretical discussion when they are looking for answers, or confronted with answers when advice is not solicited. This speaks to the value of the ethics teacher spending as much time as possible with the clinical faculty, getting to know them and building an understanding of the mutual expectations.

A second major challenge, and perhaps the most frustrating, is the problem of time. In the format of clinical rounds, one ordinarily has only five or ten minutes for each patient to raise and discuss whatever issues there are. And, of course, on rounds the clinical concerns of the patient need to be fully addressed as well. Even in a more structured conference format which focuses on one patient or a group of patients with similar concerns, time is still limited to an hour or so. Is this enough time to accomplish the goals described earlier, from basic exposure to ethical issues to a careful method of problem resolution? Is this brief amount of time enough to help students develop any kind of skill in dealing with ethical issues? To persons who have studied for years in graduate school and then as teachers of ethics, this hardly satisfies a minimum requirement for inaugurating an educational activity, much less completing it.

One of the authors has made an important distinction in this connection between "training" in medical humanities and "education." (Thomasma 1982) An education in the medical humanities requires exposure to each of the liberal arts, and even if only ethics were chosen, an "education" would require in-depth exposure to many issues and traditions of ethical reflection. Few health professionals can take the time for such a broad exposure. Their needs require a limited exposure to a few of the liberal arts and a more focused range of ethical issues and traditions, perhaps only those most applicable to the problem they actually face and focused in such a way as to more directly respond to these problems. This limited exposure is more like "training," and requires different formats and perhaps less time. But the question still remains, is there adequate time even for such training? This issue of time is perhaps even more difficult in regard to consultations. Often problems require an immediate response and there is not adequate time to convene a meeting with those involved in the case or to discuss the issue at any length.

One response, of course, is that it is better to do something than nothing, and this is certainly true. But when something is done, it is often easy for the institution, as well as its graduates, to conclude that this "something" is therefore enough, that the training in clinical ethics which students receive in our programs fully equips them for the ethical challenges they will face. So the teachers of ethics must continually raise the question about time and work with the institutions in finding even more effective ways of integrating concern for ethical issues into the program.

A third challenge is the clinical rounding format itself. As mentioned earlier, rounding sessions are not only teaching sessions, but they are also work sessions. Depending on the caseload of the attending physician and the residents, the session may well be more of a working session and less of a teaching session. Even on clinical matters there sometimes just isn't time to discuss issues of any subtlety. Great flexibility is required to adjust to the needs of the various rounding sessions. Flexibility is also required in one's schedule to accommodate changing rounding times. There is also the problem of lack of information that occurs for the ethics teacher in the clinical rounding format. The attending physician, residents, and students all have exposure to the cases on a daily basis. Often the rounding sessions do not include complete case histories, but only abbreviated discussions of only the most current information. Unless the ethicist attends morning report on a daily basis, he or she may not have heard a more complete presentation of the case. This sometimes makes it very difficult to identify and discuss relevant ethical issues. Then the ethicist must rely on the attending and residents to bring up questions for discussion, which may limit the range of ethical discussion significantly. Still it is important to keep in mind that the ethicist teaches in partnership with the attending physician; both are involved in raising ethical issues for the students. The ethicists' need for information can also be met by the team, who can explain the case history more fully when the ethicist is present than they might for one another.

This brings up an additional question of collegiality in the clinical setting. It is the attending physician who has the established credibility in the clinical format. Residents, students, nurses and others must answer to him or her. The ethics teacher seems to get credibility through the attending physician. If he or she finds the ethicist's work important and useful, it is more likely that the others will as well. This is perhaps less of a problem in a consult, when the attending physician has called for advice. But it is very difficult to feel useful at first, and perhaps for quite a while, as ethicists become more involved in this new environment. It is hard to be accepted as a teacher, when there is so much to learn about the medical setting.

Along these same lines, confidence as an instructor comes very slowly. The hospital is a new setting, and one that only a few regard as a place of work. For many, the hospital is still mainly associated with more agonizing experiences of personal illness or illness in the family. It has not yet developed the familiarity of a "workplace." On top of this, there is a tremendous emotional impact upon hearing the personal tragedies of the individuals encountered in "cases." Just as the ethicist is grappling to apply professional skills in a new setting, he or she is confronted with personal tragedies and emotions that are beyond even the most finely honed professional skills. One cannot confront life's essential questions and values with only "professional" skills. Our lives are not lived on only one level. It is a disturbing realization of the power of the workplace to stand at someone's bedside, hearing a very personal story in confidence, and realize that one is not thinking about the person at all, but rather formulating a next question for the students.

A final challenge, and perhaps the most important, concerns the appropriateness of the method of moral analysis itself that we are assuming would be used by the ethics teacher. Some would argue that this kind of structured problem resolution in ethics, sometimes referred to as an "engineering model," is too simplistic and may do a disservice to moral philosophy. (Caplan 1983) Ethics is more complicated than a "cookbook" approach would allow. A way of approaching ethical issues and of asking the appropriate questions is essential, as is a common language. But can the weighing of values in particular instances be so easily formalized? Getting *to* the essential ethical question in a particular case is one thing, but weighing the values and supporting a particular decision is quite another.

It is important for medical professionals and students to learn when they are confronting a question of patient self-determination versus established medical practice, for example. And it is important to come to a resolution in particular cases. But can we standardize the weighing of these two values? If by standardize we mean to give guidelines and reasons for their acceptance, then the answer is yes. Further reflection is, of course, required. But that is always the case in ethics. This does not stop us from making the best decisions we can at the time with the information we have available. This is what health professionals already do in medical decision-making and also what we hope to teach students and others to do while more explicitly appreciating the ethical dimensions of their decision-making.

Because we cannot be guaranteed of making *the* best decision in some absolute sense, is no reason to think that we shouldn't strive to make the best decisions possible. Medicine, like ethics, is not an exact science. We gather information, construct ideas, defend positions, change positions, and try to make the best choice with the information and experience available at the time.

As Caplan admits in his *Ethics* article, a method of analysis may be a valuable product, particularly in medicine. (Caplan 1983) Medicine already has an established decision-making procedure based on the best interests of the patient. Ethical analysis expands the consideration about these interests. It does not add anything that does not already exist. The decision-making procedure remains intact. However, it is expanded to include *all* the relevant considerations.

Ethical analysis, then, is no stranger to medical decision-making. People who worry that such ethical training will hinder physician activities are missing the point. They see physicians as making split-second decisions that will be hampered by further considerations. But what do they mean by hinder? Make less easy? Make less right? We can surely see the first, but not the second. All physician decision-making is not at the last minute, although some is. Treatment plans are made over broader periods of time with much research, thought, and revision. If this aspect were emphasized, perhaps the number of split-second decisions would itself be reduced. Errors in judgment are often the result of *not* taking advantage of adequate time to reflect. But this is not to say that split-second decisions never have to be made. However, if adequate reflection is done when the time is available, the experience will be helpful in emergencies as well. Just as physicians prepare with adequate medical information for the emergencies, they need to prepare with adequate information about the value dimensions.

7. Summary

We have accepted and supported in this paper the basic thesis that ethics teaching should occur in the clinical setting. And we have argued that clinical teaching has a unique character in that it is clearly related to ethics consulting. The ethics teacher must fulfill three roles, that of teacher/consultant, consultant/teacher, and teacher, depending on the particular circumstances. In clinical teaching it is most often required that the ethics teacher actually help decide on an appropriate course of action. This the ethics teacher does in conjunction with others involved in the case. The ethics teacher is also an ethics consultant, not as an indivdual "expert," rather as a decision facilitator. But the ethics teacher is also not exclusively as ethics consultant. He or she is also responsible at times for raising broader ethical concerns for further reflection. There are many challenges for the ethics teacher functioning in the clinical setting, but the practice of medicine can be well-served by persistent attempts to find a bridge between medical values and broader human concerns and values.

NOTES

1. One distinction we had thought about was between the physician as decision-maker and the physician as executor of the decision. The physician works with others to determine an appropriate course of action, and in that sense is a codecider with others, but the physician is also still responsible for carrying out the decision. This distinction, however, does not eliminate the tension between an individual and group responsibility. But perhaps it does point more clearly to a real problem in an understanding of the professions that seeks to open up the process of judgment and yet to maintain the idea of unique responsibility. This problem requires further examination not possible in this paper.
2. The communities with whom the ethicist is in dialogue are many. One of the ethicists' contributions is to identify the communities that are involved in a particular decision, and to help determine those that are most suited to advise in a particular case. This is a very complex idea, however, and one we can only touch on here. We hope to expand on the meaning of "community" in the decision-making process, as well as the role of the physician in interacting with communities, in a later paper.

REFERENCES

Caplan, A. L.: 1983, "Can applied ethics be effective in health care and should it strive to be?" *Ethics* **93**, 311–319.
Churchill, L. R.: 1978, "The role of the stranger, the ethicist in professional education," *The Hasting Center Report* **8**, 13–15.
Culver, CM., Clouser, K.D., Gert, B., Brody, H., Fletcher, J., Jonsen, A., Kopelman, L., Lynn, J., Siegler, M., Wikler, O.: 1985, "Basic curricular goals in medical ethics," *The New England Journal of Medicine* **312**, 253–256.
Siegler, M.: 1979, "Clinical ethics and clinical medicine," *Archives of Internal Medicine* **139**, 914–915.
Thomasma, D.: 1982, "Humanities training for health professionals, reflections in Loyola of Chicago and the University of Tennessee," *Möbius* 73–80.

Study Questions

1. What is the precise meaning of an ethics consultant as portrayed in this article?
2. What is the relationship between teaching, consulting, and actually making decisions, if any?

Teaching Medical Ethics in Other Countries

Sir Gordon Wolstenholme*

Author's abstract

In the past 20 years, around the world, there has been an explosion in the teaching of medical ethics. As the dust begins to settle, it would appear that such teaching is likely to have its most effective impact not during the undergraduate period but at the immediate postgraduate level and in continuing education. While important contributions can be made by teachers of religion, philosophy and law, probably the essential wisdom, capable of standing a doctor in good stead throughout the developments of a lifetime's career, must largely come from those who have studied both medicine and ethics. It would be appropriate if the study of medical ethics were to lead to better international understanding among doctors.

In all the countries known to me, apparently no formal teaching in medical ethics took place until at least 1965. For example, an editorial in the *Journal of the American Medical Association*[1] in 1976 contained the comment that "as an intellectual endeavor, medical ethics was virtually nonexistent in American medical schools up to less than a decade before;" and Blomquist[2] in Sweden, writing in 1975 noted that "nowhere in Europe today is there formal teaching in ethics for medical students." Up to about 20 years ago, the traditional way of learning ethical concepts in medicine from the example of distinguished and admired clinical teachers

---

* Harveian Librarian, The Royal College of Physicians

128

had seemed adequate, and what formal instruction there was, was concerned more with matters of legality or medical etiquette.

During the last two decades there have arisen, as we all know, unprecedented problems for which learning by example has everywhere become inadequate. And everywhere the spotlight of publicity has been turned by the media onto the manner in which doctors take their many unavoidable decisions.

Needless to say, the spotlight has had its greatest wattage in the United States, generating heat as well as light, incubating and hotting up arguments for which few doctors in my generation were prepared. There is still a major distinction between the U.S. and ourselves in regard to decision-making, which essentially we continue to regard as ultimately a medical responsibility, whereas in America many other disciplines believe they have an equal right not only to an opinion, but also to a power of decision in matters of life and death.

In 1963 a committee of the Association of American Medical Colleges began to make plans for a Society of Health and Human Values, which came fully into existence in 1969. With funding from the National Endowment for the Humanities, the society supports an Institute of Human Values in Medicine—its director, Dr Edmund Pellegrino, has written a great deal on the "humanizing" of medicine, a sad tautological reflection on our profession—and the society publishes a *Journal of Medicine and Philosophy*. By 1969, also, there had come into existence The Hastings Institute of Society, Ethics and Life Sciences[3] which organizes conferences and publishes reports; and also the Kennedy Institute of Human Reproduction and Bioethics, which aims to encourage an academic approach and research. By 1973 it was possible to record a "massive growth" of courses in the previous five years, many of which took the form of summer schools, with teachers drawn from law, religion and nursing, as well as medicine. Tensions were, however, even then developing as to how far those from nonscientific disciplines could contribute to discussion of highly complex medical problems, and a new breed of "ethicists" not surprisingly began to make its appearance.

In 1974, on the initiative of The Hastings Center, a national commission began a three-year study on the teaching of medical ethics in American medical schools[4]. Out of 112 schools, 107 replied to a questionnaire; 97 claimed to give special instruction in medical ethics (the other 10 schools excused themselves as new or still provisionally accredited) but of the 97, only in 6 was the course in medical ethics mandatory; it was elective in 47; ethical issues were discussed in a variety of courses in 69; 56 arranged conferences or lectures; and, interestingly, 12 schools had created clerkships of one month's duration during which ethical problems arising in any part of the hospital would be intensively studied, with the aid of an ethicist. The commission noted that in a period of two years there had been a threefold increase in the provision of courses—trust American enthusiasm—and a 50 percent increase in the number of teachers involved.

Among American developments in the 1970s, illustrative of an intensification of academic involvement in medical ethics, I may mention a collaborative effort between the Kennedy Institute and Georgetown University, Washington, D.C., providing a PhD course in bioethics and the publication of a bibliographical record of new titles in bioethics; a joint program between the Institute for the Medical Humanities in Galveston, the University of Texas at Austin and the Southern Methodist University; the institution of MA and PhD degrees in bioethics at the University of Tennessee; the introduction at Hershey Medical School, Pennsylvania, of 15 elective courses in medical ethics, two of which must be taken; a Harvard interfaculty program in medical ethics, involving the Divinity School, the School of Public Health, the Graduate School of Arts and Sciences and the Medical School; and from 1974 the foundation by the University of California, Los Angeles (UCLA) School of Medicine, its Aesculapian Society, the UCLA Committee on Public Lectures and the UCLA Medical Center, of a medical and social forums[5] providing a series of tightly organized videotapes to form the basis for small group discussions. And by 1979 the National Science Foundation had established EVIST[6], a program of Ethics and Values in Sciences and Technology.

Despite, or because of, the multiplication of courses, Brody[7], writing in the *JAMA* in 1974, was already bewailing a lack of definition of objectives and a failure to build in a process of evaluation of courses, without which students were regarding courses in ethics as unserious, irrelevant and avoidable. A course in Ohio[8], which began in 1979, seemed to go to the other extreme: it has been described as a cognitive-developmental approach, based on psychological and educational theories and philosophical rationale, and is based on six stages of moral reasoning.

Recently the State of California has legislated for the compulsory inclusion of teaching of medical ethics in its medical schools (also human sexuality and recognition of child abuse); and before leaving the U.S. I should emphasise that there is an ongoing, widespread and passionate debate on the ethics of social policies in the provision of primary health care.

I have spent much of my short time on the American ethical scene; it is inexhaustible and overwhelming in its manifestations and certain to influence, if it is not already doing so, all other countries.

In Canada, it was noted in 1982[9] that McGill had had formal undergraduate instruction in medical ethics "for some time," based in a Department of Humanities and Social Studies in Medicine. And the University of Western Ontario[10], with a neighboring Westminster College, had set up by 1978 "a center for research on ethics and the quality of life."

Coming over to Europe, Maastricht University in the Netherlands[11], which in 1975 was a new, eighth school of medicine in Holland, introduced a new curriculum based largely on problem-oriented teaching, in small groups and with a lot of student self-teaching, which includes periods of training with GPs and social workers, all aided by an ethicist, who remains available throughout clinical training. The new curriculum called for professorships in medical psychology, medical sociology and medical ethics. Most other Dutch schools provided lectures and tutorials on medical ethics ona voluntary basis, but Nijmegen[12] went further, with monthly ethical meetings and ethical discussions held regularly within six clinical departments.

West Germany, after World War II, was in a difficult, appropriately embarrassing situation in the deep shadow of Nazism and the Nuremberg trials. Up to 1979 there was no systematic teaching of ethics at the undergraduate or graduate level, or in continuing education[13]. Even the old tradition of teaching by example was in difficulties because of the excessive number of students, insufficient opportunities for clinical experience, a lack of bedside oral presentations, and a tightly packed six-year dictated curriculum. Freiburg University was perhaps the first to show an ethical initiative, devising courses for medical students, student nurses and social workers.

In France[14], although about 98 percent of the population are protected by insurance against the cost of illness, some 78 percent of doctors (46 percent of them GPs and 32 percent specialists) practice privately and gain their incomes from fees. The legal and social security background is complicated and this is reflected in some schools by the elaborate courses provided. According to Dr. J. Autin, Secretary-General, in Paris, of the Conférence Internationale des Ordres, the European Assembly of the medical regulating bodies within the European Economic Community, a single course-package may include forensic medicine, regulations of relations between doctors and other health professionals, human rights, consent to treatment, attitudes to torture, dangers to the public from alcoholism, abuse of drugs, commitment of the mentally ill, prevention of practice by the sick doctor, responsibilities of the doctor in a court of law, organization of social security systems, accuracy and validity of certification, duties in case of death, responsibilities in regard to examinations before marriage, contraception, abortion and crimes of sexual violence; and considerable instruction in health economics. The Ordre National— the equivalent of rather more than the registration responsibilities of the GMC—is active in producing video films giving examples of ethical dilemmas in practice; and the French, as many of you know, have made a praiseworthy attempt to impose a common ethical outlook on the rest of Western Europe, but unfortunately without due regard to the religious, legal and social backgrounds which still distinguish our separate countries.

Medical ethics in Italy are usually taught as part of a course on legal medicine, according to information from Dr. Rino Reggio, an officer of the Federazione Nazionale Degli Ordini Dei Medici, the equivalent in Italy of the British Medical Association. Since October 1983 the National Federation of Medical Orders has urged the provincial orders to set up courses of postgraduate continuing education about medical ethics and health legislation. The courses, which are already proving highly successful, include such topics as professional secrecy, obligation to cooperate with health authorities and the police, confidentiality of medical documentation, interruption of pregnancy, euthanasia, and experimentation on man.

Yugoslavia[15] introduced into its penal code in 1963 a Code of Ethics for Medical Workers, not only for doctors but also for all paramedicals. Undergraduates receive some 30 hours, and postgraduates some 30 to 40 hours of instruction, in which forensic medicine includes coverage of medical ethics.

In a somewhat similar way, according to Edward Shotter, Director of the Institute of Medical Ethics President Ceaucescu in Romania, when asked about medical ethics, put it simply and without argument: "A doctor shall have the same ethics as the worker."

In 1975, at a conference in Bulgaria, the Russians poured scorn on the barbarity of the British when I was unable to produce evidence of the formal teaching of ethics in our medical schools, but retreated into silence when I told them of student initiative and energy in the busy activities of the London Medical Group and the (then) Society for the Study of Medical Ethics.

Last, but very far from least, the situation in Scandinavia: according to Blomquist (2), the first academic teacher in medical ethics was appointed in 1975, but his teaching and research were to be carried out beyond his full-time duties as a clinical psychiatrist and lecturer in psychiatry. Voluntary courses for medical students were begun in 1975, but it was soon evident, as Blomquist says, that "it is easier for a medical doctor to learn ethics than for a moral philosopher to learn medicine." The Swedish Society of Medical Sciences set up a Delegation for Medical Ethics which included a representative from medicine, surgery, pediatrics, psychiatry and clinical pharmacology, four lay members and trade union and legal representatives.

Denmark shows perhaps the greatest activity, according to Dr. Povl Riis, Physician-in-Chief of the Medical Gastroenterological Department in the University Hospital, Copenhagen, possibly because they have experimented so freely in social behavior. Nevertheless, at the undergraduate level, in the three medical schools there is no formal ethical teaching. There are two small textbooks for undergraduates. However, at the postgraduate level there are no less than 40 to 50 intensive courses in which ethical considerations are much to the fore in discussion of medical and scientific methodology. A course usually lasts six days, one day being reserved for ethics and research. The Danish Medical Association also includes ethics in many courses for GPs. The Danes even export the teaching of medical ethics—under the direction of Dr. Riis, the courses have been extended to Greenland, Iceland, the Faroes, Sweden, the Netherlands, Yugoslavia, even the UK—and in April 1984 courses were held in China.

So perhaps an international outlook, which in our Western

medicine is so often lacking, may at last be opened up on a global basis, appropriately through the teaching of medical ethics.

REFERENCES

1. Anonymous. Medical ethics, education and the physician's image. [editorial]. *Journal of the American Medical Association* 1976; 235: 1043.
2. Blomquist C. The teaching of medical ethics in Sweden. *Journal of medical ethics* 1975; 1: 96–98.
3. Veatch R. M., Fenner D. The teaching of medical ethics in the United States of America. *Journal of medical ethics* 1975; 1: 99–101.
4. Veatch R. M., Sollito S. Medical ethics teaching. Report of a national medical school survey. *Journal of the American Medical Association* 1976; 235: 1030–33.
5. Anonymous. Medicine and society forum, University of California, Los Angeles. News and notes. *Journal of medical ethics* 1975; 1: 159.
6. Anonymous. Changing values in medicine. News and notes. *Journal of medical ethics* 1979; 5: 153.
7. Brody H. Teaching of medical ethics. *Journal of the American Medical Association* 1974; 229: 177–179.
8. Goldman S. A., Arbuthnot J. Teaching medical ethics: the cognitive-developmental approach. *Journal of medical ethics* 1979; 5: 170–181.
9. Lella J. Letter: Teaching of medical ethics. *Journal of medical ethics* 1982; 8: 111.
10. Anonymous. [editorial]. Ethical codes and professional conduct. *Journal of medical ethics* 1978; 4: 105.
11. Sporken P. The teaching of medical ethics in Maastricht. *Journal of medical ethics* 1975; 1: 181–183.
12. Wachter M. A. M. de. Teaching medical ethics: University of Nijmegen, the Netherlands. *Journal of medical ethics* 1978; 4: 84–88.
13. Seidler E. The teaching of medical ethics in the Federal Republic of Germany. *Journal of medical ethics* 1979; 5: 76–79.
14. Regnier F, Rouzioux J-M. Certain aspects of medical ethics in France. *Journal of medical ethics* 1983; 9: 170–174.
15. Milciuski J., Stražišćar S. Teaching medical ethics: Ljubljana School of Medicine, Yugoslavia. *Journal of medical ethics* 1980; 6: 145–148.

Study Questions

1. How could it be argued that only a medically qualified person can fully understand the application of ethics to clinical situations? *Defend* your answer with solid, logical reasons.
2. Do you consider that international discussion of the problems of medical ethics could lead to greater understanding between doctors in different countries of their shared responsibilities?

The Unruly Rise of Medical Capitalism

James A. Morone*

Everybody agrees that something dramatic is happening in the health business. The dispute is over what it is and whether we should view it with alarm, indifference, or relief.

One essential fact is clear: corporate capitalism has discovered medicine and swiftly turned enormous profits by providing it. Five companies that did not exist in 1968 now own or manage more than one out of seven hospitals in the United States. For-profit corporations made $1,160,000,000 in 1983 (before taxes); they have begun to acquire related enterprises such as nursing homes and hospital supply companies, and they continue to grow at a breathless rate. Comparing these corporations to traditional medical services is—as Bradford Gray puts it—like comparing agribusiness to the family farm.

Corporate medicine is possible today partially because of what did not happen in the past. Most industrial nations long ago defined health care as a right of citizenship, sponsored—if not provided—by the state. National programs, rooted in a firm vision of entitlement, restrict the field for medical entrepreneurs.

In the United States, however, the conception of health care as a right guaranteed by the state has been intermittently asserted, always disputed, and only partially achieved. National health insurance was proposed and defeated before World War I; it was

* James A. Morone is a professor of political science at Brown University.

135

scratched out of the Social Security Act (1935) at the last moment, served as Harry Truman's major domestic issue in the 1948 campaign, passed for a fraction of the population (as Medicare) during the Great Society (1965), and failed by growing margins in the Ford and Carter years. Despite the apparent popularity of broad entitlements to health care, reforms calling for a state-dominated health care system have been checked repeatedly by two powerful political principles.

The first is free-market enterprise, generally contrasted to tyrannical government intervention (which is fancifully known as "socialized medicine"). Senator Robert Taft challenged Harry Truman with what was already a trusty line of political reasoning: "It has always been assumed in this country that those able to pay . . . would buy their own medical service, just as under any system, except a socialistic one, they buy their own food, their own housing, their own clothing and their own automobiles." (Quoted in Robert and Rosemary Stevens, *Welfare Medicine in America*, 1974, p. 21.)

Though the issue has by now lost some of its zing, entitlement theorists continue to argue that health care is just another commodity—"like beer or panty hose." (Robert Veatch in *The New Health Care for Profit*, p. 142) It follows that health care is no more a right than any other good or service, and that the state has no business reshaping the health market through compulsory national insurance schemes. While some assistance might be provided to the poor, a broad notion of medical care as "a right of the patient . . . protected by government law . . . entails the threat of violence against physicians" and is therefore "immoral." (Robert Sade, "Medical Care as a Right: A Refutation," *The New England Journal of Medicine*, December 2, 1971, p. 1280)

The second, perhaps more important, principle standing against state action has been the almost zealous struggle of physicians to remain autonomous. For a long time, state intervention was the most obvious threat. The arguments extolling free medical markets were often made in order to protect physician autonomy from government programs.

State action, when it came, came timidly and with deference to the profession. For instance, the Medicare statute begins not with bold assertions of entitlement but with a denial that any bureaucrat would "exercise any control over the practice of medicine." (*The Social Security Act*, Section 1801) It financed care almost without constraints, paying what providers charged; and when controls were introduced, in the early 1970s, they were turned over to the profession itself. A hospital system that was generously financed but poorly controlled developed problems: relentless inflation coupled ironically with bankrupt urban hospitals and widespread claims that no one was caring for the poor. American policymakers began to grope for solutions. A half century of homage to free enterprise, a growing sense of trouble, the public eye cocked hopefully toward medical markets, and a reluctance to impose public solutions, all prepared the way for the for-profit corporations.

For-profit chains scramble the traditional discourse over American health policy by pitting the principle of free enterprise against that of physician autonomy. After five decades of mobilizing support against government threats to their autonomy, physicians are suddenly finding that free enterprise means large corporations whose profit-seeking nature and business hierarchy provide both ends and means to threaten that autonomy.

Predictably, the corporations act with a legitimacy that government action has only rarely been able to muster. For instance, when public planning boards (complete with citizen representatives) sought to reduce redundant services in neighboring hospitals, it proved easy to mobilize support against meddlesome government; when corporations buy those hospitals and do likewise, their actions—firmly grounded in property rights—are rarely disputed.

But what does the rise of the corporation mean for American health care? None of these books cleanly answers the question. It is difficult to do so because so much else is happening at the same time: both public and private payers have increasingly moved to limit their own costs (by restricting payments, setting rates prospectively, shifting costs to patients, and so on); medical care providers have, in turn, responded in a wide variety of ways. Whether the medical corporations are a cause, a consequence, or simply an instance of change is often unclear. Still, some of what they do and don't do is clear; and even where it is not the interesting questions can be put.

Money and Medicine

One thing that the for-profit corporations do not do to medicine is introduce profits. This literature repeatedly asks whether patients will be less trustful now that they think their doctors have been tainted by capitalism. However, an association between money and medicine is nothing new. Physician salaries (they averaged $93,000 in 1981) and hospital prosperity are stock items in American popular culture.

At least since the early 1950s, the *New Yorker* has specialized in a brand of cartoon humor typified by the physician smiling not so benevolently into the telephone as he murmurs (to his patient's obvious discomfort), "Buy it if you really want it, dear. We'll find the money for it somehow." Another reviewer of Wohl's book, Robert Ubell, recalls a scene from "The Man Who Knew Too Much" in which Doris Day reminds a doctor played by Jimmy Stewart that their holiday was paid for by "Mrs. Campbell's gallstones" and her pearls by "Johnny Smith's tonsils."

If some observers fret over profits, others celebrate what might be called the folklore of American capitalism. This popular view welcomes the competition and efficiency that the chains have thrust onto the health sector. American medicine is said to be getting what it really needs—no-nonsense managers disciplined by attention to the bottom line. (See, for example, *Forbes*, August 1984.)

A rejoinder emerges from Robert Siegrist's report on the view from Wall Street (in *The New Health Care for Profit*). Financial analysts generally agree that the companies are efficient. But the critical issue is what the corporations are efficient at. The answer is clear in their recipe for success: price aggressively, emphasize profitable services, increase the intensity of care, attract physicians with the latest technology and patients with private bathrooms and color televisions. In brief, provide more expensive care in more expensive facilities set as far as possible from poor people (in suburbs) or government regulators (70 percent are in the South and West). The corporate chains may be extremely efficient. But they are efficient at what they have been established to do—make money for investors. There is no obvious return on controlling hospital inflation, much less getting better care to those who cannot afford it.

Investor-owned corporations should neither be blamed for introducing profit to American medicine nor acclaimed as a managerial fix. However, it is their management of profits that makes them distinctive. Furthermore, while making money is not new to medicine, it has rarely been the providers' unabashed raison d'etre. For-profit hospitals provide health care in order to generate income. The logic of their institutions turns on satisfying consumers—a far more limited mission than hospitals have traditionally articulated.

One obvious implication affects the long-disputed right to health care. When a hospital defines itself as a business, it defines medical services as a commodity rather than a right. Business logic leads away from allocating services on the basis of need. The for-profit hospitals are not the only ones to avoid indigent patients. But corporate incentives to care mainly for the well insured are not balanced by the hospital's philosophy or its tax status.

In the past, resistance to health care rights protected physician autonomy; in the for-profit corporations resistance threatens autonomy. Wohl describes a hospital in which the chief of medicine is a PR specialist with no medical training. Lay efforts to control or reshape the practice of medicine are by no means restricted to the investor-owned chains—the new Medicare payment scheme or prepaid group practices can have a similar effect. (See "DRGs: The Counterrevolution in Health Care" by Danielle Dolenc and Charles Dougherty and "The MD and the DRG" by E. Haavi Morreim, *Hastings Center Report*, June 1985, pp. 19–38.) But again the corporation is different in both conception and capacity. The organizing principle of these hospitals is return on investment; efficient management means measuring medical practice to those ends. In different situations, different styles of medicine will prove cost-effective—today it appears to be color televisions and high technology that pay. Managers and physicians may now agree on the preferred style of medical practice. However, in a business setting the business managers are likely to influence the choice.

The threat to medical judgment can be traced not simply to *ad hoc* accounts of pressured physicians or empirical analyses measuring medical outcomes in different settings but to the logic of the organizational form itself. Furthermore, the corporations have the capacity to make their managerial judgments stick, the crux of their celebrated efficiency. They have developed the resources both to measure the financial consequences of physician behavior and—as in every corporation—to mete out sanctions and rewards. (The disposition of subsidized office space near the hospital is a well-known example.) As Siegrist's financial analysts conclude, even in a less hospitable future of tightening financial controls, "The hospital management companies will be in the best position to cope." When free enterprise clashes with physician autonomy, the money men are betting on the former.

The Politics of Corporate Medicine

Another consequence of the medical corporation—its political effects—is more significant but less often analyzed. The for-profits are powerful and well organized; they have already taken their place among the health care interest groups. Political reform in America must generally thread its way past the most affected interests. What sort of role are these new political actors likely to play?

First, they will undoubtedly seek to protect the conditions that have permitted their growth—a pastiche of reasonably generous public and private payers, free of any single overarching national program. To be sure, a generous national health entitlement, a broad extension of Medicare to the entire population, for instance, might appear to benefit them. But so extravagant an entitlement has not been seriously contemplated since the Truman administration. Rather, liberal reforms (such as those in Senator Edward Kennedy's last three national health insurance proposals) seek to limit lavish reimbursements in order to distribute health benefits more broadly. Trading off high payments ("quality of care" is the industry's argot) for increased access would not profit the chains; they are likely to oppose it lustily. Corporate medicine adds another, powerful, interest into a political equation already tilted against redistributive programs. The absence of a national health program facilitated the rise of for-profits; it is likely to be perpetuated by their power.

This is not to suggest that the corporations will fend off all governmental intervention in medicine. On the contrary, they are likely to facilitate federal regulation. A broadly regulatory approach to health care costs is not incompatible with the hospital chains; corporate industries are often characterized by extensive federal regulation. Furthermore, by placing the physician and the local hospital in a corporate setting, they undercut what were once powerful political symbols working against government intervention. The new setting may permit regulatory reformers to make "big business" the relevant symbol. It has always been sporting to bash large corporations in American politics.

In the end, the politics of corporate medicine are likely to resemble the politics of many other corporate sectors: active government regulation (driven in the health case by the government's role as a purchaser) that constrains but does not fundamentally threaten the corporation. Indeed, if the experience in other sectors is a guide, state officials may come to protect the industry, citing its economic significance and the welfare of the workers that its companies employ.

Too Soon to Tell

The eleven authors in the three volumes above take on the investor-owned hospital corporations from every angle but the political. If their works arrive at a single judgment, it is probably the sensible one—that it is too early to tell what the corporations really mean for American medicine.

Stanley Wohl's *The Medical Industrial Complex* appears, at first blush, to be the most disapproving. It is packaged in the best traditions of American muckraking: the title is a phrase popularized by Arnold Relman in the first widely circulated critique of corporate medicine; it conjures up all the insidious implications of the military industrial complex. The dust jacket asks pointedly, "Are these corporations making health profits at the expense of your health?" Wohl picks up the motif in his first chapter: "I fear that the unfettered corporate practice of medicine may well destroy" [medicine's] "commitent . . . that . . . each individual enjoy the most disease-free body that state-of-the-art knowledge allows."

It quickly becomes clear, however, that this is a very limited indictment. Wohl fears that "the wrong type of people are exerting a great measure of control over the nation's health," which is to say that "the grey flannel suit is replacing the white coat." He has no brief against the corporations—we need their "know how"—as long as they leave medical practice in medical hands and do not threaten physician incomes. Wohl is explicit about the latter, lamenting that physicians should not be blamed for medical inflation since they receive "only two dollars of every ten billed to patients." Despite the title and attendant rhetoric, Wohl is ultimately uncritical of the corporate managers; his concern is that physicians will be cut out of the action. In the end, *The Medical Industrial Complex* is more interesting as illustration than analysis— one physician's well-written concern over his profession's status within the for-profit hospital corporations.

Bradford Gray's sober volume, a product of a roundtable at the Institute of Medicine, is a far more illuminating introduction to for-profit corporations. Robert Veatch does a particularly fine job of sorting the ethical themes that attend medical profits. He neatly lays out the evolution of provider practices and the medical controversies that surrounded them. Robert Siegrist's essay on the Wall Street perspective is devoid of soft sentiments, yet full of implicit ethical issues embedded in the financiers' jargon. Harold S. Luft's essay is a carefully drawn juxtaposition of the physician and economic perspectives; it is one of the few places in the volume—in any of the volumes—where the two are linked, though social scientists may find Luft overly gentle in breaking the news to physicians that their world is becoming more like the one that economists have always seen. Jessica Townsend grounds the more theoretical discussions with a description of five corporate takeovers and the issues that they raise. Other essays examine legal aspects of the investor-owned chains (competition is blurring the differences between the profits and the not-for-profits), the dynamics of the physician's role in hospital decision making (nicely laid out by Stephen Shortell), and the physician-patient relationship in a fiduciary context.

Taken together, the volume forms a fine introduction to many of the issues. However, like many symposia, the sum is not clear. Most of the authors do not write as if they have shared a roundtable: they do not take much account or shed much light on one another. The failure may be symptomatic of a larger question that nags most discussions of for-profit hospital corporations: What exactly is the subject? Health care for profit, as the title suggests? Or, as he subtitle shifts the question, the newly competitive hospital environment that is emerging regardless of profits? It is often unclear which is thought to be causing what.

Further, overlapping issues include the role of the physicians in the changing hospital, the gray suits challenging the white coats (again, regardless of profits); large hospital chains (profit or not) with their emphasis on expansion; and, more peripherally in this collection, the aggravation of a two-tier medical system (first class and poor) or the implications of oligopoly in medicine. Despite Gray's well-crafted introduction, the volume never sorts out exactly what is affecting what and how profit (or competition) fits in. Ultimately, we get a fine series of snapshots that captures specific issues, but no real grip on what is happening to American medicine.

For that, we get a better feel from a far less analytic book. *The Healing Mission and the Business Ethic* is a collection of essays written by Robert Cunningham over 15 years (largely for the *Journal of the American Medical Association*). It is a punchy, rambunctious, streetwise, irreverent, thoroughly enjoyable ramble through recent history. The collection underscores both the swiftness with which the health care world has changed and the intractability of the stubborn problems it confronts.

One vignette, from an essay written in January 1969, describes a conference of economists and hospital administrators. The former were incredulous at the notion that "demand responds to supply in this business rather than vice versa." Finally an economist offers, "If supply increases demand we're in real trouble. If this is true, it's next to impossible to rationalize this industry."

In the end, all three books tangle not just with profits but with a rash of overlapping developments—policies, institutions, entrepreneurs—that seek to rationalize the health care delivery system, or a portion of it. The for-profit hospital corporations are one—crucial, powerful—instance in this wide rationalizing impulse. Their development makes it less likely that the impulse will take the form of redistribution from the political center; and more likely that public regulatory power will ultimately freeze into place the current health care financing melange.

Study Questions

1. From your understanding of history, how would you argue either for or against Morone's claim that, ultimately, the federal government will *protect* the new medical corporations.

2. In discussing the efficacy of the medical corporations, Morone asserts that the notion that corporate chains will provide ". . . , efficiency . . ." and ". . . no-nonsense managers disciplined by attention to the bottom line" is merely part of "the folklore of American capitalism." How would you defend this "folklore" against Morone's charges? Mention specific examples of other kinds of corporations that *have*, in fact, clearly introduced such efficiency.

Kindnesses and Duties in the Abortion Issue

Michael J. Matthis

Judith Thomson's "A Defense of Abortion"[1] bases its arguments on the claim that many of our most important obligations derive from promises and agreements made between contracting parties. For this reason, in the absence of any evidence of a voluntary commitment by the mother to allow the fetus the right to the use of her body, abortion may be justified without disputing the fetus' claim to personhood. Crucially the success of her argument relies on the premise that responsibilities to aid, assist, or improve the position of other persons all derive from the transaction of promises or agreements: I have no duty to help you at my expense unless I have assumed it voluntarily. On the other hand, I also have a duty not to interfere with the rights of others, where such interference is not requested, and this duty of restraint on my freedom does not derive from my consent but from such "natural rights" as the right to life and the right to choose the use of one's own body,[2] natural because independent of consent or agreement.

In essence, then, actions considered by Thomson to fall within the class of duties and obligations, those morally binding on any ethical agent, amount to two separate kinds: those that are morally required because voluntarily accepted or agreed to, or what Thomson terms "special responsibilities,"[3] and those that are morally required by virtue of natural rights inherent in all persons, actions we might term "general responsibilities," in the absence of any designation by Thomson. Beyond these, a large number of actions that are morally neutral, or that do not arise in a context of obligation, are discussed throughout her article: aiding distressed victims of assault out of kindness (the Good and Minimally Decent Samaritans); monstrously refusing to aid distressed victims; offering one's hand out of kindness to the fevered brow of someone who otherwise will die; refusing out of callousness to offer one's hand; giving chocolates to one's brother out of kindness; refusing out of greed to give chocolates. All of these actions, Thomson argues, contain no implications of moral responsibility; they are examples of nice or mean, decent or indecent, kind or callous behavior, falling, presumably, under some kind of social formulation of acceptable or unacceptable behavior, but are outside the universal range of moral actions. Of course, one may *agree* to some "special responsibility" out of kindness or greed, but then only subsequent acts are morally binding, the initial act itself being entirely of one's own inclination. Now while some commentators have questioned a moral foundation that would leave so large a number of human actions outside the governance of morality and justice, a claim basically that hers is too narrow a view of morality,[4] no one has examined what seems to me to be the most significant flaw in her argument, an internal inconsistency which, if pursued, will in fact commit Thomson on her own terms to a position significantly close to the antiabortion argument, thereby effectively widening her moral basis to a level perhaps acceptable by those critics. Thus my aim is to show that, by her own logic, Thomson must agree that certain basic actions that are supposed to be "morally neutral" are in fact, if we read her argument carefully, part of a large range of *general responsibilities* deriving from some nontransactional moral basis. By analyzing her position critically from within, rather than criticizing it from without through some other standard of morality, I hope to find a wider area of agreement in the abortion dispute than now seems to exist.

Thomson's principal line of attack against the antiabortion argument is directed not against the thesis that the fetus is a person, an idea she accepts for the sake of argument, but against the idea that a person's right to life is more fundamental than a person's right to choose the use of his or her own body. Thus the antiabortionist claims, according to Thomson, that the mother must consent under almost any circumstance to the use of her body by the fetus, since without it the fetus rarely has the chance to live, and "isn't the child's right ot life weightier than anything other than the mother's own right to life, which she might put forward as the ground for abortion?"[5] Thomson questions the cogency of this reasoning, doing so through the use of her celebrated analogy of the violinist who needs a woman's kidneys for nine months and is therefore hooked up with the woman mechanically for that purpose. Thomson's intuitions tell her that no woman must sacrifice nine months of her body's life for the life of someone else, unless that right has been given beforehand by agreement, that we therefore have no natural, noncontractual duty to assist others in preserving their own life: "My own view is that if a human being has any just, prior claim to anything at all, he has a just prior claim to his own body."[6]

The grounds upon which this lack of a natural social obligation rest seem at times in her argument to coincide with the inconvenience, sacrifice, or risk involved in aiding others who need our help in order to live: "I have been arguing that no person is morally required to make *large sacrifices* to sustain the life of another who has no right to demand them. . . ."[7] And further "I am suggesting that if assuming responsibility (for another's life) would require large sacrifices, then (we) may refuse."[8] The argument then seems to suggest or imply that where no large sacrifice or risk is involved, then refusal to aid others in their struggle for life is morally impermissible. But this implication would mean that we do indeed have some form of a natural social duty to others, a positive duty, and not simply a negative duty that prohibits interference in the rights of others. And once this kind of positive duty is allowed to stand, it is only a short step to the position the antiabortionists are trying to defend, that in comparison with the possible loss of another person's life, the burden of carrying even an accidental and unwanted fetus to term is small indeed, and must therefore be accepted as part of our social duty to contribute to and aid the lives of all persons if called on by circumstance to do so.

No doubt sensing the possibly crucial opening that any such natural, positive social duty would give to opponents of abortion, Thomson equivocates on the position, arguing, in what one must assume is her primary position, that no one has any *right* to demand that I help them unless I have so authorized this right through a prior agreement; that is, unless I have contractually given them a special right over me requiring my assistance. By adopting this position, Thomson wants completely to avoid any circumstance in which a woman, or anyone innocent of prior consent, must suddenly give up her own freedom to assist another person, the refusal of which would be unjust. In trying to convince us of the truth of this view, Thomson appeals to some fairly obvious cases in which we would have difficulty declaring that one's refusal to give assistance to needy parties or victims is unjust. Thus the woman who finds herself suddenly plugged into the violinist for nine months without her prior approval is not unjust if she refuses to help him. Were she to accede now to the violinist's demand and grant him the nine month stay, the woman would be what Thomson terms "kind": "No doubt it would be very nice if you did, a great kindness. But do you *have* to accede to it?"[9] Thomson's choice of words—very nice, kind—are crucial to the success of her argument, for they are chosen precisely for the purpose of showing that we do have a group of actions that lie outside the realm of moral requirements, and so must not be judged morally good or bad, just or unjust, when undertaken.

Without actually analyzing this hidden assumption in her argument, Thomson seems to have concluded that a kindness is a morally neutral kind of action, since the concept suggests an action that arises out of an agent's own generosity, a gratuity, one that goes above and beyond the required and the expected. Certainly if someone is obligated morally to perform a certain action, it would be odd to label such an action as kind without distorting what is important to the concept, its gratuitous and generous aspect. For this reason Thomson argues that a Good Samaritan, by definition, is not doing something morally expected or required, and that therefore the refusal to be kind, to be a Good Samaritan, cannot be judged morally blameworthy. If one is not required to do the act, failure to do the act cannot be labeled immoral, and as a result the thirty-eight people who did not rush out to aid Kitty Genovese from a ruthless attack are not immoral, since giving aid at the risk of one's own life is a kindness, is not morally required: "At all events it seems plain that it was not morally required of any of the thirty-eight that he rush out to give direct assistance at the risk of his own life, and that it is not morally required of anyone that he give long stretches of his life—nine years or nine months—to sustaining the life of a person who has no special right . . . to demand it."[10]

Thomson therefore recognizes that the significant claims of her argument depend on the assimilation of the abortion decision to the same kind of decision one would make with regard to any act of generosity, so that by relegating it to the status of a kindness if one refuses to abort (in the absence of special obligations to the contrary) one is simply kind, and not morally good, because more than the required has been done. In like manner, Thomson claims that Henry Fonda is not morally required to cross the country to give the touch of his cool hand to someone who needs it in order to live: "It would be *frightfully nice* of him to fly in from the West Coast to provide it,"[11] but it is not unjust for him to refuse to do so. So far our intuitions concerning the woman and the violinist, the thirty-eight bystanders and Kitty Genovese, and Henry Fonda and the ailing woman perhaps match Thomson's and we can agree that no natural, general social duties to give assistance exist in such cases. Each of these are acts of kindness; but why are they acts of kindness? Are they kindnesses, and not duties; merely because large and difficult sacrifices or risks are involved, so that in cases where less trouble is required to assist we are no longer acting under the category of kindnesses but under that of duties? Such a conclusion could plausibly be argued for in the context of her presentations, and all the more so when Thomson claims that "We have in fact to distinguish between two kinds of Samaritan: the Good Samaritan and what we might call the Minimally Decent Samaritan."[12] A Minimally Decent Samaritan apparently is not required to do anything of difficulty or danger to help Kitty Genovese—just call the police from the safety of his locked room. In this case, do we now have a noncontractual, positive, general social duty to assist another, the refusal of which is immoral or unjust? One would think so, given that "We are not morally required to be Good Samaritans or anyway Very Good Samaritans to one another,"[13] in which case it would appear that a *Minimally Decent Samaritan*, if he is actually to be distinguished from the Good, is not simply a kind person deserving our admiration and applause if he does what he does, but a morally obligated person, deserving only our condemnation if he does not do what is morally expected.

Not surprisingly, however, Thomson abandons her occasional commitment to sacrifice, or large sacrifice, as the line at which duty ends and kindness begins and so wants to have nothing whatever to do with talk about general social duties, even at the level of Minimally Decent Samaritanship. The category of kindnesses, of morally neutral actions, for Thomson, in fact has nothing to do with the distinction of sacrifice/nonsacrifice, but belongs exclusively to the category of noncontractual actions, so that any action is a kindness (nonexpected), outside of those very few natural obligations,[14] if it is not part of the group of special obligations. There are, in fact, no natural social obligations for Thomson, even at the level of the Minimally Decent Samaritan, because even where very little, if any, sacrifice is required to help or to save the life of another, Thomson refuses to classify one's failure to assist as morally *wrong* or *unjust*.

Thus in the case where a violinist might need only one hour of the woman's time for the use of her kidneys, a very small sacrifice is required, making the woman if she consents something on the order of a Minimally Decent Samaritan. Is the woman required morally, by justice, to accede to the violinist's request? No, according to Thomson, because no rights are violated by the woman's refusal, making the refusal a morally neutral act. If she refuses, she is "self-centered and callous, indecent in fact, but not unjust,"[15] indecency being the proper corollary for those who fail to be Decent Samaritans. But Thomson's point seems to be that at the moral level there is no distinction between the Decent and the Good Samaritan, despite her assertion to the contrary, that decency is also a species of kindness and therefore, like Good Samaritanship, not required by duty or the rights of others, but simply wells up freely within someone, to be offered like friendship if they choose, and to be refused if they so choose. Thus no one morally can require me to be decent, if decency is a kindness and therefore something like a gift, for which reason Thomson concludes that no one can condemn me morally for being indecent, that is, for refusing to be decent. They may call me names, such as mean, callous, selfish, but they may never appropriately call me unjust, because if decency and kindness are, by virtue of their gratuitous character, nonduties or are morally neutral, so too are indecency and unkindness, by virtue of their being the opposite of, and related conceptually to, decency and kindness.

Thomson unquestionably believes that she has created at least a logically impervious, if narrow, haven for the woman's exercise of her rights, and therefore is satisfied to accept charges of narrowness of morality and egocentricity of character, since she can always avoid the charge of being unjust and immoral within her own stated position. And the logic of her argument does have the appearance of consistency on its side: if we accept the idea that kindnesses are not duties, that gratuities cannot be expected or required, without undermining the meaning of such concepts, then a large class of actions must be accepted as morally neutral or irrelevant. Thus a kind action strikes us with a sense of awe or admiration precisely because it is the unusual, the unexpected, and the unrequired: someone has done something above and beyond the normal, the required, and expected. A morally required act cannot call up our wonder or applause, or else it would not be expected and demanded by virtue of moral law. In this way Thomson has secured a morally neutral zone of behavior for those who want to have abortions, in the absence of special obligations, and are willing to endure charges of being unkind and indecent, with the added solace of knowing that at least they are not unjust. For not having the abortion in, say, the case of pregnancy due to rape is very decent, but not morally expected, and so having the abortion is morally neutral, precisely *because* it is *unkind*, and so part of the category of kind/unkind acts.

Now while the logic supporting this position seems consistently to have made secure at least some acts of abortion, there is something logically and conceptually flawed in this reasoning process, a process that leads Thomson with a strange attraction, to the acceptance of unkind and indecent ways of behaving as morally safe kinds of action. There is admittedly something perverse about terming morally acceptable, or not unjust, an action that is also termed "monstrous,"[16] as Thomson in fact does in describing the indifference of the thirty-eight onlookers to Kitty Genovese's death. So too it is strange that the boy who refuses to share chocolates with his brother may be "greedy, stingy, callous—but not unjust."[17] And likewise it is strange that Henry Fonda, who now has only to cross a room in order to save the woman with the touch of his hand, is acting indecently but not unjustly if he refuses.[18] But the strangeness in each of these cases comes from more than any violation of our own conventional set of rights and wrongs. It derives precisely from the violation of the logic of the very terms that Thomson feels has been consistently employed. For the strategy that has enabled her to use acts of kindness as morally neutral, because gratuitous ways of behavior, does not, upon closer inspection, enable her or anyone to safeguard unkind actions from the realm of moral wrongs; the reason being that while we may logically accept acts of kindness, as unrequired, to be devoid of any connotation of duty, it does not follow that, merely because unkind acts are conceptual opposites of kind acts, they also have the same morally neutral status and so are beyond moral condemnation.

The central problem is Thomson's argument lies in the unexamined belief that unkind or indecent acts are indeed conceptual opposities of kind and decent acts, and therefore belong in the same morally neutral category. This assumption, however, is mistaken, as can easily be seen by analysis of the concepts kindness and unkindness. A kind act is indeed morally neutral, in the sense regarded as important by Thomson to her argument, because it does not derive its rationale from sources like rights and obligations outside the desire of the acting moral agent. A person is kind if he or she gives without requirement, expectation, or demand of some portion of his or her life, which gift we appropriately applaud or express gratitude toward precisely because it is not a duty. But what sort of act in fact is the conceptual opposite of a kind act, one that correctly lies on the same morally neutral plane? Assuredly it is not an unkind act, as Thomson supposes, for the important reason that unkind acts, as she herself asserts, are regarded by all as indecent, mean, and callous, among other things. But let us reflect on this. If a Good Samaritan, a Decent Samaritan, or even lower, is an object of our admiration and applause because of the *extra* effort of action employed in some nonrequired task, is it proper ever for us to condemn or disapprove of someone for failure to be a Good Samaritan, for failure to be kind? I argue that logically such disapproval is meaningless, that if a kind act, no matter how small its kindness, is in fact an unexpected gift, then no one has the right to complain that failure to be kind is unkind or indecent. Indeed, if failure to be kind is unkind, then the kind act never was a morally neutral act of pure generosity but something else, a required or expected act. And this is why unkindness is not the conceptual opposite of kindness.

Assuredly, unkindness *means* the opposite of kindness, but the exact conceptual opposite of kindness, that is, the act that signifies a *failure* to be kind, is something else. Perhaps indifference, or obliviousness, is the conceptual opposite of kindness, that wherein one chooses not to go above and beyond the expected and required, at which point one is not to be condemned by others, but only ignored by them. For if unkindness deserves our condemnation, as certainly it does, then it cannot be because one did not give an unexpected gratuity that one is unkind. A kindness is *above* and beyond, but therefore an unkindness is *below* the expected, for which reason the conceptual opposite of the unkind is the *expected*, not the generous or kind. I can never be labelled self-centered or callous because I fail to do *more* than is expected. A stranger is not unkind or indecent if he does not come over to me and give me five-unasked-for dollars; he is merely indifferent, or else kindness means nothing. He is certainly very kind if he offers me an unexpected gift, but he is not kind if he does only what is required, pays me back the five dollars he owes me. He is unkind *only* if he will not do what must be done, or what *ought* to be done, for which reason he deserves blame, censure, and disapproval if he does not pay me back for malicious reasons the money he owes me. And therefore the unkind act is never the failure to be kind, but the failure to do what is demanded, required, or expected.

Thus, if we grant Thomson that human actions fall into three categories, natural or general obligations, special or contractual obligations, and kindnesses, we are not committed to regarding unkind actions in the way she does as species of kind and morally neutral actions, but instead as part of those general obligations that merit condemnation if they are acted upon. Abortion in cases such as accidental pregnancy or rape may be, in her own words, "indecent,"[19] in which case by her own logic it must be considered immoral. For unkind actions cannot conceptually be a part of the list of kind actions, even as an opposite on that list, and must therefore be regarded as failures to act according to expected standards outside oneself. Now it may well be that not all expectations merit the status of "moral," but certainly expectations in the way intended by Thomson come close to, indeed arguably are identical with, moral expectations. That is, someone might *expect* me to arrive at eight for the meeting, but it is not really unkind of me to arrive late if the expectation is no more than the habit of a local custom with which I am not thoroughly acquainted. Again, someone might *expect* me to arrive at eight, if this is based on what I usually do, but such expectation is not moral in character, and is assuredly not what Thomson means by the concept. Someone might expect me, based on my talent, to become a violinist, but it is not unkind of me if I choose to do something else. In short, only where failure to do what is expected deserves the word *unkind* do we have a case of failure to do one's duty, that is, a case of using someone other, in the Kantian sense, as a means only, or of regarding the other person as a mere thing, rather than as a center of dignity and value, and this is exactly the way the word is used by Thomson throughout her article. That is, the boy is unkind in refusing to share his chocolates because he acts as though his brother is not there as a conscious and personal presence, acts as though he were a thing: Henry Fonda is unkind if he does not move across the room to save the woman, because he acts as though the being over there has no dignity, is a thing like a table or chair. In both cases, moral action of a positive, social nature is demanded by the context of the situation, wherein to do what is required is not a kindness but a moral expectation, and failure to do so is an unkindness, to the point of being a monstrosity in the case of Henry Fonda. Unkindness, therefore, is truly a category of moral concepts, far more so than the "agreement" complex of actions assigned by Thomson to the special category of the moral or dutiful. Thomson regards the breaking of an agreement as such as unjust, and the judgment of its monstrosity as something else, but it seems clear that the moral impact of the act is signified by words like monstrous. I may well make or break an agreement, but the judgment that such a making or breaking is monstrous or indecent is far more morally relevant, as Plato long ago perceived,[20] than the simple agreeing as such, an act that indeed seems on the face of it more morally neutral than an indecent or monstrous act would ever be. I may or may not make an agreement, but the judgment of its moral *worth* is always something separate, something to be judged by such words as monstrous and indecent, or by what is expected and required, and so forth.

In conclusion, Thomson's admission that the act of abortion, even in the absence of special obligations to the contrary, may well be labeled indecent seems to place her position nearer to that of the antiabortionists than she is clearly willing to concede. A fundamental complaint of antiabortionists against a position such as hers, I would imagine, has been the narrowness of her adopted morality that would enable her to accept indecent and selfish behavior as morally neutral, and therefore morally acceptable. I think now, by examining the presuppositions of Thomson's use of such words as kindness and unkindness, and noting carefully their real conceptual opposites, that we are entitled to argue that in terms of her own conceptual scheme, she is committed to labeling her own defense of abortion as unjust. Thomson now cannot avoid the requests of others that she broaden her moral base, because in fact she has already done precisely that, allowing us by her conceptual scheme to infer the existence of some general, noncontractual social duties, the duties not to be unkind and indecent. Ultimately Thomson might want to admit that unkind acts do indeed convey the moral overtones that kind acts do not, but that this does not nevertheless commit her to condemning abortion in, say, the case of someone who was impregnated accidentally. For surely, she might say, carrying the uninvited fetus to term for nine months cannot really be expected, since it is such a hardship, and so refusal to do so is not really unkind.

But even if we concede that an amended position accepting unkindness as morally relevant might well want to consider hardship as pertinent to the concept of kindness, we are never committed to the thesis that undergoing hardship for others always signifies a kindness, an unexpected gratuity, a morally neutral act. Kindness, as morally neutral, does indeed mean going beyond the expected and required, but nowhere is it written that difficulty and hardship are never morally expected, and when chosen are always acts of kindness. There may well be many cases where failure to undergo prolonged hardship accurately deserves the term "unkind" or "indecent," and that undergoing the hardship may not merit our applause, but only our acknowledgement that the required was met. I argue that carrying a fetus, a living person in Thomson's words, for nine months, even if the pregnancy is the product of an accident or a rape, is not simply a kindness, precisely because we must regard the act of evicting and sending a living person to a certain death as an act that is at least callous and self-centered, for which reason the bearing of that offspring is intuitively expected, and therfore normally required.

NOTES

1. *Philosophy and Public Affairs,* Vol. 1, No. 1 (1971), 47–66.
2. Cf. *Ibid.,* pp. 54 and 56.
3. Cf. *Ibid.,* p. 65.
4. Cf. John Finnis, "The Rights and Wrongs of Abortion: A Reply to Judith Thomson," *Philosophy and Public Affairs,* Vol. 2, No. 2, 117–149. Cf. also the article by Mary Anne Warren, "On the Moral and Legal Status of Abortion," *The Monist,* Vol. 57, No. 1 (1973), 43–61, wherein she attacks Thomson's article for giving up too much to the anti-abortionists; but in doing so, Warren argues that Thomson's moral base is too narrow, once personhood has been granted to the fetus, that a person's right to life cannot so easily be overridden as Thomson believes.
5. Thomson, p. 55.
6. *Ibid.,* p. 54.
7. *Ibid.,* p. 64.
8. *Ibid.,* p. 65.
9. *Ibid.,* p. 49.
10. *Ibid.,* p. 63.
11. *Ibid.,* p. 55. (Italics mine.)
12. *Ibid.,* p. 62.
13. *Ibid.,* p. 64.
14. I.e., the obligation to respect the right of others to use their bodies as they please and the obligation not to take the life of others, in the absence of any other conflict.
15. Thomson, p. 61.
16. *Ibid.,* p. 63.
17. *Ibid.,* p. 60.
18. *Ibid.,* p. 61.
19. Cf. p. 61: "And similarly, that even supposing a case in which a woman pregnant due to rape ought to allow the unborn person to use her body for the hour he needs, we should not conclude that he has a right to do so; we should conclude that she is self-centered, callous, indecent, but not unjust, if she refuses." The point is that, even though Thomson has given us a fantastic version of pregnancy in the case of rape, the term "indecency" is allowed to stand where no prior commitment or agreement to the fetus had been made. Thus nothing in principle stands in Thomson's way to admitting the in-decency of refusing to carry the offspring of a rape to term for nine months.
20. *Republic,* 331 c.

Study Questions

1. What view of the fetus, person or not a person, is assumed by both authors in this debate? Would it make any difference to their dispute

if their view of the fetus were wrong? (Engelhardt's essay may be helpful here.)

2. Distinguish carefully the concepts of general or natural responsibilities, on the one hand, and special or contractual responsibilities on the other.

Medical Ethics in the Clinical Setting: Challenging the MD Monopoly

*Janet Fleetwood, PhD**

From the time of Hippocrates to the mid-twentieth century, medical decision-making has fallen squarely on the shoulders of those thought to have the relevant medical training and technical expertise, physicians. But health care professionals were often making ethical decisions when they made *medical* ones, and frequently the difference between the issues was barely recognized. In the mid-1950s, the climate of health care began to change. The middle of the twentieth century marked the beginning of a time of great social unrest, setting the foundation for far-reaching social changes. Along with the civil rights movement and the women's movement came a more general concern for individual rights, including patients' rights in the health care "marketplace." The willingness to question authority in the social and political realm spread to a willingness to question authority in the medical realm. The burden of proof was shifted, placing on professionals a demand to justify their actions. Concurrent with the social upheaval came a great surge in available medical technology, such as the availability of ventilators to artificially produce respiration and human organ transplants. These new technological advances raised both possibilities and expectations, and gave rise to a new level of question. Doctors, once comfortably reliant on their sci-

* Janet Fleetwood received her PhD in philosophy from the University of Southern California. She was an assistant professor in the department of philosophy at Villanova University, and later moved to her present faculty position at the Medical College of Pennsylvania where she is a clinical medical ethicist.

entifically focused medical education, were suddenly faced with questions that went far beyond their training or experience. A few confused their technical competence with moral expertise and failed to see the extension of their experience that such answers would require. Most, however, recognized the scope of the dilemmas now newly exacerbated by the available technologies as well as a better informed and more assertive clientele.

As health care professionals have come to recognize the complexities of their role, many have looked to other professionals to provide education and guidance. This paper will examine the role of philosophers in the growth and development of medical ethics in the clinical setting. Although the involvement of philosophers is varied, it will focus on my work as a medical ethicist on the faculty of a medical school affiliated with an urban hospital.

I. Medical Ethics: Philosophy in Practice

Medical ethics, a branch of applied ethics, is the study of what constitutes morally justifiable conduct within the health care setting and the methods and principles by which such conduct is supported. It relies on a foundation of ethical theory as well as traditional moral principles.

Philosophers engaged as medical ethicists can make unique contributions to the health care setting. As Tom Beauchamp writes in "What Philosophers Can Offer,"[1] philosophers can be expected to make contributions to the clinical setting in four forms, including 1) "performing conceptual analysis," 2) "exposing the inadequacies and unexpected consequences of an argument," 3) "engaging in collaborative scholarly endeavors with professionals in other fields, as the basis for policy decisions," and 4) "participating in decision-making processes in institutional settings." More specifically, medical ethicists function as educators within the hospital community and as administrators for programs and policies that have far-reaching affects.

II. Educational Programs

Courses in medical ethics are frequently taught in the undergraduate curricula of both pre-medical students and nursing students, and these courses are important in establishing an interest in, and awareness of, bioethical issues. They do not, however, provide the same kind of training as medical ethics taught in the clinical context. In this section I will describe some of the educational programs in medical schools and health care facilities, and will provide an analysis of the similarities and differences between ethics education in a clinical setting and the more usual college environment. The first section discusses education programs for medical students. These programs are categorized as undergraduate medical education, or preclinical education, even though the students have already completed college. The section following the discussion of preclinical education addresses programs for new physicians who are completing their specialized clinical training, so are considered to be in their graduate years. The third section discusses programs for allied health professionals, particularly nurses, and the last section focuses upon programs for medical school faculty, most of which are themselves practicing physicians.

A. Preclinical Education

The first teaching programs in the humanities appeared in medical schools in the late 1960s, most notably at Pennsylvania State University College of Medicine, University of Florida College of Medicine, and State University of New York at Stony Brook Health Sciences Center School of Medicine.[2] A study by the Institute of Human Values in Medicine shows that in 1972, there were 11 programs in medical ethics and human values in medicine and by 1981 there were 65 such programs.[3] A 1982 survey by the AMA reported that of 127 medical schools, all but one offered courses in medical ethics, 38 of which had medical ethics as a required course.[4]

Programs that include elements of medical ethics are often broadly described as "human values courses," and include, in addition to topics in ethics, discussions of social and interpersonal aspects of patient care. Many programs have a dual approach, focusing both on ethics training and on the development of effective communication skills, thereby offering a comprehensive notion of humane medical care. While comparison between the content of various programs is difficult, a study done by Janet Bickel of the Association of American Medical Colleges shows the new and growing interest in values education.[5] That study indicates a growing commitment to teaching human values courses, broadly defined as "any course or component in which primary objectives included improvement of students' ability to examine their values in relation to those of their patients, communicate effectively with patients, or think critically about cultural, social, and ethical issues arising in medical care." Bickel's work and the 1986 survey of 126 U.S. medical schools by the AAMC showed that, of the 114 medical schools that responded, 84% require a human values course during the first or second year of medical school and 38% require one during the last two years. A 1985 article on ethics programs in medical schools, published in the Journal of the American Medical Association, states, ". . . studies give evidence of a steady progression in content and method toward more formal and rigorous ethical analysis of clinical-ethical issues."[6] It goes on to assert that these studies show that each successive graduating class of medical students is likely to have had more exposure to a structured approach to medical ethics than the preceding graduating class. This structured approach includes an analysis of the meanings of terms and theories as well as their founding assumptions, the logic of ethical argumentation, and the examination of competing courses of action. Similarly, a separate study on the status of the teaching of medical ethics concluded that, "the field is now sufficiently developed and the need for the application of ethical knowledge and skills in medicine sufficiently compelling to justify a recommendation that all medical schools require basic instruction in the subject."[7] The authors assert that such instruction should focus on common moral problems in medicine should include the clarification of concepts such as competency and consent, the elucidation and demonstrated application of decision-making procedures, and the teaching of communication skills. Clearly, interest in incorporating human values courses into the medical curriculum has increased sharply over the last two decades.

The Medical College of Pennsylvania is one of the schools that requires coursework in medical ethics for its medical students. The required ethics course, offered by the Division of Medical Humanities in the Department of Community and Preventive Medicine, is designed to introduce beginning medical students to the

complexities of medical decision-making and the moral underpinnings of such decisions. This course, codirected by an ethicist and
a physician, familiarizes students with competing moral values
and teaches them to develop and support an ethical stance with
reasoned arguments. It includes both lectures and small group
discussions and involves the active participation of various clinicians. As a medical ethicist, I work with physicians in an orientation program which precedes the course itself and which is
designed to explicate a clear method of analysis for moral dilemmas. In addition, I present selected lectures and participate in the
group discussions, which focus on cases that involve issues such
as withholding or withdrawing medical treatment, human experimentation, treatment of defective newborns, confidentiality and
disclosure, and informed consent.

Along with the formal teaching involved in the first-year required
bioethics course, my role is to develop and teach at least one
elective course in a topic in medical ethics. The topic for this
medical ethics elective might focus on competing social theories
as applied to the problem of allocation of health care resources,
or the application of ethical theory to the issue of withholding
treatment for seriously defective newborns. These electives are
part of a larger Medical Humanities Program, which includes such
courses as "History of Medicine," "Medicine and Literature," and
"Medicine and Religion," and which are available to medical students throughout their medical education.

B. Graduate Medical Education

Similarly, the concern for values education has spread to the graduate level, referred to as the residency. Recently the American
Board of Internal Medicine, the certification board for Internists,
has declared that it expects its residency program directors to
evaluate residents on such criteria as "integrity," "respect," and
"compassion." This new requirement is discussed in an article in
the Annals of Internal Medicine.[8] In support of it the authors of
the article state, "If residents are not encouraged to integrate
medical humanities into their ongoing clinical practice, they may
lose sight of the practical value of the medical humanities, and
the impact of innovative medical schools programs will be lost."

Like the American Board of Internal Medicine, the American Board of Pediatrics has mandated that "interpersonal skills and ethical decision making" will be among the areas in which candidates for board certification will be expected to show proficiency.[9]

This concern for ethics education beyond the medical school years gives rise to several types of educational programs. Graduate (residency) education largely focuses on informal conferences and formal lectures, or "Grand Rounds." Bimonthly conferences for faculty and residents that are part of the Medical Humanities Program focus on ethical issues in patient care. As an ethicist I get the opportunity to direct many of these forums. Cases are solicited from residents, and the ensuing conference, largely based on the Socratic teaching model, focuses on clarifying the competing values and working through a method of principled analysis. Discussion is often lively and residents welcome reasoned guidance, if not specific advice. Afterwards an analysis is distributed to all who attended, which discusses the case and the underlying theoretical constructs. This paper serves to synthesize the complexities of the case at hand with the general guidelines provided by the application of moral principles and methods of philosophical analysis.

Finally, studies show that clinical ethics must be integrated into the resident's daily work, and the teaching that goes on in conferences and lectures should continue at the bedside. While currently many programs, including the one at the Medical College of Pennsylvania, focus on lectures, conferences, grand rounds, and seminar lectures, recent studies indicate that physicians find bedside teaching especially helpful. An article in the Journal of the American Medical Association[10] advocates the teaching of medical ethics to medical students by philosopher/ethicists, with contribution from physicians. It goes on to argue that, beyond the early years of medical school, medical ethics ought to be taught primarily at the bedside and mostly by physicians. Thus the type and balance of instruction and instructors shifts from classroom to bedside, and from ethicist to clinician, although both are involved at every level. As the author states, "When medicine is taught at the bedside the tone of an entire medical unit changes, and there suddenly develops a pervasive atmosphere of intellectual excitement and inquiry. Further, the teaching of clinical ethics and human values in the ward and at the patient's bedside will permit the entire health care team—the physicians, medical students, nurses, social workers, chaplains, dietitians, administrators, and the patient—to participate actively in the total educational experience, including the making of clinical decisions." Bedside teaching by an ethicist must not, however, be modeled after the physician "consultation." Medical ethicists, unlike neurosurgeons for example, are not certified specialists with greater moral expertise. Because there are no clear educational or certification standards, and because ethicists do not take responsibility for ultimate outcomes, ethicists in a clinical setting should limit themselves to suggesting morally appropriate alternatives, encouraging open discussion, and facilitating clear conceptual analysis.

C. Education For Allied Health Professionals

One of my current projects is the development of a series of conferences, something like the residents' conferences, for the nursing staff. These conferences will address such issues as patient confidentiality, competency to consent/refuse medical treatment, and withholding or withdrawing life support. Such a conference was arranged when a recent conflict arose between nurses and physicians on a particular unit at my hospital, and was helpful in encouraging the participants to air their views and analyze their positions. That conference, arranged on an *ad hoc* basis, will serve as a model for future conferences. Although the issues addressed in these nursing conferences will probably be similar to those addressed in the conferences for faculty and residents, there are several good reasons to hold separate conferences. One reason is that a common characteristic of hospitals is that they are hierarchial, with physicians at the top of the pyramid. This makes it difficult for a nurse to speak freely about sensitive issues, and raises questions about the seriousness with which the nurse's views will be taken. Similarly, nurses have limited authority within the medical institution, so the recommended course of action for a physician might be quite different than that recommended for a nurse. There is, however, a clear need for such joint conferences and for creating an atmosphere of mutual respect.

D. Faculty Education

The concern about medical ethics has reached the level of medical school faculty as well. In the fall of 1987, I was invited to teach two seminars, one for faculty and residents in neurology and neurosurgery, and one for the health care professionals involved in the hemodialysis unit. Each seminar was roughly one month long, meeting weekly. The first series, for neurologists and neurosurgeons, was team-taught by a historian of medicine and me. It began with a formal lecture showing the ethical issues and historical changes in neurosurgery, and was followed up by four discussion sections. Issues such as informed consent, medical parentalism, and risk/benefit analysis were discussed and were complemented by the team approach. The second seminar series, "Ethical Issues in Dialysis," was attended by nephrologists, dialysis unit nurses, and the unit social worker and addressed issues such as informed consent, social justice and the noncompliant patient, and withholding of dialysis for patients with poor quality of life. In these sessions material was presented in the form of principles and actual cases were used to highlight and demonstrate the application of philosophic method.

III. Institutional Projects

As a medical ethicist, my role and the role of other ethicists extends beyond that of student, faculty, and staff education, as institutional projects require a substantial amount of time and effort. In general, institutional projects divide into the areas of program development, committee participation, and consulting.

A. Program Development

Program development involves revising existing programs and developing new projects. In contrast to designing a course to be taught within a department of philosophy, developing programs within a medical environment often requires the cooperation and participation of many people from different disciplines. Organization of a recent medical ethics program, for example, involved the active participation of over 30 different health care professionals. This program, designed to familiarize teachers of medical ethics in undergraduate institutions with the clinical setting, was greatly enhanced by the active participation of physicians, nurses, social workers, psychologists, administrators, and other health care professionals. As I have learned, collaborative projects are the rule rather than the exception.

B. Committee Participation

I am presently a member of several Hospital Ethics Committees, including the one at my own institution. Hospital Ethics Committees are instituted to provide policy review, education, and case consultations. Over the past months I have coordinated various committee self-education programs by suggesting articles to read and topics to discuss and then serving as a discussion director. Ethicists also participate in the ongoing review process of hospital policies, both as part of committee activities and independently. Additionally, many ethicists are active participants in Institutional Review Boards, or IRBs. These committees review research protocols within their institution and make recommendations which safeguards the fair treatment of research subjects.

C. Consulting

Other institutional projects can be loosely grouped as "consulting." They include such things as collaborating in a review of a neighboring medical school's medical ethics program, setting up a regional network of hospital ethics committees, and collaborating in the design of a pilot project on ethical issues in human experimentation for a national manufacturer of pharmaceuticals.

IV. Considering the Field: Making an Informed Decision

Philosophers considering pursuing a career in nontraditional academic employment, like patients considering surgery, should proceed only after having been informed of the benefits, risks, and burdens of such an endeavor. Informed consent in the medical context entails that one make a choice freely, with an understanding of the relevant information and alternatives. Similarly, making a career choice requires an informed stance. What are the benefits of applying ethics in the clinical setting? What are the burdens? Why would anyone choose to pursue academic life in a medical school, especially after successfully landing a position at a respected university?

My position, and similar positions at other medical schools, offer some very special advantages. First, the medical students I've worked with have been among the best and the brightest of all the students I've yet encountered. They are motivated to do well, and few are there simply because they didn't know what else to do with themselves for four years. While the students may be unfamiliar with philosophic method, they enjoy learning and seek challenges.

Second, class size is often smaller and efforts are made to keep discussion sections below a dozen students. This facilitates more personal contact and familiarity with students, as well as lively discussions. Conferences, while generally larger, are still small enough to be conducive to group discussion.

Third, because physicians demand good treatment, the treatment of medical school faculty is often better than the treatment of many university-based philosophers. At my institution, private offices are *de rigeur*, as is secretarial support, personal computers, and travel money for meetings. Many possible explanations for this exist, but the raised expectations of medical school faculty is surely an important factor.

Fourth, the opportunities for collaborative research are excellent. While my role was initially viewed by many health care professionals with curiosity, I've been fortunate to have had the chance to work with many different professionals on papers, lectures, and presentations, and have learned an enormous amount from their important insights and varying perspectives.

At what price do these benefits come? The largest price to be paid, from my own perspective, comes from having to adjust to the twelve-month calendar. Gone are those "lazy days of summer," when I was free to pursue philosophical writing and reading or participate in visiting fellowships or seminars. I now get only a month "off," and research is expected to be integrated into my regular routine. Although I am able to do some of my writing at home, it is important that I be available on a regular basis and extended periods away are viewed as vacation time. However, since actual classroom time is less, time spent in my office seeing students, revising programs, and working on special projects roughly equals the time I would normally be spending in the more

traditional academic classroom. As before, I frequently work eve-
nings and weekends, usually to a weekly total of 45 to 50 hours
per week. Although the hours are long, the work is extremely
rewarding. Revising policies to conform with ethically justifiable
standards and thereby affecting the life and well-being of many
hospital patients is important and rewarding work, and teaching
physicians and other allied health professionals ways to solve
difficult bioethical dilemmas is about as worthwhile as any work
could possibly be.

The most troubling issue for me is the uncertainty of how
effective my efforts really are. While my work is attractive because
of its perceived importance and relevance, I have real questions
about whether my influence really makes any difference in the
attitudes and behavior of health care professionals. Again, though,
this question is not a new one for ethicists. Plato specifically addressed it in the *Meno*, when he inquires of Socrates whether
virtue can be taught. Medical ethicists, as philosophers, are not
immune to the impact of such questions and recognize the problem
of evaluating programs for their effectiveness. At best, evaluation
is subjective. The study in The Journal of the American Medical
Association,[11] gives the results of a random sample of 3,000 practicing physicians who graduated medical school between 1974 and
1978. Those who had courses in medical ethics favored continuing
and expanding such programs and thought the courses were of
"substantial benefit" in confronting actual ethical issues. Respondents believed their formal training was successful because it enabled them to "identify value conflicts," increase their sensitivities
to patients' needs," and "deal more openly with moral dilemmas
with patients and fellow professionals." While the utility and relevance were perceived to be positive, the respondents indicated
a strong preference for physicians as instructors, and for seminars,
discussion groups, and bedside teaching instead of lectures. These
findings, while not surprising, should alter the way medical ethicists design educational programs and clearly emphasize the need
for ethicists to involve themselves at the clinical level.

But medical ethicists looking for evidence of their impact need
not be forced to concede that nonmeasurable results should be
equated with ineffectiveness. Learning ethics may not make someone more ethical, but if one is in doubt about what constitutes
the right course of action, a foundation in ethical theory can help

by clearing a path. Health care professionals learning medical ethics are learning a skill, but their choice to use that skill appropriately must be their own.

Other troubling questions pertain to the correctness of the solutions reached through systematic philosophical analysis. If we admit that no clear universal criteria exist for what counts as adequate justification, much less a morally acceptable course of action, then we are left seriously questioning the whole endeavor of applied ethics. Yet this problem, like the one mentioned earlier, pervades any philosophic study of ethics, especially in its applied aspects.

Philosophers with a strong interest in applied ethics and the desire to work in a clinical setting have several avenues to pursue. After obtaining a firm foundation in ethical theory, history of ethics and metaethics, it is relatively easy to move into any one of the "applied" realms such as business ethics or medical ethics. Each, however, requires knowledge about the area to which the ethical principles are being applied. While many books and excellent journals are available in medical ethics, and most schools with premed programs offer general introductory courses, I strongly believe that classroom courses and textbook readings are not enough to fully acquaint a "layperson" with the health care system. Just as homegrown "philosophers" who buy their "philosophy" books at the local drugstore are scorned by academic philosophers, homegrown "medical ethicists" have little credibility with physicians. If clinical interests are to be taken seriously, one must demonstrate a willingness to become involved in problems where they occur, in the clinical setting. Opportunities for this are increasingly available, but they take some effort to find. For example, as a graduate student in philosophy at the University of Southern California, I found a special program in medical ethics which offered not only the standard introductory level courses but also an excellent advanced course that was clinically oriented and held at the USC/Los Angeles County Medical Center. Jointly taught by a philosopher/theologian and selected clinicians, this course enabled me to gain real bedside exposure to the moral problems of modern medicine. After completing this course of study, I sought additional clinical experience by participating as a medical ethics intern, also at the USC/Los Angeles County Medical Center, for one half-day per week for a school year. During this internship, I accompanied a group of first-year medical students in their "Introduction to Clinical Medicine" course, interviewing patients and health care professionals. This internship, more than any course, changed my perception of modern medicine. It brought my view of ethical dilemmas into perspective, so much so that I felt forced to change the topic of my doctoral dissertation. Most recently, I participated as a visiting postdoctoral fellow in ethics and medicine at the Center for Ethics, Medicine, and Public Issues at Baylor College of Medicine. Programs such as the one at Baylor provide both valuable clinical experience and the opportunity to talk with other philosophers in the field.

After becoming informed about the questions and issues of medical ethics, one can pursue any number of opportunities for clinical involvement. Many hospitals have now established Hospital Ethics Committees and welcome involvement of outside professionals, especially philosophers with an interest in clinical ethics. Similarly, hospitals that perform medical research have Institutional Review Boards to review research protocols and again, the abilities of a philosopher with a medical ethics background is appreciated. Finally, if one then decides to pursue full-time academic employment in this area one can approach colleges and universities as well as respond to the APA job listings, some of which now list medical ethics as an area of desired competence.[13] Opportunities for involvement are unlimited; all it takes are some creative ideas and a willingness to approach people in ways that would be unusual for a philosopher seeking a standard academic position.

V. Reflections

In summary, this brief overview of the role of the medical ethicist in a clinical setting has focused on two major areas; educational activities and institutional projects. Challenging the MD monopoly in medical ethics requires a strong philosophic background, a familiarity with modern medicine, and a willingness to interact and collaborate with health care professionals at all levels. The newly emerging partnership between physicians and medical ethicists reflects the recognition of the need for change, as well as the strong desire on both sides to make those changes in a reasoned and systematic way.

NOTES

1. T. Beauchamp, "What Philosophers Can Offer," The Hastings Center Report, June 1982, pp. 13–14.
2. E. Pellegrino and T. McElhinney, *Teaching Ethics, the Humanities, and Human Values in Medical Schools: A Ten-Year Overview.* (Washington, D.C.: Society for Health and Human Values, 1982).
3. E. Pellegrino, R. Hart, Jr., S. Henderson, et. al., "Relevance and Utility of Courses in Medical Ethics: A Survey of Physicians' Perceptions," The Journal of the American Medical Association, volume 253, #1, January 4, 1985.
4. E. Pellegrino, "The Relevance and Utility of Courses in Medical Ethics: A Survey of Physicians' Perceptions," ibid., p. 52.
5. J. Bickle, "Human Values Teaching Programs in the Clinical Education of Medical Students," Journal of Medical Education, volume 62, #5, May 1987.
6. E. Pellegrino, "Relevance and Utility of Courses in Medical Ethics: A Survey of Physicians' Perceptions," ibid., p. 52.
7. C. Culver, K.D. Clouser, B. Gert, et al., "Basic Curricular Goals in Medical Ethics," The New England Journal of Medicine, Volume 312, #4, January 24, 1985.
8. For an interesting discussion of these criteria and the means used to fulfill and evaluate them, see R. Arnold, G. Povar, J. Howell, "The Humanities, Humanistic Behavior, and the Humane Physician: A Cautionary Note," Annuals of Internal Medicine, Volume 106, #2, February 1987.
9. The American Board of Pediatrics Ethics Subcommittee, "Teaching and Evaluation of Interpersonal Skills and Ethical Decision Making in Pediatrics," Pediatrics, volume 70, #5, May 1987.
10. M. Siegler, MD, "A Legacy of Osler—Teaching Clinical Ethics at the Bedside," The Journal of the American Medical Association, volume 239, #10, March 6, 1978.
11. E. Pellegrino, "The Relevance and Utility of Courses in Medical Ethics: A Survey of Physicians' Perceptions," ibid.
12. The December 1986 issue of American Philosophical Association's "Jobs for Philosophers," lists 161 open positions, 12 of which list "medical ethics" as an area of desired competency or specialization. Salaries for these positions, especially those in medical schools, are competitive.

Study Questions

1. Compare and contrast ethics education programs in clinical settings, such as hospitals, to those in undergraduate colleges. How are the goals and objectives different?
2. What educational preparations does the author recommend for clinical ethicists? In your opinion, is this preparation sufficient in clinical settings? Why or why not?

When Should Sick People Be Quarantined?

William B. Irvine

It was not that long ago that a significant number of people advocated a generalized quarantine of AIDS victims; and there are no doubt some who even now would advocate such a measure. Most people, however, would reject a generalized quarantine of AIDS victims as being not just inordinately expensive, but inappropriate as well.[1]

Although the debate on whether to quarantine AIDS victims has subsided, this debate leaves in its wake an interesting general question: When, if ever, is it appropriate to quarantine sick people? In this paper, I will take some steps toward answering this question. More precisely, I will present two analyses of quarantines, one from a utilitarian viewpoint and one from a libertarian (or "rights") viewpoint.[2] I will argue that, starting from either viewpoint, one will reach the conclusion that quarantines are appropriate in at least some circumstances; and I will try to isolate the factors we should consider in trying to determine the appropriateness of a quarantine. In the course of my remarks, I will make special reference to the AIDS epidemic and will offer some suggestions concerning current quarantine laws.

1. A Utilitarian Analysis of Quarantines

Let us first consider how a utilitarian will probably answer the question, "When," if ever, "should we quarantine someone?"

Chances are that he will do a cost/benefit analysis. It is true, the utilitarian will tell us, that quarantining a sick individual can benefit society by making it less likely that others will contract his illness. The utilitarian will go on to remind us, though, that these benefits are not free; for by quarantining people, we impose certain costs upon them—and perhaps on society in general as well. The utilitarian will compare the benefits generated by a policy of quarantining sick people to the costs imposed by such a policy. If the benefits outweigh the costs, he will advocate the policy in question; and if they do not, he will argue against the policy.

Let us, then, turn our attention to some of the factors that will affect the outcome of the utilitarian's cost/benefit analysis. Let us first consider the risk that the public experiences when a person with a contagious illness is allowed to move about freely in public. The amount of risk obviously depends upon such factors as the communicability and the severity of the illness. At one end of the spectrum, we find those illnesses that are highly communicable and that, if contracted, are quite debilitating or even fatal. At the other end of the spectrum are those illnesses that are not particularly communicable, and that, if contracted, are not particularly debilitating. Most illnesses, to be sure, fall somewhere in the middle of this spectrum. Colds, for example, are highly communicable, but not very debilitating; and rabies is debilitating, but not particularly communicable.

Actually, if we want to be precise in measuring risk, we should separate communicability into two components. In the first place, there are the circumstances in which a disease is transmitted. In the second place, there is the likelihood of transmission when those circumstances are present. Consider, then, two equally debilitating diseases—call them Disease A and Disease B. Disease A is transmitted only by sexual intercourse; and if you have sexual intercourse with a person who has the disease, you have a 90 percent chance of contracting it yourself. Disease B, on the other hand, is transmitted by sneezes; and if you are near a person who carries the disease when he sneezes, you have a 10 percent chance of contracting it yourself. It should be clear that Disease B is a bigger threat to society than Disease A, and thus that there is more reason to quarantine a person with Disease B than there is to quarantine a person with Disease A. After all, even though it is much easier for a person in the "relevant circumstances" to contract Disease A than Disease B, we find ourselves in the "relevant circumstances" for Disease A—the disease transmitted by sexual intercourse—far less often than we find ourselves in the "relevant circumstances" for Disease B—the disease transmitted by sneezes. Notice, too, that in a sense we have a choice whether we place ourselves in the "relevant circumstances" for Disease A: We don't have to have intercourse with someone if we don't want to. It is much more difficult, however, to avoid placing ourselves in the "relevant circumstances" for Disease B: To avoid being around sneezers, we will have to isolate ourselves.

Now let us look at the other side of the analysis, the harm done to the person who is quarantined. The amount of harm depends upon how sick the person is. If a person is laid flat on his back by an illness, then it doesn't really make much difference whether or not he is quarantined. By placing him under quarantine, we are in effect commanding him to do what he would gladly do anyway—namely, stay put. At the other end of the spectrum, we have a person who is an asymptomatic carrier of a disease. (The most famous such person is probably the notorious Typhoid Mary; more will be said about her below.) Such a person can transmit the disease to others without himself feeling its effects. Consequently, by quarantining him, we will be depriving him of all the good things that come from being able to move about freely in society.

One thing we must keep in mind when measuring the harm done to a quarantined person is that this harm is largely a function of the laws under which he is quarantined. By way of illustration, let me describe the laws currently in effect in two states, Ohio and California.

In Ohio, if a person has been exposed to a communicable disease declared quarantinable by certain health officials, he can be restricted to his place of residence or other suitable place. Once quarantined, he will be unable to leave the premises without the written permission of certain health officials; and outsiders will be prevented from coming into contact with him. A placard will be placed in a "conspicuous position on the premises"; said placard will have printed on it, in large letters, the name of the disease.[3] If necessary, health officials can employ quarantine guards to keep a person in quarantine; the guards in question are granted "police powers" and may use "all necessary means" to enforce the quarantine.[4] When the person quarantined has recovered (or died), health officials can disinfect the premises he occupied or have them destroyed.[5]

In Ohio, then, a quarantined person is harmed in several ways. His freedom to move about and associate with others is severely limited. As a result of these limitations, he will be prevented from working. He will at least lose income, and he might even lose his job. After he has recovered, he will suffer from the stigma of having been publicly labelled the victim of a certain disease. If the disease in question is one that is sexually transmitted, the stigma will be particularly harmful. Finally, when he recovers he might find that health officials have found it necessary to destroy his home.

If the quarantined person expects to get some compensation from the government for all he has been through, he will be disappointed. To begin with, *he* will have to pay for "food, fuel, and all other necessaries of life, including medical attendants, medicine, and nurses when necessary."[6] He will receive no compensation whatsoever for income lost or for having lost his job. This is not to say that he will be utterly uncompensated for his losses: If health officials find it necessary to destroy his home, he will receive "just compensation therefor."[7]

In summary, the quarantined person will receive only partial compensation for the harm done him by being quarantined. Because of this, when a sick person is quarantined, it doubles the blow he suffers: The first blow is dealt him by the disease; the second is dealt him by the government that, in some cases, deprives him of his livelihood by quarantining him.

In California, by way of contrast, the law has less to say on the compensation issue than in Ohio. The California Constitution specifies that "private property may be taken or damaged for public use only when just compensation, ascertained by a jury unless waived, has first been paid to, or into court for, the owner." Notice, however, that this clause specifies property rather than lost wages or lost jobs. It is also important to realize that there is an exception to this clause: Damages don't have to be compensated when the damages in question are inflicted in the course of a proper exercise of the state's police power;[8] and according to certain court decisions, the exercise of police power is proper if it is "reasonably necessary to 'protect the order, safety, health, morals, and general welfare of society.' '"[9] Thus, it looks as if being quarantined in California could be an even worse blow than being quarantined in Ohio.

It is, by the way, worth noting that some of the California case law dealing with the compensation of those who suffer financially as a result of quarantines came into existence as a result of the agricultural quarantines imposed to deal with an outbreak of the Mediterranean fruit fly in the early 1980s. It is a bit ironic (although not necessarily inappropriate, from a legal point of view) that legal decisions made with flies in mind could someday have an impact on how sick human beings are dealt with.

Also worth noting are the resemblances between the quarantine procedures set forth in modern law and the quarantine procedure described by Daniel Defoe in his *Journal of the Plague Year*. Things do not appear to have changed much, even though Defoe is writing about the quarantine of victims of the bubonic plague in England in 1665.

So far, only the price the quarantined person pays as a result of being quarantined has been considered. It should be clear, however, that when we quarantine someone, our society can pay a price as well. For one thing, our society loses the quarantined person's labor and the things his labor might have produced; and for another, our society will incur various costs when it imposes a quarantine—e.g., the cost of seeing that the quarantine is not broken.

Furthermore, I should emphasize that in measuring the costs and benefits of a policy of quarantining sick people, a utilitarian will not restrict himself to financial costs and benefits. For example, besides worrying about how quarantining a person will affect his pocketbook, a utilitarian will worry about whether it will cause him emotional distress. These nonfinancial costs and benefits, of course, will generally be far harder to measure than the financial ones.

Keeping the above factors in mind, let us, by way of illustration, do a cost/benefit analysis for a generalized quarantine of AIDS victims. AIDS is certainly a debilitating and even fatal disease, but it is not spread through casual contact. Indeed, it is not even spread through "intimate" contact; instead, it is spread only by a transmission of bodily fluids. On the other hand, to quarantine a victim of AIDS will be quite expensive to him and probably to the society in which he lives as well. Since AIDS is a disease that drags on for years, to quarantine an AIDS victim during his entire illness is to destroy him financially, and thereby make him a potential burden to society.

In short, AIDS does not appear to be a prime example of a disease whose victims we should quarantine; and if we are persuaded that the benefits of quarantining AIDS victims outweigh the costs, then we will be inconsistent if we fail to quarantine the victims of any number of other diseases which, though not as debilitating as AIDS, are far more contagious.

Although the case for a generalized quarantine of AIDS victims is not impressive, a case might be made for limited quarantines of AIDS victims—limited, that is, to certain groups of AIDS victims. Consider, for example, AIDS-infected prostitutes. Suppose that we have reason to believe that these people, when they engage in "unprotected" intercourse with other people, place them at great risk of contracting AIDS; suppose that the prostitutes in question realize this and realize that they have AIDS, but nevertheless continue to have "unprotected" intercourse with a variety of people; and suppose, finally, that they routinely lie to their customers and deny that they have AIDS. In such a case, someone analyzing things from a utilitarian point of view might advocate quarantining the prostitutes in question. He will admit that the quarantine will impose substantial costs on them, but he will point out that in the case described, the benefits (i.e., in terms of reduced risk to the population at large) outweigh these costs.

Furthermore, although a utilitarian probably won't advocate a generalized quarantine of AIDS victims now that the disease is widespread, he might well have advocated such a quarantine at the earliest stages of the epidemic. Notice that from a utilitarian point of view, the earlier in the course of an epidemic you quarantine people, the less are your costs and the greater are your potential benefits; and therefore, the earlier you quarantine, the more favorable the benefits-to-costs ratio will be.

2. A Libertarian Analysis of Quarantines

So far a utilitarian analysis of quarantines has been described. Suppose, however, that we are anti-utilitarian: Suppose, more precisely, that instead of thinking that we should act to maximize utility, we think that we should act to minimize rights violations—that is, should act to protect the rights of individuals. What would someone taking this libertarian approach have to say about quarantines?

Some libertarians might answer that by quarantining sick people, we violate their rights. Quarantining them is like putting them in jail; in getting ill, however, they have done nothing wrong, and hence don't deserve to be quarantined. We are doing them an injustice by quarantining them.

Consider the case of Mary Mallon, a.k.a. Typhoid Mary. She was a cook for various families in New York City in the first decade of this century. Because she was a carrier of typhoid fever, the people she cooked for had an unfortunate tendency to come down with the malady. Health authorities finally caught up with her and placed her in an isolation center. In 1910, she was released on the condition that she never work as a cook again. Since cooking was the only way she could make a living, however, she broke her promise and not only went to work as a cook, but found employment with the Sloane Maternity Hospital. She was caught in 1914 and reincarcerated. She remained in isolation until her death in 1938.[10] There are no doubt libertarians who will tell us that the government, by isolating Mary Mallon against her will, violated her rights.

Let me take a moment to try to convince libertarians that even they should advocate quarantining people under certain circumstances. After all, a person with a contagious disease can, in some circumstances, pose an unreasonable level of risk to others. If we think that it is appropriate for us to take steps to prevent people from exposing others to unreasonable levels of risk, we will be led to the conclusion that we can, in some circumstances, legitimately quarantine individuals to protect the rights of others.

To better understand this line of reasoning, consider the following cases.

Case 1. Suppose, to begin with, that Smith builds and occupies a house, and that after it is built, Jones purchases the lot next to Smith's and sets up a dynamite storage business there. A libertarian will presumably argue that even though Smith is never actually harmed by the stored dynamite, Jones's activities expose him to an unreasonable level of risk; and therefore we should take steps to make Jones stop storing dynamite next to Smith's house. In doing so, we are interfering with Jones's right to start a business, but we are doing so in order to prevent Jones from violating Smith's rights to life and property.

Case 2. Now suppose that instead of storing dynamite next to Smith's house, Jones stores hazardous biological agents. (They are stored in glass vials; if one of the vials should break, there is a significant chance that Smith would become infected by the biological agent in question and would become sick or even die.) Once again, I think that a libertarian will admit that we should intervene to protect Smith: We should force Jones to store the hazardous biological agents elsewhere.

Case 3. Now consider one last case. Suppose Jones—perhaps through no fault of his own—is storing a hazardous biological agent not on the lot next to Smith's, but *in his own body*—suppose, that is, that Jones is a carrier of some communicable disease. Suppose that Jones insists on bringing himself in close proximity to Smith and thereby exposing him to risk of infection. To be consistent with the cases described above, the libertarian should, I think, once again argue that we should intervene to protect Smith from Jones: We should forbid Jones to circulate in public. In doing so, we are not punishing Jones for being sick, which is something over which he might have no control; instead, we are curbing the activities Jones undertakes *as a sick person*, curbing them so as to lessen the chance that the rights of others are violated.

When a person has a contagious illness, there can arise a conflict of rights. On the one hand, there is the sick person's right to travel about and associate with others; and on the other hand, there are the rights of others that he not expose them to unreasonable levels of risk. In such a case, whatever we do, we will interfere with someone's rights: If we quarantine the sick person, we will interfere with his rights; and if we do not quarantine him, other people's rights will likely be violated. In such a case, it seems clear that what we should do—if, at any rate, we are concerned with protecting people's rights—is to act to minimize the extent to which the rights of individuals are violated; and this could well mean quarantining sick people.

Of course, if I *voluntarily* let a diseased person infect me or expose me to risk of infection, libertarians will probably say that I should be allowed to do so without interference from others.

From a libertarian point of view, one of the most important things about our rights is that we can choose to waive them. If I, as a sane adult, choose to expose myself to certain risks (and do not violate the rights of others in doing so), others are not justified in interfering, even though doing so would be "for my own good."

In summary, then, I think that even libertarians will want to admit that we should quarantine people under certain circumstances. The key question for them will be this: Will a certain quarantine policy minimize the extent to which people's rights are violated?

It is, by the way, likely that libertarians will agree with utilitarians that it would be inappropriate to quarantine AIDS victims in general. Libertarians might also advocate limited quarantines of AIDS victims—such as a quarantine of the deceiving prostitutes described above. (Notice that when a person has sex with a "deceiving prostitute," he is not *knowingly* exposing himself a significant health risk, and it would be wrong to think that he has chosen to waive his right to life. The case is importantly different from the case in which a person has sex with someone he knows to be a carrier of AIDS.)

3. Some Final Remarks

Before concluding, I would like to comment on two things that both utilitarians and libertarians should keep in mind when deciding on the appropriateness of a quarantine.

My first point is that the above analyses were made on the assumption that adoption of a policy of quarantining victims of a certain disease would not affect people's behavior. This assumption, however, is quite unrealistic. If we announce that anyone infected with a certain disease will be quarantined and if such a quarantine would tend to harm persons quarantined, we can expect a large number of people to take steps to evade the quarantine—i.e., we can expect people who suspect that they have the disease in question to take steps to avoid being detected and, if detected, to take steps to avoid being placed in quarantine. Whenever this is the case, adopting a policy of quarantining people with the disease in question can have the unintended effect of *increasing* the number of carriers who continue to circulate among the public. Both utilitarians and libertarians, when determining the appropriateness of quarantines, should keep in mind the fact that quarantines can be counterproductive in the manner just described.

My second point takes us back to a claim that was made above: The amount of harm done to the people we quarantine is a function of the laws under which they are quarantined. Some quarantine laws will do more harm than others; and when devising quarantine laws, we should therefore be careful to pick the ones that, from a utilitarian point of view, give us the greatest benefits for the lowest costs, or that, from a libertarian point of view, place as few restraints as possible on people's freedom.

Along these lines, let me make a pair of proposals with respect to current quarantine laws. My first proposal is that the government should compensate those who are quarantined for the losses they suffer as a result of being quarantined. More precisely, I think that the government should compensate quarantined people, not for *all* the costs incurred by them, but only for those costs that they would not have incurred if they had not been quarantined.

To my mind, the reasoning behind quarantine laws parallels that behind emminent domain laws. We give the government the right to take a person's property when doing so is in the public interest—so that a new highway can be built, for example. We don't, however, expect that person to sacrifice for the public good; instead, we compensate him for the "fair value" of the land we took. Similarly, when we quarantine someone, we do so for the public good. We shouldn't expect him to sacrifice for the public good, but should compensate him for his losses.

I would also like to make a second proposal: We should, when appropriate, alter currently existing quarantine laws to allow for partial quarantines. To partially quarantine a person is to limit his freedom in some respects, but not in others. When health officials let Mary Mallon go on the condition that she not work as a cook, they were, in effect, placing her under an informal partial quarantine. In the same way, the state might forbid the carrier of a sexually transmitted disease like AIDS to have sexual relations with others (or perhaps forbid him to have sexual relations with others without first informing them of the risks they face), and it could change his partial quarantine into a full quarantine if he disobeyed. At present, many states have essentially two options open to them: They can place someone under full quarantine or do nothing. It would be nice if health officials had a third option—namely, the partial quarantine. As they currently exist, quarantine laws tend to be a needlessly blunt instrument. By refining them in the manner described, we can retain the benefits of such laws and at the same time reduce the costs these laws impose upon those quarantined.

NOTES

1. There is evidence that people are becoming less reluctant to allow AIDS victims to circulate in the general population. In, for example, "Living with AIDS: . . ." (*Wall Street Journal*, 2 September 1988, pp. 1 and 6), Roger Ricklefs describes the increasing rate at which people diagnosed as having AIDS are returning to the workplace.
2. There are, to be sure, other viewpoints than the utilitarian and libertarian viewpoints. I focus my discussion on these two viewpoints simply because by doing so, I can appeal to the intuitions of a fairly large number of people.
3. Ohio Revised Code, 3707.08.
4. ORC, 3703.09.
5. ORC, 3707.12.
6. ORC, 3707.14.
7. ORC, 3707.13.
8. See Holtz v. Superior Court (1970) 3 Cal. 3d 296, 305.
9. Freeman v. Contra Costa County Water Dist. (1971) 18 Cal. App. 3d 404, 408.
10. Vermont Royster, "Tests vs. Rights: The Story of Mary Mallon," *Wall Street Journal*, 18 September 1986, p. 26.

Study Questions

1. After reading Irvine's article, construct an argument for quarantining a member of your family afflicted with AIDS.
2. Explain why you believe or do not believe that an adherent of the ethical philosophy of Immanuel Kant would endorse Irvine's view.

Abortion Decisions: Personal Morality

Daniel Callahan*

The strength of pluralistic societies lies in the personal freedom they afford individuals. One is free to choose among religious, philosophical, ideological and political creeds; or one can create one's own highly personal, idiosyncratic moral code and view of the universe. Increasingly, the individual is free to ignore the morals, manners and mores of society. The only limitations are upon those actions which seem to present clear and present dangers to the common good, and even there the range of prohibited actions is diminishing as more and more choices are left to personal and private decisions. I have contended that, apart from some regulatory laws, abortion and decisions should be left, finally, up to the women themselves. Whatever one may think of the morality of abortion, it cannot be established that it poses a clear and present danger to the common good. Thus society does not have the right decisively to interpose itself between a woman and the abortion she wants. It can only intervene where it can be shown that some of its own interests are at stake *qua* society. Regulatory

* Daniel Callahan, a philosopher, is the director of the Institute of Society, Ethics and the Life Sciences, usually called The Hastings Center. His numerous publications reflect an enduring concern with issues in biomedical ethics. He is, for example, the author of *Ethics and Population Limitation* (1971) and the coeditor of *Science, Ethics and Medicine* (1976). Callahan's principal work on the subject of abortion is *Abortion: Law, Choice and Morality* (1970), *from which this selection is excerpted.*

laws of a minimal kind therefore seem in order, since in a variety of ways already mentioned society will be affected by the number, kind and quality of legal abortions. In short, with a few important stipulations, what I have been urging is tantamount to saying that abortion decisions should be private decisions. It is to accept, in principle, the contention of those who believe that, in a free, pluralistic society, the woman should be allowed to make her own moral choice on abortion and be allowed to implement that choice.

But pluralistic societies also lay a few traps for the unwary. It is not a large psychological step from saying that individuals should be left free to make up their own minds on some crucial moral issues (of whom abortion is one) to an adoption of the view that one personal decision is as good as another, that any decision is a good one as long as it is honest or sincere, that a free decision equals a correct decision. However short the psychological step, the logical gap is very large. An absence of cant, hypocrisy and coercion may prepare the way for good personal decisions. But that is only to clean the room, and something must then be put in it. The hazard is that, once cleaned, it will be filled with capriciousness, sentimentality, a thinly disguised conformity to the reigning moral taste, or strongly felt but inadequately analyzed moral opinions. This is a particular danger in affluent pluralistic societies, heavily dominated by popular tastes, communication media and the absence of shared values. Philosophically, the view that all values are equally good and all private moral choices on a par is all but dead: but it still has a strong life at the popular level, where there is a tendency to act as if, once personal freedom is legally and socially achieved, moral questions cease to exist.

A considerable quantity of literature exists in the field of ethics concerned with such problems as subjective and objective values, the meaning and use of ethical principles and moral rules, the role of intentionality. That literature need not be reviewed here. But it is directly to the point to observe that a particular failing of the abortion-on-reqest literature is that it persistently scants the moral problem of how a woman, if granted the desired legal freedom to make her own decision about abortion, should go about making that decision. Up to a point, this deficiency is understandable. The immediate tactical problem has been to get the laws changed or repealed; that has been the burden of the public struggle, which has concentrated on statutes and legislators rather than on the moral contents and problems of personal decision-making. It is reasonable and legitimate to say that a woman should be left free to make the decision in the light of her own personal values; that is, I believe, the best legal solution. But it leaves totally untouched the question of how, once freedom is achieved, she ought to go about the personal business of forming a coherent, rational, sensitive moral perspective and opinion on abortion. After freedom, what then? Society may have no right to go about the personal business of forming a coherent, rational, sensitive moral perspective and opinion on abortion. After freedom, what then? Society may have no right to demand that a woman give it good reasons why she should have an abortion before permitting it. But this does not entail that the woman should not, as a morally responsible person, have good reasons to justify her desires or acts in her own eyes.

This is only to say that a solution of the legal problem is not the same as a solution to the moral problem. That the moral struggle is transferred from the public to the private sphere should not be taken to mean that the moral problem has been solved; only its public aspect, under a permissive law or repeal of all laws, has been dealt with. The personal problem will remain.

Some women will be part of a religious group or ethical tradition which they freely choose and which can offer them something, possibly very much, in the way of helpful moral insight consistent with that tradition. The obvious course in that instance is for them to turn to their tradition to see what it has to offer them on the particular problem of abortion. But what of those who have no tradition to repair to or those who find their tradition wanting on this problem? One way or another, they will have to find some way of developing a set of ethical principles and moral rules to help them act responsibly, to justify their own conduct in their own eyes. To press the problem to a finer point, what ought they think about as they try to work out their own views on abortion?

Only a few suggestions will be made here, taking the form of arguing for an ethic of personal responsibility which tries, in the process of decision-making, to make itself aware of a number of things. The biological evidence should be considered, just as the problem of methodolgy must be considered; the philosophical assumption implicit in different uses of the word "human" need to be considered; a philosophical theory of biological analysis is required; the social consequences of different kinds of analyses and different meanings of the word "human" should be thought through: consistency of meaning and use should be sought to avoid *ad hoc* and arbitrary solutions.

It is my own conviction that the "developmental school" offers the most helpful and illuminating approach to the problem of the beginning of human life, avoiding, on the one hand, a too narrow genetic criterion of human life and, on the other, a too broad and socially dangerous social definition of the "human." Yet the kinds of problems which appear in any attempt to decide upon the beginning of life suggest that no one position can be either proved or disproved from biological evidence alone. It becomes a question of trying to do justice to the evidence while, at the same time, realizing that how the evidence is approached and used will be a function of one's way of looking at reality, one's moral policy, the values and rights one believes need balancing, and the type of questions one thinks need to be asked. At the very least, however, the genetic evidence of the uniqueness of zygotes and embryos (a uniqueness of a different kind than that of the uniqueness of sperm and ova), their potentiality for development into a human person, their early development of human characteristics, their genetic and organic distinctness from the organism of the mother, appear to rule out a treatment even of zygotes, much less the more developed stages of the conceptus, as mere pieces of "tissue," of no human significance or value. The "tissue" theory of the significance of the conceptus can only be made plausible by a systematic disregard of the biological evidence. Moreover, though one may conclude that a conceptus is only potential human life, in the process of continually actualizing its potential through growth and development, a respect for the sanctity of life, with its bias in favor even of undeveloped life, it is enough to make the taking of such life a moral problem. There is a choice to be made and it is a moral choice. In the near future, it is likely that some kind of simple, safe abortifacient drug will be developed, which either prevents implantation or destroys the conceptus before it can develop. It will be tempting then to think that the moral dilemma has vanished, but I do not believe it will have.

It is possible to imagine a huge number of situations where a woman could, in good and sensitive conscience, choose abortions as a moral solution to her personal or social difficulties. But, at the very least, the bounds of morality are overstepped when either through a systematic intellectual negligence or a willful choosing of that moral solution most personally convenient, personal choice is deliberately made easy and problem-free. Yet it seems to me that a pressure in that direction is a growing part of the ethos of technological societies; it is easily possible to find people to reassure us that we need have no scruples about the way we act, whether the issue is war, the suppression of rebellion and revolution, discrimination against minorities or the use of technological advances. Pluralism makes possible the achieving of freer, more subtle moral thinking; but it is a possibility constantly endangered by cultural pressures which would simplify or dissolve moral doubts and anguish.

The question of abortion "indications" returns at the level of personal choice. I have contended that the advent of permissive laws should not mean a cessation of efforts to explore the problem of "indications." When a woman asks herself, as she ought, whether her reasons for wanting an abortion are sound reasons—which presumes abortion is a serious enough moral issue to warrant the need to provide oneself with good reasons for choosing it—she will be asking herself about justifiable indications. Thus, transposed from the legal to the personal level, the kinds of concerns adumbrated in the earlier chapters on indications remain fully pertinent. It was argued in those chapters that, with the possible exception of exceedingly rare instances of a direct threat to the physical life of the mother, one cannot speak of general categories of abortion indications as *necessitating* an abortion. In a number of circumstances, abortion may be a wise and justifiable solution to a distressed pregnancy. But when the language of necessity is used, the implication is that no other conceivable alternative is available. It may be granted, willingly enough, that some set of practical circumstances in some (possibly very many) concrete cases may indicate that abortion is the only feasible option open. But these cases cannot readily be determined in advance, and, for that reason, it is necessary to say that no formal indication as such (e.g., a psychiatric indication) entails a necessary, predetermined choice in favor of abortion.

The word "indication" remains the best word, suggesting that a number of given circumstances will bring the possibility or desirability of abortion to the fore. But to escalate the concept of an indication into that of a required procedure is to go too far. Abortion is *one* way to solve the problem of an unwanted or hazardous pregancy (physically, psychologically, economically or socially), but it is rarely the only way, at least in affluent societies (I would be considerably less certain about making the same statement about poor societies). Even in the most extreme cases—rape, incest, psychosis, for instance—alternatives will usually be available and different choices open. It is not necessarily the end of every woman's chance for a happy, meaningful life to bear an illegitimate child. It is not necessarily the automatic destruction of a family to have a seriously defective child born into it. It is not necessarily the ruination of every family living in overcrowded housing to have still another child. It is not inevitable that every immature woman would become even more so if she bore a child or another child. It is not inevitable that a gravely handicapped child can hope for nothing from life. It is not inevitable that every unwanted child is doomed to misery. It is not written in the essence of things, as a fixed law of human nature, that a woman cannot come to accept, love and be a good mother to a child who was initially unwanted. Nor is it a fixed law that she could not come to cherish a grossly deformed child. Naturally, these are only generalizations. The point is only that human beings are as a rule flexible, capable of doing more than they sometimes think they can, able to surmount serious dangers and challenges, able to grow and mature, able to transform inauspicious beginnings into satisfactory conclusions. Everything in life, even in procreative and family life, is not fixed in advance; the future is never wholly unalterable.

Yet the problem of personal question-asking must be pushed a step farther. The way the questions are answered will be very much determined by a woman's way of looking at herself and at life. A woman who has decided, as a personal moral policy, that nothing should be allowed to stand in the way of her own happiness, goals and self-interest will have no trouble solving the moral problem. For her, an unwanted pregnancy will, by definition, be a pregnancy to be terminated. But only by a Pickwickian use of words could this form of reasoning be called moral. It would preclude any need to consult the opinion of others, any need to examine the validity of one's own viewpoint, any need to, for instance, ask when human life begins, any need to interrogate oneself in any way, intellectually or morally; will and desire would be king.

Assuming, however, that most women would seek a broader

ethical horizon than that of their exclusively personal self-interest, what might they think about when faced with an abortion decision? A respect for the sanctity of human life should, I believe, incline them toward a general and strong bias against abortion. Abortion is an act of killing, the violent, direct destruction of potential human life, already in the process of development. That fact should not be disguised, or glossed over by euphemism and circumlocution. It is not the destruction of a human person—for at no stage of its development does the conceptus fulfill the definition of a person, which implies a developed capacity for reasoning, willing, desiring and relating to others—but it is the destruction of an important and valuable form of human life. Its value and it potentiality are not dependent upon the attitude of the woman toward it; it grows by its own biological dynamism and has a genetic and morphological potential distinct from that of the woman. It has its own distinctive and individual future. If contraception and abortion are both seen as forms of birth limitation, they are distinctly different acts; the former precludes the possibility of a conceptus being formed, while the latter stops a conceptus already in existence from developing. The bias implied by the principle of the sanctity of human life is toward the protection of all forms of human life, especially, in ordinary circumstances, the protection of the right to life. That right should be accorded even to doubtful life; its existence should not be wholly dependent upon the personal self-interest of the woman.

Yet she has her own rights as well, and her own set of responsibilities to those around her; that is why she may have to choose abortion. In extreme situations of overpopulation, she may also have a responsibility for the survival of the species or of a people. In many circumstances, then, a decision in favor of abortion—one which overrides the right to life of that potential human being she carries within—can be a responsible moral decision, worthy neither of the condemnation of others nor of self-condemnation. But the bias of the principle of the sanctity of life is against a routine, unthinking employment of abortion; it bends over backwards not to take life and gives the benefit of the doubt to life. It does not seek to diminish the range of responsibility toward life—potential or actual—but to extend it. It does not seek the narrowest definition of life, but the widest and the richest. It is mindful of individual possibility, on the one hand, and of destructive human tendency, on the other, to exclude from the category of "the human" or deny rights to those beings whose existence is or could prove burdensome to others.

The language used to describe abortion will have an important bearing on the sensitivities and imagination of those women who must make abortion decisions. Abortion can be talked about in the language of medical technology and technique—as, say, "a therapeutic procedure involving the emptying of the uterine contents." That language is neutral, clinical, unemotional. Or abortion can be talked about in the emotive language of relieving woman from suffering, or meeting the need for freedom among women, or saving a nation from a devastating overpopulation. Both kinds of language have their place, for abortion has more than one result and meaning and abortion can legitimately be talked about in more than one way. What is objectionable is a conscious manipulation of language to incite an irrational emotional response, to allay doubts or to mislead the imagination. Particularly misleading is one commonly employed mixture of rhetorical modes by advocates of abortion on request. That is the use of a detached, clinical language to describe the actual operation itself combined with an emotive rhetoric to evoke the personal and social goods which an abortion can bring about. Thus, when every effort is made to suggest that emotion and feeling are perfectly appropriate to describe the social and personal goals of abortion, but that a clinical language only is appropriate when the actual technique and medical objective of an abortion is described, then the moral imagination is being misled.

Any human act can be described in impersonal, technological language, just as any act can be described in emotive language. What is wanted is an equity in the language. It is fair enough and to the point to say that in many circumstances abortion will save a woman's health and her family. It only becomes misleading when the act itself, as distinguished from its therapeutic goal, it talked about in an entirely different way. For, abortion is not just an "emptying of the uterine contents." It is also an act of killing; there will be no abortion unless the conceptus is killed (or its further existence made impossible, which amounts to the same thing). If it is appropriate to evoke the imagination and elicit sympathy for those women in a distressed pregnancy who could be helped by abortion, it is no less appropriate to evoke the imagination about what actually occurs in an abortion "procedure."

Imagination should also come into play at another point. It is often argued by proponents of abortion that there is no need for a woman to take any chances in a distressed pregnancy, particularly in the instance of an otherwise healthy woman who, if she has an abortion on one occasion, could simply get pregnant again on another, more auspicious occasion. This might be termed the "replacement theory" of abortion indications: since fetus "x" can be replaced by fetus "y," then there is no reason why a woman should have any scruples about such a replacement. This way of conceiving the choices effectively dissolves them; it becomes important only to know whether a woman can get pregnant again when she wants to. But this strategy can be employed only at the price of convincing oneself that there is no difference whatever among embryos or fetuses, that they all have exactly the same potentiality. But even the sketchiest knowledge of the genetic uniqueness of each conceptus (save in the instance of monozygotic twins), and thus the different genetic potentialities of each, should raise doubts on that point. Yet, having said that, I would not want to deny that the possibility of a further pregnancy could have an important bearing on the moral reasoning of a woman whose present pregnancy was threatening. If, out of a sense of responsibility toward her present children or her present life situation, a woman decided that an abortion was the wisest, most moral course, then the possibility that she could become pregnant later, when these responsibilities would be pressing, would be a pertinent consideration.

The goal of these remarks is to keep alive in the consciences of women who have an abortion choice a moral tension; and it is to hope that they will be willing to bear the pain and the uncertainty of having to make a moral choice. It is the automatic, unthinking and unimaginative personal solution of abortion questions which women themselves should be extremely wary of, either for or against abortion. A woman can, with little trouble, find both people and books to reassure her that there is no problem about abortion at all; or people and books to convince her that she would be a moral monster if she chose abortion. A woman can choose in advance the views she will listen to and thus have her predispositions confirmed. Yet a willingness to keep alive a moral tension, and to be wary of precipitous solutions, presupposes two things. First, that the woman herself wants to do what is right, realizing that what is right may not always be that which is most convenient, most easy or most immediately apt to solve a pressing problem. It is simply the case that what one wants to do, or would like to do, or is predisposed to do is necessarily the right thing to do. A willingness seriously to entertain the moral perception—which, of course, does not in itself imply a decision for or against an abortion—is one sign of moral seriousness.

Second, moral seriousness presupposes one is concerned with the protection and furthering of life. This means that, out of respect for human life, one bends over backwards not to eliminate human life, not to desensitize oneself to the meaning and value of potential life, not to seek definitions of the "human" which serve one's self-interest only. A desire to respect human life in all of its forms means, therefore, that one voluntarily imposes upon oneself a pressure against the taking of life; that one demands of oneself serious reasons for doing so, even in the case of a very early embryo; that one use not only the mind but also the imagination when a decision is being made; that one seeks not to evade the moral issues but to face them; that one searches out the alternatives and conscientiously entertains them before turning to abortion. A bias in favor of the sanctity of human life in all of its forms would include a bias against abortion on the part of women; it would be the last rather than the first choice when unwanted pregnancies occurred. It would be an act to be avoided if at all possible.

A bias of this kind, voluntarily imposed by a woman upon herself, would not trap her; for it is also part of a respect for the dignity of life to leave the way open for an abortion when other reasonable choices are not available. For she also has duties toward herself, her family and her society. There can be good reasons for taking the life even of a very late fetus; once that also is seen and seen as a counterpoise in particular cases to the general bias against the taking of potential life the way is open to choose abortion. The bias of the moral policy implies the need for moral rules which seek to preserve life. But, as a policy which leaves room for choice—rather then entailing a fixed set of rules—it is open to flexible interpretation when the circumstances point to the wisdom of taking exception to the normal ordering of the rules in particular cases. Yet, in that case, one is not genuinely taking exception to the rules. More accurately, one would be deciding that, for the preservation or furtherance of other values or rights—species-rights, person-rights—a choice in favor of abortion would be serving the sanctity of life. That there would be, in that case, conflict between rights, with one set of rights set aside (reluctantly) to serve another set, goes without saying. A subversion of the principle occurs when it is made out that there is no conflict and thus nothing to decide.

Study Questions

1. Compare and contrast Callahan's stance on abortion with that of Matthis. Do you think Matthis could agree with Callahan? If not, why not. If so, to what extent?
2. Given Callahan's view that a fetus cannot be considered a "person," state why you think he is or is not in basic agreement with Engelhardt.

The Limits of Confidentiality

*Sissela Bok**

Doctors, lawyers, and priests have traditionally recognized the duty of professional secrecy regarding what individuals confide to them: personal matters such as alcoholism or depression, marital difficulties, corporate or political problems, and indeed most concerns that patients or clients want to share with someone, yet keep from all others[1]. Accountants, bankers, social workers, and growing numbers of professionals now invoke a similar duty to guard confidences. As codes of ethics take form in old and new professions, the duty of confidentiality serves in part to reinforce their claim to prefessional status, and in part to strenghten their capacity to offer help to clients.

Confidential information may be more or less intimate, more or less discrediting, more or less accurate and complete. No matter how false or trivial the substance of what clients or patients convey, they may ask that it be kept confidential, or assume that it will be even in the absence of such a request, taking it for granted that professionals owe them secrecy. Professionals, in turn, must not only receive and respect such confidences; the very nature of the help they can give may depend on their searching for even the most deeply buried knowledge.

* Sissela Bok is lecturer on the core curriculum at Harvard University and the author of *Lying: Moral Choice in Public and Private Life*. This article is adapted from her forthcoming book *Secrets*. Copyright © 1982 Sissela Bok. Reprinted by permission of Pantheon Books, a division of Random House, Inc.

All the pressures for and against secrecy are present in such relationships. But the duty of confidentiality is no longer what it was when lawyers or doctors simply kept to themselves the confidences of those who sought their help. How can it be, when office personnel and collaborators and team members must have access to the information as well, and when clients and patients with numerous interdependent needs consult different professionals who must in turn communicate with one another? And how can it be, given the vast increase in information collected, stored, and retrievable that has expanded the opportunities for access by outsiders? How can it be, finally, when employers, school officials, law enforcement agencies, insurance companies, tax inspectors, and credit bureaus all press to see some of this confidential information?

So much confidential information is now being gathered and recorded and requested by so many about so many that confidentiality, though as strenuously invoked as in the past, is turning out to be a weaker reed then ever. At the same time, paradoxically, a growing number of discreditable, often unlawful secrets never even entered into computer banks or medical records have come to burden lawyers, financial advisers, journalists, and many others who take themselves to be professionally bound to silence. Faced with growing demands for both revelation and secrecy, those who have to make decisions about whether or not to uphold confidentiality face numerous difficult moral quandaries. Legislation can sometimes dictate their choice. But the law differs from state to state and from nation to nation, and does not necessarily prescribe what is right from a moral point of view. Even if it did, it could never entirely resolve many of the quandaries that arise, since they often present strong moral arguments on both sides. Consider, for example, the following case:

> A forty-seven-year-old engineer has polycystic kidney disease, in his case a genetic disorder, and must have his blood purified by hemodialysis with an artificial kidney machine. Victims of the disease [at the time of his diagnosis] usually die a few years after symptoms appear, often in their forties, though dialysis and transplants can stave off death for as much as ten years.
>
> The patient has two children: a son, eighteen, just starting college, and a daughter, sixteen. Though the parents know that the disease is genetic—that their children may carry it and might trans-

mit it to their own offspring—the son and daughter are kept in the dark. The parents insist the children should not be told because it would frighten them unnecessarily, would inhibit their social life, and would make them feel hopeless about the future. They are firm in saying that the hospital staff should not tell the children; the knowledge, they believe, is privileged and must be kept secret. Yet the hospital staff worries about the children innocently involving their future spouses and victimizing their own children.[2]

It is not difficult to see the conflicting and, in themselves, quite legitimate claims on each side in this case: the parents' insistence on privacy and on the right to decide when to speak to their children about a matter of such importance to the family; and the staff members' concern for the welfare of the children. But the question of whether the parents are wrong to keep the information from the children must be separated from that of what the staff members should do about what they see as harmful secrecy. Should they reject their obligation of confidentiality in this case?

Even those who arrive at clear answers concerning the parents' responsibility may recognize that their views could change if the facts were somewhat different. If they conclude, for example, that the children have a right to be told, they might decide differently if the disease were less severe, if a cure seemed likely to be found shortly, if the chances of the illness striking the children were low, or if the children were much younger. And those who decide that the parents are right to insist on secrecy might similarly come to a different conclusion if the illness were more certain to strike the children, or to afflict them sooner. A few might hold rigidly to one choice or the other no matter what the circumstances, but many would discern cases where the conflicting claims are so nearly equal that choice is difficult. At such times, the additional weight to be placed on confidentiality becomes crucial. Should it matter at all? If so, why? And in what sorts of conflicts should it be rejected?

These questions require us to look more closely at the nature of confidentiality and its powerful hold and to ask what it is that makes so many professionals regard it as the first and most binding of their duties.

Confidentiality refers to the boundaries surrounding shared secrets and to the process of guarding these boundaries. While confidentiality protects much that is not in fact secret, personal secrets lie at its core. The innermost, the vulnerable, often the shameful: these aspects of self-disclosure help explain why one name for professional confidentiality has been "the professional secret." Such secrecy is sometimes mistakenly confused with privacy; yet it can concern many matter in no way private, but that someone wishes to keep from the knowledge of third parties.

Confidentiality must also be distinguished from the testimonial privilege that protects information possessed by spouses or members of the clergy or lawyers against coerced revelations in court. While a great many professional groups invoke confidentiality, the law recognizes the privilege only in limited cases. In some states, only lawyers can invoke it; in others, physicians and clergy can as well; more recently, psychiatrists and other professionals have been added to their number. Who ought and who ought not to be able to guarantee such a privilege is under ceaseless debate. Every newly established professional group seeks the privileges of existing ones. Established ones, on the other hand, work to exclude those whom they take to be encroaching on their territory.

The principle of confidentiality postulates a duty to protect confidences against third parties under certain circumstances. Professionals appeal to such a principle in keeping secrets from all outsiders, and seek to protect even what they would otherwise feel bound to reveal. While few regard the principle as absolute, most see the burden of proof as resting squarely on anyone who claims a reason for overriding it. Why should confidentiality bind thus? And why should it constrain professionals to silence more than, say, close friends?

Justification and Rationale

The justification for confidentiality rests on four premises, three supporting confidentiality in general and the fourth, professional secrecy in particular. They concern human autonomy regarding personal information, respect for relationships, respect for the bonds and promises that protect shared information, and the benefits of confidentiality to those in need of advice, sanctuary, and aid, and in turn to society.

The first and fundamental premise is that of individual autonomy over personal information. It asks that we respect individuals as capable of having secrets. Without some control over secrecy and openness about themselves, their thoughts and plans, their actions, and in part their property, people could neither maintain privacy nor guard against danger. But of course this control should be only partial. Matters such as contagious diseases place individual autonomy in conflict with the rights of others. And a variety of matters cannot easily be concealed. No one can maintain control, for example, over others' seeing that they have a broken leg or a perennially vile temper.[3]

The second premise is closely linked to the first. It presupposes the ligitimacy not only of having personal secrets but of sharing them, and assumes respect for relationships among human beings and for intimacy. It is rooted in loyalties that precede the formulation of moral justification and that preserve collective survival for one's tribe, one's kin, one's clan. Building on such a sense of loyalty, the premise holds that it is not only natural but often also right to respect the secrets of intimates and associates, and that human relationships could not survive without such respect.

This premise is fundamental to the marital privilege upheld in American Law, according to which one spouse cannot be forced to testify against the other; and to the ancient Chinese legal tradition, so strongly attacked in the Maoist period, that forbade relatives to report on one another's misdeeds and penalized such revelations severely.[4] No more than the first premise, however, does this second one suffice to justify all confidentiality. It can conflict with other duties, so that individuals have to choose, say, between betraying country or friend, parents or children; and it can be undercut by the nature of the secret one is asked to keep.

The third premise holds that a pledge of silence creates an obligation beyond the respect due to persons and to existing relationships. Once we promise someone secrecy, we no longer start from scratch in weighing the moral factors of a situation. They matter differently once the promise is given, so that full impartiality is no longer called for.

In promising one alienates, as Grotius said, either a thing or some portion of one's freedom of action: "To the former category belong promises to give; to the latter, promises to perform)."[5] Promises of secrecy are unusual in both respects. What they promise to give is allegiance; what they promise to perform is some action that will guard the secret—to keep silent, at least, and perhaps to do more. Just what performance is promised, and at what cost it will be carried out, are questions that go to the heart of conflicts over confidentiality.[6] To invoke a promise, therefore, while it is surely to point to a *prima facie* ground of obligation, is not to close the debate over pledges of secrecy. Rather, one must go on to ask whether it was right to make the pledge in the first place, and right to accept it; whether the promise is a binding one, and even if it is, what circumstances might nevertheless justify overriding it.[7]

Individuals vary with respect to the seriousness with which they make a promise and the consequent weight of the reasons they see as sufficient to override it. Consider the CIA agent who takes an oath of secrecy before gaining access to classified information; the White House butler who pledges never to publish confidential memoirs; the relatives who give their word to a dying author never to publish her diaries; the religious initiate who swears on all he holds sacred not to divulge the mysteries he is about to share; the engineer who signs a pledge not to give away company trade secrets as a conditon of employment. Some of these individuals take the pledge casually, others in utter seriousness. If the latter still break their pledge, they may argue that they were coerced into making their promise, or that they did not understand how it bound them. Or else they may claim that something is important enough to override their promise—as when the relatives publish the author's diaries after her death for a sum of money they cannot resist, or in the belief that the reading public would be deprived without such documents.

For many, a promise involves their integrity and can create a bond that is closer than kinship, as the ceremonies by which people become blood brothers indicate. The strength of promising is conveyed in such early practices as those in which promisors might offer as a pledge their wife, their child, or a part of their body.[8] And promises of *secrecy* have been invested with special meaning, in part because of the respect for persons and for relationships called for by the first two premises.

Taken together, the three premises give strong *prima facie* reasons to support confidentiality. With certain limitations, I accept each one binding on those who have accepted information in confidence. But of course there are reasons sufficient to override the force of all these premises, as when secrecy would allow violence to be done to innocent persons, or turn someone into an unwitting accomplice in crime. At such times, autonomy and relationship no longer provide sufficient legitimacy. And the promise of silence should never be given, or if given, can be breached.

It is here that the fourth premise enters in to add strength to the particular pledges of silence given by professionals.[9] This premise assigns weight beyond ordinary loyalty to professional confidentiality because of its utility to persons and to society. As a result, professionals grant their clients secrecy even when they would otherwise have reason to speak out: thus lawyers feel justified in concealing past crimes of clients, bankers the suspect provenance of investors' funds, and priests the sins they hear in confession.

According to this premise, individuals benefit from such confidentiality because it allows them to seek help they might otherwise fear to ask for; those most vulnerable or at risk might otherwise not go for help to doctors or lawyers or others trained to provide it. In this way, innocent persons might end up convicted of crimes for lack of competent legal defense, and disease could take a greater toll among those ashamed of the nature of their ailment. Society therefore gains in turn from allowing such professional refuge, the argument holds, in spite of the undoubted risks of not learning about certain dangers to the community; and everyone is better off when professionals can probe for the secrets that will make them more capable of providing the needed help.

The nature of the helpfulness thought to override the importance of revealing some confidences differs from one profession to another. The social worker can offer support, counsel, sometimes therapy; physicians provide means of relieving suffering and of curing disease; lawyers give assistance in self-protection against the state or other individuals. These efforts may conflict, as for many psychiatrists whenever their mission is both to receive the confidences of troubled military personnel and to serve as agents of the state, obligated to report on the condition of their patients. And the help held to justify confidentiality about informants by police and journalists is not directed to individuals in need of relief at all, but rather to society by encouraging disclosures of abuses and crime.

Such claims to individual and social utility touch on the *raison d'être* of the professions themselves; but they are also potentially treacherous. For if it were found that a professional group or subspecialty not only did not help but actually hurt individuals, and increased the social burden of, say, illness or crime, then there would be a strong case for not allowing it to promise professional confidentiality. To question its special reason for being able to promise confidentiality of unusual strength is therefore seen as an attack on its special purposes, and on the power it acquires in being able to give assurances beyond those which nonprofessionals can offer.

A purely strategic reason for stressing professional confidentiality is that, while needed by clients, it is so easily breached and under such strong pressures to begin with. In schools and in offices, at hospitals and in social gatherings, confidential information may be casually passed around. Other items are conveyed "off the record" or leaked in secret. The prohibition against breaching confidentiality must be especially strong in order to combat the pressures on insiders to do so, especially in view of the ease and frequency with which it is done.

Together with the first three premises for confidentiality, the defense of the fourth helps explain the ritualistic tone in which the duty of preserving secrets is repeatedly set forth in professional oaths and codes of ethics. Still more is needed, however, to explain the sacrosanct nature often ascribed to this duty. The ritualistic nature of confidentiality in certain religious traditions has surely has an effect on its role in law and medicine. A powerful esoteric rationale for secrecy linked the earliest practices of medicine and religion. Thus Henry Sigerist points out that in Mesopotamia medicine, like other sacred knowledge, was kept secret and not divulged to the profane; conversely, many religious texts ended with a warning that "he who does not keep the secret will not remain in health. His days will be shortened."[10]

However strong, these historical links between faith and professional practice give *no* added justification to professional confidentiality. The sacramental nature of religious confession is a matter of faith for believers. It may be respected even in secular law on grounds of religious freedom; but it adds no legitimacy to that of the four premises when it comes to what professionals conceal for clients.[11]

The four premises are not usually separated and evaluated in the context of individual cases or practices. Rather, they blend with the ritualistic nature attributed to confidentiality to support a rigid stance that I shall call the rationale of confidentiality. Not only does this rationale point to links with the most fundamental grounds of autonomy and relationships and trust and help; it also serves as a rationalization that helps deflect ethical inquiry. The very self-evidence that it claims can then expand beyond its legitimate applications. Confidentiality, like all secrecy, can then cover up for and in turn lead to a great deal of error, injury, pathology, and abuse.

When professionals advance confidentiality as a shield, their action is, to be sure, in part intentional and manipulative, but in part it also results from a failure to examine the roots of confidentiality and to spell out the limits of its application. It can lead then to sweeping claims such as that made by the World Medical Association in its 1949 International Code of Medical Ethics: "A doctor shall preserve absolute secrecy on all he knows about his patient because of the confidence entrusted in him."[12]

If such claims go too far, where and how should the lines be drawn? Granting the *prima facie* importance of the principle of confidentiality in the light of the premises which support it, when and for what reasons must it be set aside? I shall consider such limits with respect to the secrets of individual clients, of professionals themselves, and of institutional or corporate clients.

Individual Clients and Their Secrets

Among the most difficult choices for physicians and others are those which arise with respect to confidences by children, mentally incompetent persons, and those who are temporarily not fully capable of guilding their affairs. While some such confidences— as about fears or hopes—can be kept secret without difficulty, others are more troubling. Consider the following case:

> Janet M., a thirteen-year-old girl in the seventh grade of a smalltown junior high school, comes to the office of a family physician. She has known him from childhood, and he has cared for all the members of her family. She tells him that she is pregnant, and that she has had a lab test performed at an out-of-town clinic. She wants to have an abortion. She is afraid that her family, already burdened by unemployment and illness, would be thrown into a crisis by the

news. Her boyfriend, fifteen, would probably be opposed to the abortion. She asks the doctor for help in securing the abortion, and for assurance that he will not reveal her condition to anyone.

Cases such as Janet's are no longer rare. In small towns as in large cities, teenage pregnancy is on the rise, teenage abortion commonplace. Many families do provide the guidance and understanding so desperately needed at such times; but when girls request confidentiality, it is often out of fear of their families' reaction. Health professionals should clearly make every effort to help these girls communicate with their families. But sometimes there is no functioning family. Or else family members may have been so brutal or so unable to cope with crisis in the past that it is legitimate to be concerned about the risks in informing them. At times, it is even the case that a member of the girl's own family has abused her sexually.[13]

Health professionals are then caught in a conflict between their traditional obligation of confidentiality and the normal procedure of consulting with a child's parents before an irreversible step is taken. In this conflict, the premises supporting confidentiality are themselves in doubt. Just how autonomous should thirteen-year-olds be with respect to decisions about pregnancy? They are children still, but with an adult's choice to make. And what about even younger girls? In what relation does a physician stand to them, and to their parents, regarding such secrets?

Because the premises of autonomy and of relationship do not necessarily mandate secrecy at such times, deciding whether or not to pledge silence is much harder. Even the professional help that confidentiality allows is then in doubt. Pregnant young girls are in need of advice and assistance more than most others; confidentiality too routinely extended may lock them into an attitude of frightened concealment that can do permanent damage. Health professionals owe it to these patients, therefore, to encourage and help them to communicate with their families or others responsible for their support. But to *mandate*, as some seek to do, consultation with family members, no matter how brutal or psychologically abusive, would be to take a shortsighted view. Not only would it injure those pregnant girls forced into family confrontations; many others would end by not seeking professional help at all, at a time when they need it most.

Childhood and adolescent pregnancies are far from the only conditions that present professionals with conflicts over confidentiality. Veneral disease, drug and alcohol addiction among the young, as well as a great many problems of incompetent and disturbed individuals past childhood, render confidentiality similarly problematic.

Even where there is no question about maturity or competence, professionals worry about the secrecy asked of them when someone confides to them plans that seem self-injurious: to enter into a clearly disastrous business arrangement, or to give all his possessions to an exploitative "guru," or to abandon life-prolonging medical treatment. He may have no intention of hurting anyone else (though relatives and others may in fact be profoundly affected by his choice) and may be fully within his rights in acting as he does. But his judgment may itself be in doubt, depending on how self-destructive the plans are that he is confiding.

Here again, an absolute insistence on confidentiality would be unreasonable. No one would hesitate to reveal the secret of a temporarily deranged person about to do himself irreversible harm. Patients and clients do not have the requisite balance at such a time to justify silence—and thus complicity—regarding their self-destructive acts, the less so as the very revelation of such plans to a professional is often correctly interpreted as a call for help.

If, on the other hand, the act has been carefully thought through, breaches of confidentiality are much less justified, no matter how irrational the project might at first seem to outsiders. Say the person planning to give his money away wants to live the rest of his life as a contemplative; or that the patient planning to abandon medical treatment has decided to cease delaying death in view of his progressively debilitating and painful disease; it is harder to see the basis for a breach of professional confidentiality in such cases,* since it is more difficult to prove that his act is necessarily self-destructive from his point of view. Professionals are constantly at risk of assuming too readily that the purposes they take to be overriding and to which they have dedicated their careers—financial prudence, for instance—are necessarily more

---

* A number of questions having to do with paternalism arise in these cases. It is important to note, however, that breaching confidence for paternalistic reasons does not necessarily involve interfering with the persons whose confidences are revealed, nor coercing them.

rational for all others than conflicting aims. This professional bias has to be taken into account in any decision to override confidentiality on grounds of irrationality and self-harm.

Sometimes, however, a patient's insistence on confidentiality can bring quite unintended risks. Because people live longer, and often suffer from multiple chronic diseases, their records have to be accessible to many different health professionals. Their reluctance to have certain facts on their medical records may then be dangerous. One physician has pointed to some of the possible consequences of such concealment:

> The man who insists that no record be made of a psychiatric history, or the drugs that would suggest that there is one, and wants no record of his syphilis and penicillin injections and subsequent recovery, is the same man who must face squarely the risk of future syphilitic disease of the nervous system or even lethal penicillin reactions because future medical personnel never followed through in the right manner. They do not even know that the problem existed; they and the patient stumbled blindly into trouble.[14]

At times, the insistence on secrecy can become obsessive, so that confidentiality may come to surround the most trivial matters, even when less secrecy could be useful not only to oneself but to others. Thus many refuse to release information about their blood types or past illnesses, even at the cost of slowing down research that might help other sufferers. Here as always, secrecy can shut out many forms of feedback and assistance and consequently encourage poor judgment.

Do patients have the same claims to confidentiality about personal information when persons from whom it is kept run serious risks? Consider again the family mentioned earlier in which the father wishes to conceal from his children that he suffers from polycystic kidney disease. It is now two years later. The father, much closer to death, has told his two children about the genetic nature of his disease. He was prompted to do so, in part, by his daughter's plans to marry. She, however, fears disclosing to her future husband that the same disease may strike her and affect their children. Now it is her turn to insist on confidentiality, not only from her father but from all others who know the facts, including the health professionals involved.

The dilemma they face is in one sense very old, in another

quite new. It resembles all the choices through the ages about whether or not to reveal to intimates and future spouses that someone suffers from incurable venereal disease, sexual problems, a recurring psychiatric condition, or a degenerative disease as yet in its early stages. But it has taken on a new frequency because there is now so much more information, especially of a genetic nature, than even a hundred years ago. The category of problematic and troubling predictions has expanded, raising new conflicts of secrecy for parents, prospective spouses, and many others, and of confidentiality for health professionals. Lacking the genetic information, this family would not have faced the same choice in an earlier period. With increased knowledge of risks, therefore, the collective burden of confidentiality has grown as well.

Does a professional owe confidentiality to clients who reveal plans or acts that endanger other directly? Such a question arises for the lawyer whose client lets slip that he plans a bank robbery, or that he has committed an assault for which an innocent man is standing trial; for the pediatrician who suspects that a mother drugs her children to keep them quiet; and for the psychiatrist whose patient discloses that he is obsessed by jealousy and thoughts of violence to his wife. . . . [15]

Once professionals undertake to receive and even probe for information threatening to others, they can no longer ignore those others, out of concern either for their patients or for society. The *prima facie* premises supporting confidentiality are overridden at such times.

The autonomy we grant individuals over personal secrets, first of all, cannot reasonably be thought to extend to plans of violence against innocent persons; at such times, on the contrary, someone who knows of plans that endanger others owes it to them to counteract those plans, and, if he is not sure he can forestall them, to warn the potential victims. Nor, in the second place, can patients who voice serious threats against innocent persons invoke confidentiality on the basis of their relationship with therapists or anyone else without asking them to be partially complicitous. The third premise, basing confidentiality in part on a promise, is likewise overridden, since in the absence of legitimacy for the first two, it ought to be clearly understood that no one, whether professionally trained or not, should give such a pledge. The benefits invoked in the fourth premise, finally, are not only demonstrated in these cases; even if they were, they could not override the injustices done to those unwittingly placed at risk.*

Long before psychiatrists worried about these problems, Catholic theologians had studied them with a thoroughness often lacking in contemporary discussions. The distinctions they worked out over the centuries concerning different types of secrets and the obligations of professionals were detailed and well reasoned. Most theologians agreed that certain types of secrets were not binding on professional recipients, foremost among them grave threats against the public good or against innocent third persons.[16]

An example they often described is the following: What should a doctor do if he has a patient who suffers from an incurable and highly contagious venereal disease and who plans to marry without disclosing this fact to his fiancée? According to many theologians, the doctor's obligation of secrecy would then cease; the young man forfeits such consideration through his intent to act in a way that might gravely injure his fiancée. The doctor is therefore free to speak, but with certain limitations: he must reveal only so much of the secret as is necessary to avert the harm, and only to the person threatened, who has a right to this information, rather than to family members, neighbors, or the curious or gossip-hungry at large.

These commentators also discussed a subject that still divides the contemporary debate: should the breach of secrecy to avert grave harm be obligatory, or merely permitted? Should the professional feel free to choose whether or not to warn the endangered person, or acknowledge a duty to do so? It is one thing to say that he no longer owes the client confidentiality; but does he also *owe* the endangered person the information? Do lawyers, for example, owe any information to persons who may be injured by their clients' unlawful tax schemes, plans for extortion, or threats of violence? And if they do recognize some such obligation, how does it weigh against that of confidentiality?

The duty of confidentiality clearly has some weight; as a result, the obligation to warn potential victims is not as great for profes-

---

* Such a conclusion carries with it line-drawing problems: how likely the danger should be before one assumes serious risk, how sure one should be about the identity of the potential victim, how much this individual already knows about the risk, the degree of precautions already in place, etc. But line-drawing problems would occur no matter what the conclusion unless one postulated either no duty to breach confidentiality under any conditions whatsoever, or, on the contrary, no obligation of confidentiality at all.

sionals as it might be for others who happen to hear of the danger. Yet it is a strong one nevertheless, especially where serious harm is likely to occur. In such cases, the duty to warn ought to be overriding. Professionals should not then be free to promise confidentiality, nor should a client expect to be able to entrust them with such projects, any more than with stolen goods or lethal weapons.[17]

The same is true for confidences regarding past crimes. Here, too, confidentiality counts; but it must be weighed against other aims—of social justice and restitution. It is therefore hard to agree with lawyers who argue as a matter of course that they owe clients silence about past, unsolved murders; it is equally hard to agree with Swiss bankers claiming that confidentiality suffices to legitimate the secret bank accounts that attract so many depositors enriched through crime, conspiracy, and political exploitation.

Secrecy as a Shield

The greatest burden of secrecy imposed by confidentiality, however, is that of the secrets professionals keep to protect themselves rather than patients and clients. Confidentiality can be used, here as elsewhere, as a shield for activities that could ill afford to see the light of day. An example of how dangerous such shielding can be is afforded by the story of the death in 1976 of Anneliese Michel, a young German student, after ten months of exorcism.[18]

Anneliese Michel had been under periodic medical care since she was 16 years old. She had been diagnosed as suffering both from recurrent epileptic seizures and from anorexia nervosa. When she was 22, her parents persuaded her to withdraw from university studies. Ernst Alt, the local parish priest, suspected that she might be posessed by devils and that exorcism might cure her. He saw the seizures as evidence of such possession rather than of epilepsy, and decided to consult Germany's leading "satanologist," the 83-year-old Adolf Rodewyk, S.J. Father Rodewyk concluded that the convulsions were trancelike states of possession in which, among other manifestations, a devil calling himself Judas made no secret of his identity.

Father Rodewyk recommended exorcism. The *Rituale Romanum* of 1614, still followed in cases of exorcism, prescribes that a bishop must agree to the procedure before it can be undertaken, and that the person thus treated must be beyond medical help. Father Rodewyk assured Bishop Joseph Stangl of Wurzburg that Anneliese's case was one for exorcists, not for doctors; and the bishop authorized the rites, ordering "strictest secrecy and total discretion."

For ten months, the young woman took part in lengthy sessions with the parish priest and Father Wilhelm Renz, an expert called in for the exorcism. The two prayed with her and tried, by means by holy water, adjurations, and commands, to drive out the devils—by then thought to number at least six and calling themselves, in addition to Judas, by such names as Lucifer, Nero, and Hitler. Anneliese was convinced that she was thus possessed and that the powers of good and of evil were fighting over her soul. She wrote in her diary that the Savior had told her she was a great saint. Fearing that doctors might diagnose her voices and seizures as psychiatric symptoms and send her to a mental hospital, she avoided health professionals. As the months wore on, she grew weaker, eating and drinking next to nothing. During one particularly stormy session of exorcism, she rushed head first against the wall facing her bed, they lay back exhausted. The devils were finally declared to have left. The next morning, she was found dead in her bed.

In April 1978, her parents and the two priests who had conducted the exorcism were brought to trial. They were convicted of negligent homicide for having failed to seek medical help up to the very end. Physicians testified that, even as late as a few days before Anneliese died, her life could have been saved had she had medical attention. The four accused were sentenced to six months imprisonment.

The priests sincerely believed that they were doing their best to save Anneliese Michel. Insofar as they believed Father Rodewyk's attesting to the presence of devils, they could hardly think medical treatment appropriate. But they knew their belief that Anneliese was possessed by devils would be shared by few, and so they conspired with her parents to keep the sessions of exorcism secret to the very end. Two kinds of confidentiality come together here: that between priest and penitent, and that between caretaker and patient. But neither one should have been honored in this case, for while they protect much that is spoken by penitents and by patients, they were never intended to protect all that is done by priests or caretakers in response, least of all when it constitutes treatment of very sick persons by dangerous methods without medical assistance.

The case is an extreme one. Strict adherence to the stipulation in the *Rituale Romanum* of 1614 that someone must be beyond medical help would have required much more careful consultation with physicians before leaping to the conclusion that exorcism was called for. When publicity about the case arose, Catholics and non-Catholics alike were distressed at how the young woman had been treated. What is worth noting, however, is that her need for medical help went unnoticed because of the secrecy in which the exorcism was conducted. The case illustrates, therefore, what can happen in almost any system of advising and helping those in need whenever secrecy shrouds what is done to them. And it raises broader questions about confidentiality: Exactly whose secret should it protect? The patient's or client's alone? Or the professional's? Or all that transpires between them?

In principle, confidentiality should protect only the first. But in practice, it can expand, like all other practices of secrecy, to cover much more. It may even be stretched so far as to include what professionals hide *from* patients, clients, and the public at large.

The sick, the poor, the mentally ill, the aged, and the very young are in a paradoxical situation in this respect. While their right to confidentiality is often breached and their most intimate problems openly bandied about, the poor care they may receive is just as often covered up under the same name of confidentiality. That is the shield held forth to prevent outsiders from finding out about negligence, overcharging, unnecessary surgery, or institutionalization. And far more than individual mistakes and misdeeds are thus covered up, for confidentiality is also the shield that professionals invoke to protect incompetent colleagues and negligence and unexpected accidents in, for instance, hospitals, factories, or entire industries.

The word "confidentiality" has by now become a means of covering up a multitude of questionable and often dangerous practices. When lawyers use it to justify keeping secret their client's plans to construct housing so shoddy as to be life-threatening, or when government officials invoke it in concealing the risks of nuclear weapons, confidentiality no longer serves the purpose for which it was intended; it has become, rather, a means for deflecting legitimate public attention.

Such invocations of confidentiality are facilitated by the ease with which many transpose the confidentiality owed to individuals to the collective level. Consider, for example, the prolonged collaboration between asbestos manufacturers and company physicians to conceal the risks from exposure to asbestos dust. These risks were kept secret from the public, from workers in plants manufacturing asbestos insulation, and even from those workers found in medical checkups to be in the early stages of asbestos-induced disease. When a reporter approached a physician associated with the concealment as consultant for a large manufacturer, the physician turned down his request for an interview on grounds of confidentiality owned as a matter of "the patient's rights," and explained, when the astonished reporter inquired who the "patient" was, that it was the *company*.[19]

The step from patient confidentiality to institutional confidentiality is a large one, but it is often lightly taken in arguments that ignore the differences between the two. The first two premises underlying confidentiality, of autonomy regarding personal information and the respect for intimacy and human bonds, are obviously applicable, if at all, in a different manner when it comes to institutions. And the fourth premise, concerning the benefit to individuals from having somewhere to turn when vulnerable and in need of help, and the indirect benefit to society from allowing professionals to give counsel in strict confidence, must be scrutinized with care whenever the claim is made that it applies to government agencies, law firms, or corporations. We ask of them a much higher degree of accountability.

To be sure, these institutions should be able to invoke confidentiality for legitimate activities such as internal memoranda and personnel files; but it is a different matter altogether to claim confidentiality for plans that endanger others. Such protection attracts all who seek surreptitious assistance with bribery, tax evasion, and similar schemes. And because corporate or consulting law is so lucrative, the power to exercise confidentiality for such secrets then shields not merely the company and the client but the lawyer's own links to, and rewards from, highly questionable practices.

The premises supporting confidentiality are strong, but they cannot support practices of secrecy—whether by individual clients, institutions, or professionals—that undermine and contradict the very respect for persons and for human bonds that confidentiality was meant to protect.

NOTES

1. See Robert E. Regan, *Professional Secrecy in the Light of Moral Principles* (Washington, D.C.: Augustinian Press, 1943); Alan H. Goldman, *The Moral Foundations of Professional Ethics* (Totowa, N.J.: Rowman & Littlefield, 1980); LeRoy Walters, "Ethical Aspects of Medical Confidentiality," in Tom L. Beauchamp and LeRoy Walters, eds., *Contemporary Issues in Bioethics* (Encino, Calif.: Dickenson Publishing Co., 1978), pp. 169–75; Susanna J.Wilson, *Confidentiality in Social Work* (New York: Free Press, 1978); William Harold Tiemann, *The Right to Silence: Priviledged Communication and the Pastor* (Richmond, Va.: John Knox Press, 1964); William W. Meissner, "Threats to Confidentiality," *Psychiatric Annals* 2 (1979):54–71.
2. From the newsletter *Hard Choices,* of the Office for Radio and Television for Learning (Boston, 1980), p. 9.
3. For a discussion of whether this partial autonomy over personal information should be defended in terms of property, see Authur R. Miller, *The Assault in Privacy* (Ann Arbor: University of Michigan Press, 1971), pp. 211–16.
4. For the marital privilege, see Sanford Levinson, *The State and Structures of Intimacy* (New York: Basic Books, forthcoming). For the Chinese tradition, see Derk Bodde and Clarence Morris, *Law in Imperial China* (Cambridge, Mass.: Harvard University Press, 1967), p. 40.
5. Hugo Grotius, *The Law of War and Peace*, trans. Francis Kelsey (Indianapolis: Bobbs-Merrill Co., 1925), bk. 2, chap. 11, p. 331.
6. I discussed the question of lying to protect confidences in *Lying: Moral Choice in Public and Private Life* (New York: Pantheon Books, 1978), chap. 11.
7. For different views on the binding force of promises, see William Godwin, *Enquiry Concerning Political Justice* (1793; 3rd ed. 1798), bk. 3, chap. 3; Richard Price, *A Review of the Principal Questions in Morals* (1758; 3rd ed. 1787), chap. 7 (both in D. H. Munro, ed., *A Guide to the British Moralists* [London: William Collins, Sons & Co., 1972], pp. 187–97, 180–96). For more general treatments of promising, see Grotius, *Law of War and Peace,* bk. 2, chap. 11, pp. 328–42; John Searle, *Speech Acts* (Cambridge: Cambridge University Press, 1969); Charles Fried, *Contract as Promise* (Cambridge, Mass.: Harvard University Press, 1981).
8. Nietzsche, in *Ecce Homo,* trans. Kaufmann, p. 64, relates such pledges to the bond between debtor and creditor; he argues that the memory

necessary for people to keep promises only developed through such painful, often cruel experiences.

9. For discussions of whether some or all of these premises should be accepted, and whether they are grounded on utilitarian or deontological considerations, see Goldman, *The Moral Foundations of Professional Ethics*; Leo J. Cass and William J. Curran, "Rights of Privacy in Medical Practice," partially reprinted in Samuel Gorovitz, et al., *Moral Problems in Medicine* (Englewood Cliffs, N.J.: Prentice-Hall, 1976), pp. 82–85; Benjamin Freedman, "A Meta-Ethics for Professional Morality," *Ethics* 89 (1978):1–79; Benjamin Freedman, "What Really Makes Professional Morality Different: Response to Martin," *Ethics* 91 (1981): 626–30; Mike W. Martin, "Rights and the Meta-Ethics of Professional Morality," *Ethics* 91 (1981): 619–25.

10. Henry E. Sigerist, *A History of Medicine*, vol. 1, *Primitive and Archaic Medicine* (New York: Oxford University Press, 1951), p. 433.

11. Jeremy Bentham, otherwise opposed to testimonial privileges for professionals, argues in favor of "excluding the evidence of a Catholic priest respecting the confessions intrusted to him," holding that freedom of religion outweighs the social costs of such practices. See *Works of Jeremy Bentham*, 7:366–68.

12. Code of Ethics, 1949 World Medical Association, In *Encyclopedia of Bioethics* (New York: Free Press, 1978), pp. 1749–50.

13. I have discussed abortion in "Ethical Problems of Abortion," *Hastings Center Studies* 2 (1974):33–52.

14. Lawrence Weed, *Your Health Care and How to Manage it* (Arlington, Vt.: Essex Publishing Co., 1978), p. 79.

15. The conflicts that psychotherapists face in this respect were brought to public attention by the murder of a young student, Tatiana Tarasoff, and the subsequent lawsuits brought by her parents against the university, the campus police, and the psychotherapists who had failed to warn her of threats against her life by her murderer. See Judge Tobriner, *Tarasoff v. Regents of the Universtiy of California*, Opinion #551, 1. 2d 334, 131 Cal. Rptr. 14(1979). See also Harvey L. Ruben and Diana D. Ruben, "Confidentiality and Privileged Communication: The Psychotherapeutic Relationship Revisited," *Medical Annals of the District of Columbia* 41 (1972):365; Alan A. Stone, "The Tarasoff Decisions: Suing Psychotherapists to Safeguard Society," *Harvard Law Review* 90 (1976): 1358–78; and David Wechsler, in "Patients, Therapists, and Third Parties: The Victimological Virtues of Tarasoff," *International Journal of Law and Psychiatry* 2 (1979):1–28.

16. See Regan, *Professional Secrecy*, pp. 104–13.

17. For diverging views of the lawyer's responsibility of confidentiality, see American Bar Association, Proposed Final Draft, Model Rules of Professional Conduct, 1981, pp. 37–47; and the Roscoe Pound–American Trial Lawyers Foundation, Discussion Draft, The American Lawyer's Code of Conduct, June 1980, pp. 101–10.

18. For accounts of the story of Anneliese Michel and of the trial after her death, I have relied on *Die Zeit*, July 30, 1976, and April 7, 1978;

Der Spiegel, July 2, 1976, and April 3, 1978, and *Süddeutsche Zeitung*, which had stories almost daily during the period of the trial, Mar. 30–April 24, 1978.
19. See Paul Brodeur, *Expendable Americans* (New York: Viking Press, 1973).

Study Questions

1. After reading Bok's article, would you withhold information on a terminal illness if a member of your own family was involved?
2. Among all the types of confidentiality relationships discussed, which do you think should have the greatest protection from, say, an obligation to legal disclosure. (Doctor-patient, priest-confessioner, etc.)

Feminist Ethics and In Vitro Fertilization[1]

*Susan Sherwin**

New technology in human reproduction has provoked wide ranging arguments about the desirability and moral justifiability of
many of these efforts. Authors of biomedical ethics have ventured
into the field to offer the insight of moral theory to these complex
moral problems of contemporary life. I believe, however, that the
moral theories most widely endorsed today are problematic and
that a new approach to ethics is necessary if we are to address
the concerns and perspectives identified by feminist theorists in
our considerations of such topics. Hence, I propose to look at one
particular technique in the growing repertoire of new reproductive
technologies, in vitro fertilization (IVF), in order to consider the
insight which the mainstream approaches to moral theory have
offered to this debate, and to see the difference made by a feminist
approach to ethics.

I have argued elsewhere that the most widely accepted moral
theories of our time are inadequate for addressing many of the
moral issues we encounter in our lives, since they focus entirely
on such abstract qualities of moral agents as autonomy or quan-
tities of happiness, and they are addressed to agents who are
conceived of as independent, non-tuistic individuals. In contrast,
I claimed, we need a theory which places the locus of ethical

* Dalhousie University
Halifax, NS
Canada B3H 3J5

concerns in a complex social network of interrelated persons who are involved in special sorts of relations with one another. Such a theory, as I envision it, would be influenced by the insights and concerns of feminist theory, and hence, I have called it feminist ethics.[2]

In this paper, I propose to explore the differences between a feminist approach to ethics and other, more traditional approaches in examining the propriety of developing and implementing in vitro fertilization and related technologies. This is a complicated task, since each sort of ethical theory admits of a variety of interpretations and hence of a variety of conclusions on concrete ethical issues. Nonetheless, certain themes and trends can be seen to emerge. Feminist thinking is also ambivalent in application, for feminists are quite torn about their response to this sort of technology. It is my hope that a systematic theoretic evaluation of IVF from the point of view of a feminist ethical theory will help feminists like myself sort through our uncertainty on these matters.

Let me begin with a quick description of IVF for the uninitiated. In vitro fertilization is the technology responsible for what the media likes to call "test tube babies." It circumvents, rather than cures, a variety of barriers to conception, primarily those of blocked fallopian tubes and low sperm counts. In vitro fertilization involves removing ova from the woman's body, collecting sperm from the man's, combining them to achieve conception in the laboratory, and, a few days later, implanting some number of the newly fertilized eggs directly into the woman's womb with the hope that pregnancy will continue normally from this point on. This process requires that a variety of hormones be administered to the women—which involve profound emotional and physical changes—that her blood and urine be monitored daily, and then at three hour intervals, that ultrasound be used to determine when ovulation occurs. In some clinics, implantation requires that she remain immobile for 48 hours (including 24 hours in the head down position). IVF is successful in about 10–15% of the cases selected as suitable, and commonly involves multiple efforts at implantation.

Let us turn now to the responses that philosophers working within the traditional approaches to ethics have offered on this subject. A review of the literature in bioethics identifies a variety of concerns with this technology. Philosophers who adopt a theological perspectve tend to object that such technology is wrong because it is not "natural" and undermines God's plan for the family. Paul Ramsey, for instance, is concerned about the artificiality of IVF and other sorts of reproductive technology with which it is potentially associated, e.g., embryo transfer, ova as well as sperm donation or sale, increased eugenic control, etc:

> But there is as yet no discernable evidence that we are recovering a sense for man [sic] as a natural object . . . toward whom a . . . form of "natural piety" is appropriate . . . parenthood is certainly one of those "courses of action" natural to man, which cannot without violation be disassembled and put together again.[3]

Leon Kass argues a smiliar line in "Making Babies Revisited."[4] He worries that our conception of humanness will not survive the technological permutations before us, and that we will treat these new artificially conceived embryos more as objects than as subjects; he also fears that we will be unable to track traditional human categories of parenthood and lineage, and that this loss would cause us to loose track of important aspects of our identity. The recent position paper of the Catholic Church on reproductive technology reflects related concerns:

> It is through the secure and recognized relationship to his [sic] own parents that the child can discover his own identity and achieve his own proper human development . . .
>   Heterologous artificial fertilization violates the rights of the child; it deprives him of his filial relationship with his parental origins and can hinder the maturing of his personal identity.[5]

Philosophers partial to utilitarianism prefer a more scientific approach; they treat these sorts of concerns as sheer superstition. They carefully explain to their theological colleagues that there is no clear sense of "natural" and certainly no sense that demands special moral status. All medical activity, and perhaps all human activity, can be seen in some sense as being "interference with nature," but that is hardly grounds for avoiding such action. "Humanness," too, is a concept that admits of many interpretations; generally, it does not provide satisfactory grounds for moral distinctions. Further, it is no longer thought appropriate to focus too strictly on questions of lineage and strict biological parentage, and, they note, most theories of personal identity do not rely on such matters.

Where some theologians object that "fertilization achieved outside the bodies of the couple remains by this very fact deprived of the meanings of the values which are expressed in the language of the body and in the union of human persons,"[6] utilitarians quickly dismiss the objection against reproduction without sexuality in a properly sanctified marriage. See, for instance, Michael Bayles in *Reproductive Ethics*: " . . . even if reproduction should occur only within a context of marital love, the point of that requirement is the nurturance of offspring. Such nurturance does not depend on the sexual act itself. The argument confuses the biological act with the familial context."[7]

Another area of disagreement between theological ethicists and their philosophical critics is the significance of the wedge argument to the debate about IVF. IVF is already a complex technology involving research on superovulation, "harvesting" of ova, fertilization, and embryo implants. It is readily adaptable to technology involving the transfer of ova and embryos, and hence their donation or sale, as well as to the "rental of womb space;" it also contributes to an increasing ability to foster fetal growth outside of the womb and, potentially, to the development of artificial wombs covering the whole period of gestation. It is already sometimes combined with artificial insemination and is frequently used to produce surplus fertilized eggs to be frozen for later use. Theological ethicists worry that such activity, and further reproductive developments we can anticipate (such as human cloning), violate God's plan for human reproduction. They worry about the cultural shift involved in viewing reproduction as a scientific enterprise, rather than the "miracle of love" which religious proponents prefer: "[He] cannot be desired or conceived as the product of an intervention of medical or biological techniques; that would be equivalent to reducing him to an object of scientific technology."[8] And, worse, they note, we cannot anticipate the ultimate outcome of this rapidly expanding technology.

The where-will-it-all-end hand-wringing that comes with this sort of religious futurology is rejected by most analytical philosophers; they urge us to realize that few slopes are as slippery as the pessimists would have us believe, that scientists are moral people and quite capable of evaluating each new form of technology on its own merits, and that IVF must be judged by its own consequences and not the possible result of some future technology with which it may be linked. Samuel Gorovitz is typical:

> It is not enough to show that disaster awaits if the process is not controlled. A man walking East in Omaha will drown in the Atlantic—if he does not stop. The argument must also rest on the evidence about the likelihood that judgment and control will be exercised responsibly . . . Collectively we have significant capacity to exercise judgment and control . . . our record has been rather good in regard to medical treatment and research.[9]

The question of the moral status of the fertilized eggs is more controversial. Since the superovulation involved in producing eggs for collection tends to produce several at once, and the process of collecting eggs is so difficult, and since the odds against conception on any given attempt are so slim, several eggs are usually collected and ferlitized at once. A number of these fertilized eggs will be introduced to the womb with the hope that at least one will implant and gestation will begin, but there are frequently some "extras." Moral problems arise as to what should be done with these surplus eggs. They can be frozen for future use (since odds are against the first attempt "taking"), or they can be used as research material, or simply discarded. Canadian clinics get around the awkwardness of their ambivalence on the moral status of these cells by putting them all into the woman's womb. This poses the devastating threat of six or eight "successfully" implanting, and a woman being put into the position of carrying a litter; something, we might note, her body is not constructed to do.

Those who take a hard line against abortion and argue that the embryo is a person from the moment of conception object to all these procedures, and, hence, they argue, there is no morally acceptable means of conducting IVF. To this line, utilitarians offer the standard responses. Personhood involves moral, not biological categories. A being neither sentient nor conscious is not a person in any meaningful sense. For example, Gorovitz argues, "Surely the concept of person involves in some fundamental way the capacity for sentience, or an awareness of sensations at the very least."[10] Bayles says, "For fetuses to have moral status they must be capable of good or bad in their lives . . . What happens to them must make a difference to them. Consequently some form of awareness is necessary for moral status."[11] (Apparently, clinicians in the field have been trying to avoid this whole issue by coining a new term in the hopes of identifying a new ontological category, that of the "pre-embryo.")[12]

Many bioethicists have agreed here, as they have in the abortion debate, that the principal moral question of IVF is the moral status and rights of the embryo. Once they resolve that question, they can, like Englehardt, conclude that since fetuses are not persons, and since reproductive processes occurring outside a human body pose no special moral problems, "there will be no sustainable moral arguments in principle . . . against in vitro fertilization."[13] He argues,

> in vitro fertilization and techniques that will allow us to study and control human reproduction are morally neutral instruments for the realization of profoundly important human goals, which are bound up with the realization of the good of others: children for infertile parents and greater health for the children that will be born.[14]

Moral theorists also express worries about the safety of the process, and by that they tend to mean the safety to fetuses that may result from this technique. Those fears have largely been put to rest in the years since the first IVF baby was born in 1978, for the couple of thousand infants reportedly produced by this technique to date seem no more prone to apparent birth defects than the population at large, and, in fact, there seems to be evidence that birth defects may be less common in this group—presumably because of better monitoring and pre- and post-natal care. (There is concern expressed, however, in some circles outside of the bioethical literature about the long-term effect of some of the hormones involved, in light of our belated discoveries of the effect of DES usage on offspring. This concern is aggravated by the chemical similarity of clomid, one of the hormones used in IVF, to DES.)[15]

Most of the literature tends to omit comment on the uncertainties associated with the effect of drugs inducing superovulation in the woman concerned, or with the dangers posed by the general anaesthetic required for the laparoscopy procedure; the emotional costs associated with this therapy are also overlooked, even though there is evidence that it is extremely stressful in the 85–

90% of the attempts that fail, and that those who succeed have difficulty in dealing with common parental feelings of anger and frustration with a child they tried so hard to get. Nonetheless, utilitarian theory could readily accommodate such concerns, should the philosophers involved think to look for them. In principle, no new moral theory is yet called for, although a widening of perspective (to include the effects on the women involved) would certainly be appropriate.

The easiest solution to the IVF question seems to be available to ethicists of a deontological orientation who are keen on autonomy and rights and free of religious prejudice. For the, IVF is simply a private matter, to be decided by the couple concerned together with a medical specialist. The desire to have and raise children is a very common one and generally thought to be a paradigm case of a purely private matter. Couples seeking this technology face medical complications that require the assistance of a third party, and it is thought, "it would be unfair to make infertile couples pass up the joys of rearing infants or suffer the burdens of rearing handicapped chidren."[16] Certainly, meeting individuals' desires/needs is the most widely accepted argument in favor of the use of this technology.

What is left, then, in the more traditional ethical discussions, is usually some handwaving about costs. This is an extremely expensive procedure; estimates range from $1500 to $6000 per attempt. Gorovitz says, for instance, "there is the question of the distribution of costs, a question that has heightened impact if we consider the use of public funds to pay for medical treatment."[17] Debate tends to end here in the mystery of how to balance soaring medical costs of various sorts and a comment that no new ethical problems are posed.

Feminists share many of these concerns, but they find many other moral issues involved in the development and use of such technology and note the silence of the standard moral approaches in addressing these matters. Further, feminism does not identify the issues just cited as the primary areas of moral concern. Nonetheless, IVF is a difficult issue for feminists.

On the one hand, most feminists share the concern for autonomy held by most moral theorists, and they are interested in allowing women freedom of choice in reproductive matters. This freedom is most widely discussed in connection with access to safe and effective contraception and, when necessary, to abortion services. For women who are unable to conceive because of blocked fallopian tubes, or certain fertility problems of their partners, IVF provides the technology to permit pregnancy which is otherwise impossible. Certainly most of the women seeking IVF perceive it to be technology that increases their reproductive freedom of choice. So, it would seem that feminists should support this sort of technology as part of our general concern to foster the degree of reproductive control women may have over their own bodies. Some feminists have chosen this route. But feminists must also note that IVF as practiced does not altogether satisfy the motivation of fostering individual autonomy.

It is, after all, the sort of technology that requires medical intervention, and hence it is not really controlled by the women seeking it, but rather by the medical staff providing this "service." IVF is not available to every woman who is medically suitable, but only to those who are judged to be worthy by the medical specialists concerned. To be a candidate for this procedure, a woman must have a husband and an apparently stable marriage. She must satisfy those specialists that she and her husband have appropriate resources to support any children produced by this arrangement (in addition, of course, to the funds required to purchase the treatment in the first place), and that they generally "deserve" this support. IVF is not available to single women, lesbian women, or women not securely placed in the middle class or beyond. Nor is it available to women whom the controlling medical practitioners judge to be deviant with respect to their norms of who makes a good mother. The supposed freedom of choice, then, is provided only to selected women who have been screened by the personal values of those administering the technology.

Further, even for these women, the record on their degree of choice is unclear. Consider, for instance, that this treatment has always been very experimental: it was introduced without the prior primate studies which are required for most new forms of medical technology, and it continues to be carried out under constantly shifting protocols, with little empirical testing, as clinics try to raise their very poor success rates. Moreover, consent forms are perceived by patients to be quite restrictive procedures and women seeking this technology are not in a particularly strong position to bargain to revise the terms; there is no alternate clinic down the street to choose if a woman dislikes her treatment at some clinic, but there are usually many other women waiting for access to her place in the clinic should she choose to withdraw.

Some recent studies indicate that few of the women participating in current programs really know how low the success rates are.[18] And it is not apparent that participants are encouraged to ponder the medical unknowns associated with various aspects of the technique, such as the long-term consequences of superovulation and the use of hormones chemically similar to DES. Nor is it the case that the consent procedure involves consultation on how to handle the disposal of 'surplus' zygotes. It is doubtful that the women concerned have much real choice about which procedure is followed with the eggs they will not need. These policy decisions are usually made at the level of the clinic. It should be noted here that at least one feminist argues that neither the woman, nor the doctors have the right to choose to destroy these embryos: " . . . because no one, not even its parents, owns the embryo/fetus, no one has the *right* to destroy it, even at a very early developmental stage . . . to destroy an embryo is not an automatic entitlement held by anyone, including its genetic parents."[19]

Moreover, some participants reflect deep seated ambivalence on the part of many women about the procedure—they indicate that their marriage and status depends on a determination to do "whatever is possible" in pursuit of their "natural" childbearing function—and they are not helped to work through the seeming imponderables associated with their long-term well-being. Thus, IVF as practiced involves significant limits on the degree of autonomy deontologists insist on in other medical contexts, though the nonfeminst literature is insensitive to this anomaly.

From the perspective of consequentialism, feminists take a long view and try to see IVF in the context of the burgeoning range of techniques in the area of human reproductive technology. While some of this technology seems to hold the potential of benefitting women generally—by leading to better understanding of conception and contraception, for instance—there is a wary suspicion that this research will help foster new techniques and products such as human cloning and the development of artificial wombs which can, in principle, make the majority of women superfluous.

(This is not a wholly paranoid fear in a woman-hating culture: we can anticipate that there will be great pressure for such techniques in subsequent generations, since one of the "successes" of reproductive technology to date has been to allow parents to control the sex of their offspring; the "choice" now made possible clearly threatens to result in significant imbalances in the ratio of boy to girl infants. Thus, it appears, there will likely be significant shortages of women to bear children in the future, and we can anticipate pressures for further technological solutions to the "new" problem of reproduction that will follow.)

Many authors from all traditions consider it necessary to ask why it is that some couples seek this technology so desperately. Why is it so important to so many people to produce their "own" child? On this question, theorists in the analytic tradition seem to shift to previously rejected ground and suggest that this is a natural, or at least a proper, desire. Englehardt, for example, says, "The use of technology in the fashioning of children is integral to the goal of rendering the world congenial to persons."[20] Bayles more cautiously observes that "A desire to beget for its own sake . . . is probably irrational;" nonetheless, he immediately concludes, "these techniques for fulfilling that desire have been found ethically permissible."[21] R.G. Edwards and David Sharpe state the case most strongly: "the desire to have children must be among the most basic of human instincts, and denying it can lead to considerable psychological and social difficulties."[22] Interestingly, although the recent pronouncement of the Catholic Church assumes that "the desire for a child is natural,"[23] it denies that a couple has a right to a child: "The child is not an object to which one has a right."[24]

Here, I believe, it becomes clear why we need a deeper sort of feminist analysis. We must look at the sort of social arrangements and cultural values that underlie the drive to assume such risks for the sake of biological parenthood. We find that the capitalism, racism, sexism, and elitism of our culture have combined to create a set of attitudes which views children as commodities whose value is derived from their possession of parental chromosomes. Children are valued as privatized commodities, reflecting the virility and heredity of their parents. They are also viewed as the responsibility of their parents and are not seen as the social treasure and burden that they are. Parents must tend their needs on pain of prosecution, and, in return, they get to keep complete control over them. Other adults are inhibited from having warm, stable interactions with the children of others—it is as suspect to try to hug and talk regularly with a child who is not one's own as it is to fondle and hang longingly about a car or a bicycle which belongs to someone else—so those who wish to know children well often find they must have their own.

Women are persuaded that their most important purpose in life is to bear and raise children; they are told repeatedly that their life is incomplete, that they are lacking in fulfillment if they do not have children. And, in fact, many women do face a barren existence without children. Few women have access to meaningful, satisfying jobs. Most do not find themselves in the center of the romantic personal relationships which the culture pretends is the norm for heterosexual couples. And they have been socialized to be fearful of close friendships with others—they are taught to distrust other women, and to avoid the danger of friendship with men other than their husbands. Children remain the one hope for real intimacy and for the sense of accomplishment which comes from doing work one judges to be valuable.

To be sure, chilren can provide that sense of self-worth, although for many women (and probably for all mothers at some times) motherhood is not the romanticized satisfaction they are led to expect. But there is something very wrong with a culture where childrearing is the only outlet available to most women in which to pursue fulfillment. Moreover, there is something wrong with the ownership theory of children that keeps other adults at a distance from children. There ought to be a variety of close relationships possible between children and adults so that we all recognize that we have a stake in the well-being of the young, and we all benefit from contact with their view of the world.

In such a world, it would not be necessary to spend the huge sums on designer children which IVF requires while millions of other children starve to death each year. Adults who enjoyed children could be involved in caring for them whether or not they produced them biologically. And, if the institution of marriage survives, women and men would marry because they wished to share their lives together, not because the men needed someone to produce heirs for them and women needed financial support for their children. That would be a world in which we might have reproductive freedom of choice. The world we now live in has so limited women's options and self-esteem, it is legitimate to question the freedom behind women's demand for this technology, for it may well be largely a reflection of constraining social perspectives.

Nonetheless, I must acknowledge that some couples today genuinely mourn their incapacity to produce children without IVF and there are very significant and unique joys which can be found in producing and raising one's own children which are not accessible to persons in infertile relationships. We must sympathize with these people. None of us shall live to see the implementation of the ideal cultural values outlined above which would make the demand for IVF less severe. It is with real concern that some feminists suggest that the personal wishes of couples with fertility difficulties may not be compatible with the overall interests of women and children.

Feminist thought, then, helps us to focus on different dimensions of the problem then do other sorts of approaches. But, with this perspective, we still have difficulty in reaching a final conclusion on whether to encourage, tolerate, modify, or restrict this sort of reproductive technology. I suggest that we turn to the developing theories of feminist ethics for guidance in resolving this question.[25]

In my view, a feminist ethics is a moral theory that focuses on relations among persons as well as on individuals. It has as a model an interconnected social fabric, rather than the familiar one of isolated, independent atoms; and it gives primacy to bonds among people rather than to rights to independence. It is a theory that focusses on concrete situations and persons and not on free-floating abstract actions.[26] Although many details have yet to be worked out, we can see some of its implications in particular problem areas such as this.

It is a theory that is explicitly conscious of the social, political, and economic relations that exist among persons; in particular, as a feminist theory, it attends to the implications of actions or policies on the status of women. Hence, it is necessary to ask questions from the perspective of feminist ethics in addition to those which are normally asked from the perspective of mainstream ethical theories. We must view issues such as this one in the context of the social and political realities in which they arise, and resist the attempt to evaluate actions or practices in isolation (as traditional responses in biomedical ethics often do). Thus, we cannot just address the question of IVF per se without asking how IVF contributes to general patterns of women's oppression. As Kathryn Payne Addleson has argued about abortion,[27] a feminist perspective raises questions that are inadmissable within the traditional ethical frameworks, and yet, for women in a patriarchal society, they are value questions of greater urgency. In particular, a feminist ethics, in contrast to other approaches in biomedical ethics, would take seriously the concerns just reviewed which are part of the debate in the feminist literature.

A feminist ethics would also include components of theories that have been developed as "feminine ethics," as sketched out by the empirical work of Carol Gilligan.[28] (The best example of such a theory is the work of Nel Noddings in her influential book *Caring*.)[29] In other words, it would be a theory that gives primacy to interpersonal relationships and woman-centered values such as nurturing, empathy, and cooperation. Hence, in the case of IVF, we must care for the women and men who are so despairing about their infertility as to want to spend the vast sums and risk the associated physical and emotional costs of the treatment, in pursuit of "their own children." That is, we should, in Noddings' terms, see their reality as our own and address their very real sense of loss. In so doing, however, we must also consider the implications of this sort of solution to their difficulty. While meeting the perceived desires of some women—desires which are problematic in themselves, since they are so compatible with the values of a culture deeply oppressive to women—this technology threatens to further entrench those values which are responsible for that oppression. A larger vision suggests that the technology offered may, in reality, reduce women's freedom and, if so, it should be avoided.

A feminist ethics will not support a wholly negative response, however, for that would not address our obligation to care for those suffering from infertility; it is the responsibility of those who oppose further implementation of this technology to work towards the changes in the social arrangements that will lead to a reduction of the sense of need for this sort of solution. On the medical front, research and treatment ought to be stepped up to reduce the rates of peral sepsis and gonorrhea which often result in tubal blockage, more attention should be directed at the causes and possible cures for male infertility, and we should pursue techniques that will permit safe reversible sterilization providing women with better alternatives to tubal ligation as a means of fertility control; these sorts of technology would increase the control of many women over their own fertility and would be compatible with feminist objectives. On the social front, we must continue the social pressure to change the status of women and children in our society from that of breeder and possession respectively; hence, we must develop a vision of society as community where all participants are valued members, regardless of age or gender. And we must challenge the notion that having one's wife produce a child with his own genes is sufficient cause for the wives of men with low sperm counts to be expected to undergo the physical and emotional assault such technology involves.

Further, a feminist ethics will attend to the nature of the relationships among those concerned. Annette Baier has eloquently argued for the importance of developing an ethics of trust,[30] and I believe a feminist ethics must address the question of the degree of trust appropriate to the relationships involved. Feminists have noted that women have little reason to trust the medical specialists who offer to respond to their reproductive desires, for, commonly women's interests have not come first from the medical point of view.[31] In fact, it is accurate to perceive feminist attacks on reproductive technology as expressions of the lack of trust feminists have in those who control the technology. Few feminists object to reproductive technology per se; rather they express concern about who controls it and how it can be used to further exploit women. The problem with reproductive technology is that it concentrates power in reproductive matters in the hands of those who are not directly involved in the actual bearing and rearing of the child; i.e., in men who relate to their clients in a technical, professional, authoritarian manner. It is a further step in the medicalization of pregnancy and birth which, in North America, is marked by relationships between pregnant women and their doctors which are very different from the traditional relationships between pregnant women and midwives. The latter relationships fostered an atmosphere of mutual trust which is impossible to replicate in hospital deliveries today. In fact, current approaches to pregnancy, labor, and birth tend to view the mother as a threat to the fetus who must be coerced to comply with medical procedures designed to ensure delivery of healthy babies at whatever cost necessary to the mother. Frequently, the fetus-mother relationship is medically characterized as adversarial and the physicians choose to foster a sense of alienation and passivity in the role they permit the mother. However well IVF may serve the interests of the few women with access to it, it more clearly serves the interests (be they commercial, professional, scholarly, or purely patriarchal) of those who control it.

Questions such as these are a puzzle to those engaged in the traditional approaches to ethics, for they always urge us to separate the question of evaluating the morality of various forms of reproductive technology in themselves, from questions about particular uses of that technology. From the perspective of a feminist ethics, however, no such distinction can be meaningfully made. Reproductive technology is not an abstract activity, it is an activity done in particular contexts and it is those contexts which must be addressed.

Feminist concerns cited earlier made clear the difficulties we have with some of our traditional ethical concepts; hence, feminist ethics directs us to rethink our basic ethical notions. Autonomy, or freedom of choice, is not a matter to be determined in isolated instances, as is commonly assumed in many approaches to applied ethics. Rather it is a matter that evolves reflection on one's whole life situation. The freedom of choice feminists appeal to in the abortion situation is freedom to define one's status as childbearer, given the social, economic, and political significance of reproduction for women. A feminist perspective permits us to understand that reproductive freedom includes control of one's sexuality, protection against coerced sterilization (or iatrogenic sterilization, e.g., as caused by the Dalkon Shield), and the existence of a social and economic network of support for the children we may choose to bear. It is the freedom to redefine our roles in society according to our concerns and needs as women.

In contrast, the consumer freedom to purchase technology, allowed only to a few couples of the privileged classes (in traditionally approved relationships), seems to entrench further the patriarchal notions of woman's role as childbearer and of heterosexual monogamy as the only acceptable intimate relationship. In other words, this sort of choice does not seem to foster autonomy for women on the broad scale. IVF is a practice which seems to reinforce sexist, classist, and often racist assumptions of our culture; therefore, on our revised understanding of freedom, the contribution of this technology to the general autonomy of women is largely negative.

We can now see the advantage of a feminist ethics over mainstream ethical theories, for a feminist analysis explicitly accepts the need for a political component to our understanding of ethical issues. In this, it differs from traditional ethical theories and it also differs from a simply feminine ethics approach, such as the one Noddings offers, for Noddings seems to rely on individual relations exclusively and is deeply suspicious of political alliances as potential threats to the pure relation of caring. Yet, a full understanding of both the threat of IVF, and the alternative action necessary should we decide to reject IVF, is possible only if it includes a political dimension reflecting on the role of women in society.

From the point of view of feminist ethics, the primary question to consider is whether this and other forms of reproductive technology threaten to reinforce the lack of autonomy which women now experience in our culture—even as they appear, in the short run, to be increasing freedom. We must recognize that the interconnections among the social forces oppressive to women underlie feminists' mistrust of this technology which advertises itself as increasing women's autonomy.[32] The political perspective which directs us to look at how this technology fits in with general patterns of treatment for women is not readily accessible to traditional moral theories, for it involves categories of concern not accounted for in those theories—e.g., the complexity of issues which makes it inappropriate to study them in isolation from one another, the role of oppression in shaping individual desires, and potential differences in moral status which are connected with differences in treatment.

It is the set of connections constituting women's continued oppression in our society which inspires feminists to resurrect the old slippery slope arguments to warn against IVF. We must recognize that women's existing lack of control in reproductive matters begins the debate on a pretty steep incline. Technology with the potential to further remove control of reproduction from women makes the slope very slippery indeed. This new technology, though offered under the guise of increasing reproductive freedom, threatens to result, in fact, in a significant decrease in freedom, especially since it is a technology that will always include the active involvement of designated specialists and will not ever be a private matter for the couple or women concerned.

Ethics ought not to direct us to evaluate individual cases without also looking at the implications of our decisions from a wide perspective. My argument is that a theory of feminist ethics provides that wider perspective, for its different sort of methodology is sensitive to both the personal and the social dimensions of issues. For that reason, I believe it is the only ethical perspective suitable for evaluating issues of this sort.

NOTES

1. I appreciate the helpful criticism I have received from colleagues in the Dalhousie Department of Philosophy, the Canadian Society for Women in Philosophy, and the Women's Studies program of the University of Alberta where earlier versions of this paper were read. I am particularly grateful for the careful criticism it has received from Linda Williams and Christine Overall.
2. Susan Sherwin, "A Feminist Approach to Ethics," *Dalhousie Review* **64**, 4 (Winter 1984–85) 704–13.
3. Paul Ramsey, "Shall We Reproduce?" *Journal of American Medical Association* **220** (June 12, 1972), 1484.
4. Leon Kass, "Making Babies Revisited," *The Public Interest* **54** (Winter 1979), 32–60..
5. Joseph Card Ratzinger and Alberto Bovone, "Instruction on Respect for Human Life in its Origin and on the Dignity of Procreation: Replies to Certain Questions of the Day" (Vatican City: Vatican Polyglot Press 1987), 23–4.
6. *Ibid.*, 28.
7. Michael Bayles, *Reproductive Ethics* (Englewood Cliffs, NJ: Prentice-Hall 1984) 15.
8. Ratzinger and Bovone, 28.
9. Samuel Gorovitz, *Doctors' Dilemmas: Moral Conflict and Medical Care* (New York: Oxford University Press 1982), 168.
10. *Ibid.*, 173.
11. Bayles, 66.
12. I owe this observation to Linda Williams..
13. H. Tristram Englehardt, *The Foundations of Bioethics* (Oxford: Oxford University Press 1986), 237.
14. *Ibid.*, 241.

15. Anita Direcks, "Has the Lesson Been Learned?" *DES Action Voice* **28** (Spring 1986), 1–4; and Nikita A. Crook. "Clomid," DES Action/ Toronto Factsheet **#442** (available from 60 Grosvenor St., Toronto, M5S 1B6).

16. Bayles, 32. Though Bayles is not a deontologist, he does concisely express a deontological concern here.

17. Gorovitz, 177.

18. Michael Soules, "The In Vitro Fertilization Pregnancy Rate: Let's Be Honest with One Another," *Fertility and Sterility* **43**, 4 (1985) 511–13.

19. Christine Overall, *Ethics and Human Reproduction: A Feminist Analysis* (Allen and Unwin, forthcoming), 104 ms.

20. Englehardt, 239.

21. Bayles, 31.

22. Robert G. Edwards and David J. Sharpe, "Social Values and Research in Human Embryology," *Nature* **231** (May 14, 1971), 87.

23. Ratzinger and Bovone, 33.

24. *Ibid.*, 34.

25. Many authors are now working on an understanding of what feminist ethics entail. Among the Canadian papers I am familiar with, are Kathryn Morgan's "Women and Moral Madness," Sheila Mullett's "Only Connect: The Place of Self-Knowledge in Ethics," both in this volume, and Leslie Wilson's "Is a Feminine Ethics Enough?" *Atlantis* (forthcoming).

26. Sherwin, "A Feminist Approach to Ethics."

27. Kathryn Payne Addelson, "Moral Revolution," in Marilyn Pearsall, ed., *Women and Values* (Belmont, CA: Wadsworth 1986), 291–309.

28. Carol Gilligan, *In a Different Voice* (Cambridge, MA: Harvard University Press 1982).

29. Nel Noddings, *Caring* (Berkeley: University of California Press 1984).

30. Annette Baier, "What Do Women Want in a Moral Theory?" *Nous* **19** (March 1985) 53–64, and "Trust and Antitrust," *Ethics* **96** (January 1986) 231–60.

31. Linda Williams presents this position particularly clearly in her invaluable work "But What Will They Mean for Women? Feminist Concerns About the New Reproductive Technologies," No. 6 in the *Feminist Perspective* Series. CRIAW.

32. Marilyn Frye vividly describes the phenomenon of interrelatedness which supports sexist oppression by appeal to the metaphor of a bird cage composed of thin wires, each relatively harmless in itself, but, collectively, the wires constitute an overwhelming barrier to the inhabitant of the cage. Marilyn Frye, *The Politics of Reality: Essays in Feminist Theory* (Trumansburg, NY: The Crossing Press 1983), 4–7.

Study Questions

1. State why you agree or disagree with Sherwin's contention that the perspective of feminism can contribute to our understanding of ethical issues in in vitro fertilization.
2. State how you might try and apply Sherwin's analysis to other issues in medical ethics, such as abortion or AID. (Artificial insemination by donor, a practice also condemned by some as being "against nature.")

Active and Passive Euthanasia

*James Rachels**

The distinction between active and passive euthanasia is thought to be crucial for medical ethics. The idea is that it is permissible, at least in some cases, to withhold treatment and allow a patient to die, but it is never permissible to take any direct action designed to kill the patient. This doctrine seems to be accepted by most doctors, and it is endorsed in a statement adopted by the House of Delegates of the American Medical Association on December 4, 1973:

> The intentional termination of the life of one human being by another—mercy killing—is contrary to that for which the medical profession stands and is contrary to the policy of the American Medical Association.
> The cessation of the employment of extraordinary means to prolong the life of the body when there is irrefutable evidence that biological death is imminent is the decision of the patient and/or his immediate family. The advice and judgment of the physician should be freely available to the patient and/or his immediate family.

Reprinted by permission from *The New England Journal of Medicine*, vol. 292, no. 2 (Jan. 9, 1975), pp. 78–80.
* *James Rachels is professor of philosophy at the University of Alabama in Birmingham. Specializing in ethics, he is the author of such articles as "Why Privacy is Important," "On Moral Absolutism," and "Can Ethics Provide Answers?" He is also the editor of* Moral Problems: A Collection of Philosophical Essays *(1971, 3d ed., 1979) and* Understanding Moral Philosophy *(1976).*

However, a strong case can be made against this doctrine. In what follows, I will set out some of the relevant arguments, and urge doctors to reconsider their views on this matter.

To begin with a familiar type of situation, a patient who is dying of incurable cancer of the throat is in terrible pain, which can no longer be satisfactorily alleviated. He is certain to die within a few days, even if present treatment is continued, but he does not want to go on living for those days since the pain is unbearable. So he asks the doctor for an end to it, and his family joins in the request.

Suppose the doctor agrees to withhold treatment, as the conventional doctrine says he may. The justification for his doing so is that the patient is in terrible agony, and since he is going to die anyway, it would be wrong to prolong his suffering needlessly. But now notice this. If one simply withholds treatment, it may take the patient longer to die, and so he may suffer more than he would if more direct action were taken and a lethal injection given. This fact provides strong reason for thinking that, once the initial decision not to prolong his agony has been made, active euthanasia is actually preferable to passive euthanasia, rather than the reverse. To say otherwise is to endorse the option that leads to more suffering rather than less, and is contrary to the humanitarian impulse that prompts the decision not to prolong his life in the first place.

Part of my point is that the process of being "allowed to die" can be relatively slow and painful, whereas being given a lethal injection is relatively quick and painless. Let me give a different sort of example. In the United States about one in 600 babies is born with Down's syndrome. Most of these babies are otherwise healthy—that is, with only the usual pediatric care, they will proceed to an otherwise normal infancy. Some, however, are born with congenital defects such as intestinal obstructions that require operations if they are to live. Sometimes, the parents and the doctor will decide not to operate, and let the infant die. Anthony Shaw describes what happens then:

> . . . When surgery is denied [the doctor] must try to keep the infant from suffering while natural forces sap the baby's life away. As a surgeon whose natural inclination is to use the scalpel to fight off death, standing by and watching a salvageable baby die is the most

emotionally exhausting experience I know. It is easy at a conference, in a theoretical discussion, to decide that such infants should be allowed to die. It is altogether different to stand by in the nursery and watch as dehydration and infection wither a tiny being over hours and days. This is a terrible ordeal for me and the hospital staff—much more so than for the parents who never set foot in the nursery.[1]

I can understand why some people are opposed to all euthanasia, and insist that such infants must be allowed to live. I think I can also understand why other people favor destroying these babies quickly and painlessly. But why should anyone favor letting "dehydration and infection wither a tiny being over hours and days?" The doctrine that says that a baby may be allowed to dehydrate and wither, but may not be given an injection that would end its life without suffering, seems so patently cruel as to require no further refutation. The strong language is not intended to offend, but only to put the point in the clearest possible way.

My second argument is that the conventional doctrine leads to decisions concerning life and death made on irrelevant grounds.

Consider again the case of the infants with Down's syndrome who need operations for congenital defects unrelated to the syndrome to live. Sometimes, there is no operation, and the baby dies, but when there is no such defect, the baby lives on. Now, an operation such as that to remove an intestinal obstruction is not prohibitively difficult. The reason why such operations are not performed in these cases is, clearly, that the child has Down's syndrome and the parents and doctor judge that because of that fact it is better for the child to die.

But notice that this situation is absurd, no matter what view one takes of the lives and potentials of such babies. If the life of such an infant is worth preserving, what does it matter if it needs a simple operation? Or, if one thinks it better that such a baby should not live on, what difference does it make that it happens to have an unobstructed intestinal tract? In either case, the matter of life and death is being decided on irrelevant grounds. It is the Down's syndrome, and not the intestines, that is the issue. The matter should be decided, if at all, on that basis, and not be allowed to depend on the essentially irrelevant question of whether the intestinal tract is blocked.

What makes this situation possible, of course, is the idea that when there is an intestinal blockage, one can "let the baby die," but when there is no such defect there is nothing that can be done, for one must not "kill" it. The fact that this idea leads to such results as deciding life or death on irrelevant grounds is another good reason why the doctrine should be rejected.

One reason why so many people think that there is an important moral difference between active and passive euthanasia is that they think killing someone is morally worse than letting someone die. But is it? Is killing, in itself, worse than letting die? To investigate this issue, two cases may be considered that are exactly alike except that one involves killing whereas the other involves letting someone die. Then, it can be asked whether this difference makes any difference to the moral assessments. It is important that the cases be exactly alike, except for this one difference, since otherwise one cannot be confident that it is this difference and not some other that accounts for any variation in the assessments of the two cases. So, let us consider this pair of cases:

In the first, Smith stands to gain a large inheritance if anything should happen to his six-year-old cousin. One evening while the child is taking his bath, Smith sneaks into the bathroom and drowns the child, and then arranges things so that it will look like an accident.

In the second, Jones also stands to gain if anything should happen to his six-year-old cousin. Like Smith, Jones sneaks in planning to drown the child in his bath. However, just as he enters the bathroom Jones sees the child slip and hit his head, and fall face down in the water. Jones is delighted; he stands by, ready to push the child's head back under if it is necessary, but it is not necessary. With only a little thrashing about the child drowns all by himself, "accidentally," as Jones watches and does nothing.

Now Smith killed the child, whereas Jones "merely" let the child die. That is the only difference between them. Did either man behave better, from a moral point of view? If the difference between killing and letting die were in itself a morally important matter, one should say that Jones's behavior was less reprehensible than Smith's. But does one really want to say that? I think not. In the first place, both men acted from the same motive, personal gain, and both had exactly the same end in view when they acted. It may be inferred from Smith's conduct that he is a bad man, although that judgment may be withdrawn or modified if certain further facts are learned about him—for example, that he is mentally deranged. But would not the very same thing be inferred about Jones from his conduct? And would not the same further considerations also be relevant to any modification of this judgment? Moreover, suppose Jones pleaded, in his own defense, "After all, I didn't do anything except just stand there and watch the child drown. I didn't kill him; I only let him die." Again, if letting die were in itself less bad than killing, this defense should have at least some weight. But it does not. Such a "defense" can only be regarded as a grotesque perversion of moral reasoning. Morally speaking, it is no defense at all.

Now, it may be pointed out, quite properly, that the cases of euthanasia with which doctors are concerned are not like this at all. They do not involve personal gain or the destruction of normally healthy children. Doctors are concerned only with cases in which the patient's life is of no further use to him, or in which the patient's life has become or will soon become a terrible burden. However, the point is the same in these cases: the bare difference between killing and letting die does not, in itself, make a moral difference. If a doctor lets a patient die, for humane reasons, he is in the same moral position as if he had given the patient a lethal injection for humane reasons. If his decision was wrong—if, for example, the patient's illness was in fact curable—the decision would be equally regrettable no matter which method was used to carry it out. And if the doctor's decision was the right one, the method used is not in itself important.

The AMA policy statement isolates the crucial issue very well; the crucial issue is "the intentional termination of the life of one human being by another." But after identifying this issue, and forbidding "mercy killing," the statement goes on to deny that the cessation of treatment is the intentional termination of a life. This is where the mistake comes in, for what is the cessation of treatment, in these circumstances, if it is not "the intentional termination of the life of one human being by another?" Of course, it is exactly that, and if it were not, there would be no point to it.

Many people will find this judgment hard to accept. One reason, I think, is that it is very easy to conflate the question of whether killing is, in itself, worse than letting die, with the very different question of whether most actual cases of killing are more reprehensible than most actual cases of letting die. Most actual cases of killing are clearly terrible (think, for example, of all the murders reported in the newspapers), and one hears of such cases every day. On the other hand, one hardly ever hears of a case of letting die, except for the actions of doctors who are motivated by humanitarian reasons. So one learns to think of killing in a much worse light than of letting die. But this does not mean that there is something about killing that makes it in itself worse than letting die, for it is not the bare difference between killing and letting die that makes the difference in these cases. Rather, the other factors—the murderer's motive of personal gain, for example, contrasted with the doctor's humanitarian motivation—account for different reactions to the different cases.

I have argued that killing is not in itself any worse than letting die; if my contention is right, it follows that active euthanasia is not any worse than passive euthanasia. What arguments can be given on the other side? The most common, I believe, is the following:

"The important difference between active and passive euthanasia is that, in passive euthanasia, the doctor does not do anything to bring about the patient's death. The doctor does nothing, and the patient dies of whatever ills already afflict him. In active euthanasia, however, the doctor does something to bring about the patient's death: he kills him. The doctor who gives the patient with cancer a lethal injection has himself caused his patient's death; whereas if he merely ceases treatment, the cancer is the cause of death."

A number of points need to be made here. The first is that it is not exactly correct to say that in passive euthanasia the doctor does nothing, for he does do one thing that is very important: he lets the patient die. "Letting someone die" is certainly different, in some respects, from other types of action—mainly in that it is a kind of action that one may perform by way of not performing certain other actions. For example, one may let a patient die by way of not giving medication, just as one may insult someone by way of not shaking his hand. But for any purpose of moral assessment, it is a type of action nonetheless. The decision to let a patient die is subject to moral appraisal in the same way that a decision to kill him would be subject to moral appraisal: it may be assessed as wise or unwise, compassionate or sadistic, right or wrong. If a doctor deliberately let a patient die who was suffering from a routinely curable illness, the doctor would certainly be to blame for what he had done, just as he would be to blame if he had needlessly killed the patient. Charges against him would then be appropriate. If so, it would be no defense at all for him to insist that he didn't "do anything." He would have done something very serious indeed, for he let his patient die.

Fixing the cause of death may be very important from a legal point of view, for it may determine whether criminal charges are brought against the doctor. But I do not think that this notion can be used to show a moral difference between active and passive euthanasia. The reason why it is considered bad to be the cause of someone's death is that death is regarded as a great evil—and so it is. However, if it has been decided that euthanasia—even passive euthanasia—is desirable in a given case, it has also been decided that in this instance death is no greater an evil than the patient's continued existence. And if this is true, the usual reason for not wanting to be the cause of someone's death simply does not apply.

Finally, doctors may think that all of this is only of academic interest—the sort of thing that philosophers may worry about but that has no practical bearing on their own work. After all, doctors must be concerned about the legal consequences of what they do, and active euthanasia is clearly forbidden by the law. But even so, doctors should also be concerned with the fact that the law is forcing upon them a moral doctrine that may well be indefensible, and has a considerable effect on their practices. Of course, most doctors are not now in the position of being coerced in this matter, for they do not regard themselves as merely going along with what the law requires. Rather, in statements such as the AMA policy statement that I have quoted, they are endorsing this doctrine as a central point of medical ethics. In that statement, active euthanasia is condemned not merely as illegal but as "contrary to that for which the medical profession stands," whereas passive euthanasia is approved. However, the preceding considerations suggest that there is really no moral difference between the two, considered in themselves (there may be important moral differences in some cases in their *consequences*, but, as I pointed out, these differences may make active euthanasia, and not passive euthanasia, the morally preferable option). So, whereas doctors may have to discriminate between active and passive euthanasia to satisfy the law, they should not do any more than that. In particular, they should not give the distinction any added authority and weight by writing it into official statements of medical ethics.

NOTES

1. A. Shaw: "Doctor, Do We Have a Choice?" *The New York Times Magazine*, Jan. 30, 1972, p. 54.

Study Questions

1. After reading Rachel's article, do you believe there is any important difference between the two forms of euthanasia?
2. If a member of your family were dying a painful death, would you—assuming ou believe in euthanasia—prefer that they starve to death, or actively take a role by requesting a physician or nurse to give them a lethal injection of some painless, fast-acting substance?

Euthanasia and the Care of the Dying

Sissela Bok

Our century has seen great advances in the knowledge about the human life cycle and in the power to combat disease and death. But with this increased power, new dilemmas have sprung up for physicians, and new anguish on the part of patients and those who are close to them. How far should a physician go in delaying death? Which of the many techniques for prolonging life can he in good conscience omit in caring for a terminally ill patient? What can a patient ask his doctor to do and to forbear, in those cases where there is a conflict between prolonging life and easing suffering? Is there anything a person can do *before* he becomes a patient, in order to decrease the chances of being reduced to intolerable levels of suffering, loneliness, and dehumanization?

These dilemmas have often been discussed under the heading of euthanasia. The discussion, however, has been hampered by a dearth of relevant empirical information and by a lack of careful definitions, often resulting in conflicting assertions, impossible either to prove or to disprove, and expressing, rather, value premises of the most general kind. The articles in this series represent an effort to examine the existing practices and the concepts which underlie them, and to indicate what can be done to help patients cope with dying without breaking the fundamental restrictions which our society justly places on the taking of lives.

Definitions

The Oxford English Dictionary (1971) defines euthanasia as: "The action of inducing a quiet and easy death."

Webster's Third New International Dictionary (1967) defines it as an "act or practice of painlessly putting to death persons suffering from incurable conditions or diseases."

And Lord Moynihan, in the 1936 British Parliamentary Debates, arguing for the introduction of a bill to remove the prohibition of voluntary euthanasia, held that:

Briefly our desire is to obtain legal recognition for the principle that in cases of advanced and inevitable fatal disease, attended by agony which reaches, or oversteps, the boundaries of human endurance, the sufferer, after legal inquiry and after due observance of all safeguards, shall have the right to demand and be entitled to release.

These three definitions are representative of many others. They reflect interesting differences regarding the following questions: Must the patient necessarily be suffering? Must the disease be considered to be fatal? Must the patient be close to dying? Must the patient have requested help in dying? And is euthanasia an act of putting the patient to death, or can it also describe suicide and omission or cessation of care?

The first definition does not mention suffering or incurable illness and does, therefore, not exclude the kind of "euthanasia program" practiced in Nazi Germany. The second and third definitions are more reflective, in this sense, of the intentions which have motivated the concern with euthanasia in this country during the last decades. Mercy for the suffering patient has been the primary reason given by those who would change the law to allow a limited form of euthanasia.

The Nazi practices made clear the need to guard against abuses of several kinds. The proposals for changes in legislation have, therefore, often added a proviso that the patient's condition should be an incurable one, or that he should actually be dying (Williams 1957; Downing 1969). Ehrhardt (1965) considers this last proviso the main distinction between what he calls "aid in dying" and the Nazi extermination programs. This distinction, however, ex-

cludes persons who are suffering so much that they request euthanasia, but who could be kept alive by medical technology. Are
we meant to be concerned only with speeding or assisting the
process of dying, or are we to consider merciful death wherever
there is unbearable suffering, even when the patient is chronically
ill but not about to die? Since the appeal to mercy is the basic
argument for euthanasia, it is not immediately clear why only
patients who are actually dying should be shown mercy, whereas
those who face much longer periods of suffering must continue
without relief.

The proviso that the patient be dying, furthermore, is not without ambiguity. In a sense, any patient who is seriously ill might
or might not be dying. And even in those cases where death
seems *likely* in days or weeks (Brown 1970), its probability varies.
Thus, one patient may be thought of as having one chance in a
hundred of surviving, the estimate based upon a comparison with
past cases. Another may be considered to have two chances in a
hundred, or five, of surviving. Where does one draw the line and
determine that the patient is definitely dying? Nowhere in the
long history of disagreement among doctors about the certainty
of the prognosis of death has this question been resolved.

A third difference between the three definitions stems from the
nature of the action involved in euthanasia and illustrates the
tension and hesitation regarding how such a death is to come to
the suffering person. Can it be through an intentional act on the
part of another, or through suicide, assisted or unassisted, or
through omitting acts to prolong life? Suicide presents separate
problems which will not be discussed here. But the distinction
between omission and commission is one which some consider
central, whereas others see it as impossible to maintain and, therefore, to be discarded. Is there any difference between killing a
person and letting him die through omitting a remedy, so long
as his death is intended in both cases and comes about in both?

In order to answer this question, we must look at the whole
continuum running from natural death to homicide. Countless
cases can be imagined between a completely natural death, neither
intended nor brought about by another in any way, and a death
actively and intentionally caused, as by a dose of lethal pills.
Somewhere in the center of this continuum lie the acts of intentional omission which result in death. There *are* borderline cases

where the distinction is nearly impossible to make. Thus G. Williams (1966) asks whether there is a meaningful difference between pulling out the plug from an oxygen machine keeping an otherwise dying patient alive, and simply not replacing the tank of oxygen when the machine has run out. Such an example demonstrates that there are no clear lines of demarcation between some acts of omission and of commission. It does *not* in my opinion come close to showing that most acts cannot be so distinguished. There are a number of acts which are clearly acts of killing, and others which are just as clearly acts of omitting support for life. When a person is close to dying, a great many omissions of support he would not otherwise need can result in death. Even those who are not terminally ill may die as a result of the omission of essential life support when they are in need.

Legislative Proposals

Proposals to legalize euthanasia would permit both acts of omission and commission resulting in death, given certain safeguards. The requirement that the patient should have *requested or consented* ♦ *expressly* to the act of euthanasia is clearly the most important of these safeguards. It is held by some to provide a simple and clearcut distinction between voluntary and nonvoluntary euthanasia. But it raises problems—always present when consent is involved—that are especially grave when a person's life is a stake. Is there not an important distinction between request and consent in the first place? Might there be a danger of slipping from request to resigned acquiescence? Might there be a risk of someone's asking to die out of a concern for the burden he places on his family? How does one determine whether the request or the consent is not the result of a temporary aberration or of medication-induced confusion or depression? Or what if the desire to die is based upon an unrealistic view of the present situation, or of the prognosis for the future, based on false or insufficient information? And how is the situation altered if the patient requesting to die has dependents (Cantor 1973)?

In order to meet some of these concerns, a number of additional requirements, beyond mere consent or request, are, therefore, present in legislative proposals: The patient must be over the age

√of 21; the agent must be a physician who should have consulted with another physician or with some specified authority; sometimes a period of time is required between the request for euthanasia and the act itself during which the patient's possible change of mind must be heeded.

Given these safeguards, the proponents of new legislation argue *
that it is cruel to prolong intense suffering on the part of someone who is mortally ill and desires to die. Mercy dictates intervention. A secondary argument holds that a person has the *right* to decide whether he should continue to live or not, and that such a decision can be reached after rationally weighing the benefits of continued living against the suffering involved. If a person has such a right, it is held, then it cannot be wrong for him to ask another to help him carry out his desire, nor can it be wrong for another to do so.

A case which would correspond to the safeguards against hasty or erroneous euthanasia elaborated by the legislative proposals, and which illustrates the predicament of the patient asking for help, is that of a well-known physicist, Percy Williams Bridgman, described in the *Bulletin of Atomic Scientists* (Holton 1962). He was dying in an advanced stage of cancer in the eightieth year of his life. He had, with the best medical help available, exhausted all avenues of cure. He was in "considerable pain," with little or no hope of alleviation. He requested euthanasia from his physicians; when they refused, he committed suicide, leaving a note reading:

> It isn't decent for society to make a man do this thing himself. Probably this is the last day I will be able to do it myself.

The opponents of bills to legalize voluntary euthanasia argue as follows: First they dispute whether acts of killing would always truly *be merciful* for patients requesting them. There are risks that patients might then die as a result of an error in the prognosis of their disease. Others might die who could have recovered as a result of a new approach to their illness such as that provided when penicillin came into use. Still others might die who did not really wish to die, given the difficulties already mentioned of knowing whether the request for euthanasia is genuine, and, even if genuine, is truly in the best interest of the patient. They point to the familiar cases where patients have pleaded to be allowed to die, only to recover with gratitude that the physician did not respond to their plea.

Secondly, critics argue that, even where dying would be more merciful, and even if patients have the right to determine whether they want to continue to live or not, such a right provides the justification for *suicide*, and for the *refusal of life-prolonging treatment*, but not for another to engage in an act of killing. "Helping" a person to end his life is seen as fundamentally different from helping him to build a house or to find his way; and the question of whether the killing is helpful or harmful, lawful or prohibited, cannot, therefore, be decided merely by establishing that the victim asked for help.

The third argument stresses the small numbers of those who would actually be helped by new legislation. There is general agreement that very few of the cases publicly debated under the rubric of euthanasia would fit the requirements suggested in the different proposals (Weisman 1972; Glaser and Strauss 1965; Kamisar 1958). True, many persons suffer, and many are near death. But those who suffer *and* are near death and who are willing and able to express a desire to die in a manner acceptable to courts and to physicians constitute a much smaller group. All acts of euthanasia contemplated by relatives or friends would be ruled out. And the familiar cases of infanticide often referred to as euthanasia—such as the Liege "Thalidomide" case where a mother and a physician killed a newborn (D'Otremont 1964)—would also be ruled out, both because of the absence of consent by the victim and because the victim was under the age of 21.

Most important, those *not competent* to give consent, even if they are over the age of 21, would not fit the requirements. Those who are legally incompetent—such as great numbers of retarded— have not been held capable of initiating procedures to resist medical treatment, nor have their guardians been held so capable. Much less, then, would they be able to request euthanasia. Those who are physically unable to communicate, such as the patients whose brains have ceased to respond, would likewise be excluded from consideration by euthanasia legislation, in spite of the fact that much public concern with euthanasia stems from an awareness of the conditions under which their lives are prolonged.

Fourth, risks are feared for society stemming from the possibility of abuses and errors which might result from a relaxation in the present strong prohibitions against killing. Rules may be misapplied. Practices may be extended to groups of patients beyond the original few that fit the strict requirements. Distinctions may be blurred, so that patients may come to die without having requested euthanasia, perhaps even against their wishes. These fears are supported by a concern for the defenselessness on the part of groups such as the newborn or the senile, and by a lack of confidence in social resistance to violence done to the vulnerable. Given the increased efficiency of different methods of pain relief, and the already lawful ways of ceasing treatment for a patient who so desires, the benefits of euthanasia to the few who would fit the requirements listed in the legislative proposals do not outweigh the social risks which would be incurred.[1]

I believe that one must accept both the need for mercy and help on the part of the suffering individual *and* the caution expressed over the risks in changing the legislation. The conflict which results is both sharp and poignant. The arguments against euthanasia are scarcely such as to be persuasive to an individual who is suffering so much that death seems preferable to a continuation of his agony. His receiving voluntary euthanasia would not directly harm anyone else. Yet he is asked to suffer on the grounds that allowing euthanasia may deprive other individuals of their lives against their wishes or their best interest.

It is impossible to arrive at an irrefutable balancing of these factors. I believe that the wisest course is to continue the prohibition or active euthanasia, but to reduce the suffering of patients through a much greater concern for the humane care of the dying, for the rights of patients to refuse medical care, and for lawful termination of those aspects of treatment which cause suffering with no cure or relief. It is to these that the rest of my paper is devoted. For the public concern with dying is more *pervasive* than in the past and seeks, rather than a new law to benefit a few, a more humane approach to dying within the existing laws. This concern stems both from the growth in the extent to which the plight of the dying is seen as wrongful and to be mitigated, and from an increasing awareness that the conditions under which people die have greatly changed.

The Growing Concern Over Dying ⱱ

The easing of material circumstances for many in Western societies has brought a decrease in early deaths and in physical suffering. Before this century, the peoples of Europe were haunted by famine, epidemics, gruesome infant and child mortality, and the ever-present threat of indigence. Not many could "afford" the luxury of worrying about the possibility of suffering at the end of life. It is easy to forget that the need for sheer physical survival prevented and still prevents the majority of mankind from a primary concern with the suffering in dying. In addition, suffering was often taken for granted as being the inevitable lot of mankind, most probably willed by God; an example of this view is the intense resistance in the nineteenth century to anesthesia, on the grounds that God intended the suffering of human beings, especially of women in childbirth.

In addition to a new awareness of suffering at the end of life, the present concern for the way in which people die is heightened by the fact that dying has *changed* so drastically with advancing techniques of medical care. It has changed from three points of view.

First of all, the illnesses of which people die have changed in relative importance since the turn of the century.

> One of the most significant changes in the mortality experience of this country since 1900 has been the decline in the major communicable diseases as leading causes of death and the consequent increase *in relative importance* of the so-called chronic degenerative diseases occurring mainly later in life and generally thought to be associated in some way with the aging process. (Lerner 1970)

These changes have had an immense impact on the public concern for dying, and on the way in which the process of dying is seen by patients and by those who take care of them.

Second, the fact that death now not only stems from degenerative diseases more often than from communicable ones, but also comes much later in life adds to these concerns. The average life expectancy in the United States has gone from around 40 years at the turn of the century to around 70 years now. Cerebral degeneration and cardiovascular disease are increasingly common before death. As a result, the fear of senility has come to accompany the fear of a long and possibly painful death.

Third, the location and circumstances in which death takes place have changed. At the turn of the century, most Americans died in their familiar lodgings. In 1958, 60.9 percent of all deaths in America occurred in hospitals or other institutions such as nursing homes (Lerner 1970) and estimates now range near 80 percent (*Medical World News* 1971). Among the reasons for this great shift are the increased urbanization of our population and the much higher proportion of people who live in small apartments, with no extra room available as a "sick-room," and often no one at home to care for a sick person. The family units have shrunk; many elderly live alone. Among those relatives who might take them in and care for them, many fewer now feel up to coping with their medical and other needs, either financially or emotionally. Finally, among those relatives who *could* cope, fewer are willing to do so or have any sense of obligation to do so. It is easy to overestimate the frequency with which patients have died in the past surrounded by loving family and comforted by religious and other rites; it is nevertheless clear that the shift to dying in institutions has greatly increased the loneliness of the patient and his estrangement from his familiar surroundings.

These factors all contribute to the lowered sense of meaningful *humanity* characterizing the end of life. Studies have shown how not only nurses and physicians, but also relatives tend to *avoid* dying patients. Instead of keeping the dying patient company, the physician, often hard-pressed to attend other patients, may prescribe life-sustaining techniques he knows will not provide a cure. The dehumanization is then increased by electrical wiring, machines, and intravenous administration of liquids, which create additional barriers between the patient and any human beings who are near. They sometimes even lead to what has been called "the intensive care syndrome," characterized by sometimes acute psychological and behavioral disturbances resulting from sleep deprivation, unfamiliar and impersonal surroundings, mechanization, and uncertainty (McKegney 1966, Hackett et al. 1968). Improvements in diagnosis and treatment have done so much for the possibilities of helping the curable patient that such psychological distance and distress may be well worth enduring. But for the dying patient, these aids create the distance and the distress *without* providing any cure. In fact they then become a *substitute* for comforting human acts.

There has likewise been a growing tendency for physicians to look at the disease rather than at the whole patient. A continuing controversy in the history of medicine has centered around the question of whether illness is a state involving all or part of one's body. The sharper focusing upon disease in the nineteenth century, first upon the anatomical lesion and then upon the micro-organism, has led doctors to concentrate their efforts upon the disease, more and more minutely localized, rather than on the whole patient. And while there are signs indicating a change, we are still a long way from a generally accepted focus on the whole human being, rather than on aspects of his health.[2] Fragmented care may be justified in terms of the cures now available for many patients. But it is completely unjustifiable where there is *no* cure. There are too few checks on the humane concern with which dying patients are treated; a concern not just for *what* is done for them, but also for *how* it is done (Strauss and Glaser 1964).

Krant (1973) notes that:

> Medical students, house officers and staff physicians, especially in universities and large teaching hospitals, are held accountable to senior staff and consequently to each other, for a vigorous biologic model of disease . . . The knowledge of disease, of dying and of death is defined in terms of physical and chemical faltering and deficit. Mortality conferences are directed toward a search for potential deficit or default . . . The medical student, the house officer or the staff physician is not accountable for the human dimension of living and dying. Therefore, the question at a staff conference or at mortality rounds is not directed toward whether a patient died peacefully or in control of his limited options.

The focus on the disease rather than on the patient is illuminated at those times when a patient, near death and suffering from one disease such as cancer, develops another, treatable disease such as pneumonia. If medical care is viewed simply as the fight against disease, even in a dying patient, then medication will routinely be recommended, perhaps even (though unlawfully) forced upon the patient, since pneumonia is one condition which can be combated in the patient. If his well-being is also considered, then the fact that he is dying, and the necessity and humanity of helping him to have as good a death as possible, will permit greater flexibility, and much will depend on the anticipated course of the two illnesses and on the patient's wishes and plans (Ramsey 1970).

Dilemmas for Physicians

Physicians are not unaware of these factors underlying the public concern with dying. But they see great obstacles, in practice, to simply relinquishing the prolongation of the lives of terminally ill patients.

The two central functions of the medical profession are the struggle against death and disease, and the alleviation of suffering. Where they conflict, as in surgical operations, for instance, the first is most often held to have priority, both by patients and by physicians. But when these functions conflict for patients who are terminally ill, the dilemma is much more difficult, because so much uncertainty surrounds the two functions themselves in the context of terminal illness.

The first function—the struggle against death and disease—must be shown to be unattainable if it is to be given up without regret by physicians. Yet it is difficult *ever* to be certain that it is unattainable in a particular case; to know that death is inevitable for a patient. The chance of a misdiagnosis is always present; even the best diagnosticians make errors in predicting death (Kamisar 1958). And where the diagnosis is correct, the prognosis may still be affected by a new medical development. (It must be said, however, that such developments have been much more spectacular in saving lives which would otherwise have been cut short in childhood or maturity; their utility for persons having chronic degenerative diseases in advanced stages is doubtful. Nevertheless, the fact remains that it is not always easy in practice to say that a patient will definitely die soon.)

The second traditional function of the medical profession—that of alleviating suffering—is equally difficult to clarify in the context of the terminally ill. The methods of pain relief are more adequate now than in the 1930s when the euthanasia debate was growing in strength. They will undoubtedly be increasingly so if they can be made available to all those who need them. As a result, many patients and physicians may choose the relief of pain rather than the irrevocability of letting death come. Yet the *degree of suffering* is a factor which has not yet received adequate empirical treatment in discussions of dying.

It has long been argued that prolonging life is not a great cause of distress to the patient since physical suffering is actually uncommon among the dying. Epstein (forthcoming) holds that:

> Most terminal patients, contrary to lay belief, do not suffer pain. Excruciating pain is almost never present in dying patients and when it is, it can be controlled.

In the past, the discussions of the painlessness of dying have frequently referred to the very last stages of death. But, as has been pointed out, we must take into account the much longer periods of discomfort and deterioration which most patients endure, as well as the anxiety resulting from removal from familiar surroundings and the lack of meaningful personal contacts.

Those who maintain that there is very little suffering also often mean only physical pain. Beecher (1957) and others have demonstrated that the "psychic" reaction to the pain stimulus can be extremely important:

> Not much imagination is needed to suppose that the sickbed of the patient in pain with its ominous threat against happiness, his security, his very life, provides a milieu *and reaction* entirely removed from the laboratory.

In considering suffering of terminal patients, therefore, one cannot exclude from consideration the anguish due to fear or uncertainty or loneliness. Nor must the pain be underestimated that is thought to be bearable, such as that in the intervals between doses of medication, or resulting from incessant injections or blood tests, or from bedsores or simply from being turned over in bed. Much too little is still known about what is actually experienced by patients as they approach death.

Even where a physician is certain about the relative weights to be given to a patient's suffering and nearness to death, however, and where he is prepared not to battle death to the last, it is still very difficult for him to know where, in practice, to draw the line—which aspects of therapy to cease, and how to cease them. Should he discontinue certain kinds of medication? Intravenous nourishment? Should he decide against additional surgery? Should he fail to resuscitate the patient after a cardiac arrest? Should he turn off life-supporting equipment, instituted while the chances for recovery were higher? Diana Crane's study, reported in this series, makes clear the number of possible choices and the disagreement within the medical specialities as to what ought to be done in difficult cases. The facile phrases about "ceasing unnecessary life support" simply fail to apply.

Before a consensus is established with respect to such decisions, physicians will continue to be concerned lest they do less than they might to combat death in the eyes of their profession and of the hospital committees or rounds which consider each patient's death. Few peers will fault a physician for doing more than he might have to prolong life. But the fear of disapproval and of litigation can be present in decisions to do *less*.

The Refusal of Treatment by Patients

Cutting across the dilemmas physicians face in weighing the battle against death, on the one hand, and suffering on the other hand, are those situations where patients themselves refuse to consent to further treatment. It is clear that a patient's decision to ask for a cessation in treatment, reflecting his own preference for death rather than for a continuation of discomfort or suffering, must be respected, barring exceptional circumstances. We are all familiar with cases where death might be preferable to intense suffering, or to treason, or to torture. We also know that individuals differ in the amount of suffering they can tolerate. Some may wish to live longer thanks to the use of kidney dialysis, whereas others may not. Some might prefer death over the amputation of both legs whereas others might not. Even the latter might prefer it to the amputation of both arms and legs. These preferences have to do with a person's level of tolerance and with his sense of his integrity *as a person*—what constitutes an unbearable inroad upon it, and upon his freedom to live his life.

In order to make such decisions, however, the patient's requests for information concerning his condition must be respected. The dangers of paternalism for those near death are great. It is tempting to do for them what is thought to be in their best interest without consulting them, and sometimes even against their wishes. And it is standard medical practice—though one under increasing attack—to keep dying patients in the dark concerning their condition (Oken 1961, Waitzkin and Stoeckle 1972).

If a patient is aware of the fact that he is approaching death and if he wishes to discontinue further treatment, what can he do? He can refuse to be hospitalized, or to enter a home for the aged. But such a refusal presupposes that there is another place to be ill, and persons to care for him, and, as indicated before, this is all too rarely the case. Once within the hospital or the institution, a patient may attempt to learn the facts about his condition and then refuse those procedures he considers undesirable. But his power to do so is very limited and will depend to a large extent on whether the medical personnel and his family choose to comply with his wishes.

Because of this powerlessness of terminal patients, some have chosen to try to influence what might be done to them *in advance* while they are still in good health. They can do so by talking over with their physician and their family what they would wish to have done should they be disabled by disease or by an accident or confronted by a painful and lingering death. They may even sign a statement, such as a Living Will, declaring that under certain circumstances they do not wish to have their lives prolonged. Such wills are not legally binding, but they can serve to remove doubts and feelings of guilt on the part of relatives and physicians which so often underlie the prolongation of life.

Treatment, Care, and Cure

The great majority of dying patients, however, have not had the opportunity to affect the end of their lives in advance or to stay away from institutions. Some are not able to refuse treatment even when it causes them to suffer, or to ask for a change in treatment. Others are not willing to do so and have hopes for recovery until the very end. Still others would appreciate a change in treatment, but are afraid of seeming troublesome or losing their slender contact with physicians or nurses by appearing to question what is being done for them.

Efforts to make the end of their lives as good as possible must, therefore, come from the outside—from all those who are involved in their care. The care of sick patients involves many activities, ranging from assistance in the ordinary tasks required for survival and everyday life to providing increasingly unusual or expensive treatment. Where the dying are concerned, the different tasks of "care," "cure," "healing," or "treating" assume a different meaning, and two different distinctions then tend to become confused: the distinction between caring for a patient and abandoning all care, and that between keeping up efforts to cure the patient and abandoning these efforts.

Dying patients today are often *abandoned* from the point of view of human care and family concern, whereas, paradoxically, efforts to cure may still be kept up. The patient's comfort and welfare may then be sacrificed in order to maintain the illusion that efforts to cure him may yet prove successful. Relatives and medical personnel are less frequently present, and when they are, the mechanical and chemical effects of the efforts to cure provide a barrier which is difficult to surmount. As a result, once it has been established that a patient is close to a death which cannot be avoided, continued efforts to cure should be abandoned, while a great deal more *human care* should be devoted to the patient in order to make the end of his life as comfortable as possible while helping him to fear death less.

If these conclusions were accepted, dying could become a different experience from the ordeal which rightly troubles so many now. The location would be chosen with a view to the patient's comfort; in many cases the familiar home surroundings supplemented by whatever is needed from the medical point of view would be appropriate; at other times a small hospital or other institution designed to provide humane care without fear of unnecessary operations or other procedures. All necessary pain relief would be permitted with no concern about addiction—a baseless fear with so few days left to live—and a recognition that increased dosages required to keep pain away are available even if they might speed death. All possible remaining pleasures and activities would be permitted, and all visits desired by the patient encouraged. There would be no useless surgery, and no prolongation of life, but rather a cooperation between the patient and his physician, nurses, and family in confronting death. One institution which shows how these ways of treating dying patients can operate has been receiving increasing public notice—the Saint Christopher's Hospice in London, run by Cicely Saunders (Neale (1972). Others are springing up or are in the planning stages. While they will not be large enough to care for more than a fraction of all those who need help, they may serve as models for the humane care which so many are interested in providing.

Our social norms concerning death and dying have to be brought into the open, and compared with what we see today of the reality of dying. We must ask ourselves the ancient question of what a good death might be. We must ask what kinds of community efforts can insure adequate housing, nourishment, and medical care for patients, and also how we can preserve and strengthen a humane approach to the dying on the part of medical personnel, family and friends.

Acknowledgements

I acknowledge with gratitude the comments by Franklin Epstein, MD, Melvin Krant, MD, and Stanley Reiser, MD upon a draft of this article.

REFERENCES

Beecher, H.K. 1957. The measurement of pain, *Pharmacological Review*, 9:168.

Boke, S. 1970. Voluntary Euthanasia. Unpublished Dissertation, Harvard University.

British Parliamentary Debates. 1936. House of Lords, Vol. 103.

Brown, N.K., R.J. Bulger, E.H. Laws and D.J. Thompson, 1970. The preservation of life. *Journal of the American Medical Association*, **211**: 76–81.

Cantor, N. 1973. A patient's decision to decline life-saving medical treatment: Bodily integrity versus the preservation of life. *Rutgers Law Review*, **26**: 228–264.

Downing, A.B., ed. 1969. Euthanasia and the Right to Death. Owen, London.

Ehrhardt, H. 1965. Euthanasie und Vernichtung "Lebensunwerten" Lebens (Euthanasia and the Taking of Lives "Unworthy of Being Lived"). Ferdinard Elke Verlag, Stuttgart. p. 5–6.

Epstein, F. The role of the physician in the prolongation of life, **Page 2**: *in:* F. Ingelfinger, ed. Controversy in Medicine, II. W. B. Saunders Co., Philadelphia. (in press)

Glaser, B. and A. Strauss. 1965. Awareness of Dying. Aldine-Atherton, Chicago.

Hackett, T., N. Cassem and H. Wishnie. 1968. The Coronary-Care Unit. An appraisal of its psychologic hazards. *New England Journal of Medicine*, **279**: 1365–1370.

Holton, G. 1969. Percy Williams Bridgman. *Bulletin of Atomic Scientists*, **18**(2): 22–23.

Kamisar, Y. 1958. Some non-religious views against proposed "mercy-killing" legislation. *Minnesota Law Review*, **42**: 969–1042.

Krant, M. 1973. The physician and the dying patient—A problem. *PRISM*. (in press)

Lerner, M. 1970. When, why, and where people die. Pages 5–29 *in:* O. Brim, et al. *The Dying Patient*. Russell Sage Foundation, New York.

McKegney, F. 1966. The intensive care syndrome. *Connecticut Medicine*, **30**: 633–644.

Medical World News. 1971. Dealing with death. **12**: May 21):30.

Neale, R.E. 1972. A Place to Live, A Place to Die. *Hastings Center Report* No. 2.

Oken, D. 1961. What to tell cancer patients: A study of medical attitudes. *Journal of the American Medical Association*, **175**: 1120–1128.

D'Otremont, S. 1964. Peut-on Tuer? (May One Kill?). La Mobilisation des Consciencies, Belgium.

Oxford English Dictionary. 1971. Oxford University Press, London.

Ramsey, P. 1970. The Patient as Person. Yale University Press, New Haven, p. 115.

Strauss, A. and B. Glaser. 1964. The non-accountability of the terminal case. *Hospitals*, **38**: 73–87.

Waitzkin, H. and J. Stoeckle. 1972. The communication of information about illness. *Adv. Psychosom, Med.*, **8**: 180–215.

Webster's Third New International Dictionary. 1967. G. & G. Merriam Co., Springfield, Massachusetts.

Weisman, A. 1972. On Dying and Denying. Behavioral Publications, Inc., New York. p. 23–41.

Williams, G. 1957. The Sanctity of Life and the Criminal Law. Alfred A. Knopf, New York, p. 339–340.

———. 1966. Euthanasia and abortion. *Colorado Law Review*, **38**: 183.

NOTES

1. Space permits only this brief treatment of the complex arguments of all sides of the legalization question. For a fuller account and for a discussion of the religious and natural law arguments omitted here,

see S. Bok, Voluntary Euthanasia, unpublished dissertation, Harvard University, 1970.

2. I am indebted for this thought to Stanley Reiser.

Study Questions

1. After reading Bok's article, what would you do if a member of your own family was terminally ill, but with an *extremely* slight chance of recovering.
2. Given all the problems Bok raises with consent, do you still believe a patient has the right to demand his or her own death in the event of terminal disease?

Medicine and The Concept of Person*

H.T. Engelhardt, Jr.

Recent advances in medicine and the biomedical sciences have raised a number of ethical issues that medical ethics, or, more broadly, bioethics have treated. Ingredient in such considerations, however, are fundamentally conceptual and ontological issues. To talk of the sanctity of life, for example, presupposes that one knows (1) what life is, and (2) what makes for its sanctity. More importantly, to talk of the rights of persons presupposes that one knows what counts as a person. In this paper I will provide an examination of the concept of person and will argue that the terms "human life" and even "human person" are complex and heterogeneous terms. I will hold that human life has more than one meaning and that there is more than one sense of human person. I will then indicate how the recognition of these multiple meanings has important implications for medicine.

I. Kinds of Life and Sanctity of Life

Whatever is meant by life's being sacred, it is rarely held that all life is equally sacred. Most people would find the life of bacteria,

* An earlier version of this paper was read as a part of the Matchette Foundation Series, "The Expanding Universe of Modern Medicine," The Kennedy Institute and the Department of Philosophy, Georgetown University, Washington D.C., November 19, 1974. I wish to express my debt to George Agich, Thomas J. Bole, III, Edmund L. Erde, Laurence B. McCullough, and John Moskop for their discussion and criticism of the ancestral drafts of this paper.

for example, to be less valuable or sacred than the life of fellow humans. In fact, there appears to be a spectrum of increasing value to life (I will presume that the term sanctity of life signifies that life has either special values or rights). All else being equal, plants seem to be valued less than lower animals, lower animals less than higher animals (such as primates other than humans), and humans are ususally held to have the highest value. Moreover, distinctions are made with respect to humans. Not all human life has the same sanctity. The issue of brain death, for example, turns on such a distinction. Brain-dead, but otherwise alive, human beings do not have the sanctity of normal adult human beings. That is, the indices of brain death have been selected in order to measure the death of a person. As a legal issue, it is a question of when a human being ceases to be a person before the law. In a sense, the older definition of death measured the point of which organismic death occurred, when there was a complete cessation of vital functions.[1] The life of the human organism was taken as a necessary condition for being a person, and, therefore, such a definition allowed one to identify cases in which humans ceased to be persons.

The brain-oriented concept of death is more directly concerned with human *personal life*.[2] It makes three presuppositions: (1) that being a person involves more than mere vegetative life, (2) that merely vegetative life may have value but it has no rights, (3) that a sensory-motor organ such as the brain is a necessary condition for the possibility of experience and actions in the world, that is, for being a person living in the world. Thus in the absence of the possibility of brain function, one has the absence of the possibility of personal life—that is, the person is dead. Of course, the presence of some brain activity (or more than vegetative function) does not imply the presence of a person—a necessary condition for the life of a person is not a sufficient condition for the life of a person. The brain-oriented concept of death is of philosophical significance, for, among other things, it implies a distinction between human biological life and human personal life, between the life of a human organism and the life of a human person. The human biological life continues after brain death is fairly clear: the body continues to circulate blood, the kidneys function; in fact, there is no reason why the organism would not continue to be cross-fertile (e.g., produce viable sperm) and, thus, satisfy yet one more criterion for biological life. Such a body can be a biologically integrated reproductive unit even if the level of integration is very low. And, if such a body is an instance of human biological but not human personal life, then it is open to use merely as a subject of experimentation without the constraints of a second status as a person. Thus Dr. Willard Gaylin has argued that living but brain-dead bodies could provide an excellent source of subjects for medical experimentation and education.[3] and recommends "sustaining life in the brain-dead."[4] To avoid what would otherwise be an oxymoronic position, he is legitimately pressed to distinguish, as he does in fact, between "aliveness" and "personhood,"[5] or, to use more precise terminology, between human biological and human personal life. In short, a distinction between the status of human biological and personal life is presupposed.

We are brought then to a set of distinctions: first, human life must be distinguished as human personal and human biological life. Not all instances of human biological life are instances of human personal life. Brain-dead (but otherwise alive) human beings, human gametes, cells in human cell cultures, all count as instances of human biological life. Further, not only are some humans not persons, there is no reason to hold that all persons are humans, as the possibility of extraterrestrial self-conscious life suggests.

Second, the concept of the sanctity of life comes to refer in different ways to the value of biological life and the dignity of persons. Probably much that is associated with arguments concerning the sanctity of life really refers to the dignity of the life of persons. In any event, there is no unambiguous sense of being simply "pro-life" or a defender of the sanctity of life—one must decide what sort of life one wishes to defend and on what grounds. To begin with, the morally significant difference between biological and personal life lies in the fact, to use Kant's idiom, that persons are ends in themselves. Rational, self-conscious agents can make claims to treatment as ends in themselves because they can experience themselves, can know that they experience themselves, and can determine and control the circumstances of such experience. Self-conscious agents are self-determining and can claim respect as such. That is, they can claim the right to be respected as free agents. Such a claim is to the effect that self-respect and mutual respect turn on self-determination, on the fact that self-conscious beings are necessary for the existence of a moral order—a kingdom of ends, a community based on mutual self-respect, not force. Only self-conscious agents can be held accountable for their actions and thus be bound together solely in terms of mutual respect of each other's autonomy.

What I intend here is no more than an exegesis of what we could mean by "respecting persons." Kant, for example, argued that rational beings are "persons, because their very nature [as rational beings] points them out as ends in themselves."[6] In this fashion, Kant developed a distinction between things that have only "a worth *for us*" and persons "whose existence is an end in itself."[7] As a result, Kant drew a stark and clear distinction between persons and non-persons.

> "A person is [a] subject whose actions are capable of being imputed [that is, one who can act responsibly]. Accordingly, moral personality is nothing but the freedom of a rational being under moral laws (whereas psychological personality is merely the capacity to be conscious of the identity of one's self in the various conditions of one's existence) . . . . [In contrast], a thing is that which is not capable of any imputation [that is, of acting responsibly]."[8]

To be respected as a moral agent is precisely to be respected as a free self-conscious being capable of being blamed and praised, of being held responsible for its actions. The language of respect in the sense of recognizing others as free to determine themselves (i.e., as ends in themselves) rather than as beings to be determined by others (i.e., to be used as means, instruments to good and values) turns upon acknowledging others as free, as moral agents.

This somewhat obvious exegesis (or tautological point) is an account of the nature of the language of obligation. Talk of obligation functions (1) to remind us that certain actions cannot be reconciled with the notion of a moral community, and (2) to enjoin others to pursue particular values or goods. The only actions that strictly contradict the notion of a moral community are those that are incompatible with the notion of such a community—actions that treat moral agents as if they were objects. Morality as mutual respect of autonomy (i.e., more than conjoint pursuit of particular goods or goals) can be consistently pursued only if persons in the strict sense (i.e., self-conscious agents, entities able to be self-legislative) are treated with respect for their autonomy. Though we may treat other entities with a form of respect, that respect is never central to the notion of a community of moral agents. Insofar as we identify persons with moral agents, we exclude from the range of the concept person those entities which are not self-conscious. Which is to say, only those beings are unqualified bearers of rights and duties who can both claim to be acknowledged as having a dignity beyond a value (i.e., as being ends in themselves) and can be responsible for their actions. Of course, this strict sense of person is not unlike that often used in the law.[9] And, as Kant suggests in the passage above, it requires as well an experience of self-identity through time.

It is only respect for persons in this strict sense that cannot be violated without contradicting the idea of a moral order in the sense of the living with others on the basis of a mutual respect of autonomy. The point to be emphasized is a distinction between value and dignity, between biological life and personal life. These distinctions provide a basis for the differentiation between biological or merely animal life, and personal life, and turn on the rather commonsense criterion of respect being given that which can be respected—that is, blamed or praised. Moral treatment comes to depend, not implausibly, on moral agency. The importance of such distinctions for medicine is that they can be employed in treating medical ethical issues. As arguments, they are attempts to sort out everyday distinctions between moral agents, other animals, and just plain things. They provide a conceptual apparatus based on the meaning of obligations as respect due that which can have obligations.

The distinctions between human biological life and human personal life, and between the value of human biological life and the dignity of human personal life, involve a basic conceptual distinction that modern medical science presses as an issue of practical importance. Medicine after all is not merely the enterprise of preserving human life—if that were the case, medicine would confuse human cell cultures with patients who are persons. In fact, a maxim "to treat patients as persons" presupposes that we do or can indeed know who the persons are. These distinctions focus not only on the newly problematic issue of the definition of death, but on the question of abortion as well: issues that turn on when persons end and when they begin. In the case of the definition of death, one is saying that even though genetic continuity, organic function, and reproductive capability may extend beyond brain death, personal life does not. Sentience in an appropriate embodiment is a necessary condition for being a person.[10] One, thus, finds that persons die when this embodiment is undermined.

With regard to abortion, many have argued similarly that the fetus is not a person, though it is surely an instance of human biological life. Even if the fetus is a human organism that will probably be genetically and organically continuous with a human person, it is not yet such a person.[11] Simply put, fetuses are not rational, self-conscious beings—that is, given a strict definition of persons, fetuses do not qualify as persons. One sees this when comparing talk about dead men with talk about fetuses. When speaking of a dead man, one knows of whom one speaks, the one who died, the person whom one knew before his death. But in speaking of the fetus, one has no such person to whom one can refer. There is not yet a person, a "who," to whom one can refer to in the case of the fetus (compare: one can keep promises to dead men but not to men yet unborn). In short, the fetus in no way singles itself out as, or shows itself to be, a person. This conclusion has theoretical advantages, since many zygotes never implant and some divide into two.[12] It offers as well a moral clarification of the practice of using intrauterine contraceptive devices and abortion. Whatever these practices involve, they do not involve the taking of the life of a person.[13] This position in short involves recurring to a distinction forged by both Aristotle and St. Thomas—between biological life and personal life,[14] between life that has value and life that has dignity.

But this distinction does too much, as the arguments by Michael Tooley on behalf of infanticide show.[15] By the terms of the argument, infants, as well as fetuses are left open to abortion. The question then is whether one can recoup something for infants or perhaps even for fetuses. One might think that a counterargument, or at least a mitigating argument, could be made on the basis of potentiality—the potentiality of infants or the potentiality of fetuses. That argument, though, fails because one must distinguish the potentialities of a person from the potentiality to become a person. If, for example, one holds that a fetus has the potentiality of a person, one begs the very question at issue—whether fetuses are persons. But, on the other hand, if one succeeds in arguing that a fetus or infant has the potentiality to become a person, one has conceded the point that the fetus or infant is not a person. One may value a dozen eggs or a handful of acorns because they can become chickens or oak trees. But a dozen eggs is not a flock of chickens, a handful of acorns is not a stand of oaks. In, short, the potentiality of X's to become Y's may cause us to value X's very highly because Y's are valued very highly, but until X's are Y's they do not have the value of Y's.[16]

Which is to say, given our judgments concerning brain-dead humans and concerning zygotes, embryos, and fetuses, we are left in a quandary with regard to infants. How, if at all, are we to understand them to be persons, beings to whom we might have obligations? One should remember that these questions arise against the backdrop of issues concerning the disposition of deformed neonates—whether they should all be given maximal treatment, or whether some should be allowed to die, or even have their deaths expedited.[17]

In short, though we have sorted out a distinction between the value of human biological life and the dignity of human personal life, this distinction does not do all we want, or rather it may do too much. That is, it goes against an intuitive appreciation of children, even neonates, as not being open to destruction or request. We may not in the end be able to support that intuition, for it may simply be a cultural prejudice; but I will now try to give a reasonable exegesis of its significance.

II. Two Concepts of Person

I shall argue in this section that a confusion arises out of a false presupposition that we have only one concept of person: we have a least two concepts (probably many more) of person. I will restrict myself to examining the two that are most relevant here. First, there is the sense of person that we use in identifying moral agents: individual, living bearers of rights and duties. That sense singles out entities who can participate in the language of morals, who can make claims and have those claims respected: the strict sense we have examined above. We would, for example, understand "person" in this sense to be used properly if we found another group of self-conscious agents in the universe and called them persons even if they were not human, though it is a term that usually applies to normal adult humans. This sense of person I shall term the strict sense, one which is used in reference to self-conscious, rational agents. But what of the respect accorded to infants and other examples of non-self-conscious or not-yet-self-conscious human life? How are such entities to be understood?

A plausible analysis can, I believe, be given in terms of a second concept or use of person—a social concept or social role of person that is invoked when certain instances of human biological life are treated as if they were persons strictly, even though they are not. A good example is the mother-child or parent-child relationship in which the infant is treated as a person even though it is not one strictly. That is, the infant is treated as if it had the wants and desires of a person—its cries are treated as a call for food, attention, care, etc., and the infant is socialized, placed within a social structure, the family, and becomes a child. The shift is from merely biological to social significance. The shift is made on the basis that the infant is a human and is able to engage in a minimum of social interaction. With regard to the latter point, severely anencephalic infants may not qualify for the role *person* just as brain-dead adults would fail to qualify; both lack the ability to engage in minimal social interaction.[18] This use of person is, after all, one employed with instances of human biological life that are enmeshed in social roles as if they were persons. Further, one finds a difference between the biological mother-fetus relation and the social mother-child relation. The first relation can continue whether or not there is social recognition of the fetus, the second cannot. The mother-child relation is essentially a social practice.[19]

This practice can be justified as a means of preserving trust in families, of nurturing important virtues of care and solicitude towards the weak, and of assuring the healthy development of children. Further, it has a special value because it is difficult to determine specifically when in human ontogeny persons strictly emerge. Socializing infants into the role *person* draws the line conservatively. Humans do not become persons strictly until sometime after birth. Moreover, there is a considerable value in protecting anything that looks and acts in a reasonably human fashion, especially when it falls within an established human social role as infants do within the role *child*. This ascription of the role *person* constitutes a social practice that allows the rights of a person to be imputed to forms of human life that can engage in at least a minimum of social interaction. The interest is in guarding anything that could reasonably play the role *person* and thus to strengthen the social position of persons generally.

The social sense of person appears as well to structure the treatment of the senile, the mentally retarded, and the otherwise severely mentally infirm. Though they are not moral agents, persons strictly, they are treated as if they were persons. The social sense of person identifies their place in a social relationship with persons strictly. It is, in short, a practice that gives to instances of human biological life the status of persons. Unlike persons strictly, who are bearers of both rights and duties, persons in the social sense have rights but no duties. That is, they are not morally responsible agents, but are treated with respect (i.e., rights are imputed to them) in order to establish a practice of considerable utility to moral agents: a society where kind treatment of the infirm and weak is an established practice. The central element of the utility of this practice lies in the fact that it is often difficult to tell when an individual is a person strictly (i.e., how senile need one be in order no longer to be able to be a person strictly), and persons strictly might need to fear concerning their treatment (as well as the inadvertent mistreatment of other persons strictly) were such a practice not established. The social sense of person is a way of treating certain instances of human life in order to secure the life of persons strictly.

To recapitulate, we value children and our feelings of care of them, and we seek ways to make these commitments perdure. That is, social roles are ways in which we give an enduring fabric to our often inconstant passions. This is not to say that the social role person is merely a convention. To the contrary, it represents a fabric of ways of nurturing the high value we place on human life, especially the life that will come to be persons such as we. That fabric constitutes a practice of giving great value to instances of human biological life that can in some measure act as if they were persons, so that (1) the dignity of persons strictly is guarded against erosion during the various vicissitudes of health and disease, (2) virtues of care and attention to the dependent are nurtured, and (3) important social goals such as the successful rearing of children (and care of the aged) succeed. In the case of infants, one can add in passing a special consideration (4) that with luck they will become persons strictly, and that actions taken against infants could injure the persons they will eventually become.[20]

It should be stressed that the social sense of person is primarily a utilitarian construct. A person in this sense is not a person strictly, and hence not an unqualified object of respect. Rather, one treats certain instances of human life as person for the good of those individuals who are persons strictly. As a consequence, exactly where one draws the line between persons in the social sense and merely human biological life is not crucial as long as the integrity of persons strictly is preserved. Thus there is a somewhat arbitrary quality about the distinction between fetuses and infants. One draws a line where the practice of treating human life as human personal life is practical and useful. Birth, including the production of a viable fetus through an abortion procedure provides a somewhat natural line at which to begin to treat human biological life as human personal life. One might report, why not include fetuses as persons in a social sense? The answer is, Only if there are good reasons to do so in terms of utility. One would have to measure the utility of abortions for the convenience of women and families, for the prevention of the birth of infants with serious genetic diseases, and for the control of population growth against whatever increased goods would come from treating fetuses as persons. In addition, there would have to be consideration of the woman's right to choose freely concerning her body, and this would weigh heavily against any purely utilitarian considerations for restricting abortions. Early abortions would probably have to be allowed in any case in order to give respect due to the woman as a moral agent. But if these considerations are met, the exact point at which the line is drawn between a fetus and an infant is arbitrary in that utility considerations rarely produce absolute lines of demarcation. The best that one can say is that treating infants as persons in a social sense supports many central human values that abortion does not undermine, and that allowing at least early abortions acknowledges a woman's freedom to determine whether or not she wishes to be a mother.

One is thus left with at least two concepts of person. On the one hand, persons strictly can and usually do identify themselves as such—they are self-conscious, rational agents, respect for whom is part of valuing freedom, assigning blame and praise, and understanding obligation. That is, one's duty to respect persons strictly is the core of morality itself. The social concept of person is, on the other hand, more mediate, it turns on central values but is not the same as respect for the dignity of persons strictly. It allows us to value highly certain but not all instances of human biological life, without confusing that value with the dignity of persons strictly. That is, we can maintain the distinction between human biological and human personal life. We must recognize, though, that some human biological life is treated as human personal life even though it does not involve the existence of a person in the strict sense.

III. Conclusions

I wish to conclude now with a number of reflections reviewing the implications of distinguishing between human biological and human personal life, and between social and strict senses of person. First, it would seem that one can appreciate the general value of human biological life as just that. Human sperm, human ova, human cell cultures, human zygotes, embryos, and fetuses can have value, but they lack the dignity of persons. They are thus, all else being equal, open to socially justifiable experimentation in a way persons in either the strict or social sense should never be. That is, they can be used as means merely.

With infants, one finds human biological life already playing the social role of person. An element of this is the propriety of parents' controlling the destiny of their very young children insofar as this does not undermine the role *child*. That is, parents are given broad powers of control over their children as long as they do not abuse them, because very young children do in fact live in and through their families. Very young children are more in the possession of their families than in their own possession— they are not self-possessed, they are not yet moral agents. They do not yet belong to themselves. In fact, though persons strictly have both rights and duties, persons in the social sense are given moral rights but have no duties. Moreover, others must act in their behalf since they are not self-determining entities. And when they act in their behalf, they need not to do so in a manner that respects them as moral agents (i.e., there is not moral autonomy to respect), but in terms of what in general would be their best interests. Further, the duty to pursue those best interests can be defeated.

At least some puzzles about parental choice with regard to the treatment of their deformed infants or experimentation on their very young children can be resolved in these terms. Parents become the obvious ones to decide concerning the treatment of their very young children as long as that choice does not erode the care of children generally, or injure the persons strictly those children will become. And parents can properly refuse life-prolonging treatment of their deformed infants if such treatment would entail a substantial investment of their economic and psychological resources. They can be morally justified if they calculate expenses against the expected life-style of the child if treated, and the probability of success. Such a utility calculus is justified (i.e., it is in accord with general social interests in preserving the role child) insofar as it involves a sufficiently serous acknowledgment of the value of the role child (i.e., as long as such choices are not capricious and there is a substantial hardship involved so that such investment is "not worth it"[21] in order to maintain the practice of the social sense of person. Further, one can justify social intervention in the form of legal injunctions to treat where such calculations by the parents are not convincing.

As to using very young children in experiments, they can be used in a fashion that adults may not, since they are not persons strictly. By that I mean someone can consent on their behalf when the risk is minimal, the value pursued substantial, when such experiments cannot in fact be performed on adults, and when such treatment does not erode the use of the social sense of person. One might picture here the trial of rubella vaccine on children that was not intended to be of direct benefit to those children, especially those who would grow to be misanthropic bachelors and thus never want to protect fetuses from damage. Nor need one presume anything except that most small children who are vaccinated have in some fashion been coerced or coopted into being vaccinated.

Consequently, with very young children one need not respect caprice in order to maintain the social sense of person. With free agents that is a different matter. Part of the freedom of self-determination is the latitude to act with caprice. For example, adults should be able, all else being equal, to refuse life-prolonging treatment; very young children should not. Surely difficult issues arise with older children and adolescents.[22] But the problems of dealing with free choice on the part of older children and adolescents attest to the validity of the rule rather than defeating it. With adults one is primarily concerned with the dignity of free agents, and what is problematic with respect to adolescents is that they are very much free agents.[23] In contrast, with small children one is concerned with their value (and the value of the social sense of person) and with not damaging the persons the children will become. In intermediate cases (i.e., older children) one must respect what freedom and self-possession does exist.

In summary, fetuses appear in no sense to be persons, children appear in some sense to be persons, normal adult humans show themselves to be persons. Is anything lost by these distinctions? I would argue not and that only clarity is gained. For those who hold some variety of homunculus theory of potentiality, it may appear that something is lost, for example, by saying that infants are not persons strictly. But how they could be such is, on the view I have advanced, at best a mystery. In this respect I would like to add a caveat lest in some fashion my distinction between persons strictly and persons socially be taken to imply that those humans who are only (!) persons socially are somehow set in jeopardy. It is one thing to say that an entity lacks the dignity of being a person strictly, and another thing to say that it does not have great value. For example, the argument with regard to the social role *child* has been that a child is a person socially because it does indeed have great value and because the social sense of person has general value. Children receive the social sense of person because we value children, and moreover because the social sense of person has a general utility in protecting persons strictly. In short, there is no universal way of speaking of the sanctity of life; some life (personal life) has dignity, all life can have value, and human biological life that plays the social role person has a special value and is treated as human personal life.

What I have offered is, in short, an examination of the ways in which the biomedical sciences have caused the concept of person to be reexamined, and some of the conclusions of these examinations. These analyses lead us to speak not only of human biological versus human personal life, of strict versus social concepts of person, but to distinguish, with regard to the sanctity of life, the value of biological life, the dignity of strictly personal life, and the care due to human biological life that can assume the social role of a person.

NOTES

1. *Black's Law Dictionary*, 4th ed., rev., s.v. "death."
2. For the first such statutory definition of death see: "Definition of Death," Kan. Stat. Ann., secs. 77–202 (1970).
3. Willard Gaylin, "Harvesting the Dead," *Harper's Magazine*, 249 (September 1974), 23–30.
4. *Ibid,*. p. 28.
5. *Ibid*.
6. Immanuel Kant, *Fundamental Principles of the Metaphysic of Morals*, in *Kant's Critique of Practical Reason and Other Works on the Theory of Ethics*, trans. Thomas K. Abbott, 6th ed. (1873); rpt. London: Longmans, Green and Co., 1909), p. 46; *Kants gesammelte Schriften*, 23 vols., Preussische Akademie der Wissenshaften, eds. (Berlin: Walter de Gruyter, 1902–1956), IV, 428.
7. *Ibid*.
8. Immanuel Kant, *The Metaphysical Principals of Virtue: Part II of The Metaphysics of Morals*, trans. James Ellington (New York: Bobbs-Merrill, 1964), p. 23; Akademie Textausgabe, VI, 223.
9. *Black's Law Dictionary*, 4th ed., rev., s.v. "person."
10. Strictly, the present brain-oriented definition of death distinguishes between a vegetative level of biological life and all higher levels. Report of the Ad Hoc Committee of the Harvard Medical School to Examine the Definition of Brain Death, "A Definition of Irreversible Coma," *Journal of the American Medical Association*, 205 (August 5, 1968), 85–88; Report of the Ad Hoc Committe of the American Electroencephalographic Society on EEG Criteria for Determination of Cerebral Death, "Cerebral Death and the Electroencephalogram," *Journal of the American Medical Association*, 209 (September 8, 1969), 1505–10. The point of this definition (at least in part) is to be conservative, not to make the mistake of prematurely pronouncing someone dead. On that ground, it is better to draw the line between vegetative life and sentient life, rather than between sentient life and self-conscious life. Moreover, non-self conscious human life can, as will be argued, be treated as a person in other than a strict sense of that concept.
11. I have treated these issues more fully elsewhere. H. Tristram Engelhardt, Jr., "The Ontology of Abortion," *Ethics*, 84 (April 1974), 217–34.
12. If one held that zygotes were persons (i.e., that persons begin at conception), one would have to account for how persons can split

into two (i.e., monozygous twins), and for the fact that perhaps half of all persons die *in utero*. That is, there is evidence to indicate that perhaps up to 50 percent of all zygotes never implant. Arthur T. Hertig, "Human Trophoblast: Normal and Abnormal," *American Journal of Clinical Pathology*, 47 (March 1967), 249–68.

13. That is, even if such practices might involve some disvalue, it would surely not be that of taking the life of a person. Also, one must recognize that if intrauterine contraceptive devices act by preventing the implantation of the zygote they would count as a form of abortion.

14. Both Aristotle and St. Thomas held that human persons developed at some point after conception. See Aristotle, *Historia Animalium*, Book II, Chapter 3, 583 b, and St. Thomas Aquinas, *Summa Theologica*, Part 1, Q 118, art. 2, reply to obj. 2. See also St. Thomas Aquinas, *Opera Omnia*, XXVI (Paris: Vives, 1875), in *Aristoteles Stagiritae: Politicorum seu de Rebus Civilibus*, Book II, Lectio XII, p. 484, and *Opera Omnia*, XI, *Commentum in Quartum Librum Sententiarium Magistri Petri Lombardi*, Distinctio XXXI, Expositio Textus, p. 127.

15. Michael Tooley, "A Defense of Abortion and Infanticide," in *The Problem of Abortion*, ed. Joel Feinberg (Belmont, Calif.: Wadsworth Publishing Company, 1973), pp. 51–91.

16. One might think that a counterexample exists in the case of sleeping persons. That is, a person while asleep is not self-conscious and rational, and would seem in the absence of a doctrine of potentiality not to be a person and to be therefore open to being used by others. A sleeping person is, though, a person in three senses in which a fetus or infant is not. First, in speaking of the sleeping person, one can know of whom one speaks in the sense of having previously known him before sleep. One therefore can know whose rights would be violated should that "person" be killed while asleep. His right to his life would *in part* be analogous to a dead man's right to have a promise kept that had been made to him when he was a self-conscious living person. In contrast, the fetus is not yet a person, an entity of whom, for example, promises can be made in anything but a metaphorical sense. Second, the sleeping man has a concrete presence in the world that is uniquely his, a fully intact functioning brain. Though asleep, the fully developed physical presence of the person continues. Third, the gap of sleep will be woven together by the life of the person involved: he goes to sleep expecting to awake and awakes to bring those past expectations into his present life. In short, one is not dealing with the potentiality of something to become a person, but with the potentiality of a person to resume his life after sleep.

17. See, for example, John M. Freeman, "To Treat or Not to Treat," *Practical Management of Meningomyelocele*, ed. John Freeman (Baltimore: University Park Press, 1974), pp. 13–22, and John Lorber, "Selective Treatment of Myelomeningocele: To Treat or Not to Treat," *Pediatrics* 53 (March 1974), 307–8. Arguments such as Professor Tooley's imply that one may fairly freely employ positive and negative euthanasia

in such cases, in that infants are not yet persons. Tooley, "A Defense of Abortion and Infanticide," p. 91.
18. It is important to note that severely anencephalic infants and brain-dead adults fail to be persons in a social sense because they lack the ability for social interaction, not because they lack the potentiality to become persons.

Study Questions

1. State why you believe that Haber would agree or not agree with Engelhardt's description of what a "person" is.
2. State why you believe Engelhardt's piece could or could not be used to justify an abortion of child known to be severely mentally defective.

What is Suicide?*

Tom L. Beauchamp

Although debate about the legality, rationality, and morality of
suicide has increased in recent years, only fragmentary attention
has been devoted to the development of an adequate definition
of suicide. Because significantly different moral, social, and legal
sanctions will be implied by the classification of an act as suicide,
euthanasia, murder, or accidental death, the development of an
adequate definition will have important practical consequences.
The way we classify actions is indicative of the way we think
about them, and in the present case such classifications have
immediate relevance for medicine, ethics, and law.

A start in the direction of a definition of "suicide" is the following: The death of a person is a suicide only if: (1) the person's
own death is intentionally self-caused, and (2) the person's action
is noncoerced. However, two special problems prevent this simple
definition from being fully adequate.

The Problem of Treatment Refusal

The first class of difficult cases for the above definition involve
persons who suffer from a terminal illness or mortal injury, and
who refuse some medical therapy without which they will die,

* Copyright © 1977 by Tom L. Beauchamp.

277

but with which they could live for some period beyond the point they would die without the therapy. For example, refusal to allow a blood transfusion, or an amputation, or refusal of further kidney dialysis are now familiar facts of hospital life. But are they suicides? Two facts about such cases are noteworthy. First, these acts certainly *can* be suicides, because *any* means productive of death potentially can be used to the end of suicide. Pulling the plug on one's respirator is not relevantly different from plunging a knife into one's heart, if the reason for putting an end to life is identical in the two cases. Second, suicidal acts can also be sacrificial. For example, if a person were suffering from a costly terminal disease, then it would be an altruistic (even if perhaps misguided) action to take his own life in order to spare his family the inordinate cost of providing the care; but it would nonetheless be suicide.

Still, the seriously suffering person with end-stage renal disease who refuses to continue dialysis and dies a "natural" death does not strike most as a suicide. Why not? Three features of such situations need to be distinguished in order to answer this question:

1. whether the death is *intended* by the agent,
2. whether an *active* means to death is selected,
3. whether a *nonfatal condition* is present
   (no terminal disease or mortal injury exists).

The more we have unmistakable cases of actions by an agent that involve an *intentionally caused death* using an *active* means where there is a *nonfatal* condition, the more inclined we are to classify such acts as suicides, whereas the more such conditions are absent the less inclined we are to call the acts suicides. For example, if a seriously but not mortally wounded soldier turns his rifle on himself and intentionally brings about his death, it is a suicide. But what about the seriously ill patient of ambiguous intentions, suffering from a terminal illness, and refusing yet another blood transfusion?

Although considerations of terminal illness and of intention are important, the main source of our present definitional problem is the active/passive distinction. A passively allowed, "natural" death seems foreign to the notion of suicide, both because the death is at least in part not caused by the agent and because the "cide" part of "suicide" entails "killing," which is commonly contrasted with allowing to die. In the face of this complex mixture of elements the following generalization may be offered about such cases: An act is *not* a suicide if the person who dies suffers from a terminal disease or from a mortal injury which, by refusal of treatment, he passively allows to cause his death—even if the person intends his death. However, this analysis does not seem adequate for all cases; for example, think of a patient with a terminal condition who could easily avoid dying for a long time but who chooses to end his life immediately by not taking cheap and painless medication. This counterexample might incline us toward the view that a time restriction is also needed. But this restriction probably could not be reasonably formulated, and I am inclined to think that we have reached the conceptual boundaries of our notion of suicide. If in the end the analysis offered has become slightly reforming (one that requires that we change the ordinary meaning of "suicide" somewhat), the vagaries of the concept itself are perhaps responsible.

The Problem of Sacrificial Deaths

There remains the problem of so-called "altruistically motivated (or other-regarding) suicide." Here the key notion responsible for our not classifying some intentional self-killings as suicides seems to some to be that of *sacrifice*. Perhaps those who sacrifice their lives are not conceived as "suicides" for an interesting reason: because we see such actions as from the suicide's point of view having plausible claim to being justified for *other-regarding*—not *self-regarding*—reasons, and hence we logically exclude them from the realm of the suicidal.

Sadly, exclusions based on self-sacrificial acts will not help much in structuring a definition of suicide unless further qualifications are introduced. The monk in Vietnam who pours gasoline over his body and burns himself to death as a protest against his government does not do so for his own sake but for the sake of his beloved countrymen, just as the father who kills himself in the midst of a famine so that his wife and children may have enough to eat acts from self-sacrificial motives. Many cases of this general description provide paradigms of suicidal actions but would have to be declared nonsuicides if the approach were taken that other-regarding, sacrificial acts fail to qualify as suicides.

In the face of this new complexity, a course paralleling the one for refusal-of-treatment cases may be taken: An act is *not* a suicide if the person is caused to die by a life-threatening condition he does not intend to bring about through his own actions. Interestingly, this approach does not turn on the notion of sacrifice, the original problem compelling consideration of these cases. It makes no difference whether the action is sacrificial or nonsacrificial, so long as the condition causing death is not brought about *by the agent* for the purpose of ending his life. This conclusion is somewhat troublesome, because the agent does intend his death in those cases of sacrifice where a person has the option either to save his life or to act in protection of others' lives, and then specifically chooses a course of action that brings about his own death. Nonetheless, in such cases *it cannot be said that he brings about the life-threatening condition causing his death in order to cause his death*, and that fact is the crucial matter.

There are further parallels between this kind of case and the refusal of treatment cases previously discussed. Three relevant ingredients can again be distinguished:

1. whether the death is *intended* by the agent,
2. whether the death is *caused by* the agent (or is caused to the agent),
3. whether the action is *self-regarding* (or is other-regarding).

Here the main source of confusion is not the "active/passive" distinction, but rather is the parallel "caused by/caused to" distinction. To cause one's own death in order to die is to kill oneself, but to have death caused by some alien condition in the course of an action with multiple objectives may not be. Here we might say that the killing/being killed distinction is involved, and that it functions rather like the killing/letting die distinction previously discussed. At any rate, we have again reached the boundaries of our concept of suicide, which is here being contrasted with the concept of an externally caused death. A person might be using an externally caused means as a socially acceptable and convenient way of ending his life, and hence it might be a suicide. But we have seen that this is true of any means to death whatsoever.

A good test case for the above analysis is the now classic case of Captain Oates, who walked into the Antarctic snow to die, because he was suffering from an illness that hindered the progress of a party attempting to make its way out of a severe blizzard.[1] According to R.F. Holland, Oates was not a suicide because: "in Oates's case I can say, 'No [he didn't kill himself]; the blizzard killed him.' Had Oates taken out a revolver and shot himself I should have agreed he was a suicide."[2] I cannot agree with Holland's estimate. On the analysis offered above, Oates' heroic sacrifice is a suicide because of the active steps that he took to bring about his death. Although the climatic conditions proximately caused his death, he *brought about* the relevant life-threatening condition causing his death (exposure to the weather) in order that he die. There is no relevant difference between death by revolver and death by exposure to freezing weather when both equally are life-threatening conditions used to cause one's own death. However, the Oates case is not an easy one to declare a suicide. It is a close call precisely because there is both multiple causation and multiple intent: the action is an heroic way of being *causally responsible* for placing oneself in *conditions which cause* death, and death was intended as a merciful release from an intolerable burden, not only because of Oates' suffering but also because of his knowledge that he was imperilling the lives of his colleagues. Moreover, his release from these burdens is apparently his major objective. No wonder the Oates case has become a classic in literature on the definition of suicides; it is hard to imagine a case sitting more astride the boundaries between suicide and non-suicide.

Although the analysis proposed above does not differ in some respects from that of Joseph Margolis', the point at which we part company is now evident, for he argues as follows:

> The Buddhist monk who sets fire to himself in order to protest the war that he might have resisted in another way will not be said to have committed suicide if the *overriding* characterization of what he did fixes on the ulterior objective of influencing his countrymen. . . . [If there is] some further purpose that he serves instrumentally, then we normally refuse to say he has suicided; . . .[3]

Margolis thinks there is a decisive difference between whether one's overriding reason is some sacrificial objective or the objective of ending one's life. In my view the matter is more complicated and has little to do with the notions of sacrifice, martyrdom, and patriotism. It has rather to do with whether death is caused by one's own arrangement of the life-threatening conditions causing death for the purpose of bringing about death (whether this purpose be the overriding reason or not). Since the monk arranges the conditions, precisely for this purpose (though for others as well), he is a suicide.

Conclusion

We have arrived, then, at an understanding of suicide that is fairly simple, even if somewhat more complicated than the definitions with which we began: An act is a suicide if a person intentionally brings about his own death in circumstances where others do not coerce him to the action, except in those cases where death occurs through an agent's intentional decision but is caused by conditions not specifically arranged by the agent for the purpose of bringing about his own death. However, in concluding, we should ask whether anything useful has been accomplished by this analysis, and especially whether such a definition of the ordinary language meaning of "suicide" is a proper one for moral philosophy. Terms in their ordinary meaning often contain evaluative accretions due to social attitudes that render them difficult for purposes of moral analysis; and the meaning we have located for "suicide" appears to be a premiere instance of this problem: Because self-caused deaths are often revolting and inexplicable, an emotive meaning of disapproval has been incorporated into our use of "suicide." More importantly, because of this already attached disapproval we find it hard to accept as "suicides" acts of which we approve, or at least do not disapprove. We thus by the very logic of the term prejudice any pending moral analysis of the action of a suicide as being right or wrong, let alone praiseworthy or blameworthy.

NOTES

1. See *Scott's Last Expedition* (London: 1935), Vol. I, p. 462.
2. "Suicide," in J. Rachels, ed., *Moral Problems* (New York: Harper and Row, 1971), pp. 352–53.
3. Margolis, *"Suicide,"* in *Negativities* (Columbus, Ohio: Charles E. Merrill Co., 1975), pp. 27–28. Cf. his final definition on p. 33. [Reprinted above.]

Study Questions

1. State Beauchamp's refined definition of suicide. Do you agree with it? Does it improve on more traditional definitions?
2. Would you say the death of Captain Oates (p. 000) was a suicide or a sacrificial death? Explain.

Ethics, Advertising and the Definition of a Profession

*Allen R. Dyer**

The status of medicine as a profession has long gone unchallenged. If anything was a profession, it was medicine. Medicine, along with law and the clergy, the so-called "learned professions," were defined by the knowledge held by their members and by the application of that knowledge to the needs of fellow citizens. The relationship between the professional and those served was considered of special importance, and societies have traditionally placed sanctions on that relationship, such as the protection of confidentiality, notable in English common law dating back to medieval times. But the sanctity of relationships with professionals has always existed alongside an uneasiness about the mercantile aspects of professional practice. In the contemporary era, the criticisms of the medical profession have become so widespread that the idea of a profession being defined primarily by an ethic of service shared by its members is no longer entirely convincing. More prominent is the idea of a profession being defined by technical services traded in the marketplace.

This paper attempts to assess the meaning of contemporary challenges to the profession of medicine by looking at what it means for medicine to be considered a profession as distinct from a trade. Specifically it considers the role codes and traditions of ethics play in defining medicine as a profession.

* Departments of Psychiatry and Community and Family Medicine, Duke University Medical Center, Durham, North Carolina, U.S.

284

The Definition of a Profession

Originally the word profession meant "to profess" religious vows. Medicine was a profession along with the clergy because its members shared a common "calling," and law was considered professional through a similar educational background in the medieval university.[1] University "professors" (the masters at the University of Paris) were first allowed to incorporate in the thirteenth century,[2] and the debate about whether guilds and guild-like groups exert true monopoly power over prices has yet to be settled.[3]

What is considered professional might best be understood in contrast with what is not. In athletics as in sexual activity, the designation "professional" merely implies getting paid for what others do for free.[4] But the professional is also distinguished from the amateur by a greater level of proficiency which merits the monetary compensation. Thus some level of skill or expertise is generally held to be requisite for professional status. Reiser, Dyck and Curran extend this consideration in a particularly useful definition of profession. They suggest that "self-conscious reflection on standards of conduct is one of the defining characteristics of a profession".[5]

The dual themes relating professions to knowledge on the one hand and its application to practice on the other place professions in an intermediate position between sciences and trades with features in common with both, but also distinct from both.[6] The literature distinguishing professions from trades is abundant,[7,8,9] but in the twentieth century, as knowledge has come to mean scientific knowledge, the medical profession is increasingly identified with technical expertise. But technical expertise is not sufficient to characterize a profession, as sociologists of the professions have demonstrated. The ethical dimension is also required.

The Sociology of Professions

A popular generalization of the sociological literature is that occupations are becoming "professionalized." But specialization, technical skills and expertise do not suffice to establish a work group as a profession. What does? According to Wilensky, any occupation wishing to exercise professional authority must find a technical basis for it, assert an exclusive jurisdiction, link both skill and jurisdiction to standards of training and convince the public that its services are uniquely trustworthy.[10]

The theme of trustiworthiness is the pivotal criterion of professional status. The understanding of someone as a "professional" ultimately depends on the ability to trust that individual with personal matters. The various articulated codes of ethics of professional groups all stress the maintenance of the trustworthiness of members of the professional group through control of entry into and exit from the professional group and discipline of deviant members if necessary (for example censure or removal from membership of the group, or removal of license). Table 1 (overleaf) illustrates the process of professionalization of a number of professions and would-be professions in the United States. It demonstrates that the route to professional status includes the establishment of university training programs, the formation of professional associations, and the presence of formal codes of ethics.

Profession and Monopoly

One of the most noticeable features of professional organizations, viewed in sociological perspective, is their attempt to control markets and promote self-interest. The theory of professional monopoly was developed by Max Weber, who described the following steps by which the medical profession, as all commercial classes, achieves monopoly power: creation of commodities, separation of the performance of services from the satisfaction of the client's interest (i.e., doctors get paid whether or not the therapies work), creation of scarcity, monopolization of supply, restriction of group membership, elimination of external competition, price fixation above the theoretical competitive market value, unification of suppliers, elimination of internal competition, and development of group solidarity and co-operation.[11] Such careful delineation of an economic component to human motivation was truly radical in its time, but today it has become commonplace to reduce all human motivation to economic considerations. The problem with this analysis of professional monopoly is that it is one-dimensional; it considers only economic motives and overlooks the benefit to the public which occurs from such things as the promotion of scientific medicine and efforts to maintain professional standards.

The basic issue is whether physicians can place concern for the public good ahead of their own self-interest. Trust or trustworthiness is the keystone of medical virtue in the traditional canons of medical ethics from the Hippocratic Oath to Percival's code to the various versions of the AMA codes (see Table 2, page 77). Trust is the basis of what it means to be a professional, what it means to be ethical. From the antitrust point of view, any trust, even basic human trust is suspect as a form of monopoly.

Berlant, applying Weber's theory of monopoly to the medical profession, states the case very cogently:

> [The] trust-inducing devices of the Percivalian code increase the market value of medical services and help convert them into commodities . . . It also creates a paternalistic relationship toward the patient, which may undermine consumer organization for mutual self-protection, thereby maintaining consumer atomization. . . . Through atomization of the public into vulnerable patients, paternalism results in the profession's dealing with fragmented individuals rather than bargaining groups. Moreover, by appealing to patient salvation fantasies, trust inducement can stimulate inter-patient competition by increasing each patient's desire to see that nothing stand between doctor and himself. Much of the emotional power of the sentiment of the doctor-patient relationship resides in this wish of the patient to save himself at any cost to himself or others.[12]

Berlant offers a sharp attack on professional ethics from a particular ideological perspective. But basically this attack is not just on professional ethics, it is also an attack on a kind of community in which people may not be autonomous and independent, but in which people may be dependent and in need of help which they willingly seek. This argument introduces a note of almost cynical suspiciousness into a society whose members seem almost too willing to trust and to place themselves in the care of others. This is a crisis of confidence—both for medicine and for our civic life in general: to what extent is it possible and necessary to trust and rely on others and to what extent is it possible to remain isolated, self-reliant and autonomous human beings?

It is because of such challenges to the medical profession's codes and traditions of ethics that a closer look at the form and substance of those codes is necessary.

The Antitrust Challenge to the Professions

A profession's service ideal has several manifestations: a formal code of ethics, more personal ethical outlooks, and certain activities, such as licensure, specialty certification and the accreditation of institutions and training programs, undertaken by a professional association to maintain standards of the group. It can be argued that such professional gate-keeping is an essential aspect of professional responsibility, but there is a widespread perception that the restrictions that the learned professions have placed on themselves under the *aegis* of professional ethics have been motivated not in fact by "ethics" in the sense of a desire to achieve a higher plane of moral conduct, but rather to serve the self-interest of the existing members of the profession.

Perhaps because of the ambiguous relationship of public interest and professional self-interest, the learned professions were considered exempt from the antitrust laws from the time of the passing of the Sherman Antitrust act in 1891 until the Supreme Court's *Goldfarb* decision in 1975, in which Virginia lawyers were found liable to charges of price-fixing of the fees charged for title searches. The *Goldfarb* decision heralded a flurry of antitrust activity, most notably the suit by the Federal Trade Commission against the American Medical Association, charging that these professional organizations were in restraint of trade because their code of ethics prohibited advertising. After a seven-year legal battle, this case was settled on March 23, 1982, when the Supreme Court split 4–4 leaving in place the lower court ruling that barred the AMA from making any reference to advertising and the solicitation of patients, and further prohibiting the AMA from "formulating, adopting and disseminating" any ethical guidelines without first obtaining "permission from and approval of the guidelines by the Federal Trade Commission".[13] Though advertising is the focal issue in this particular case, the ethics of the profession both as explicitly formulated in the AMA's *Principles of Medical Ethics* and as implicitly practiced, as well as the right and

TABLE 1   THE PROCESS OF PROFESSIONALIZATION*

	Became Full-time Occupation	First Training School	First University School	First Local Professional Association	First National Professional Association	First State License Law	Formal Code of Ethics
Established:							
Accounting (CPA)	19th cent	1881	1881	1882	1887	1896	1917
Architecture	18th cent	1865	1868	1815	1857	1897	1909
Civil engineering	18th cent	1819	1847	1848	1852	1908	ca. 1910
Dentistry	18th cent	1840	1867	1844	1840	1868	1866
Law	17th cent	1784	1817	1802	1878	1732	1908
Medicine	ca. 1700	1765	1779	1735	1847	Before 1780	1847
Others in process, some marginal:							
Librarianship	1732	1887	1897	1885	1876	Before 1917	1938
Nursing	17th cent	1861	1909	1885	1896	1903	1950
Optometry		1892	1910	1896	1897	1901	ca. 1935
Pharmacy	1646	1821	1868	1821	1852	1874	ca. 1850
School teaching	17th cent	1823	1879	1794	1857	1781	1929
Social work	1898	1898	1904	1918	1874	1940	1948
Veterinary medicine	1803	1852	1879	1854	1863	1886	1866
New:							
City management	1912	1921	1948	After 1914	1914	None	1924
City planning	19th cent	1909	1909	1947	1917	1963	1948
Hospital Administration	19th cent	1926	1926		1933	1957	1939
Doubtful:							
Advertising	1841	1900	1909	1894	1917	None	1924
Funeral direction	19th cent	ca. 1870	1914	1864	1822	1894	1884

*Modified after Wilensky

propriety of a professional association to formulate its own code of ethics, are being called into question.[14, 15]

The FTC suit hinged on the questions of cost, advertising, and the mercantile aspects of the medical profession. The position of the FTC is that the reason costs are high is because doctors have a monopoly on health care delivery and can thus maintain artificially high costs for their own profit. If doctors were not prohibited from advertising, it is argued, prices would come down because patients could shop for the best deals. FTC chairman, Michael B. Pertschuk, stated the case as follows: "One possible way to control the seemingly uncontrollable health sector could be to treat it as a business and make it respond to the same marketplace influences as other American business and industries".[16] In other words, medicine could better be controlled if it were understood as a trade and not as a profession.

The categorization of medicine as a trade is obviously an oversimplification. The profession is inescapably concerned with the public well-being. Medicine is both a trade and a profession. It is certainly appropriate for the commercial aspects of medical practice to be regulated (or deregulated), but it would be a catastrophic mistake to assume that medicine is merely a trade and subject all aspects of professional regulation either to market influences or to the crude tools of antitrust litigation.

The courts have clearly recognized that professions have trade aspects. They have not eliminated the responsibility for professional self-regulation except in such instances in which such self-regulation may be in restraint of trade. For medicine the issue the Supreme Court decided in FTC v. AMA is that the AMA's code of ethics cannot prohibit advertising. It remains for conscientious physicians to decide what constitutes ethical advertising.

The Ethics of Advertising

Medical advertising is at the crossroads of two very different philosophies about what medicine should be and how professions should be regulated. The traditional view opposes advertising in order to protect the public from physicians who are too commercially oriented. The more prevalent contemporary view holds that medicine is indeed commercially oriented and thus cannot be trusted to regulate itself. In order to reconcile the best aspects of traditional professionalism with the need for greater public accountability, it is necessary to consider what might be ethical and unethical in advertising.

Would advertising of physicians' fees and services be a desirable and ethical thing? If increased competition through advertising could reduce medical costs, then it would be socially desirable *unless* lowered costs were achieved through a lowering of the quality of service or *unless* increased advertising created a demand for more services further straining the economy beyond the approximately ten per cent of the U.S. Gross National Product which currently goes to health care. The cost/quality equation is always a delicate balance, and although costs are easy to measure, the values by which we assess quality are impossible to quantify.

Advertising is a multifaceted issue. It serves two very distinct objectives: 1) the dissemination of information and 2) product differentiation, which economists define as public perception of differences between two products, even though such differences may not in fact exist. The AMA has traditionally held that dissemination of information is acceptable, but that product differentiation or solicitation of patients is not.[17] The physician was to be distinguished from the itinerant merchant of nostrums by deemphasizing the commercial aspects of practice and emphasizing professional ethics (actually standards which minimized the difference between physicians similarly credentialed and certified). Thus if someone were to develop appendicitis while traveling in an unfamiliar part of the country, it would not be necessary to shop for a physician who believed in the germ theory or a hospital that maintained antiseptic standards. This shopping would be taken care of by credentialing procedures. The physician would obtain patients, not by direct appeal to the public but by building a reputation in a community. Although the distinction between dissemination of information and product differentiation was dropped in the 1980 revision of the AMA *Principles of Medical Ethics* it remains an important distinction for physicians to keep in mind when contemplating the ethics of advertising. Advertising which provides information to consumers is ethical; creation of the illusion of differences through product differentiation is as unethical in medicine as it is in any business.

TABLE 2
THE CODES OF ETHICS ON ADVERTISING

The Hippocratic Oath: Nowhere in the surviving Hippocratic writings do we find anything about advertising or self-promotion, but we do find a clearly established concept of the profession as a fraternity in the following statement: "I swear . . . to regard my teacher in this art as equal to my parents; to make him partner in my livelihood, and when he is in need of money to share mine with him; to consider his offspring equal to my brothers; to teach them this art, if they require to learn it, without fee or indenture; and to impart precept, oral instruction, and all the other learning, to my sons, to the sons of my teacher, and to pupils who have signed the indenture and sworn obedience to the physicians' Law, but to none other."

Percival's Medical Ethics: Percival apparently had no occasion to refer explicitly to advertising on the part of English physicians, though his code is concerned throughout with maintaining the dignity, honor, and reputation of the profession.

American Medical Association, 1847 code: Duties of physicians for the support of professional character: "It is derogatory to the dignity of the profession, to resort to public advertisements or private cards or handbills, inviting the attention of individuals affected with particular diseases—publicly offering advice and medicine to the poor gratis, or promising radical cures; or to publish cases and operations in the daily prints or suffer such publications to be made; —to invite laymen to be present at operations, —to boast of cures and remedies—to adduce certificates of skill and success, or to perform any other similar acts. These are the ordinary practices of empirics, and are highly reprehensible in a regular physician."

AMA, 1903 revision: In this first revision after the Sherman Act the caption "Principles of Medical Ethics" is substituted for "Code of Medical Ethics" leaving broader discretion to the State and territorial medical societies. The strictures against advertising specify methods to be avoided: "It is incompatible with honorable standing in the profession to resort to public advertisement or private cards inviting the attention of persons affected with particular diseases; to promise radical cures; to publish cases or operations in the daily prints, or to suffer such publication to be made; to invite laymen (other than relatives he may desire to be at hand) to be present at operations; to boast of cures and remedies; to adduce certificates of skill and success, or to employ any of the other methods of charlatans."

AMA, 1912 revision: "Solicitation of patients by circulars or advertisements, or by personal communications or interviews, not warranted by personal relations, is unprofessional. It is equally unprofessional to procure patients by indirection through solicitors or agents of any kind, or by indirect advertisement, or by furnishing or inspiring newspaper or magazine comments concerning cases in which the physician has been or is concerned. All other like self-adulations defy the traditions and lower the tone of any profession and so are intolerable. The most worthy and effective advertisement possible, . . . is the establishment of a well-merited reputation for professional ability and fidelity. This cannot be forced, but must be the outcome of character and conduct."

AMA, 1957 revision: A physician "shall not solicit patients." (A physician shall not attempt to obtain patients by deception.)

AMA, 1980 revision: No comment on advertising in the *Principles of Medical Ethics*, as per FTC order. The *Current Opinions of the Judicial Council* (1982) offers the following comment: "Competition between and among physicians and other health care practitioners on the basis of competitive factors such as quality of services, skill, experience, miscellaneous conveniences offered to patients, credit terms, fees charged, etc, is not only ethical but is encouraged."

British Medical Association: *Handbook of Medical Ethics* (1984): (Quoting the General Medical Council booklet *Professional Conduct and Discipline: Fitness to Practise*—1983) "The medical profession in this country has long accepted the tradition that doctors should refrain from self-advertisement. In the Council's opinion advertising is not only incompatible with the principles which should govern relations between members but could be a source of danger to the public. A doctor successful at achieving publicity may not be the most appropriate doctor for a patient to consult. In extreme cases advertising may raise illusory hopes of a cure."

L'Ordre des Medecins, *Code de Deontologie Medicale* (Belgium, 1975): Publicity, direct or indirect, is forbidden. The reputation of the physician is founded on his professional competence and on his integrity.

Canadian Medical Association, *Code of Ethics:* An ethical physician . . . will build a professional reputation based only on his ability and integrity, will avoid advertising in any form and make professional announcements according to local custom.

World Medical Association, *International Code of Medical Ethics:* Any self advertisement except such as is expressly authorized by the national code of medical ethics [is deemed unethical].

It could be debated whether advertising is ever ethical, but it is an accepted feature of capitalist societies. The ethical issue for advertising is whether advertising is truthful and whether there can be objectively measurable standards for judging the truthfulness of advertising claims. A more problematic concern is the way in which advertising plays upon peoples' unconscious wishes and fantasies: sex, greed, the quest for power, status, and perfection. The scientific basis for advertising rests on the ability to identify and manipulate such longings and fears. When we speak of "the market" or "market forces" or "demand," we are generally talking about human wants and wishes.

Truthfulness in advertising was the concern when the field of advertising itself attempted to follow the course of professionalism in the early part of the twentieth century (see Table 1). At issue were the values which distinguished the professional advertisers from the retail-space merchants. The American Marketing Association (another AMA) established university training programs and codes of ethics which promoted the scientific ideal of detachment and statistical analysis. This scientific vision of community and definition of man (as consumer) replaced the older, empathic, rural, and value-laden world in which a merchant had a feel for what his customers (not consumers) wanted because he lived with them in the same community.[18, 19]

That example of professional advertising is illustrative for the medical profession, not only because advertising promises (threatens?) to be such a conspicuous feature of contemporary medicine, but also because medicine's traditions of professionalism derive from an era in which the physician participated in the life of the community in which he practiced. Knowledge of the patient as a person, the patient's life history and social situation, have traditionally been deemed essential to quality care. At issue today for the profession of medicine is whether it will be possible to preserve the values of personal care which characterized the ideals of an earlier era. The ethics of medicine derive from the time when medicine was a cottage industry. Will it be possible to maintain such ethics if medicine is transformed to assembly-line efficiency?

Conclusion

It is paradoxical that medical ethics should be at the center of controversy about what is in the public interest. Ethical strictures against professional advertisement have a long and venerable tradition in the Western world, which stems from a view of professional life which cannot be easily reduced to economic analysis. The traditions represented by professional ethics stress the personal nature of professional practice. In the traditional model, trust is essential, for the patient/client must trust the professional in order to reveal such confidences as may be necessary to understand the problem. The professional is worthy of that trust according to (i) knowledge possessed and (ii) such "professional" attributes as ability to keep confidences, to refrain from taking advantage of vulnerable patients, to put the patient's interests before his/her own, and to refrain from self-aggrandizement at the patient's expense. It is out of such a view of professionalism that strictures against advertising arose.

The question of whether physicians should advertise and how the profession should be regulated cannot be settled until the prior question of what it means to be a profession is addressed. The economic analysis of market forces addresses a different concern from the concerns of professional ethics. The question is not whether doctors should be allowed to advertise, but what are the trade-offs of a strictly economic analysis of professional activities.

From the economic standpoint the question is this: Are there any reasons not to allow market forces to solve pricing and other problems? In other words, government regulation or professional self-regulation would be warranted only if the market failed. This is not the only question of interest, however. The ethical concern must also be addressed, namely can quality care be maintained if the economically most efficient methods of health care delivery are adopted? From this point of view, the FTC strategy of reforming the medical profession by treating it as a business fails at the outset because it fails to consider the issues of quality care which are so much the concern of physicians and patients alike.

The message for the medical profession from the current round of antitrust litigation is clear: Unfair trade practices will not be tolerated. A more subtle message must also be recognized: The reputation of the profession and its ethics has become tarnished as the public has come to perceive professional ethics as a protective mantle under which professionals cloak self-interest. This does not mean that the old ethics should be abandoned, but rather that they should be taken more seriously.

The doctor-patient relationship, spoken of almost religiously as the keystone of medical practice, has traditionally been a dyad in which the doctor answered directly only to the patient and his own conscience:

DOCTOR ↔ PATIENT

In the modern era, financial considerations, even more than changes in technology, have transformed all parties in this relationship and added new ones:

PROVIDERS ↔ CONSUMERS
THIRD
PARTIES

Patients have become "consumers;" doctors have become "providers;" health care has become a commodity; and "third parties," including insurance companies, social service agencies, and allied health professionals, are very much part of the picture. The patient seldom appears privately (and confidentially) before the doctor for help. Likewise the physician does not answer only to the patient. The conscientious physician concerned about cost containment may be put in the position of limiting the resources given to a demanding or anxious patient. Still, however, the appeal of a person in need of help and the response of a concerned physician remain the essence of medical practice. Though some would suggest that medicine should, in the interests of efficiency, be limited to treating just physical ailments, most responsible physicians still concern themselves with the impact of disease and illness on people's lives and not just with the disease itself.

It is this broader concern of medical practice which professional ethics attempts to address, and which is generally not understood to be an essential feature of a trade. The attempt to regulate the medical profession as a trade comes at a time when the activities of physicians are largely perceived as commercial and impersonal. Physicians must bear the responsibility for maintaining a broader concern for the patient as a person as part of their professional identity. To the extent that medicine fails in maintaining its professional ethical standards of public service and personal care, it is vulnerable to the criticism of self-serving commercialism. To the extent that medicine relies merely on technique and not on an ethic of service, it becomes merely a trade and not a profession.

Acknowledgment

This work is supported by fellowships from the Kellogg Foundation and National Humanities Center and by grants from the Roy A. Hunt Foundation and the Josiah Charles Trent Memorial Foundation.

NOTES

1. La Vopa, A. J. Humanism and professional education: historical background. In: Dyer, A. R. ed. *The humanities and the profession of medicine.* Research Triangle Park, NC: National Humanities Center, 1982.
2. Post, G. Parisian masters as a corporation, 1200–1246. *Spectrum* 1934; 9: 421–445.
3. Thrupp, S. L. *The guilds, Cambridge economic history of Europe.* Cambridge: Cambridge University Press, 1963.
4. Moline, J. On professionals and professions. See reference (1):
5. Reiser, S. J., Dyck, A. J., Curran, W. J., eds. *Ethics in medicine.* Cambridge: MIT Press, 1977: 1.
6. Michels, R. Professional ethics and social value. *International review of psychoanalysis* 1976; 3: 377–384.
7. Friedson, E. *Profession of medicine: a study of the sociology of applied knowledge.* New York: Dodd, Mead, 1970.
8. Larson, M. S. *The rise of professionalism: a sociological analysis.* Berkeley: University of California Press, 1977.
9. Haskell, T. L. *The emergence of professional social science.* Urbana: University of Illinois Press, 1977.

10. Wilensky, H. The professionalization of everyone? *The American journal of sociology* 1964; 70: 137ff.
11. Weber, M. *On the methodology of social sciences.* Translated and edited by Shils, E. A., Finch, H. A. Glencoe: The Free Press, 1949.
12. Berlant, J. *Profession and monopoly: a study of medicine in the United States and Great Britain.* Berkeley: University of California Press, 1975.
13. Greenhouse, J. Justices uphold right of doctors to solicit trade. *New York Times* 1982 Mar 24: 10.
14. Lee, R. E. Application of antitrust laws to the professions. *Journal of legal medicine* 1979; 1(2): 143–153.
15. Havighurst, C. Antitrust enforcement in the medical services industry: what does it all mean? *Milbank Memorial Fund quarterly/health and society* 1980; 58(1): 89–124.
16. Pertschuk, M. FTC Conference, 1977, Jun 1–2. Quoted in: Rosoff, A. J. Antitrust laws and the health care industry: new warriors into an old battle. *Saint Louis University law journal* 1979; 23: 478. Also quoted in Ballentine, T. H., Jr. Annual discourse—the crisis in ethics, anno domini 1979. *New England journal of medicine* 1979; 301: 634.
17. Relman, A. S. Professional directories—but not commercial advertising—as a public service. *New England journal of medicine* 1978; 299: 476–478.
18. Christians, C. G., Schultze, Q. J., Simms, N. H. Community, epistemology, and mass media ethics. *Journalism history* 1978; 5: 38–41, 65–67.
19. Schultze, Q J. Professionalism in advertising: the origin of ethical codes. *Journal of communication* 1981; 31: 64–71.

Study Questions

1. Why does the author feel that there would be greater benefit to society by considering medicine a profession rather than transforming it into a business?
2. What are the net gains or losses to society by allowing physicians to advertise?

PART III

Business Ethics

It is difficult to imagine any sphere of American life that is so often and so consistently the target of moral assault than business. Yet the formal, academic study of ethical values in business—business ethics—has appeared only in recent years. It is not fully accepted, at least by the academic community, even today. To many, the very phrase "business ethics" seems to many to be nothing more than a simple contradiction in terms.

Actually, it is surprising that it has taken this long to formulate. For even the idea of economic survival itself reflects a set of philosophical and ethical commitments. This, of course, is the concept of capitalism that erupted in the nineteenth century in Europe and England. It is this system that Dickens attacked in *Hard Times* and *Dombey and Son*. It is, too, the system and the slavery it spawned that Dickens attacked without mercy in *American Notes*. It is the social system that Veblen rejected in *The Theory of the Leisure Class*.

Another philosophical system, socialism, holds to the opposing view, that the government should guarantee a minimally adequate living. This too has had its assaulters, critics most recently from the cradle of socialism itself by such authors as Solzhenitsyn in *Cancer Ward, August 1914* and other works.

It should be no shock, therefore, to learn that during the last decade the intensity of interest in the subject of business ethics has surprised even the most ardent defenders of the movement to study them. It is easy for a practitioner to become ecstatic over such developments. But the fact is that the movement stands at a crossroads. The key to success is dependent upon a multidisciplinary approach that relies on cooperation among faculty in the academy and in business. This will ensure a mix of theory and practice.

Yet it's not so easy as that. One obstacle to this is a credibility gap of long standing. Business itself is too often thought to be *un*ethical.

It is hardly surprising that many have noticed the problem. I hear often from my students that insofar as businessmen have any ethics at all, they twist ethical ideals to suit their particular needs, as the occasion demands. Whether this is true or not is, of course, debatable. And even to the extent that it is true, such ethical sins are surely a direct result of market pressures not to mention sheer survival. Often, the company that plays it strictly by the ethical rules simply cannot survive the competition. But the negative portrait can be overdone: most companies do not go out of their way to be unethical. Certainly most corporate officers do not go out of their way to harm anyone. Indeed many corporations, especially those dealing with dangerous products, do go to unusual lengths to protect both workers and the public. (Mobil is a notable example.)

Whatever the reality, business—large or small—is a pillar of the American way of life. To some extent, they are even synonomous: business *is* America and, increasingly, the world.

All well and good: Indeed, some may wonder what all the fuss is about. We all know what is ethical and unethical: Why do we need special courses in "business ethics?" Surely, some will say, the principles of ethics—such as "treat people as ends and never merely as means" and "do not cause unnecessary harm"—apply in nearly every aspect of life, and in every nation and culture.

But most of ethics requires a more specific grasp of the practices in which human beings participate. The rules of one activity are often very different from that of another.

Yet even with this renewed interest in ethics and business, much remains to be done along a variety of lines and approaches. Very little has been done, for example, to find out what business has done to build values into their organizations. In a survey of 1984 "Fortune" 1000 industrial and service companies, the Center for Business Ethics reveals some facts regarding codes of ethics, ethics programs, boards of directors, and other areas where corporations might implement ethical codes. Based on the survey, the Center for Business Ethics believes that corporations are beginning to take steps, while recognizing that in most cases more enforcement is needed.

From the religious perspective, work needs to be done along theological lines. Some, such as Professor De George, have already taken bold steps. Others, like Paul Camenisch, have taken up the challenge as shown by his excellent article, "On Monopoly in Business Ethics: Can Philosophy Do It All?" In this essay, he suggests that theological ethics can provide a uniquely different perspective on business ethics. In a similar vein, Brian Sullivan in "Laborem Exercens" has argued for an examination of business ethics using Pope John II's encyclical "Laborem Exercens" as a framework. (See the comment on De George below.) Theological ethics is concerned with the good life. De George has criticized such approaches, while John Leahy has suggested, in "Embodied Ethics: Some Common Concerns of Religion and Business," that a revisionist model of theology can avoid De George's criticisms and make fruitful contributions to business ethics.

Perhaps the fundamental problem is that the field of ethics as defined by the philosophers of the past five centuries is too abstract to do justice to business.

In this anthology some attention has also been given to the ethical problems involved in dealing with Third World countries. Professor De George, who is one of the few philosophers in recent years to give some attention to this problem is again turned to. Some other topics in business ethics discussed in this work include corporate responsibility and punishment, the nature of business ethics itself, the ethical role of the corporation in other nations, preferential hiring, worker's rights, advertising, government regulation of business and the teaching of business ethics.

Jeffrey Burkhardt, in "Business Ethics: Ideology or Utopia," points out that for some thinkers—e.g., Marxist critics, all "justification" or defense of the ethics of this-or-that business practice is little more than a thinly veiled defense of the "oppressive capitalist superstructure." And among the philosophers Burkhardt discusses is De George, so the latter's paper should be read first. Also, Burkhardt briefly mentions "whistle-blowing," so it would be helpful to look at Professor Elliston's more extensive paper on that topic. (It is also the case that virtually all business ethics analyses are subject to the critique Burkhardt provides, including the pieces in this anthology.) Professor Burkhardt's tactic is to admit there is a "kernel of truth" in this view, while yet proposing a conception of business ethics, following the views of Mannheim, that he believes can lead to a useful and socially beneficial system of business practice in the near future if individuals take action right now.

It is difficult to critique this piece, as so much of it is speculative—as, indeed Burkhardt himself admits. Burkhardt has faith that, through the actions of committed individuals, a humane and just society can be brought about.

Kenneth Goodpaster is one of the giants in business ethics, well-known for his acumen in applying concepts from other disciplines to the problems of business ethics. And in his essay, "Toward an Integrated Approach to Business Ethics," he does not disappoint. The essay offers an interpretation of accountability in business ethics on three scales or levels of analysis—the person, the organization, and the economic system. Inasmuch as the author discusses the question of what, precisely, "business ethics is," his paper should be studied in conjunction with Burkhardt's essay. As Professor Goodpaster relies to some extent on the work of Gewirth, Professor Allen's paper should also be studied with it. Finally, in the spirit of this anthology's intention to link the various branches of professional ethics with one another, the reader should find it enlightening to study Goodpaster's paper along with Professor Elliston's paper, since the latter extends the brief analysis of "whistle-blowing" that Professor Goodpaster gives.

Utilizing innovative work in mathematics on "fractals," Goodpaster suggests both descriptive and prescriptive implications of this conceptual model. Relationships of this model to recent literature in business ethics are indicated, as well as its classical roots. Professor Goodpaster invites theorists and practitioners alike to expand and apply the ideas presented with a view toward future research.

His paper is ingenious and daring, so far as Goodpaster tries to "map" an important concept from mathematics onto business ethics. How useful is it? Some of the suggested possible applications are difficult to see. So far as ethical relativism is concerned, there seems to be no possible application, if one is talking about the classical and radical, nonpropositional account of moral language such as proposed by Professor Ayer in *Language, Truth and Logic*. Surely, if ethics does not consist of propositions as Ayer suggests, then one cannot have "universal" cross-cultural truths of ethics. This is an old-fashioned view of course, though still respectable in some quarters. But with a less radical kind of relativism—one which treats moral assertions as genuine propositions—Goodpaster may be on to something. However, since he admits these are merely suggestions for future research, any effort to answer it *à priori* here is rather pointless. Only time will determine whether the application of fractals will have the usefulness Professor Goodpaster believes they will. On the other hand, it would certainly be good to consider this claim in the context of Professor Allen's paper, who argues for the view that moral judgments can, indeed, be "universal," and, one would suppose, cross-cultural.

"Publicity and the Control of Corporate Conduct: Hester Prynne's New Image" is Professor French's much discussed proposal for an effective way of punishing corporations. In French's suggestion, a penal sanction for corporate wrongdoing can be imposed, based in the concept of shame which French calls the "Hester Prynne Sanction" [From, of course, N. Hawthorne's novel, *The Scarlet Letter*, which the reader should also study.]. Quite obviously, Professor Corlett's paper is the one to study in connection with this one, as it directly attacks the value of French's "Hester Prynne Sanction."

One of the great benefits of the "Hester Prynne" sanction, according to the author, would be its power to not only generate adverse publicity and social contempt, but as an incentive to generate the types of adjustments of policy necessary for the corporation to regain moral worth "both in its own eyes and those of the community."

One possible fundamental problem with French's view is his uncritical assumption that the corporation is a moral "person," which can, thereby, be expected to behave like a person, in that it will "feel" shame, be "embarassed," etc. It may well be that *individual officers* of the corporation might feel shame, but the corporation as an entity transcending the individuals within it, will not, whatever "feeling" shame might mean with respect to a corporation. (An excellent article relevant to this question, incidentally, is "Corporations, Persons and Moral Responsibility," which appeared in the journal *Thought* in the summer, 1986 issue.)

Questions of this sort, however, are taken up more completely by Professor Corlett in the next article in this anthology.

J. Angelo Corlett is a versatile philosopher who has published in various fields including ethics and the history of philosophy. He shows his erudition in "French on Corporate Punishment: Some Problems." In this paper he discusses French's argument that corporate-collectives found guilty of wrongdoing ought to be punished by an institutionalized form of adverse publicity. Since Professor De George also deals with the question of corporate responsibility and since both papers discuss corporate responsibility in foreign nations, both pieces should be studied together. (Interestingly Corlett seems to endorse, to some extent, the pessimism regarding the possibility of business behaving "ethically," and for similar reasons ideas expressed by Professor Eversluis.)

Corlett argues that there are at least eight reasons why the "Hester Prynne Sanction" is problematic. Even if French's premise regarding corporate-collective, moral personhood is granted, it does not follow that the "Hester Prynne Sanction" is an adequate way by which to punish corporate-collectives found guilty of wrongdoing.

If French's theory of corporate responsibility and punishment is plausible, then he must explain just how it is that his "sanction" provides an adequate technique of punishment to alter unethical corporate behavior.

Business Ethics: Ideology or Utopia?

Jeffrey Burkhardt

In more extreme versions of Marxist criticism of capitalist society, normative moral philosophizing is regarded as veiled apologetics. Talk of justice or rights or fairness is thought to be at best mystification, at worst insidious rationalization for a decadent social order, if that talk is not premised upon the destruction of capitalist society. Indeed, the work of philosophers and social scientists, theologians and other intellectuals in capitalist society is seen as having been pressed into the service of the capitalist class. Intellectuals have become ideologues, and their philosophies ideology. For the Marxist, ideologies must be rejected, or at least shown for what they are—an attempt by capitalists to maintain hegemony over the terms and conditions of social life.

Given this orientation, normative moral philosophizing about business ethics, or business social responsibility, has to receive the strongest of replies: Pigs! Ideologues! Lackeys! For business practice, in our era, is capitalism; and if general normative moral philosophizing under the capitalist order is insidious ideologizing, so much the worse must be talk of morals in business, or of ethical business practice.

It may be that no reflective critic of capitalism actually holds the extreme version of this position. But there is a range of criticism of the idea of business ethics, including skepticism about the whole idea and passive disdain for particular notions like that of corporate social responsibility, which may have some elements of the "dogmatic" view presented. In fact, it may be that even "right-wing" critics of business ethics could acknowledge an underlying "ideology-critique" in their positions. That is, the real reason why "business and ethics don't mix" is that talk of ethics is meaningless fluff, or a marketing strategy.

My aim in this paper is to utilize what I take to be the "kernels of truth" in the dogmatic view, and, borrowing from Karl Mannheim's analysis in *Ideology and Utopia*, present an alternative view of business ethics, or rather, of talk of business ethics. I wish to leave what I mean by the phrase "business ethics" somewhat open-ended for the moment, so that it can include any content in the phrase, "Business (or corporations, businesspeople, etc.) morally ought to ＿＿＿ ," *except* " . . . blow themselves up," or "close down," or "give all property to the people," and the like. What I wish to argue is that Mannheim's distinction between ideologies proper and utopian ideologies is useful for seeing talk of business ethics as implying a vision which is capable of realizing its content in practice. That is, business ethics is a Mannheimian utopia.

I. The Nature of Ideologies and Utopias

Despite difficulties which have been well-noted since the publication of *Ideology and Utopia*, Karl Mannheim's account of the function of ideologies in the development, legitimation, and maintenance of a society's institutions is particularly useful for understanding the talk about business ethics. In particular, the distinction between ideology proper and utopia has the advantage over an orthodox Marxist model in better accounting for how a system or set of ideas might come to have progressive force.

Ideologies proper are ideologies in the "standard" Marxist sense. A dominant political or economic or religious group utilizes institutions to promulgate its vision of the "ideal world." A number of factors including social instability makes institutionalization of this vision possible, since people, out of fear or anxiety, accept, or acquiesce in, the legal, moral, and ontological norms of the dominant group. Hegemony of the dominant group is secured by having the ideals embodies in institutional practice either so closely "resemble" actual institutional practices as to make the existing order "best by default." In both cases, little is done by the existing power-structure to actually implement the ideals in the institutions of society. Without an implementation plan, the ideology never succeeds in the concrete realization of what it projects as a vision of the ideal world, although it may succeed for a good while in securing the political-economic establishment in power.

What distinguishes a utopia from an ideology is that in a utopian ideology, this vision has "progressive force." While "representatives of a given order will label as utopian all conceptions . . . which *from their point of view* can in principle never be realized," both the content of and the political dynamics underlying *some* sets of ideas do have such capabilities. (*Ideology and Utopia*, pp. 195–99)

Utopias arise in response to the conservative force of the dominant ideology. A dominant vision which continues to reinforce its own legitimacy even though historical conditions have altered must face challenges. Some of those challenges may be met through force, some through stepped-up persuasion or "ideologizing," some through "repressive tolerance." But depending upon the fears, frustrations, and unfulfilled needs of people in a given situation, alternative idea-systems can arise which might even gain some "institutional" form. A new political party may be created; members of the establishment may become disaffected; information media representatives may find themselves talking and conducting themselves in ways inimical to the existing order. Most importantly, however, will the "out groups" begin to talk among themselves in terms of this new vision.

In Mannheim's analysis, one can judge the progressive force of this vision only after its institutionalization. However, given his model, we should be able to identify as utopian, ideologies which have emerged, but which have not yet reached their full realization in practice. There are four points or foci which follow from his analysis, which reduce, though not completely, the speculative nature of an answer to the question, "Is this ideology utopian?" First, the source of the ideology. Has it emerged from the dominant political group, or has it sprung up in response to the prevailing ideology? While utopias might arise from within a prevailing ideological framework, it is more likely that they come from without. Second, the content. Are the ideals "too realistic" or "too unrealistic?" Since these are tacks of a conservative ideology's self-maintenance, we should be careful if the ideals appear incapable of realization, or set sights too low. Third, institutional prospects. Could the ideology generate a different set of relationships if institutionalized? Would changes occur in conduct as well as attitude or belief? And finally, conflict resolution. Would institutionalization of the ideology precipitate conflicts both among individuals and within an individual, or would a basis be provided for conflict resolution? An ideology which fails to resolve both kinds of conflicts will fail to maintain itself for very long, let alone generate a "new order."

With these points in mind, we can, I believe, see how talk of business ethics has the marks of a utopian ideology.

II. Business Ethics as a Utopia

People who talk about business ethics are a diverse lot, as are the theories, analyses, orientations, methods, styles, etc., which go under the general heading "business ethics." Yet, I find three reasons to think that talk about business ethics forms a more or less coherent ideological orientation. (1) Nearly all business ethicists are involved in attempts to show how, with a suitable moral consciousness or with suitable legal or ethical constraints, business practice can be a morally acceptable thing for people to engage in. (2) Whatever normative foundation is given or assumed, nearly all business ethicists seem committed to an ideal of business social responsibility. And (3) most important, whether explicit in this regard or not, most business ethics talk has the characteristic of using what might be called "capitalist language" in a way which attempts to alter—and even undermine—the "ordinary meaning" of such language. We might put this a little differently by stating that business ethics talk is engaged in a game of persuasive definition—substituting new definitions for concepts "near and dear" to business practitioners, in order to affect changes in the way these practioners "see the world."

(1) Even a cursory review of the recent literature in business ethics will reveal the fact that most business ethicists are concerned with particular kinds of practices within the general context of business. Typically, moral arguments are offered concerning the unjustifiability of sex discrimination on the job, or the suitability of "whistle-blowing" under certain circumstances, or the prefer-

ability of the control of extreme pollutants becoming the responsibility of the polluting firm, and so on. What emphasis upon these various issues suggests is that the context in which they occur, namely, business practice—the practice of trade, sales, manufacture, profit-taking, etc.—is not fundamentally immoral or unethical. Granted, discussions of business ethics both in the literature and at meetings of the various institutes and societies concerned with business ethics occasionally include representatives of the "antibusiness" point of view. More often than not, however, even the apparently anti-business position is fundamentally probusiness: critics point to abuses, by large corporations of the business-government connection, of basically justifiable business practices.

This orientation toward business is reflected further in what appears a general attitude that despite the moral dilemmas that might arise for particular people involved in business, including problems of integrity, community responsibilities, role obligations, and the like, businesspeople can remain in business without completely sacrificing moral values or personal integrity. Businesspeople can be moral, that is, and still be businesspeople, although certain changes in particular courses of action or attitudes toward certain practices might have to occur. The nature of these changes, or of the constraints that might have to be placed on business institutions by governments, certainly vary from writer to writer, depending both upon the ethical orientation of the analyst and upon his or her assessment of the facts. Still, I think it not a gross generalization to say that the majority of business ethicists subscribe to a belief that business practice can be, or at least could be, a morally legitimate activity for people to engage in.

(2) I said that most, if not all, business ethicists seem committed to an ideal, namely, the social responsibility of business. There are two major problems with this claim. The first is that certain business ethicists, or more precisely, writers on business ethics, attempt to deny that business has any unique social responsibilities. Milton Friedman and Theodore Levitt immediately come to mind. The second problem is that some writers, notably Richard De George, want to separate moral and social responsibilities, and argue that while business (like everyone) has moral responsibilities, "social responsibility" is more correctly understood as including a range of options which business may or may not act

upon. That is, social responsibilities are not really *responsibilities*.

Friedman's argument is well known. He maintains that if firms attempt to maximize profits, using whatever means possible within the law and the limits of sound business judgment, they are in fact acting "socially responsibly." Since the purpose of business is to provide goods and services to consumers, and returns on investment to investors, any activities that a business could engage in which would not be strictly cost-effective are irresponsible. One might say that society charters business to be cost effective relative to consumers and investors. That's all there is to what business has to do.

What is interesting is that Friedman's argument has a decidedly utilitarian ring, despite the value of freedom which permeates his analysis. As such, the real argument is not that business has no social responsibilities, or very limited social responsibilities, rather, that it can't be shown that other socially responsible activities produce results as good as simply pursuing profits. But *if* it could be shown, either on a utilitarian or even an "enlightened egoist" basis, that, say, a more active role in internalizing externalities like pollution were cost-effective, then these other socially responsible activities could not be rejected by his position. In other words, Friedman doesn't seem to be against social responsibility, only skeptical of its extent. A factual argument would presumably change his mind.

Theodore Levitt's argument is more extreme. Levitt stresses the "Dangers of Social Responsibility," although he concedes that businesses do have two responsibilities, to "seek material gain and to respect the canons of civility." His main argument is that business social responsibility may have the effect of muddying the boundaries between business and the government, and in fact, may force a situation where both intrude on the other's legitimate "turf." But again, there is an interesting twist in Levitt's argument. Seeking material gain and respecting canons of civility are first of all, socially responsible things to do, á lá Friedman's "utilitarian" argument: and further, if certain precautions were in effect to better protect the respective "turfs" of government and business, certain business activities like refusing to deal with countries that indiscriminately kill porpoises while tuna fishing could be justifiable. So it seems that Levitt's argument is concerned only with the dangers of taking social responsibility too far, and not with denying that businesses do have, or ought to have, certain social responsibilities.

De George's argument is more difficult to deal with, precisely because he includes under the category "moral responsibility" a good many of the activities that others would categorize as social responsibilities. His argument is basically that we should not expect too much of business in regard to solving societal problems. Clearly business, like every person and other institutions in our society, has an obligation to "do no harm." But beyond providing the necessary goods and services for our economy, business has no *obligation* to "maximize welfare." If a firm voluntarily wants to advertise its products in not only nondiscriminatory, but in fact antidiscriminatory ways, so much the better for them. These kinds of things are, however, supererogatory.

The main point about De George's position is that he does not deny that there are social responsibilities, only that those things for which a business could be responsible are not always obligatory. There is a certain similarity in his approach to those of Friedman and Levitt—despite differing conclusions about the extent of social responsibility—in so far as it might always be shown that something which was previously not a moral obligation, though on the list of "social responsibility issues," is now a moral obligation. It is not exactly a utilitarian argument: rather, it is an historical argument. As circumstances change, or perhaps as information increases, we alter our obligations to correspond to the recognition of new harms we are causing. The point is that those harms are for the most part drawn from the list of things which business does affecting society at large, and for which a business could be responsible.

There are probably many others who appear to reject a strong notion of the social responsibility of business. I think, however, that these three positions represent the best "challenges." For the most part, business ethicists subscribe, explicitly, to a notion that business institutions have responsibilities or obligations to society, although the specific obligations may vary. Although a utilitarian or enlightened egoist framework can provide a justification for such responsibilities, the strongest justification comes from the "social contractarian" camp.

A number of authors now hold that business institutions, especially corporations since they are legally chartered, have a "contract with society." In return for legal protection, a certain status, money making, and so forth, corporations are responsible to keep harm production to the absolute minimum, while at the same time contributing to the maintenance of values within the community in which the institution operates. In some cases this may require limiting profit-making activities in order to protect the environment; in other cases, to positively contribute toward rectifying racial or sexual injustices which are not at all the result of the business' activities. Underlying both sorts of activities is the view that there are values which the community finds important enough to demand that all "members" of the community contribute toward actualizing, and that businesses and business institutions are members of the community.

It is actually this notion of businesses as "members of the community" which permeates all business ethics talk, even if not explicitly, and, in my judgment, even if the ethicist is not contractarian, utilitarian, or any other "denomination" of ethical theorist. This is what, in the final analysis, I see as most indicative of the commitment to the "ideal of social responsibility of business" which I am suggesting generally exists. At the very least, businesses have to *respond* to the community and the community's values, and are held accountable for actions within the community. In fact, it is the idea that business *ought* to be an active and circumspective member of a broader society which permeates business ethics talk. This is a positive ideal throughout business ethics talk, even if the extent of responsibility may differ among ethicists.

It is partly because of this positive ideal in business ethics talk that I believe it has the markings of a utopian ideology. Ideologies posit norms for conduct, define legitimate relationships and so forth. Talk of social contracts or social responsibilities or even of the effect of business practice on social and economic welfare begins to articulate those norms and definitions. We still have to decide whether such talk is sincerely meant. My belief is that it is, at least generally. There is a further aspect of business ethics talk which bears on the reasonableness of this belief, however, and that is the "ontology" of business ethics talk. For, if the world of business ethics retains so much of the capitalist language as to undeniably legitimate current practices, or if it posits ethical ideals totally incapable of realization, we should remain skeptical—or in my case, become more so.

(3) Talk about business ethics, or at least the proliferation of it, has emerged in an era of advanced capitalism. Perhaps business-people or capitalists have existed for all time; capitalism is now, however, the dominant form of social-economic relation, at least in most Western societies. And, even though talk of morals in trade or commerce appears in literature throughout the ages, it is only in recent years that a whole area of discourse called "business ethics" has emerged. One has to conclude that "something is up:" practices within the dominant form of social-economic relationship are being subjected to some measure of critical scrutiny.

There are two points related to the emergence and proliferation of business ethics that I want to focus upon. The first is the question of why such talk has grown at such a rapid rate. The second is why, if as I have suggested, business ethics talk is a utopian ideology, so much of business talk retains decidedly "capitalistic" language.

Atwell and Beardsley give three reasons for the emergence of business ethics talk. These are:

1. An increasing number of philosophers are coming to appreciate the value of making our discipline constructively available to those whose lives are chiefly focused on some form of practical activity.
2. Practitioners in various fields have for several complex reasons turned their attention to the ethical dimensions of their own activities.
3. There is a growing tendency of students to think of themselves as persons who do or will have certain occupational roles. (*Business Ethics*, pp. ix–x)

These seem fairly typical of explanations offered throughout the business and professional ethics (and even general applied ethics) literature. And on the surface, they seem true, although (3) is less an explanation for the emergence of a concern for ethics than an explanation for the emergence of a concern for practical and specialized courses and skill development. In any event, the problem with all three, but especially 1 and 2, is that they might attest to the truth of the "standard" Marxist explanation I began this paper by referring to. Why business ethics?

Because as capitalism increasingly finds itself in trouble as a social and economic system, manifest internally in stagflation, unemployment, lack of productivity, faltering urban economies, and externally by the attractiveness of socialist alternatives to peoples of the Third World, some "new" ideology appears required. The ideology of laissez-faire capitalism, of the meritoriousness of the entrepreneur, of the Horatio Alger success story, and the beneficence of the huge corporate conglomerates, no longer seems to work. Thus, leaders in business and industry, and academic sycophants of the economic establishment, conjure up images of socially responsible business, of business as a noble enterprise, and harmonious intercourse among businesses, government, labor and consumers essentially to shore up the position of the capitalist elite.

This is a crucial point, but there are basically two replies. The first is that for the most part challenges to capitalism are met not with ideological pronouncements of the latter sort; instead, there is only more fervent recourse to the traditional ideological position. In the face of faltering urban economies, business and government leaders invoke the idea of "free enterprise zones." Lack of productivity and unemployment are met with notions of harder work, retraining, and entrepreneurship. Socialist challenges in the Third World are decried as external—i.e., Soviet—interference in the free working of the indigenous political-economic system, i.e., the market system. Not only is no "new" ideology officially invoked, the old one is paraded even more strongly before the public. Witness Reaganomics.

Second, and more important, the ideas of socially responsible business and morals in the workplace do have, at least in the minds of some of those promoting the vision, serious critical foundations. Some business ethicists outside of the business establishment, even if still employed in colleges and universities receiving funding from corporate sources, challenge the fundamental assumptions of business practice while in the very process of talking to businesspeople, or researching materials for corporations. How many do this, would, of course, be a matter for empirical investigation, *if* the information concerning the critical foundations for work in business ethics were even forthcoming in the first place. Simply put, despite appearances, notions of social responsibility in business can be extremely critical of even fundamental notions such as profit, entrepreneurship, or competition.

But the move from "appearances" to "reality" is always a tricky, even dangerous, one. The language of business ethics makes my last claim tricky in this very way. Arguments to the effect that the corporation is a "moral agent" and not simply a legal fiction, for example, seem to smuggle connotations of "respect for persons" into "ordinary" discourse. Conjunctions like "Ethics, Free Enterprise and Public Policy" suggest an essential compatibility of morality and the political-economic institutions of capitalist society. Even in a mandatory "criticisms of capitalism" section in business ethics texts, there is a conspicuous lack of serious discussion about noncapitalist political-economic systems. Where, for instance, does one find an in-depth discussion of Yugoslavia or China or Zimbabwe or of traditional Native American economic relationships? Business ethics' concern, it has to be concluded, is with maintaining *categories* of life in capitalism, by using the language of capitalist relationships, and by refusing to take seriously alternative visions of human relationships and social institutions.

But again, I think this is incorrect. The terminology of business ethics talk is decidedly capitalistic in appearance. To say this is not, however, to say that the meaning, the concrete content, of such talk is as it appears.

Consider, for example, talk of respect for employee rights in the workplace, or for more employee input into decision making, or for ESOPs (Employee Stock Option Plans), or for pregnancy leave that may take as a given the primary function of the firm, profit maximization. The "best" arguments in favor of such measures, at least from the business perspective, are "increased productivity" arguments. What is interesting is that if norms specifying these measures were taken seriously, the quality of the workplace would be transformed; and it just might turn out that the primary focus of the workplace shifts from profit maximization to "humanization-maximization." It is in fact almost *despite* the productivity arguments that "respect for human dignity" enters the workplace under such arrangements. Similar kinds of shifts in meaning occur in such notions as the "social audit." Presumably a cost-benefit accounting device, the social audit smuggles into cost-benefit analysis notions of respect for the environment, antidiscrimination, improved quality in products and services delivered to the public.

Discrepancies between what might be called the "surface structure" and the "deep structure" in business ethics talk should not be overestimated. Still, underlying much of the talk are notions of individuals as members of a broader community; of corporations as public trusts and public trustees, of workers and management as equal sharers in the transformation of materials and time into useful commodities and services for human consumption and so on. One might even go so far as to say that talk of business ethics, despite its capitalist appearance, is fundamentally socialistic, meaning not politically or economically designed to promote Socialism, but rather, reflective of an underlying assumption that business, or, perhaps better termed, "commerce," is at base a social activity, implying ideals of community, global family, ecological interdependence.

It is with this interpretation of the real significance of the "capitalist" ontology in business ethics talk that the utopian character of the ideology comes forth. Consider again the four focal points for discerning ideologies from utopias in the present age: The Source. Business ethics may have supporters in the business establishment. Even if Atwell and Beardsley overestimate the importance of such talk within the business establishment or business schools, there are indications that managers, consultants, and even workers in corporations are interested in some of the concerns voiced throughout the "philosophical" business ethics literature. As I mentioned above, it is not impossible that some members of a dominant political-ideological power should come to hold beliefs inimical to the dominant ideology. But most importantly, it is "out-groups" who are increasingly demanding business social responsibility, humanization of economic activities, participation in corporate decision-making. Some black activists, antinukes, women's groups, and academic ethicists and social scientists are the most prominent sources of the "new" ideology.

Second, Content. I mentioned above that the content of business ethics talk includes norms which may require a very different set of behaviors and especially attitudes than those now actually practiced in business. Are these norms "too realistic?" I think not. To expect candor, honesty, sympathetic understanding and non-manipulation from, for example, an advertising concern, is to posit ideals for ethical practice the adherence to which would demand major changes throughout advertising practice. Are these ideals "too unrealistic?" Again, I think not. Demands for ethics in business, while stressing a deeper sense of community, or of recognition of the social nature of economic practices, can point to some actual manifestations of these in some business practice. Examples are probably clearer in smaller businesses, local establishments, local chambers of commerce, and the like. The point is that there are some already noticed, and at least partially actualized, ideals from business ethics talk in actual business practice.

Third, Institutional Prospects. The idea of business ethics, if institutionalized in business practice and social and governmental expectations, would radically transform the kinds of relationships, attitudes, and beliefs, of people both within and outside of business. Take environmental responsibility as an example. Business ethicists call for increased circumspection about the environmental impact of ordinary productive activities. Certainly some businesses have begun to institutionalize, through policy and corporate strategy, environmental responsibility. If we imagine responsibility of this sort becoming institutionalized across the board, the general climate of opinion and extrabusiness pressure would have to change. Needless to say, relationships between business and environmental groups, or between corporate executives and the EPA would have to change. And, of course, the environment would noticeably improve. This leads to the final point.

Conflict Resolution. Sociologists and moral philosophers often talk of the point of a moral theory or moral ideology in terms of its providing a framework for the settling of disagreement. I think that we can see that the institutionalization of the ideology of business ethics would indeed provide such a framework. On the one hand, the kinds of pressures and even litigation brought upon businesses by the government and citizen-action groups would "soften," or even disappear, if ethical responsibility were actualized in policy and practice. On the other hand, the climate within particular corporations would change from one of tension and rigid adherence to certain canons of competition, productivity, and "bottom line" performance to a more humane, probably less stressful, atmosphere. A good bit of the difficulty in maintaining an efficient and productive organization, organization theorists tell us, is the "moral climate" within the firm. Presumably that means that introducing more "morality" into the firm will cut down on the kinds of real and potential conflicts among interests which often do grind the productive wheels to a halt. Conflicts of personality, and even interpretation and expectation regarding others' behaving in accordance with moral standards may remain; such conflicts pale in comparison to the kind of competitive conflicts which mark contemporary business practice.

Admittedly, the above paragraphs contain some speculation. What I am getting at is, however, not at all speculative. I am claiming that there is progressive force in the notion of ethical practice in business which surpasses skeptical doubts about its utility or even its source. Interestingly, to borrow again from Mannheim's analysis, even if the original idea of business ethics were simply ideological, that the idea is capable of providing a framework for transforming business practice suggests that it is utopian, and in that fact, positive and progressive in its vision. It remains for us to reflect on the role of this utopian vision in current business practice.

III. Conclusion: Validating Utopia

A utopian vision fails when it simply cannot be acted upon; even with the best of intentions to act in accordance with its ideals, a person cannot actualize the vision. If this is so, a utopian vision must be said to be successful when it can be acted upon, when the best of intentions do help to bring its ideals into real practice. My final point is that it is precisely the "best of intentions" which present us with the possibility that the ideals of ethical, socially responsible, and humane business practice can be validated: those ideals can be acted upon.

In *Socialism, Utopian and Scientific*, Frederick Engels argued that utopians like Robert Owen had to fail to bring about thier vision of "no place:" if social and economic conditions are "ripe" for radical institutional and attitudinal changes, social reformers, social engineers, or even "incrementalists" would not be necessary. If conditions are not ripe, no amount of planning, engineering, or even reforming zeal would make them ripe. Scientific socialists, said Engels, document, study, trace the emergence of the conditions wherein major socioeconomic changes can occur. When they arrive, the scientific socialists "seize the moment." Only then can changes really work.

A similar argument could be made in regard to socially responsible business practice. Up until now, and even for a good while into the future, the conditions are not right for ethical business practice. Too many problems exist within business, within government, among businesses, and among governments. Too many problems exist among people even in more democratic—and hence more "ethically enlightened"—societies. Those with a clear vision of the just society, the humane society, have to wait until the actual conditions are more confused, contradictory, for a true revolution in institutions and attitudes to take place. Until that time, we should simply weather the dark ages.

But this argument is self-defeating, besides being naive. When it comes to institutions and social and economic conditions emerging, nature does not simply "take its course." For, it is through the actions of individual people, within groups of individual people, that society's course develops. To wait to seize the moment, is to fail to recognize that for any given vision of a better life, a possible life, the moment is always now. Marx wrote that it is the "concrete actions of concrete living individuals which make history." In this regard, we should be prepared to recognize, support, and take steps to further, those actions by concrete individuals, which seek to actualize and institutionalize the ideals of an emerging progressive ideology.

In the final analysis, a utopia remains but a dream if those whose intentions are "best" are not actively supported by those who are in a position to help clarify that vision, give credence to those intentions, and draw out in fullest detail the practical, institutional and attitudinal implications of the general "sense" of that vision. This, I suppose, is a challenge to the contemporary ideologue—to go beyond a simple "cultivation of his garden" to the kind of positive, visionary, and ultimately political action to which a utopian vision like that of humane, socially responsible, economic institutions in a society demands response.

REFERENCES

Anshen, Melvin. "Changing the Social Contract: A Role for Business," *The Columbia Journal of World Business* V, Number 6 (November–December, 1970).

Atwell, John, and Beardsley, Elizabeth. "Occupational Ethics Series Introduction," in N. Bowie, *Business Ethics* (Englewood Cliffs, NJ: Prentice-Hall, 1982).

Bowie, Norman, and Beauchamp, Tom. *Ethical Theory and Business* (Englewood Cliffs NJ: Prentice-Hall, 1982).

De George, Richard T. *Business Ethics* (New York: Macmillan, 1982).

Engels, Frederick. *Socialism, Utopian and Scientific*, in Marx, Karl and Engels, Frederick, *Selected Works*, Volume III (Moscow: Progress Publishers, 1976).

Friedman, Milton. *Capitalism and Freedom* (Chicago: University of Chicago Press, 1982).

Levitt, Theodore. "The Dangers of Social Responsibility," *Harvard Business Review* (September–October, 1958).

Mannheim, Karl. *Ideology or Utopia?* (New York: Harcourt Brace Jovanovich, 1936).

Marcuse, Herbert. "Repressive Tolerance," in Marcuse, Herbert, Wolff, Robert Paul, and Moore, Barringtón, *A Critique of Pure Tolerance* (Boston: Beacon Press, 1969).

Marx, Karl, and Engels, Frederick. *The German Ideology* (Moscow: Progress Publishers, 1976).

Stevenson, Charles. *Ethics and Language* (New Haven: Yale University Press, 1976).

Study Questions

1. Of what value is Burkhardt's distinction between a utopia and an ideology?
2. State why you agree or disagree with the author in his claim that some writers on business ethics, De George particularly, unjustifiably separate social and moral responsibilities.

Toward an Integrated Approach to Business Ethics

Kenneth E. Goodpaster

What are the practical limits of moral imagination and vision? Is there a collective or institutional ethic beyond the ethics of the individual? (McCoy 106)

The aim of this essay is to outline a framework or model for accountability in business ethics. To help motivate such an undertaking, I will sketch in *Part I* an overview of the field and then suggest some basic categories for classifying research.

Part II will go beyond classification toward an integrated approach to issues in the field. A geometrical analogue will be presented—the concept of a *fractal*—and it will be related to ethics with the help of a case study.

Part III will then draw out some of the theoretical and practical implications of "moral fractals," along with directions for future research.

Part I. Motivating the Model

There is today a growing network of educators in business ethics that includes not only philosophers and theologians, but also humanities scholars, social scientists, and managers—all of whom are as interested in applying practice to theory as they are in applying theory to practice. The discussion that follows is intended for this growing audience and seeks to develop a vocabulary for dialogue that is interdisciplinary without sacrificing precision and clarity of thought.

A Field Both Old and New

Interest in the subject matter of business ethics has, by most accounts, grown dramatically over the past two decades. Business managers, academicians, and the general public have come to appreciate in new ways the importance of the relationship between economic excellence and ethical judgment. Speculation abounds, of course, as to why this interest has developed: institutional self-examination after Watergate, the environmental movement, concern over employee rights, the increased number of working women, affirmative action regarding minorities, new challenges on the health and safety front, competition and comparisons with European and Asian business practices, and so on. Probably none of these factors is a sufficient explanation, but jointly they explain a lot.

Many of the concerns that are now being addressed under the rubric of "business ethics" were addressed during earlier decades under different names. Some were called "business and society." Others were called "human relations in organizations." Still others focused on "business-government relations" or "international business." There is, therefore, considerable *topical* continuity and history to what is now called business ethics.

If there is a new twist, it has to do with a more sustained and systematic push in the seventies and eighties for an application of the tools and concepts of the humanities. Whereas in previous decades, it was largely the social sciences (psychology, sociology, economics, and political science) to which management studies turned, we see today increasing attention to disciplines such as philosophy and theology. An awareness seems to be growing that there are as many untapped resources in the disciplines that focus on frameworks for ethical thought as in those that focus on individual and group behavior.[1]

Ethics: Three Ways of Thinking About Morality

"Ethics" and "moral philosophy" refer to a domain of inquiry, a discipline in which matters of right and wrong, good and evil, virtue and vice, are systematically (or at least carefully) examined, "Morality," by contrast, most often refers not to a discipline but to a pattern of thought and action "in place" in an individual or a group or a whole society. Thus morality is what the discipline of ethics is *about*—and business morality is what business ethics is about.

Understood in this way, ethical inquiry may take one of three forms: *descriptive, normative,* or *analytical*. It is useful to distinguish these forms not just to maintain precise terminology but because discussions that ignore their differences create confusion. A comment like "for Americans bribery is unethical but for others not so" illustrates how such confusion can arise.

If the intention is descriptive, the speaker would (correctly or not) be claiming that there are differences in moral beliefs about bribery across societies. If the intention is analytical, the speaker would (again, correctly or not) be saying something about the lack of an objective or crosscultural ethical standard. Finally, if the intention is normative, the speaker would be expressing a conviction about the moral unacceptability of bribery, at least for Americans. Any agreement or disagreement that we might have with the speaker, then, depends a great deal on how we understand the comment.

Much philosophical effort has been devoted in this country to the analytical form of ethical inquiry (also referred to as *metaethics*). Some have sought to make normative ethics objective by defining "good" and "right" in empirically verifiable terms. Others, convinced that such definitions involved an "is/ought" fallacy, found themselves unable to offer an alternative account of objectivity and lapsed into ethical relativism.

While a primary task of this essay will be analytical, in the sense of providing a *model* or *conceptual framework*, equally important are the descriptive and prescriptive tasks that it seeks to advance, i.e., understanding the values that can and should guide persons and organizations in the context of democratic capitalism as a socioeconomic system.

Moral Transactions: The Subject Matter of Ethics

If morality, as the subject matter of ethics, refers to a pattern of thought and action in the real world, what kind of pattern might this be? Following philosopher Alan Gewirth, we can say that morality has to do with *transactions* between "agents" and "recipients" in which

> what is affected is the recipient's freedom and well-being, and hence his capacity for action. Such modes of affecting in transactions can be most readily recognized in their negative forms: when one person coerces another, hence preventing him from participating purposively or with well-being in the transaction. (78)

At the core of morality, then, is the idea of a transaction between parties in which the freedom and well-being of each is at stake. One of the merits of this characterization is that it implies two importantly different functions for ethical reflection:

1) understanding the nature of the *parties* to moral transactions and the criteria for identifying members of each group (agents and recipients); and

2) giving critical attention to the *transactions* themselves (either prospectively or retrospectively), using frameworks such as those implicit in Gewirth's mention of the "freedom and well-being" of the parties.

Unforunately, the first of these two functions has been insufficiently explored by philosophers. There is a tendency to assume that the parties to moral transactions are easily identified or that ethical problems come prepackaged with respect to "agent" and "recipient." Since the conventional paradigm is one in which the parties are individual persons, e.g., "Cain strikes Abel," one could easily overlook the fact that an initial process of interpretation takes place, and that such a process might have ethical ramifications of its own. The moral point of view or conscience, after identifying Cain and Abel as relevant parties, moves directly to the challenge of evaluating the transaction between them.

Debates over the morality of abortion illustrate the importance of distinguishing these two functions of ethical reflection, for it becomes clear that a question of the first type—"Is the fetus a human life in the morally relevant sense?"—lies behind the question of the second type—"How are we to evaluate the taking of this life?"

Conventional wisdom about the parties to various moral trans-actions can be and has been called into question in recent years. Concerns about the environment as well as concerns about busi-ness and professional ethics have led many to ask: "What are the criteria for including something in the range of morally "consid-erable" recipients or in the domain of morally "accountable" agents? Who or what might count as considerable from the moral point of view? Obviously contemporary individual persons, but what about other possibilities: future persons? developing per-sons? animals? whole systems of living things? Such questioning is at the foundation of what is now called environmental ethics, and is leading us to a deeper understanding of the roots of Western moral thought.[2]

More important for present purposes is the question: What might count as an "agent" or morally accountable in the basic ethical transaction? Again, the conventional paradigm tells us that individual persons count. But what about organizations and na-tions or whole social systems? Are these not significant actors on the human stage and are they not in some sense "more than the sums of their parts (individual members)?" Might corporate or government policy decisions and various forms of resource allo-cation be thought of as "transactions" on an institutional scale?[3]

In the context of business ethics, what I have called the con-ventional paradigm has led many researchers to focus on business transactions (e.g., employment, production, investment, market-ing, accounting, etc.) without identifying the morally accountable parties in such transactions.[4] There is a danger, however, in re-lying solely upon this approach in defining our subject matter. We shall see that it can lead to a kind of myopia or narrowness of vision with respect to the full complexity of the issues involved.

Figure 1 depicts the basic moral transaction, labelling the class to which the agent belongs, the "domain of moral accountability" and the class to which the recipient belongs, the "range of moral considerability." It leaves open questions regarding who or what might belong to each of these two classes.

Mapping the Domain of Moral Accountability

While business ethics can and should include questions about considerability (e.g., Do organizations have rights?), primary at-

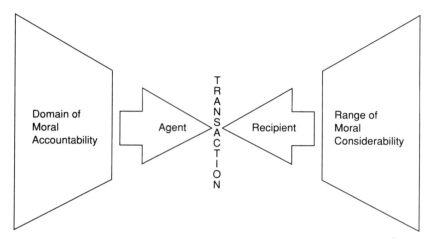

Fig. 1 Morality as a transaction.

tention naturally turns to the domain of moral accountability in exploring the conventional paradigm for business transactions. The three most plausible candidates for moral accountability are the choices and characters of *persons*, the policies and cultures of *organizations*, and the arrangements and ideologies of entire social *systems* (such as democratic capitalism).

Much if not all recent research in business ethics can be classified as descriptive, normative, or analytical with respect to issues on one of these three levels, though as we have seen, most writers use a more transaction-oriented classification scheme. The problem of "whistle-blowing" illustrates the ethics of the person, for example, and might be examined descriptively through case studies (How and to whom does it become an issue?), normatively through moral arguments (When is it right and when is it wrong?), or analytically through inquiries into meaning and justification (Can we define and defend it as a practice?).[5]

Issues such as employee rights, product safety, and environmental protection illustrate the ethics of the organization and, again, can be investigated along descriptive, normative, and analytical lines.[6] The ethics of the social system itself can come under scrutiny in the arena of international business practices such as questionable payments or exports of hazardous substances.[7]

Figure 2 depicts the distinctions so far discussed, arranging the levels of moral accountability to indicate a broadening of scope as one moves upward from the level of the person.

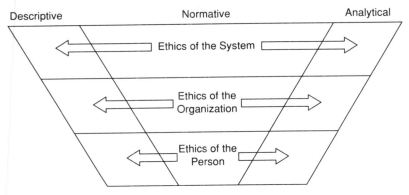

Fig. 2   The domain of moral accountability.

One senses in this multiplicity of issues and levels a somewhat disordered "state of the art" in the field of business ethics. Part II will outline a framework or model that not only helps to classify research in the field but also illuminates linkages between research efforts and results on different levels.

Part II. Explicating the Model

Metaphysics aside, we think naturally of the domain of players on the human stage as populated by several "levels" of accountability. The institutional structures that we both form and are formed by admit of meaningful description and evaluation in terms analogous to those applied to individual persons. Once we begin to move in this direction, however, we are moving beyond simply "classifying" problems and issues in the field of business ethics.

Beyond Classification

What might it mean to go "beyond classification" in the direction of a unified framework for business ethics? We get a hint about an answer to this question when we ask another: Might there be relationships among the three levels of moral accountability that contribute to our understanding of *each* issue or problem that we meet—much as when we look through different lenses on a microscope or camera, we reveal successive layers of detail and various kinds of kinship among them?

If so, then specific issues in business ethics might turn out to have several scales or levels of moral detail to them (system, organization, person). And we might inquire as to whether there were useful generalizations or patterns to be found from level to level for a given problem or kind of problem. One might seek not only to identify and address issues consistently on any given level, but also to relate the levels themselves in ways that might have implications for both philosophical understanding and management practice. Phenomena on one level might be expected to *illuminate* or even *explain* phenomena on other levels.[8]

Such an approach is what I will propose—going beyond classification in the direction of a unified framework by taking cues from a branch of contemporary mathematics: the theory of "fractals." I will argue later that this approach has significant heuristic value for the three kinds of ethical inquiry mentioned earlier: descriptive, normative, and analytical.

An Integrating Image: Fractals in Geometry

There seems to be wide consensus in the mathematical community that the inventor of "fractals" is Benoit B. Mandelbrot, whose original essays on the subject have been refined in his book *The Fractal Geometry of Nature*. Mandelbrot coined the term "fractal" a decade ago (from the Latin *fractus*: broken or fragmented) to refer to geometrical objects that have a unique property, unlike ordinary Euclidean curves. If you look at a circle, Mandelbrot explains,

> then look at it more and more closely, you will see a smaller and smaller segment of the curve and it will appear to become straight and straighter. There is no new structure in a circle at higher magnifications. It simply looks more and more like a straight line. But imagine a shape in which increasing detail is revealed with increasing magnification, and the newly revealed structure looks the same as what you have seen at lower magnifications. This shape is a fractal. (McDermott 112)

Not all fractals are strictly "self-similar" in the sense of being assembled out of smaller identical copies of themselves (like the classic "Koch Snowflake" in *Figure 3*, courtesy of B. Mandelbrot).

In some cases the similiarity is only statistical. Mandelbrot points out, for example, that

Fig. 3   A fractal produced by adding more and more triangles to the sides of triangles.

> the coast of Britain is not an exact copy of parts of itself. However, if you magnify a section of the coastline, it looks like a plausible piece of coastline from somewhere. Its pattern of wiggles is the same; there are the same number, roughly, of big wiggles and medium wiggles and small wiggles. In a statistical sense, it looks just like it did before. Just as a twig resembles a branch and a branch resembles the tree, each part of a fractal is like the whole. This property, that the statistical nature of the object remains the same if it is magnified, is known as statistical self-similarity, and it is very common indeed in nature. (Prince 48)

The concept of a fractal, sketched here in only the most elementary terms, has opened up new vistas in science and mathematics for two basics reasons: *manageability* and *explanatory utility*. By manageability, I mean simply the technical capacity to generate representations of hitherto "chaotic" phenomena—to see them as possessing an unexpected regularity:

> Until recently, scientists believed that the only shares that were useful in science were those simple Euclidean shapes, lines, planes, and spheres; all else was chaos. There was order and there was disorder. Now there is order (simple shapes), manageable chaos (fractals) and unmanageable chaos. (McDermott 115)

By explanatory utility I mean that fractal geometry often enables us to predict the behavior of natural objects better than conventional constructs. Mandelbrot believed that fractals described nature better than any Euclidean shapes and he set out to prove it:

> (Mandelbrot) scavenged problems that scientists had swept under the rugs of their disciplines, problems that did not fit conventional thinking. He characterized price jumps in the stock market, turbulence in the weather, the distribution of galaxies, the flooding of the Nile, even the length of coastlines. (McDermott 114)

The contexts in which the theory of fractals has found application, therefore, are many and varied—including meteorology, geography, metallurgy, computer science, and economics. While I have been unable to discover any previous applications in the field of ethics, it is my hope that in the future such an idea will not seem strange. The suggestion of this essay is that the notion of a fractal has as much power in the context of moral subjects as in the context of natural objects.[9]

Giving Meaning to "Moral Fractals"

To clarify this latter suggestion, and thus to give meaning to the notion of a "moral fractal," three features of our geometrical analogue need to be emphasized. Each represents a condition or requirement for the transferability of the notion of a fractal to the field of ethics.

(1) The first feature is that our ordinary intuitions about space permit mathematical objects to have similar properties at various "scales"—and therefore to be *self*-similar. While this may seem obvious for geometry, it is less obvious in the domain of moral accountability and therefore deserves special notice.

It is necessary for the intelligibility of moral fractals that ethical attributes be meaningful at different "scales" (person, organization, system). Without some constancy of meaning across levels of attribution, similarity between levels cannot be defined. And without the availability of similarity as a relation among levels, the idea of fractal self-similarity cannot be understood.

Thus concepts like "right" and "wrong," "good" and "evil," "responsible" and "virtuous," must have analogous meaning as applied to moral subjects on the personal, organizational, and systematic levels. Otherwise the fractal comparison cannot even get a foothold.

This way of thinking is already implicit in our use of persons, organizations, and systems as units of analysis in social scientific description and explanation. It is not only logically possible, but often quite illuminating, to view them as agents in transactions with other persons, organizations, and systems, particularly when they manifest symptoms of rationality and self-interest. We speak, for example, of the goals and purposes of individuals like Tom and Mary, the interests and strategies of organizations like IBM, and the directions of entire social systems including nations and groups of nations (e.g., "the West").

I have argued elsewhere that it is meaningful to attribute general moral characteristics to organizations by analogy with individual persons.[10] Extending this line of thought to social systems by analogy with organizations, of course, requires certain qualifications (having to do with the sense in which such systems can be "managed" as unified wholes), but raises no insurmountable obstacles.

(2) The second feature of our geometrical analogue that needs emphasis is that it is a theory about "full-scale" objects. That is, while it is possible to distinguish between scales from the point of view of the scientific observer, objects come packaged in nature with all scales in place at once.

The corresponding feature of moral accountability is illuminating, for it represents a condition (in fact satisfied) that persons, organizations, and systems do not come separated neatly in real life. They are inevitably and inextricably linked. A moral fractal is a complex reality made up of persons-in-organizations-in-systems that manifests more or less self-similarity with respect to a given set of ethical characteristics. It is not enough in trying to understand problem situations to focus on individuals or organizations or systems in isolation from one another. This point will be clarified further in the next section with the help of a case study.

(3) The third feature of our geometrical analogue that should be emphasized is that not all fractals are strictly self-similar. One should not interpret the claim that certain persons or organizations are parts of moral fractals to mean that precisely the same attributes will be found in one that are found in the other. It may be that the attributes are only remotely similar—or indeed it may be that they are not similar at all, but *eventually will be* given the playing out of certain social or psychological dynamics.

In the context of moral accountability, this last feature of fractal geometry requires that we be able to make sense of partial similarities as well as tendencies toward congruence from one level to another. That this condition is satisfied can be seen from such observations as the following by psychiatrist M. Scott Peck, writing of the infamous massacre at My Lai:

For many years it has seemed to me that human groups tend to behave in much the same ways as human individuals—except at a level that is more primitive and immature than one might expect.

Why this is so, Peck says, he does not know. But he adds:

It is an extremely important question, deserving great thought and research. It is an issue not only specific to group evil in general—as if that were not enough—but crucial to the understanding of all human group phenomena, from international relations to the nature of the family. (216)

Up to this point, we have been exploring the meaningfulness of the notion of a moral fractal in terms of three key features of its geometrical analogue. These features add up to the simultaneous presence in real world situations of different levels of moral accountability and different degrees of self-similarity. Let us now enrich this somewhat abstract analogy with the help of a case study, and then (in Part III) explore some of its philosophical and managerial implications.

Moral Fractals in Business Ethics: A Case Study

Consider the (disguised but real) case of John Reed, president of the Food Products Division of Diversified Industries, Inc., a large multinational corporation headquartered in Atlanta, Georgia:

It had been a very profitable year, but Reed was under pressure to misrepresent his division's financial success by asking several major suppliers to bill him in advance for amounts totalling $1 million in future goods and services. This would reduce profits just enough to make his division's goal for the year, while not encouraging corporate headquarters to increase the goal too much for next year. Forty percent of Reed's compensation, as well as the compensation of a significant number of his best managers, depended upon the bonus allocated for achieving the division's annual financial goals.

Each year Reed was expected to sign a document attesting to his compliance with Diversified's Code of Ethics, a code that explicitly mentioned honest financial reporting. Nevertheless, he was aware that his ambitious counterparts in other divisions understated their income regularly as a kind of "savings account" for future success.

What, and on what level, is the ethical problem in this case? It is possible to view the case as a study in the ethics of the person—John Reed—as he struggled to maintain his integrity in the face of significant pressures to compromise. It is also possible to view it as a study in the ethics of the organization—Diversified Industries, Inc.—as it sought to encourage both ethical behavior and dependable growth through a management incentive system. On still a third level, it is possible to view the case as a study in the values and competitive dynamics of capitalism itself: large and small investors guide their resource-allocation decisions by the quarterly and annual earnings reported by large organizations.

To ask "On what level is the ethical problem in this case?" is, in a sense, to do violence to the moral reality of the situation. It is to look at the level structure depicted earlier in *Figure 2* from a classificatory rather than a fractal point of view. A full understanding of John Reed's problem and meaningful suggestions for resolving it demand that we look at the issues on all three levels at once and that we see the relationships between them. The "problem" does not *exist* on only one level—any more than objects in nature exist on only one "scale"—even though they must of course *present* themselves to us at a given scale.

Thus it would be accurate—but misleading—to say that this is a case about whistle-blowing, or about corporate management incentive systems and ethical codes, or about the values implicit in capital markets. In reality, it is a case about all three—and about their "connectedness." What is more, we can see certain structural similarities on each level of moral accountability; the person, the organization, and the system each confront circumstances in which "breaking ranks" in the name of ethical values could be costly. We cannot fully understand the moral transactions (and hence responsibilities) in this case until we see them as resonating through several levels of moral accountability.[11]

Part III. Some Implications of the Model

I shall call the strategic or methodological principle that I am proposing here the "Moral Fractal Principle" (MFP).[12] In its simplest form it can be stated as follows:

(MFP) Persons, organizations, and social systems can usefully be
seen from the fractal point of view as aspects of self-similar coalitions
of moral accountability.

Just as many phenomena in nature can usefully be seen as
complex unities which copy themselves when one enlarges or
reduces their scale, the MFP asserts that certain ethical "patterns"
reappear in the domain of moral accountability at the "scale" of
the person, the organization, and the system as a whole. Morally
accountable "coalitions" in transactions, like "players" in game
theory, can be understood and analyzed similarly on multiple
levels—not in "perceptual" space, as with geometrical fractals, but
in "conceptual" space.[13]

To try to set out the full implications of the fractal point of view
in business ethics would take us beyond the scope of this essay,
but we can get a sense of its heuristic value for three primary
groups whose interests in the field are significant—social scientists, managers, and ethical theorists. The perspectives of these
groups, it should be noted, correspond roughly to the branches
of ethical inquiry mentioned in Part I—descriptive, normative,
and analytical.

In the three sections that follow, I will discuss some of the
implications of the MFP for these branches of inquiry—touching
upon directions for future research. No attempt will be made to
be comprehensive in these discussions; rather, the purpose is to
indicate the fertility of the notion of a "moral fractal" for each
branch. Such fertility is, in the end, the strongest argument for
any methodological principle.

The Social Sciences

The MFP has two general implications for the *descriptive* study of
business ethics, carried on largely by the social sciences. First of
all, it supports certain broad similarities in research methods across
persons, organizations, and social systems. Sociologist Philip Selznick has observed that

> the study of institutions is in some ways comparable to the clinical
> study of personality. It requires a genetic and developmental ap-
> proach, an emphasis on historical origins and growth stages. There
> is a need to see the enterprise as a whole and to see how it is

transformed as new ways of dealing with a changing environment evolve. As in the case of personality, effective diagnosis depends upon locating the special problems that go along with a particular character-structure; and we can understand character better when we see it as the product of self-preserving efforts to deal with inner impulses and external demands. In both personality and institutions "self-preservation" means more than bare organic or material survival. Self-preservation has to do with the maintenance of basic identity, with the integrity of a personal or institutional "self." (141)

Selznick's point has been echoed in other quarters and applied even more directly to quasimoral characteristics in Robert Axelrod's game-theoretic study of cooperation. Axelrod writes:

> The emergence, growth, and maintenance of cooperation do require some assumptions about the individuals and the social setting. . . . Actually, these requirements (for recognition and recall) are not so strong as they might seem. Even bacteria can fulfill them by interacting with only one other organism and using a strategy which responds only to the recent behavior of the other player. And if bacteria can play games, so can people and nations. (174)

Both Selznick and Axelrod reinforce the suggestion of the MFP that categories such as "self-preservation" and "cooperation" display empirical similarities from person to organization to system. Further research is needed that focuses directly on the moral aspects of such characteristics as perception, reasoning, coordination, and implementation.[14]

The second general implication of the MFP for social-scientific research goes beyond similarities of *method* from one level to another and focuses on the *connections* between empirical findings on each level. Once we understand that John Reed (in our case study) is faced with a personal moral dilemma and that Diversified Products, Inc. is also faced with an organizational moral dilemma, we can explore the relationships between them.

If we generalize from individual cases, and pursue *causal* regularities, it becomes natural to ask such questions as whether capitalism as a system confers virtues or vices on the organizations and institutions that comprise it; and whether the organizations and institutions that comprise it confer virtues or vices on the persons that work for them. Similar questions might be raised in the reverse direction (from persons, through organizations, to the system itself).

Research of this sort has been conducted during the past decade by psychoanalyst Michael Maccoby, for example, who suggests that certain character traits of responsible executives are selected against by the "psychostructure" of many corporations leading in turn to effects on the overall character of the organizations themselves.

Some of the questions in this branch of inquiry to which the MFP naturally gives rise are:

What are the most reliable "indicators" of the various moral characteristics in which we are interested at each level?

To what extent do the moral values of managers and employees at various levels in the organizational hierarchy influence the moral values of the organization as a whole—and conversely?

To what extent do the moral values of organizations of various sizes in various sectors influence the moral values of the system as a whole—and conversely?

What are the mechanisms by which ethical "accommodation" takes place between individuals and an organization, between organizations and a system, and among systems in a global social economy?

The research challenges that lie ahead here will involve understanding patterns that more conventional research agendas would overlook. Selznick's observations over 25 years ago still apply, especially if we interpret "diagnosis" (if not "therapy") in ethical terms:

> In approaching these problems, there is necessarily a close connection between clinical diagnosis of particular cases and the development of sound general knowledge. Our problem is to discover the characteristic ways in which *types* of institutions respond to *types* of circumstances. The significant classifications may well depart from common-sense distinctions among enterprises according to whether they perform economic, political, religious, or military functions. . . . Students of personality have had similar objectives and have made greater, although still very crude, efforts to get away from common-sense rubrics. Yet, despite theoretical difficulties, real progress has been made, and clinical success in diagnosis and therapy lends confidence to the larger scientific quest. (142)

In summary, the MFP does have both methodological and substantive heuristic value for the study of business ethics by social scientists. Let us now turn to the most concrete purposes that such studies might serve, the normative decision making of managers themselves.

Business Administration

We have seen that "moral fractals" both merit and encourage further social-scientific inquiry. But business managers must make and act upon *normative* ethical judgments about right and wrong, good and evil, virtue and vice. What implications and heuristic value might the MFP have in the executive suite?

A number of contemporary observers of management have expressed the view that human values are increasingly becoming a part of the business of business. The extraordinary popularity of the book *In Search of Excellence* by Peters and Waterman is some testimony to the wide following that such a view possesses. Another well-received book, *The Art of Japanese Management* by Pascale and Athos, expands on the point:

> Two forces are at work: employees seeking more meaning from their jobs and demanding more concern from the corporation, and legislative pressures enforcing a broad range of personal services, including employee rights to counseling. (193)

Management that is responsive to these forces will give special attention to the formulation and implementation of corporate policies for securing "shared values" among employees. The MFP suggests that this process may be analogous to the process that system-level regulators face in dealing with corporations. If so, then corporate executives might consider a kind of "Golden Rule" in order to avoid ethical dissonance: "Regulate internally as you would be regulated externally—no more but no less."

A related point about dissonance is that very seldom is it possible in an administrative situation to "do just one thing"—so that conflict and internal inconsistency must be guarded against. Policies may not only conflict with one another at a given level (as in the case of the incentive system and the ethics code at Diversified Industries) but they may interact from one level to the next as well (e.g., ethical "anarchy" in the name of toleration leading to organizational amorality).

The MFP suggests that the policies governing ethical decisions for the organization as a whole should be similar to the policies governing the ethical behavior of individuals and/or the larger system. In other words, the normative ethical role of the administrator may involve not only the avoidance of conflict on or between levels but the more positive task of developing a set of moral principles or "superordinate goals" for the organization analogous to those he or she would define and defend for an individual or conversely. To quote Pascale and Athos again:

> What is needed in the West is a nondefined, nonreligious "spiritualism" that enables a firm's superordinate goals to respond truly to the inner meanings that many people seek in their work—or, alternatively, seek in their lives and could find at work if only that were more culturally acceptable. (193)

Some of the questions in this arena to which the MFP naturally gives rise are:

Is it desirable for a chief executive to try to articulate a statement or formulation of a corporation's moral beliefs, especially if they run the risk of disadvantaging the company with respect to one or more of its many constituencies?

What are the most effective techniques for implementing such a statement (if desirable) to foster an ethical environment in the corporation (management succession, hiring policies, reward systems, organizational structure, etc.)?

What is an appropriate degree of "value tolerance" in an organization, avoiding both indifference and dogmatism?

What is an appropriate degree of "value tolerance" in a social system, made up of organizations and institutions?

Leadership in administration has a profoundly normative aspect to it that reaches from the level of the organization to both the person and the wider social system. Managers who ignore this aspect of their role do so not only at their own peril but at the peril of those—either within or outside—whose lives are touched by the corporation. Selznick summarizes this line of thought eloquently when he writes:

> The lesson is this: Those who deal with the more obvious ideals—such as education, science, creativity, or freedom—should more fully recognize the dependence of these ideals on congenial though often mundane administrative arrangements. On the other hand, those who deal with more restricted values, such as the maintenance of a particular industrial competence, should be aware that these values too involve ideals of excellence, ideals that must be built into the social structure of the enterprise and become part of its basic character. In either case, a too ready acceptance of neutral techniques of efficiency, whatever their other merits, will contribute little to this institutional development and may even retard it. (141)

The MFP, then, in addition to its heuristic value for descriptive ethics in the realm of business, offers normative guidance for those who struggle with the legitimacy and content of the administrative point of view.

Ethical Theory

We turn now to ethical theory, which, while it includes some of the normative concerns of the previous section, embraces as well the conceptual foundations of moral thought. Here we discover that the MFP has deep classical roots and that Plato long ago appreciated (and presupposed) it in his discussion of justice (*Republic*, Book II). The language is richly suggestive in the context of fractals:

> SOCRATES: This investigation we are undertaking is not easy, but requires keen eyesight. As we are not very clever, I think we should adopt a method like this: if men who did not have keen eyesight were told to read small letters from a distance, and then someone noticed that these same letters were to be found somewhere else on a larger scale and on a larger object, it would be considered a piece of luck that they could read these first and then examine the smaller letters to see if they were the same.
> FRIENDS: That is certainly true, but what relevance do you see in it to our present search for justice?
> SOCRATES: I will tell you. There is, we say, the justice of one man, and also the justice of a whole city. And a city is larger than one man. Perhaps there is more justice in the larger unit, and it may be easier to grasp. So if you are willing, let us first investigate what

justice is in the cities, and afterwards let us look for it in the individual, observing the similarities to the larger in the smaller.

Plato's strategy in the above passage represents a rather direct application of the MFP to the problem of analyzing the concept of justice. Similar moves might be made with respect to other key moral concepts such as responsibility, virtue, rationality, and respect—as well as into the *conditions* presupposed by such concepts, such as unity of consciousness, centralization of control, perception, freedom, action, etc.

Beyond the heuristic value of the MFP for the analysis of moral concepts and their conditions, however, we can begin to see its value for deepening our understanding of certain recurrent "conundrums" in ethical theory. Four such issues have been the topic of much discussion in the twentieth century:

Ethical Relativism. Can there be a cross-cultural standard of moral judgment based on certain universal human characteristics? Or are we reduced to either moral imperialism on the one hand or what one author calls "moral isolationism" on the other? What are the organizational and systemic analogues to this problem in the context of multinational corporations and are they related?[15]

Ethical Egoism. Is it possible to provide a satisfactory account of rationality that incorporates nonegoistic elements such as respect for others? How would such an account test against competitive dilemmas in game theory: Is the problem of egoism present in the same way at each level of moral accountability?[16]

The Naturalistic Fallacy. Does the temptation to supply a reductivistic "definition" of the moral point of view manifest itself at each level of moral accountability? Can we see in the tendency of corporations to substitute various "stakeholder" interests for conscience an analogue to this temptation? If so, does the organizational analogue afford any insight into the issue on the personal and systemic levels?

Collective Responsibility. How are we to understand the attribution of responsibility (in various senses of that term) to individuals and collectives? Does one imply or exclude the other?

In connection with the last mentioned issue, it is perhaps worth mentioning that the MFP may help resolve recent debates over the implications of ascribing moral responsibility to corporations. Some have argued, for example, that if we were to take the notion of corporate (let alone systemic!) responsibility seriously, we would either be logically or morally forced to ignore individual or personal responsibility—that attribution of responsibility at one level precludes attribution at the other.[17]

If we take the fractal point of view, however, we can see that there is no pressure in the direction of exclusivity as we attribute moral characteristics across levels. Indeed, fractal geometry (in contrast to Euclidean geometry) helps us to understand precisely how it is possible for characteristics at one level or scale to be present simultaneously at others without exclusion.[18] Recalling our case study, this translates into the observation that John Reed's personal responsibility for honest financial reporting is not removed by the acknowledgment of responsibilities on the part of Diversified Industries for ethical incentive policies or the attribution of responsibility to the social system for the regulation of capital markets.

We should note, in reflecting on the fundamental issues mentioned here, that the MFP stimulates new questions and points out new directions for seeking answers in ethical theory. It does this by forcing us to consider whether and in what sense corporations and social systems, like persons, can be regarded as agents and recipients in moral transactions. The answers to such questions are not simply logical truths about moral discourse. They have to do not with possible worlds but with the actual world in which we live out the moral life.

Nor are they *ontological* truths about individuals and organizations. The "furniture" of the moral world, like that in one's study, needn't be regarded as ontologically primitive or irreducible in order to be used for sitting, writing, storing information, etc. It serves its purpose if it helps one to get on with the business of living well. The ontological status of persons, corporations, and systems can remain open while ethical theorists explore the similarities and differences among the levels of moral accountability.

Thus the MFP suggests a kind of "metaphysics of morals," but without the trappings of logical or ontological ultimacy. It helps the ethical theorist to appreciate the multidimensional structure of practical problems that call for moral judgment.

Conclusion

This essay has sought to integrate moral accountability on three scales or levels of analysis—the person, the organization, and the economic system. Utilizing innovative work in mathematics on "fractals," I have suggested some of the implications of this conceptual model for social scientists, business managers, and ethical theorists. Linkages to recent literature in business ethics have been indicated, as well as to classical sources.

The concept of a moral fractal is *not* offered as a device for easy solutions to ethical problems. On this point, I am inclined to echo Mandelbrot's own words on the subject:

> Most emphatically, I do not consider the fractal point of view a panacea, and each case analysis should be assessed by the criteria holding in its field, that is, mostly upon the basis of its powers of organization, explanation, and prediction. . . . (3)

Nevertheless, the potential relevance of the Moral Fractal Principle to business ethics is dramatic. It presents an image of great heuristic power for understanding the multiple levels of moral accountability. This means that there may be a way to integrate the field—in the sense of providing researchable descriptive, normative, and analytical hypotheses—hypotheses that if false, will be interestingly false and if true will be importantly true. Theorists and practitioners alike are invited to expand and apply these ideas with a view toward an integrated approach to business ethics.

REFERENCES

Axelrod, Robt. *The Evolution of Cooperation*. New York: Basic, 1984.

Barry, V. *Moral Issues in Business*. Belmont, CA: Wadsworth, 1979.

Beauchamp, T.L. *Case Studies in Business, Society, and Ethics*. Englewood Cliffs: Prentice, 1983.

Beauchamp, T.L., and N. Bowie, *Ethical Theory and Business*. 2nd ed. Englewood Cliffs: Prentice, 1983.

Bowie, N. *Business Ethics*. Englewood Cliffs: Prentice, 1982.

Braybrooke, D. *Ethics in the World of Business*. Totowa, NJ: Rowman and Allanheld, 1983.

Davis, Morton D. *Game Theory: A Nontechnical Introduction*. New York: Harper, 1970.

De George, R. *Business Ethics*. New York: Macmillan, 1982.

DesJardins and McCall. *Contemporary Issues in Business Ethics*. Belmont, CA: Wadsworth, 1985.

Donaldson, T. *Case Studies in Business Ethics*. Englewood Cliffs: Prentice, 1984.

————. *Corporations and Morality*. Englewood Cliffs: Prentice, 1982.

Donaldson, T. and P. Werhane, *Ethical Issues in Business: A Philosophical Approach*. 2nd ed. Englewood Cliffs, Prentice, 1983.

Evans, W. *Management Ethics: An Intercultural Perspective*. Hingham, MA: Martinus Nijhoff, 1981.

Ewing, D. *Do It My Way or You're Fired!* New York: Wiley, 1983.

————. *Freedom Inside the Organization*. New York: McGraw, 1977.

Gewirth, Alan. *Reason and Morality*. Chicago: U of Chicago P, 1978.

Goodpaster, K. "Commentary." *Business and Professional Ethics Journal* 2.4 (1984): 100–3.

————. "The Concept of Corporate Responsibility." *Journal of Business Ethics* 2.1 (1983): 1–22. Also in T. Regan. *Just Business*. New York: Random, 1984.

————. *Ethics in Management*. Boston, MA: Harvard Business School Case Services, 1984.

————. "From Egoism to Environmentalism." *Ethics and Problems of the 21st Century*. Ed. K. Goodpaster and K. Sayre. Notre Dame: U of Notre Dame P, 1979: 21–35.

————. "Morality and Organizations." *Ethical Issues in Business*. Ed. T. Donaldson and P. Werhane. Englewood Cliffs: Prentice, 1983: 137–45.

————. "Morality as a System of Categorical Imperatives." *Journal of Value Inquiry* (1981): 179–97.

————. "On Being Morally Considerable." *Journal of Philosophy* 75 (1978): 308–?

Hoffman, W., and J. Moore. *Business Ethics: Readings in Corporate Morality*. New York: McGraw, 1983.

Jones, D. *Doing Ethics in Business*. Cambridge, MA: Oelgeschlager, Gunn & Hain, 1982.

Ladd, ?. "Corporate Mythology and Individual Responsibility." *Journal of Applied Philosophy* 2.2 (1984): 1–22.

Lodge, G.C. *The New American Ideology*. New York: Knopf, 1979.

Maccoby, Michael. "The Corporate Climber Has to Find His Heart." *Fortune* (Dec. 1976): 98–101.

————. *The Gamesman*. New York: Simon, 1976.

————. *The Leader*. New York: Simon, 1981.

Mandelbrot, B. *The Fractal Geometry of Nature*. New York: Freeman, 1983.

Matthews, JB., K. Goodpaster and L. Nash. *Policies and Persons: A Casebook in Business Ethics*. New York: McGraw, 1985.

McCoy, Bowen, H. "The Parable of the Sadhu." *Harvard Business Review* Sept.–Oct. (1983): 106.

McDermott, Jeanne. "Geometrical Forms Known as Fractals Find Sense in Chaos." *Smithsonian* (November 1983): 110–7.

Midgley, M. *Heart and Mind: The Varieties of Moral Experience*. New York: St. Martin's P, 1981.

Novak, M. *The Spirit of Democratic Capitalism*. New York: Simon, 1982.

Pascale, R. and A. Athos. *The Art of Japanese Management*. New York: Simon, 1981.

Peck, M. Scott. *People of the Lie*. New York: Simon, 1982.

Peters, T. and R. Waterman, Jr. *In Search of Excellence*. New York: Harper, 1982.

Prince, S.D. "On the Mind of Dr. Benoit Mandelbrot." *Computer Pictures* (May–June, 1984): 46–52.

Regan, T. *Just Business: New Introductory Essays in Business Ethics*. New York: Random, 1984.

Selznick, P. *Leadership in Administration*. New York: Harper, 1957.

Solomon, R.C. and K. Hanson. *Above the Bottom Line*. San Diego, CA: Harcourt, 1983.

Stone, C. *Where the Law Ends: The Social Control of Corporate Behavior*. New York: Harper, 1975.

Velasquez, M. *Business Ethics: Concepts and Cases*. Englewood Cliffs: Prentice, 1982.

————. "Why Corporations Are Not Responsible for Anything They Do." *Business and Professional Ethics Journal* 2.3 (1984): 1–18.

Werhane, P. *Persons, Rights, and Corporations*. Englewood Cliffs: Prentice, 1985.

Westin, A. *Whistleblowing!* New York: McGraw, 1981.

Williams, O. and J. Houck. *The Judeo-Christian Vision and the Modern Corporation*. Notre Dame: U of Notre Dame P, 1982.

NOTES

1. Some notable examples of recent texts, anthologies, and casebooks are: Bowie, *Business Ethics*; DeGeorge, *Business Ethics*; Donaldson, *Corporations and Morality*; Barry, *Moral Issues in Business*; Beauchamp and Bowie, *Ethical Theory and Business*; Des Jardins and McCall, *Contemporary Issues in Business Ethics*; Donaldson and Werhane, *Ethical Issues in Business: A Philosophical Approach*; Hoffman and Moore, *Business Ethics: Readings and Cases in Corporate Morality*; Regan, *Just Business: New Introductory Essays in Business Ethics*; Williams and Houck, *The Judeo-Christian Vision and the Modern Corporation*; Velasquez, *Business Ethics: Concepts and Cases*; Werhane, *Persons, Rights, and Corporations*; Beauchamp, *Case Studies in Business, Society, and Ethics*; Donaldson, *Case Studies in Business Ethics*; Goodpaster, *Ethics in Management*; Matthews, Goodpaster, and Nash, *Policies and Persons: A Casebook in Business Ethics*.

2. For further discussion of the range of moral considerability, see Goodpaster, 1978 and 1979.

3. For further discussion of the domain of moral accountability, see Goodpaster, "Morality and Organizations," and "The Concept of Corporate Responsibility."

4. An examination of the tables of contents of the books listed in footnote #1 will confirm this point. Also see Braybrooke, *Ethics in the World of Business*; Jones, *Doing Ethics in Business*; and Solomon and Hanson, *Above the Bottom Line*.

5. See Westin, *Whistleblowing!*; Maccoby, *The Gamesman* and *The Leader*.
6. See Ewing, *Freedom Inside the Organization* and *Do It My Way Or You're Fired!*; also Stone, *Where the Law Ends: The Social Control of Corporate Behavior*.
7. See Evans, *Management Ethics: An Intercultural Perspective*. Also see Heilbroner, *Business Civilization in Decline*; Lodge, *The New American Ideology*; and Novak, *The Spirit of Democratic Capitalism*.
8. One is reminded here of Hume's relations of resemblance, contiguity, and causality (*Treatise*, Book I, 4).
9. See Mandelbrot, especially Chapter XII, for connections between fractal geometry and certain base themes in classical philosophical and scientific thought.
10. Goodpaster, "The Concept of Corporate Responsibility."
11. Greater detail on this and several other case studies that invite ethical analysis from a fractal point of view can be found in Goodpaster, *Ethics in Management*.
12. Readers of Goodpaster, "The Concept of Corporate Responsibility" will see in the MFP a generalization of what I there called the "Principle of Moral Projection" (see §8). Readers will also see that a corresponding "Fractal Principle of Moral Considerability" might be developed on the other side of the transaction in *Figure 1*. The seeds for such a corresponding principle were planted in the essay "From Egoism to Environmentalism."
13. One might view the "level independence" of the notion of a "player" in game theory as an illustration of the relevance of the fractal point of view to nonmoral studies of decision making. See, for example, Davis, *Game Theory: A Nontechnical Introduction:*

   The word "player," incidentally, does not have quite the meaning one would expect. A player need not be one person; he may be a team, a corporation, a nation. It is useful to regard any group of individuals who have identical interests with respect to the game as a single player. (xvi).

14. See Goodpaster, "The Concept of Corporate Responsibility" §§6, 7, 9.
15. See Midgley, *Heart and Mind: The Varieties of Moral Experience*.
16. See Axelrod; also see Goodpaster, "Morality as a System of Categorical Imperatives."
17. See Velasquez. "Why Corporations Are Not Responsible for Anything They Do," and "Commentary" article by Goodpaster in the following issue of the same journal.
18. Arguments like the following from a recent article by Philosopher John Ladd can thus seem to be flawed: Just as Greek mythology relieved individuals of responsibility for their actions and projected it onto the gods, so also the corporate mythology enables individuals to abdicate their responsibility for collective action and to "project" responsibility instead onto the corporation.

In the same journal issue, see a reply by Goodpaster, "Testing Morality in Organizations", 35–8.

Study Questions

1. Explain in your own words what Goodpaster means by the "Moral Fractal Principle." (MFP)
2. Do you think corporations could operate with the same moral "shape" (principles, values) as ordinary persons? Why? Why not?

Publicity and the Control of Corporate Conduct: Hester Prynne's New Image

Peter A. French

Perhaps the most quoted line in the long history of the discussion of corporate criminal liability is attributed to Edward, First Baron Thurlow, Lord Chancellor of England. The line is:

> "Did you ever expect a corporation to have a conscience, when it has no soul to be damned, and no body to be kicked?"[1]

Baron Thurlow was concerned with how to effectively punish a corporation that had committed a serious crime even though corporations cannot be thrown into jail and the cost of large fines can often be passed on to consumers. This is an important issue because the idea of corporate criminality will be an empty one if the law has no effective means of punishing a corporation that has been found guilty of a criminal violation, and the courts have been busy lately in hearing corporate criminal cases.[2] ("Corporate crimes" are not to be confused with crimes perpetrated by managers, accountants, etc., against their own corporations but, as I use the term, are those offenses that involve general corporate policy or decisionmaking, e.g., the manufacture of defective, life-threatening products, pollution of the environment, wrongful death in certain airline disasters, antitrust violations, and price-fixing.)[3]

347

Baron Thurlow's dictum is cemented in the foundation of the retributive views that, by and large, sustain our penal system. The firm hand of retribution, with its biblical "eye for an eye" authority, still commands the high ground of our thinking about the punishment of criminals,[4] and I think that it should. If a corporation has no body to kick (leaving to God the business of souls and eternal damnation), how can it retribute its felonious behavior? It has no eye to be exchanged for an eye it has blinded by unsafe working conditions. It has no neck to stretch for the wrongful deaths it has caused in product explosion. Or so the story is meant to go.

Retributivism, however, does not have to be understood in biblical bloodlust terms. Repayment need not always be made in kind. Capital punishment in the case of human murderers, for example, has in many jurisdictions been replaced by life sentences that carry possible parole stipulations, and the old Anglo-Saxon notion of *wergeld* is frequently utilized in settling wrongful death suits. The price of a human life may not always come cheap, but it is being set by the courts and paid by corporate offenders or their insurance carriers.

The idea that a corporation can pay a fine or a set sum to the relatives of its victim in a homicide case and thereby expiate its guilt is, however, regarded by many people as an affront to justice.[5] After all, the price of such punishment can be written off as another cost of business and, in the normal course of events, be passed on to the consumers of the corporation's products or services. Certainly, a whole corporation cannot, as Baron Thurlow knew, be tossed in jail. But, if the crime is a truly corporate one, it will also be an affront to justice to punish any individual employee or manager to director when such persons usually can demonstrate that they did not have the relevant intention nor the required capacities to constitute the *mens rea* required by the law for successful prosecution.[6] Vicarious liability or guilt by association in these instances is hardly likely to satisfy the demands of justice. Frankly, very few of these cases are really reducible to individual negligence, let alone intention or recklessness.[7] Most of the existing penal options such as license or charter revocation are usually ineffective. Fines and forced closings frequently hurt those who are the least closely associated with corporate decisionmaking, namely, low-level employees and stockholders.

Stockholders, of course, are protected by SEC regulations, and if they suffer from corporate punishment, that is a risk they undertook when entering the market. Often stockholders benefit from the undetected crime and may do so for a period of time. I see no reason why they ought not bear some of the burden of punishment. The stockholder, after all, is free to trade his or her holdings in the market and is never assured of a clear profit. Also, the stockholder might consider pressing a civil suit against the corporation that cost him or her a significant value in stock due to its criminal behavior. A class action suit by stockholders who claim damage under such conditions could have a second level retributive result. And if the corporation were forced to pay stockholders for losses due to corporate crime, additional deterrent aims of punishment might be accomplished.

Heavy fines, as we know, are likely to be recovered from the consumer in the form of higher prices. The limit to that practice, however, is set by the marketplace. The exceptions would be in public utilities or in other monopoly or semimonopolistic enterprises where consumers must deal with the criminal corporation or forego the service. Such corporations are generally regulated by goverment agencies, and pricing increases to offset penalties could be prevented if those agencies act in the best interests of the community at large.

It should also be mentioned with respect to the harming of innocent employees that when a human being is convicted of a felony and punished, his or her family and dependents are frequently cast into dire financial straits. The harm done to them, though they may be totally innocent of any complicity in the crime, may in fact far outweigh that done to the incarcerated felon. After all, the convicted criminal receives three meals a day and lodging. The family may be reduced to penury and find that meals are only a sometime thing, and then hardly nutritious. In many jurisdictions, little or no official interest is paid to these innocent sufferers. Why should it be paid to employees who work for offending corporations?[8]

Returning to the efficacy of punishment, the fining of corporations is just not perceived by the corporate world as punishment comparable to incarceration of the human felon. Therefore, many believe that at least as a practical matter and regardless of whether punishment is morally justified, corporations should not even be subject to the criminal law.[9] Such a view, however, is remarkably shortsighted and, worse yet, can lead to a number of socially unacceptable outcomes. If, as earlier noted, we can only punish individuals, and if we must do so in a defensibly just fashion, then many offenses must go unpunished because the offense will be peculiarly corporate. We will then lose an important avenue of social control over the most powerful institutions in our social system.

We are, however, not as restricted or unimaginative as many have been assumed. I propose to commend an alternative corporate punishment—adverse publicity—though I must stress that in isolation from other available sanctions (e.g., fines, probation orders), the punishment I have in mind will not likely have the full reformative or deterrent effects a concerned citizenry would desire. In some cases it will best be used only to augment other sentences, but in many cases it may have all of the desired punitive effects, retributive and deterrent.

The moral psychology of our criminal legal system surely is guilt-based.[10] Guilt historically is viewed as a form of debt either to the specific victim harmed or to the society as a whole. To expiate guilt, the guilty party must repay. Hence, the fine system. Punishment is an institutional vehicle of repayment and restoration. When the debt is retired the original *status quo* is restored. The Latin *debitum* in the Lord's Prayer and in Matthew 18:27 is translated in Old English as *gylt*. The substantive sense of *gylt* as debt is usually treated as the primary sense of the term. Hence, the popular expression "paying one's debt to society." There are, of course, a number of things one can do with debts that one cannot do with guilt. For example, debts can be transferred, guilt cannot. The family of the deceased may be bound to pay his outstanding debts, but they do not assume his criminal guilt.

Our notion of guilt, because it so directly associates with law violation, is a threshold notion. Either the defendant in a criminal case is guilty as charged or not guilty. Guilt is a minimum maintenance notion. Guilt avoidance involves meeting very basic standards of behavior. As should be expected, guilt-based moralities are statute-dominated and the primary concern is to be in a state of nonviolation. The spotlight is on the drawing of the boundaries of acceptable behavior, at the minimal level.

In contrast to a guilt-based morality, certain societies, and in part our own, emphasize development and maintenance of personal worth and image in comparison to exemplary models of behavior. In such moralities the central notion is shame rather than guilt.[11]

In a shame-based morality, evaluation of behavior is not made against rules or laws that set minimal constraints. Moral worth is measured against role or type models. Do you remember how your mother or your grandmother ingrained this type of morality in you? "Act like a human being, only a pig would do that," or "your brother or sister would never behave like that." To feel shame or to be shameful a person must come to regard one's behavior as having fallen below or short of what is expected of or associated with the role, station, or type to which one belongs. The feeling of shame is the feeling of inadequacy or inferiority.

A crucial element in a shame-based morality is stress on the individual's self-conception as measured against ideal models that are accepted by the person as appropriate to that individual's way of life. (Shame, by the way, is much more of a biblical notion than guilt, both in the Old and New Testament.) Shame is a visual concept. Its root meaning is to cover one's face or hide. It relates to the way one is seen, the way one's actions look to oneself and to others. Interestingly, the language indicates that being without any shame is not a respectable thing, while being guiltless is. That is because shame depends on a sensibility to oneself. The most dangerous persons are the brazen incorrigibles who, in Zephaniah's words, "knoweth no shame."[12] To be unaffected by shame is to be antisocial and, worse than that, to have no concern for self-image. Shame operates in the field of honor and self-respect rather than being associated with meeting legal and social obligations.

An adept penal system, I should think, would be one that could induce shame when there has been a notable incongruity with the accepted models and could utilize the visual and media capabilities of the society to heighten the awareness in the offending individual or corporation, as well as the community at large, of a serious discrepancy between actual behavior and the identity or image thought to be possessed or projected.[13] Importantly, shame cannot be purged by repayment. Shame is not translatable to debt. It is not a matter of paying a fine and restoring the *status quo*. To regain one's sense of worth, to reclaim one's desired identity, the shameful person must act in positive, creative, and even heroic ways so that he or she may again feel and be seen as worthy. Often the shameful persons must go well beyond what is ordinarily required to again value themselves. The greater the shame the more extraordinary and prolonged must be the behavior that reestablishes worth. Our current penal system only incidentally, accidentally, produces such a response in an offender. But there is a form of punishment that specifically derives from the concept of shame and that may again be utilized in this country: the Hester Prynne Sanction. Recall *The Scarlet Letter?*[14]

> The penalty thereof is death. But in their great mercy and tenderness of heart, they have doomed Mistress Prynne to stand only a space of three hours on the platform of the pilory, and then and thereafter, for the remainder of her natural life, to wear a mark of shame upon her bosom. "A wise sentence!" remarked the stranger gravely bowing his head. "Thus she will be a living sermon against sin."[15]

The Hester Prynne Sanction surely is not directly a monetary penalty. Adverse publicity, however, could contribute to the achievement of monetary deterrent and retributive effects by costing the corporation business when customers refuse to purchase products or services, but that cost may be negligible and so not constitute a real repayment for the crime. When applied to a corporate offender it threatens the company's prestige, its image.[16] The Hester Prynne Sanction, in fact, will be effective only if the criminal either or both regards social stigmatization as a matter of grave concern, or is concerned with personal moral worth, i.e., is not shameless. For the Hester Prynne Sanction to really work, the offenders must regard themselves as having acted disgracefully, as having significantly reduced their status in the community by their behavior. The criminals must think of themselves as unworthy of the kind of respect and consideration they previously enjoyed, as having fallen short of what can be legitimately expected of them. They must come to view the sanction as a legitimate damaging blot on their reputations; as a mark of their failure; as an exposure of their moral shortcomings; as an indicator of the disgust of others; as a signal that they must rebuild their identity.

The Hester Prynne Sanction is particularly suited to corporate offenders, because image and reputation are at the very heart of modern corporate life.[17] Little sustained success has ever been enjoyed by a company with a bad reputation. Official censure is not an inconsequential matter when corporate achievement depends on communal standing. In fact, the Hester Prynne Sanction might be far more effective in dealing with corporate offenders than with human criminals.

It is worth noting that in a recent study of seventeen major corporations that have suffered adverse publicity over an offense or serious incident (though such publicity was not court-ordered), executives at the middle and higher levels of management reported that loss of corporate prestige was regarded as a very major corporate concern.[18] Indeed, the loss of prestige was regarded as far more serious than the payment of a fine.

For a corporation to survive it simply must garner and nurture a good image among the constituents of its marketplace. Furthermore, framing a corporate punishments in terms of adverse publicity orders is more likely to minimize the kinds of unwanted externalities that plague the kinds of sanctions now used by the courts against corporate offenders.[19] It is noteworthy that the U.S. National Committee on Reform of Federal Criminal Laws in their 1970 *Study Draft* supported use of something that sounds remarkably like Hester Prynne. The proposal was this:

> When an organization is convicted of an offense, the court may in addition or in lieu of imposing other authorised sanctions . . . require the organization to give appropriate publicity to the conviction . . . by advertising in designated areas or in designated media . . .[20]

Sadly, the Commission's *Final Report*[21] lacked this recommendation due to strong corporate lobbying. My argument is directed toward a revival of the basic idea.

The almost universal corporate aversion to a tarnished image is, however, insufficient by itself to ground the Hester Prynne Sanction as a penal device. "Bad Press" may be repugnant, but it is hardly penal and can be countered by corporate media campaigns intended "to put a different face on the matter." Quite simply, if this sanction is to be retributively penal, the convicted corporation must regard the adverse publicity to be not only noxious, but a justified communal revelation of the corporation's disgrace, its failure to "measure up."

Measure up to what? Against what standard, what model identity is a corporation to judge itself and be judged by the institutions of social order and justice? *The Scarlet Letter* provides only the structural or formal aspects of the matter. Hester is judged unworthy against a model of human fidelity that was deeply embedded in the puritanical society of early Boston. That model was understood and internalized throughout her community. It was not a product of law, though surely many of the Bostonian laws were derived from the same set of conceptions that engendered the model. In the eyes of Boston, Hester was not just guilty of lawbreaking, she should be ashamed. The willful breaking of law in itself does not generate shame. Very few people, for example, who are caught driving at 60 miles per hour in a 55 mile zone, under ordinary conditions, report feeling ashamed of what they have done.

We have throughout the centuries articulated human ideal models.[22] They are a part of our history, legend, education, religion, and literature. But there surely are corporate ideal models as well. The content of those models need not here be specified, though we should expect to find such features as being profitable, socially responsive, and humane in them. Each corporation, just as each human being, formulates its own conception of worth and associates itself with an ideal of behavior. Just as human beings are disposed to be the kind of persons they value, corporations are guided, at least in part, by an attempt to successfully realize the corporate images they have adopted and to be viewed by the community as having the characteristics of ideal corporate models. Public relations and advertising departments, of course, play focal roles in every corporation's attempt to establish and nurture its social standing and its exemplary image in the community.

The courts have both the authority and the social credibility to force persons and corporations to confront their failures, to live up to the ideals of their types. Court-ordered adverse publicity should provide an institutionalized revelatory apparatus, the modern substitute for the pillory, where the offender stands contemptible before the community, forced to confront the fact of his or her, or its, inadequacy. Shame is, after all, an identity crisis.

The exciting aspect of the Hester Prynne Sanction, however, is that the suffering of adverse publicity alone does not restore the offender to communal grace and relieve the shame. Only positive corrective acts can do that, as Hester proved by her exceeding good deeds. But look where this gets us: the imposition of the Hester Prynne Sanction on a corporation can institutionalize and broadcast a corporate offender's behavior, thus arousing the appropriate social contempt, an internal approbation, and it can be the spark to ignite the kind of adjustments of its operating procedures, policies, and practices that are required for that corporation to again appropriate the model identity and regain moral worth in both its own eyes an those of the community.[23]

The Hester Prynne Sanction might have significant retributive and deterrent effects on corporations, but as a primary penal device some have thought it prone to fail for a number of practical reasons. In the first place, as we all know, government is a rather poor propagandist.[24] It is not very persuasive, and very rarely is it pithy. (Have you ever seen a catchy piece of government-written prose that could rival the output of Madison Avenue?) For the adverse publicity sanction to have the desired *in terrorem* effects, and when used, for it to have a genuine impact on an offending corporation's established image, the court will have to employ clever writers and publicists, not the run-of-the-mill bureaucratic scribblers who crank out the government's literature. Courts also risk soiling their own images by descending to the Madison Avenue level in order to produce effective penal outcomes.

Such concerns can be easily addressed. Courts have the power to write their orders in such a way that the cost of the adverse publicity is paid by the criminal corporation from its own advertising budget to a competitive agency (other than ones that carry its accounts) which will then manage a campaign as approved by an officer of the court (perhaps a college professor trained in advertising and marketing). The corporation will have to submit its previous year's advertising budget to be used as a starting line, a percentage of the advertising budget will be set aside for the adverse publicity campaign, and that percentage will be carried through all annual budgets until the expiration of the order. In this way, even if the corporation increases its advertising budget to attempt to entice sales, it will have to pay a higher adverse publicity cost. The court-appointed overseer will instruct the agency to expend all funds in the adverse publicity budget annually and to do so in outlets roughly equivalent to those used by the usual corporate advertising agencies, e.g., the agency will not be allowed to place adverse publicity in obscure small-town newspapers if the corporation does not generally advertise in such ways. The private sector would then be actively engaged in the penal process, and a whole new respectable area of advertising will provide jobs and new paths of expression for the creative imagination to wander.

A frequently voiced second concern is that the level of anti-corporate "noise" in our society is so great as to devalue the effect of specific adverse publicity orders.[25] The newspaper editorialists, the campaigning politicians, the special interest groups, the conservationists, the Naderites, the assorted movie and TV actors and actresses with various causes all contribute to a confusing cacophony of charges that are usually indirect, often unsubstantiated, and certainly not properly adjudicated. Can this noise be controlled? Probably not, and it is not a good idea to pursue such a line in a free country. The corporations attacked in such ways have the option of legal action to counter unfair criticism. Against this noise, however, a well-developed adverse publicity campaign against a particular corporate offender, identified clearly as court-ordered, is still likely to draw attention. The public may never be very discriminating, but generally the fact that a court has ordered a certain publicity campaign as punishment for a particular criminal offense should pierce the shield of apathy behind which the public hides from the onslaught of ordinary corporate criticism.

It will be suggested that corporations can dilute the Hester Prynne Sanction through counterpublicity.[26] There is no denying the power of Madison Avenue agencies to create clever and effective image-building, even in the face of severe public or government criticism. But the sanction can be written in such a way, as suggested above, to offset any corporate counterattack. Furthermore, the court has the power to order the corporation not to engage in any advertising directed specifically towards rebutting or diluting the sentence. If the corporation were to promote its own case after having lost in court and having received an adverse publicity sentence, it would be in contempt of the court and sterner measures would be justified. Oil companies such as Mobil mounted effective replies to the charges leveled against them during the energy crisis. Also corporations after *Central Hudson Gas & Electric Corp.* v. *Public Service Commission*[27] clearly have First Amendment rights to express opinions on matters of public concern.[28] Corporate rebuttals to adverse publicity orders, however, are not necessarily protected by *Central Hudson,* and the Mobil commercials were certainly not attempts to minimize the effectiveness of any adverse publicity court orders. The oil companies were only charged in the court of public opinion, and the response was a totally appropriate defense in that venue.

The Hester Prynne Sanction may prove efficacious in fraud, public safety, and felony cases, but some doubt it can be equally effective in regulatory cases. Gulf Oil, it will be remembered, made illegal campaign contributions in connection with the Watergate scandals.[29] The publicity was profuse, but there is little evidence that it hurt Gulf Oil sales. There are two things that seem appropriate in response. The first is to point out that in the regulatory cases questioned adverse publicity occurred in the ordinary media coverage of the events. It was not court-ordered in lieu of or in addition to some other penal sanction, e.g., a stiff fine. In effect, it was incidental, and as the story faded from the front page or the first 15 minutes of the telecast, its intensity diminished. But it just may be the case that the Hester Prynne Sanction does not produce significant desired effects in the case of certain crimes. I make no claim that adverse publicity orders will always suffice to achieve the retributive or deterrent ends of the legal system. A mix of sanctions will undoubtedly be required. I would argue that adverse publicity orders are more likely than most other sanctions to produce what might be called rehabilitative outcomes, reformed corporations. Fines certainly are too easily assimilated to business costs.

The Hester Prynne Sanction, however, may produce much the same externalities as fines.[30] After all, if it is really effective, some say that it should lead to decreased sales, and the corporation's employees at the lowest levels could be made to suffer layoffs and other unwanted effects.[31] This should not overly concern us. Such externalities plague penal sanctions of all kinds. More to the point, however, the true question is whether the Hester Prynne Sanction is justifiable over the simple assessment of a fine when both produce basically equivalent externalities. I think that I have offered some firm reasons for the court to prefer, at least with regard to certain crimes, the Hester Prynne Sanction rather than or in addition to fines. The payment of a fine and the suffering of court-ordered and supervised adverse publicity are simply not equivalent punishment.

The celebrated case of *United States* v. *Allied Chemical Company,*[32] in which Allied Chemical was fined $13.24 million after a no-contest plea to 940 counts of pollution of the James River and other Virginia waterways, is often cited as an example of creative sentencing leading to the development of an alternative to the traditional sanctions.[33] The Allied Chemical fine was reduced to $5 million when the company agreed to give more than $8 million to the Virginia Environmental Endowment. Strictly speaking, the court did not order community service, but it did accept the company's establishment of the endowment as mitigatory. In another case, *United States* v *Olin Mathieson*,[34] the company pleaded no contest to the charge of conspiracy involving the shipment of rifles to South Africa. The judge imposed a $45,000 fine after Olin Mathieson agreed to set up a $500,000 New Haven Community Betterment Fund. (The maximum penalty could have been $510,000.)

Although neither of these cases really involved the imposition of a community service sanction (the defendants essentially wrote a check), some legal theorists have recently argued that the lesson learned in them indicate the desirability of providing the court with such a sentencing option.[35] There are certain practical problems with this approach that warrant only brief mention. Perhaps the most serious is that the corporation's costs in buying or performing community service are tax deductible charity contributions, and standard court-imposed fines are, of course, nondeductible. Legislation, however, could correct this deficiency.

It must also be realized that the performance of community service is a positive, image-enhancing action. It can be expected to elevate the public opinion of the criminal corporation. In fact, the results of corporate community service projects and charitable contributions are likely to make a rather favorable impression on members of society, while the reasons why the donor-corporation embarked on its apparently altruistic ventures are likely to be forgotten or lost in the outpouring of grateful sentiment. An obvious corrective for this difficulty, is to invoke Hester Prynne in conjunction with community service sentencing. Simply, the court can require that the service project be clearly identified as court-ordered as a penalty for a specific criminal offense. Every association drawn by the corporation to its beneficence would have to include an adverse publicity reference to its criminal conviction as the reason for the service.

Although community service does not seem to stand on a par

with Hester Prynne and the traditional sentencing options, should it be encouraged? I think there are reasons why its use should be very restricted and that is should never be used in isolation from other penal sanctions.

The socially conciliatory aspect of community service, the fact that such endeavors can restore lost prestige and polish tarnished images, makes such civic contributions a major avenue for corporations to regain status and acceptance lost through conviction and broadcast in accord with the imposition of a Hester Prynne sentence. A shamed company, as earlier noted, cannot simply buy its way back to social grace. It needs to perform especially worthy deeds to achieve restoration. Community service is cerainly a type of action it needs to perform to achieve such ends. But for there to be worth in the doing of such deeds, they must be voluntary. If they are performed under a form of duress, they are not actions of the person compelled to perform them. Insofar as none of our principles of responsibility capture them for that purpose, they do not accrue to the moral credit of that person. They would seem to be extended acts of the judge who decided to whom and how much. The convicted corporation is little more than an instrument of the court's conception of social need. A recent Nebraska sentence is a case in point. A corporation convicted of bid-rigging in highway construction contracts was ordered to donate $1.4 million to establish a permanent professional chair in business ethics at the state university.[36]

The community service sanction, when conjoined to Hester Prynne (ideally) or to a fine, can, however, have a certain morally desirable outcome, beside the fact that some good was done (the service was performed or the donation to a worthy cause was made), regardless of the reasons for its performance. Forced charitable deeds might serve to inculcate a habit of social concern in the corporation. At the very least, the sentenced corporation might come to view a continuation of community involvement as a way to curry future judicial favor. Aristotle maintained that a person is good by doing good deeds, by getting into the habit of doing such things.[37] A community service sentence could start a corporation on the path to virtue. Hence, there may be a rehabilitative value in the sanction despite the involuntary nature of the service performed by the convicted company.

There is, however, a notable amount of uncertainty that such an outcome will ensue from this type of sentencing. It does not seem likely enough to be a justifying reason to use the sanction. In fact, the best reason for a judge to order community service would be to achieve the charitable ends themselves. The rehabilitation of the offending corporation would seem to be an incidental upshot. Judges, however, are not necessarily in the best position to decide on our social or charitable needs. Furthermore, other than monetary or time loss, the penalty relationship of the sentence to the crime may be remote.[38]

All of these factors militate against the use of community service orders in corporate criminal cases, unless they are augmented by stiff fines and/or Hester Prynne. In comparison with the other discussed sanctions, adverse publicity, with its primary shaming function, would seem to be preferable on both practical and moral grounds. In any event, it is clear that there are effective and morally justifiable sentencing options (though community service is the least preferable) that support the inclusion of corporate entities among those persons who are subject to the criminal law. Baron Thurlow's demurral on the notion of corporate criminal liability may be set aside. Corporations are not only intentional agents, moral persons, they are proper subjects of the criminal law and all of its fury. They can be stigmatized and they can be "kicked" in ways comparable to those imposed on human offenders.

NOTES

1. The *Oxford Dictionary of Quotations*, 2d ed. (Oxford: Oxford University Press, 1966), 547.
2. See generally Marshall B. Clinard and Peter C. Yeager, *Corporate Crime* (New York: Free Press, 1980).
3. See e.g., Brent Fisse and John Braithwaite, *The Impact of Publicity on Corporate Offenders* (Albany: State University of New York Press, 1983), Chs. 2–18, 317.
4. See e.g., J. Murphy, *Retribution, Justice, and Therapy* (Boston: D. Reidel Pub. Co., 1979); R. Singer, *Just Deserts: Sentencing Based on Equality and Desert* (Cambridge, Mass.: Ballinger Pub. Co., 1979); A. Von Hirsch, *Doing Justice: The Choice of Punishments* (New York: Hill and Wang, 1976). But see John Braithwaite, "Challenging Just Deserts: Punishing White-Collar Criminals," *Journal of Criminal Law and Criminology* 73 (1982): 723–63.

5. See generally Victoria Lynn Swigert and Ronald A. Farrell, "Corporate Homicide: Definitional Processes in the Creation of Deviance," *Law & Society Review* 15 (1980): 161–82; Brent Fisse, "Reconstructing Corporate Criminal Law: Deterrence, Retribution, Fault, and Sanctions," *Southern California Law Review* 56 (1983): 1141–1246.
6. See further Peter A. French, *Collective and Corporate Responsibility* (New York: Columbia University Press, 1984), Ch. 11.
7. See e.g., Fisse and Braithwaite, *The Impact of Publicity on Corporate Offenders*, 303.
8. See generally John C. Coffee, Jr., " 'No Soul to Damn: No Body to Kick': An Unscandalized Inquiry into the Problem of Corporate Punishment," *Michigan Law Review* 79 (1981): 401–02.
9. See e.g., Gerhard Mueller, *"Mens Rea* and the Corporation," *University of Pittsburgh Law Review* 19 (1957): 21–50.
10. See generally Walter Kaufmann, *Without Guilt and Justice* (New York: Delta, 1973).
11. See further Peter A. French, "It's a Damn Shame" (unpublished manuscript 1984). For a psychodynamic analysis of shame, see Helen M. Lynd, *On Shame and the Search for Identity* (London: Routledge & Kegan Paul, 1958).
12. Zephaniah 3:5.
13. See e.g., Fisse and Braithwaite, *The Impact of Publicity on Corporate Offenders*, 75–76, 214–215, 227, 298, 302.
14. Nathaniel Hawthorne, *The Scarlet Letter* (New York: Pocket Books, 1954; originally published in 1850).
15. Ibid., 63.
16. See generally Fisse and Braithwaite, *The Impact of Publicity on Corporate Offenders*.
17. See e.g., Wally Olins, *The Corporate Personality: An Inquiry into the Nature of Corporate Identity* (New York: Mayflower Books, 1981); Charles Channon, "Corporations and the Politics of Perception," *Advertising Quarterly* 60(2) (1981): 12–15; Nancy Yashihara, "$1 Billion Spent on Identity: Companies Push Image of Selves, Not Products," *Los Angeles Times* (10 May 1981): pt. 6, pp. 1, 17.
18. See Fisse and Braithwaite, *The Impact of Publicity on Corporate Offenders*, Ch. 19.
19. Ibid., 308–09.
20. U.S., National Commission on Reform of Federal Criminal Laws, *Study Draft* (Washington, D.C.: U.S. Government Printing Office, 1970), 405.
21. U.S., National Commission on Reform of Federal Criminal Laws, *Final Report* (Washington D.C.: U.S. Government Printing Office, 1971), 3007.
22. See generally Kaufmann, *Without Guilt and Justice*; Fred L. Polak, *The Image of the Future: Enlightening the Past, Orienting the Present, Forecasting the Future*, vols. 1 and 2 (New York: Oceana Publications, 1961).
23. See references at Note 13 above.
24. See further, Coffee, " 'No Soul to Damn: No Body to Kick' ": 425–

26; Fisse and Braithwaite, *The Impact of Publicity on Corporate Offenders*, 291–92.

25. Ibid., 426. See further Fisse and Braithwaite, *The Impact of Publicity on Corporate Offenders*, 294–95.

26. See further Coffee, " 'No Soul to Damn: No Body to Kick' ": 426: Fisse and Braithwaite, *The Impact of Publicity on Corporate Offenders*, 295–98.

27. 447 U.S. 557 (1980).

28. See generally Herbert Schmertz, *Corporations and the First Amendment* (New York: Amacom, 1978); William Patton and Randall Bartlett, "Corporate 'Persons' and Freedom of Speech: The Political Impact of Legal Mythology," *Wisconsin Law Review* (1981): 494–512.

29. See John J.McCloy, *The Great Oil Spill* (New York: Chelsea House, 1976).

30. Coffee, " 'No Soul to Damn: No Body to Kick' ": 427–28.

31. But see Fisse and Braithwaite, *The Impact of Publicity on Corporate Offenders*, 306–09.

32. 420 F. Supp. 122 (1976).

33. See further Brent Fisse, "Community Service as a Sanction against Corporations," *Wisconsin Law Review* (1981): 970–1017.

34. Criminal No. 78–30, slip. op. (D. Conn., June 1, 1978).

35. Fisse, "Community Service as a Sanction against Corporations." See also Ch. 7.

36. *New York Times* (29 July 1983): 1.

37. Aristotle, *Nicomachean Ethics*, tran. M. Ostwald (Indianapolis: Bobbs-Merrill, 1962), 33.

38. But see Fisse, "Community Service as a Sanction against Corporations," 1008–16.

Study Questions

1. What is the "Hester Prynne" sanction? Do you believe that French has correctly understood Hawthorne's point?

2. For what *types* of corporations do you think the sanction might be most effective (i.e., supermarket chains, insurance companies, newspaper publishers, etc.), assuming it can, in fact, be effective at all?

French on Corporate Punishment: Some Problems

*J. Angelo Corlett**

In *Corporate and Collective Responsibility* (New York: Columbia University Press, 1984), Peter A. French argues that corporations as well as corporate-individuals can and should be held morally responsible for untoward events of which they are intentional agents. Moreover, he argues, guilty corporations can and ought to be punished for their wrongdoings. The purpose of this paper is to examine his theory of corporate punishment, and to show why it is problematic. One assumption I shall make is that corporations can be guilty of and responsible for wrongdoing.

The punishment of corporations, which I shall refer to as corporate punishment, is a primary stumbling block to French's collective and corporate responsibility theory. Retribution, he states, need not always be made in kind. The reason why this is so is because the corporation has no eye to exchange for an eye that it might have destroyed. Straightaway, then, there is a difficulty in effectively and sufficiently punishing a corporation which is responsible and guilty for causing an untoward event (French, 188).

Take the recent Union Carbide toxic chemical leakage in Bhopal, India, where Union Carbide is reponsible (I shall assume) for approximately 2,000 deaths and several more short- and long-term illnesses of Indian people. The question here is how to administer punishment to Union Carbide so that both parties are treated

* Philosophy Department, University of California, Santa Barbara

justly. Thus a main question regarding the punishment of guilty corporations is how to effectively and sufficiently deal with corporations that are found guilty of untoward events.

French explores some proposed methods of corporate punishment and notes why these are problematic. First, he argues that fining a guilty corporation is inadequate because the cost of the fines can be easily absorbed by raising consumer prices. Second, French argues that the revocation of a guilty corporation's charter or license to operate in a given locale is problematic for at least two reasons: a) The corporation might be able to reconstruct itself under a new charter, management and a new name in that locale or elsewhere in order to resume corporate activities; b) Innocent employees of the corporation are likely to be adversely affected economically by a charter revocation (French, 188). Insofar as the Bhopal incident is concerned, fining Union Carbide or revoking its charter are inadequate penalties for its wrongdoing. For both such punishments are likely to be passed on to the consumer in the form of higher prices for Union Carbide products. What, then, can be done to effectively and sufficiently punish corporations that are found guilty of untoward events?

As a remedy for this puzzle of corporate punishment French suggests what he calls the "Hester Prynne Sanction." The Hester Prynne Sanction consists largely of an institutionalized psychological punishment administered to the corporation that is found guilty of wrongdoing. It takes the form of a court ordered adverse publication of the corporation the cost of which is paid by the guilty corporation. The aim of the sanction is to create a psychological disposition of shame within the corporation for that of which it is guilty. French thinks that such shame, when the guilt of the corporation is made public, is most fatal to any corporation because public shame damages a corporation's prestige. According to higher-level management, a corporation's loss of prestige is the worst thing that can happen to it (French, 200).

There are, however, a number of difficulties which plague the utilization of the Hester Prynne Sanction against guilty corporations. First, the loss of prestige of a corporation may contribute to the financial failure of that corporation. In turn, this will adversely affect the economic condition of that corporation's work force, causing undue immiseration to its workers. (Here I assume that the work force does not play a primary role in that which make the corporation guilty of wrongdoing.)

To this criticism French replies that the adverse economic effects that the Hester Prynne Sanction might have on a guilty corporation's work force "should not overly concern us" (French 200). But this *is* a concern unless and until French can provide a successful argument which shows that it ought to be of no concern. Such an argument would at least have to consist in his showing that there is a genuine and significant causal connection between the untoward event and the work force of the corporation that is found guilty of that untoward event. If this is not shown, and if the Hester Prynne Sanction is imposed on a corporation the work force of which is not causally related to an untoward event in question, then the work force is punished unfairly. French himself uses this criticism against the suggestion of charter revocations and fines for corporations that are found guilty of wrongdoing. But he fails to see that this criticism also applies to his suggestion that the adverse economic effects the Hester Prynne Sanction might have on a corporation's work force ought not to overly concern one.

A second problem with the use of the sanction against guilty corporations is that the corporation might escape such financial loss and the immiseration of its workers by passing on the cost of the sanction to consumers in the form of higher prices. French uses this as an argument against the suggestion of fining corporations that are found guilty of wrongdoing. However, he does not see that the adverse effects of the Hester Prynne Sanction may be evaded by a corporation in the same manner. If a corporation is punished by means of French's sanction, then it may raise the prices of its products to the consumers in order to make up for the loss of profit due to the adverse publicity brought on by the sanction. On French's view, there is nothing which ensures against this possibility.

A third problem with the use of the Hester Prynne Sanction against guilty corporations is that the guilty corporation can simply, if it knows that it is economically advantageous for it to do so, recharter itself under another name, management, etc., in order to avoid the shame occasioned by the sanction. That is, the corporation can simply file bankruptcy and reorganize itself in such a way that one would not recognize the new corporation as being (for the most part) the same as the previous corporation, rather than suffer the embarrassment and costliness of the sanction. There are at least two ways that a corporation might recharter itself. First, it can recharter itself under a new name while continuing to do business in the same industry. Second, it can recharter itself under a new name while taking up business in another industry. An example of the first sort of reorganization would be an oil company simply changing its name in order to avoid the social stigma attached to it by the Hester Prynne Sanction. An example of the second sort would be that oil company's rechartering and entering into a different field of business altogether, say, computer technology. In this latter case, a corporation could escape the adverse effects of the sanction by making itself unrecognizable to both the media (which is said to be the primary tool used by the court to execute the Hester Prynne Sanction) and to the public. On French's view, there seems to be nothing stopping a guilty corporation from evading the effects of the sanction in this manner. Moreover, French argues against the revocation of charters for guilty corporations on the ground that innocent people related to the corporation are negatively affected. But he fails to realize that this argument also applies to the Hester Prynne Sanction. French provides no reason why a corporation found guilty of wrongdoing could not recharter itself in order to avoid the humiliation of the sanction. Again, French's arguments are turned against him.

A fourth weakness of the Hester Prynne Sanction against guilty corporations is that it depends too much on the reliability of the media to effectively carry out the sanction insofar as publicity is concerned. This is especially true if the corporation in question has significant ties with the media. Under such conditions the media might be prone to tone down its coverage of the corporation in question out of either a loyalty to the guilty corporation or out of a fear that the sanction might spell the demise of that corporation upon which the media is itself financially dependent. Thus any damage to the reputation of the guilty corporation by the sanction might also lead to the demise of the media itself because of its significant economic ties to the guilty corporation. On French's view, there seems to be no doubt about the media's motives or ability to carry out the Hester Prynne Sanction effectively.

A fifth puzzle with the use of the Hester Prynne Sanction against guilty corporations is that its scope is limited. It may indeed work in a situation where a corporation is found guilty of systematically abusing its workers, or where a corporation is found guilty of producing and selling, say, automobiles which malfunction slightly. In these cases the sanction might serve well as a deterrent to the continuation of such unacceptable business procedures. However, the sanction is unable to effectively and sufficiently punish corporations that are found guilty of gross forms of negligence. For example, the effects of the Hester Prynne Sanction on Union Carbide for the Bhopal incident would in no way do justice to the immensity of Union Carbide's responsibility to the families of those who were killed and severely injured by the toxic chemical leakage. The public shame of Union Carbide is at best only a necessary punishment. It is not a sufficient punishment for the incident of which Union Carbide is responsible. Neither the short- nor long-term effects of the Hester Prynne Sanction on Union Carbide could begin to render a just punishment for the fatal occurence at Bhopal.

Furthermore, even if it is a statistical fact that, generally speaking, corporate management thinks that the loss of prestige resulting from the Hester Prynne Sanction (or something akin to it) is the most devastating punishment that a corporation guilty of wrongdoing can receive, this is irrelevant. In the case of Union Carbide it is certainly in the corporation's best interest to be publically shamed because justice actually requires that somehow the corporation ought to recompense for the deaths and illnesses of thousands of Indian people. In such a case Union Carbide would obviously accept public shame over a much more severe punishment, say, the death penalty or long-term imprisonment with no chance of parole for certain constituents of the corporation who are the primary responsible agents of the Bhopal incident. So it is simply a mistake to punish corporations according to a standard with which they agree or find acceptable. The very fact that the management of such corporations considers the publicity of guilty corporations and the shame that ensues to be an acceptable punishment might serve to destroy or severely limit the deterrent force of the Hester Prynne Sanction. Punishing guilty corporations according to a standard which their membership accepts is akin to punishing a criminal according to what that criminal finds to be an acceptable punishment! The Hester Prynne Sanction is only useful in cases of minor corporate offences, it is an ineffective and insufficient punishment for instances of more significant corporate wrongdoing.

To this French might reply that the implementation of more

stringent penalties on corporations that are found guilty of gross forms of wrongdoing would tend to render such corporations impotent in the marketplace of trade and competition. Moreover, it might stifle business and technological growth altogether if corporations are to be severely punished for the unfortunate results of what are otherwise quite "natural" business practices. To this reply I simply answer that justice cannot be tailored to the methods of business or technological manifest destiny. This is the sort of morality that leads to corporate wrongdoing in the first place. Rather, corporations must themselves act according to the dictates of what justice requires in given circumstances. The circumstances of justice must determine the practices of corporations, not vice versa.

French states that the Hester Prynne Sanction might be more effective as a punishment for corporate wrongdoing if it is coupled with a planned and enforced community service project the cost of which is covered by the guilty corporation (French, 200–1). An example of this might be punishing an oil company guilty of environmental pollution by having it pay for high-level research in ecological and environmental preservation.

But there are puzzles with French's suggestion. One is that the financial status of such research is directly dependent on the financial stability of the funding corporation. But if the corporation is adversely affected by the sanction, then it might fall on economic hard times, threatening the operation of the environmental research. Moreover, since the corporation funds the research, it can in some way influence and hence bias the reports coming out of the research so that such reports do not further complicate the adverse conditions of the corporation or industry. For example, the corporation might strongly suggest or even dictate that the research be done in areas of environmental studies which reflect a positive outlook toward the corporation rather than a negative one. Even if this is not the case, the researchers might come to the realization that their wages can be threatened if they produce and publicize any environmentally negative studies related to the guilty corporation. And if the public considers these studies, the stock of that corporation could drop to a drastic level, not to mention the fact that the public could boycott the purchase of that corporation's manufactured products enough to force it into dire financial conditions, leaving its research institute and its employees without funding. A further problem with French's position on this matter of a guilty corporation's being punished by having to fund research projects is that such a penalty in no way serves as a recompense for gross forms of corporate wrongdoing. For example, forcing Union Carbide to fund, say, chemical engineering research in no way amounts to a fair punishment for its responsibility and guilt regarding the Bhopal incident. Even if such research is not problematic in the ways I describe, and even if such a punishment is coupled with the Hester Prynne Sanction, a punishment much more severe is needed to effectively and sufficiently penalize Union Carbide for the magnitude of the untoward event of which it is responsible. Moreover, linking the Hester Prynne Sanction with community service might yield another undesirable consequence. French is concerned with creating an attitude of corporate shame for corporate wrongdoing. But he fails to realize that linking the sanction to community service (whether it be environmental research, support of the arts, or whatever) may serve as a guilty corporation's opportunity to boast—as is often done—of its community service achievements, thereby deceiving the public regarding the actual reason why the corporation is performing such services.

A seventh problem with the Hester Prynne Sanction is that it is to some degree hypocritical. It is the context of corporate competition that creates a problem of hypocrisy for corporate punishment theories like French's. The same system that encourages corporate competition and corporate success is the same one which seeks to punish corporations for pursuing such ideals. The hypocritical nature of the Hester Prynne Sanction, then, consists in the fact that it seeks to punish corporations for doing what they are encouraged to do (i.e., making a profit and bettering the economic achievements of all other corporations) as corporate enterprises.

Since French takes the name of his sanction from Hawthorne's *The Scarlet Letter*, an illustration from that story will suffice to suggest the hypocritical nature of the Hester Prynne Sanction. The reader will recall that in Hawthorne's story Hester Prynne commits adultery with the town cleric. She is "tried" and sentenced to the humiliation of having to wear a scarlet letter in order to publicize her wrongdoing. Now there are several things to note about this story. First, Hawthorne is widely known as a *critic* of the Puritan culture. The point of his story, secondly, is to suggest the hypocritical nature of that culture. The townspeople are not genuinely concerned about the welfare of this woman who is caught in the web of a most complex human relationship. Their concern is punishment. They are unconcerned with the fact that Hester Prynne is a victim of the social situation in which she finds herself. They are unconcerned with the fact that the society is "set up" in such a manner that only certain "crimes" (or "sins") are socially apparent (i.e., adultery in the case of some women) while other "crimes" are not obvious to the public, but are regularly practiced by the very persons who condemn Hester Prynne. Certainly the story of Hester Prynne is a seething indictment of the intolerance and self-righteousness of the Puritan culture. Just as the Puritan culture fosters a way of life which gives rise to various wrongdoing, so does the social order in which corporations operate. And just as it is hypocritical for the Puritans to adversely publicize the "sinful" deed of Hester Prynne, it is also hypocritical for corporations to be adversely publicized for socially unacceptable practices. How can French suggest punishment for guilty corporations when the "free market" system itself forces corporations (if they desire to be successful) to compete under terms which encourage such abuses? Will the corporations which are without sin cast the first stone?

Now I am in no way hinting that French intends to punish corporations guilty of wrongdoing in an intolerant or self-righteous way. However, French does not explain the court's procedural fairness in punishing corporations that are found guilty of causing untoward events. He does not show how the system will operate in a fair manner when punishing such corporations. There seems to be no reason why one should not expect to find the same arbitrary and politically and economically motivated procedures in punishing guilty corporations which exists presently, i.e., where a corporation is punished for wrongdoing, but other corporations which contributed indirectly to the same untoward event are not punished. Certainly equal punishment under the law applies to the corporate realm. Moreover, French's utilization of the term "Hester Prynne Sanction" perhaps betrays an ignorance regarding the fundamental points of Hawthorne's story. Hester Prynne, according to Hawthorne, is treated *wrongly* for her "offence," suggesting that any mode of punishment akin to that which she receives is equally wrong. Perhaps French ought to rename his suggested method of corporate punishment.

Furthermore, French states that the Hester Prynne Sanction is an effective means of corporate punishment in a shame based society like our own (French, 192–3). It is true that the success of the sanction depends on the guilty corporation's ability to feel shame for what it has done wrong. But what if it has little or no capacity for such a feeling under any circumstance? What if, moreover, the corporation is perfectly willing to delude the courts, media and the public into thinking that it is shameful about doing a wrongful deed, but it in fact places more emphasis on profit-making than on moral practices in business? What if a guilty corporation is perfectly willing to undergo the Hester Prynne Sanction so long as it does not interfere with significant profit-making? Does not the sanction then lose its sting? Can the Hester Prynne Sanction be of help in punishing such corporations? French seems to have assumed, rather naively, that all corporations will feel shameful regarding their corporate wrongdoing. Moreover, he assumes that in the light of such shame corporations will be deterred from repeat offences by way of the sanction. I believe this is false at least in some cases. The primary reason that some corporations feel shameful for doing something which is deemed unacceptable is because they are caught. This can, however, hardly be seen as shame if by "shame" one means a genuine remorse for one's actions and a genuine effort to change one's ways. I submit, then, that corporations are not automatically shameful of their wrong actions. A case in point is Union Carbide, which (as far as I am aware) offers no more than $2,000 to the surviving families of each dead victim of the Bhopal incident, while it offers nothing to the thousands of surviving victims of that disaster. Obviously, a corporation which is clearly responsible for, and feels genuine remorse for, an untoward event of this magnitude would make a much more generous offer to both the families of those who died and to those who survived the chemical leakage. Thus, the Hester Prynne Sanction assumes that guilty corporations will feel shameful about their wrongful acts, but it is by no means clear that corporations will or do exhibit such a feeling. As long as a guilty corporation can find avenues to increase its profits, there seems to be no reason for that corporation not to continue in its wrongful ways, despite the effects on it as a result of the

Hester Prynne Sanction. This undercuts the sanction because if there is no guarrantee that guilty corporations will feel such shame, then the possibility of corporate rehabilitation is wanting, making the Hester Prynne Sanction an ineffective means of corporate punishment.

In conclusion, nothing on French's view of the use of the Hester Prynne Sanction against guilty corporations ensures against the following: 1) The unjust immiseration of the guilty corporation's work force; 2) The ability of the guilty corporation to escape the financial penalty of the sanction by raising its prices for the consumer; 3) The ability of the guilty corporation to reorganize itself and thereby escape the public shame of the sanction; 4) The possibility of the media's ineffectiveness in carrying out the sanction; 5) The limited scope of the sanction on those corporations guilty of gross forms of wrongdoing; 6) The guilty corporation's ability to control the findings and operations of its court appointed research facility; 7) The hypocritical nature of the sanction; 8) The possibility that some corporations will not feel shameful about their wrongful deeds. These are eight reasons why the utilization of French's Hester Prynne Sanction is problematic as a punishment for corporate wrongdoing.

Although the Hester Prynne Sanction is useful in some cases of minor corporate wrongdoing, it is not useful as a punishment for corporations guilty of gross wrongdoing, such as the Union Carbide incident in Bhopal. What French needs in order to ensure the success of his claims regarding corporate punishment is a general theory of punishment which is capable of giving an effective and sufficient punishment to corporations guilty of gross wrongdoing. What he needs is a theory of corporate punishment which: 1) does not permit a corporation found guilty of wrongdoing to evade the guilt, shame and negative effects of the punishment; 2) does not permit the punishment to adversely effect (in any way) innocent employees or the general public in any significant manner; 3) does not permit the guilty corporation a way by which to benefit financially from the punishment; and 4) has a genuine rehabilitative intent and effect (instead of a crippling one) on the punished corporation. Moreover, such a theory of corporate punishment must be based on an adequate concept of corporate moral personhood. How such a theory might be explicated is the subject of another paper.

(I am grateful to Burleigh T. Wilkins, Philosophy Department, University of California, Santa Barbara, and B. Celeste Corlett, Psychology Department, University of California, Santa Barbara, for their comments on earlier drafts of this paper.)

Study Questions

1. Granted that Corlett's analysis of French's "Hester Prynne Sanction" is correct, how might French's theory of corporate punishment be reconstructed to evade Corlett's criticisms?
2. Do corporations tend to have a sense of moral personhood, guilt or shame as French claims that they do? Or is Corlett correct in arguing that this is a dubious claim? State your reasons for your answer.
3. How valuable do you think the Hester Prynne Sanction still is, after all of Corlett's arguments against its alleged value as a tool for punishing serious corporate wrongdoing? Is there any reason to have any faith in it?

Five Moral Rules for Multinationals Operating Overseas

*Richard T. De George**

Can a multinational corporation operate ethically in a country whose structure is basically immoral—either because of oppression of the poor, gross government corruption or immoral legal structures?

Even people who believe that ethics may have a role to play in business within the United States, often argue that it has no role to play in international business. As Howard Schaefer writes:

> The view that there is some form of universal . . . standard to which multinational corporations (MNCs) are subject is incorrect. This is not the way the world works. That decision is made strictly on the basis of economic power. . . . The real question has to be . . . what are the standards MNCs are following?

Or Charles Nevill:

> If a business loses a competitive advantage because of giving vent to morality, then the very reason for the existence of a business is defeated. . . . The golden rule does not apply in international business because they do not play by the rules that we make.

* Richard T. De George is University Distinguished Professor at the University of Kansas. He is the coeditor of Ethics, Free Enterprise and Public Policy and the author of Business Ethics, now in a second edition and also available in Japanese translation. In 1987, he was one of three Americans who negotiated the first American-USSR philosophical exchange.

Yet the view that ethics applies to business on the national but not on the international level is both inconsistent and untenable. There are moral values that undergird international business, just as there are moral values that undergird American business, and ethics is not out of place in either of them.

All countries hold that it is wrong for one person to arbitrarily kill another. Unless this were the case the lives of all foreigners, including all business people, would be at risk in any foreign country—which is clearly not the case. Nor are lying and stealing morally acceptable in any country. If these actions were morally acceptable, the society would soon fall into disarray and cease to exist.

As for business, unless there is some minimum of trust between buyer and seller on the international level, commercial transactions would prove impossible. Hence truthfulness, respect for contracts, and respect for the lives and personal integrity of those with whom one does business are all essential and necessary for business to take place.

Multinationals do not operate in a Hobbesian state of nature in which no rules apply. Because the existing laws that do apply are frequently minimal, however, there is clearly a need for moral rules.

What follows are five moral norms that might be generated and defended with respect to the actions of multinationals in less developed countries (LDCs). We concentrate on LDCs because these nations—unlike the developed countries—often lack the background institutions, i.e., laws, customs, and institutionalized practices, to regulate business so that it operates under conditions of reasonable equality and recioprocity.

First Norm: The "Moral Minimum"

The first norm, which has been called the "moral minimum," is the norm to do no direct intentional harm. This moral minimum applies to all actions of all people, corporations and countries. To do intentional harm is to willfully harm another, and unless done in self defense or with some similar overriding reason, it is generally immoral and widely recognized as such. When appplied with respect to relations of U.S. companies and LDCs, it has a number of obvious implications. Dumping toxic products, such as selling in African markets the asbestos pajamas for children that were prohibited for sale in the United States and Europe, is one example of doing harm knowingly and willingly and taking advantage of the lack of legal restraints to the detriment of the consumer. Similarly, selling pesticides and drugs that the seller knows will be misused or, even if properly used, will cause harm—an action of which some American multinationals have been guilty—are prohibited by this rule.

Obviously, precluded is gross pollution of air, land and water. Less obviously precluded is the acquisition of the prime farmland previously used for growing local foodstuffs, and its conversion to cash export crops, if this leads to starvation or serious malnutrition for the local population.

This first norm *does not* hold that whatever the FDA or some other U.S. agency prohibits from sale in the U.S. may not morally be sold abroad. The norm can be interpreted independently of U.S. regulations. Yet if there are U.S. prohibitions, then those engaged in selling such products abroad should be able to show that they are not causing direct intentional harm and that there are valid reasons why the U.S. standards—which are not in themselves moral standards—may morally be ignored in the country of sale. The norm also requires U.S. companies to examine the effects of their actions on the host country, and not simply to look only at the self-interest of the company.

Second Norm: Trade Must Benefit Host Country

The second norm builds on the first. Although the injunction to do no direct intentional harm applies to all companies in both developed and less developed countries, business by a multinational in the LDCs must take into account the differences between the country of origin and the host country. Given the great disparities, not only should the multinational do no direct intentional harm, but if its activity is to be morally justified, it activity must benefit the host country. This means that the multinational's activities must not only benefit the multinational, but also the host country; and that good to the multinational cannot be traded off against harm—even unintentional, indirect harm—to the host country. A typcial utilitarian analysis might seem to justify a transaction that produced great good to the multinational and serious harm to the host country as long as the good was greater than the harm. But if one takes a broader view, given the already poor condition of the host country, to make its lot worse in order to better the position of the United States or an American multinational is to deepen that country's problems and to make the gap between developed and less developed countries greater rather than less. Hence, the justification for this second norm.

A corollary to this norm is that the good of the country is not the same as the good of the corrupt leader or the good of an oppressive elite. The good of the country must include the good of the ordinary people of the country. This distinction is crucial. Trade that increases the wealth of a Marcos but does not help the Philippine people is not trade that helps the country in the sense required by this norm.

Third Norm: Respect for Workers, Consumers

The third norm is to respect the human rights of the workers and consumers in the host country. Like the first norm, this applies to all companies operating in all countries. But it is primarily in the LDCs that multinationals tend to violate the norm, primarily because of the great poverty and high unemployment rates found there and because of the lack of protective legislation. This norm would clearly prevent any company from engaging in slavery. It also precludes their practicing apartheid, paying less than subsistence wages or failing to provide adequate and safe working conditions. Paying more than the going wage may cause problems for a multinational and open it up to charges that it is draining off the best workers or forcing local industries to raise wages beyond what they can afford, thus in effect driving them out of business. All these considerations must be weighed. Yet none of them justifies failure to respect the human rights of workers. If local companies are guilty of this, that cannot be taken as justification for acting in like manner.

Once again, the argument leads not to the conclusion that if others violate rights we are allowed to do so also; but to the conclusion that if others violate rights and we cannot compete effectively without also violating rights, either we do not compete or we attempt to get background institutions that protect the human rights of all.

Fourth Norm: Promote Background Institutions

This leads to the next two norms. The fourth norm is to promote the development of just background institutions (e.g., minimum wage laws, protection of unions and the right to strike, legal guarantees of safety standards) internally within the country as well as on the international level. The fifth norm requires a multinational to respect the laws of a host country and to respect as well its culture and local values, providing these do not violate human rights or impose immoral laws. If apartheid is immoral, then, even if legal, a multinational has no more right to engage in the practice than do local firms. Yet multinationals should respect the other local laws and cultures, and seek neither to undermine them nor to replace them. To do either would be a violation of the first norm of doing no harm, and this fifth norm is simply an application of that first one. Moreover, as guests in a foreign land, an outside multinational generally has no right to interfere with the local government, and should not stand in the way of or lobby against reforms or laws that protect the workers or consumers, even if such laws make operating in these countries less profitable.

There is a narrow line between working toward just background institutions—both in LDCs and on an international level—on the one hand, and observing one's proper place in not interfering with the internal affairs of a country and respecting its culture and values on the other. Nonetheless, it should be clear that supporting a government's efforts in establishing just laws, protecting workers' rights and welfare, and the life, constitues neither inappropriate interference nor the promotion of self-interest at the expense and good of the host country.

Following these rules will preclude the kind of exploitation that multinationals are so often charged with—exploitation of both resources and labor. An American multinational interested in acting ethically can go a long way toward reaching that goal by taking such norms seriously.

Model Codes Already Exist

The preconditions and mechanisms for establishing rules by mutual agreement exist, and we have several models for doing so. The World Health Organization has formulated an international code for the sale of infant milk formula. The U.N. has been working for many years on a set of guidelines for the operations of multinationals, and this is just one of many codes being considered. A number of church-sponsored groups have drawn up codes of international business conduct. Some individual corporations have devised their own codes; and others, such as General Motors, with its Sullivan Principles, have led the way in attempting to deal with the issue of apartheid and the conditions under which companies might morally operate in South Africa.

Thus, we have a basis for developing some moral rules that apply to all international business.

Finally, the American business system and the international system are inextricably intertwined. Ethics in international business involves ethics in American business and vice versa.

Consider only the question of the export of industry. Some people complain when a company moves its factory from the northern part of the United States to the Sun Belt, where it can find cheaper labor. Many others argue this is morally and economically acceptable. Yet when the same company—for the same reasons—namely to lower labor costs—moves from the United States to a foreign country, then many of the latter group condemn the action as immoral. The reason for the difference, they claim, is that although the northern states may be adversely affected by the first move, the Sun Belt states benefit, and the overall benefit to the country balances out the harm done. When industry is exported, however, then Americans lose jobs and harm is done to the country as a whole from the loss of industry as well as jobs. This adds to unemployment, reduces the national tax base, and benefits the company at the expense of the country.

Not Only American Jobs Must Be Considered

The argument is, however, a one-sided view. For it considers only the company and the United States. It fails to consider the fact that exporting industry in this way helps provide jobs for people in the host country, where typically the unemployment rate is staggering. Are jobs more important for Americans than for the unemployed of other countries? To argue only in terms of the benefits to America and Americans is not to take a broad enough perspective. I am not now claiming that the export of industry is necessarily moral or immoral; I am only claiming that from a moral point of view not only are the interests of Americans to count, but the interests of others are to count as well. If America can prosper while others also prosper, so much the better. If in order for the disadvantaged to prosper at all the standard of living of Americans must be somewhat reduced, then that is the cost that morality may impose and that Americans as well as others similarly affected may be morally required to pay.

In sum, those who argue that since others act immorally we should act immorally draw the wrong conclusion from the facts they cite. If others act immorally and that results in our disadvantage, we should try to establish rules that preclude their so acting, rather than act as they do. That is the way we proceed on the national level, and it is appropriate to proceed in that way on the international level as well. If American business suffers a competitive disadvantage because it is legally prevented from paying bribes, and if bribery is harmful to business in general by making it unfair, then there is good reason to seek international regulations prohibiting bribery. When formal international agreements are impossible, joint action by concerned firms (e.g., the joint action of American firms in South Africa), joint protests to local governments (e.g., American firms that protested petty bribery in Mexico), and similar actions are possible and place the burden of morality on no one company.

Ethics for international business constitutes one more layer of analysis that business must consider in any business activity. Ethics by itself will not tell a business how to act. In this sense, it is a sieve through which business decisions must pass. Only those that pass through are morally acceptable. But which of those that pass through are the best from a business point of view must of course be decided by those in business.

Study Questions

1. Since, as argued by others (Prof. Merrill, e.g.), newspaper codes of ethics appear to be a failure, do you still agree with Professor De George that corporate codes can succeed? If so, what might be the important differences between the world of journalism and business generally that might allow for successful ethical codes with the latter where they failed with the former?
2. Contrary to several fashionable approaches to ethics (so-called "situation ethics," e.g.) De George takes a bold step in arguing that there are "universal" ethical principles—principles that transcend any individual culture and apply to all. Is this true? (He says, for example, that "All countries hold that it is wrong for one person to arbitrarily kill another.") Try to find counterexamples to De George's claim (a nation or culture that does sanction wonton killing).

An Ethical Analysis of Deception in Advertising

Thomas L. Carson
Richard E. Wokutch
*James E. Cox, Jr.**

It is almost always assumed that deceptive advertising is morally objectionable. However the grounds for this are seldom, if ever, stated. It is also taken for granted by many that deceptive advertising should be prohibited by law. In fact most definitions of "deception" and "deception in advertising" are simply proposals of criteria for when advertising should be prohibited on account of being deceptive. This is the case with FTC usage of these terms and it is also the case with definitions of these terms found in the

* Thomas L. Carson is Assistant Professor of Philosophy at the Virginia Polytechnic Institute and State University. He was previously Lecturer at the University of California at Los Angeles and was holder of an NEH Fellowship for College Teachers. His most important publication is *The Status of Morality*, Reidel, Dordrecht, 1984. Forthcoming (in *Philosophy and Public Affairs*) is: "Bribery, Extortion, and The Foreign Current Corrupt Practices Act."

Richard L. Wokutch is Associate Professor of Management at the Virginia Polytechnic Institute and State University where he teaches in the social issues and policy areas. He previously held positions as Visiting Assistant Research Professor at the Values Center, University of Delaware, and as Visiting Fulbright Research Fellow, Science Center, Berlin, West Germany. He has published several recent articles in the areas of bluffing and deception in business and 'ethical'/social investing.

James E. Cox, Jr., is Assistant Professor of Management and Marketing at Illinois State University. Formerly, he was at the Virginia Polytechnic Institute and State University (from September 1979 until August 1983). He was a fellow at the 1979 American Marketing Association PhD Consortium and his research has been published in the *Journal of Forecasting*, the *Journal of Marketing Education*, the *Proceedings of the American Marketing Association*, and the *Proceedings of the National Council of Physical Distribution Management*. He is also coauthor of the book *Sales Forecasting Methods: A Survey of Recent Developments*.

marketing literature. Rarely, if ever, definitions of these terms are presented in the sense that they are used in everyday language.

The purposes of this paper are threefold. First, we will suggest criticisms of a widely discussed definition of deception in advertising. Second, we will attempt to show how discussion of the moral and legal aspects of deception in advertising can be illuminated by a discussion of the everyday concept of deception. We will argue that it is not enough to consider only the concepts of deception discussed in the marketing literature which are, in effect, proposals for when the law should prohibit deceptive advertising. Our third and most important aim is to give a plausible explanation of why deceptive advertising is morally objectionable. We will argue that deceptive advertising can be shown to be morally wrong given the rather weak and noncontroversial assumption that there is a moral presumption against harming others, i.e. there is a *presumption* for thinking that any act that harms others is morally wrong.

Both industry and government leaders have recognized the need to avoid deception in advertising. In 1937 the Wheeler-Lea Amendments extended the regulatory powers of the FTC beyond the prohibition of unfair methods of competition. These acts authorized the FTC to forbid unfair or deceptive practices. This placed the identification of deceptive advertising under the FTC's jurisdiction. In 1962 the American Association of Advertising Agencies published a *Creative Code* discouraging deceptive or misleading advertising. Since the early 1900s the American Advertising Federation has waged a truth-in-advertising campaign to set guidelines for the industry. In its *Advertising Code of American Business*[1] it declares that "advertising shall tell the truth, and shall reveal significant facts, the concealment of which would mislead the public."[2]

There has been no problem in making industry and government leaders aware of the need to avoid deception in advertising. The real problem has been to agree on a definition of "deception" and consequently how to measure it.

It is becoming increasingly important to find an acceptable definition of deception. This is because the 1980 FTC Amendment Act deemphasizes the use of the "unfairness" criterion in regulating advertising.[3] Thus even with the current policy of the FTC to rely more on market forces and less on regulation to influence advertisers, regulations concerning deception will more likely be the basis of complaint if FTC action is taken against advertisers. However the criteria for deception are not very precise and there are no clear guidelines for determining its existence.[4]

Barbour and Gardner give an overview of attempts at defining and measuring deception:

> In recent years a number of articles have attempted to broaden and increase the understanding of deception in advertising, especially from a behavioral perspective. There have been several attempts to define deception in advertising.
>
> Conceptually, with the exception of Haefner, these attempts have defined deception in terms of consumer information processing. The differences between these conceptual definitions are relatively minor. For instance, Gardner argues for veridical perception as the conceptual basis while Olson and Dover argue that demonstrably false beliefs must be acquired. Based on these definitions, attempts have been made to measure deception in advertising.[5]

It would be impossible in a paper of this length to compare and contrast all previous definitions of deception. However as Barbour and Gardner point out above "the differences between these conceptual definitions are relatively minor." Thus, in this paper we have chosen a representative definition of deceptive advertising as the basis for discussion. Since Gardner's definition seems to be the most frequently cited in the literature we will use this definition.

Gardner's definition of deception

David Gardner proposes the following definition of deception in advertising:

> If an advertisement (or advertising campaign) leaves the consumer with (an) impression(s) and/or belief(s) different from what would normally be expected if the consumer had reasonable knowledge, and that impression(s) and/or belief(s) is factually untrue or potentially misleading, then deception is said to exist.[6]

It is unclear to us whether this is intended as: (1) a strict definition of the English phrase "deceptive advertising," as used in everyday conversation, or (2) just a definition for legal purposes, i.e., a definition picking out those instances of deceptive advertising that ought to be prohibited by law, or (3) both (1) and (2). We shall argue that his definition is unsatisfactory for any of these purposes. Then we will offer a definition of deceptive advertising for legal purposes (a standard for determining when deceptive advertising ought to be prohibited) and a strict semantic definition of "deceptive advertising."

According to Gardner's definition, if an advertisement or ad campaign leaves consumers with other than reasonable knowledge (i.e., the knowledge required in order to make an informed purchasing decision) about the product in question then it is to be considered deceptive. This definition is open to clear counter-examples such as the following case. Suppose that a consumer is completely ignorant about a certain type of product. For example, a refugee from Indochina might be completely ignorant about the functioning of automobiles: their maintenance requirements, susceptibility to rust, fuel and oil consumption etc. According to Gardner's definition a brief, totally honest, television commercial emphasizing the gasoline mileage and warranty of a particular car would count as deceptive. (After viewing the commercial, the refugee's beliefs about automobiles would still be other than they would be if he had reasonable knowledge about them and his beliefs would be potentially misleading.) Surely it would be unfair to label an advertisement deceptive just because it fails to educate the ignorant up to the level of "reasonable knowledge." Gardner's definition equates the failure of an ad to provide one with the knowledge required in order to make a reasonable choice with the ad's being deceptive. This is surely not the case; in order to count as deceptive an ad must be the cause of one's misinformation or lack of reasonable knowledge. (As we shall see shortly, Gardner's methods for measuring deception also run afoul of this requirement.) Ads that picture beautiful women cavorting with the product are uninformative but they are surely not deceptive.

The automobile ad (from our earlier example) which Gardner's definition counts as deceptive actually may have had a positive effect on the man's knowledge of the product—it may have moved him in the direction of reasonable knowledge. This suggests the following revised definition of deceptive advertising:

> An advertisement can be said to have deceived consumer if and
> only if as a result of the ad he has a less reasonable knowledge of
> the product than he would have had otherwise.

This definition, however, is also inadequate. For an advertisement
containing two pieces of valuable and little known information
and one outright lie could not count as deceptive under this definition because such an advertisement would still constitute a net
gain in terms of knowledge.

Our purported counterexample to Gardner's definition appeals
to the very atypical case of an immigrant who is completely ignorant of the nature of the product being advertised, i.e., someone
fitting the FTC's "least reasonable man" or "ignorant man" description. It might be suggested that Gardner can easily avoid this
objection by incorporating the FTC's "reasonable man standard"
into his definition, and as we pointed out in Note 6, Gardner may
be implying this in his definition. According to the reasonable
man standard an ad cannot be considered deceptive unless it
misleads (or has the potential to mislead) reasonable intelligent
and well informed adults. Any advertisement can mislead someone, but in order to count as deceptive an ad must mislead reasonably intelligent and well-informed people. Gardner's definition
can be revised along these lines as follows:

> If an advertisement or advertising campaign leaves intelligent and
> knowledgeable adults (or a significant percentage of intelligent and
> knowledgeable adults) with (an) impression(s) and/or belief(s) dif-
> ferent from what would normally be expected if the consumer had
> reasonable knowledge, and that impression(s) and/or belief(s) is
> factually untrue or potentially misleading, then deception is said to
> exist.

Some might argue that this is what Gardner really means; we
disagree (see Note 6). In any case our argument does not depend
on accepting the first interpretation of the definition as the correct
reading of Gardner, since we argue the definition is inadequate
in either event.

As Gardner claims, for such definitions as that above to be of
operational utility, agreement would need to be reached on the
meaning of such terms as "intelligent and well-informed" and
"significant percentage." Such agreement, however, may not in

general be possible and the meaning of these terms is likely to be dependent on the circumstances. If the consequences of being misled are sufficiently bad (e.g., resulting in a person's death) then we would seem to be justified in setting a very low percentage criterion for "significant."[7] The above revision of Gardner's definition and any other definition that makes "the reasonable man standard" *a necessary condition* of deceptive advertising are implausible. For all such definitions imply that many of the kinds of objectionable and misleading advertisements aimed at children are not deceptive because such advertisements would not mislead very many adults.

An Alternative Definition of Deception

To account for the problem of commercials aimed at children we suggest the following definition of deception (*for legal purposes*):

> An advertisement is deceptive if it causes a significant percentage of potential consumers (i.e., those at whom it is directed or whose consumption behavior is likely to be influenced by it) to have false beliefs about the product.

The situational determination of what constitutes a "significant percentage" would still be necessary.

It should be stressed that this is not a strict definition of deception for everyday usage but a criterion of deception for legal purposes. It might be more appropriately considered a strict definition of "misleading advertising," since a strict definition of "deception" must make some reference to the intention of the deceiver as we will argue below. Both the FTC and the FDA have in fact used the terms interchangeably disregarding the issue of intention.[8] We suggest the above as the legal norm for determining when ads should count as deceptive. We feel the government is justified in forcing advertisers to stop any such ads and in fining them for deceptive ads (fines may be used to finance "corrective advertising" or to compensate consumers and/or competitors).

It might be objected that this violates one of the most elementary principles of legal justice—that one should be punished only for actions that are deliberate or intentional. For example, in order to punish someone for murder, it is necessary to prove that he killed someone *intentionally*. But, this objection is mistaken for several reasons. First, it can be justifiable to punish people for unintentional actions if those actions involve negligence. The drunken driver who unintentionally kills someone is still liable to be punished for negligent homicide (and rightly so). The penalty for this is, however, less severe than for murder.

Second, and more fundamentally, an individual or organization may be rightfully compelled to cease harmful activity and to compensate others for that harm, even if the harms are completely unintended, e.g., it is justifiable to compel someone to cease an activity and to compensate others for the unintentional destruction of their property. Proof of intent or negligence is only necessary in cases of criminal prosecution which involve the possibility of imprisonment and punitive fines. We believe that cease and desist orders, corrective advertising, and compensation to victims of deception are appropriate penalties for both intentional and unintentional deception. Punitive fines would be appropriate only for cases of intentional deception.

As stated above, the FTC and FDA typically have not been concerned with the issue of intent. However in matters pertaining to the related field of product liability, the intent of manufacturers has been a matter of courtroom deliberation. The most notable instance of this was the Ford Pinto case where Ford was charged with criminal negligence for allegedly having knowingly put an unsafe car on the market. While Ford was acquitted on this count, it is likely that this is a legal precedent that will be repeated. It seems reasonable to the authors that in an extreme case of deceptive advertising involving large dollar amounts of consumer purchases that this matter of intention can and should be raised in court as well.

Measuring Deception

Gardner proposes a number of techniques for measuring deception. One of these is what he calls the "normative belief technique." The normative belief technique involves testing people's beliefs and expectations about a product after they have been subjected to advertisements for it. If there is a discrepancy between these beliefs and the actual features of the product then the advertisement is to be considered deceptive. As Gardner notes, if unfulfilled consumer expectations for a product are often caused by favorable associations with a particular brand name, any advertisements for that product must be considered deceptive by his criteria. Suppose, for example, that Gerbers markets a new line of inexpensive baby food with a simple ad saying that this is Gerbers' new line. Gerbers has a reputation for being the best and most reliable baby food and consumers will expect the new line to have all of these virtues. Let us suppose that these expectations are unfounded and that the new line of baby foods is actually inferior in quality to other less expensive brands. Gardner is committed to saying that any advertisement for this product must be considered deceptive. He admits that this seems to be implausible:

> The advertiser need only mention the brand name and a substantial percentage of the audience may *understand* the message as, 'Here we are again, old reliable Gerbers, the safest, most nutritious, most reliable baby food your baby can eat.' If that claim were made explicitly, it would be deceptive. But Gerbers does not have to make the claim; consumers get the message without being told. It is quite possible that the procedures mentioned here will find such advertising deceptive in some manner. Why should an advertisement that merely repeats the brand name be judged deceptive? But why should this be any less 'deceptive', if you go along with the Gerbers example, than a campaign for a *new* baby food product that explicitly makes such a claim? No ready solution to this dilemma can be advanced. However, the dilemma cries out for research.[9]

However, there is a ready solution to this problem. If an advertisement merely repeats the product's brand name, the advertisement, in and of itself, cannot be said to have caused or brought about the unfulfilled expectations of the consumers. These expectations are based on consumers' past experience with Gerbers, not on the current advertising. Whereas, if a commercial explicitly makes false claims about the quality of a product, it may be responsible for creating unrealized expectations. An advertisement cannot be considered deceptive unless it, of *itself*, causes people to be misled.

The Concept of Deception in Everyday Life

We will attempt to give a definition of "deception" that is faithful to its everyday meaning in English. Before proceeding with this it would be helpful to distinguish deception from lying. A lie is a deliberate false statement made orally, in writing or through some other use of language. Deception need not involve any false statements or any other use of language. My confident demeanor as I raise the pot in a game of poker may deceive you into thinking that I have a good hand, but it does not involve the making of any statement (whether true or false). So, not all cases of deception involve lying. Likewise, not all lying involves deception. If a lie is not believed then the liar has not succeeded in deceiving anyone. According to the standard definition of lying, lying only involves the *attempt* to deceive others.[10] The relationship between lying and deception can be illustrated as follows:

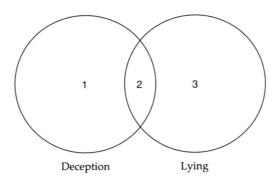

The left circle includes all instances of deception; the right circle includes all instances of lying. Area 1 represents non-verbal or non-linguistic deception, area 2 represents successful lies (lies that do deceive others) and area 3 represents unsuccessful lies (lies that fail to deceive others).

The foregoing points out an important feature of the concept of deception—unlike "lying" the word 'deception' connotes success. An act must actually mislead someone if it is to count as a case of deception. If my bluff fails to deceive you then it cannot be described as a case of deception, however, it could be considered an attempt at deception which many would consider no less morally objectionable than deception itself.

The root meaning of the word "deceive" is simply to cause another person to have false beliefs. However, this definition is not adequate to cover all cases. For one might cause another to have false beliefs in indirect ways that we would not be willing to allow as cases of deception. For example, by telling you about a sale at the local bookstore I might cause you to notice and purchase a book containing numerous false claims about the life of Elvis Presley that you would believe. I will have indirectly caused you to believe such things as that Elvis practiced cannibalism, but it would not be correct to say that I deceived you. A perfectly clear and truthful statement is likely to be misinterpreted by inattentive listeners or readers but we don't call it deceptive if my lecture on World War I causes a student dozing in the back of the classroom to come to the mistaken belief that Germany and Turkey fought on opposing sides in the war. It won't do to define deception as *directly* causing someone else to have false beliefs. Not only are the notions of direct and indirect causation too obscure for the purposes of definition, but some of the subtler forms of deception involve indirection.

It might be argued that the reason why cases of this sort should not count as instances of deception is that they involve no *intention* that the other person be led to have false beliefs. This suggests the following definition:

> *x* deceives *y* if and only if *x* intentionally causes *y* to have false beliefs.

This definition, while a clear improvement over those that preceded it, is also inadequate. For according to it, no matter how false or misleading an advertisement is, it cannot be considered a case of deception provided that those who are responsible for producing it believe that it is true because in that case there is no intent to cause false beliefs. Moreover, if this defintion were correct, then an advertiser would have no need to attempt to determine if a claim is in fact true in order to avoid deception. If an automobile dealer's advertisement mistakenly claims that his model cars have the best safety record of any American-made car, the ad is deceptive, the dealer has committed an act of deception, even if he believes that it's true. We may wish to say that his moral culpability for the deception depends on whether or not he believes this claim and whether or not he made a good faith effort to verify it, but that is another matter. We propose the following definition of deception:

> x deceives y if and only if: x causes y to have certain false beliefs (b) and x intends or expects his actions to cause y to believe b.

This definition does not require that x believe that b is false, although, of course, he may. The reader will note that this definition differs from the earlier legalistic one in an important respect. The present definition only attempts to define what it is for one individual to deceive another. A given act (or advertisement) might mislead some people but not others. We need to provide additional standards in order to determine whether the ad *per se* should be considered deceptive. Thus our defintion would not provide adequate guidance to an FTC administrative law judge who would need to rule on whether or not an advertisement was likely to deceive enough people that, on the whole, it should be viewed as deceptive. However, our definition can (and we think should) be incorporated into guidelines for the regulation of advertising. Any definition of deception in advertising must be based upon an understanding of what it means to deceive an individual. An advertisement is said to be deceptive on account of its propensity to deceive or mislead individuals, and the intention or expectation on the part of the advertiser that it would do so. As we argued previously, intention is an issue that should be considered in important cases. For less important cases it might be considered sufficient to show that an advertiser expected (or should have expected) that a given percentage of people would be misled by the ad.

What's Wrong with Deception?

Here we will attempt to give an explanation of why deceptive advertising is wrong. We will argue that there are strong reasons for thinking that deceptive advertising is morally objectionable given the very weak assumption that it is wrong to hurt others.

(1) Our first and most important reason for thinking that deceptive advertisements are wrong is that they are harmful to consumers. Deceptive ads harm consumers by causing them to have false beliefs about the nature of the products being advertised and thereby cause some consumers to make different purchasing decisions than they would have made otherwise. For example, my being deceived into believing that eating Wheaties will make me a champion athlete may cause me to buy Wheaties instead of Kroger's Wheat Flakes which are of equal nutritional value and cheaper in price. I would have been better off if I'd bought the Kroger cereal. (My true interests are determined by what I would have done if I had been fully informed; and if I had been fully informed, I would have bought the Kroger Wheat Flakes.) Deceptive advertisements also harm one's competitors by reducing their sales.

Of course, there is no absolute moral prohibition against harming others. One is perfectly justified in harming someone else in self-defense. Similarly, a newspaper editor would be justified in printing an exposé harmful to the interests of corrupt official. However, harming others is *prima facie* wrong, or wrong, other things being equal. We may also put this by saying that there is a presumption for supposing that harming others is wrong. We need to be able to give a special justification in order for it to be right for us to harm others. For example, in the second case above, the general presumption against harming others is overridden by the public's interest in good government and the potential removal of the harms caused by the official.

So, the fact that deceptive advertisements harm consumers and competitors gives us a presumption for thinking that such advertisements are unethical. Are there any conceivable justifications for deceptive advertising that might override this presumption? Deceptive ads might cause someone to purchase a product which is of value to him which he would not have bought otherwise. For example in the Wheaties case, some might argue that the satisfaction derived from being associated with the Wheaties image more than compensates the consumer for the higher price paid. Or consider the hypothetical case of a well-meaning bureaucrat who decides to exaggerate the evidence linking cigarette smoking to cancer in a government sponsored antismoking campaign.

In the first case we have what is clearly a self-serving argument. Since the image projected depends on the fact that consumers are deceived. It is hard to see how the consumer benefits from the image. This case is unlike the case of those who purchase certain products (e.g., designer jeans) for their snob appeal. The image of Wheaties is itself dependent on a lie or falsehood, namely that Wheaties has special nutritional properties that help to produce champion athletes. A child is almost certainly better off in the long run if he realizes that athletic prowess can only be achieved by a combination of long hard training and natural ability rather than have his hopes dashed when he finds out that eating Wheaties will not make him a great athlete.[11] Even if there was some benefit, it is not clear that this benefit would be sufficient to justify the deception.

The second case (as well as the first) constitutes a type of paternalism typically rejected in the United States. The freedom for individuals to make decisions about their own consumption activities based upon accurate and complete information is generally thought to be more important than the consequences of their making the "wrong" decision. In extreme cases there are options other than deception to control consumption. Thus we have bans on the purchase of certain drugs and requirements that certain safety devices be purchased (e.g., automobile safety requirements). These other approaches appear superior to deception in attempting to promote the public good since they do not have the negative side effects discussed below that lying and deception (even for benevolent motives) do. Paternalism, if acceptable at all, should at least be practiced in the open.

Another possible justification for deception is that the benefits derived by the advertiser outweigh the harms that his ads cause others. This seems unlikely since all the deceptive advertiser's *economic* gains must come from somewhere—and this will be either from inflated prices paid by consumers and/or sales lost by competitors. Also economic theory tells us that in a free society economic welfare will be promoted through the efficient allocation of resources brought about by people making free choices on the basis of full information. Perfect (or at least adequate) information is not only an assumption of economic theory, it is a prerequisite for the operation of the "invisible hand" of capitalism. Unless consumers can tell which is the better of two products at a given price, there will be little incentive for the producer to make a better product and an inefficient allocation of resources will result. A firm that needs to deceive the public about the nature of its goods or services in order to stay in business is of dubious value to society—the resources that it utilizes could be put to better use in some other way. One possible exception to this is a case in which deceptive practices of a firm's competitors do financial damage to the firm. While deception by this beleaguered firm might then be justifiable from an economic standpoint, exposing the guilty firm would seem as effective and more morally acceptable. With the recent increase in comparative advertising we have in fact seen more firms attempt to expose alleged deception through their own ads and through the courts.[12]

The proposed justification of deceptive advertising is also untenable for reasons independent of the dubious empirical claim that harms to others are less than benefits to the deceiver. For, in general, the fact that harming someone else will benefit oneself is a very feeble justification for harming him. For example, the fact that my stealing your money would benefit me economically as much as it harms you would not justify me in stealing your money. Similarly, even if the economic benefits to a firm that presents deceptive advertisements about its products are roughly equal to the economic harms that it causes others, it is still clearly wrong for the firm to run the ads. The same reasoning applies in the typical case of deceptive advertising of relatively inexpensive consumer products leading to a small harm to each of many consumers, but cumulatively a great benefit to the producer. It's hard to see why cheating 100 people out of $1 is any less reprehensible than cheating one person out of $100, especially since the probable cumulative effect of both of these types of deceptive advertising would be the same for the typical consumer.

So, we have seen that on the weak and scarcely debatable assumption that it is *prima facie* wrong to harm others we can show that there is a strong presumption for supposing that deceptive advertising is morally wrong, irrespective of its legality.

(2) Sissela Bok[13] argues that, apart from its immediate bad consequences, lying (and by extension, deception) lowers the general level of trust and truthfulness so essential to the proper functioning of our society and its economic system. Because of this she claims that there is a strong presumption against lying and deception, even when they do no immediate harm.

Richard De George[14] and Norman Bowie[15] appeal to the same claims about the importance of honesty for creating an atmosphere of trust and cooperation in order to construct a different kind of argument for the claim that lying and dishonesty in business are morally objectionable. They argue that the practices of lying and deception would be self-defeating if everyone engaged in them, because the general climate of trust that makes these practices advantageous to those who engage in them would no longer prevail. De George writes the following:

> If everyone in business—buyers, sellers, producers, management, workers and consumers—acted immorally or even amorally (i.e., without concern for whether their actions were moral or immoral), business would soon grind to a halt. Morality is the oil as well as the glue of society and business. It is only against the background of morality that immorality can not only be profitable but even possible. Lying would not succeed if most people were not truthful and did not tend to believe others. A breach of trust requires a background of trust.[16]

Both De George and Bowie appeal to the views of the German philosopher Immanuel Kant who proposed what he called the "categorical imperative" as a standard for the rightness or wrongness of actions. The categorical imperative can be stated roughly as follows:

> An act is morally right if and only if the person who does it would be willing to have everyone else do the same thing or have everyone else follow the same principles that he does.[17]

Kant's argument in the case of deception in advertising would be that the person who engages in deceptive advertising would not be willing to have everyone else do the same, since if everyone did so the background of trust that makes his deception both possible and advantageous would no longer exist. Kant also proposes the following principle as a criterion of right and wrong:

> An act is wrong if it could not become a universal practice without being self-defeating.[18]

Bowie argues that making deceptive advertisements in order to gain a competitive advantage is morally wrong according to this criterion. If deception in advertising were a universal practice, no one would trust advertising and no one could gain an advantage by means of deceptive advertising.[19]

Suppose that we accept Kant's general principles. Do we have an additional argument for thinking that deceptive advertising is morally objectionable? Perhaps not. For there *already* exists a great distrust of advertising, but this has not rendered advertising ineffective or futile. However, while this argument may not succeed in establishing the immorality of the milder forms of deceptive advertising prevalent in our society, one can still imagine blatant forms of deceptive advertising that would make advertising futile if they became a universal practice. Suppose, for example that all ads grossly misrepresented the price and characteristics of the products being advertised. In that case, advertising would cease to provide consumers with useful information and would be unable to exert any significant effect on consumer behavior. Kant's principles would seem to provide us with an argument against blatantly false advertising. It is well to remember the degree to which we *can* trust the claims and descriptions we encounter in most ads. For example, if a margarine is advertised as being "100% corn oil with no cholesterol" hardly anyone questions this claim.

It might be argued that the *moderate* level of distrust fostered by advertising is something that is desirable and beneficial. Advertising helps to foster a "healthy skepticism" not only for the claims of other advertisers, but for the claims of politicians and government officials also. There is no doubt that a certain measure of distrust is desirable and little doubt that advertising helps to instill this distrust. However, we are not persuaded that such considerations could ever justify deceptive advertising. One cannot justify unethical conduct on the grounds that it helps to warn others to be on guard against conduct of that very sort. A mugger cannot justify his actions on the grounds that he makes people more cautious about where and how they travel. Similarly, a politician cannot justify lying to the public on the grounds that doing so will help instill prudent distrust of politicians in the average person.

(3) So far, our argument has depended on an appeal to utilitarian or quasi-utilitarian considerations about the undesirable consequences of deceptive advertising. Many people hold that certain acts (e.g., lying, promise breaking) are inherently *prima facie* wrong apart from any of their consequences. This view finds

its classic formulation in the writings of the British philosopher Sir W.D. Ross.[20] Ross holds that lying is *prima facie* wrong apart from any bad consequences that it may have, i.e., in the absence of any special justification it is wrong to lie, even if doing so won't result in any bad consequences. For example, it is wrong to lie about one's age to a stranger in a train station, even though no harm will come of this. Ross would claim that a utilitarian must say that lying is permissible in this case. (This is not entirely clear, since the utilitarian might try to avoid this conclusion by pushing Bok's argument that all lying undermines trust. But for the sake of argument let us assume that this lie will go undetected and will not have any negative consequences.) Ross identifies his own view about this matter with the morality of common sense. Here we think that he is clearly right. Most of us do believe that such things as lying and deception are inherently wrong. If common sense morality is right about this, then we have still further reasons for thinking that deceptive advertising is immoral. Our arguments in this paper do not commit us to any particular stance in the debate between Ross and the utilitarian. We simply assume something that both agree on, namely it is *prima facie* wrong to harm others.

New Directions in the Regulation of Deception

The FTC has recently enacted controversial new standards pertaining to the regulation of deception.[21] According to these new regulations, before the FTC would consider an advertisement to be deceptive, it must be found to have the capacity to mislead *and* to cause harm to "reasonable" consumers. This policy is supported and extended by FTC Chairman James Miller's contention that all FTC advertising regulations should be subjected to cost-benefit analysis. Since such regulatory activities can be quite costly, it is possible that the costs of regulating deception (which the consumer will pay in higher taxes or higher product prices) will exceed the benefits. This he feels is likely to be the case with low cost consumer goods which are repurchased frequently. He contends that the desire for repeat business and the threat of legal action for harmful deceptive advertisements will keep deception to a minimum.

This seems to the authors to be an overly optimistic view of the power of the marketplace to curb deception since it is unlikely that we would have so many well-documented cases of deception if it were unprofitable. The idea of regulating on the basis of cost-benefit criteria presupposes a commitment to utilitarianism and is open to question for that reason. But even if we accept the utilitarian presuppositions on which Miller's argument depends, it's still not clear that his proposed guidelines are appropriate. A utilitarian would caution that *all* of the costs and benefits need to be considered. Thus such factors as the decline of trust in society would be relevant. Also a utilitarian would recommend protecting children and ignorant adults from deceptive ads if the benefits of doing so exceeded the costs (see our earlier arguments regarding these special cases). A utilitarian would also be bound to recommend action whenever the costs of deception exceed the costs of regulation regardless of whether the deception costs a great many consumers only a few pennies or a few consumers a great amount. And finally the utilitarian would recommend that that vehicle (government regulation, government litigation or consumer litigation) which could alleviate the problem most cost-effectively should be used.

Summary

In the above analysis we have tried to point out weaknesses in proposed definitions of deception in advertising and have suggested ways of correcting these deficiencies. In addition, we have proposed an explanation of why deceptive advertising is wrong. Finally, new FTC approaches for regulating deception were examined in the light of these ethical considerations. It is hoped that a better understanding by academics, practitioners, and government officials of the concepts presented in this paper will provide a better basis for the consideration and the measurement of deception in advertising.

NOTES

1. *Creative Code* (American Association of Advertising Agencies, 1962).
2. *The Advertising Code of American Business* (American Advertising Federation, n.d.).
3. D. Cohen, "Unfairness in Advertising Revisited," *Journal of Marketing* **46** (Winter 1982), p. 77.
4. Cohen, *ibid*.
5. F.L. Barbour II and D.M. Gardner, "Deceptive Advertising: A Practical Approach to Measurement," *Journal of Advertising*, **11** (1982), p. 21. In this quotation the following references are cited: D.A. Aaker, "Deceptive Advertising," in *Consumerism: Search for the Consumer Interest*, 2nd ed., D.A. Aaker and G.S. Day (eds.) (The Free Press, New York, 1974), pp. 137–156; G.M. Armstrong, M.N. Gurol and F.A. Russ, "Detecting and Correcting Deceptive Advertising," *Journal of Consumer Research* **6** (December 1978), pp. 237–246; G.M. Armstrong, C.L. Kendall and F.A. Russ, "Applications of Consumer Information Processing Research to Public Policy Issues," *Communications Research* **2** (July 1975), pp. 232–245; G.M. Armstrong and F.A. Russ, "Detecting Deception in Advertising," *MSU Business Topics* **23** (Spring 1975), pp. 21–32; G.T. Ford, P.G. Keuhl and O. Reksten, "Classifying and Measuring Deceptive Advertising: An Experimental Approach," *American Marketing Association 1975 Combined Proceedings*, E.M. Mazze (ed.) (1975), pp. 493–497; D.M. Gardner, "Deception in Advertising: A Conceptual Approach," *Journal of Marketing* **39** (January 1975), pp. 40–46; D.M. Gardner, "Deception in Advertising: A Receiver Oriented Approach to Understanding," *Journal of Advertising* **5** (Fall 1976), pp. 5–11; J.E. Haefner, "The Perception of Deception in Television Advertising: An Exploratory Investigation," unpublished doctoral dissertation (University of Minnesota, Minneapolis, 1972); J.E. Haefner, "The Legal Versus the Behavioral Meaning of Deception," *Proceedings of the Association for Consumer Research, 3rd Annual Conference* **17**, Venkatesan (ed.) Cincinnati (1972), pp. 356–360; J.A. Howard and J. Hulbert, *Advertising and the Public Interest* (Crain Communications, Inc., Chicago 1973); J. Jacoby and C. Small, "The FDA Approach to Defining Misleading Advertising," *Journal of Marketing* **39** (October 1975), pp. 65–68; P.G. Keuhl and R.F. Dyer, "Broad Belief Measures in Deceptive-Corrective Advertising: An Experimental Assessment," *Proceedings of the 1976 American Marketing Association Fall Conference*, K.L. Benhardt (ed.) (1976), pp. 373–379; P.G. Keuhl and R.F. Dyer, "Applications of the 'Normative Belief' Technique for Measuring the Effectiveness of Deceptive and Corrective Advertisements," *Advances in Consumer Research* **IV**, W.D. Perrault, Jr. (ed.) (1977), pp. 204–212; J.C. Olson and P.A. Dover, "Cognitive Effects of Deceptive Advertising," *Journal of Marketing Research* **15** (February 1978), pp. 29–38; I.L. Preston, "Researchers at the Federal Trade Commission: Peril and Promise," *Current Issues and Research in Advertising*, J.H. Leigh

and Claude R. Martin, Jr. (eds.) (Division of Research, Graduate School of Business Administration, University of Michigan, Ann Arbor, 1980), pp. 1–16.

6. Gardner (1975), *op. cit.*, p. 42. This definition is ambiguous in the use of the term "reasonable knowledge." It is unclear whether Gardner means: (1) the consumer has reasonable knowledge about the product after seeing the ad or (2) the consumer is a reasonably intelligent individual. A strict reading of Gardner's definition strongly suggests the first interpretation. According to Gardner we test the deceptiveness of an ad by reference to the impressions and beliefs people are left with after seeing it. An ad is deceptive if after seeing it people have less than adequate knowledge about the product. We use this first interpretation here and discuss a definition which incorporates this second interpretation below.

7. Jacoby and Small, *op. cit.*

8. I.L Preston, "A Comment on 'Defining Misleading Advertising' and 'Deception in Advertising'," *Journal of Marketing* 40 (July 1976), pp. 54–60.

9. Gardner (1975), op. cit., p. 46.

10. The standard definition of lying is "a lie is a deliberate false statement that is intended to deceive others." (*Oxford English Dictionary*). We have argued in other contexts that this definition is implausible and proposed the following definition instead:

A lie is a deliberate false statement which is either intended to deceive others or foreseen to be likely to deceive others. (from: T. Carson, R. Wokutch and K. Murrmann, "Bluffing in Labor Negotiations: Legal and Ethical Issues," *Journal of Business Ethics* 1 (February 1982), p. 17.)

Nothing that we have to say in this paper depends on this dispute about the definition of lying.

11. It must be conceded that sometimes people can be made better off by being deceived and led to believe that things are better than they actually are. For example, the parents of a dead man might be happier if they falsely believe that their son was not a murderer. But such cases are very atypical and the proof of this is that very few are willing to be deceived "for our own good." We resent those who deceive us or conceal information from us. In order to act effectively and achieve our goals we need to operate on the basis of true beliefs. Others seldom benefit us by deceiving us. It should also be stressed that the benefits of such deception are likely to be short-lived and outweighed by subsequent disappointment upon learning the truth.

12. D. Kneale, "Remedy Ruckus: Tylenol, the Painkiller, Gives Rivals Headache in Stores and in Court," *The Wall Street Journal* 10 (September 2, 1982), p. 1.

13. S. Bok, *Lying: Moral Choice in Public and Private Life* (Vintage Books, New York, 1979).

14. R. De George, *Business Ethics* (MacMillan, New York, 1982).

15. N. Bowie, *Business Ethics* (Prentice-Hall, Englewood Cliffs, 1982), pp. 61–64.
16. De George, *ibid.*, p. 6.
17. I. Kant, *Groundwork of the Metaphysics of Morals*, translation, H.J. Paton (Harper and Row, New York, 1964), pp. 88–89.
18. Kant, *ibid.*, p. 70.
19. Bowie, *ibid.*
20. W.D. Ross, *The Right and the Good* (Oxford, England, 1930).
21. M. Isikoff, "FTC Narrows Definition of Deceptive Ads," *The Washington Post* (October 22, 1983), pp. A1, A7: J. Saddler, "FTC Alters Its Policy on Deceptive Ads by 3–2 Vote. Sparks Congressional Outcry," *The Wall Street Journal* (October 24, 1983), p. 41.

Study Questions

1. Why do the authors criticize "The Reasonable Man Standard?" Do you agree? Why or why not?
2. How can deceptive ads harm consumers? Are deceptive ads wrong when they don't cause harm?
3. Do you agree with the author's claim that deceptive advertising is morally objectionable on the grounds that there is a moral presumption against harming others?
4. What do you think of the authors attempt to distinguish deception from *lying*? How would your own view affect the general conclusions of the paper?

Business Ethics, Interdisciplinarity and Higher Education

Peter Madsen

The following discussion can be taken as a challenge to philosophers and others who are responsible for the planning and the execution of courses of instruction or educational programs which fall under the rubric of "business ethics." First, some remarks directed toward a clarification of the concept of "interdisciplinarity" are offered, since much of the terminology in this area is used in different shades of senses by educators in different locales. Next, an argument that the most fruitful form of the business ethics course or program is one which incorporates interdisciplinarity is advanced and sustained. Last, a number of suggestions for an undergraduate business ethics course are made in which the concept of interdisciplinarity is central. The challenge which this paper poses consists in a criticism of the current method of teaching business ethics which is characterized by the traditional disciplinary approach and in pointing out that such an approach does not adequately treat the complexity of the problems and issues in business ethics. What is offered instead is a course of instruction in business ethics based upon the concept of interdisciplinarity as one which does adequately address these problems and issues and as one which fulfills the needs of students which is, after all, the chief goal of any course or program of instruction.

Three Propositions

There are, however, three propositions which function as assumptions or, more accurately, as givens in this paper which need be raised and accepted if an educational activity like business ethics built upon the concept of interdisciplinarity is to be at all possible. These three are: 1) that ethics *per se* and thereby business ethics specifically can be taught and hence learned, 2) that business ethics courses and programs are valuable components of college curriculums and should be encouraged and 3) that interdisciplinarity is itself inherently valuable as an educational tool and should likewise be encouraged. Cogent and persuasive arguments for each of these propositions have been advanced numerous times in the literature of philosophy and education, so no long, in-depth defense of them is necessary here. A few summary remarks about them should suffice.

To claim that business ethics is teachable and learnable is to claim that descriptions, normative principles and analytic activities can be presented to students in such a way that they can gain a new perspective on business not available to them elsewhere. This is not to claim, though, that students will necessarily become more ethical, moral or virtuous after enrolling in such a course. They will have acquired a body of knowledge that will help them understand the ethical dimensions of their future conduct as business practitioners or as citizens, but this is no guarantee of future ethical behavior. This is, of course, the main objection to the teaching of business ethics, viz., that it will not make and cannot make students more ethical. But such an objection is misdirected. Ethics courses share knowledge and are not activities or endeavors designed to legislate values or legitimize a particular set of ethical principles which should be adopted by students so that they may lead ethical lives. Rather, alternative forms of ethical theories, principles and guidelines are presented as examples which increase a student's awareness of the realm of ethics. To expect that business ethics courses will legislate values or legitimize a particular set of ethical principles is to expect the instructor of business ethics to be a proselytizer and not a teacher. Enrollment in Business Ethics 201 is no guarantee of future ethical behavior on the part of the student, just as enrollment in Business Management 201 is no guarantee of good future managerial behavior on the part of the student. Both behaviors rely upon any number of contingencies and the best that such college and universtiy courses can do is a sharing of the knowledge base of that area as it grows, develops and expands.

What then is the value of a business ethics component of a college, university or business school curriculum? The value is that they speak to the kinds of issues that students in business, as well as other student majors, need to know if they are to have a framework within which to make ethical decisions in business or about business. In other words, since every ethical judgement requires a knowledge base which is pertinent to that judgement and its context, then the business decisions which have ethical ramifications will have their own particular knowledge bases out of which those judgements can be intelligently performed. Business ethics courses can provide the knowledge which may function as the point of departure or knowledge base for ethical decision-making in or about business and this is the primary value of them. And, since knowledge imparting is the business of colleges, universities and business schools, business ethics courses are to be encouraged in their curriculums as significant and important kinds of knowledge-imparting experiences. If Plato is right that knowledge and virtue are indivisible and that one can act unethically only from out of ignorance, then higher education has a duty to share the knowledge that business ethicists have complied and researched.

The final given of this paper, that interdisciplinarity is a valuable educational strategy and should be encouraged, is one which has enjoyed a wide discussion in educational circles. The main reasons why interdisciplinarity is so valued are: 1) that the individual disciplinary approach succeeds in yielding only narrow, incomplete and one-sided perspectives, 2) that the complex problems of the day require a more general and integrated understanding given their intricacy and 3) that interdisciplinarity breeds creativity, whereas disciplinarity only leads to a stultifying accumulation of fragmented data and bits of knowledge in search of some coordination. For these reasons among others, the trend toward interdisciplinarity has been pronounced and it has become a norm in educational strategies. One main point in this paper, then, will be that this trend should be extended to the business ethics offerings of higher education since the subject matter of business ethics is itself highly complex and in need of an integration of the disciplines which have a stake in it and which can contribute to such a course when they are presented in a synergetic fashion.

Now, although it appears awkward, the term "interdisciplinarity" is useful to describe in a rudimentary and general way a number of educational strategies found in many college curriculums today. "Interdisciplinarity" is used herein to signify and convey more than just "interdisciplinary study." The latter term may be taken in two distinct senses. First, an interdisciplinary study may be one which brings the principles and *modus operandi* of two or more separate disciplines together for a concerted investigatory effort. Social psychology, biochemistry and astrophysics would count as examples of this first sense of interdisciplinary study. Another possibility is the merging of two or more traditional disciplines which then emerges as a separate discipline on its own right. Here women's studies, urban studies and Afro-American studies would be prime examples. Yet both of these senses of interdisciplinary studies—the joining of principles and methods for investigatory purposes and the merging of disciplines to create a new discipline—are based upon the more general concept of interdisciplinarity.

And these two formulations are not the only possible examples which exhaust the meaning of interdisciplinarity. In addition, there are such educational phenomena as crossdisciplinarity, transdisciplinarity, multidisciplinarity and pluridisciplinarity. Each of these can be subsumed under the concept of interdisciplinarity.[1] What these and the above two senses of interdisciplinary study have in common in some converging of distinct disciplines in a particular way to achieve a particularly desired result. Their movement is away from the strict compartmentalization of knowledge, method and subject matter which characterizes the pure disciplinary approach and toward an integration of knowledge, method and subject matter. Interdisciplinarity, then, is any educational attempt to supplant specialization in favor of holism and by seeing a value in synthesis as well an in analysis. Interdisciplinarity is therefore a useful signpost of many directions, not one of which completely exhausts its meaning.

Now, one might want to automatically label the study of business ethics as a study which is in herently based upon the concept of interdisciplinarity. After all, this field of interest brings together two separate realms—ethics, on the one hand and business, on the other. As such it can count as an integrative analysis which merges these two distinct disciplines in order to achieve a particular result, viz., to share the knowledge of what might constitute morally blameworthy conduct in business as opposed to what might constitute morally praiseworthy conduct there. Furthermore, one might argue, business ethics is by nature based upon the concept of interdisciplinarity, since it presents itself as an interdisciplinary study in the second of the two senses outlined above. It is the merging of disciplines to create a new discipline on its own right worthy of it own place in the curriculum. Hence, it might be concluded, business ethics is a good example of interdisciplinarity.

However, in practical terms, all of this is but partially true in higher education. Business ethics, on the undergraduate level in particular, is a specialized study which relies heavily upon the specialized discipline of philosophy. Business ethics courses are usually designed and offered by philosophy departments and they are usually taught by philosophers. They normally award college credit hours in philosophy and in certain curriculums they may fulfill a philosophy distribution requirement. Sometimes, however, they are offered by other college departments, yet when this is the case usually those departments—theology or busines management for example—have their own disciplines at heart and are no less specialized than the philosophy business ethics course.[2]

Strictly speaking, then, business ethics offerings to undergraduate students are discipline-bound and as such are only pseudo-examples of interdisciplinarity. They are more akin to survey courses with a specialized flavor. In fact, most courses offered by philosophers begin with a survey of traditional ethical theories which have been formulated at various times in the history of philosophy. Often this survey occupies more than a goodly portion of the course and less attention is paid to the application of traditional theory to business matters. The phrase "applied philosophy" is a correct one to describe business ethics courses which do give attention to the ways in which teleological, deontological and other ethical theories are important in business decision-making, but this alone is not enough to call them examples of interdisciplinarity. Rather, the standard business ethics course in philosophy departments is a disciplinary approach to particular ethical matters and business ethics is thereby best described as a sub-discipline of applied philosophy which itself is a subdiscipline of the discipline of philosophy. Nowhere in this description is there room for interdisciplinarity.

The Call for Change

While this is the typical scene in most undergraduate curriculums, it is interesting to note the critical call for a change in the rigid specialized disciplinary approach to education that is currently enjoying a wide hearing in evaluations of business school curriculums. This criticism has been directed primarily at MBA programs which have been taken to task for employing educational techniques which tend to graduate people who are particularly adept in specific areas such as accounting, marketing, corporate planning, etc., but who are unable to integrate these skills and creatively see a unified picture of the tasks an executive must perform.[3] The point being made in these evaluations is that the MBA program is overly specialized and that the disciplinary approach is an inadequate preparation for future business men and women inasmuch as the executive's position requires an ability to perceive the universal and not just the particular. Furthermore, an additional criticism is that business schools are excellent in graduating students who possess fine quantitative skills, but who lack qualitative decision-making skills such as that which would be required in making ethical business decisions.

Among the most recent critics of business school in this regard are J.N. Behrman and R.I. Levin in their scathing "Are Business Schools Doing Their Job?"[4] The answer to this not so rhetorical question by Behrman and Levin is a resounding no. According to them, business schools of management deserve failing grades because of their rigidity, over-specialization and over emphasis on quantitative analysis. If Behrman and Levin are accurate in their judgments, then it would appear that little has changed since the first business program was founded in an American university in 1898. The Wharton School of Accounts [sic] and Finance of the University of Pennsylvania was little more than a center where students learned techniques of accurately reporting accounts in a quantitative fashion.[5]

Given their level of appreciation of the standard MBA program in America, Behrman and Levin call for a movement to "deparochialize" the quantitatively oriented business schools so as to ". . . develop 'management scholars' who can talk broadly with managers about business philosophy, business environment, business planning and business decision-making without esoteric language and methodologies . . ."[6] And with respect to the role of interdisciplinarity, their message is quite clear: "Cross-disciplinary teaching and research should be required and rewarded; this will ensure that faculties can recognize, research and prescribe for complex problems. All teaching should make visible the 'limits of the discipline' and the 'useful life' of what is being taught."[7] Further they argue that: "teaching areas should be coordinated so that professors can remove their disciplinary blinders—which limit them technologically, internationally, ethically, culturally and politically—and begin to think in policy and strategy terms."[8] In short, the fetishism with quantitative analysis and the strictly disciplinary approach to education is a disability in business education according to these and many other critics and a movement toward interdisciplinarity is recommeneded as its cure.

This call for a change from disciplinarity to interdisciplinarity in MBA programs is one which should be instructive to educators on the undergraduate level. If the trend towards interdisciplinarity takes hold in graduate business school as it most likely will, then the traditional discipline-bound business ethics course on the undergraduate level will be poor preparation for business students who comprise a large percentage of the students who take business ethics. Also, since the problems of business ethics are so complex and since they would lend themselves readily to the virtues of interdisciplinarity, this might just be the correct educational strategy for the standard undergraduate business ethics course. In fact, the disciplinary study of business ethics is not adequate to encompass all the various perspectives that are to be found in the typical business ethics problem. For a philosopher, a theologian or a business management instructor to believe that their own disciplinary preparation is enough from which to adeptly address the many economic, social, political, legal, governmental or consumer problems which are covered in their business ethics courses is just self-deception. There is, therefore, a need that undergraduate educators develop a business ethics program which is based squarely upon the principles of interdisciplinarity so as to over-come the many difficulties which are present in the traditional disciplinary approach.

What shape might such a business ethics course take? What example of interdisciplinarity is best suited for the study of busi-ness ethics? How will students learn the subject matter of business ethics in a way that does justice to the concept of interdiscipli-narity? Perhaps the best strategy here is that educators consider the introduction of the crossdisciplinary method since it possesses two important features. First, it is based squarely upon the notion of interdisciplinarity in that it brings together many perspectives found in the distinct disciplines and second it incorporates the notion of centralization within the presentation of these perspec-tives. The crossdisciplinary method provides for many analyses from many directions, while at the same time providing for a centralizing synthesis of these independent perspectives. Hence, it can be both instructive on a multiple of levels and enriching on a single level which serves to unify the others.

Another reason why adoption of the crossdisciplinary method makes sense in business ethics is that its problems, issues and questions truly cross disciplinary lines and borders. The problems which comprise the issue of discrimination in hiring and the use of a quota system to rectify past discriminatory practices is a prime example of the complexity which can be found in business ethics courses. First of all, and perhaps foremost, there are various ethical arguments about discrimination as well as various arguments about the use of quota systems based upon ethical principles. Next, there are statistical facts about discrimination and quota systems which are pertinent to the issue in that they demonstrate the widespread nature of the problem. This data can be interpreted in any number of ways as is the case with statistics. And then there are arguments about the rights of individual versus the rights of businesses to hire whomever they regard as the best candidate for a position. Also, the question of whether governments have any duty to impose quota systems or to regulate businesses gen-erally is another separate issue. There are likewise many social, political, legal and historical themes all present in this area as well. In short, there is a whole range of distinct disciplinary issues that this one problem will raise and given this complexity, a crossdis-ciplinary approach to it would be an intelligent strategy.

The Cross-Disciplinary Method

A fine description of cross-disciplinarity is offered by Robert L. Scott.[9] For Scott, the cross-disciplinary method is primarily problem oriented, i.e., various educators address and analyze those aspects of a particular problem which have a relevance to their own discipline and share the results of that discipline's treatment of the problem. According to Scott, cross-disciplinary methods are significant as examples of interdisciplinarity because: ". . . they bring to bear several lines of disciplinary inquiry in some common context for some particular purpose."[10] Moreover, the cross-disciplinary, problem-orientation style of education is worthy of attention because: "In general the aims of cross-disciplinarity seems to be to create persons whose first allegiance is to responding to immediate, socially relevant problems, and for whom the various disciplines are existing resources to be tapped when they promise to yield applicable tools, insights or evidence, and never learned simply for their own sakes."[11] So Scott suggests a definition of cross-disciplinarity by means of a business metaphor: "If one were discussing these issues in the metaphor of the stockbrokers, one might offer cross-disciplinary studies, in which sequences of courses or learning experiences are organized so as to focus on some current social-political-economic problem, as a growth issue."[12]

As can be observed from these observations, instructors who teach business ethics might well be advised to consider cross-disciplinarity as a possible vehicle in their own efforts. A structuring of the business ethics course in a series of learning experiences for students where diverse individuals from diverse disciplines provide problem analysis of the course material might do a great deal to underscore the importance of this material in a student's mind. It would also do much to enchance a student's understanding of the complexity of such material and foster a creative response from them. And if Scott is right and the cross-disciplinary method is best suited to intricate problems which are immediate and socially relevant, then it may be just the best method for a successful ethics course which takes so much of its subject matter from recent cases of corporate practices.

The cross-disciplinary approach is also appropriate in the field of business ethics inasmuch as it requires a "common context" as

Scott has put it. In other words, a series of learning experiences *per se* and for its own sake is not adequate as a good educational procedure. Without some focal point or some central framework within which the series is presented, the result is likely to be student confusion rather than student understanding. The beauty of cross-disciplinarity is that it brings together the best from both the disciplinary approach and the concept of interdisciplinarity. It is both analytic and synthetic. Philosophers, theologians and business management instructors can utilize their own preparations as the necessary context, synthesis or focus for a wide ranging analysis of issues from colleagues in other departments who contribute to the series of learning experiences. For example, a philosopher may use the traditional theories of ethics as a central focus and at the same time invite sociologists, political scientists, economists, business instructors, psychologists, etc., etc. to develop the nonethical aspects of the course in a cogent series of learning experiences. Or a theologian may use religious principles, or a business management instructor may use theories of management as the central focus and at the same time have others develop issues not necessarily emerging out of that focus. In this way, rigidity, overspecialization, the fragmentation of knowledge and the tendency for self-deception on the part of the business ethics instructor may be eliminated.

One strong recommendation of the cross-disciplinary method has been made in the field of "business and society" which has emerged as an area of intense study in business schools and departments and which can be taken as a field allied to business ethics. Its emphasis is usually on business management theories and executive decision-making with an eye toward the social ramifications of decisions in business. Liam Fahey and Richard E. Wokutch have offered an alternative to the current disciplinary strategy of business and society courses which is an alternative because it is built upon a model of cross-disciplinarity.[13] They suggest that certain exchanges between businesses and other social institutions can be observed and described, then it makes sense for business and society theorists to analyze these exchanges from one system to another in their courses. With the institution of business as the focal point, they argue that the exchanges between business and institutions active in the political, social, legal, economic and social systems can be utilized as the basis for study.

This means that political scientists, governmental analysts, lawyers, economists, sociologists and public policy analysts among others have a potential contribution to make to research and teaching in the field of business and society. In thereby recommending this cross-disciplinary approach which this exchange analysis mandates, they conclude that: "The proposed framework is essentially transdisciplinary in that it encompasses the multiplicity of perspectives which have contributed to the development of the field; yet it provides a unifying theme to integrate these diverse efforts."[14]

This work may likewise be instructive to business ethicists. First, it again alerts one to the change from the purely disciplinary to the concept of interdisciplinarity that is gaining momentum in higher education. Further, it underscores the fact that the cross-disciplinary approach cannot succeed without some unifying central focus. Interdisciplinarity for the sake of interdisciplinarity is no virtue. There is a need for an overview in the implementation of a cross-disciplinary study which provides for consistency of course content, cogency of thought and a common point of reference. Without this unifying principle, the cross-disciplinary business ethics course will be doomed to failure as it accumulates uncoordinated facts for students who will find it difficult to bring them together into some useful and integrated whole.

The cross-disciplinary method in a business ethics course can be summarized as a transcending of disciplinary boundaries to create a series of interdisciplinary learning experiences in the classroom each of which is grounded in some overall disciplinary perspective be that philosophy, theology or business management. The emphasis is placed on the problems of business ethics such that students are given a number of views of a typical problem in business ethics which encourages them to respond with creativity and to appreciate the complexity of the issues. The series of learning experiences and the individual disciplines which should be included in it will be determined by the specific problem being addressed and analyzed. Often there will be many specializations which can be brought to bear upon a single problem. Sometimes there will be few. But the main point is that hardly ever is only one discipline appropriate for a complete treatment of a given business ethics problem. The cross-disciplinary method, then, is a proper vehicle for those responsible for the planning and execution of the business ethics course in higher education since it is both analytic and synthetic, since it is best suited to treat immediate and socially relevant issues and since it will encourage student creativity and learning.

One final suggestion can be made to instructors of business ethics as worthy of their consideration in their attempt to give students the best possible course of instruction. The facts of the matter are that the problems and issues in business ethics are such as not only to cross disciplinary lines, but also they literally cross institutional lines and boundaries. The business ethics class is not just merely a reflection and study within the institution of academia. It likewise relates to the activities of corporations, governments and governmental regulatory agencies, the legal system and various social systems among others. In other words, instructors of business ethics can enhance their courses by opening the forum of the classroom to representatives of institutions other than their own colleges or universities. Business men and women, directors of governmental agencies, lawyers, labor leaders, consumer advocates, etc., each has had firsthand experience with the issues typically found on the business ethics syllabus. It would be a smart move to include some of these representatives in the series of learning experiences which would comprise the crossdisciplinary business ethics offering. The chance for students—not to mention instructors—of business ethics courses to exchange ideas, question and dialogue with corporate executives, government authorities, etc., would be an invaluable addition to the series of learning experiences. Here textbooks would come alive, problems would not be merely academic, issues would have faces and become personalized and students would gain a real access to the "real world." Hence, cross-disciplinarity can become the parent of cross-institutional education.

Cross-institutional education can be implemented in a number of ways. Often a telephone call to a corporate headquarters will uncover a speaker's bureau in the public relations or corporate communications department. These bureaus offer company representatives to discuss various issues which the corporation feels is important enough to it that it wishes to communicate its own position to the public. Not infrequently these issues will be the same ones which a business ethics course will find worthy of investigation. Although one can expect a more formal presentation from a corporate speaker's bureau and a presentation that will be one-sided, there is usually a chance for questions and some discussion. But even given these limitations, this possibility would do much to enhance the business ethics class.

Another possibility for cross-institutional education is for the instructor to write a corporate officer or board of directors member who have had expertise with ethical issues in business and are responsible for the ethical conduct of the corporation in a certain area, say employee relations, and invite them to join the class and share their knowledge and expertise. Often this invitation will be flattering to the executive and they will be anxious to make such connections with a college or university. Another way to achieve this result is to invite a corporate executive who sits on the academic institution's board of trustees. Since they are already friends of higher education, they might be even more willing to take the time to address the business ethics class.

Instructors can also participate in the "executive-in-residence" programs that many campuses have become involved with and invite this individual to their course for a discussion of a pertinent topic. These programs are gaining in numbers of participating executives and institutions of higher education. Two well-known executive-in-residence programs are sponsored by the Woodrow Wilson National Fellowship Foundation in Princeton and by the American Council of Life Insurance (ACLI) which has offices in Washington, D.C. In these novel experiences, a corporate executive visits a campus for an extended period to enter into dialogue with students, faculty, administration and staff so that his or her own experiences as an executive can be shared with the members of the academic institution. If one's campus is not already involved in an executive-in-residence program, perhaps the business ethics instructor might take the initiative and begin one on their campus. Also, other possible cross-institutional, educative experiences will occur to the creative instructor.

Conclusion

This paper has called for a change in the *status quo*. It is a recommendation and a challenge to philosophers, theologians, business management instructors and others to restructure the way in which they teach business ethics. It has argued that while business ethics is teachable and learnable and that while business ethics is a valuable component within the curriculums of higher education for the kind of knowledge that it can impart, it has also called into question the kind of teaching and imparting of knowledge that usually takes place in higher education. It finds little value in the traditional disciplinary approach of higher education which tends to fragment knowledge into compartments that have little useful applications for students. It is further argued that the business ethics course should avoid this fragmentation and proceed upon the basis of interdisciplinarity which is seen as a more creative educational tool. It recommends that the cross-disciplinary method be implemented since it allows for a proper treatment of the complexity of the problems, issues and questions of business ethics. It encourages students to become involved creatively and it enhances their learning experience. Cross-disciplinarity is valuable also because it requires a central focus or common context which can be provided by philosophy, theology, business management or another regular discipline. Furthermore, it is suggested that the cross-disciplinary method be utilized with cross-institutional education where representatives of corporations, government, labor, consumer advocacy, etc., provide their expertise and knowledge along side of representatives from the traditional academic disciplines. Such a series of cogent learning experiences will have the effect of underscoring the importance of the issues in business ethics, or demonstrating their complexity and of integrating that which gets lost in a purely disciplinary teaching of business ethics. And, most importantly, such a strategy will foster student involvement, creativity and understanding by providing useful, coordinated knowledge that they can draw upon in the future as business men and women or as citizens of the modern corporate world.

NOTES

1. For an examination of the history, development and problems of interdisciplinarity and the associated concepts see Kockelmans, Joseph J. (ed.), *Interdisciplinarity and Higher Education*, (University Park: The Pennsylvania University Press, 1979).

2. Cf. Hoffman, W. Michael and Moore, Jennifer Mills, "Results of a Business Ethics Curriculum Survey by the Center for Business Ethics," *Journal of Business Ethics*, Vol. 1, May 1982, pp. 81–83.
3. Cf. "Are MBAs More Than Quantitative Robots?" in *Business and Society Review*, No. 44, Winter 1983, pp. 4–12.
4. Behrman, J.N. and Levin, R.I., "Are Business Schools Doing Their Job?" *Harvard Business Review*, Vol. 62, No. 1, January–February 1984, pp. 140–147.
5. Jacoby, Neil H., *Corporate Power and Social Responsibility*, (New York: Macmillan Publishing Co., Inc. 1973), pp. 61–62.
6. Behrman, J.N. and Levin, R.I., p. 144.
7. *Ibid.*, p. 144.
8. *Ibid.*, p. 144.
9. Scott, Robert L., "Personal and Institutional Problems Encountered in Being Interdisciplinary" in Kockelmans, Joseph J. (ed.), *Interdisciplinarity and Higher Education*, Op. Cit., pp. 306–327.
10. *Ibid.*, p. 314.
11. *Ibid.*, p. 314.
12. *Ibid.*, p. 314.
13. Fahey, Liam and Wokutch, Richard E., "Business and Society Exchanges: A Framework for Analysis," *California Management Review*, Vol. XXV, No. 4, Summer 1983, pp. 128–142.
14. *Ibid.*, pp. 141–142.

Study Questions

1. State why you agree or disagree with the author that courses such as business ethics are no guarantee that students who attend them will be ethical in their future careers?
2. What is your evaluation of the author's contention that courses in business ethics should be based upon an interdisciplinary approach?

The Profit Motive in Medicine

*Dan W. Brock and Allen E. Buchanan**

The American health care system is undergoing a rapid socioeconomic revolution. Within a general environment of heightening competition, the number of investor-owned for-profit hospitals has more than doubled in the past ten years.[1] Although the increase in investor-owned hospitals has been most dramatic and publicized, a rise in investor-owned health care facilities of other types, from dialysis clinics to outpatient surgery and "urgent care" centers has also occurred.[2]

Investor-owned-for-profit corporations are controlled ultimately by stockholders who appropriate surplus revenues either in the form of stock dividends or increased stock values. Independent proprietary institutions are for-profit entities owned by an individual, a partnership, or a corporation, but which are not controlled by stockholders. Nonprofit corporations are tax-exempt and are controlled ultimately by boards of trustees who are prohibited by law from appropriating surplus revenues after expenses (including salaries) are paid.

The above definitions treat "for-profit" rather narrowly as a legal status term referring to investor-owned and independent proprietary institutions. However, much of the current concern

* Dan W. Brock, PhD, Professor, Department of Philosophy, Brown University, Providence, Rhode Island 02912, U.S.
Allen E. Buchanan, PhD, Professor, Department of Philosophy, University of Arizona, Tucson, Arizona 85721, U.S.
The Journal of Medicine and Philosophy **12** (1987), 1–35. © 1987 by D. Reidel Publishing Company.

over "for-profit health care" has a wider, though much less clear, focus. It is often said, for instance, that health care in America is being transformed from a profession into a business like any other because of the growing dominance of those types of motivation, decision-making techniques, and organizational structures that are characteristic of large-scale commercial enterprises.

A recent book published by the Institute of Medicine (1983) bears the title *The New Health Care for Profit*, with the subtitle *Doctors and Hospitals in a Competitive Environment*. The difference in scope between the title and subtitle is but one example of a widespread tendency of discussions of "for-profit health care" to run together concerns about the effects of increasing competition in health care, which affects both "for-profit" and "nonprofit" institutions in the legal sense, and special concerns about the growth of those health care institutions that have the distinctive "for-profit" legal status.

This essay will focus primarily on the ethical implications of the growth of for-profit health care institutions in the legal sense. However, although the ethical problems we shall explore have been brought to public attention by the rapid rise of for-profit institutions (in the legal sense), it would be a mistake to assume that they are all peculiar to institutions that have this legal form. They are problems that stem from increasing competition and cost-conscious management throughout the health care sector.

There has been a sharp polarization in the responses of observers to this apparent trend toward increased profit seeking in medicine. Some view profit motives in any form and at any place as wholly inappropriate for medicine. This has led in at least two states to legislation or proposed legislation limiting or banning for-profit health care institutions from operating in the state.[3] Opponents of for-profit medicine are a diverse group and include representatives of the medical profession seeking to preserve their professional autonomy, advocates concerned to prevent a worsening of access to health care for the poor and uninsured, those concerned about the impact of profit seeking on quality of care, and many others. Proponents of the growth of for-profits are likewise diverse and include, among others, representatives of the investor-owned firms concerned to protect their economic interests as well as health policy analysts who look to the for-profits to introduce more competition into health care and to help contain rising health care costs.

The polarization of positions on the influx of profit seeking in medicine has often generated more heat than light. Serious moral criticisms of for-profit health care have been voiced, but often in overstated, rhetorical terms. Before they can be evaluated, these criticisms must be more carefully articulated than has usually been done. In this paper, we seek to clarify and evaluate two of the central ethical criticisms of profit motivations and for-profit institutions in medicine: (1) for-profit health care institutions fail to fulfill their obligations to do their fair share in providing health care to the poor and so exacerbate the problem of access to health care; and (2) profit seeking in medicine will damage the physician-patient relationship, creating conflicts of interest that will diminish the quality of care and erode patients' trust in their physicians and the public's trust in the medical profession.

I. For-Profits Exacerbate the Problem of Access to Health Care

Twenty-two to twenty-five million Americans have no health care coverage, either through private insurance or through government programs including Medicare, Medicaid, and the Veterans Administration. Another twenty million have coverage that is inadequate by any reasonable standards (President's Commission, pp. 92–101). The charge that for-profits are exacerbating this already serious problem takes at least two forms. First, it is said that for-profits contribute directly to the problem by not providing care for nonpaying patients. The data are not fully consistent on whether for-profit hospitals provide less or as much uncompensated care as do nonprofit hospitals; data from several states show that they provide less, but national data show minimal differences between for-profits and nonprofits, both of which do much less than publicly owned hospitals. In any event, our concern here is to analyze the arguments that have been advanced regarding the issue of uncompensated care. In particular, we shall examine the assumption that if for-profit hospitals provide less indigent care, then they thereby fail to fulfill an important obligation and act unfairly.

Second, it is also alleged that for-profits worsen the problem of access to care in an indirect way because the competition they provide makes it more difficult for nonprofits to continue their long-standing practices of "cross-subsidization." Cross-subsidization is of two distinct types: nonprofits have traditionally financed some indigent care by inflating the prices they charge for paying patients, and they have subsidized more costly types of services by revenues from those that are less costly relative to the revenues they generate.

It is sometimes assumed that in general for-profits are more efficient in the sense of producing the same services at lower costs and that these production efficiencies will be reflected in lower prices. At present, however, there is insufficient empirical evidence to show that for-profits on the whole are providing significant price competition by offering the same services at lower prices, though this may change in the future. In fact, what little data there are at present indicate that costs, especially of ancillary services, tend to be higher, not lower, in the for-profits (Brown and Klosterman 1986; Watt *et al.* 1986).

However, the argument that for-profits are making it more difficult for nonprofits to continue the practice of cross-subsidization does not depend upon the assumption that for-profits are successful price competitors in that sense. Instead, it is argued that for-profits "skim the cream" in two distinct ways. First, they capture the most attractive segment of the patient population by locating in more affluent areas, leaving nonprofits with a correspondingly smaller proportion of paying patients from which to subsidize care for nonpaying patients. Second, by concentrating on those services that generate higher revenues relative to the costs of supplying them, for-profits can achieve greater revenue surpluses, which provide opportunities either for lower prices or for investment in higher quality or more attractive facilities, both of which may worsen the competitive position of nonprofits, making it more difficult for them to cross-subsidize.

Critics of for-profits predict that access to care will suffer in two ways: fewer nonpaying patients will be able to get care and some paying patients, i.e., some who are covered by public or private insurance, will be unable to find providers who will treat them for certain "unprofitable" conditions. Although these predications have a certain *a priori* plausibility, they should be tempered by several important considerations. First, as already indicated, there is at present a dearth of supporting data concerning differences in the behavior of for-profits and nonprofits, and this is hardly surprising since the expansion of the for-profit sector has been so recent and rapid. However, preliminary data do support two hypotheses that tend to weaken the force of the criticism that for-profits are exacerbating the problem of access to care by making it more difficult for nonprofits to continue cross-subsidization. One is that at present there seems to be no substantial difference in the proportion of nonpaying care rendered by for-profits and non-profits (Committee Report, Ch. 5). The other is that at present the proportion of nonpaying care rendered by nonprofits is on average only about 4% of their total patient care expenditures (Committee Report, Ch. 5). Here again, however, it may be important to separate from the overall data for nonprofits the public hospitals in which the proportion of nonpaying care is both higher than in the for-profits and substantially in excess of 3% of overall total patient care expenditures (California Association of Public Hospitals, unpublished). If the public hospitals experience a decrease in their paying patients, their ability to carry out their mission of serving the indigent could be seriously jeopardized.

A third reason for viewing predictions about the effects of for-profits on access to care with caution is that there are other variables at work that may be having a much more serious impact. In particular, the advent of a prospective reimbursement system for Medicare hospital services (Diagnostic Related Groups [DRGs]) and other efforts for cost-containment of state and federal regulatory bodies and businesses, as well as the general increase in competition throughout the health care sector, are making it more difficult for any institution to cross-subsidize.

In addition, as defenders of for-profits have been quick to point out, in some cases for-profits have actually improved access to care not only by locating facilities in previously underserved areas thus making it more convenient for patients to use them, but also by making certain services more affordable to more people by removing them from the more expensive hospital setting. The growth of outpatient surgical facilities in suburban areas, for example, has improved access to care in both respects. Indeed, there is some reason to believe that by making decisions on the basis of the preferences of their boards of trustees (which may be shaped more by their own particular tastes or considerations of prestige rather than by demands of sound medical practice or response to accurate perceptions of consumer demand), nonprofits have in some cases duplicated each other's services and passed up opportunities for improving access by failing to expand into underserved areas.

This latter point drives home the complexity of the access issue and the need for careful distinctions. For-profits may improve access to care in the sense of better meeting some previously unmet demand for services by paying patients, while at the same time exacerbating the problem of access to care for nonpaying patients. However, there is clearly a sense in which the latter effect on access is of greater moral concern. We assume here that the members of a society as affluent as ours have a collective moral obligation to ensure that all have access to some "decent minimum" or "adequate level" of care, even if they are not able to pay for it themselves. Surely, providing basic care for those who lack any coverage whatsoever then should take priority over efforts to make access to care more convenient for those who already enjoy coverage and over efforts to reduce further the financial burdens of those who already have coverage by providing services for which they are already insured in less costly non-hospital settings.

So far we have examined the statement that "cream skimming" by for-profits exacerbates the problem of access to care. Ultimately, this is largely an empirical question about which current data are inconclusive. There is another way in which the "cream skimming" charge can be understood. Sometimes it is suggested that for-profits are acting irresponsibly or are not fulfilling their social obligations by failing to provide their "fair share" of indigent care and unprofitable care, as well as making it more difficult for nonprofits to bear their fair share through cross-subsidization. To this allegation of unfairness, defenders of for-profits have a ready reply: "No one is *entitled* to the cream; so for-profits do no wrong when they skim it. Further, for-profits discharge *their* social obligations by paying taxes. Finally, since the surplus revenues that nonprofits use to subsidize nonpaying or unprofitable care are themselves the result of overcharging—charging higher prices than would have existed in a genuinely competitive market—then it is all the more implausible to say that they are entitled to them."

While this reply is not a debate-stopper, it should give the critic of for-profits pause since it draws attention to the unstated—and controversial—premises underlying the contention that cream skimming by for-profits is unfair because it constitutes a failure to bear a fair share of the costs of nonpaying or unprofitable patients. The most obvious of these is the assumption that in general nonprofits are (or have been) bearing their fair share.

To determine whether for-profits or nonprofits are discharging their obligations, we must distinguish between two different types of obligations—general and special. For-profit corporations, like individual citizens, can argue that they are discharging their *general* obligation to subsidize health care for the poor by paying taxes. To see this, assume that the fairness of the overall tax system is not in question, and in particular its taxation of corporate profits. For-profits can then reasonably claim that they are doing their fair share to support *overall* government expenditures by paying taxes. If the government is subsidizing health care for the poor as part of overall government expenditures, then for-profits would appear to be doing their fair share towards supporting subsidized health care for the poor. If the government is providing inadequate subsidization of health care for the poor, then the fair share funded by the for-profits' taxes will in turn be inadequate, but proportionately no more so than every other taxpayer's share is inadequate, and *not unfair* relative to the subsidization by other taxpayers. The responsibility for this inadequacy, in any case, would be the government's or society's, not that of the for-profit health care corporation's.

A for-profit hospital chain cannot say that if it is paying, for example, $30 million in taxes, it is providing $30 million towards funding health care for the poor. Its taxes, whether at the federal, state, or local level should be understood as a contribution to the overall array of tax-supported programs at those levels. But it can claim to be subsidizing health care for the poor with the portion of its taxes proportionate to the portion of overall government expenditures devoted to subsidizing health care for the poor.

On the other hand, those who raise the issue of fairness have apparently assumed that health care institutions have *special* obligations to help care for indigents. Even if this assumption is accepted, however, it is not obvious that in general nonprofits have been discharging the alleged special obligation successfully for the reasons already indicated. First, even if cross-subsidization is widespread among nonprofits, the proportion of nonpaying and unprofitable care that is actually provided by many nonprofits appears not to be large. Second, some of the revenues from "overcharging" paying patients apparently are not channeled into care for nonpaying patients or patients with unprofitable conditions.

It was noted earlier that while many *publicly owned* nonprofit hospitals provide a substantial proportion of care for nonpaying patients, non-publicly owned nonprofits ("voluntaries") as a group do not provide significantly more uncompensated care than for-profits. One rationale for granting tax-exempt status is that this benefit is bestowed in exchange for the public service of providing care for the indigent. If it turns out that many nonprofit health care institutions are in fact not providing this public service at a level commensurate with the benefit they receive from being tax exempt, then this justification for granting them tax-exempt status is undermined.

It is also crucial to question the assumption that for-profit health care institutions have special obligations to help subsidize care for the needy over and above their general obligation as taxpayers. As the for-profits are quick to point out, supermarkets are not expected to provide free food to the hungry poor, real estate developers are not expected to let the poor live rent-free in their housing, and so forth. Yet food and housing, like health care, are basic necessities for even minimal subsistence. If there are basic human rights or welfare rights to some adequate level of health care, it is reasonable to think there are such rights to food and shelter as well as health care.

Whose obligation is it, then, to secure some basic health care for those unable to secure it for themselves?[4] Assuming that private markets and charity leave some without access to whatever amount of health care that justice requires be available to all, there are several reasons to believe that the obligation ultimately rests with the federal government. First, the obligation to secure a just of fair overall distribution of benefits and burdens across society is usually understood to be a general societal obligation. Second, the federal government is the institution society commonly employs to meet societywide distributive requirements. The federal government has two sorts of powers generally lacking in other institutions, including state and local governments, that are necessary to meeting this obligation fairly. With its taxing power, it has the revenue-raising capacities to finance what would be a massively expensive program on any reasonable account for an adequate level of health care to be guaranteed to all. This taxing power also allows the burden of financing health care for the poor to be spread fairly across the members of society and not to depend on the vagaries of how wealthy or poor a state or local area happens to be. With its nationwide scope, it also has the power to coordinate programs guaranteeing access to health care for the poor across local and state boundaries. This is necessary both for reducing inefficiencies that allow substantial numbers of the poor to fall between the cracks of the patchwork of local and state programs, and for ensuring that there are not great differences in the minimum of health care guaranteed to all in different locales within our country.

If we are one society, a *United* States, then the level of health care required by justice for all citizens should not vary greatly in different locales because of political and economic contingencies of a particular locale. It is worth noting that food stamp programs and housing subsidies, also aimed at basic necessities, similarly are largely a federal, not a state or local, responsibility. These are reasons for the federal government having the obligation to guarantee access to health care for those unable to secure it for themselves. It might do this by directly providing the care itself, or by providing vouchers to be used by the poor in the health care marketplace. *How* access should be guaranteed and secured—and in particular, to what extent market mechanisms ought to be utilized—is a separate question.

Granted that the obligation to provide access to health care for the poor rests ultimately with the federal government, is there any reason to hold that for-profit health care institutions, such as hospitals, have any special obligations to provide such care? The usual reason offered is that health care institutions, whether nonprofit or for-profit, are heavily subsidized directly or indirectly by public expenditures for medical education and research and by Medicare and Medicaid reimbursement, which have created the enormous predictable demand for health care services that has enabled health care institutions to flourish and expand so dramatically since the advent of these programs in 1965. However, we believe it is less clear than is commonly supposed that these subsidies redound to the benefit of the for-profit institution in such a way as to ground a special institutional obligation to subsidize health care for the poor.

The legal obligation of nonprofit hospitals to provide free care to the poor is principally derived from their receipt of Hill-Burton federal funds for hospital construction. However, the for-profit hospital chains secure capital for construction costs in private capital markets and do not rely on special federal subsidies. Even when they purchase hospitals that have in the past received Hill-Burton monies, they presumably now pay full market value for the hospitals. If there is a subsidy that has not been worked off in free care, that redounds to the nonprofit seller, not the for-profit purchaser. What of other subsidies?

There is heavy governmental subsidy of medical education; it is widely agreed that physicians do not pay the full costs of their medical education. Perhaps then they have a reciprocal duty later to pay back that subsidy, though it would need to be shown why the form that duty should take is to provide free care to the poor as opposed, for example, to reimbursing the government directly. However that may be, it is physicians and not the for-profit hospitals who are the beneficiaries of medical education subsidies. Physicians are the owners of these publicly subsidized capital investments in their skills and training, and are able to sell their subsidized skills at their full market value. Physicians, and not the owners of for-profit health care institutions in which they practice or are employed, are the beneficiaries of education subsidies and so are the ones who have any obligation there may be to return those subsidies by in turn subsidizing free care for the poor.

Another important area of public subsidy in the health care field is medical research. Much medical research has many of the features of a public good, providing good reason for it to be publicly supported and funded. (Where these reasons do not apply, as, for example, in drug research, the research is largely privately funded by the drug companies.) Medical research makes possible new forms of medical technology, knowledge, and treatment. Because it is publicly funded, and once developed is generally freely available for use by the medical profession, for-profit health care institutions are able to make use of the benefits of that research in their delivery of health care without sharing in its cost. But who ultimately are the principal beneficiaries of this public subsidy of research? Not, we believe, the for-profits, but rather the patients who are the consumers of the new or improved treatments generated by medical research. It may or may not be true that for-profits will not bear the research costs of these treatments as part of their delivery costs. But if, as is increasingly the case, the for-profits operate in a competitive environment concerning health care costs or charges, they will be forced to pass on these subsidies to consumers or patients. (And if they operate in a largely noncompetitive environment, there will be a strong case for some form of regulation of their rates.) The price that patients pay for health care treatments whose research costs were subsidized by the government will not include those research costs and so will not reflect true costs. It is then consumers of health care, not the for-profits, who principally benefit from research subsidies, and any obligation arising from this subsidy presumably lies on them.

Finally, consider the large public subsidy represented by Medicare and Medicaid. These programs created a vast expansion in the market for health care that many for-profits serve and from which they benefit. This is new health care business that heretofore did not exist and on which they make a profit. Perhaps this benefit grounds a special obligation of for-profit institutions to provide subsidized care for the poor. The most obvious difficulty with such a view is that the subsidized health care consumers, not the deliverers of the health care, are by far the principal beneficiaries of Medicare and Medicaid. Any profit that the for-profits receive from serving Medicare and Medicaid patients is only a small proportion of the overall cost of their care.

It must be granted, nevertheless, that the for-profits do earn profits from these subsidized patients. But it is difficult to see how this fact by itself is sufficient to ground a special obligation of the for-profits to subsidize free care for the poor. In the first place, for-profits can again respond that they pay taxes on these profits, like other profit-making enterprises. Moreover, they can point out that in no other cases of government-generated business of for-profit enterprises it is held that merely earning a profit from such business grounds a special obligation similar to that claimed for for-profit health care enterprises. Virtually no one holds that defense contractors, supermarkets who sell to food stamp recipients, highway builders, and so forth have any analogous special obligation based on the fact that their business is created by government funds. Nor is it ever made clear why this fact should itself ground any special obligation of for-profits in health care to provide access to health care for the poor. Thus, we conclude that none of the current forms of public subsidy of health care will establish any significant *special* obligation of for-profits to provide free care, and so the claim cannot be sustained that for-profits do not do their fair share in providing access to health care for the poor. We emphasize that we believe there *is* an obligation to guarantee some adequate level of health care for all, but the obligation is society's and ultimately the federal government's and not a special obligation of for-profit health care institutions.

Even if there are insufficient grounds for the assumption that for-profit health care institutions, or health care institutions as such, have special obligations to provide a "fair share" of uncompensated care, it can be argued that a nation or a community, operating through a democratic process, can impose such a special obligation on the institutions in question as a condition of their being allowed to operate. According to this line of thinking, a community may, through its elected representatives, require that any hospital doing business in that community provide some specified amount of indigent care, either directly or by contributing to an indigent care fund through a special tax on health care institutions (so far as they are not legally exempt from taxes) or through a licensing fee.

Whether such an arrangement would be constitutional or compatible with statutory law in various jurisdictions is not our concern here. One basic ethical issue is whether the imposition of such special obligations would unduly infringe on individuals' occupational and economic freedoms. Although no attempt to examine this question will be made here, this much can be said: a community's authority to impose a special obligation to contribute a portion of revenues (as opposed to an obligation to contribute services) for indigent care seems no more (or less) ethically problematic than its authority to levy taxes in general.

A second basic ethical issue is then whether such taxes, or requirements to provide uncompensated care as conditions of doing business for health care institutions, fairly distribute the costs of providing care to the indigent. That will depend on the details of the particular tax or requirement to provide uncompensated care, but since any are likely to be ultimately a tax on the sick, it is doubtful that such provisions will be fairer than financing care for the indigent through general tax revenues.

There is, moreover, an additional difficulty with any claim that, by skimming the cream, for-profits fail to fulfill an existing special obligation to bear a fair share of the burden of providing at least some minimum level of care for all who need it but cannot afford it. This is the assumption that in the current U.S. health care system any determinate sense can be given to the notion of a "fair share" of the burden of ensuring access to care (in the absence of specific legislation such as the Hill-Burton Act). Unless a rather specific content can be supplied for the notion of a fair share, the nature and extent of an institution's alleged special obligation will be correspondingly indeterminate. In particular, it will be difficult if not impossible to determine whether for-profits have met such a special obligation. But it will also be problematic to assert what some defenders of nonprofits imply, namely that nonprofits have in the past done their fair share through cross-subsidization.

The current U.S. health care system is a patchwork—or, less charitably, a crazy quilt—of private insurance and public program entitlements. There is no generally accepted standard for a "decent minimum" or "adequate level" of care to be ensured for all, no systemwide plan for coordinating local, state, and federal programs, charity, and private insurance so as to achieve it, and no overall plan for distributing the costs of providing care for those who are unable to afford it from their own resources. Absent all of this, no determinate sense can be given to the notion of an institution's special obligation to provide a "fair share" of the burden of ensuring an "adequate level" or "decent minimum" of care for everyone.

Furthermore, even if it were possible at present to determine, if only in some rough-and-ready way, what an institution's "fair share" is, this would still not be enough. Whether an institution has an *obligation*—a duty whose fulfillment society can require—will depend upon whether it can do so without unreasonable risks to its own financial well-being. But in a competitive environment, whether one institution's contributing its "fair share" will be unreasonably risky for it will depend upon whether other institutions are doing *their* "fair share."

The establishment of a coordinated systemwide scheme in which institutions share the costs of providing some minimum level of care for all is a "public good" in the economist's sense. Even if every governing board of every institution agrees that it is desirable or even imperative to ensure some level of care for all, so long as contribution to this good is strictly voluntary, each potential institutional contributor may attempt to take a free ride on the contribution of others with the result that the good will not be achieved.

It is important to understand that failure to produce the public good of a fair system for distributing the costs of care by voluntary efforts does *not* depend upon the assumption that potential contributors are crass egoists. Even if the potential contributor has no intention to take a free ride on the contributions of others, he may nonetheless be unwilling to contribute his fair share unless he has *assurance* that others will do their fair share. For unless he has this assurance, to expect him to contribute his fair share is to expect him to bear an unreasonable risk—a cost that might put him at a serious competitive disadvantage. In the absence of an *enforced* scheme for fairly distributing the costs of care for the needy, the current vogue for containing costs by increasing competition in health care will only exacerbate this free-rider and assurance problem. And unless an institution can shoulder its fair share without unreasonable risk to itself, it cannot be said that it has an *obligation* that it has failed to fulfill. Granted that this is so, what is needed is an effective mechanism for enforcing a coordinated scheme for distributing the costs of providing some minimal level of care for all without imposing unreasonable competitive disadvantages on particular institutions.

It is important not to overstate this point. Although the notion of unreasonable risk is not sharply defined, it is almost certainly true that many for-profit (and nonprofit) institutions could be spending more than they currently are for nonpaying or unprofitable patients without compromising their financial viability. So it is incorrect to conclude simply from this that in the current state of affairs institutions have no special obligations whatsoever. The point, rather, is that debates over which institutions are or are not fulfilling their obligation are of limited value and that the energy they consume could be more productively used to develop a system in which institutional obligations could be more concretely specified and in which society would be morally justified in holding those who control the institutions, whether governmental or private, accountable for the fulfillment of those obligations.

Moreover, there is at least one obligation that *now* can be justifiably imputed to for-profit (and nonprofit) health care institutions and that is the obligation to cooperate in developing a system in which determinate obligations (whether general or special) can be fairly assigned and enforced. It is much less plausible to argue that the initial efforts needed *to develop* a coordinated, enforced system would undermine an institution's competitive position, even if it is true that in the absence of such a system an institution's acting on a strictly voluntary basis to help fund indigent care would subject it to unreasonable risks.

Assuming that, as members of this society, we all share a collective obligation to ensure an "adequate level" or "decent minimum" of health care for the needy, those who control health care institutions, as individuals, have the same obligations the rest of us do. However, because of their special knowledge of the health care system and the disproportionate influence they can wield in health policy debates and decisions, health care professionals may indeed have an additional *special* obligation beyond the general obligations of ordinary citizens to help ensure that a just system of access to health care is established.

It can still be argued that whether or not they fail to fulfill their obligations, for-profits have at least contributed to the decline of cross-subsidization and that the cross-subsidization system has made some contribution toward coping with the problem of access to care. Whether this provides a good reason for social policy designed to restrain or modify the behavior of for-profits will depend upon the answer to two further questions: (1) Are cross-subsidization arrangements the best way of coping wih the access problem? And, just as importantly, (2) is it now feasible in an increasingly competitive environment to preserve cross-subsidization even if we wish to do so?

Objections to cross-subsidization are not hard to find. On the one hand, cross-subsidization can be viewed as an inefficient, uncoordinated welfare system hidden from public view and unaccountable to the public or to its representatives in government. Further, it can be argued that widespread cross-subsidization is incompatible with effective efforts to curb costs. Surely an effective solution to both the access and cost-containment problems requires a more integrated, comprehensive, and publicly accountable approach. Consequently, the demise of cross-subsidization should be welcomed, not lamented.

This last conclusion, however, is simplistic. It assumes that an explicit public policy designed to improve access for those not covered by private or public insurance is presently or in the foreseeable future politically feasible. Perhaps the strongest argument for cross-subsidization is the claim that it does—though admittedly in a haphazard and inefficient way—what is not likely to be done through more explicit social policies.

It might be tempting to protest that even if this is so, cross-subsidization ought to be rejected as an unauthorized welfare system since it did not come about through the democratic political process as a conscious social policy. However, if providing some minimum of care for the needy is a matter of right or enforceable societal obligation and not a matter of discretion, then the lack of a democratic pedigree may not be fatal, since rights and obligations place limitations on the scope of the democratic process.

Controversy over the ethical status of cross-subsidization may soon become moot if a point is reached where it is no longer feasible to store up or rebuild an environment in which cross-subsidization is economically viable for health care institutions. So even if cross-subsidization has been the best feasible way of coping with the problem of access it does not follow that it will continue to be a viable option. Perhaps too much energy has already been wasted in policy debates defending or attacking cross-subsidization when the real issue is: How can we now best achieve the purpose that cross-subsidization was supposed to serve?

Our focus thus far has been on the charge that for-profit health care institutions fail to fulfill their obligations to provide care for the poor. We have seen that a close examination of this criticism of for-profit institutions raises more general issues about the relationship between self-interested institutional behavior—whether in for-profit or nonprofit institutions—and the access problem. One important conclusion reached was that it is incorrect to understand the access problems as the result of a failure to fulfill institutional obligations because at present there is no social mechanism that specifies, fairly distributes, and enforces such institutional obligations.

It seems likely that competition and cost-containment pressures will continue to lead to further increases in commercial or profit-maximizing motivation and behavior in all forms of health care institutions, for-profit and nonprofit as well. If this is the case, then the crucial question is this: How can the pursuit of institutional self-interest be made to serve the social goal of improving access?

The preceding discussions of the free-rider and assurance problems suggest, respectively, two distinct approaches. The first, proceeding on the assumption that a sense of collective moral responsibility will not serve as a significant constraint on the pursuit of profit by institutions, is to change the incentive structure under which institutions operate so that they can best serve their own interests by serving the poor. This might be achieved by providing the poor with health-care vouchers at financial levels comparable to those of current insurance reimbursements or by expanding eligibility for Medicaid and increasing Medicaid reimbursement rates. A second, quite different, approach proceeds on the more charitable assumption that a collective sense of moral responsibility can serve as a significant constraint on an institution's pursuit of profit if the cost of acting morally, though not eliminated, is kept at acceptable levels. One important way of lowering the cost an institution incurs when it aids the poor is to provide it with assurance that competing institutions will reciprocate by bearing their fair share of the burden. To prevent the pursuit of profit by health care institutions from worsening an already shameful access problem, a combination of both types of approaches will probably be needed.

II. For-Profits Damage the Physician-Patient Relationship, Erode Trust, Create New Conflicts of Interest, and Diminish Quality of Care

The second broad concern about the growth of profit seeking in medicine is that it will damage the physician-patient relationship, erode the trust necessary to that relationship, create new conflicts of interest and ultimately diminish the quality of care. Physicians have, of course, always sought to earn a living from the practice of medicine. The concern about increased profit-oriented behavior is commonly that new profit-oriented institutions, most commonly large for-profit hospital chains, will alter the behavior of physicians that work for or in them in ways to produce the bad effects noted above. We shall continue to use here for-profit hospitals as the paradigm of the rise in profit seeking at the institutional level in exploring its potential effects on the behavior of individual physicians and on the physician-patient relationship. It is undeniable that for-profit health care involves potential conflicts between the interests of providers (physicians, managers, administrators, and stockholders) and those of patients. In the most general terms, the conflict is simply this: An institution with a strong, if not an overriding, commitment to maximizing profit may sometimes find that the best way to do this is not to act in its patients' best interests.

This fundamental potential conflict of interest is said to be of special concern in health care, not only because health care interests are so important, but also because the "consumer" of health care, unlike the consumer of most other goods and services provided by profit-seeking firms, is in an especially vulnerable position for two reasons. First, patients will often lack the special knowledge and expertise needed for judging whether a particular health service is necessary or would be beneficial, whether it is being rendered in an appropriate way, and even in some cases whether it has been successful. Second, because illness or injury can result in anxiety, dependence and loss of self-confidence, the patient may find it difficult to engage in the sort of self-protective bargaining behavior expressed in the admonition "caveat emptor."

Whether this conflict of interest will damage the physician/patient relationship will depend on the extent to which it already exists outside profit-seeking settings. And it is quite clear that a fundamental potential for conflict of interest is not peculiar to for-profit health care. A health care institution may exhibit a strong commitment to maximizing profit, and this commitment may result in practices that are not in patients' best interests, even if the institution is of nonprofit form. When we ask whether an institution's or an individual's pursuit of profits is prejudicial to the patient's interests, the appropriate sense of the phrase "pursuit of profits" is quite broad, not the narrower legal sense in which nonprofit institutions do not by definition pursue profits. After all, the issue is whether the opportunities for attaining *benefits* for themselves provide incentives that influence behavior on the part of providers that is not in patients' best interest. Whatever form these incentives take and whatever kinds of benefits are pursued, they may all run counter to the patients' interests.

In any form of medical practice operating under a fee-for-service system, under any system of prepayment (as in Health Maintenance Organizations [HMOs]), and under any system of capitation, where physicians are paid a salary determined by the number of patients they treat (as in Independent Practice Associations [IPAs]), a basic conflict of interest will exist, regardless of whether the organization is for-profit or nonprofit. In a fee-for-service system, the conflict is obvious: physicians have an incentive to overutilize services because their financial return will thereby be increased. The incentive for overutilization of services can conflict with the patient's interest in three distinct ways: it can lead physicians to (1) provide services whose *medical costs* to the patient outweight their *medical benefits* (as in the case of surgery or x-rays which actually do more medical harm than good), (2) impose financial costs on the patient that exceed the medical benefits provided (greater out-of-pocket expenses for the patient), and (3) contribute to higher health care costs (including higher insurance premiums) for everyone, including the patient.

In prepayment or capitation systems, providers are subject to conflicts of interest because of incentives to underutilize care. In HMOs, providers have an incentive to limit care because the overall financial well-being of the organization requires it and because salary increases and year-end bonuses as well as new personnel, new equipment, and new services are all financed by these savings. In IPAs and other organizations that operate on a capitation system, conflicts of interest due to the incentive for underutilization are equally clear: spending less time and using fewer scarce resources enables physicians to handle a larger number of patients, and this results in a larger salary. Whether, or to what extent, these incentives actually result in reduced quality of care is an extremely difficult question. But what is clear is that they create conflicts of interest in both for-profit and nonprofit settings.

The nature of the concern about physicians acting to further their own economic interests will change as the settings in which they practice increasingly shift from fee-for-service with its incentives for *over*utilization to various forms of capitation with their incentives for *under*utilization. The most obvious harm to patients from overutilization is the financial waste of resources in comparison with other more beneficial uses. However, there are probably also serious and widespread health harms to patients from overutilization of treatments (for example, unnecessary coronary artery by-pass operations that have significant mortality rates), procedures (for example, overuse of x-rays and mammograms linked to cancer), and hospitalization with its attendant risks including infection. The harm to patients from underutilization, on the other hand, is principally to their health and well-being, or even life, when needed and potentially beneficial but unprofitable health care is withheld. Neither over- nor underutilization will be easily detectable by the patients who suffer them. Patients' consent is commonly needed for the additional treatment of overutilization and so they will usually be aware of receiving the treatment, but they will commonly be in a poor position to evaluate for themselves their need for the care. Incentives for underutilization may lead the physician never to mention possibly beneficial but unprofitable treatment, and so leave the patient unaware of it. Thus, shifting incentives from over- towards underutilization will alter the likely effects and concerns about conflicts of interest, though we lack the data to say whether overutilization or underutilization is on balance a more serious problem.

Some analysts have recognized that the preceding sorts of conflicts of interest are unavoidable because they result from two features that will be found in any form of health care institution or organization: (1) the patient's special vulnerability and (2) the need to provide some form of incentive for providers that is related in some fashion to the amount and kind of services they provide. They have then gone on to argue that what makes conflicts of interest especially serious in for-profits is that for-profits provide physicians with opportunities for *secondary income*. This secondary income may come either from charges for services which they themselves do not provide but which they recommend or which are provided by others under their supervision, or from being a shareholder in the for-profit health care corporation.

Secondary income, however, and the conflict of interest it involves, is also neither a new phenomenon in health care nor peculiar to for-profits. While "fee-splitting" traditionally has been condemned by organized medicine, several forms of practice of physicians receive a percentage of the fee charged for x-rays, laboratory tests, other diagnostic procedures, physical therapy, or drug or alcohol counseling that they recommend but which are performed by people they employ or supervise. In some cases, licensing and certification laws and reimbursement eligibility requirements for Medicare, Medicaid, and private insurance require nonphysician health care professionals to be supervised by a physician, thus creating a dependence which makes it possible for physicians to reap this secondary income. Physicians may also charge fees for interpreting diagnostic tests, such as electrocardiograms, that they recommend and which are performed by others even if they do not split the fee for the procedure itself.

It may still be the case that the opportunities for secondary income and other conflicts of interest tend to be *greater* in most for-profit institutions than in most nonprofit institutions. While there is some data suggesting higher usage rates for profitable ancillary services in for-profit hospitals, at present neither the extent of these differences, nor, more importantly, the extent to which they are taken advantage of in ways that reduce quality of care, increase costs, or otherwise compromise patients' interests is well-documented. It may also be the case that even though serious conflicts of interest, from secondary income and other sources, already exist in nonprofit health care, the continued growth of for-profits, both in their own activities and the influence they have on the behavior of nonprofits, will result in a significant worsening of the problem. The current paucity of data, however, makes it premature to predict that this will happen or when it will happen.

There is another form of the charge that profit-seeking health care institutions create new conflicts of interest or exacerbate old ones. Some fear that even if physicians' behavior toward patients is not distorted by incentives for secondary income or by equity ownership, physicians in profit-making institutions will be subject to greater control by management and that this control will make it more difficult for physicians to serve the patient's interests rather than the corporation's. There can be little doubt that American physicians are increasingly subject to control by others, especially by managers and administrators, many of whom are not physicians.

There are two major factors that have led to this loss of "professional dominance" that are quite independent of the growth of profit-seeking institutions in health care (Starr, 1982). One is the institutionalization of medicine that itself arose from a variety of factors, including the proliferation of technologies and specializations that call for large-scale social cooperation and cannot be rendered efficiently, if they can be rendered at all, by independent practitioners. The other is the increased pressure for cost-containment in a more competitive environment, which has led to a greater reliance on professional management techniques within health care institutions and more extensive regulatory controls by government. At most, the growth of profit-seeking institutions may be accelerating this loss of professional dominance.

It should not simply be assumed, however, that diminished physician control will result in an overall lowering of the quality of care or a worsening of the problem of conflict of interests. Whether it will depends upon the answer to three difficult questions. To what extent will management or shareholders of for-profits exercise their control over physicians in the pursuit of profit and at the expense of patient interests, unrestrained by ethical considerations? To what extent will management and stockholders act on the belief that in the long-run profits will be maximized by serving patients' interests? To what extent have physicians, in the physician-dominated system that has existed up until recently, actually acted in the best interests of their patients? The answers to the first two questions await data not yet available.

The third question is especially difficult to answer because of an ambiguity in the notion of the "patient's best interests." In a fee-for-service, third-party payment system in which physicians exercise a great deal of control in ordering treatments and procedures, a physician who makes decisions according to what is in the individual patient's best medical interests will tend to order any treatment or test whose expected net medical benefit is greater than zero, no matter how small the net benefit may be. Under such a system, the traditional ethical principles of the medical profession, which require the physician to do what is best for the patient (or to minimize harm to him), and the principle of self-interest speak with one voice, at least so long as the patient's interests are restricted to his medical interests. Indeed, even if the physician considers the patient's overall interests—financial as well as medical—so long as a third party is picking up the major portion of the bill, the physician may still conclude that acting in the patient's best interest requires doing anything that can be expected to yield a nonzero net medical benefit. Yet, as has often been noted, the cumulative result of large numbers of such decisions, each of which may be in the best interest of the particular patient, is that health care is overutilized and a cost crisis results.

"Overutilization" here does not mean the use of medically unnecessary care, i.e., care that is of no net medical benefit, or that is positively harmful; instead what is meant is what one author has called "non-costworthy care"—care that yields less benefit than some alternative use to which the same resources could be put, either for other health care services or for nonhealth care goods (Menzel 1983, p. 17). Overutilization of health care in this sense, not just overutilization as nonbeneficial care, is clearly contrary to everyone's interest. If continued professional dominance means perpetuation of this problem of overutilization, then even if a further loss of professional dominance will lead to medical decisions that are not, considered in isolation, in the individual patient's best interest, it may nevertheless result in the elimination of one important conflict of interest and one source of collective irrationality in the current system. This does not rule out the possibility, of course, that greater control by nonphysicians will also lead to overutilization. If this occurs, then one system that works against everyone's best interest will merely have been replaced by another that does the same thing.

We have seen that in the fee-for-service, third-party payment system in nonprofit as well as for-profit settings the cumulative result of many physicians acting on the desire to do what is best for the individual patient can result in overutilization that is contrary to all patients' best interests. Some critics of for-profits suggest that we must either pay the price of this overutilization or cope with it by methods that do not undermine physicians' commitments to doing what is best for their individual patients. They then conclude that even if it could be shown that the growth of for-profits would restrain overutilization by introducing greater price competition into health care, the price would be too high to pay because the physician's all-important commitment to do his best for each patient would eventually be eroded by the increasing "commercialization" of health care that is being accelerated if not caused by the growth of profit-seeking enterprise in medicine.

The force of this objection to for-profits depends, of course, not only upon the correctness of the prediction that the growth of for-profits will in fact contribute to a weakening of the physician's commitment to do the best he can for each patient; it also depends upon the assumption that under the current system that commitment has been a dominant force in physician behavior. This last point may be cast in a slightly different way. How concerned we should be about the tendency for the behavior of physicians to become more like that of businessmen depends upon how great the difference in behavior of the two groups is and has been. If one assumes that as a group physicians have been significantly more altruistic than businessmen and if one also assumes that altruism is the only effective safeguard against exploitation of the patient's special vulnerability, then one will oppose any development, including the growth of for-profit health care, which can be expected to make physicians more like businessmen.

Many outside the medical profession and some within it greet the claim that physicians as a class are especially altruistic and committed to patient interests at the expense of their own with some skepticism. This attitude is not groundless. One of the difficulties of determining the strength of altruistic patient-centered motivation among physicians, as we have already noted, is that until very recently, the fee-for-service, third-party payment system has produced a situation in which altruism and self-interest converge: doing what is best for the patient (pursuing all treatment that promises nonzero benefits) was often doing what was financially best for the physician. Nevertheless, critics of the thesis that physicians are especially altruistic can marshal a good deal of evidence to support their view—such as the profession's historical opposition to HMOs and to Medicare and Medicaid—each of which promised significant extensions of access to health care (Starr 1982), its failure to overcome the chronic geographical maldistribution of physicians in this country, its support of strict entry controls to the profession through medical licensure together with relatively weak oversight of the continuing competence of those already licensed, and the refusal of many physicians to treat Medicaid patients because Medicaid reimbursements are lower than those of private insurance. We can make no attempt to evaluate such evidence here, but the self-interest of the profession seems a better prima facie explanation for much of this behavior than does an altruistic concern for the ill. It is important to emphasize that explanations of these phenomena need not assume that self-interest here is exclusively or even primarily *financial* self-interest. The profession's resistance to Medicare, for example, was probably more an attempt to preserve physician *autonomy*, as well as to protect the physician-patient relationship from outside intrusion by government.

In assessing these questions of conflict of interest and physician motivations we think it is helpful to distinguish the behavior of physicians acting as an organized profession addressing matters of health policy from the behavior of individual physicians toward individual patients. As we have noted above, much behavior of medicine as an organized profession (as reflected for example in the political role played by the American Medical Association [AMA]) in seeking to maintain physician dominance in the health care profession, to protect and enhance physician incomes, and so forth, has served the self-interest of physicians. Controversial is the extent to which the self-interested function of the motivation for supporting such practices as medical licensure is manifest or latent, explicit or implicit. In considering the conduct of professional trade associations such as the AMA, we believe that forwarding the economic and other interests of the members of the profession is often the explicit, conscious and indeed often legitimate intent of the representatives of the profession. To the extent that the profession has been successful in furthering its members' interest, we would expect to find an institutional, organizational, and legal structure shaping the practice of medicine that serves the economic and other interests of members of the profession.

It would be hard to look back over the evolution in this century of the position and structure of the medical profession without concluding that the profession has in fact had considerable success in promoting its interests. It would be completely implausible to attribute a high level of altruism to the medical profession if that was interpreted to mean a high level of economic self-sacrifice in favor of the public's health needs. The exceptionally high levels of physician incomes would belie that. Nor is it plausible to claim that the organized profession had led efforts to address some of the most serious moral deficiencies in our health care system, such as the continued lack of access to health care of large numbers of the poor. As we noted above, the history of the profession's opposition to national health insurance and to Medicare and Medicaid belies any such role of altruism or moral leadership. Nor finally have many members of the profession acting as individuals been remarkably self-sacrificing or acted as moral leaders in addressing these problems. Occasional physicians have, of course, located in undesirable geographical areas to meet pressing health care needs or provided substantial unpaid care to the poor, but such behavior has not been sufficiently widespread to have a major impact on these problems.

Despite the extent that the profession has promoted its members' interests and that individual members have not been self-sacrificing in addressing the most serious deficiencies in the health care system, we believe it would be a serious mistake to conclude that the patient-centered ethic that has defined the traditional physician-patient relationship is mere sham and rhetoric, a thin guise overlaying the physician's self-interest.

An alternative, and we believe more plausible, interpretation is that in part just because the medical profession has been exceptionally successful in promoting and protecting an institutional and organizational setting that serves well physicians' economic and other interests, individual physicians have thereby been freed to follow the traditional patient-centered ethic in their relations with their individual patients. Put oversimply, a physician whose overall practice structure assures him a high income need not be so concerned to weight economic benefits to himself when considering treatment recommendations for his individual patients. As we have argued above, conflicts of interest between physicians and patients have long existed and are hardly a heretofore unknown consequence of for-profit health care institutions. As one commentator has argued, much of medicine can be viewed as a conflict for the physician between self-interest and altruism, requiring a balancing of these sometimes conflicting motivations, (Jonson 1983).

What we are suggesting is that the self-interested organized professional behavior and institutional structure of medicine may have helped protect the possibility of altruistic behavior on the part of the physician when guiding treatment with his individual patients. (This hypothesis, of course, requires careful qualification. In some cases the self-interested behavior of organized medicine has clearly had a negative impact on patient interests. For example, licensure and other forms of self-regulation by the profession have often failed to protect patients from chemically dependent or otherwise incompetent physicians and have exacerbated the problem of access by inhibiting the development of less expensive forms of care utilizing nonphysician providers such as midwives and nurse practitioners.)

One virtue of this more complex perspective is that it allows us to accommodate the elements of truth that exist in each of two otherwise seemingly incompatible perspectives, each of which taken only by itself appears extreme and incomplete. One perspective views the physician simply as an economically self-interested businessman in his dealings with patients. Those who support this perspective can point to the various ways in which the actions of the medical profession and the institutional and financing structure in which medicine is practiced serve the interests of physicians, as we have done above, but they often go on to deny any significant reality to physicians' commitment to promoting their patients' best interests. On the other hand, many defenders of physicians viewed as devoted professionals committed to the well-being of their patients seem also to feel it necessary to deny the extent to which medical practices and institutional structures serve physicians' interests. Either perspective is by itself stubbornly one-sided in its view of physicians simply as self-interested economic accumulators or as devoted altruists. We favor a view which recognizes that these two perspectives are *not* incompatible and accepts the elements of truth in each of them.

One advantage of this more balanced perspective is that it permits the recognition of the reality and great importance of the traditional patient-centered ethic, without denying the conflicts of interest between physician and patient that we have discussed above or the important historical role played by the economic interests of physicians. A perspective that encompasses a balance between self-interested and altruistic motivations on the part of physicians can help articulate the concern of many observers that the rise of for-profit medicine while *not* representing an entirely new phenomenon nevertheless *does* pose a danger to the traditional physician-patient relationship by shifting the traditional *balance* between self-interested and altruistic motivations and by bringing motivations of economic self-interest more directly and substantially into the physician's relations with individual patients.

What, more specifically, is the worry about the erosion of the physician-patient relatinship by the rise of for-profit health care institutions? We think that worry can be most pointedly brought out by initially overstating the possible effect. The traditional account of the patient-centered ethic makes the physician the agent of the patient, whose "highest commitment is the patient (American College of Physicians, p. 17)." The physician is to seek to determine together with the patient that course of treatment that will best promote the patient's well-being, setting aside effects of others, including effects on the physician, the patient's family, or society. This commitment to the patient's well-being responds to the various respects discussed above in which patients are in a very poor position to determine for themselves what health care, if any, they need. It is not just a function of more traditional paternalistic forms of physician-patient relations. Among the many increasingly common accounts of shared decision-making between physician and patient, the more plausible versions recognize that many of the inequalities in the physician-patient relation are probably to a significant extent unavoidable. Because many patients are and wish to be significantly dependent on their physicians, it is especially important to the success of this physician-patient partnership in the service of the patient's well-being that the patient believe that the physician will be guided in his recommendation solely by the patient's best interests. Patients have compelling reasons to want the physician-patient relationship to be one in which this trust is both warranted and fostered, quite apart from the putative therapeutic benefits of such trust.

Suppose the rise of for-profit health care so eroded this traditional relationship, and in its place substituted a commercial relationship, that patients came to view their physicians as they commonly now view used-car salesmen. We emphasize that such a radical shift in view is not to be expected. We use this "worst-case" example of a caveat emptor commercial relationship only because it focuses most pointedly the worry about the effect on the physician-patient relationship of the increasing commercialization of health care. Many factors will inhabit such a shift from actually taking place in patients' views of their physicians, including traditional codes of ethics in medicine, requirements of informed consent, fiduciary obligations of physicians, as well as powerful traditions of professionalism in medicine. Recognizing that the unsavory stereotype of the used-car salesman substantially overstates what there is any reason to expect in medicine, nevertheless what would a shift in this direction do to the physician-patient relationship?

Most obviously and perhaps also most importantly, it would undermine the trust that many patients are prepared to place in their physicians' commitment to seek the patient's best interests. In general, there is no such trust of a used-car salesman, but rather his claims and advice are commonly greeted with a cool skepticism. He is viewed as pursuing his own economic interests, with no commitment to the customer's welfare. It is the rare (and probably in the end sorry) consumer who places himself in the hands of the car salesman. Anything like the fiduciary relationship in which a patient trusts the physician's commitment to put the patient's interests first is quite absent with the used-car salesman.

This is not to say that some additional consumer skepticism of physician recommendations and increased attempts by patients to become knowledgeable health care consumers would not be a good thing—they would. It is rather to say as already noted, that many of the various inequalities in the physician-patient relationship are sufficiently deep and difficult to eradicate that some substantial trust of the physician's commitment to the patient is likely to remain necessary and valuable. The commercial model of arm's-length, caveat emptor bargaining is not well-suited to the physician-patient relation.

While historically there has been some deception of patients by physicians, it seems to have markedly decreased in recent decades, and this deception in medicine was justified as for the patient's own good (even if in fact it often was not). However, one does not expect the truth, the whole truth, and nothing but the truth from a used-car salesman, nor that shadings of the truth are done for the customer's own good. We expect some concealment and distortion of information in order to make the sale, although this is not to say that some outright deception in commerce may not be fraudulent and immoral.

It is also commonly accepted that businessmen are in business to sell as much of their product as possible, however much the customer may not "need" the expensive car being pushed by the salesman. Businessmen respond to consumer wants, not needs, and will do their best to manufacture such wants where they do not already exist. Physicians, on the other hand, are expected not to encourage needless consumption. Commercialized medicine may respond increasingly to consumer wants for health care even if they are for frivolous amenities such as champagne breakfasts for obstetric patients and however unrelated they may be to the patient's true health care needs. Because health care consumers are commonly in a poor position to evaluate for themselves their own need for health care, their actual health care wants will often be both ill-informed and unusually vulnerable to influence and manipulation by health care professionals. However, not all increased responsiveness to consumer wants would constitute a shift from serving patients' true health needs to serving their mere wants. To the extent that a treatment, if indeed there is one, best promotes a patient's well-being depends at least in part on that patient's particular aims and values, increased responsiveness to consumer wants can make a genuine contribution to patient well-being.

A shift towards commercialization of health care could also be expected to result in increasing emphasis on marketing strategies to secure profitable segments of the market. Moreover, we expect no unprofitable products or service from a car salesman in response to consumer need. And most clearly, persons who lack the ability to pay for commercial goods and services simply do not receive them. We have argued that the moral obligation to ensure access to health care for the poor is ultimately the government's, not an individual physician's or hospital's by way of cross-subsidization. Nevertheless, in the face of unmet need, some physicians and health care institutions do, and are often expected to, respond to that need by furnishing the needed care. Increasing commercialization of health care is likely to weaken this disposition of some physicians to respond to people's health care needs without regard to their ability to pay.

Other norms important to the practice of medicine also have a weakened or nonexistent role in most commercial transactions, such as the requirement of confidentiality concerning information about the patient. Like the commitment to put the patient's interests first, the norm of confidentiality concerning patient information is both fragile and under increasing pressure from many forces, such as the growing specialization within health care, besides rising commercialism.

One must be careful not to overstate the contrast between medicine and commerce. It is certainly not the case that commerce takes place in the absence of any ethical constraints (or legal constraints, reflecting ethical norms) nor that the medical profession is never moved by self-interest. Our society does in fact expect, and in some cases enforces by the power of the law, significant restrictions on the pursuit of profit by "mere businessmen." One would not want a physician who has motivated exclusively by financial reward, but then one would not want an electrician who was either. In fact, it can be argued that the moral obligations of businessmen to their customers are not significantly less demanding than those of physicians toward their patients *when equally important interests are at stake.* However, important interests may be more frequently potentially at stake in health care than in ordinary business transactions. And even if there is a tendency to overstate the contrast between ethical and legal constraints on business transactions and the physician-patient relationship, we typically do expect a somewhat higher standard of conduct from physicians.

We believe there is, moreover, a genuine and important difference in the ethos of the two enterprises that plays out in important differences in the physician-patient and businessman-consumer transaction. The ethos of medicine is one of commitment and service to others. While medicine has, of course, contained physicians primarily concerned with their own economic and other interests, they are viewed and condemned as deviants by that ethos. Not so, however, in commerce. Oversimplifying, it is commonly believed that in business transactions, individuals pursuing their own interests, though admittedly within some ethical and legal constraints, will best promote the overall social good. It is this view of the motivation of self-interest as ethically acceptable that quite reasonably worries many as medicine becomes increasingly commercialized.

Since physicians are, of course, human like the rest of us and quite naturally concerned with their own interests, it is reasonable to view their primary commitment to the patient's well-being as inevitably fragile and always in danger of being undermined. In that light, it is unnecessary to view for-profit institutions as introducing a qualitatively new dimension of commercialization and new set of conflicts of interest into health care. As we have argued, such a view is indefensible. Nor need it be expected that physicians' concern with their patients' well-being will just disappear as soon as they go on the payroll of a for-profit hospital or, more likely, establish other types of contractual relations with it. That view too would be indefensible, indeed downright silly.

The realistic worry, concerning which the data are not yet in, is rather that over time the increased importance of investor-owned for-profit institutions may permit considerations of economic self-interest increasingly to invade the heretofore somewhat protected sphere of the physician-patient relationship, and thereby weaken the patient-centered ethic on which that relationship importantly depends. The difference would only be one of degree, but no less important for that. As we have noted above, there are other independent factors putting similar pressures on the relationship such as the expected oversupply of physicians. It would be a mistake to think that these possible adverse effects on the physician-patient relationship are uniquely due to the rise of for-profits. However, that is no reason to be unconcerned with these effects of for-profits, but only a reason not to focus solely on for-profits.

We emphasize that the traditional patient-centered ethic need not be incompatible with greater attention to costs in health care utilization decisions and practices. Utilization of health care should reflect the financial costs as well as benefits of care, but that will not be appropriately achieved by, nor need it inevitably lead to, physicians making utilization decisions solely according to their own economic self-interest. Whatever the right mix of incentives for reasonably limiting health care utilization and costs, simply making physicians fully subject to incentives of economic self-interest by breaking down the patient-centered ethic seems not the path to that mix. A physician weighing the true financial costs of care against its medical benefits *to the patient* is entirely different from one who simply weighs the economic consequences *to himself* of the patient utilizing care.

The most obvious worry, then, is that the increasing prominence for for-profits may contribute to a shift in physicians' patient-oriented *behavior*, which may in turn affect the patient trust important to a well-functioning physician-patient relationship. The test of that hypothesis would then be the extent to which physician behavior is actually different within for-profit settings. But it is important to realize that patient trust may be eroded, and so the

physician-patient relationship adversely affected, even in the absence of any actual shift toward more self-interested behavior by
physicians. Even if outward behavior does not change, a change
in the motivations of the behavior, and in turn of perceptions by
others of those motivations, may be important. If physicians are
increasingly perceived by patients as motivated by self-interest
rather than by a commitment to serving their patient, then even
in the absence of a change in physicians' behavior, it is reasonable
to expect an erosion in patient *trust* that physicians will act for
their patients' best interests. Part of what is important to patients
in health care is the reassurance that the professional *cares* about
them and their plight. (This is one respect in which other health
care professionals, for example nurses, are often more important
than physicians in patient care.) A change in physicians' motivations, may be enough to affect patients' beliefs about whether
their physicians "really care" about them. This point should give
pause to those who propose to test the effects of for-profits on
the physician-patient relationship and on patient trust by looking
only at changes in physician behavior.

III. Concluding Remarks

Any summary conclusion of our examination of two of the principal ethical issues in the growth of profit seeking in health care
will inevitably oversimplify. A continuing theme running through
our analysis is that the moral objections commonly voiced against
profit motives and for-profit institutions need to be both framed
and evaluated more carefully than they usually are. At many
places, these objections also rest on empirical claims for which
the data are not yet available. We have been generally critical of
the argument that for-profits fail to do their fair share in providing
health care to poor or unprofitable patients. That argument assumes that for-profits have special obligations to care for these
patients, that a determinate content can now be given to that
obligation, and that the obligation can be discharged without unreasonable sacrifice on the part of the for-profit. These assumptions are all problematic. It is a mistake to focus on how for-profits
exacerbate or ameliorate access. The debate could more profitably
concentrate on the need for a coordinated societal response to the
serious injustices in access to health care that now exist.

We believe that the potential adverse effects of the growth of for-profits on the physician-patient relationship and on the quality of care is of serious ethical concern. The potential conflicts of interest between patient and provider are not new. Indeed, they are fundamental to the physician-patient relationship in either for-profit or nonprofit settings. Moreover, the other powerful forces besides the growth of for-profits, in particular cost-containment efforts and increased competition, are impinging on the physician-patient relationship. But the importance of the patient's trust in his physician, and the fragile balance between the physician's commitment to serve the patient and his natural concern with his own interests, give reason for serious continuing attention to this potential effect of increased profit seeking in health care.

NOTES

* This paper is drawn, with revisions, from our longer paper, "Ethical Issues in For-Profit Health Care" (Brock and Buchanan 1986).
1. While the number of *investor-owned*, as opposed to *independent*, for-profit hospitals has risen, hospital ownership, classified by broad categories—federal, state, and local government, nonprofit and for-profit—has changed little in the past decade (Gray 1984).
2. Investor-owned for-profit corporations are controlled ultimately by stockholders who appropriate surplus revenues either in the form of stock dividends or increased stock values. Nonprofit corporations are tax-exempt and are controlled ultimately by boards of trustees who are prohibited by law from appropriating surplus revenues after expenses (including salaries) are paid.
3. At this writing, New York has legislation limiting the operation of for-profits in the state and the Rhode Island legislature is considering proposed legislation to ban their operation.
4. The argument in this and the next paragraph is drawn directly from the President's Commission for the Study of Ethical Problems in Medicine report, *Securing Access to Health Care* (1983), which both the present authors helped to write.

REFERENCES

American College of Physicians: 1984, *Ethics Manual*, Philadelphia, Pennsylvania.
Brock, D.W. and Buchanan, A.E.: 1986, "Ethical issues in for-profit health care" in B.H. Gray (ed.), *For-Profit Enterprise in Health Care*, National Academy Press, Washington, D.C., pp. 224–249.

Brown, K.J. and Klosterman, R.E.: 1986, "Hospital acquisitions and their effects: an analysis of Florida data, 1979–1982," in B. Gray (ed.), *For-Profit Enterprise in Health Care*, National Academy Press, Washington, D.C., pp. 303–321.

California Association of Public Hospitals: unpublished, "Health care in the 80's—can the safety net survive?" California Association of Public Hospitals White Paper on the Unique Contributions and Needs of California's Public Hospitals, prepared for the Institute of Medicine.

Committee Report on Implications for For-Profit Enterprise in Health Care: 1986, in B.H. Gray (ed.), *For-Profit Enterprise in Health Care*, National Academy Press, Washington, D.C.

Gray, B.: 1984, "Overview: origins and trends," Keynote Address, Annual Health Conference, The New Entrepreneurialism in Health Care, held by the Committee on Medicine in Society of the New York Academy of Medicine (May), *Bulletin of the New York Academy of Medicine* (2nd series) 61, 7–22.

Institute of Medicine; 1983, *The New Health Care For Profit: Doctors and Hospitals in a Competitive Environment*, U.S. Government Printing Office, Washington, D.C.

Jonson, A.: 1983, "Watching the doctor," *New England Journal of Medicine* 308, 1531–1535.

Menzel, P.: 1983, *Medical Costs, Moral Choices*, Yale University Press, New Haven, Connecticut.

President's Commission for the Study of Ethical Problems in Medicine and Biomedical and Behavioral Research: 1983, *Securing Access to Health Care*, U.S. Government Printing Office. Washington, D.C.

Starr, P.: 1982, *The Social Transformation of American Medicine*, Basic Books, New York.

Watt, J.M. *et al.*: 1986, "The comparative economic performance of investor-owned chain and not-for-profit hospitals," *New England Journal of Medicine* 314, 89–92.

Study Questions

1. Considering the precipitous decline in medical school applications and the continuing drop in the public's estimate and trust of the medical community, how would you defend or attack the authors' general position?
2. The authors appear to believe that medicine and commerce are more alike than most people believe. State why you agree or disagree with this position.

The Nature of
the State

*John Hospers**

Most academicians, somewhat isolated from the marketplace which ultimately pays their salaries, still appear to think of the State as a benevolent agent which may have gone wrong in this way or that, but still to be trusted and admired (and in any case, used by them). My own attitude toward the State, based on its workings and the experience of myself and many others with its representatives, is very different.

It is difficult to communicate briefly an attitude toward the State which took many years of reading and reflection to develop. I shall begin with the thesis of Franz Oppenheimer's book *The State* (1908). There are, he said, two ways of obtaining the things one needs and wants: the first method is production and exchange—to produce something out of nature's raw materials or transform them into a product (or service) desired by others, and to take the surplus of one's own production of one thing and exchange it for another kind of surplus from the production of others. This method of survival, production and exchange, he called the *economic* means. But there is also a second means: not to produce anything at all but to seize by force the things that others have

* John Hospers is professor of philosophy at the University of Southern California and editor of *Pacific Philosophical Quarterly*. Specializing in aesthetics, ethics, and political philosophy, Hospers has written a number of books, including *Human Conduct: Problems of Ethics* (1972), *Introduction to Philosophical Analysis* (1967), and *Libertarianism: A Political Philosophy for Tomorrow* (1971). Reprinted with permission of the author and the publisher from *The Personalist*, vol. 59, no. 4 (October 1978), pp. 398–404.

produced—the method of plunder. This he called the *political means*.

Not everyone, of course, can use the second means, since one cannot seize from others something they have not already created or produced. But some people can and do, siphoning off the fruits of other people's labor for themselves. In the end, the supply is destroyed if this means is used too extensively, since it does not add to but rather subtracts from the totality of production: the more that is used up by the predator, the more must be created by others to replenish the supply. And of course the systematic plunder of the goods that someone has produced considerably reduces his motivation for producing any more.

Now the State, said Oppenheimer, is *the organization of the political means*. It is the systematic use of the predatory process over a given territory. Crimes committed by individuals, e.g., murder and theft, are sporadic and uncertain in their outcome: the victims may resist and even win. But the State provides a legal, orderly, systematic channel for the seizure of the fruits of other men's labor, and through the use of force it renders secure the parasitic caste in society.

> The classic paradigm was a conquering tribe pausing in its time-honored method of looting and murdering a conquered tribe, to realize that the time-span of plunder would be longer and more secure, and the situation more pleasant, if the conquered tribe were allowed to live and produce, with the conquerors settling among them as the rulers exacting a steady annual tribute. One method of the birth of a State may be illustrated as follows: in the hills of southern Ruritania, a bandit group manages to obtain physical control over the territory, and finally the bandit chieftain proclaims himself "King of the sovereign and independent government of South Ruritania"; and, if he and his men have the force to maintain this rule for a while, lo and behold! a new State has joined the "family of nations," and the former bandit leaders have been transformed into the lawful nobility of the realm.[1]

The State cannot keep the process of extortion going indefinitely unless it also confers some benefits (people might sooner or later revolt). One such benefit is protection—protection against other tribes, and protection against aggressors within the tribe. The State seldom manages this efficiently (what *does* it do efficiently?)—e.g., it protects only heads of state, and with everyone else it punishes (if at all) only after the aggression has been committed. And of course it increases its levy on all citizens to pay for this protection. But the State well knows that people also desire other benefits, specifically economic benefits. And these the State endeavors to supply, if for no other reason than to keep them peaceful, and, in the case of a democracy, to win their votes.

But this presents a problem, for the State has no resources of its own with which to confer these benefits. It can give to one person only by first seizing it from another; if one person gets something for nothing, another must get nothing for something. But the citizen-voter's attention is so centered on the attractiveness of the things being promised that he forgets that the politician making the promises doesn't have any of these things to give— and that he will have none of them after he gets into office; he will seize the earnings of one special interest group and distribute those earnings to another such group (minus the government's 40% handling fee, of course). And thus

. . . the promises continue to give their votes to the candidate making the biggest promises. One candidate promises to get sufficient federal funds for urban transportation to maintain the artificially low-priced subway ride in New York City. Another promises sufficient funds to guarantee Kansas wheat farmers more income for less wheat than the open market gives. Both candidates win. They meet in the cloak room on Capitol Hill, confess their sins to each other, and each one pledges to help the other deliver on his promise.

As the farmer collects the higher price for his wheat and the New Yorker enjoys his subsidized subway ride, each of them takes pride in the fine representative he has in Washington. As the farmer and the subway rider see it, each representative has just demonstrated that free servants are available, and that the honest citizen can get something for nothing if he will vote for the right candidate. The New Yorker fails to see that his own taxes have been increased in order to pay the Kansas farmer to cut down on his wheat production so the farmer can get a higher price for what he sells; so the New Yorker will have to pay a higher price for his bread. In like manner, the farmer doesn't seem to realize that his taxes have been increased in order to subsidize the urban transportation system, so the city dweller can enjoy a higher standard of living while lowering his own level of production; so the farmer will have the dubious privilege of paying the higher prices for the tools and machinery he has to buy. The farmer and the subway rider are expropriating each other's productive capacity and paying a handsome royalty to an unruly bureaucracy for the privilege of doing it. In the marketplace that would be called plundering. In the political arena it is known as social progress.[2]

Particularly profitable for the State is the "discovery" of scapegoats, those whose earnings it can systematically loot, and gain public approval for doing so through an incessant barrage of propaganda against them. Such scapegoats are not difficult to find: any person who wishes to be independent of the State; anyone who is a "self-made man," and most of all anyone who has produced and marketed something and attained wealth. Those who have not succeeded in open competition tend to envy those who have, and the State fans this envy.[3] Thus the majority of the population actually come to applaud the State for taking it away from those who have been more successful than they. Like those that killed the goose that laid the golden egg, they do not see ahead to the time when there will be no more eggs forthcoming. There will be little incentive to produce if years of effort are confiscated by the State, and many people who were employed before will now find themselves without work. The general standard of living of course will decline—most citizens do not see the inevitability of this, and some politicians do but don't mind, preferring to have a subservient and poverty-stricken population. In some States the process goes so far that the State itself becomes the sole owner of land, the sole employer of everyone (e.g., the Soviet Union); determining the profession and salary of every worker; and anyone who tries to save anything for himself, or earn anything other than through the State, is subject to interrogation, torture, and death by shooting or exile or the Gulag. Yet so successful, often, is the propaganda of the State on its own behalf, that even with this ultimate control over the life of every citizen, some people applaud the State as their protector and security ("the sanction of the victim"). As if the State could supply security, instead of (as it does) taking away from its subjects that much chance of ever taking steps to achieve their own security! But the process continues:

> As the competition for votes increases, each candidate finds it necessary to broaden his base. He must make more promises to more people. As these promises are fulfilled, more and more people find it advantageous to lower their own level of production so they can qualify for large appropriations from the public till. Direct payments

to farmers for producing less is an example of this. So are rent subsidies and food stamps for the lower income groups . . . [And] some of the less skilled members of society learn that it is more profitable to them to cease production altogether and rely upon the relief rolls for everything. . . . [Increasingly] the expectations of some special interest group have not been met, and the government is called upon to supply the shortage. That is to say, the government is called upon to supply some "free" services. Unfortunately, the government has nothing to give any special group except what it expropriates through taxation or otherwise from some other group.

The contest becomes a contest between producers and non-producers, with the government aligned on the side of the non-producers. This result has nothing to do with whether government officials are honest or dishonest, wise or stupid. They are mere agents administering a system which the citizens, acting in their capacity as voters, have demanded. It is a system that includes in its own mechanism the seeds of its own destruction. The marginal producer, whether he is a laborer or a manager, cannot avoid seeing the advantages of allowing himself to fall below the survival line, cease his contributions to those who are still further below, and qualify for a claim upon his government, and through his government upon more successful competitors, for his own support. And each individual or business enterprise that takes that step will automatically draw the producer who is only slightly higher on the economic scale just a little closer to that same survival line. Eventually all are pulled below it and are faced with the necessity of beginning over again without any prosperous neighbors upon whom they can call for help, and without any backlog of capital they can use as a starting point.[4]

And thus does the State, once it goes into the business of conferring economic benefits, cause a state of splendidly equalized destitution for everyone. The State itself rises from the ashes more powerful than ever: with every economic crisis a new emergency is declared, giving the State more power with the full approval of the majority of its citizens ("only for the duration of the emergency"—whose end is never in sight), until it ends up in total control of everything and everyone—which of course is just what the State wanted all along. But by that time it is too late for anyone to object.

The full story is far too long even to outline here. I shall mention only a few chapter headings in the saga of The State:

1. *Taxation.* It can usually be relied upon to increase until the point of total collapse ("take till there's nothing left to be taken").

2. *Inflation.* Even high taxation is not enough to pay for what the politicians have promised the voters, so the State increases the money supply to meet the deficit. This of course decreases the value of each dollar saved, and ultimately destroys savings, penalizes thrift, wrecks incentive, bankrupts business enterprises and creates huge unemployment. But this is only the beginning.
3. *Dictatorship.* As prices rise out of sight, demand for price controls increases. Price controls create shortages (men cannot continue to produce at a loss). Shortages create strikes, hunger riots, civil commotion as the shortages spread. From this arises a Caesar, to "take a firm hand" and "restore law and order." The economy is now totally controlled from the center (with all the inefficiency and waste that this implies), and each individual, including his wages and conditions of work (and what he may work at), is thoroughly regimented. Liberty has now been lost. Most of this scenario is probably inevitable for the U.S. in the next two decades.[5]

Other chapter headings along the way would include: (4) Depressions. The State, through its interventionist policies, is solely responsible for economic depressions.[6] (5) Poverty. The State is the cause of most of the poverty that there is in this country. If you want to eliminate poverty, eliminate State intervention in the marketplace.[7]—There are others, but the point is aptly summarized by Rose Wilder Lane, commenting on the slogan "Government should do for people what people can not do for themselves":

Would persons who adopt such resolutions (and say the same thing again and again, all the time, everywhere) put that idea in realistic terms and say, "Government should do nothing but compel other persons, by force, to do what those persons do not want to do?" Because, obviously, if those other persons *want* to do it, they *will* do it, if it can possibly be done; so it will be done, if it can be—if they're simply let alone.

"The people" have in fact done everything that *is* done; they built the houses and roads and railroads and telephones and planes, they organized the oil companies, the banks, the postal services, the schools—what didn't "the people" do? What happens is that, after they do it, the Government *takes* it. The Government takes the roads, the postal service, the systems of communications, the banks, the markets, the stock exchange, insurance companies, schools, building trades, telegraphs and telephones, *after* "the people" have done all these things for themselves.[8]

Small children are prolific with their spending proposals because their eyes are on the goodies to be attained, and they do not see the labor, the cost, the hardship and deprivation which their spending schemes would entail. Social planners are as a whole in the same category; they see the end but not the means.

These views have often been accused of being un-humanitarian. (Though President Ford was also among the big spenders—what else would you call a hundred billion dollar deficit in one year? which was more than all the profits of all American corporations put together—he occasionally vetoed a particularly virulent piece of legislation, and was accused of being un-humanitarian.) What is humanitarian about seizing other people's earnings and using them for purposes which *you* think they should be used for? While others think of the "great social gains" to be achieved (which will not occur anyway, since the State employees waste most of it—what poverty has been ended by poverty programs?), I think of the corner shopkeeper, already forced to the wall by confiscatory taxation, government inflation, and endless government regulation, trying to keep his head above water, and the effect of one government scheme after another to spend his money—what will be the effect of all this on him and others like him? Much more humanitarian are the words of the great French economist Frederic Bastiat, written in 1848:

> How is legal plunder to be identified? Quite simply. See if the law takes from some persons what belongs to them, and gives it to the other persons to whom it does not belong. See if the law benefits one citizen at the expense of another by doing what the citizen himself cannot do without committing a crime.[9]

The State, implemented by all the channels of communications which it controls, will use all its powers to resist such advice; and every economic incentive (and threat of deprivation) at its command will be used as well. But this in no way alters the fact that

> ... The State is no proper agency for social welfare, and never will be, for exactly the same reason that an ivory paperknife is nothing to shave with. The interests of society and of the State do not coincide; any pretense that they can be made to coincide is sheer nonsense. Society gets on best when people are most happy and contented, which they are when freest to do as they please and what they please; hence society's interest is in having as little government as possible, and in keeping it as decentralized as possible. The State, on the other hand, is administered by job-holders; hence its interest is in having as much government as possible. It is hard to imagine two sets of interests more directly opposed than these.[10]

Those who ignore these remarks, and seek to use the coercive power of the State to impose their ideas of welfare or utopia on others, must bear a heavy moral burden—the burden of the suffering they impose (however inadvertently) on others by their actions, of the incalculable loss in human well-being.

According to Rawls, man's primary social goods are "rights and liberties, opportunities and powers, income and wealth."[11] But some of these, when put into practice, would negate others. Rawls advocates (to take one example among many) government ownership of the means of production (though not necessarily all of them). This entails not only the inefficiency and waste and corruption that regularly characterize enterprises handled by the State, from the post office on down (or up?), but the huge bureaucracy required to administer it, which always seeks to increase its own numbers and power, and over which the citizen has no direct control.[12] When one spells out the full implications of all of this, very little is left of liberty; and the ostensible reason for placing such things in the hands of government—"so that everyone can have it"—ends up as its very opposite, "there's nothing left to distribute." Any resemblance between Rawls' theory and justice is strictly coincidental.

Dr. Burrill, like most of his colleagues, considers some ends so important that he would use the coercive apparatus of the State to enforce his ideals on everyone. He concludes that the marketplace is in need of improvement through State intervention (presumably along the lines of his own ideals), and that we need "a general justification of the entrepreneurial system as it stands." As it stands! As if there were anything left of the entrepreneurial system in this country but a mangled hulk, with a few crumbs thrown out by omnipotent government to produce and make money so that the State could confiscate it! as if this country still had a live and functioning "entrepreneurial system" instead of what we have now, a fascist-type State in which the State has a life-and-death stranglehold on every industry, every trade, every farm, every enterprise that exists! Is this battered ruin to be "improved" by still further interventions by the State? And what justifies one person in imposing *his* ideals on *everyone* through the coercive machinery of the State?[13]

It matters little whether Oppenheimer's account of the origins of the State is correct. (It surely is in most cases, but there are very significant differences in the case of the origin of the U.S.) It matters much more what the State is doing *now*. Whether the State was conceived and born in sin is less important than whether it is involved in sin now. And there is little doubt that, whatever its origin, sinning is currently its principal activity.

In a remarkably prescient letter to one H.S. Randall of New York, the British historian Thomas Macaulay wrote (May 23, 1857):

> The day will come when . . . a multitude of people will choose the legislature. Is it possible to doubt what sort of legislature will be chosen? On the one side is a statesman preaching patience, respect for rights, strict observance of the public faith. On the other is the demagogue ranting about the tyranny of capitalism . . . Which of the Candidates is likely to be preferred . . . ? I seriously apprehend that you will, in some season of adversity, do things which will prevent prosperity from returning; that you will act like some people in a year of scarcity: devour all the seed corn and thus make next year a year, not of scarcity but of absolute failure. There will be, I fear, spoliation. This spoliation will increase distress. The distress will produce fresh spoliation. There is nothing to stay you. Your Constitution is all sail and no anchor. When Society has entered on this downward progress, either civilization or liberty must perish. Either some Caesar or Napoleon will seize the reins of government with a strong hand, or your Republic will be as fearfully plundered and laid waste by barbarians in the twentieth century as the Roman Empire in the fifth: with this difference, that the Huns and Vandals who ravaged the Roman Empire came from without, and that your Huns and Vandals will have been engendered within your country, by your own institutions.[14]

The State, says Robert Paul Wolff in his *In Defense of Anarchism*, wields great *power* over us—but whence derives its *authority* (the moral right to wield that power)? In a telling exposition of the distinction, he finds no basis for any such authority; nor does he succeed in solving this problem in the later (more pragmatic) sections of the book. (Even if a contract theory would help—and as Hume cogently argued, it wouldn't—there was in fact no such contract. Unlike other organizations such as churches and clubs, no one contracted to be ruled by the State.)

In all existing States, some individuals (through their representatives) get hold of the State apparatus to enforce their ideas of a good society on others, including those who find it useless, repellent, or immoral. A would like to impose his plan on B and C (they would be pawns on *his* chessboard); B would impose his plan on A and C; and so on. But, observed Bastiat,

> . . . by what right does the law force me to conform to the social plan of Mr. A or Mr. B or Mr. C? If the law has a moral right to do this, why does it not, then, force these gentlemen to submit to *my* plans? Is it logical to suppose that nature has not given *me* sufficient imagination to dream up a utopia also? Should the law choose one fantasy among many, and put the organized force of government at its service only?[15]

Am I then committed to anarchism? Not necessarily, though as it has been worked out in detail by numerous writers, with provisions for a system of private defense and courts, I consider it greatly preferable to the leviathan we have today.[16] One of the greatest and least appreciated of political philosophers, Herbert Spencer, was not an anarchist.[17] He set forth "The Law of Equal Freedom": "Each man should be free to act as he chooses, provided he trenches not on the equal freedom of each other man to act as he chooses." Then he attempted to resolve the "problem of political authority" as follows, in the chapter "The Right to Ignore the State" (omitted from most subsequent editions) of his book *Social Statics*:

> . . . we can not choose but admit the right of the citizen to adopt a condition of *voluntary outlawry*. If every man has freedom to do all that he wills, provided he infringes not on the equal freedom of any others, then he is free to *drop connection with the State*—to relinquish its protection and to refuse paying toward its support. It is self-evident that in so behaving he in no way trenches upon the liberty of others, for his position is a passive one, and while

passive he cannot become an aggressor . . . He cannot be compelled to continue one of a political corporation without a breach of the moral law, seeing that citizenship involves payment of taxes; and the taking away of a man's property against his will is an infringement of his rights. *Government being simply an agent employed in common by a number of individuals to secure to them certain advantages, the very nature of the connection implies that it is for each to say whether he will employ such an agent or not.* If any one of them determines to ignore this mutual-safety confederation, nothing can be said except that he loses all claim to its good offices and exposes himself to the danger of maltreatment—a thing he is quite at liberty to do if he likes. He cannot be coerced into political combination without breach of the Law of Equal Freedom; he *can* withdraw from it without committing any such breach, and he has therefore a right so to withdraw.[18]

These words of Spencer seem to me to contain the core of any political philosophy worthy of the name. No other provides sufficiently for voluntary consent and human liberty (or as Wolff says, autonomy), not to mention such other human values as individuality, enduring prosperity, creative opportunity, and peace.

NOTES

1. Murray Rothbard, *Egalitarianism and Other Essays* (New York: Laissez Faire Press, 1973), p. 37. See also the opening pages of Richard Taylor, *Freedom, Anarchy and the Law* (Prentice-Hall, 1973).
2. Bertel Sparks, "How Many Servants Can You Afford?" *The Freeman*, October 1976, p. 593.
3. See Helmut Schoeck, *Envy*.
4. Bertel Sparks, *op. cit.*, pp. 593–5.
5. See Irwin Schiff, *The Biggest Con* (Arlington House, 1976), C.V. Myers, *The Coming Deflation* (Arlington House, 1976), Clarence B. Carson, *The War on the Poor* (Arlington House, 1970), and others.
6. See, for example, Lionel Robbins, *The Great Depression*, and Murray Rothbard, *The Great Depression*.
7. See, e.g., Clarence B. Carson, *The War on the Poor*, and Shirley Scheibla, *Poverty Is Where the Money Is*.
8. Rose Wilder Lane, in Roger L. MacBride (ed.), *The Lady and the Tycoon* (Caxton Press, 1973), pp. 332–3.
9. Frederic Bastiat, *The Law* (Foundation for Economic Education edition, p. 21).
10. Albert Jay Nock, *Cogitations*, p. 40.
11. John Rawls, *A Theory of Justice* (Harvard University Press, 1971), p. 91.

12. For many examples of this, in the context of American history, see William Wooldridge, *Uncle Sam the Monopoly Man* (Arlington House, 1970).
13. See John Hospers, *Libertarianism* (Nash, 1971); also Robert Nozick, *Anarchy, State, and Utopia* (Basic Books, 1975); Frederic Bastiat, *The Law*; Henry Hazlitt, *Economics in One Lesson* (Harper, 1946); Ludwig von Mises' books *Socialism; Bureaucracy, and Omnipotent Government* (all Yale University Press).
14. For similar predictions, see Alexis de Tocqueville, *Democracy in America*, 1840.
15. Bastiat, *The Law*, p. 71.
16. See, for example, Morris and Linda Tannehill, *The Market for Liberty*, 1970; David Friedman, *The Machinery of Freedom* (Anchor Doubleday, 1973); Leonard Krimerman and Lewis Perry (eds.), *Patterns of Anarchy* (Anchor Doubleday, 1966); Lysander Spooner, *The Constitution of No Authority*; James J. Martin (ed.), *Men against the State* (De Kalb, Ill.: Adrian Allen Associates, 1953); also Chapter 11 of J. Hospers, *Libertarianism* (Nash, 1971).
17. See his monumental work, *The Man versus the State* (1884; reprinted by Caxton Press, 1940).

Study Questions

1. Explain, after reading Hosper's essay, what he sees as the obligations (if any) of the *state* to the *individual*.
2. Do you agree with the libertarian contention that without a very large measure of *economic* freedom our democratic liberties as we know them would cease to exist? Support your answer.

Should Sponsors Screen for Moral Values?

*Kenneth E. Goodpaster**

Mid-January 1981. Top management at Consolidated Foods Corporation in Chicago was concerned. Some consumers were complaining and threatening boycotts because of the television and print ad content of the company's recently acquired Hanes division; others objected to its sponsorship of television programs thought to portray excessive sex or violence. Organized groups had adopted progressively more sophisticated tactics; simple letter-writing campaigns had evolved into elaborate TV monitoring and publicity efforts. In addition, the groups had shifted their targets from the networks to advertisers and their parent companies.

John Bryan, chief executive officer of Consolidated Foods, had been receiving numerous complaint letters as well as communications from organized groups. The most recent was an invitation to attend a press conference in Washington, D.C., to announce the formation of the "Coalition for Better Television." Lurking behind the invitation was a veiled threat of boycott publicity against Hanes hosiery products (Hanes, L'eggs, L'Erin cosmetics) as well as other Consolidated Foods consumer products (Shasta, Electrolux, Sara Lee, Kahn's meats, Monarch foods, and others). Hanes had been listed in some of the TV monitoring results as the top "user of sex in commercials."

* **KENNETH E. GOODPASTER** is a philosopher who teaches business ethics at the graduate school of business administration, Harvard University.

Bryan did not know the magnitude of the threat. His staff estimated that the impact of a boycott would be very small, yet the issues involved were clearly receiving press attention, and possibly the company could be hurt. Perhaps more important, Bryan himself faced a personal conflict in this situation.

Like many of the people in the civic and religious groups forming the coalition, Bryan was raised in the conservative Christian South. He shared many of the protesters' values. Yet his corporate role demanded that he look at the issues more broadly. He did not watch much television, though on occasion he had been dismayed by what was passing for "entertainment" on the networks. Sex and violence were being depicted with increasing boldness to attract viewers and ultimately to sell consumer products. Once, when a letter writer complained about a particularly offensive program (and his company's sponsorship in it), he responded with an embarrassed apology and a memo to the advertising agency, asking for more careful guidelines.

Bryan felt strongly that advertisers, from self-interest if from no other motive, had to exercise great care in choosing both ads and programs for sponsorship. Good taste and social awareness were essential to the marketing effectiveness of any consumer goods company. On the other hand, the products (women's hosiery) and target markets of the Hanes division seemed to demand a somewhat "sexy" image. Nielsen ratings were important indicators of what the relevant public apparently enjoyed watching on television. The consumer was, in some sense, getting no more and no less than she wanted. Ought a corporation do anything but "follow" the market?

Even if the Moral Majority and other groups thought corporations ought to change their policies, they were probably in the minority. Yet other important groups that had challenged establishment values, including civil rights groups in the sixties, had also been minorities. Such groups can work through the political process for change—or they can bring their concerns to the public through protests and boycotts. In this case, no one wanted government censorship of networks and the advertisers. That left the networks and the advertisers as targets. Bryan knew this, and as much as he would have liked to be rid of the problem, it persisted. Corporations were being challenged to re-examine their largely quantitative, market-following media policies in favor of more qualitative, value-sensitive policies. The marketplace was speaking, but with profoundly mixed messages.

Complicating Bryan's situation was Hanes's status as a recent acquisition. Its own corporate culture, which had evolved independently over many successful years, was less conservative than that of its new parent company. Hanes had systematically cultivated a "glamorous" image that was less cautious and conventional than the profile of the other divisions in Consolidated Foods. Some aspects of this difference were welcomed, even sought, in the acquisition. New managerial talent from Hanes would enliven the entire corporation. But now the cultural factors seemed to be an unforeseen drawback. The game of mergers and acquisitions involved more than balance sheets and income statements and business unit synergies. It also involved values in subtle, but very real, ways.*

Moral Agents and Moral Environments

The issues that faced John Bryan in 1981 reveal in microcosm most, if not all, the central issues in contemporary business ethics, and indeed in professional ethics more generally. Quite apart from the intensely important *topical* issues involved, to which I shall return shortly, the basic *structural* issues that emerge are worth careful attention.

First, Consolidated Foods is both a "moral agent" in a wider social environment and itself a "moral environment" for its subunits, managers, and employees. John Bryan's responsibilities, therefore, extended in both outward and inward directions—like the image of Janus at the gates of ancient Roman cities.

Second, as a moral agent, the corporation in this case confronted the apparent insufficiency of the two primary "systemic surrogates" for value awareness or conscience: the visible hand of law and government intervention and the invisible hand of market competition. The problem that confronted John Bryan resisted resolution through either of these standard channels. In fact, it was in a sense the product of the undesirability of the first sur-

---

* The case material is drawn from three studies by the author, available through HBS Case Services (9–382–158, 9–382–159, and 9–382–160), Harvard Business School, Boston, MA 02163.

rogate (law and government) combined with the relative insensitivity of the second (the marketplace). The corporation and its leadership seemed called upon to exercise value judgments that were "systemically underdetermined."

Third, as a moral environment, the corporation in this case faced questions about its own culture. Can a highly diversified corporation effectively maintain the different, perhaps competing internal value systems of its components? If so, can the corporate leaders avoid both the Scylla of standing for nothing and the Charybdis of moral imperialism toward employees? If not, what are the implications for corporate ethics as more and more large organizations grow by merger and acquisition?

Fourth, if corporate ethics demands, as it appears to, that managers and their organizations "institutionalize" more than the values implicit in law and the market-place, where are these larger values to be sought and how are they to be appropriately implemented? What structures, systems, and management styles does this process require?

Fifth, and finally, if we seek guidance on these issues by looking to the natural analogy between the moral life of the individual and the "moral life" of the organization, do we gain clarity or lose it? As individuals, we regularly recognize that the imperatives of law and self-interest (the "market") are insufficient for moral judgment. Both in our relationships with others and in our inner lives we are called upon to balance and weigh values that are "underdetermined" by such forces. Can we project not only darkness but also light from this individual challenge to the level of organizational policy and governance?

John Bryan's situation as a corporate executive is paradigmatic in many ways of the situations of business leaders everywhere. The issues can vary from advertising policies through environmental impacts of more ordinary kinds, to employee rights and international business practices. At the core of such issues lie questions about the legitimacy, the authority, and the content of the moral point of view in the management of institutions—questions with which philosophers and theologians have struggled for centuries, at least in their more individualistic manifestations.

More Cautious Programming

Many chief executive officers of large corporations did more or less what John Bryan did: they quietly directed the "tightening up" of advertising and programming guidelines, while "lying low" to avoid media attention and boycott "hit lists."

One major advertiser, however, Procter & Gamble, adopted a different posture. Owen Butler, chairman of the corporation made the television issue the central theme in a widely quoted speech to the Academy of Television Arts and Sciences (June 1981). After cautiously acknowledging the basic validity of the protests of the Coalition for Better Television, Butler asserted:

> For sound commercial reasons, we are not going to let our advertising messages appear in an environment which we think many of our potential customers will find distasteful. Beyond that, we are going to be guided by our conscience on the kind of material we sponsor. A corporation is not without personality and character and conscience. A corporation like ours has a character which is the sum of all the tens of thousands of people who have made up that corporation for more than 140 years, and our defintion of the kind of media which we would support with our advertising has always involved some moral considerations. . . . It is completely within our character not only to screen out problem programs, but also to actively seek programs of exceptional artistic quality, which are truly inspirational and which challenge the very best in human nature.

Many applauded Butler's public stand; some, pointing to certain afternoon soap operas sponsored by P&G, were more cynical. In any case, many felt that his significant statement actually improved network performance over the following year.

In November 1981, another influential figure added some potent reflections to the debate over sex and violence on television. Daniel Yankelovich, president of the social-research firm Yankelovich, Skelly, and White, wrote in *Psychology Today*:

> I am convinced that many Americans, especially parents, are increasingly uncomfortable with the sweeping permissiveness that their own pursuit of permissiveness has created for young people. . . . We need to confront the possibility that adults who now live a life of choice while keeping their own moral center intact are capable of doing so because their upbringing instilled in them a

clear sense of right and wrong. We need to recognize that we have been neglecting the question, broadly put, of what is best for our children because we have been too busy with the question of what is best for us as adults, assuming—all too comfortably—that the same answer would do for both questions. It will not.

Beyond the Market Ethic

Yankelovich's concerns, expressed by others as well, captured the public mood. The general public (and business leaders) were perhaps not as conservative as the Moral Majority, but neither were they blind to the moral significance of the television debate. The market ethic had not served public values well. Government regulation was even less likely to serve these values effectively. Mature moral judgment seemed to be the only answer, and this judgment was called for not only in the family, but also in corporate offices.

According to some commentators, the 1982 television season brought "giggle instead of jiggle," much more cautious sponsoring policies on the part of advertisers, and correspondingly more cautious programming by the networks. The issue was far from settled, however. Today communities across the country are beginning to face the thorny value issues raised by cable television technology. Concerns for corporate responsibility, new avenues of video "freedom" (including sex and violence), and rights of free expression will doubtless intensify.

But perhaps we are learning in the process—not only about business ethics and its basic structure, but about ourselves. And perhaps the dialogue between business and the humanities that such learning requires will leave us better off. There is not just one "economy" to which corporations need address themselves. There are several, and each has a kind of "market" of its own. If business ethics is to be an intellectual and moral force for good of society, it will be because it has helped us discover and serve the economy of values that lies beneath our more conventional transactions.

BIOGRAPHICAL INFORMATION ON AUTHOR—see "Toward an Integrated Approach to Business Ethics" by the same author.

Study Questions

1. Explain in your own words Goodpaster's distinction between moral agents and moral environments.
2. Do you agree that the market and the law are insufficient substitutes for corporate conscience? Why? Why not?

PART IV

Journalistic Ethics

Journalists have been studying journalistic ethics now for a good many years, though even their concern with such issues has increased with such dramatic and controversial episodes as the Janet Cooke case, the Pentagon Papers, the Myron Farber case and so forth. These national tragedies, accompanied as they were by fierce and even ruthless interest among journalists in ethical questions. This has led to a new interest in journalistic ethics within journalism programs.

Philosophers, however, have displayed only marginal interest in such questions, and when they do take up these issues, they usually restrict themselves to questions about privacy or freedom of expression. And even here, their analyses do not necessarily relate these matters specifically to journalism. Thus, the particular skills of the philosopher have not been applied to such questions and the consequences of such neglect have been disastrous. As Professor Anita Silvers points out in her article, "How To Avoid Resting Journalistic Ethics On A Mistake": ". . . when so much has been accomplished during the last decade in many of the areas of professional and applied ethics, the study of journalistic ethics appears anemic at best . . . Compared to the study of medical and business ethics . . . the investigation of journalistic ethics has had relatively little impact either on philosophy or journalism."

This seems unquestionably true and, of course, part of the purpose of this book is to at least make a start towards rectifying

473

that situation. Despite the honest efforts of journalists, the skills of the philosopher need to be brought to bear as well, both on the above-mentioned ethical issues and on many others, including first versus sixth amendment questions (free press versus fair trial), whistle-blowing, blackmail, the pedagogy of journalism, reporters' relationships to their sources, and the vexing question of journalistic objectivity.

While the number of good articles penned by journalists is small, there have been some outstanding ones. A number of them have been included, along side essays by philosophers. My hope is that the various essays in this section will further contribute to an understanding of the nature of, and possible solutions for, the great problems in journalistic ethics.

In the piece, "Contemporary Approaches to Journalistic Ethics," John Ferré discusses the various approaches to journalistic ethics, especially during the 1970s. According to his analysis, interest rose during the 1970s after nearly half a century of silence. Since he discusses Professor Merrill's work at some length, this piece should be read in conjunction with Merrill's. Also important is Silvers' analysis since the fundamental distinction she draws between special "professional rights" and general moral imperatives (e.g., promise keeping) have ramifications throughout the approaches Ferré surveys.

Professor Ferré believes it is essential to step back and survey the recent literature in journalistic ethics in order to "suggest the direction it must go to reach its goal." He goes on to point out that journalistic ethics has been approached in two ways—via questions that analyze ethical dilemmas and conundrums, and through theories which attempt to build the foundations for practical ethical decisions. As a good example of the latter, he briefly discusses Professor John Merrill's work. He concludes by urging that both approaches are important in order to make further progress in journalistic ethics.

While Ferré has done an excellent survey, not all will agree with some of his interpretations. In his discussion of Kant, for example, he appears to regard the "hypothetical imperative" as having moral force, although Kant does not believe so. (It is not clear whether Kant is correct in this, but that is his official view). Other than that, Ferré's survey is comprehensive and a reliable "map" through the jungle of varying approaches to journalistic ethics.

In "How to Avoid Resting Journalistic Ethics on a Mistake," Professor Anita Silvers argues that discussions of professional ethics typically assume that there are special rights and responsibilities which pertain to persons by virtue of their professions. But some philosophers dispute this assumption by insisting that the principles of ordinary morality suffice for determining professional rights and duties. If they are correct, there is no such thing as professional ethics. In the practice of any profession, people's rights and duties result simply from the "application of ordinary morality to the profession's special circumstances."

Silvers, however, disputes this widely held view. The essay thus contains a justification for believing that professional rights and duties are not reducible to ordinary rights and duties. She makes a strong case for supposing that professionals do have specialized obligations, and accepting this view has consequences for assigning them specialized rights as well. Moreover, if we are to have a claim on journalists to practice their profession morally, we must be able to appeal to moral considerations which do not bind everyone equally.

This piece, therefore, applies to nearly all the pieces in this selection to the extent that they make the false assumption mentioned above (which they do). Professor Good's paper, however, appears to be an exception, as is Professor Murphy's and one or two others. Perhaps McDonald's paper exhibits this sort of instructive and tempting error. (A useful exercise for the student, incidentally, is to search the essays in this section to see if they agree or disagree with my comments here.)

Later in her argument, Silvers argues, doubtless controversially, that, in a sense, journalists are relatively "uninformed" people. That is, unlike in law or medicine, there is, nothing like a "body of knowledge" that constitutes the field of journalism. Thus, journalists' views and opinions, especially moral opinions, have no special supportive credentials. At the finish of this unusually insightful and well-argued piece, Professor Silvers calls for much greater study of the metaethics of journalism and not just "applied" analyses.

Now, while one can see Silvers' point that ". . . journalists do not appear to possess any specialized knowledge," it is arguable that they possess specialized *skills*. Presumably, they have skills as interviewers, researchers and writers, among others. And in that sense, it is hard to see how journalists differ so much from, say, a skilled surgeon or psychiatrist. This issue needs further study, especially inasmuch as the answers to it will obviously affect the *education* of journalists.

In "Liberty and its Limits," Professor Michael Levin defends a version of liberty and free choice which is at variance with a number of classical approaches, including the traditional utilitarian arguments for liberty. Since Professor Allen deals with the same issues and, indeed, defends his view of rights in a Kantian context, his piece should be read in connection with Levin's. He argues the interesting view that we have rights to "negative" liberty but no rights to "positive" liberty. That is, he holds that we all have a right to do as we please without interference by the will of another. But we do not necessarily and automatically have any rights of "positive" liberty. E.g., two or more persons cannot logically claim the positive right to speak from the same podium. All this is defended in a deontological context.

Levin's distinction between a "negative" and "positive" freedom seems quite sound (although it is not entirely a new one, of course). It is surely true that my "negative" right to your non-interference with my exercise of the franchise is surely consistent with a similar claim by everyone else.

What should concern us are some of the supporting arguments in his piece. He says, e.g., "Michael Jackson is not being rewarded for possessing those talents but for using them. He is being remunerated for what *is* in his control, not an accident of birth." This goes down hard: my problem with the distinction is simply that the connection with having talent and *using* it is so tight. Using a talent does, after all, logically presuppose having been born with it. Further, in Jackson's case, using the "talent" (if that is the right word) is a comparatively trivial exercise. Perhaps I would find Levin's distinction more palatable were he talking of, say, an accomplished violinist like Erica Morini who, while admittedly having been born with talent, needed years of hard study to actualize it. In Jackson's case, it seems that it is perfectly consistent with our linguistic intuitions to describe Jackson as being rewarded for his "talent." Indeed, I have heard just such descriptions of Jackson by my students on numerous (highly unpleasant) occasions. I do not see that ordinary usage warrants the implied premise that one can be rewarded only for *doings* or activities, and not for "havings" (traits one is born with). There is no necessary or *conceptual* connection between the two.

In "Speech, Expression and the Constitution," Professor Morrow engages in considerable subtle and delicate analyses of several amendments of the constitution, particularly the First, Fifth, and Ninth. That being the case, his piece deals with the same issues as Berger's, and to some extent Elliston's and Richard's, especially considering that the latter, like Morrow, also touches on the vexing question of pornography and freedom.

In the early stages of his argument, Morrow suggests that while the first amendment protects speech, it does not necessarily confer absolute protection on just any type of expression (wearing unusual hairstyles or unorthodox clothing, e.g.). By making further distinctions, he argues that the first amendment protects political speech, but cannot be construed as conferring protection on purely private speech. However, private speech can be thought of as a liberty similar to the right to hold property. This, however, is not absolute, as government can suspend such rights under Fifth-amendment conditions of due process.

Finally, he argues that "expression," understood in its widest possible sense, may be protected by the ninth amendment, and that it is to this amendment, rather than to the first (as is usually done) that persons should look for such protection.

One interesting feature of his analysis concerns the suggestion that the first amendment protects "political" speech, but not "private" speech. Still, one might argue that, at any given instant when something is said, it might be unclear whether that utterance is "private" or "political." I may say something against my state senator in the privacy of my own home and to my best friend. Is this an instance of "private" speech?! It seems so: Yet, if my friend turns to me, and reports back to the senator, clearly my "private" remarks could be used for political purposes. What was "private" at one point, can later become "political." True, Morrow deals extensively with these kinds of questions, but I believe they are fertile ground for further exploration.

In "Whistleblowing: The Reporter's Role" by Frederick A. Elliston, the author first examines several classic approaches to whistleblowing, including what he deems the self-help, exposé, personal, legal and philosophical ones. Since he is inspired in part by De George's work, the latter's article should be read along with this one. (Sissela Bok has written on this issue also.) Indeed, selected this piece as it is another example of the close ties between the various fields of professional ethics—business and journalistic ethics in this case. It is closely linked with business ethics generally inasmuch as a large aspect of the whistle-blowing issue involves disclosing such information about corporations which is in the public interest to know (that a company is polluting the water supply with dangerous chemicals, for example.) In that connection, Professors Corlett and French's pieces in the business ethics section are relevant, inasmuch as they suggest how to correct and prevent such dangerous and irresponsible behavior by corporations.

Elliston then examines the concept of whistleblowing and how it may fairly be judged. He discusses also the reporter's particular and special role in whistleblowing, what factors that make approaching the press an appropriate strategy and when it might be inappropriate. He concludes with a brief discussion of the ethics of whistleblowing, arguing that anyone considering this method of exposing wrongdoing should consider the costs of doing so. He should also be fully informed on the facts, laws and regulations governing the situation at issue. Additionally, he should define it carefully, weigh its importance, verify the facts, consider the possibility of retaliation and, finally, ask whether, in fact, whistleblowing in that case will be effective. Though he does not dwell on them, it is clear that Professor Elliston has few problems with "codes of ethics." Yet it is worth keeping in mind that, according to many press critics, such as Merrill and Rick Pullen, such codes simply have not worked. Also worth noting is the fact that Elliston seems to endorse a consequentialist approach rather uncritically, although he succeeds very well in spelling out the relevant practical factors in ethical decisions of this kind.

Professor Murphy's piece is a paradigm of close analysis, much in the style of philosophers such as Norman Malcolm. Like Malcolm, Murphy asks over and over, "what could, be meant by various concepts," probing ever more deeply into the mist to clarify the notion of blackmail. "Blackmail: A Preliminary Inquiry," argues that the traditional view of blackmail as something intrinsically "sleazy" and clearly immoral is premature. It should be noted that Professor Silvers' piece, to the extent that it, like Murphy's, touches on the rights of public persons, is relevant to Murphy's work. Also, since questions of constitutional freedoms and rights are dealt with, Professor Morrow's should be read with this one.

To clarify some of the basic issues (and he states clearly that he hopes to do no more than make a start towards doing so), Murphy examines some widely differing notions of blackmail as, for example, those held by Marxists and Libertarians. He also discusses the view that what seems to be wrong with blackmail has to do with privacy, rather than economic benefit. Later in the piece he argues that with respect to public persons, where there is an economic market for information about them, anyone having that information should not be charged with blackmail so long as he "asks no more than the going market value."

In general, Professor Murphy argues that there are good reasons for making blackmail a criminal act when private individuals are concerned; and there are reasons for making blackmail a criminal act when public persons are involved *only*, as indicated above, when the person in possession of the information charges more than what, e.g., the press would be willing to pay.

A Marxist critic would, of course have trouble with this, insofar as it in effect extends the free market economy into intimate and vulnerable areas of people's lives. Beyond that general caveat, there are interesting and serious questions about the rights of "public" persons. Ever since *Linus Pauling vs. National Review* (which effectively extended New York *Times vs. Sullivan* to cover public persons as well as elected officials) it is not at all clear that public persons have been fairly treated by the press. Perhaps the question here is whether all information about public persons (their sex lives, e.g.) is "up for grabs" on the free market, or whether only that information that the public needs to know should be made public. And how does one *draw* that distinction? If adequate criteria for doing the latter cannot be given, then Judge Silverman's decision in *Linus Pauling vs. National Review* may not be well-founded. It would have been interesting to see Professor Murphy discuss that case in this context.

The editor's own contribution, first published in *The International Journal of Applied Philosophy* in 1987, argues that there are numerous close affinities between the fields of philosophy and journalism, much as Professors Merrill and Odell have argued in their recent book, *Philosophy and Journalism*. Among these are the relationships to language and logic, as well as the mutual importance of various kinds of epistemological problems. The piece then suggests that the education of journalists would be improved if the curricula in schools of journalism were broadened to include teachers and scholars in other areas—especially philosophy.

Such being the case, it is recommended that Professor Silvers' piece be read alongside mine. Also, the pieces on the subject of pedagogy in the business and medical ethics sections should be read. Professor Madsen's article is relevant also in comparing the philosophy of teaching in business and journalistic ethics.

It may be that the biggest problem with this view is that it may simply be unrealistic to suppose one could undertake the massive reorganization of journalistic programs in universities as suggested. And that leaves aside the question of whether the other branches of knowledge have as much relevance to journalism as is claimed. If Professor Silvers is right, for example, in the claim that there just isn't a "body of knowledge" associated with journalism—and I, for one, believe she is right—then attempts to "fabricate" one may not work. That is, while it may be in general a good thing for journalists to, e.g., know some science, it may not be qua *journalists* that such knowledge is a good thing, but merely qua human beings living in civilized society that it is good to know science. There may be no *special* reason for journalists to know any science, unless, of course, they are specifically science journalists).

In "The Press, the government, and the ethics vacuum," Professor John C. Merrill takes on a substantial number of problems in the media. In the course of doing this, he covers a large number of issues of varying importance. Since he focuses some of his discussion on journalistic freedom, his paper should be studied in connection with Professor Morrow's. He also expresses dismay at the lack of fixed ethical codes (Though in other works, such as *Philosophy and Journalism*, written with Professor Jack Odell, he clearly expresses his view that they do not work anyway). Fundamentally, however, he bemoans the lack of a fixed, formalistic Kantian ethic in both government and the press, and feels there is too much concern with a vacuous, relativistic ethics which can be used/abused to "justify" virtually any individual decision, no matter how capricious. More importantly, according to Merrill, this unfortunate state of affairs exists because neither the government nor the press really *desire* any reasonably fixed ethical standards—protestations to the contrary notwithstanding. Yet Merrill goes deeper, urging that the reason for all this confusion is "that there is really no consistent and logical philosophy of journalism."

Following this he offers a complex analysis of two press notions, the idea that the press and government are adversaries, and that the people have a 'right to know." His discussion of freedom is possibly controversial. He seems to speak disparagingly of journalists' fears about freedom with responsibility; as he puts it, "Most journalists . . . see the escalated talk and concern about press responsibility as a potential danger to press freedom. . . ."

A real concern is that this fear might, in fact, *be* a real danger. As a former newspaper editor myself, I've sometimes been accused by readers of discussing an issue "irresponsibly," or "presenting only one side," etc. In my experience, usually someone hurls such charges only when you have been unfavorable to their position.

In "Foundations and Limits of Freedom of the Press," Judith Lichtenberg argues in various ways that most of the arguments traditionally used by journalists in defense of a free press do not work. She points out, for example, that contemporary news organizations usually belong to big companies that, in effect, dictate what gets covered and what does not. Also, she indicates that even the form of the media governs what is covered; television, e.g., is well-suited for action, rather than analysis of events. (In this respect, she follows the spirit of press critic Edward Jay Epstein in *News From Nowhere*.) Perhaps her most valuable and original contribution is the suggestion that, while freedom of speech should be virtually unconditional, freedom of the *press*—the two are usually and erroneously lumped together—should not be.

Interestingly, there are similarities between the arguments in her piece and those in Professor Rachels, on euthanasia though, of course, the issues treated are quite different. Both Rachels and Lichtenberg touch on the concept of an "action," and for those interested in that issue alone, it would be worthwhile to compare their respective analyses. Also, her analysis should be compared and contrasted with Professor Levin's, inasmuch as both philosophers appear to endorse some kind of "negative" freedom—i.e., both endorse some right of noninterference.

Donald McDonald's "Is Objectivity Possible?" is surely one of the classics on this question, and the author's probing insights and comprehensive analysis are well worth careful study. Since he deals so extensively with the issue of objectivity, my own analysis would seem relevant here, especially since, as the reader will see, I differ from McDonald on some critical points, especially regarding the role and nature of language.

Mr. McDonald covers most of the usual issues raised in discussions of objectivity, such as the definition of newsworthiness, the scope of the reporter's task, the responsibilities of the *reader* in the reporting process (an issue often overlooked by other critics), the importance of "bare facts" vis-à-vis study and reflection on matters of great importance, the relationship of fact gathering and interpretation, the relationship of reporters to their sources and so forth.

Most of his argument is quite winning, but some points, here and there, seem arguable or vague. Early on he defines "objectivity," for example, as ". . . simply an essential correspondence between knowledge of a thing and the thing itself." This is perhaps more aptly called a definition of "truth," rather than a definition of "objectivity." Indeed, what McDonald has given us is a fair statement of the classic theories of truth, the so-called "correspondence" theory. (See the Austin-Strawson debates on this topic.)

Also—and this has been stated by other journalistic critics— McDonald argues against a conventioinal conception of "news," the notion ". . . that a thing is not newsworthy until it becomes an event; that is, until something happens . . . significant phenomena that are not events (e.g., situations, trends, conditions) go largely unreported; second, often the context which can make even an event meaningful, is either not reported or reported inadequately."

While this sounds compelling, McDonald may be asking too much. To approach it from a Wittgensteinian perspective, one might respond very simply by pointing out that "events," are just part of what we *mean* by news. McDonald may simply be suggesting that there should not *be* news at all in the conventional sense. Whether this would be a good thing for society is something else altogether. In any case, to urge a new definition of "news" along his lines would likely exacerbate the problem of objectivity considerably. In my view, it is far more difficult to spot important trends than important events; while there are admittedly hundreds of events to pick from every day, surely there are *thousands* if not millions of "trends" in progress all the time—trends toward upward mobility, to second jobs, to greater spending by the government, to more vacationing in Australia than Europe, toward wider ties, etc. And while all of these *may* lead to significant "events," it is not clear why a reporter should spend time trying to select from and report on, say, a trend towards vacationing in Australia until something (i.e., an event) dramatic occurs which gives some reason to believe that that trend, rather than some other, is important enough for the public to want to know about. (The collapse of a major European airline due to a decline in tourism, for example.)

Some of McDonald's comments on the nature of language are unconvincing as well. He urges that "[The Thomists] showed that language and meaning depend on the past experiences of men; that different words can mean different things to different men . . ." This is really a gross exaggeration though, of course it is true that this occurs, say, where regional dialects are involved. In black English, to say that so-and-so is "on," has a very precise meaning, where as in British high society it may be meaningless. Even so, the majority of words in a language are quite fixed. All native speakers of English know that "bank" has a precise and fixed range of meanings—'financial institution" and, e.g., "riverbank." And anyone who thought that "bank" referred to ice-cream cones or condoms would be simply *mistaken* about the meaning of the word. Indeed, if words did not have at least relatively stable meanings, we would all live in an Alice-in-Wonderland world where communication would be impossible.

In general, McDonald's article, for all its comprehensiveness and fine writing, suffers from the same defects that virtually all treatments of "objectivity" suffer from at the hands of many journalists: a lack of philosophical sophistication as well as a lack of background knowledge of treatments of the key issues by philosophers of language and philosophers of science. Language is an issue that has been seriously studied by philosophers, linguists, anthropologists and physical scientists. Much the same applies to the concept of "objectivity" itself. All of this is ignored by McDonald and most writers on objectivity.

Thus the greatest value of the article is the extent to which it illustrates how a fine mind and a fine journalist can wander aimlessly through the philosophical problems related to his subject. This, in its turn, argues powerfully for the introduction of philosophers, historians, scientists, etc., into the faculty ranks of journalism schools, as I have myself argued on other occasions.

Pulitzer Prize-winning author James Michener, scarcely needs an introduction, having been one of the world's most distinguished writers for many years. He deals with the disastrous Janet Cooke hoax, where she wrote a story about a child heroin addict that was pure mythology.

In his essay, Michener, of couse, laments the entire event, but also tries to clarify it and suggest possible remedies. He argues, for example, that a big part of the problem with this and many other stories in journalism is the ability of reporters to conceal their sources. This is precisely the phenomenon Edward Jay Epstein deals with, and it will be useful for the reader to compare their two analyses. (See my discussion of Epstein's article for more on this comparison.) My only reservation about Michener's suggestions is whether they are realistic, given the pressures of daily journalism. For example, when I was editor of the tiny *Fairfield Chronicle*, in Fairfield, New Jersey, there were some stories I had to omit because I did not have the time to check them to my satisfaction.) And even if smaller papers could afford the resources to undertake such investigations and make writers prove the truth of their sources, there is, among other things, the "script" problem that critics like Edward Epstein in *News From Nowhere* mentions. No matter how many true facts one might accumulate, a news organization *has* to mold them into a form palatable to readers and unoffensive to advertisers, lest they go bankrupt.

The main point to be drawn from Mr. Michener's analysis doubtless is that many newspapers could do considerably better than they are currently doing in verifying sources.

"Privacy and the Right to Privacy" by Professor H.J. McCloskey is classical ordinary-language philosophy in the grand tradition of Wittgenstein, Warnock, Austin, Malcolm, etc. McCloskey wades carefully through the complexities of our use of the term "privacy," taking pains to distinguish one sense from another, and to show how a person may or not have such a "right" to privacy, depending on what the correct analysis of the term is. In doing this, McCloskey suggests that we may not depend on the great liberal philosphers, such as Mill, Locke, etc., since they virtually ignore the concept. This essay may be profitably studied with Epstein's essay, since both Epstein and McCloskey seem to agree that maintaining an open society is of critical importance.

Perhaps more central to McCloskey's main argument is Murphy's piece on blackmail, since the latter phenomenon involves what at least appear to be gross intrusions on a person's privacy. Relevant also are those pieces which discuss the concept of a "person," such as Engelhardt's piece does. This is because the concept of "personhood" has often been linked with privacy as the philosophical basis for it—though McCloskey remains unconvinced by such attempts.

In the course of his analysis, then, McCloskey discusses privacy as ". . . consisting in being let alone," as ". . . the lack of disclosure, and the right to privacy as the right to selective disclosure," "privacy and secrecy," ". . . exclusive access, . . . respect for personal autonomy," etc. Most of what McCloskey says appears both correct and helpful, as when he suggests that efforts to analyze privacy in terms of trust and respect for persons are ". . . more plausibly and accurately to be construed as attempts to explain the importance of privacy and of how privacy relates to our basic values." This seems right: contrary to Rachels' account (which McCloskey discusses), it does seem that privacy is not *based* upon, say, the fact that it may make love possible, but rather the existence and possibility of love (and friendship) show why privacy is *important*. Indeed, privacy would probably be possible in a world where it was simply the case that no one ever fell in love with, or become friends with one another. (A bizarre world but, not, I should think, a conceptually inconceivable world.) In such a world, privacy would be possible, but might, as McCloskey suggests, simply be unimportant to most people. McCloskey's own view is that there is no such thing as a basic moral right to privacy, in the sense which "liberty" is often construed as a basic moral right. As he expresses it, "If this contention is that privacy has no intrinsic worth or moral value—and to rebut it much more than has been done to date will be needed. . . . then there can be no basic moral right to privacy which parallels the traditionally recognized rights to life, self-development, moral integrity, liberty. Any right to privacy will be a derivative one from other rights and other goods."

Part of the reason for McCloskey's conclusion is his contention that "privacy" has an essentially negative meaning. As he puts it, "Privacy relates to the lack of something. Its definition must be essentially negative. How can the absence of something have intrinsic value? Any value it has must relate to the absence of evils or to this absence being a condition of goods, or the like." My problem with this is that while it seems correct that privacy is the absence of something, as McCloskey claims, it also seems that such a "negative" definition could be given even of the virtues McCloskey will admit *are* basic rights. "Liberty," for example, can be defined "negatively," at least in part, merely by saying that it is the "absence of interference with action or expression."(See Levin's paper, for example.) In a similar vein, the "right to life" might be defined—at least in part—negatively by suggesting that it is the "right to" a "noninterference with one's life." Thus it may be that McCloskey's argument, if correct, also shows that neither "privacy" nor any other right can be a "basic" one.

In "Myron Farber's Confidential Sources," by Christians, et al., the authors approach the delicate and difficult question of reporters' relationships with sources. As they point out, this case is an instance of the problems that arise when First Amendment questions (free press) collide with Sixth Amendment issues (right to a fair trial). Despite the need of his notes and source information, Myron Farber refused to turn them over to the judge in a murder trial—a trial generated by the story and accusations Farber had himself written. This helps highlight why the important article to be studied here is Anita Silvers' "How To Avoid Resting Journalistic Ethics on A Mistake." This is because Christians, et al., may have committed precisely the mistake Silvers mentions which will be discussed below. Also, Good's article, because it too deals with journalistic freedom, should be studied in conjunction with this piece. And Judith Lichtenberg, because she argues for more government control over the press, is also relevant to the Farber case. Dyer's piece on defining a profession is also to the point, inasmuch as one of the questions at issue in the Farber case is the worth of his claim to "professional confidentiality" to his sources. Finally, Professor Bok's "The Limits of Confidentiality," because it deals precisely with such questions as the Farber case raises, should also be studied closely.

Much of the analysis in the Farber article is sound and insightful—particularly the author's criticisms of a Kantian approach to the case. However, the force of the author's claim that the real basis for Farber's actions were "special privilege," rather than an imperative to "promise-keeping," is incomplete. The reason is that it does not even consider some relevant and important arguments against such a view.

This is where Silvers' analysis is particularly valuable, and the fact that Christians, et al. do not even consider these elements is a stunning example of the lack of communication between journalists and philosophers working on the same issues. (This, of course, is part of the reason why I assembled this volume in the first place.) A main theme in Silvers' analysis is the fact that some philosophers have argued that, in effect, there is no such thing as "professional rights and duties" (or "special privileges," such as the confidentiality duties of reporters to the kind of sources that Christians discusses). Such philosophers further argue that in the practice of any profession, the principles of ordinary morality are the only ones applicable to a professional's special circumstances.

Silvers rejects this view, but a key issue, ultimately, as she recognizes it, is whether *journalists* have any such "special" rights, above and beyond ordinary moral rights and duties. Christians, et al. appear to be unaware of the discussion and literature already existing on this problem—the problem of "special," professional rights and duties vs. ordinary rights, as described above. (Often, such discussion take place along Kantian or deontological lines; Professor Paul Allen's in the first section of this work is also relevant here.)

Contemporary Approaches to Journalistic Ethics

*John P. Ferré**

Although the discipline of journalistic ethics has recently regained scholarly attention, the field has been largely ignored and the literature has usually lacked moral and intellectual depth. According to Clifford Christians, the scientific study of the morals of journalism emerged in the 1920s when journalists set standards for relations between organizations and between newspapers and their publics.[1] After those journalists produced many codes of ethics, interest in the ethics of journalism waned.[2]

Forty years of virtual silence passed before attention to journalistic ethics revived in the 1970s. Contemporary arguments concern implications of the widely accepted social responsibility theory of the press, since its two major proponents did not generate an ethic.[3] Rivers and Schramm prepared the way for an ethic by saying that mass communication is responsible for producing "the highest-quality product it can, which requires that it develop an awareness of the depth and breadth of the public's needs and interests."[4] They also describe forces such as codes of ethics, liberal education, media critics and press councils, which discourage unethical media practices, but they offer little guidance for ethical decision making.

Christians also notes a current trend toward legalization: Be-

* John P. Ferré (PhD, University of Illinois; 1986) is a graduate student at the University of Chicago and a visiting instructor in the Department of English and Philosophy at Purdue University, Calumet.

cause constraints are provided by law, that which is not illegal is ethically acceptable.[5] Richard Harwood of the *Washington Post* may be correct when he labels journalistic ethics a "no-man's land" in which there is "utter confusion . . . over such simple concepts as conflict of interest."[6]

The present study proposes to assess the currrent status of journalistic ethics by the major statements of the 1970s. The concern here is to analyze and assess contemporary journalistic ethics and indicate the direction a journalistic ethic must travel in order to approach its goal of guiding journalists towards consistently moral reporting methods. The relationship between law and the mass media is not emphasized here, since it does not address the primary questions within ethics.

Those who comment on journalistic ethics usually lament the apparent impotency of codes of ethics, and their criticisms are mostly valid. Codified ideals tend to be weak because they cannot take the very real contexts and constraints into account. The usual criticisms are destructive, though, because they are not followed by ethics; that is, they describe moral ambiguities that involve journalists but provide little constructive theory for concerned journalists to use to discern the moral among the vile. The small remainder of literature that theorizes about the moral obligations inherent to the media tends to be too general to be useful. The mass media still need an ethic from which principles can be drawn to be applied to most every situation that journalists encounter.

The Issue Approach

According to Robert Cirino, the American press is responsible for providing citizens with an accurate picture of reality so that democracy can function. Cirino blames media distortions on a staunchly conservative hierarchy, their profit motivations, and the subjective nature of reporting. The union of these pressures lead the media to produce a twisted, establishment view of reality to the American people. This bias, in turn, encourages such atrocities as the Vietnam War which the media helped cause and support. Cirino maintains that if the media did not suppress anti-establishment information and opinion, but instead presented it with equal favor alongside conservative propaganda, the American people would support responsible activity while condemning the inhumane.[7]

In order to insure a minimum of bias, and thus moral, democratic reporting. Cirino supports legislation to insure equal access to all media by all groups. Cirino, however, is no more specific. Furthermore, his faith in legislation seems ironic, since the establishment he wants to counter is the same one he calls upon to police the press. The media he wishes to create have the potential to become more immoral than the ones he assaults. In the end, Cirino replaces the dysfunctional with the utopian.

Hillier Krieghbaum of New York University offers a more reasonable commentary on press morality than does Cirino. Like Cirino, Krieghbaum cites distortion as the moral problem of the media. Distortion is inevitable, though, because of time and space constraints and because of individual and corporate biases of those who report the news. Krieghbaum proposes local, regional, and national media review agencies to help the media "serve the public interest," by "the power of publicity rather than any form of compulsion or penalty":

> By establishing minimum standards for reporting, editing, and dissemination of news, such machinery could protect media from being tarred by the irresponsible actions of their own less reliable members and could guard the people from repetitions of such defects in the future.[8]

Krieghbaum's approach has two strengths: He thoroughly describes many of the coercive forces that act upon the media, and his solution avoids legal difficulties. But he errs by transferring moral responsibility from journalists to outside agencies. Placing responsibility anywhere other than on the individual reporter and the institution is to establish scapegoats for journalists to blame for their moral lapses.

It can be argued that Krieghbaum and Cirino are merely describing moral problems, that they are not attempting to write ethics. True enough. But by citing problems and proposing solutions, they make moral judgments which carry the responsibility to differentiate between right and wrong, and to justify their arguments.

John Hulteng of Stanford University approaches journalistic

ethics more comprehensively than do either Cirino or Krieghbaum. He adopts the social responsibility model for mass communication, saying that since the modern situation prohibits the effectual working of libertarian theory, the American press must be responsible to society. Hulteng finds responsibility, practically, by distilling various codes of ethics. The responsible journalist adheres to the following guidelines:

> —Journalists must observe a responsibility to the public welfare; their impressive power should be employed for the general good, not for private advantage.
> —Journalists should provide a news report that is sincere, true, and accurate; accounts should be thorough, balanced, and complete.
> —Journalists should be impartial: they should function as the public's representatives, not as mouthpieces of partisan groups or special interests.
> —Journalists must be fair: they must give space or air time to the several sides of a dispute; private rights should not be invaded; corrections of errors should be prompt and wholehearted.
> —Journalists should respect the canons of decency, insofar as those canons can be identified in a society with changing values.[9]

"The central ethic of journalism," he says, is "to report the news the public needs to know, as honestly and as fully as possible."[10]

Hulteng's method illuminates the over-riding problem of contemporary treatments of journalistic ethics: Few justify the good that reporters are to actualize. Hulteng seems to assume that codes of ethics are *eo ipso* right, and that to distill their essence is to be right most assuredly. To justify the good of journalism requires a definitive concept of social responsibility with an understanding of media and social constraints. When the function of the press in relation to its society has been defined, mass media principals can be formulated. From these ethical principles for the press, principles for journalists can be drawn.

According to Hulteng, the primary moral problem is one of character. Ethical codes "without teeth" are written by and for the already good; they do not affect the immoral. Media critics such as Ben H. Bagdikian and the *Columbia Journalism Review*, journalism schools and texts, ombudsmen and press councils help lead journalists to the good, but the journalists must make the decisions. Hulteng's position still raises the question: What is the good, and why? Good people do good things, but even the good are accosted by morally ambiguous situations. Therein lies the need for a sound ethic which will tell journalists not so much what acts are good, but rather what constitutes good acts. On this point Hulteng is silent.

One further writer, who approaches journalistic ethics similarly to Hulteng, must be mentioned. Bruce Swain of the University of Georgia describes the moral haze of journalism through interviews with 67 reporters from midwestern and eastern newspapers.[11] Swain dismisses the possibility of providing any kind of universal maxim, save the direction to "be truthful storytellers"; instead, in contemporary journalistic style, he provides various sides of various issues in order to clarify issues and positions so that the reader may draw positive conclusions. The difficulty with Swain's treatment is that he does not seem to understand that the function of an ethic is to provide a sound, persuasive theory for moral decision-making. Like Hulteng, Swain notes the weakness of codes of ethics. Both do not realize that ethical codes often lack clout because they offer principles or rules with little justification. This deficiency is precisely the problem of modern journalistic ethics: They readily describe problems, often make judgments, but rarely provide theory with adequate justification.

The Theory Approach

The most prolific writer who approaches journalistic ethics theoretically is John Merrill of the Louisiana State University who, in an attempt to write an ethic of journalism as a part of his philosophy of journalistic autonomy, draws from a wide body of philosophical ethics.[12] Merrill adopts Kant's categorical imperative ("Act only on that maxim through which you can at the same time will that it should become a universal law."),[13] since it transcends antinomianism, legalism, and relativism, encompasses the virtues of reason, courage, temperance, and proportional justice, and urges the journalist to report truthfully. Merrill is also attracted to the categorical imperative because, though it is universal, it is intensely personal.[14] Following Merrill's program, the moral reporter is both free and responsible, and has a tool to help maintain this status.

Merrill's ethic is less than convincing, however. First, he tends to be superficial; in a span of 20 pages, he defines ethics, proclaims its importance, discusses teleological and deontological theories, and decides that Kant's categorical imperative provides the best ethical guidance. For purposes both philosophical and rhetorical, Merrill needs to be much more cautious and thorough. Second, Merrill's unquestioning acceptance of the categorical imperative is naive, since Kant leaves little room for the situational considerations which need to be taken into acount before ethical decisions can be made. Merrill does not answer Kant's critics. Third, Merrill needs to illustrate how the categorical imperative can work for journalists; he needs to be more specific. Finally, Merrill's program is inconsistent, for he wants to have a universal ethic while maintaining a personal ethic where "the individual journalist frame(s) his own code in his own words, internally, and change(s) it from time to time and in his own way" (italics in original).[15] Kant was not an existentialist.

Two misunderstandings can be corrected to improve Merrill's program. First, Merrill confuses the journalist as person with the journalist as reporter. He offers little guidance for journalists that those in other professions could not use. In other words, Merrill's is not an ethic of *journalism*. The second misunderstanding is related to the former: Kant's categorical imperative is general; his hypothetical imperatives are more specific. Kant differentiated between the two this way:

> If the action would be good solely as a means *to something else*, the imperative is *hypothetical*; if the action is represented as good *in itself* and therefore as necessary, in virtue of its principle, for a will which of itself accords with reason, then the imperative is *categorical*. (Italics in original)[16]

Interpreted by Kant's system, journalism is not good in itself; rather, it is good in relation to a modern society to which it is responsible. Therefore, if his ethic is to be adapted for journalism, then hypothetical, not categorical, imperatives are needed. Instead of acting "only on that maxim which you can at the same time will that it should become a universal law," the journalist as reporter uses the form, "If I will this end, I will do this act."

The ethicist who probably comes the closest to appropriating hypothetical imperatives is James Capo of Fordham University.[17]

Following an analysis of the three major networks' Watergate coverage, which diverged because of their different concepts of the underlying national values, Capo concludes that truth, objectivity, and freedom are insufficient guiding principles for journalists in a democratic society. Instead, he offers a principle which is grounded on "observable action": The good is democratic interchange, that which is most fully shared by the community. Such a principle will not inhibit freedom, credibility, or audience interest. "Good reporting," says Capo, "enables the news audience to become involved thoughtfully and actively in the important events and decisions which face their society." Following Capo's principle, the news media would emphasize societal trends and legislative activities more than they do.

Although Capo admits that his principle of democratic interchange is preliminary, his method seems sound. A complete, rationally established journalistic ethic must determine the function of the press in a democratic society, define news, extract the implicit ethical principles in the definition of news, and apply these principles in context. Capo's ground work meets these criteria.

In addition to the need for fully developed theories, the status of journalistic ethics can also be enhanced by empirical investigation. Explaining the morals involved in news gathering and dissemination will reveal the status of media morality, its achievements, and its shortcomings. Whether or not journalists act according to a moral hierarchy,[18] for instance, would help guide the construction of journalistic ethics. And researching how journalists apply their morality will illuminate the instrumentality of any given ethic.

Conclusion

Journalists can only hope that the current production of journalistic ethics will not ebb as it did around 1930, because the preliminary work for an ethic has been done. Several commentators have systematically defined the issues which confront journalists, and alternative approaches to the problems have been offered. What is missing are rationally justifiable theories that painstakingly define the good and encompass the multifarious moral issues within journalism.

NOTES

1. Clifford G. Christians, "Fifty Years of Scholarship in Media Ethics," *Journal of Communication*, 27 (1977), 19–29.
2. *Ethics* is the theoretical task of reflecting on the assumptions and presuppositions of moral action. *Morals* refers to the practical task of directing human behavior according to what people believe to be right or good. See James M. Gustafson, *Christian Ethics and the Community* (Philadelphia: Pilgrim Press, 1971), p. 85.
3. J.E. Gerald, *Social Responsibility of the Press* (Minneapolis: University of Minnesota Press, 1963) and W.L. Rivers and W. Schramm, *Responsibility in Mass Communication* (New York: Harper & Row, 1969).
4. Rivers and Schramm, p. 238.
5. Christians, p. 26.
6. Laura L. Babb, ed., *Of the Press, By the Press, For the Press (And Others, Too)* (Washington, D.C.: Washington Post Company, 1974), p. 153.
7. Robert Cirino, *Don't Blame the People: How the News Media Use Bias, Distortion & Censorship to Manipulate Public Opinion* (New York: Vintage, 1972).
8. Hillier Kreighbaum, *Pressures on the Press* (New York: Thomas Y. Crowell Co. 1972), p. 218.
9. John L. Hulteng, *The Messenger's Motives: Ethical Problems of the News Media* (Englewood Cliffs, NJ: Prentice-Hall, 1976), p. 23.
10. *Ibid.*, p. 101.
11. Bruce M. Swain, *Reporters' Ethics* (Ames, Iowa: Iowa State University Press, 1978).
12. John C. Merrill, *The Imperative of Freedom: A Philosophy of Journalistic Autonomy* (New York: Hastings House, 1974), pp. 163–182; also in John C. Merrill and Ralph D. Barney, eds., *Ethics and the Press: Readings in Mass Media Morality* (New York: Hastings House, 1975), pp. 117–131.
13. Immanuel Kant, *Groundwork of the Metaphysic of Morals*, trans. H.J. Paton (New York: Harper Torchbooks, 1964), p. 88.
14. John C. Merrill, *Existential Journalism* (New York: Hastings House, 1977), pp. 129–137.
15. *Ibid.*, p. 132.
16. Kant, p. 82.
17. James A. Capo, "Democratic Interchange as a Principle for Responsible News," paper presented at the Social Ethics Seminar, New York City, 1979.
18. Benjamin Freedman, "A Meta-Ethics for Professional Morality," *Ethics*, 89 (1979), 1–19.

Study Questions

1. How might one attack Ferré's view that Krieghbaum's approach errs in shifting moral responsibility from journalists to outside agencies?
2. Ferré claims that Merrill's view of journalistic ethics is mistaken in that he confuses the journalist as person with the journalist as reporter? Defend, using concise, well-conceived arguments, either Merrill's or Ferré's position.

How to Avoid Resting Journalistic Ethics On a Mistake

Anita Silvers

Does journalistic ethics rest on a mistake? Perhaps it does, and perhaps the mistake made by those who explore journalistic ethics explains why, when so much has been accomplished during the last decade in many of the areas of professional and applied ethics, the study of journalistic ethics appears anemic at best, despite the central role which print and broadcast journalists play in the evolution of public attitudes toward national events, and despite the ethical issues which some behavior of some journalists recurrently evokes. Compared to the study of medical, legal and business ethics, and even of the ethics of engineers, the investigation of journalistic ethics has had relatively little impact either on philosophy or on journalism. There have been created no recognized bodies of research literature nor revitalized curricula, nor has the practice of journalism been subject to any institutionalized reforms.

Some explain the comparative weakness of research in journalistic ethics by presenting an *ad hominem* argument to the effect that journalists care less about being moral than other professionals do. Journalists, this story goes, prefer to ignore or to refuse the struggle with moral problems, or else they set up diversions by intimating that no group—either of professionals or of laypersons—displays rectitude sufficient to put putatively erring journalists to shame. But this reputed behavior of journalists should make no difference to the philosophical study of journalistic ethics.

497

After all, most philosophers probably would say, what we study should be the logic and limits of moral concepts, not how individuals or groups of individuals behave.

Regardless of what philosophers usually suppose they are doing when they study ethics, it now seems to me that those who study professional ethics rarely even attempt to delineate or analyze the fundamental nature of the object of their study. For reasons which I shall present in this essay, such obscurity so far has not proven fatal to research or teaching about the ethics of some professions, medicine and law being the paradigmatic cases. In contrast, because of certain dimensions along which journalism diverges from other professions, whether or not philosophical examination of journalistic ethics is worthwhile may depend entirely, or almost entirely, upon how the subject matter of professional ethics is construed.

Those who urge the study of professional ethics sometimes tend to eschew discussions which have a metaethical ring. At least more often than not, they assume rather than analyze the logical nature and status of the obligations and rights they profess to explore. Of course, there are notable and powerful exceptions to this indictment. Let me exemplify my point by citing one of the few works on professional ethics *per se* by a proponent who insists on the existence and the significance of the subject.

In *Ethics Teaching in Higher Education*, William May contributes a long essay called "Professional Ethics." He gives the following reasons in the course of "justifying professional ethics as a discipline:"[1]

> a) The uses to which a professional puts her/his specialized knowledge are subject to the conditions which promote research and development in the field. (In other words, May suggests, if research in a field is carried on under a particular banner, such as an appeal about how the specialized knowledge discovered in the field benefits mankind, the use of this knowledge by practitioners who acquire it is conditioned by this goal.)

> b) Professionals are publicly accountable for their professional judgments because they are citizens.

> c) Professionals must teach and dispense their knowledge.

Although May makes much of professionals' specialized knowledge in justifying the discipline of professionals ethics, he fails to make clear whether he is claiming that professional ethics should take as its subject special duties and rights which pertain to professionals but not to laypersons by virtue of professionals' special knowledge, or whether he is claiming that professional ethics should take as its subject the understanding of how professionals' specialized knowledge complicates how the ordinary duties and rights of everyone pertain to them. As I will try to show, which construal is adopted does make a difference. For most professions, the difference lies in how investigations should proceed. But, for journalistic ethics, the difference is more serious. For journalistic ethics, which construal one adopts may determine whether there is any point at all in proceeding with an investigation.

Let me hasten to include my own earlier work in journalistic ethics as falling under this indictment condemning the inattention paid to the nature of the subject matter of professional ethics. Nearly a decade ago, in writing about journalistic ethics, I analyzed the arguments traditionally used to justify attributing to journalists certain duties and rights. In doing so, I did not ask, and so I did not answer, basic questions about what these obligations and rights might be like. Now I wish to reconsider my earlier treatment, not necessarily to recant the conclusions I reached in my essay, but to examine what, in my earlier attempt, I assumed, rather than demonstrated, was the case.

In my first effort to understand the ethics of journalism, I argued that the traditional considerations attributing special rights and obligations to journalists contained the seeds of inconsistency.[2] Consequently, I maintained, cynicism about the rational defensibility of moral judgments based on journalists' appeals to such special rights and obligations was understandable because the conceptual scheme supporting these appeals sometimes yielded equally well-argued, but inconsistent, guides. The difficulty did not result from a problem within the moral decision structure. It was not caused by a set of *prima facie* obligations and rights sometimes or often brought into conflict by the configuration of actual events. Instead, I thought, the inconsistency was epistemic rather than ethical in origin. Journalists' special rights and obligations derived from their special professional commitment to communicate truth, but what was supposed to be involved in their truth telling was obscure. What actions are permitted or required in communicating truth depends to some extent upon what account of truth finding and truth telling one accepts. Over the centuries during which our models of journalistic probity have evolved, several different epistemological theories have held sway at different times. These conflicting views have been incorporated uncritically into the traditions of journalism, such that, supposing journalists to possess a special duty to be objective, there remains confusion about the concomitant rights journalists may justifiably claim.

In constructing my argument, I assumed the truth of two conditionals, and I also assumed that the antecedent of both these two conditionals held. First, I assumed:

> If journalists have moral duties and concomitant rights which differentiate them from those agents not identified as members of the profession of journalism, it is plausible to conduct a philosophical inquiry into the ethics of journalism in order to assess the adequacy of the conceptual structure which supports the attribution of these rights and duties.

Second, I assumed:

> If journalists' moral duties and concomitant rights differ in some respects from those of other agents, the source or justification of the differentiation is derived from considerations of the benefits journalism, as a profession, provides equally for everyone, or, at least, equally for a society that accords to journalists any special moral role.

These assumptions were prompted by my unexamined acceptance that the ethics of journalism was analogous to the ethics of medicine and law. In the latter occupations, identification as a professional appears to bring with it certain rights and duties which seem not to be at issue for laypeople as well as a propensity to be faced with certain moral dilemmas which laypeople seem not to have to face. In law and medicine, there exist exceptional relationships between practitioner and client that, on the face of it, generate both peculiar moral privileges for practitioners and place them in unique moral plights.

We might generalize about this aspect of such professions as medicine and law by observing that, for them, the power to do good brings with it the capacity to do harm, so that professionals are subject to moral temptation and failure in ways the layperson may neither experience nor understand. The physician is able, either by omission or commission, to render physical harm to the patient. Similarly, the lawyer can impede the justice due a client. Lawyers would not characteristically be able to impede justice were they not charged professionally with securing justice. Doctors would not *characteristically* be in a position to omit or commit actions so as to cause physical damage were they not required to minister to their patients' physical complaints.

Defenders of the attribution of professional rights to doctors and lawyers often contend that the moral dilemmas which characterize medicine and law occur precisely because practitioners, being in a special position to help their clients, concomitantly have special opportunities to do them harm, they thus insist that the benefits which all of us, equally, can expect from the medical and legal tribes call for doctors and lawyers to bear unique moral burdens. They also insist that those who do not share such burdens must allow those who do the autonomy to impose professional standards upon themselves.

To extend this line of thought, it is as if some persons who benefited from the institution of promisemaking never were called upon themselves to make and keep promises, but never having experienced the rigor of forcing one's self to keep a promise, such persons might not appreciate the complex moral phenomenology of promisekeeping that enables them, at least sometimes, to depend on a promisemaker's word in the absence of external sanctions of guarantees. Similarly, persons uncommitted to the professional ideals of medicine or law may not comprehend the moral phenomenology that renders doctors and lawyers suitable recipients of our trust. Nevertheless, it is argued, we all should be willing to proffer that trust in order to enjoy the benefits rendered to us by the institutions and the practitioners of medicine and law.

Regardless of whether this line of argument ultimately turns out to be impeccable or flawed, it reflects, I think, the prevalent perspective whereby professionals in medicine and law convince themselves and laypersons that their professional status subjects them to distinctive professional ethics or to specialized moral codes. In initiating my exploration of journalistic ethics, I took journalists to claim that they possessed analogous professional rights and duties. (For those unfamiliar with the practices of print and electronic journalism, let me note that there is ample evidence of journalists making such claims.) Moreover, it also seemed plausible to hold that the (sincere) claims of these practitioners to have professional rights and duties actually served as *prima facie* reasons for attributing such rights and duties to them because their beliefs about their special moral status constituted an effective motive in selecting their own acts and in directing their colleagues' acts through the expression of moral approbation and blame.

Appealing once again to the model of promisemaking, as it seems plausible to afford the right of promisemaking to those committed to the moral obligation of keeping promises but to deny that right to those who refuse to acknowledge any obligation to keep promises, so it also seems *prima facie* plausible to allow doctors and lawyers and journalists to subject themselves to certain obligations which they take to be constitutive of their identity as professionals, and, consequently, to afford them any concomitant rights, should any such rights exist. In other words, if doctors and lawyers and journalists believe themselves to be morally obligated to take certain actions in cases where nonprofessionals in otherwise similar circumstances are not similarly obligated, and if, in virtue of their commitment to their profession, they autonomously impose what they take to be a moral requirement upon themselves, it is *prima facie* reasonable to allow that doctors and lawyers and journalists have moral duties and concomitant rights which differentiate them, *qua* professionals, with those agents not identified as members of the professions.

As a result of this tacit line of reasoning, I assumed the antecedents of the aforementioned conditionals—to wit, that journalists have moral duties and concomitant rights which differentiate them from those agents not identified as members of the profession. My adoption of this antecedent was prompted by my supposing that construing journalists as possessing special moral obligations should be analogous to the similar construals typically made on behalf of doctors and lawyers. Thereupon, I presumed journalists would not be subject to professional moral obligations unless, like doctors and lawyers, by virtue of their profession they characteristically were faced with moral dilemmas where their professional capacity to benefit others also offered exceptional opportunity to harm.

At this point, a disparity between the situation of doctors and lawyers and that of journalists appeared (or would have appeared, had I examined the premises instead of assuming them). As indicated earlier, the moral dilemmas typically encountered by doctors and lawyers characteristically involve the potential to benefit or harm specific individuals placed in the patient or client relationship to the doctor or lawyer. In becoming a patient or client, the potential beneficiary or victim placed him or herself in a position of trust, dependent upon the practitioner's integrity. In other words, from the client's or patient's point of view, acceding to the risk of being harmed appears to be a condition of seizing the opportunity for legal or medical gain. If this account of the patient client practitioner relationship resembles what is the case, we can understand the importance of the expectation that professional practitioner and patient client agree about the practitioner's possessing special obligations to the patient client. The expectation that such a view is shared may be what makes the patient client decide that the potential benefits of trusting the practitioner outweigh the potential risks. Thus, the institution of being a patient client, upon which both practitioners and patient clients depend, may be the foundation of any differential moral obligations and concomitant rights which may accrue to doctors and lawyers *qua* practitioners of their professions.

Journalists, however, do not seem to operate in analogous moral situations. Usually, we cannot identify specific individuals who stand as clients to journalists. Indeed, those whom journalists have the greatest opportunity to harm may be precisely those whom journalists consider themselves under the weakest rather than the strongest obligation to serve. If there is a single specialized moral appeal journalists are prone to make, its source is the conception of the profession according to which journalists benefit the public by disseminating information about individuals who cannot be considered as part of the public. These are persons who, through fortune or misfortune, have become newsworthy and thereby are "in the public's eye"—a figure of speech which renders such persons as objects of public perception rather than as members of that perceiving public which journalists say they serve. Prominent among the moral dilemmas which journalists typically or characteristically face are situations in which considerations of good or harm to specific individuals are countered by considerations of benefit to no individual in particular, situations in which the journalist is thought to be obligated not by the rights of any identifiable individual but instead by the public's right to know. Appealing to the public's right to know suggests that, although it is the individual subjects of the news whom journalists have the opportunity to harm through violation of privacy, publication of inadequately founded charges, deception in the course of posing and so on, the potential for harm is not outweighed by potential benefits to these same individual subjects. Instead, if journalism does offer potential benefits which mitigate its potential risks, its beneficiary usually is thought to be the public or the society or some such abstract entity, not the individuals with whom journalists most directly deal. The kind of relationship expressed in the legal profession's *Code of Professional Responsibility*, which prohibits lawyers from being "more concerned with the establishment or extension of legal principles than in the immediate protection of the rights of the lawyer's individual client,"[3] seems to have no analogue for journalists.

Of course, this disanalogy between journalism and the professions I took as paradigms, medicine and law, need not suffice to obscure the argument I intended to make. First, one might observe that individuals, as well as society in general, may benefit from the attention of journalists. At least sometimes, journalists publicize a good cause, eliciting support for deserving individuals. Moreover, a not inconsequential segment of individuals who claim to be victimized by the professional ministrations of journalists are also those who, in other circumstances, sought out such ministrations to get their views before the public or enhance their careers.

Second, even if we cannot find many individuals for whom the practice of journalism promises potential personal benefits as well as threatens potential personal harm, we might argue that the institution of journalism does benefit all the individual members of society. According to the traditional libertarian reasoning used to justify journalistic practies, the activities of journalists guard all citizens against repressive domination by sovereign governments and against other institutionalized tyrannies or unchecked constraints. According to the traditional utilitarian reasoning used to justify journalistic practices, the activities of journalists test belief claims and help to promote the acquisition of new truths. Other things being equal, surely any individual is better off for being guarded against governmental repression and for being able to acquire better tested beliefs and new truths. Thus, there is a sense in which journalists may construe themselves as benefiting the individual members of society as well as society in general.

Third, whether or not the professional obligations and concomitant rights of journalists are analogous to those of doctors and lawyers, it still may be useful to examine whether journalism possesses any characteristic professional goals. If there are such, then journalists may be expected to strive to achieve these goals, and philosophical investigation may illuminate how the means and ends of these goal-directed professional activities relate. Thus, though my argument rested on unexamined assumptions about the existence of special journalistic obligations and concomitant rights, even if these assumptions turned out to be implausible, it remained possible for my conclusion to retain some value. On the basis of my assumptions, I developed a position according to which journalists' special obligations and concomitant rights derive from the special capacity of the institution of journalism to secure and disseminate truths. However, I argued, journalistic traditions called upon different conceptions of truth, with the result that the same action might be a means to securing and disseminating truth under one epistemological construal while it impeded securing and disseminating truth on an alternative epistemological view. Such epistemological confusion accounts for the profound differences of judgment which arise when journalists attempt to satisfy such professional standards as the requirement to be objective. Finally, I urged that journalists should not claim the protection of special professional rights without clarifying the epistemological basis on which they supposed the special status of journalism to rest. So, even though my argument assumed rather than proved the existence of journalist's special obligations and rights, it at least might have had the viture of forcing consistency upon the many practitioners who accepted this assumption.

Nevertheless, J.O. Urmson took me to task for assuming without argument that there are obligations and rights attaching specifically to journalism. Urmson maintained that the rights and obligations of journalists differ not at all from the rights and obligations of butchers, bakers, candlestick-makers and all other agents.[4] Journalists have no special obligations and concomitant rights in virtue of a professional commitment to secure and disseminate truth, Urmson declared. Rather, there are merely "fascinating problems about how journalists can best discharage their common human duties of honesty and sincerity."[5] Moreover, Urmson said, the institution of journalism enjoys no special status derived from the social benefits it affords. Urmson observed that "if it be true that free criticism by the press can act as a check on the repressiveness of governments, then so can free criticism by others."[6] Urmson thereby suggested that professional journalists can do little to benefit laypersons which laypersons cannot do for themselves.

Apparently believing that the burden of proof should rest on those who complicate accounts of moral judgment, Urmson did not argue for his position. Nevertheless, his view must be addressed, for, if true, it bears an impact extending beyond the study of journalistic ethics to all philosophical investigations designed to understand the moral point of view of agents occupying specialized roles. Should Urmson be right, and should there be no moral obligations and concomitant rights which agents accept as a consequence of their identifying themselves in specialized roles, moral decision-making, including the attribution of moral praise and blame, would turn out to operate quite differently, and to result in different particular judgments, than it would, should some but not all agents be subject to specialized moral permissions and demands.

To assess Urmson's view properly, we should understand what he denies and what he does not. As I understand him, he never insists that persons occupying specialized roles always ought to do what everyone else, in the same situation, ought to do. Urmson's remarks are concise, but I believe I can expand upon them a bit without distorting what he would agree to say.

Urmson, I think, may contend that agents occupying specialized professional roles, although they apply the same moral principles as laypersons, sometimes correctly draw different moral conclusions from laypersons because they possess specialized knowledge or powers or skills. Applying the same moral principle of not harming others, a mother might believe herself permitted to stuff her child with vitamins because she believes that the more vitamins, the healthier and stronger the child will be, while a doctor might believe himself obligated to prevent the child from swallowing the vitamins because he knows that excessive vitamin consumption may damage the child's health. Here, both agents appeal to the same general evaluative principle, but the different roles they occupy function as a source of different factual premises, such that the agents arrive at antithetical conclusions about what acts are warranted or prohibited. Moreover, neither the mother nor the doctor is subject to moral blame, even though the acts of permitting and preventing the child from swallowing the vitamins are incompatible with each other. In fact, if the mother believed that the more vitamins the stronger her child would be and yet also claimed she was prohibited from giving her child vitamins, in the absence of any countervailing reasons we would question her moral position.

No doubt, in respect to many professions, there is some plausibility in analysing deviations between the moral conclusions of practitioners and those of laypeople as resulting from the inclusion of different factual premises when the professional and the layperson reasons morally. Doctors are supposed to possess extraordinary knowledge about the operation of the body, engineers about the operation of design and construction, businesspersons about the operation of the marketplace, lawyers about the operation of the judicial system, and even teachers are supposed to possess extraordinary knowledge of how learning operates. Not only does their knowledge provide special factual premises, but professionals sometimes have the skill to perform required acts, such as saving a life, from which laypersons are excused because they can't perform.

However, compared to most other professions, journalists do not appear to possess any specialized knowledge. Despite the existence of programs for professional training, journalism differs from the aforementioned fields by acknowledging that qualified practitioners need not have pursued any designated course of study. Of course, journalists may consider themselves more worldly than other folks, but it is hard to delineate any professionally related set of facts or theories which journalists characteristically are expected to know.

Notice, then, that unlike most other professionals, journalists cannot claim to differentiate their moral conclusions from those of other agents by appeal to their being in a better or at least a different position by virtue of specialized knowledge. Of course, journalists may claim that they know more about the world or about the details of particular cases. But such a defense lacks plausibility because, *qua* professionals, journalists have institutionalized no special testing or training to demonstrate how much wiser they are in the ways of the world. They thus have not provided themselves with a cognitive base for diverging from other people in moral judgment.

If, faced with any moral situation, journalists are not justified in relying upon either moral principles or factual premises different from those of other agents, are journalists ever justified in maintaining they are morally required to do what nonjournalists are morally permitted to omit or are morally permitted to do what nonjournalists are morally prohibited from doing? Urmson, I think, must reply in the negative. Indeed, I suspect, the primary objective of the approach he adopts is to answer this question with a "No!" Urmson proposes that "freedom of speech is a sacred cow"[6] and is employed as a justification for violating such fundamental legal rights as the right to a fair trial and to defend such inutile acts as the dissemination of information which harms individuals or society. For Urmson, journalists must not be permitted to escape the requirements to which other agents are bound, and therefore there must be no special professional obligations which have the potential for excusing journalists whose publicizing results in changing attitudes toward a defendant or in making it harder for a government to survive.

Suppose that members of a profession regularly diverge in moral judgment from nonprofessionals, even though the same moral principles apply and even though they appear to have no justified cognitive basis for regularly supplying divergent factual premises. Suppose that, in diverging morally, these anomalous professionals appeal to the standards of their profession as if this were a sacred trust. Suppose they note the special oaths of office they had sworn or drew attention to their profession's hagiology, and suppose they describe their actions as required by their oaths or as modelled on praiseworthy actions of the saints and heroes of their special vocation. Most probably, Urmson would be unimpressed. On his view, I think, appeals to professional standards, ideals or goals must count as nonmoral appeals.

Thus, in such cases when the conclusion ordinary moral agents should draw conflicts with the conclusion professional principles demand, Urmson most likely would maintain the supremacy of the nonprofessional point of view. This is because, for Urmson, professional principles, standards, goals, or ideals cannot make any fundamental moral difference. Only the provision of more sophisticated or reliable factual premises can shift the balance of moral approbation in favor of the professional's judgment. In the case of journalism, where no such superior factual access appears to obtain, Urmson presumably would not accept journalists' claims that their professional commitments permit actions which, for other agents, would count as moral violations. Thus, on Urmson's account, our moral expectations of journalists should be precisely the same as those of any other agents. We should neither permit them actions for which others would be condemned, nor should we demand that they act unless all other agents are equally subject to such a demand.

Many treatments of the ethics of particular professions are ambiguous between Urmson's position and mine. That is, they do not distinguish between defining the ethics of the profession as the discipline which studies the special moral concepts pertaining to the profession, and defining the ethics of the profession as the discipline of studying the moral problems which practitioners encounter when they try to practice their profession and to adhere to ordinary moral principles at the same time. For instance, the following definition of business ethics, quite typical of commentary in this genre, is excerpted from The Hastings Center's *Ethics In the Education of Business Managers:* "Business ethics, then, is a type of applied ethics which is concerned to clarify the obligations and dilemmas of actors (managers) who make business decisions."[7] And The Hastings Center's *Ethics and Engineering Curricula* contains the following account of its subject matter: ". . . "engineering ethics" is defined quite narrowly as dealing with judgments and decisions concerning the actions of engineers (individually or collectively) which involve moral principles of one sort or another."[8] Note that these putative definitions do nothing more than recommend the listing of the moral problems which are most likely to face each type of practitioner.

Why should certain problems occur more frequently for practitioners of the respective professions than for other agents? Does the answer lie solely in the high frequency with which these practitioners are tempted to violate moral prescriptions? Or are professionals bound by moral commitments from which other agents are free? Let us continue exploring the first alternative by supposing that the difference between the ethics of any profession and the ethics of all agents alike lies solely in the increased frequency with which the practitioners face one or more identifiable kinds of moral problems. Surely, to say the practitioners face certain problems more often is to admit that they have more opportunity to fail to do the relevant duty. Thus, for example, we might say the rich person probably faces more temptation to commit the sin of gluttony than the beggar. If someone is more tempted than others are, and fails to act as ordinary moral considerations require, we do not excuse the person but simply advise him or her to move out of temptation's way. On the other hand, should someone tempted more than others nevertheless act as obligation demands, we afford special approbation, praising the staunch agent as a minor or major saint or hero. Thus, if professionals, in the face of moral temptation, do not violate their moral obligations more often, it would seem they qualify as saints or heroes for doing their ordinary job.

This counterintuitive result constitutes at least one reason for avoiding Urmson's approach. To make the point more explicit, let us consider a summary of Urmson's own account of saints and heroes, derived from his famous essay of the same name: if someone does her/his duty regularly, in contexts in which other agents would not,[9] or if someone does actions beyond the limits of what others can claim to be her/his duty because, regardless of the judgments of others, she/he perceives it to be her/his duty, she/he is a saint or hero.[10] By conjoining this definition with Urmson's view that only the usual duties and no specialized ones pertain to professionals, it seems to me we are forced to conclude that practitioners of at least some professions, simply in virtue of regularly engaging in their usual line of work, qualify as saints or heroes. Pleasing as this result may be to the members of those professions, it may not be wise to adopt a metaethical analysis excessive in its award of accolades. To deem a practitioner as hero or saint for doing what we regularly expect of anyone identified as a member of the profession may be to weaken professional standards to the extent that what once were thought to be duties become supererogatory acts.

Let me extend this argument with illustrations. In these illustrations, I select actions described such that ordinary agents as well as professionals are capable of performance. These are not cases in which laypersons may be excused because "ought implies can," and they cannot. Regardless of inclination or fear, doctors typically expose themselves to the unpleasant sights and smells of illness. If doctors are motivated only by the same considerations of beneficence which would encourage other agents to aid the ill, but if we expect doctors regularly to render such aid while we expect other agents to take only intermittent advantage of opportunities to do so, then presumably we expect doctors to be saints or heroes, given Urmson's analysis of saintly and heroic states. Similarly, if journalists are motivated only by the same considerations of honesty which encourage other agents to tell the truth, but if we expect journalists not only to assert what is true but also, regardless of impediments, to ensure that the rest of us learn the truth as well, then, on Urmson's criteria, we expect journalists to be saints or heroes as well.

It seems to me that such an account distorts what is the case. First, saintly and heroic actions are such because, although they are judged by their agent, by other agents, or by both to be duties, their omission is not subject to moral condemnation. In other words, the agents of such actions are saints or heroes precisely because others, who have similar opportunities to act but do not, count not as demons or cowards but as merely ordinary men. However, surely this cannot be the case in respect to the illustrations we just examined. While we would not condemn ordinary agents who allowed the unpleasant sights and smells of illness to deter them from aiding the ill, surely we would blame doctors who failed to render aid. Similarly, although we would not condemn ordinary agents who neglected to disseminate the truth, surely journalists who failed to publish what they had learned are at least *prima facie* candidates for blame. This assertion requires qualification. Depending on what view one adopts about the special benefits the institution of journalism is expected to provide, what journalists are expected to disseminate may be truths about the government, or claims which enable others to test and refine their beliefs, or some other subset of beneficial cognitive objects.

If doctors and journalists are to be blamed for omissions of certain actions, where ordinary agents are not, it seems implausible to treat their commission of these actions not as instances of duty but rather as instances of supererogation. It seems to me much more plausible to treat our expectations that professionals must meet standards of performance to which other agents are not held as indicative of their being subject to specialized duties as a result of their commitment to their profession.

Second, if the expected behavior of doctors and journalists (and other professionals) qualifies them as saints or heroes, how are we to distinguish from among practitioners the saints and heroes of these professions themselves? Surely (even on Urmson's rendering of saints and heroes) a Schweitzer or a Zenger should be set apart from the ordinary practitioner as recipient of special moral praise. Let us note, of course, that the praiseworthy actions of Schweitzer and Zenger fit the illustrations we are considering. Schweitzer rendered aid to the ill where the ordinary doctor might be deterred; Zenger disseminated truths when ordinary journalists might not have persevered. Therefore, unless we are willing to recognize that ordinary practitioners act out of duty rather than supererogation, the status of Schweitzer and Zenger will be obscured. We will need to distinguish how much of their saintly or heroic behavior is usual for members of their profession and how much deserves praise for acting beyond the call.

Once again, it seems, denying that professionals may be subject to specialized moral obligations leads us to contort what it usually is straightforward to say. If we continue to insist that professionals are subject only to such duties as also pertain to all other agents, we apparently will find ourselves having to describe Schweitzer and Zenger not as saints or heroes but as the saints' saint or the heroes' hero. Fortunately, nothing appears to prevent us from eschewing such contortions by admitting that special professional duties exist.

For every class of actions which members of certain professional groups but not laypersons are required to perform, several alternative analyses might be tried. Reductionist alternatives attempt to explain such phenomena away, contending that agents in these classes satisfy conditions such that they are more rigorously bound to ordinary duties than are other agents. As I have tried to show, reducing talk about every special "ought" by which practitioners of a profession must abide to talk about some special "is" which describes those practitioners alone prevents us from saying what we usually want to say and forces us into employing artificial, awkward locutions. Even though this observation does not suffice to establish the existence of specialized professional duties (or concomitant rights), on balance, I believe it preferable to accept their existence as the antecedent of philosophical exploration in this field.

None of this, of course, produces insight into what the metaethics of professional ethics is like. It does not even address the question of whether the ethics of each profession has the same formal structure as the ethics of other professions and as the ethics of every person alike. There actually is some point to raising this question because some professions have practices which might affect the moral conceptual structure. For instance, suppose the legal profession makes the ethics section on bar exams the test of a practitioner's moral qualification. This certainly differs from our usual means of assessing an individual's moral perspicuity, integrity, and strength. In fact, it seems to disassociate moral action from moral judgment to a much greater degree than our ordinary concepts permit.

Similarly, in considering how the moral conceptual structure which pertains to journalism conforms or diverges from what we might call our ordinary moral conceptual scheme, we might begin by noticing that it seems impossible for journalists to possess the character defect known as "officiousness." I am not claiming, of course, that journalists are inclined to or actually have a history of "sticking their noses in other people's business." But what is a character defect for others is a character virtue for journalists.

How does this come about? Does it suggest that, in some cases, those who are prone to certain types of character defects (from the ordinary moral point of view) should consider choosing a profession where (from the point of view of the ethics of that profession) her/his tendencies count as a character virtue rather than a character defect? The answers to these questions might elucidate the logic of judgments about character.

More important, if a defect becomes a virtue from the point of view of the ethics of a profession, does that entail the obviation of the potential for harm which the behavior characterized as defective bears in ordinary contexts. I do not believe this is likely to be so. Ordinarily, the harm rendered by officious activity lies either in the subjection of persons to questioning or other forms of inquiry by persons who have no business asking, and/or to the publication of information which others have no business acquiring. I suppose one might hold that journalists, by virtue of their profession, always have a business finding things out, but this does not solve the problem. It is at least possible, and is indeed highly probable, that each of us possesses some properties whose revelation will in no way advantage anyone else but will disadvantage (at least psychologically) the properties' bearer. If we cannot use the usual character imprecation of officiousness to curb journalists from prying, does this entail that the conceptual scheme of the ethics of journalism leaves us entirely unprotected in this regard?

The answers to these questions, and others, await a much more thorough investigation of the logic of professional ethics. In my view, the distaste with which some scholars of the ethics of professions consider metaethical research impedes rather than serves their ultimate goal. The purpose of my essay has been to indicate how important metaethical argument, including the comparison and contrast of the structure of the ethics of various professions, is to supporting both ethical and casuistical conclusions about the obligations, rights and virtues which agents, *qua* practitioners of a particular profession, have. As I have tried to show, it is plausible to rest the ethics of professions on the contention that professionals possess differential obligations and rights. However, in the case of journalistic ethics, it is essential to do so, for otherwise the study of a special field called journalistic ethics may not be possible to do.

NOTES

1. May, William. "Professional Ethics" in *Ethics Teaching in Higher Education,* edited by Daniel Callahan and Sissela Bok (New York and London: Plenum Press, 1980), pp. 208–211.
2. Silvers, Anita. "Professional Press Ethics—A Case of Conflicting Concepts," in *Social Responsibility of the Mass Media,* edited by Allan Casebier and Janet Jenkins Casebier (Washington, D.C., University Press of America, 1978), pp. 49–64 passim.
3. Canon 5E C23.
4. Urmson, J.O. "Comments by J.O. Urmson" in *Social Responsibility of the Mass Media,* edited by Allan Casebier and Janet Jenkins Casebier (Washington, D.C., University Press of America, 1978), p. 65.
5. *Ibid.,* p. 65.

6. *Ibid.*, p. 66.
7. Power, Charles and Vogil, David. *Ethics in the Education of Business Managers* (Hastings-on-Hudson, NY: The Hastings Center, 1980), p. 2.
8. Baum, Robert. *Ethics and the Engineering Curricula* (Hastings-on-Hudson, NY: The Hastings Center, 1980), p. 2.
9. Urmson, J.O. "Saints and Heroes," reprinted in *Moral Concepts* (London: Oxford University Press, 1969), p. 61.
10. *Ibid.*, pp. 62–63.

Study Questions

1. What are the reasons for believing that there are specialized professional moralities? Do you think these are sufficient to establish that professionals are bound by moral codes, and enjoy moral latitudes different from that of laypersons?
2. What special obligations, if any, do journalists have? Do they have any special rights?

Liberty and Its Limits

Michael Levin

There is wide consensus that liberty is a value second to none. A more difficult matter is whether liberty is peerless. Liberty so often conflicts with other values—aggregated utility, social cohesion—that to press it as the only value to protect, or as a value which always outranks competitors, smacks of fanaticism. Yet we do tolerate considerable sacrifice of competing values on behalf of liberty. By opposing the preventive detention of "statistically likely murderers," for example, we permit preventable murders of innocents. We are to that extent all libertarians. The question is how far we are willing to go. Defining the limits of liberty leads even to the spiritual bases of political order: Irving Kristol among others has argued that liberty alone is not sufficiently inspiring, that democratic capitalism will founder without a showing that people generally put their liberty to admirable uses. The results of market competition must be and be seen to be congruent with some prior notion of propriety.

It is useful to begin with some provisional account of liberty. The present author is an unabashed negative libertarian, who construes liberty in its normative sense—the liberty we have a right to—as the ability to do what one pleases without interference by the will of another. Such liberty is distinct from liberty in the metaphysical sense, which I take to be the ability to do what one pleases (with the second-order restriction that one is pleased at one's pleasures). A man not strong enough to lift a stone that fell

516

on him during a naturally occurring avalanche is "politically" free but metaphysically bound. On the other hand, political freedom does entail metaphysical freedom, for if one is restrained by the will of another, one is restrained *tout cours*. I obviously differ from those negative libertarians who take freedom to be exhausted by the absence of coercion. A man trapped by a rock is, in a perfectly straightforward sense, not free to move; what needs stressing, and what is stressed by calling him nonetheless "politically" free, is that his unfreedom is no one's fault. He has no complaint against anyone. Were an unbudgeable rock placed upon him by an ill-wisher, he would be unfree in a normatively significant as well as metaphysically significant sense (omitting complications about inadvertence and negligence). This is not by itself to deny that there may be reasons for the state to divert public resources to aid a man accidentally trapped, but it is to deny that among those reasons is the need to restore to the man any liberty he is entitled to.

We have rights to negative liberty but no rights to positive liberty. The state may protect us from interference, but it has no business seeing that we have the means to get what we want (so long as impairments in our powers are not the result of the invasions of others). Only negative rights to liberty are basic, or "human rights," because they alone can be simultaneously held by everyone. Rights to noninterference are consistent with the categorical imperative while putative rights to positive liberty are not. Every member of a political community can exercise a right of noninterference without restricting the symmetrical exercise of that right by others. Your having a right to be allowed to speak by me is consistent with my having the same right to be allowed to speak by you. The material constraints on the simultaneous exercise of this right—we cannot both harangue a crowd from the same small region of spacetime—do not raise the issue of principle raised by a would-be speaker's claim to a right to a podium. For if anyone has this positive right, no one else can have the same right to that podium. Even positing more podiums than speakers simply defers the problem, for Smith's right to some podium or other must be realized as a right to some particular podium, a right which excludes all others. This is yet more obvious in connection with rights to a portion of the aggregate social product: some can exercise such an unconditional right only if others, working to produce a social product, do not. *Perhaps* limited, conditional positive rights can be embedded within a wider system of rights,[1] but only negative rights can be unconditional.

The relative preeminence of negative over positive liberty does not explain the absolute value of negative liberty. Nor do the familiar utilitarian arguments for liberty cut to the essence of the matter. No doubt, given the way the world is, the greatest number of wants will be satisfied if people act with the greatest amount of mutual liberty. Individuals remain the best judges of what they want, and the market's invisible hand distributes resources satisfyingly, if not optimally. Yet this does not seem to me *why* it is good for people to pursue their own destinies. I suggest we continue to look along Kantian lines for a transcendental basis for the value of liberty. My own hunch is that freedom is valued because free action is the most direct expression of the self, and we are selves. It is easy enough to understand why we think selves worth cultivating; as the behavioral counterpart to valuing something is willingness to defend it, the tendency to value one's self—or related selves, had an obvious adaptive function.

We experience ourselves as a cluster of sensations and appetites, the latter continuous with values. Appetites themselves divide into those we don't mind having and those we do, the latter being regarded as alien influences while the former are taken to constitute the self. Action as opposed to behavior is what flows from impulses properly our own; we regard these impulses as at least acceptable and so must regard as at least acceptable their causal consequences in the world. As to whether selves and their manifestations *really are* good things may be an unanswerable question. It presupposes a perspective outside ourselves from which we can cancel our deepest innate propensities and perceptions. But being the creature I am, I cannot make real to myself the supposition that the world would be no worse a place if my own rational preferences were suppressed. I can of course understand why other selves whose preferences deviate from mine should be suppressed, but that's because those preferences aren't mine. Here we may have hit the transcendental limits of ethics.

Before using this broadly Kantian conception of liberty as a guide in balancing liberty against other values, it is important to distinguish two kinds of conflict.

The first pits liberty against something else, as when the

thought of preventively detaining potential felons forces a choice between liberty and safety. Conflicts of this sort exist, but often enough alleged examples vanish before our eyes. Take the problem of "collective goods." A modestly individualistic methodology sees only particular human beings with particular preferences (and—perhaps—rights). A "collective" good can be mathematically aggregated from these individual preferences, but its moral significance is unclear. Since respect for liberty can diminish the aggregate good only by diminishing some individual's well-being, diminution of the aggregate is unacceptable only if some invidi-dual's loss is unacceptable. Reducing air pollution by restraining potential polluters is worth the attendant loss in liberty just in case the well-being of particular lungs outweighs other particular persons' freedom to act. Any conflict between liberty and collective goods reduces to conflicts among individuals.

Free-riders do not change matters. Perhaps the state *should* administer "public" goods like lighthouses lest unscrupulous sea-farers help themselves to the inevitable stray photons sent out by private lighthouse keepers trying to contract with shippers. This good that justifies state action still comes down to preventing particular wrongs to particular persons. The majority forces me to contribute to the lighthouse's upkeep because it is practically impossible to stop me from stealing the lighthouse's services. This reason does not involve a good possessed by an entity called the "public."

The conflict between freedom and justice is no clearer. Taking the disparity between your income and Michael Jackson's as ty-pifying this conflict, the grounds for calling this disparity unfair, as opposed to merely depressing, are highly unstable. Perhaps the problem is Michael Jackson's never having done anything to deserve those talents so many pay so much to hear exercised. True but irrelevant: Michael Jackson is not being rewarded for possessing those talents but for using them. He is being remu-nerated for what *is* in his control, not an accident of birth. Or perhaps the problem is Michael Jackson's lack of a conspicuously outstanding moral character to match his conspicuous income. Some writers apparently believe that reward should be propor-tional to traits like unselfishness and kindness. Yet it is hard to see what justice has to do with moral fibre. No one has a *com-pensatory* right to income proportioned to character since, I take it, virtue is not acquired through deprivation of what by independent standards one ought to own. And Michael Jackson's holdings are *distributively* unjust only if those doing the distributing—his fans—are obliged to trade only with the upright. Perhaps if I can buy the same goods at the same price from a good-natured merchant and a curmudgeon I ought to patronize the former, but this is not a matter of equity, and the obligation not to subsidize grumpiness is certainly not so important that others can force it on me.

Like comments scout the suggestion that Michael Jackson's success is not justly congruent with his skills. Mr. Jackson's skills, not acquired at anyone's expense, violate no canons of compensation. Moreover, the sound precept never to encourage video rock is neither enforcable nor a matter of equity. Anyway, absent a proof of the premised inferiority of Michael Jackson's talents, the case against the Jackson fortune can't get started.

The genuinely hard conflicts for liberty all involve someone worse off as a result of free bargaining than he would have been under constrained bargaining. Some naive buyers cannot resist noncoercive and nonfraudulent but nonetheless questionable tactics like bait-and-switch. Should high pressure salesmen be forbidden to use them? The Kantian line against such paternalism runs that, since each of us must respect his own judgment, to restrict another's exercise of his judgment implies lack of the same "respect" for him we show ourselves. I myself am more impressed by how self-defeating the arguments *for* paternalism are, which, in my experience, always represent the salesman as coercing the buyer, "forcing" him to buy out of a sense of embarrassment. This not only misdescribes the bargain, it implicitly concedes that coercion, not one's own bad judgment, is what one needs protection from.

The hardest case concerns the unappealing vagabond; he comes to town with a little money, but hostelers won't put him up and grocers throw him out of their stores. Should people be *forced* to deal with him to avoid his having to sleep in a ditch, or, failing that, should they be taxed to keep him at a minimum level of subsistence? I feel the pull toward a positive answer while seeing an explanation of this pull that does not involve its legitimacy. People who have grown up in welfare states tend to support coercive transfers of resources because the transfer is done so insensibly they don't regard it as coercive. Taxes are withheld—most people automatically deduct taxes when reckoning their income—and, far down the line, food stamps are issued. People might feel differently if the police collected taxes at gunpoint, as they do now in principle. (If you don't pay your taxes you go to jail, if necessary at gunpoint.)

Of the positive reasons usually offered for coercive transfer, I've already recorded my doubts about any right to subsistence, which extend to any putative right the vagabond may have to assistance from me. Where could he have gotten it? I didn't push him into the ditch; I merely refused to render a service which, if rendered, would have resulted in his not sleeping in the ditch. He is unquestionably worse off that he would have been, but I have *wronged* him only if we already assume he has a right to be dealt with more helpfully, the very point at issue.

Conservatives argue that the bonds of community will dissolve if people mean-spiritedly ignore the vagabond. But if people are indeed so selfish, so alienated, as not to aid those in distress, the bonds of community have long since dissolved. Coercion will not repair them; compulsory compassion is an oxymoron.

A second, conceptually more interesting sort of conflict pits liberty against itself. If a democracy can repel a totalitarian invader only by conscription, it must choose between liberty as an absolute "side constraint," in Robert Nozick's terms, and liberty as a good to be maximized. Is the relevant rule "Never coerce" (which forbids conscription), or "Minimize coercion overall" (which sanctions and may command conscription)? What may be called the "sociological preconditions" for a system of liberty raise a similar problem, although not quite so pointedly. Suppose—a not absurd hypothesis—that pornography, by accustoming him to masturbation, hinders a man's capacity to bond with women and thereby disrupts family formation. Suppose too that children raised in unstable households are psychologically unfit for participation in a liberal democracy. Can the state forbid the free dissemination of pornography in the name of preserving the liberal order?

"The liberal order," to be sure, does not name a superpersonal entity for whose sake the liberty of individuals is to be sacrificed. Individuals are to be coerced so that perhaps they but mainly other individuals may enjoy liberty in the future. Sometimes this is *obviously* proper. I do not see how anyone can protest conscription should it prove necessary to counter the Soviets' present military capabilities, or the torture of a terrorist's innocent child to make him tell where he put the atomic bomb. The hard question is why the imperative of liberty commands us to maximize it, not, as Nozick holds, to categorically refrain from invading it.

It is easy to understand why Nozick wrongly found ordinary morality to include side-constraints instead of maximizing principles. Nozick himself tends to conflate the use of individual A to safeguard the liberty of B, . . . , N with the use of A to secure for B, . . . , N positive benefits to which they have no right. The will of A is bypassed in both cases, but it needs argument to show that wronging A to safeguard rights is just as bad as wronging A to shower benefits. Second—to mimic a utilitarian argument—in virtually every situation the ordinary person is likely to face, coercion will be minimized if he acts on the maxim "Don't you coerce." The best bred coercion-minimizers are children socialized to be noncoercers. Because "Don't coerce" has been selected in as a libertarian rule of thumb, it looks like an absolute side-constraint.

Nozick's main positive argument for the side-constraint view draws on the observation that each of us has his own separate life to lead. Despite Nozick's brave talk of "an argument from moral form to moral content," however, no fact, including this one, can entail a particular categorical command. The problem is not the global is-ought gap. That each of us is an autonomous being capable of acting on reflective choices does undeniably suggest that individual liberty is valuable and that individuals are not to be used as resources for each other. By why is the proper imperative embodiment of this norm "Don't you exploit anyone no matter what" rather than "Seek above all to minimize coercion." If as I suggested earlier the ultimate basis of the value of freedom is that free actions are the most direct expressions of selves, then the *most natural* view is that freedom is a quantum to be maximized. If the manifestation of the self is a good thing, the more of it the better. In any case, the fact of our separate existences does not select a side-constraint as opposed to a teleological structure for morality.

As Nozick rightly notes, Kant's second version of the categorical imperative runs "Always treat humanity, whether in your own person or in the person of any other, never simply as a means," rather than "Minimize the treatment of people as means." Now, the status of the person principle is very vexed: *some* principle about treating people as ends in themselves is entailed by the universalization principle, as Kant thought, if the latter is supplemented by some form of the truism that no one can will himself to be a means only. But the universalization principle entails the side-constraint form of the personality principle just in case one cannot will the maxim of minimizing coercion to be a universal law. We may imagine, this maxim lying behind my advocacy of the draft. Now the cheater's maxim, "Win by taking advantage of others' obeying the rules" is immoral because it tacitly supposes that everyone else will fail to act on it. If everybody cheated to take advantage of others' obeying the rule, there would be no advantage to breaking the rules. The universalized cheater's maxim is logically self-defeating. The maxim of minimizing coercion has no comparable flaw. If everyone went around coercing people to minimize coercion overall, why would it be impossible to minimize coercion overall by coercing people? If everyone stood ready to advocate conscription in the face of totalitarian threats, conscription would still deter totalitarians.

Not only is the universalized minimization maxim not logically self-defeating, there appears to be no absurdity in my *willing* it, as there is an absurdity in my willing my own suicide "because I'll be better off dead." It is indeed a virtually *à priori* truth that I cannot will myself to be a means only to some other person P's goal, since if I *consent* to help secure that goal, I have *embraced* P's pursuit of that goal and my will is not completely bypassed. But this cannot entail the impossibility of anyone's voluntarily surrendering his liberty, for people often do it and sometimes with good reason. Unless I am the victim of a remarkably complete illusion about what I am capable of willing, I'm sure I can will being drafted for the sake of the liberty of others significantly related to me (as for example being citizens of the same country). I can even imagine myself willing to be a slave to avert a considerable enough catastrophe.

Some rights-utilitarians I have read try to paper over the profound difference between the side-constraint and utilitarian view of rights. The Nazis tell a judge in occupied France that if he doesn't find 10 innocent men guilty of treason, they will execute 100. The writers I have in mind, like Ernest van den Haag, argue that whatever decision the judge makes, he will be sending some innocent men to their deaths. (So he might as well send the 10 and save a net total of 90.) Either he condemns them or lets the Nazis condemn them. But of course if he lets the Nazis condemn any innocent men, he is in no way responsible for their deaths. The Nazis are. Of course the French jurist knows that the Nazis will kill the innocent hundred. The behavior of the Nazis is as predictable as a force of nature (and one may occasionally be in a position to halt a force of nature if one wants to). But it is clear enough by now that the predictability of the Nazis' behavior has no tendency to show that the behavior is not the product of the Nazis' free will. Siccing the Nazis on a town is not like tossing a vial of plague germs into the town. To refrain from framing the 10 is to conform to the side-constraint principle of liberty, but to violate the maximization form. I am not comfortable advocating that the French jurist should frame the 10 (assuming the Nazis keep their word), but perhaps no path is comfortable through a moral dilemma. That's what makes it a moral dilemma.

NOTES

1. I no longer think this is possible; see my "Conditional Rights", forthcoming in *Philosophical Studies*.

Study Questions

1. Do you accept Levin's view that political freedom entails metaphysical freedom? Explain your answer.
2. Do you agree with Levin's view that all conflicts between liberty and collective goods reduces to conflicts among individuals?" Explain your answer.

Speech, Expression, and the Constitution

*Frank A. Morrow**

Lon Fuller suggests that one function of legal philosophy is to give "a profitable and satisfying direction to the application of human energies in the law."[1] This paper is a proposal and defense of a theory about the place of speech and expression in our constitutional scheme. I do not know that any sitting justice of the Supreme Court shares these views, and what is said here ought not be confused with settled constitutional law by anyone. But I believe these proposals do suggest a worthwhile direction for the application of our energies in the law, and if so they modestly satisfy Professor Fuller's criterion.

Mr. Justice Holmes in 1919 formulated for a majority of the Supreme Court the clear and present danger doctrine,"[3] which is in a refined form still the balance upon which the freedom of speech allegedly afforded by the First Amendment is weighed. The freedom of speech clause contains just fourteen words; but the history of their interpretation, as evidenced both by the work of the Court and of such legal philosophers as Alexander Meiklejohn and Thomas Emerson, makes plain that some theory is required if this language is to be understood intelligently and applied consistently. This essay is intended as a step toward such a theory.

Recall the words of the First Amendment: "Congress shall make no law respecting the establishment of religion, or prohib-

* Western Washington State College, Bellingham

iting the free exercise thereof; or abridging the freedom of speech or of the press; or the right of the people peaceably to assemble, and to petition the government for a redress of grievances." I will argue that the First Amendment is a plan to insure the workability of the scheme of self-government embraced by the Constitution and that its purpose is not merely to secure some important individual rights, but more particularly to buttress certain conditions deemed essential to the working of the system itself. As the Court has said, freedom of speech and press is the "matrix, the indispensable condition, of nearly every other form of freedom."[3] The problem which has plagued both men of the law and philosophers of law is determining the meaning of the phrase "freedom of speech [and] press," and I will urge that the key to that problem is discernible in the language of the *Butts* case quoted just above.

The extent of my debt to Meiklejohn is obvious, but I do not know that he would agree with all that I shall say.[4] I understand the scope of the First Amendment to be less broad than it is claimed to be under the current official view—a view which still revolves around the "clear and present danger" language penned by Holmes over half a century ago. I concur in the "absolutism" of Justice Black, but I construe the First Amendment more narrowly than he did and leave unprotected by its umbrella some kinds of speech which he believed with his whole heart to be shielded by it from abridgment by government.

Much recent rhetoric about the First Amendment suggests that it extends beyond speech proper to expression generally, and I join Justice Black in opposing this interpretation. The First Amendment binds state governments only by virtue of the assistance rendered by the Fourteenth Amendment, but in the interest of stylistic felicity I will not recur to this point. Whenever reference to the Fourteenth Amendment is required to render strictly correct something that I say, please construe my words to incorporate that reference. I have restricted my discussion to "speech," but I define that term so as to incorporate the Fourth Estate automatically.

By "speech" I understand the deliberate communication of ideas, beliefs, questions and queries, reminders and attitudes, by means which are broadly linguistic—verbally, by writing or printing, or by some other conventional mode of signaling such as semaphore, telegraphy, head nodding or gesturing—including attempts so to communicate but excluding the calculated dissemination of propositions believed by the speaker to be false.[5] Note that I am here trying to characterize a special "First Amendment sense" of "speech" and that I have not claimed, for example, that intent is an element of speech *simpliciter*. Speech is expression, of course, insofar as the speaker is, by speaking, expressing opinion, doubt, outrage, uncertainty, etc. Perhaps we could say, correctly and more generally—if we needed to—that speech is an "expression of the speaker's mind," or maybe on occasion "an expression of the speaker's *instructions*" (here I am thinking of a speaker who merely communicates *another's* views, as an intermediary). I suspect that this last suggestion (in terms of expressing instructions) is strained and that there are some kinds of speech which cannot comfortably be classified as expressions at all. But nothing turns on this question as far as I can tell, and I do not much care whether or not all cases of speech, as I use that term, are also cases of expression.

What is clear is that not all instances of expression are instances of speech. And it disturbs me that writers who mean to discuss the speech and press clause of the First Amendment sometimes frame their discourse in terms of "expression" without bothering to examine the relationship between expression and speech. This disquiets because the First Amendment does not mention "expression" at all. Thus, if "expression" is made the key term in a discussion of that famous directive, the likelihood is increased that the discussion will mislead or go astray.

Some examples of nonspeech expression are these:

1. A man alone at home smiles as he strokes his beard. He is later shown a film of this episode, made without his knowledge, and is accused of smiling because he was pleased that some evil scheme was then being executed by a confederate. He objects that his smile merely expressed his satisfaction after a good meal. Whatever the true explanation, such private smiles of satisfaction (supposed by the smil*er* to be private) would not be instances of speech but would be cases of expression.

2. One might wear bell-bottomed trousers, or not wear a bra, simply as an "expression of one's personality." In the absence of any motive of protest or other intention to communicate or "make a point," there would be expression here but not speech.

3. A woman alone in her office strikes her desk in outrage upon reading of the alleged activities of Mr. Segretti. This is an expression of outrage, but it is not speech.

4. Finally, consider a person who wears a particular hairstyle "because it expresses what I am," or "just because I feel this way." *Ex hypothesi* there is no attempt to communicate—a case of expression but not of speech.

It is fortunately unnecessary here to offer a definition of "expression"; I merely wish to insist on the obvious point that expression is no more coextensive with speech than is piety coextensive with justice. I labor it only because it is currently fashionable to use "expression" in this context and I think that noticing the distinction at the outset may contribute to the clarity of our discussion.

The notion of "symbolic speech"—of which Mary Beth Tinker's black armband is the paradigm[6]—figures prominently in recent First Amendment law. The wearing of these armbands was an apparently successful attempt, by several Iowa children, to communicate the idea that our policy in Vietnam was wrong, or that it should be reexamined in the light of its toll in lives and suffering. A lesson of *Tinker* and similar cases is that some (prima facie) nonspeech expression may be assimilated to speech, or relabeled or reclassified as speech, for First Amendment purposes, by means of the "symbolic speech" device. We need not further refine the notion of "symbolic speech," except to note that *deliberate communication* seems to be the key and that under our definition of speech such cases qualify straightforwardly for First Amendment protection without recourse to a special doctrine. I have in mind here some of the sit-in[7] and haircut[8] cases, as well as cases like *Burnside* v. *Byars*[9] (freedom buttons) and *Schact* v. *United States*[10] (performer wearing military uniform).

I want now to interpose an exhaustive and exclusive disjunction between *political* speech and *private* speech. Most students of the First Amendment recognize this distinction or something akin to it, although they are not as one about its significance for First Amendment purposes. It corresponds closely to what Chafee calls the social and individual interests in free speech[11] and to Meiklejohn's well-known distinction between the *freedom* of speech and the *liberty* of speech.[12] I selected the label "political" in order to emphasize that the speech with which we are here concerned *is* political in the broad, classic sense of that term. It involves matters which concern the body politic *as such*—public matters which relate to the public viewed corporately or *politically*. The tag "private" on the other hand is intended to suggest the individual, as distinguished from the public or political, nature of the concerns to which it applies. It is not meant to suggest that such concerns may not be those of many individuals, even corporately, but only that they are private in nature in the sense in which we distinguish "private affairs," even of a business corporation, from "public affairs," even of a small-town registrar of voters. Political speech is, in Ciceronian terms, speech concerned with the *res publica*— the public business: with policy, government, procedure, officials, education, or with social organization (as distinguished from the organization of a private business, e.g.). That is, it is speech concerned with matters political, in a broad sense as distinguished from matters personal or individual.

The notion of "political speech" is very broad, since it includes speech which is necessary to *prepare* for political life (the life of the citizen)—that is, general intellectual and moral education. It is therefore plausible to argue that "political speech" occupies the entire range of speech and that no speech is "private" in the sense given that term here. But that is too large a topic for this essay, and having pointed it out I will leave the question for another time.

Private speech is all speech that is not political. It is concerned only with personal (nonpolitical) matters, such as Jones's opinion of Beethoven's piano concertos, or of the ancestry of his nonpolitician neighbor. It would thus include nonpolitical libel and nonpolitical pornography, although using pornography as a medium to criticize the president would constitute political speech. Many instances of speech concerning business or commercial matters are properly considered public; and with respect to "symbolic speech" it is apparent that it might be of either the political or private variety.

It is my thesis that the First Amendment should be understood to bar absolutely every abridgment by government of *political* speech; but that it does not reach either private speech or nonspeech expression.[13] Thus, the view offered here is consistent with the Supreme Court's express holding in *Roth* "that obscenity is not within the area of constitutionally protected speech or press."[14] Although *Roth* does not embrace the First Amendment theory advocated in this paper, that holding would be a consequence of this theory insofar as the obscenity contemplated is "nonpolitical."

Those who discuss the First Amendment in terms of "the freedom of expression" are generally much concerned with distinguishing between expression and action.[15] It is sometimes claimed that the freedom of speech clause protects expression but not action. I think it unnecessary to decide whether our private smiler and the special hairstyle wearer, for example, are or are not engaging in "actions." Their expressions (or acts of expression) are, *ex hypothesi*, nonspeech in nature and thus are not, on my view, within the ambit of the First Amendment. To interpret the First Amendment primarily in terms of expression is to invite unclarity and confusion and to suggest that the protection of that amendment extends to expression generally, including the nonspeech kinds of expression we have noticed. The route proposed here has the attractive advantage of avoiding the expression-action quagmire.

I suggest that the First Amendment was intended to secure certain genuinely fundamental conditions of self-government. One such condition is that the people, in their public capacity, be able freely to discuss the public business.[16] Another is that they be able to assemble or gather together to discuss such matters, organize information, air criticism, and plan strategy. If their governors are their agents, communication with them must be available—it must be possible to petition the government to redress grievances. The state is endangered when this opportunity is denied because the likelihood of violence, as the only feasible form of political communication, is vastly increased. Hence, in a system such as the founders envisioned for us freedom of speech, assembly, and petition are not three personal rights thrown together by an accident of constitutional drafting; they are connected faces of a cornerstone of our constitutional system of self-government.

The religion clauses invite a similar understanding. Direct involvement by the state in religious matters would threaten seriously the underlying unity upon which the new system depended. The temptation of the state to influence or prescribe such matters is great and is frankly advocated by Plato, Hobbes, and Rousseau. Madison's *Memorial and Remonstrance* remarks on the pernicious effects of ecclesiastical establishments on civil society, and Justice Douglas has more recently insisted upon this same point.[17]

It was not the purpose of the First Amendment merely to secure a handful of "human rights," although I do not mean at all by this remark to disparage such rights. The rights collected under and protected by that amendment are closely related in virtue of a common focus: the viability of the political system itself. Other basic rights are dealt with elsewhere—the right to a jury trial, to counsel, and the right not to have troops quartered in your living room under ordinary circumstances. According to Emerson, "freedom of expression, while not the sole or sufficient end of society, is a good in itself, or at least an essential element in a good society."[18] Hence, a major (perhaps controlling) reason for protecting expression is its own intrinsic value. With this general view I have no quarrel at all, as long as it is not intended as a description of the function of the First Amendment.

On the contrary, I see the First Amendment as a guardian of the system rather than as a shield for certain individual rights which are merely good in themselves. Further, I believe the First Amendment protects speech only (as I here use that term) and not expression generally. With deference to Justice Black, I think that the speech protected by the First Amendment is only that public or social sort of speech which I have called "political." I conceded earlier, of course, that this might encompass all speech; but that question is left open in this paper.

Some plusses which seem to accrue to this theory are these:

1. It avoids the expression-action problem without, I think, any compensating disadvantage.

2. Insisting on the political function of the entire amendment helps to make secure important systemic values which are essential to the maintenance of our constitutional plan of self-government.

3. By focusing attention on political or public speech, the case for "absolutism"—in this area—is, I think, made both clearer and stronger. Temptations to balance away this protection, engendered and encouraged by the convictions of many persons that the First Amendment was not intended to be an umbrella for smut and slander or for the shouting of "Fire!" under standard Holmesian conditions, are removed by removing these problems from the First Amendment area.

A major objection to this account is that the line between what is political and what is private is unclear—and the scope of First Amendment protection is correspondingly in doubt. At least two considerations are in point here: first, the "no contest" area is vastly greater and more important than the contested borderline; and second, the fact that we are even now under a similar disability, due to the uncertainties of the clear-and-present-danger test and to the vicissitudes of interest balancing, must deprive this objection of much of its force. As Berkeley noted, "That which bears equally hard on two contrary opinions is proof against neither."[19] The main difference would be that, whereas at present the protection afforded even to political speech is subject to these vagaries, under the proposed account all speech which is clearly political is protected absolutely. The "preferred status" which the First Amendment employs under current doctrine[20] transposes nicely into a presumption favoring the political or public nature of challenged speech. Similarly, the test of obscenity which the Court has applied since the "Fanny Hill" case, that the material be "utterly without redeeming social value,"[21] suggests a corresponding test for private speech: that it lack any discernible bearing upon the public business. The Supreme Court has recently abandoned this part of the "Fanny Hill" test, of course, but my point here is unaffected by that fact.[22]

The asset of securing absolutely all political speech seems to me easily to outweigh the concomitant liabilities. Meiklejohn was surely correct in thinking that the free exchange of ideas and information about the public business is an essential condition of self-government. He thought that the freedom of speech clause was intended to promote that exchange. I suggest that the First Amendment *as a whole* is an integrated attempt to secure that end.

I agree with Emerson that expression is a hugely important value and maybe even a basic human right. But expression *in general* is less important systematically than is that special form of expression I have called "political speech." *That* kind of expression the First Amendment protects *because* of its special importance to the system. We are then left to consider private speech and, finally, such nonspeech expression as the solitary smile and the bell-bottomed pants.

With respect to private speech, I accept Meiklejohn's argument that this shield is properly sought in the Fifth Amendment[23] rather than in the First. He held that private speech is a "liberty," analogous to a property right, which government may infringe upon or restrict for good reason and given due process of law. This is, after all, a substantial protection—property rights are not unimportant in our society. I suspect that frank recognition of the Fifth

Amendment-abridgable nature of private speech would leave its position no weaker than it now is under the First Amendment with the clear and present danger with imminence and balancing qualifications. Shouting "Fire!" in a crowded theater just for fun would still be a no-no, and some pornography and libel might be subject to strictures.[24] But it would be an important gain to remove these battles from the First Amendment area and thus to withdraw the strong temptation engendered by these social issues to intrude balancing into the realm of *political* speech.

Given this dichotomy, more justices might be inclined to construe the First Amendment as did Justice Black and to affirm that "Congress shall make no law . . ." just means, with respect to political speech, that Congress shall make *no law*. I am persuaded that this would be a gain much worth achieving.

As an alternative to Meiklejohn's analysis of the constitutional status of private speech, a respectable argument can be made that the Ninth Amendment protects all speech, political and private, and that the First Amendment overlaps it in the political sphere because of the peculiar importance of political speech in our constitutional scheme.[25] Thus, the Ninth Amendment can support arguments urging that nonpolitical libel and pornography are constitutionally protected, while conceding that the First Amendment does not insulate these kinds of speech. Indeed, what has been called the basic right of expression, at least of nonspeech expression, would seem to be housed there if it has any accommodation in the constitutional mansion. The Ninth Amendment may protect a wide variety of expression, speech and nonspeech, with the First Amendment overlap emphasizing the absolute and unqualified protection afforded to political speech. But this is another argument, and I will not pursue it here.

By way of recapitulation, I have argued as follows:

1. that the First Amendment protects speech (as I have defined it for this context), and not expression generally;

2. that the First Amendment protects political speech but not private speech, and that its protection of political speech is absolute;

3. that private speech may be construed either as a "liberty" analogous to a property right, which government can abridge but only under Fifth Amendment conditions of due process, or as a Ninth Amendment right, arguably absolute and unqualified;

4. that expression generally, although not protected by the First

Amendment, may yet be a right secured by the Ninth, and that the Ninth Amendment—not the First—is the appropriate place in which to seek protection for such nonspeech expression as the wearing of unusual hairstyles or unorthodox clothing.

NOTES

1. Lon Fuller, *The Law in Quest of Itself* (Boston: Beacon Press, 1966), p. 2.
2. Schenck v. United States, 1919, 249 U.S. 47.
3. Curtis Pub. Co. v. Butts, 1967, 388 U.S. 130, 145; Palko v. Connecticut, 1937, 302 U.S. 319, 327.
4. Meiklejohn's "Free Speech and Its Relation to Self-Government" is basic reading for students of the First Amendment. It is reprinted in his *Political Freedom* (Oxford, 1965).
5. On this point I agree with Justice Brennan's observation for the Court in Time v. Hill, 1967, 385 U.S. 374, 389, that "the constitutional guarantees can tolerate sanctions against *calculated* falsehood without significant impairment of their essential function."
6. Tinker v. Des Moines Independent School District, 1969, 393 U.S. 503. Justice Fortas wrote the majority opinion.
7. E.g., Brown v. Louisiana, 1966, 383 U.S. 131.
8. See, e.g., the Court's suggestion in Massie v. Henry (4th Cir. 1972) 455 F. 2d 779, 783 that "the length of one's hair may be symbolic speech which under some circumstances is entitled to the protection of the First Amendment."
9. 363 F. 2d 744 (5th Cir. 1966).
10. 398 U.S. 58 (1970).
11. Zechariah Chafee, Jr., *Free Speech in the United States* (New York: Atheneum Publishers, 1969), p. 33.
12. "Free Speech and Its Relation to Self-Government."
13. Justice Brennan, writing for the majority in Time v. Hill, 1967, 385 U.S. 374, 388, states that "the guarantees for speech and press are not the preserve of political expression or comment upon public affairs. . . ." This is consistent with my position if "political expression" is taken in its usual sense—which is plainly a much narrower sense than I have given to "political speech."
14. Roth v. United States, 1957, 354 U.S. 476, 485.
15. Consider Professor Emerson's claim that "the state is entitled to exercise control over action . . . on an entirely different and vastly more extensive basis" (*Toward a General Theory of the First Amendment* [New York: Random House, 1966], p. 6; see also his more recent book, *The System of Freedom of Expression* [New York: Random House, 1970]).
16. Professor Tussman's conception of the citizen as a member of the "electoral tribunal," performing a public function, is instructive here

(Joseph Tussman, *Obligation and the Body Politic* [Oxford, 1960], pp. 120–21).

17. William O. Douglas, *A Living Bill of Rights* (New York: Doubleday & Co., 1961), p. 44.
18. Emerson, *Toward a General Theory of the First Amendment*, p. 6.
19. George Berkeley, "Three Dialogues between Hylas and Philonous," in *The Works of George Berkeley*, ed. T.E. Jessop (Edinburgh: Nelson, 1949), 2: 259–60.
20. Marsh v. Alabama, 1946, 326 U.S. 501, 509 (per Black), Thomas v. Collins, 1945, 323 U.S. 516, 530 (per Rutledge), Follett v. Town of McCormick, 1944, 321 U.S. 573, 575 (per Douglas).
21. A Book Named "John Cleland's Memoirs of a Woman of Pleasure" v. Massachusetts, 1966, 383 U.S. 413, 418.
22. Miller v. California, 1973, 413 U.S. 15, reh. den. 418 U.S. 881.
23. ". . . [N]or shall any person . . . be deprived of life, liberty or property without due process of law."
24. Justice Black has expressed the view that the First Amendment renders all obscenity and libel laws unconstitutional (*A Constitutional Faith* [New York: Alfred A. Knopf, 1968], pp. 48, 53). But in Rosenbloom v. Metromedia, 1971, 403 U.S. 29, he cautioned that state libel laws are not likely to be struck down.
25. The Ninth Amendment provides that "the enumeration in the Constitution of certain rights shall not be construed to deny or disparage others retained by the people." So far the Court has determined no case on Ninth Amendment grounds, and its content and scope therefore remain speculative. But see the discussion in Griswold v. Connecticut, 1965, 381 U.S. 479.

Study Questions

1. How might one assault the author's view that, contrary to many legal scholars, First Amendment guarantees do not extend beyond speech to just *any* kind of expression? (Wearing odd clothes, adopting strange mannerisms, etc.)
2. What do you think of the author's view that the First Amendment should be understood to bar every interference with *political* speech, but not *private* speech?
3. On the basis of the author's arguments, where do you believe the protection of private speech and nonspeech expression (if, indeed such protection exists at all) resides—in the first amendment or in the fifth? Explain?

Whistleblowing: The Reporter's Role

Dr. Frederick A. Elliston

Introduction

Whistleblowing has received considerable attention over the past decade. Newspapers, magazines, and television contain daily accounts of employees who go public to disclose illegal, immoral or questionable practices in the workplace. These employees, popularly known as whistleblowers, are part of a venerable tradition in our times. They bear the mantle of the civil disobedients of the 1960s—carrying their voice of dissent from the war in Vietnam to the boardrooms of corporate America. Today, protest in the workplace about corporate wrongdoing has eclipsed political protest about government wrongdoing. This transition to the monetary arena is both natural and inevitable.[1] Big business, like big government, is one locus of power in America. It is not surprising, then, that in both institutions, we find individuals conscientiously objecting to practices they consider wrong and bringing them to light in the hope that they will thereby cease or be changed—and thereby running the risk of jeopardizing not just their jobs but their careers in order to speak their conscience.

In the literature to date there are several approaches to whistleblowing.[2] Let me mention them very briefly in order to distinguish my approach from various alternatives.[3]

One approach could be called *self-help*. Writers like Tekla Perry[4], Peter Broida[5] and Peter Raven-Hansen[6], as well as the members of the Government Accountability Project[7] have offered employees advice on how to blow the whistle—and get away with it.

A second approach could be termed the *expose*. The work of Kermit Vandivier[8] and Ernest Fitzgerald[9] fall into this category, as do the writings of newspaper columnist Jack Anderson and various other investigative reporters.

Ralph Nader's group—and the report that came out of it[10]—illustrates a third approach, the *political*. Their primary objective is to change government actions or policy.

A fourth approach is the *personal*, as illustrated by Greg Mitchell's *Truth . . . And Consequences*[11] and Alan Westin's fine collection.[12] These are largely biographical and anecdotal. They tell a personal story of discovery and protest from the point of view of the individual whistleblower."

A fifth approach is the *legal* one. A number of scholars such as Blumburg[13], Conway[14], and Blades[15] have dealt with the question of employee rights, largely in terms of the common law employment-at-will doctrine. They have analyzed the various state and federal statutes designed to provide public and private employees with a measure of protection and relief if they are discharged for revealing waste, inefficiency or corruption in their organization.

A sixth approach could be termed *philosophical*, or more precisely ethical. Here the main question is: When, if ever, is whistleblowing right (or wrong), and why? Norman Bowie[16], Tom Donaldson[17], Gene James[18] and Richard DeGeorge[19] have all looked at whistleblowing from this moral point of view.

By contrast, the approach that we adopted in our National Science Foundation (NSF) project could be termed *strategic*. In analyzing our materials, we discovered that—quite by chance—each case illustrated a distinct way of dealing with organizational wrongdoing. So we decided to focus our attention on the different ways to blow the whistle. Altogether we discovered seven different strategies for blowing the whistle. One of the most common and effective ways to blow the whistle is, of course, through the media. But before examining this strategy, let me pause briefly to examine what whistleblowing is and how one can judge it.

The Concept of Whistleblowing

In the popular literature, some of which I just cited, the term "whistleblowing" covers a multitude of sins. At the bottom end, it includes squealing, muckraking or leaking information to the press. At the high end, it refers to conscientious disclosure of threats to the safety or health of the public. To conduct our NSF project, we needed a neutral definition that did not load the dice at the outset for or against the whistleblower. We decided to define whistleblowing as an action (or process) that satisfies the following four conditions:[20]

1. the individual makes a conscious *moral decision*, or a series of decisions with a moral rationale;

2. the decision is to *disclose information*, that is, to make it accessible to others by creating a public record;

3. the information concerns actual, potential or probable *wrongdoing* by organizational members;

4. the wrongdoing was caused by an organization of which one is or was an *employee*.

Let me comment briefly on each of these four conditions for an action's counting as whistleblowing.

The whistleblower, like the civil disobedient, must act for *moral reasons*. The difference between political protest and crime is that the first has the weight of moral principles behind it whereas the second is driven mostly by self-interest. Similarly, the difference between disgruntled employees complaining about how poorly they were treated and whistleblowers protesting corporate policies is that the former are primarily concerned about themselves whereas the latter are engaged in principled moral action. Whether one accepts or rejects the principles and values of the whistleblower, their presence marks an important conceptual difference.

Whistleblowers are trying to *disclose information*, that is, to make it a matter of public record. Has one blown the whistle if one gets information into the hands of reporters who do nothing with it? I think not—it must get printed so that it is accessible to all members of the public. When the reporter runs with the story, the employee becomes a whistleblower.

The information concerns *corporate wrongdoing*. Theirs is not simply—and sometimes not at all—a personal grievance about the way they were treated but a protest against immoral, illegal or questionable corporate practices or policies, of which they may or may not be the victim.

Finally, one conceptual difference between the whistleblowers and the reporter is that the whistleblower is (or was) an *employee* of the organization whose wrongdoing is reported—whereas the

reporter is not. Thus reporters can assist employees in whistleblowing, indeed confer this status on them—but they are not
whistleblowers themselves. Organizational membership is a fourth
and final condition that distinguishes employees' whistleblowing from reporters' "muckracking," spying investigators or paid
informants.

Does an employee have to cross the organizational boundaries
before he or she counts as a whistleblower in the true sense? In
the public's mind, those who jump the chain of command within
the organization in order to redress wrongdoing are frequently
seen as whistleblowers too. These "internal whistleblowers"—for
reasons I shall list shortly—should be cautious about contacting
reporters, or anyone else, outside the organization before attempting to resolve problems from within. Conversely, reporters should
be sanguine about publicizing incidents where no internal remedies have been attempted. There are three exceptions to this rule:
first, when the internal mechanisms either do not exist or are
unlikely to work; second, when they are slow or cumbersome and
the problem requires swift, immediate action; and third, when the
personal costs to the whistleblower are likely to be so exorbitant
that no one could reasonably require such self-sacrifice. The most
appropriate place to begin to redress wrongdoing is one's immediate environment—the organization itself. Why should the
whistleblower begin within? There are several reasons to start
here.

The first reason is *pragmatic*. Doing so will strengthen one's
case. Airing the problem within the organization provides an opportunity to test one's suspicions and hear the counterevidence.
It gives others an opportunity to correct mistaken assumptions or
redress any wrongs. Dissidents who attempt to persuade management must present evidence of their claims and thereby give
their employers a chance to respond. By the time the employee
goes public, he or she will probably have constructed a stronger
and more convincing case.

The second reason is *prudential*. Most whistleblowers pay a high
price for "speaking their conscience." Retaliation in the form of
demotion, loss of pay or status and even dismissal is not uncommon. Employees can protect themselves from counterattacks by
voicing their concerns within the organization and giving management a chance to respond. Managenment may very well come

to see a problem they previously ignored or were unaware of, and decide to correct it.

The third reason is *legal*. Sometimes the use of internal mechanisms is mandated under the "exhaustion of remedies" principle of law. Before litigants can be heard in court, they must seek relief from all internal avenues and appropriate administrative agencies. Failure to do so will preclude legal redress.

The fourth reason is *moral*. Loyalty to one's organization requires that one provide its members with an opportunity to address the matter internally. It allows them to avoid public embarrassment and ridicule. Employees who have exhausted the internal avenues of dissent are less likely to be accused of acting in an unfair or disloyal manner. If they have given their accusers an opportunity to respond to their charges, they cannot be denigrated for squealing on them behind their backs.

Of course, it takes no small measure of courage to confront someone within the boundaries of the corporation, where typically the manager accused has power over the employee protesting. And indeed, there are risks involved—the manager may retaliate by attacking verbally, haranguing, demoting or firing the employee. I shall say more about the moral weight of these risks later, and their role in justifying anonymity. Here I wish only to point out the legitimate demand of corporate loyalty, while granting that this demand may be overridden under the three exceptions listed above.

Despite one's best efforts, these internal discussions may fail to solve the problems. Employees must then decide where to turn next. As they contemplate crossing the boundaries of the organization, they face a moral and conceptual boundary. They break the traditional ties of loyalty when they go outside the organization and become whistleblowers in the full sense. If one is going to go outside the organization, to whom can one turn for help?

Strategies for Blowing the Whistle

The familiar first answer to this question is: Troubled employees can turn to reporters. When one thinks of whistleblowing, one thinks inevitably of the press, and for good reason. If one's goal is to make information public, they are perhaps the most familiar and effective means to do so. But, they are not the only means and to appreciate the reporter's role in whistleblowing one must bear the alternatives in mind. Let me therefore list briefly five other ways to blow the whistle.

Community Groups. In one of the cases we studied under our NSF grant, the regional director of a government environmental agency accused his employer of disregarding serious environmental threats connected with the storage of chemical waste below ground. He attempted to block the planned disposal of the waste by contacting a community action group who shared his concerns. The community group offered expertise, anonymity and public pressure. So he leaked information not to the press—but to an environmental group. In turn, they applied pressure on the agency to hold a public hearing at which their members could testify and call the public officials to public account. Through the community group, the director was able to enlist the support he needed to prevent the agency from burying the waste in his portion of the state—thereby displacing if not solving the problem.

Professional Associations. In another case, a computer scientist employed by a criminal justice agency feared that the installation of a new case monitoring system for the district attorney's office would overload the main computer. It threatened to slow down the response time for dispatching police cars so that the crime victims might not receive the emergency help they need and suspects might escape. After voicing her concerns, both to her superior and then to the coordinating council, she was fired for insubordination. So, she contacted her professional association, the Institute for Electrical and Electronic Engineers (IEEE). A committee set up by the IEEE to investigate her allegations found that her concerns, and the actions she took to report them, were fully justified and accorded with their Code of Ethics. What did the professional association, the IEEE, have to offer?

First, it was a way to bring external pressure to bear on the organization, to persuade them to examine the situation more carefully. An IEEE committee was established to investigate the alleged harm to its members for adhering to their professional code. The committee made a determination in support of the computer scientist and put pressure on the organization by publishing the incident, along with names.

Second, it provided technical expertise. The issues were highly technical and could only be fully understood and evaluated by professionals with the requisite knowledge and expertise. The professional assocation offered her a hearing with her peers, who could appreciate the technical and moral dimensions of her dilemma.

Third, it provided moral authority. Her professional objections were justified by citing sections of her professional association's code of ethics. While such a code supported her actions, it does not have the power of enforcement but serves more as a mouthpiece than a whip. In her case, the code's stipulation that she protect the safety of the public conferred moral legitimacy on her actions.

The Inspector General. Another case involved an engineer for a major government construction project, the winter Olympics in upstate New York. He accused his department of overlooking numerous structural safety hazards. Unable to resolve the matter internally, he contacted the Inspector General. She ordered a full-scale investigation which eventually substantiated many of the engineer's charges.

The Office of the Inspector General was established in 1978 by Public Law 95–452 in response to evidence indicating massive fraud, waste, and abuse of federally funded programs. It provides for the consolidation of auditing and investigative responsibilities, under a single high-level official. The office investigates accusations of fraud, abuse, waste, and mismanagement in 12 federal departments, each with its own Inspector General.

The Inspector General offers several benefits. First, it establishes a focal point in each agency to deal with fraud. Second, the Inspector General is independent—a presidential appointment, located under the head of the 12 federal departments so as to allow maximum, independent judgment and autonomy. Third, his sole responsibility is the coordination of audits and investigations—a clear objective without conflicts.

The Courts. In another case a research scientist was concerned that her employer, a pharmaceutical company, not market a drug that she considered dangerous. After her internal efforts failed, she resigned. She sued the company for damages claiming that she had been 'constructively discharged.'

What did the court have to offer her? First, it provided a structured forum for airing disputes. Each side was given an opportunity to support its claims. Second, it was objective—and favored neither side, but served as an impartial arbiter. Third, the publicity of the court case informed not only those present but the public generally—especially the medical and legal communities, the consumers, the drug industry and the government. Fourth, the court provided a final determination that was binding and enforceable. Fifth, the court, relying as it does on the principle of *stare decisis*, would establish a precedent that she hoped could be cited in any similar case.

Congress. Another case took place in the early years of the antinuclear movement. At that time the prospect of abundant and inexpensive fuel in the face of diminishing resources was very attractive. A systems engineer responsible for safety inspections charged that the nuclear industry was not checking reactor work carefully enough, that some designs contained safety defects. His case was heard before a Senate Subcommittee.

Clearly, Congress possesses power on a national level that can be put to tremendous effect. But Congress' desire to step forward, without the backing of its voting constituency, can be abated by political considerations—lost votes and friends. Once a movement is clearly established and supported by many followers it becomes safe for politicans to support the cause. But before that time they are risking their political career by initiating unsupported action.

The Reporter's Role

It is against this backdrop that I now turn to the role of the reporter in whistleblowing. I will begin by describing one case and then ask: What makes going to the press an appropriate strategy—and what makes it inappropriate? Then, I will ask about the moral responsibilities of whistleblowers and reporters: When is whistleblowing through the press justified—and when is it not?

The case we examined involved a wildlife pathologist for a state environmental agency who charged his employer with contributing to the state's environmental problems by allowing industry to discharge large amounts of chemical waste into rivers and streams. He sent more than 100 memoranda to various senior members of the agency over a five-year period, warning them of the hazards. He got no action, and became thoroughly disgruntled and frustrated. Then, one day, he heard a story on the radio. A federal scientist had provided a *New York Times* reporter with information on the very same chemical waste problem he had been fighting from within the agency to no avail for many years. Where his memoranda had gone unheeded, the federal scientist's story caught the attention of the commissioner who ordered the discharge halted pending an investigation.

So the wildlife pathologist decided that the press was the answer. He decided to go public by informing local reporters of other cases he had tried unsuccessfully to correct from within. Needless to say, upper-level management disapproved. They limited his resources—cutting back his laboratory staff and budget until he found himself washing his own sinks and sweeping his floors. But, as a result of his actions, the department forced a halt to dumping certain toxic chemicals into the rivers.

What did the media offer this pathologist? Why did this strategy work for him? Several factors are relevant to explaining what makes the press an appropriate vehicle for publicizing organizational wrongdoing.

First, the pathologist enjoyed a great deal of *autonomy*, both as a professional and a civil servant. Consequently, press coverage did not threaten his livelihood. Not everyone is so lucky. Some employees may decide not to go to the press because it would jeopardize their jobs. Others, notably "Deep Throat" in *All the President's Men*, go to the press but remain anonymous in order to safeguard their position.

Second, the media *trusted* the accuracy of his reports. He took pains to develop a solid reputation as a person who exercised sound scientific judgment. Also, he had easy access to material data which increased his value as an informant. His personal credibility, based in part on his credentials and in part on his integrity, allowed him to use the press effectively.

Third, the head office was extremely *sensitive to political pressure*. Though he personally had little or no political savvy, he could effectively use the media to bring public pressure to bear on the administration. The press can be an effective tool for whistleblowers in public agencies because—unlike many private corporations—they are more sensitive and accountable to the public at large.

Fourth, he *enjoyed publicity* and the public recognition it brought. A shy, inarticulate and introspective person would not find the press as attractive as alternative strategies (unless he or she remained anonymous). Our whistleblower found the media engaging, entertaining and colorful. They provided an ideal setting for a dramatic performance—which he willingly provided.

Fifth, the press swiftly address a *wide audience*—precisely the pathologist's aim. Unlike bureaucratic mechanisms—which can take months to work through—the press can quickly seize the public's attention and bring public pressure to bear on agency heads.

Sixth, it allows the release of information to be *timed* for maximum impact. The media can time stories for the maximum impact according to the discretion of the reporter and the whistleblower—unlike the courts or community groups where decisions rest in the hands of others or are fixed by cumbersome organizational processes. The press can run stories at that moment when the public is most likely to hear and hearken, or when public officials are most vulnerable.

Finally, the issue was *fashionable* at the time, one that easily engaged the public's attention. The disposal of toxic waste has become a popular topic in the minds of many citizens because of its potential impact on the quality of their lives.

But, the press is not without its disadvantages. First, it is difficult to secure the public's attention on important issues—because they are too complicated, the solutions too tenuous, or the people involved too boring. Second, even when you capture the public's attention, it is difficult to sustain it. They are fickle and easily lose interest in important topics. Third, the story may not find a wide appeal, and may affect insufficient numbers of people to be newsworthy.

Yet, the whistleblower we studied who used the press was one of our few success stories. He did indeed succeed in informing the public, mobilizing resources, preventing wrongdoing, causing policy to change, preventing people from becoming victimized, and protecting the environment.

Other Avenues of Dissent

When is it appropriate to go to the press, and when is it not? This question calls for two kinds of answers: first, a comparative appraisal of the media versus other ways to blow the whistle; and second, a statement of the conditions under which whistleblowing is ethically justified. Let me identity the factors that affect the selection of a strategy.

The Nature of the Issue. Are the problems local or national; are they political or technical; do they affect just a few people or many members of the public generally? Technical engineering or scientific concerns are perhaps best understood by fellow professionals—consultants or professional groups—rather than the media. The misappropriation of government monies, on the other hand, would appropriately be brought to the attention of voters through the media through the media, so that they can pressure government officials to remedy the situation or oust them from office. If the issue is sexy, pervasive or national in scope, then a major newspaper or network may be the appropriate mechanism to bring it to the public's attention. A regional issue might be publicized through a local newspaper or radio station that can be induced to cover it. The ensuing publicity can curtail actions by government officials or lead to a change in public policy.

The Nature of the Organization. Organizations are tall (hierarchical), or flat (matrix), with a wide or narrow span of authority and a centralized or decentralized focus of power. They may be old or young, growing or falling, stable or unstable. These factors affect the procedures that are available within the organization to change policy, and the locus of pressure points. Private organizations that are flat, decentralized and far flung may be less vulnerable to public pressure brought about through the press. Public organizations, on the other hand, especially those that are hierarchical, may be more vulnerable to a newspaper or television story since their leaders are more accountable to the public at large.

One's Organizational Role. Whistleblowers typically occupy a privileged position within the organization. They usually have access to information that provides the "larger picture" of what is going on, or is supposed to be going on; and usually they enjoy considerable discretion and autonomy. Other employees—with a more limited, incomplete or partial perspective—seldom push their worries far enough to blow the whistle.

Whistleblowers, standing on the fringes of the corporation, span the boundary between it and other organizations—especially other branches of government and the community. Whistleblowers need to seek out reporters who can help them get information to members of the community at large, and to see this information dissemination function as part of their job.

Individual Personality Traits. An individual's personality affects his or her choice of strategies. As noted earlier, a quiet, task-oriented person is unlikely to go to the press—they do not want to be caught in the limelight. On the other hand those with a dramatic flair who cultivate rather than shun the limelight may seek out reporters as a congenial way to protect wrongdoing. The press works best for those who are articulate, extroverted and credible.

Recent Trends. Which stories reporters decide to run with depends in part on the historical context out of which they write. Various trends, fads, and the fluctuating political atmosphere affect not only whether or not others will be sympatic to their cause but also which medium will be most effective in getting action. For example, antinuclear groups were barely visible 20 years ago, but today they have become well-organized and gained national recognition. The consumer movement has raised our consciousness about dangerous drugs or products. And the increasing democratization of the workplace has made us sensitive to employee rights and protections for those who speak out. These three trends work in favor of the whistleblower using the media to draw attention to organizational wrongs.

A newspaper reporter will be more interested in issues that are currently on the minds of the public at large, or which he or she thinks can be made to engage their attention. The newsworthiness of a story is another factor to bear in mind in selecting a strategy.

Appraising Whistleblowing

There are several terms in which one can appraise whistleblowers—whether it be through the press or some other mechanism: pragmatic, strategic and moral. One question to be raised is: What is the best way to blow the whistle? This is a question I have already addressed in examining the different ways to blow the whistle. A second question is: Has one succeeded in blowing the whistle? This question raises troublesome questions about which counts as success and how one measures it, which I shall consider in a moment. A third question is: Was whistleblowing morally or ethically justified? I shall consider this question last, and consider some special problems that the media pose.

Whistleblowing—and the reporters who work with them—may succeed or fail at several levels. If one thinks literally of whistleblowing, one can break the process down into three stages: blowing, making a noise, and being heard.

Imagine a child who picks up a whistle, looks at it, plays with it but does nothing more. This child is like the employee who becomes concerned about illegal or immoral corporate practices, frets about what to do, perhaps loses some sleep worrying about it, and decides to do nothing—or, more simply and realistically, never decides quite what to do. As a whistleblower this person is a failure, so much so that he or she may not be regarded as a whistleblower at all. To protest successfully, one must gather enough facts to make a reasonable and informed judgment whether wrongdoing has occurred, whether one should do something about it, and the most effective path to follow.

Next consider the child who attempts to blow the whistle, but fails because he does not blow hard enough: He does not make any noise. Likewise employees may become concerned, talk to their friends or coworkers, but never put enough effort into what they are doing to sound an alarm. As with the child who huffs and puffs, nothing happens.

Finally, the child may succeed in making noises, but fail to be heard: no one is listening, or willing to listen. Employees may write memos to their boss or contact reporters, and yet nothing happens. Their concerns are dismissed as needless worries or frivolous complaints rather than legitimate causes of concern. They have blown the whistle, but not successfully. To voice one's concerns successfully, one has to overcome three hurdles:

1. one must become genuinely concerned with wrongdoing, and take positive steps to voice one's concerns;
2. one must put sufficient effort into alerting others that one sounds the alarm because something is wrong;
3. one's message must be sufficiently loud and clear that it is correctly heard by others.

If all three hurdles are cleared, the employee has successfully voiced his or her concern.

Each of these conditions has implications for the reporter who is looking for a good story. First, reporters should be wary of those employees who come to them with complaints where they have made no effort to deal with them within the organization, or have taken no concrete actions to voice them outside. If it is all talk and no show, the story may dissolve upon investigation and end up wasting the reporter's time. Likewise, if others are confused about what the problem is, if communications have gotten garbled, then the reporters may find a weak story has been dumped in their lap. So, a careful look at what the employee has done and how well others have understood the problem can protect the reporter against stories that fall apart.

Whether or not a whistleblower and a reporter succeed depends in large measure on the responses of others. What others do, in turn, depends on several factors: the kinds of concerns voiced, the reputations of the individuals involved, the nature of the organization, the whistleblower's position and reputation, the people addressed, the evidence gathered and the solutions available. Several questions need to be answered.

First, one can ask whether others heard the whistle? Did they read the story or watch the program on TV? Did people become aware of problems or dangers which previously were unknown to them? This question focuses attention on the flow of information. Insofar as whistleblowing is an effort to inform others, the whistleblower and the reporter have failed if the facts are distorted, key bits of information omitted, or the problem misinterpreted. They have succeeded if the information is conveyed accurately to enough people or the right people to make a difference.

Second, the reporter and the whistleblower can ask whether the warning was taken seriously. Did others, when they became aware of the problem, mobilize any of their resources in response? Or did the warning fall on deaf ears? They have succeeded at blowing the whistle to the extent that others are moved to act in a deliberate and responsible way—perhaps to reconsider or reexamine an organizational practice or policy.

Whistleblowers and reporters are more successful still if corporate practices are changed. If they are concerned with wrongdoing that occurred in the past, they obviously cannot change it: the past is past and as such unalterable. But they can change the policies or procedures that allow the past wrong to occur, and thereby reduce the probable incidence of similar wrongs in the future.

They can redress past wrongs by punishing those who are

responsible for them. The punishment may range from a reprimand to a firing, from a corporate sanction imposed strictly from within to a trial by jury with civil or criminal penalties. If those who have caused the wrong receive their just desserts, the whistleblower has succeeded.

The reporter and the whistleblower can redress past injustices by compensating the victims. If chemical pollution has lead to a devaluation of the property value of homeowners, the government can purchase their homes at fair market value. If dangerous gas tanks have made a car unsafe, victims of automobile accidents (or their heirs) can be awarded damages. Such reparations do not change the past wrongs, but they do mitigate their net harm. They may also serve as a deterrent that warns others against similar wrongdoing.

No wrong may yet have occurred but may be likely to occur in the near future. The reporter and the whistleblower have achieved a measure of success if the probability of its occurring or recurring is diminished. This reduction in possible harm may take the form of informing the public about risks so that they can take steps to avoid jeopardizing their health or safety. Or it may take the form of a new corporate practice that places the public less at risk.

It may turn out that their prior assessment of the risk, though reasonable given the evidence at the time, is incorrect. New findings may show that the harm is less likely, the danger more remote or the wrong far less serious. If the worries were reasonable and the new evidence reliable, then to disprove these worries is a measure of success. A balanced, responsible and thorough inquiry that alleviates reasonable concerns constitutes a measure of success for the reporter and the whistleblower.

Finally, their actions will be judged successful if dissension is diminshed. If the disagreement was rooted in mistaken assumptions, the correction of these mistakes will resolve it. But if the disagreement was rooted in conflicting value judgments, it may be impossible to achieve consensus. One can ony hope for tolerance and understanding and respect for alternative viewpoints that allows those who disagree nevertheless to work together.

The Ethics of Whistleblowing

There are several factors to bear in mind before deciding whether or not whistleblowing, or a reporter's assisting a whistleblower, is justified. Both the individual whistleblower and the reporter who will assist the whistleblower should bear these in mind as they make their decision.

First, consider the costs carefully. Blowing the whistle may exact a heavy toll on the whistleblower and other members of the organization. It can cost an individual employee not just a job but an entire career. Frequently friends will start to avoid you and colleagues will not talk to you. You will lose some sleep and perhaps some fortunes. Socrates said that the unexamined life is not worth living, and Kant claimed that we have moral obligations to ourselves. From both points of view, whistleblowers should know that they are gambling and that the odds are against them. Reporters too should know that they are gambling with other people's livelihood and sometimes their lives (as the case of Karen Silkwood dramatically illustrates)—and help them to realize it.

Second, research the facts, laws and regulations. Are there any laws, regulations, codes of ethics, special statutory provisions, or documented job descriptions which will support your cause? If so, clearly identify them and plan a strategy which will include them. Doing so serves three purposes: it enhances the prospects for success; it demonstrates that one is acting in a morally responsible way; and it protects one against charges of negligence.

Third, define the issue clearly. What is the nature of the issue—political, scientific, administrative? How broad a scope does it cover? Who has a stake in it? Who caused it? Who has the responsibility for dealing with it? Who has the power and authority to deal with it?

The answers to such questions serve two purposes—strategic and moral. First, they enable one to communicate the nature of the problem clearly to others. And second, they enable one to see where the locus of power and responsibility lie.

Fourth, weigh the importance of the issue, to determine how important the issue it, ask yourself: "If nothing were to be done about it what would happen?" The greater the potential harm which would result if you did nothing, the more reason you should speak out.

The seriousness of the issue is perhaps the main moral factor to weigh in deciding whether or not whistleblowing is justified. To counter the legitimate demands for organizational loyalty, one must document a case of serious wrongdoing. Don't blow the whistle just because someone steals paperclips. But if they are stealing thousands of dollars from the company, the wrongdoing is more serious and its disclosure more warranted.

Fifth, research the options. Carefully consider the alternative strategies. You will increase your chances of winning by choosing a strategy which best suits the situation. Generally we found that the lower the level at which the problem was addressed, the more satisfactory to all the outcome was likely to be. If you can solve a problem within the organization, do so: you will get faster and more effective solutions because the people know the problem and context better. Bearing this in mind, a reporter might well advise an employee to talk to other people in the organization first. They arguably have a right to be told and given an opportunity to redress the problem. And it may save the reporter the embarrassment of losing a story that gets resolved as it is about to break!

Sixth, verify your information. The burden of proof is on the individual and so it is important to verify the claims to be made by gathering documentation in the form of lab reports, memoranda, expert opinions or photographs. The evidence marshalled performs several functions: it protects other members of the organization from false accusations; it gives people an opportunity to correct misinformation and to become informed about wrongdoings they may not have known about; and it protects the whistleblower from accusations of being negligent or irresponsible.

Confidentiality and Anonymity

Reporters have to deal with a special problem that other avenues of dissent typically do not raise, at least in the same form or to the same extent. Should reporters keep the sources of their information confidential? This problem is the other side of the whistleblower's problem: Whether or not to try to remain anonymous? Let me, in concluding, identify some of the moral factors that enter into this two-fold issue.

Consent. Did the whistleblower ask the reporter that his identity not be made public—perhaps as a condition of providing the information he gave. If the information is gathered with this understanding, then the reporter has a prima facie obligation not to reveal the source. This obligation may arguably be overriden by other considerations—like a court order or the obligations of reporters as citizens to obey the law. But, nothing is likely to encourage anonymous whistleblowing quite as much as the sight of a reporter going off to jail to protect the identity of his informant.

Retaliation. What are the prospects for unfair retaliation? Frequently whistleblowers occupy vulnerable positions within the organization. They lack the power to change the situation, otherwise they would not need to blow the whistle. They need to defend themselves against those whose actions they protest. Consequently, they need and sometimes deserve, the protection which anonymity or confidentiality can sometimes provide.

Effectiveness. Will the prospects for bringing about change be increased or diminished by promises of anonymity? Sometimes members of the public question the integrity of someone who will not stand up and face those he accuses. They feel that the whistleblowers' own moral principles are in question if they identify others as wrongdoers while refusing to be identified themselves. Consequently, individual whistleblowers may be more effective if they do not seek anonymity.

Conversely, whistleblowing as a practice may be encouraged if whistleblowers are guaranteed the protection that anonymity brings. People may be encouraged to report wrongdoing if they do not have to fear for their jobs and careers in the process.

NOTES

1. See Frederick Elliston, "Civil Disobedience and Whistleblowing: A Comparative Appraisal of Two Forms of Dissent." *Journal of Business Ethics*, 1 (Spring 1982), 23–28.
2. See James Bowman, Frederick Elliston and Paula Lockhart, *Whistleblowing: An Annotated Bibligraphy and Resource Guide* (New York: Garland, 1984).
3. See *Whistleblowing: Managing Dissent in the Workplace* and *Whistleblowing Research: Methodological and Moral Issues* (New York: Garland, 1984).
4. Tekla Perry, "Knowing How to Blow the Whistle." *IEEE Spectrum*, 18 (September 1981), 56–61.

5. Peter B. Broida, "How to Whistle," *The Government Standard*, 37 (August 1979), 14.
6. Peter Raven-Hansen, "Do's and Don'ts for Whistleblowers: Planning for Trouble," *Technology Review*, 82 (May 1980), 34–44.
7. Government Accountability Project. *A Whistleblower's Guide to the Federal Bureaucracy*, Washington, D.C.: Institute for Policy Studies, 1977.
8. Kermit Vandivier, "The Aircraft Brake Scandal," *Harper's Magazine*, April 1972, pp. 24–52.
9. Ernest A. Fitzgerald, *The High Priests of Waste*, New York: W.W. Norton, 1972.
10. Ralph Nader, Peter J. Petkas, and Kate Blackwell, eds., *Whistle-Blowing: The Report of the Conference on Professional Responsibility*, New York: Grossman Publishers, 1972.
11. Greg Mitchell, *Truth . . . And Consequences: Seven Who Would Not Be Silenced*, New York, Dembner Books, 1981.
12. Alan F. Westin, ed., *Whistle-blowing: Loyalty and Dissent in the Corporation*, New York: McGraw-Hill, 1980. See also Peter Maas, *Serpico*, New York: Basic Books, 1973 and Albert L. Hirshman, *Exit, Voice, and Loyalty*, Cambridge: Harvard University Press, 1970. For an account more focused on whistleblowing than whistleblowers see Robert M. Anderson; Robert Perrucci; Dan E. Schendel; and Leon E. Trachtman; eds., *Divided Loyalties: Whistle-Blowing at BART*, West Lafayette, IN: Purdue University, 1980.
13. See for example, Phillip I. Blumberg, "Corporate Responsibility and the Employer's Duty of Loyalty and Obedience: A Preliminary Inquiry," *Oklahoma Law Review*, 24 (August 1971), 279–318.
14. John Conway, "Protecting the Private Sector At-Will Employee Who 'Blows the Whistle': A Cause of Action Based Upon Determinants of Public Policy." *Wisconsin Law Review*, 77 (1977), 777–812.
15. Lawrence Blades, "Employment At Will vs. Individual Freedom: On Limiting the Abusive Exercise of Employer Power." *Columbia Law Review*, 67 (December 1967), 1404–1435. See as well Mitchell J. Lindauer, "Government Employee Disclosures of Agency Wrongdoing: Protecting the Right to Blow the Whistle," *University of Chicago Law Review*, 42 (Spring 1975), 530–561. For one of the earliest statements of the employment at will doctrine is that of the Tennessee Supreme Court in *Payne v. Western & Atlantic R.R. Co.*, 81 Tenn. 507 (1884).
16. Norman Bowie, "Blowing the Whistle and Other 'Why Be Moral Questions,' " *Business Ethics*, Englewood Cliffs, N.J.: Prentice-Hall, 1982, Chapter 7, pp. 138–149.
17. Thomas Donaldson, "Employee Rights." *Corporations and Morality*, Englewood Cliffs, N.J.: Prentice-Hall, 1981, Chapter 7, pp. 129–157.

Study Questions

1. In a well-constructed essay, appraise the importance of the different factors the author lists as relevant to the morality of "whistleblowing." (For example, is the prospect of *retaliation* relevant to the morality of it?)

Blackmail: A Preliminary Inquiry

Jeffrie G. Murphy

Of all the forms of crime, blackmailing is surely the most vicious, vile and villainous; it is even lower and more contemptible than cheating at cards.

J.K. Ferrier[1]

Introduction: Blackmail and Coercion

Most of us are inclined to believe that blackmail is clearly immoral (even a particularly sleazy kind of immorality) and are thus quite content that it be criminalized.[2] Justifying this belief, however, turns out to be more of a problem than it might at first seem. In particular, it is difficult if not impossible to distinguish cases of blackmail (which we prohibit) from other hard economic transactions (which, even if we do not totally approve to them, we do not criminalize).

Consider a paradigm blackmail case: I have innocently acquired some nonobscene pictures of you (a respected person and family man) on the beach in Acapulco with your mistress.[3] I approach you and inform you that I shall circulate these photos among your friends and family members (or have them published in *National Enquirer* where they will become available to your friends and family) unless you pay me the sum of $500.

Why is this proposal wrong? Why should it be criminalized? One's initial inclination is to suggest the following: This is just a kind of *stickup*, and that is why it must be criminalized.[4] Taking money through threats is *coercion*, and coercion of one citizen by another is the very thing which it is the criminal law's primary job to prevent.

Tempting as this suggestion is, it is too quick. For the paradigm coercion case is the following: "Give me your money or I will shoot you." What is central here is that I am proposing to do to

556

you *something which I have no right to do* (I have no right to shoot you). As Vinit Haksar has suggested, coercive threats are normally ones in which the threatener's unilateral plan of action (what he proposes to do if the demanded performance is not forthcoming) is morally impermissible.[5] And this does indeed work for our gunman case. But does it work for the blackmailer? Not obviously. It is certainly not illegal for me to circulate the pictures in question (or to sell them to a scandal magazine); and, even if circulating them does not seem very morally decent, it does not seem immoral to any greater degree than portions of other economic transactions which our system permits—e.g., "I know that your son, whom you love more than anything else in the world, is dying of leukemia. I also know two other things: (1) that he is a great baseball fan who would love to have a baseball autographed by Babe Ruth to cheer him during his final days and (2) that $6000 is all the money you have in the world. Now I happen to own the last such baseball available in the world, and I will make you a proposition—namely, to sell you this baseball for $6000."

The above proposal is not merely immoral; it is so lacking in even minimal decency that it revolts the conscience.[6] But, in a system such as ours, this proposal is *tolerated*—as are countless others like it.[7] Why, then, not tolerate blackmail? The blackmailer normally does not put any greater psychological pressure on his victim than that described above, nor does he take any more of an unfair advantage of the vulnerability of the person who desparately wants what he has to offer.[8] If the baseball is mine. I have the right to sell if for whatever I want. I have the legal right to do many things which are not very nice. Why, then, cannot I reason comparably about the incriminating pictures? Why do I not have a comparable right in the blackmail case?

It is the question which produces what Glanville Williams has identified as the paradox of blackmail—where "two things that taken separately are moral and legal whites together make a moral and legal black."[9] It is permissible to circulate the photographs. It is permissible to ask you for money for the photographs. What is *not* permissible (and thus what becomes blackmail) is to conjoin these two activities:

> Although D has a liberty to demand money and a liberty to speak the truth concerning others, and even to threaten to speak the truth, he is not at liberty to demand money under threat of speaking the

truth. The position would be the same even if [the demanded sum of money] were in fact owing to D: the threat of publicity would not be a proper mode of collecting the debt.[10]

To return to the pictures: I may circulate them or not as I choose. I may threaten to circulate them. I may sell them to you (or someone else) or not as I choose. What I may *not* do is inform you that I will circulate them unless you buy them from me. Is this coherent?

In this paper I hope to make a *start* (and nothing but a start) toward sorting out the problems involved in answering this difficult question. These problems have a profundity not immediately obvious when the topic of blackmail is first raised, for they force us to look at the morality of a whole range of economic transactions. Such an examination will have an impact on some deep ideological divisions within social philosophy—e.g., on the conflict between libertarians (who argue that any economic transaction between consenting adults, including blackmail, should be allowed[11]) and Marxists (who argue that all capitalistic economic transactions should, because they are really blackmail, be prohibited[12]). There is a sense, therefore, in which libertarians and Marxists agree on something quite basic—namely, the claim that the blackmail transaction is a nondeviant transaction within a capitalistic economic system. The libertarian says: "Blackmail is just another capitalistic tranaction, so leave it alone." The Marxist says: "Capitalistic economic transactions are all blackmail, so down with the lot of them." And the liberal (always the great moderate compromiser) says something like the following: "Blackmail can be distinguished in principle from these other economic transactions and thus can properly be prohibited even when the others are allowed." The main task of this paper is to examine claims of this latter sort, to see if a principled distinction (or indeed any interesting distinction) can really be made out. The blackmailer, of course, *threatens*. But not all threats are wrong—e.g., "Start coming to work on time on I will fire you" has an acceptability which "Sleep with me or I will fire you" normally lacks.[13] Thus is the concept of an *illegitimate threat* (to expose) which must be explicated if we are to gain illumination on the topic of blackmail. It is to this worry that I shall now pass.

Blackmail and Economics

Robert Nozick has suggested that we can identify what is particularly unacceptable about blackmail in economic terms—of the concept of a *productive economic exchange*.[14] Put very informally, a productive economic exchange between A and B occurs when and only when neither A nor B would have been better off if *the other person had had nothing whatever to do with him or had never existed at all*. On this model, argues Nozick, blackmail should be prohibited because it is an *un*productive economic exchange—it being the case that, if you are being blackmailed by me, you would be better off if I did not even exist.[15]

Nozick's suggestion is interesting, but I think it fails to work for three reasons: (1) It is not obvious on its face (and thus requires argument) that unproductive economic exchanges are *immoral*. Nozick gives no such argument, and I am sceptical that one can be given. (2) Even if such exchanges are immoral or open to criticism on other grounds, it does not follow from this alone that they should be *criminalized* or prohibited. If we feel we must do *something*, why not simply void such contracts as "unconscionable" or even—as with libel and slander—allow suit for damages in tort?[16] (3) Not all blackmail exchanges are unproductive in Nozick's sense. For example: I own, publish, and edit a scandal magazine. Compromising pictures of you come to my desk. I am all set to have them published, but then I would get from increased revenue from circulation. So I go to you and make you the following offer: "I will sell you these pictures for $500." Let us suppose that you are fairly wealthy and that a loss of $500, though a sacrifice, is no grave hardship—that, indeed, as you assess the situation (exposure or loss of $500) you are *glad* to have the chance to buy them for this price. Given this, are you not better off that the world contains me (a blackmailer) than you would be if instead it contained an honorable publisher who, in my place, would simply publish the pictures he has every right to publish? Of course, you may be very sorry that the world contains the *whole situation* which makes blackmail possible (your past indiscretion, that pictures were taken of it, that the pictures now have a chance of becoming public, etc.); but this generalized regret is, of course, present in many tolerated economic transactions—e.g., a high price charged for a drug to control a disease you would prefer not to have.[17]

It thus looks as though Nozick has not given us the principle we were looking for. Indeed, Nozick's suggestion and the reasons why it fails bring to light another perplexing question about blackmail: Who is its *victim*? Who is actually being *protected* by the laws which criminalize it? Since in many cases the person being blackmailed is willing to pay the asked price, and far prefers paying the price to having the blackmailer expose him (which, remember, he has a right to do), the "victim" may well be upset rather than grateful if his blackmailer is successfully prevented from offering him his services—a state of affairs one tends not to find when such crimes as rape and robbery are prevented.

Blackmail and Privacy

At this point someone might well suggest that so far the entire point of condemning and preventing blackmail has been missed, blackmail is not just immoral; it is immoral in a particularly sleazy and disgusting way—a way which cannot be captured by a purely economic analysis. Indeed, the whole problem here (it might be argued) is viewing the issue in economic terms in the first place.[18] Here we are dealing with an issue of *privacy* (a sacred right of persons); and what is wrong with blackmail is that it involves turning a portion of a person's life into an economic commodity— something which a person has a right to do only with his own life (e.g., if he chooses to publish an autobiographical account of his sexual escapades). The person himself has a right to control which information about his private life shall become a public matter because, in a sense, he *owns* his own life.[19] Thus the blackmailer, by making into a commodity and trying to sell back to the victim something which is really his already (his life), is a rights-violator and his conduct should thus be criminalized. This is not because he is simply proposing an unjust economic transaction, but because he is economizing a part of life which he has no right to economize and (like the murderer, the rapist, the thief) is violating a right of his victim.

The above line of argument has a plausible ring to it; and, as I shall later argue, the protection of privacy does play a role in justifying the criminalization of blackmail. In the form just presented, however, the argument simply does not work. And the reason for this is quite simple: If our primary goal was indeed the protection of privacy, the blackmailer would not have the right to do what he threatens; for the publishing and broadcasting of private information would itself be illegal. But, as the open existence of such magazines as *National Enquirer* clearly demonstrates, it is *not*. Furthermore, I do not suspect that most persons pursuing the privacy argument on the blackmail issue really think it should be either. For, though they may be equally or even more concerned with the First Amendment rights of speech and press to publish the truth.[20] And if the economically big and powerful publisher (the press) gets to make money by trading in people's private lives, why deny this right to the blackmailer as small businessman? The blackmailer perhaps seems even more worthy of our protection than the press because he (unlike the press) gives the victim the chance to buy his way out of disgrace—a valued opportunity if the price is not too bad.

This, then, returns us to our original paradox: Since all the blackmailer threatens to do is something which he has the right to do, why should we prohibit him from making the threat and trying the threat to a demand for money—particularly since the victim, given the legally permitted alternative, is often happy to have the opportunity to respond to such a threat? Indeed, we can complicate the matter a bit more: Sometimes the blackmailer threatens to do that which he not only has a right to do but, in some sense, has a *duty* to do—e.g., "Pay me $500 or I shall reveal to the Internal Revenue Service that you lied on your income tax return last year (or shall report to the police the crime of which you are guilty)." Or consider this (said to Jones by a lawyer employed by Jones's wife): "Unless you settle out of court and agree to the divorce and a generous alimony settlement we shall have to go to court and charge adultery—a charge which we shall, of course, have to support with evidence (see enclosed pictures)."[21] I *should* (as a good citizen) report fraud to the Internal Revenue Service or crime to the police. I *should* (as a good lawyer) bring into the courtroom the best relevant evidence in support of my case. Why, then, do I become a criminal when, in a certain economic context, I threaten to do these things? The mist thickens.

Blackmail and Harm

At this point, someone might suggest that there is one obvious difference between all the blackmail cases cited and the case of the nasty seller of autographed baseballs—namely, that as a black-mailer I threaten *to do you harm;* whereas in my role as baseball merchant I threaten simply *to bring it about that you fail to receive a benefit.*[22] But this suggestion will be helpful only to the extent that we can answer two questions: (1) Can the distinction between *harming* and *nonbenefiting* be made clear? (2) Will the resulting distinction make any interesting *moral* or *legal* difference?

I believe that the answer to both of the above questions is *No.* The person who holds that some simple version of a harm/not-benefit distinction alone will distinguish blackmail (prohibted) from refusing to sell the baseball at any but an unfair price (al-lowed) is probably assuming some principle of the following sort: One never has a right to harm; and one always (or almost always) has a right to withhold benefits.[23] But, on at least one common-sense notion of "harm," this principle is unacceptable. I sometimes have a right to harm you (shoot you because you are attempting to kill me) and sometimes not (shoot you for sport). I sometimes have a right to bring it about that a benefit is withheld from you (reveal that the scientific work which got you a Nobel Price nom-ination was plagiarized from me) and sometimes not (falsify sales records so that you do not get the "Salesperson of the Month" award). Thus one begins to wonder how the distinction, even if it is granted, can be put to any morally or legally useful work on the issue of blackmail.

Let us look at this matter a bit more closely: What is a harm and how does it differ from a withheld benefit? Informally, a harm may be understood as anything which brings a person below his normal baseline and a benefit as anything which brings a persons above his normal baseline.[24] And, as the above discussion shows, it will sometimes be permissible to bring about either, sometimes not. The only problem with this is that there is some tendency (with which I sympathize) to describe Smith as *harmed* by Jones (even if all Jones did was to act or omit to do something with the result that Smith failed to rise above his baseline) when Smith has a *right* to the rise in question. Thus my destroying your bonus money before it reaches you is a harm in the way that my destroying all the flowers on my property which you so enjoy looking at is not. Of course, if this is correct, then it seems that the harm/ not-benefit distinction cannot yield any moral conclusions (e.g., that blackmail is wrong in a way that offering to sell the baseball is not), because a moral concept (*a right*) is required for the explication of the concept of harm itself. Thus it is the concept (*a right*) which must be at the center of attention.

Consider this example: I know that a certain piece of information would, if it came to the attention of the other members of the committee, deprive you of the title "Miss Congeniality" which (along with its financial benefits) you have been coveting. I threaten to inform the other members unless you pay me $500 or provide me with some functional equivalent. Surely my threat is to attempt to make it the case that a certain benefit does not come your way. But this way of describing the case seems to have no bearing on whether we want to call it blackmail or condemn it morally and legally. These issues will be a function of such questions as the following: Do you have a *right* to the title (e.g., on the basis of your satisfaction of certain relevant criteria)? Do I have a *right* to convey the information (e.g., is this a legitimate part of my institutional role)? These are important questions—*not* questions of the form "Is this a harming or a not-benefiting?"

To return to our earlier cases: Neither you nor your son have a right to the baseball I own; and thus, in withholding it from your child, I violate no rights (and thus do no harm in the morally loaded sense). Is the situation any different in the blackmail case? I think not. I am threatening to harm your reputation (or, perhaps, threatening to withhold from you the benefits of a good reputation if you are just on the verge of earning one) by telling the truth.[25] But *do you have a right to a good reputation?* (Note that only if the answer is *Yes* will the parallel between this and the baseball case break down). I think that the answer is No, and I would defend this answer with two reasons? (1) It is unclear to me how you can have a right to the reputation of being a person of type X if in fact you have performed acts of type Y where Y acts are inconsistent with being an X person.[26] (To what extent does the philanderer *deserve* or have a *right* to a reputation as a loyal husband?) (2) As brought out in the earlier discussion, the fact that (e.g.) the press may reveal that you have performed acts of type Y shows that your right to a good reputation is, at most, a fairly weak right. And if the press may trade in such matters, then why not the blackmailer?

We come, then, to the end of yet another attempt at finding some simple principle which distinguishes blackmail from hard but permitted economic transactions. (The others, you will recall, were the following distinctions: (1) coerced versus uncoerced choices, (2) productive versus unproductive economic exchanges, and (3) economic commodities versus privacy as a noneconomic right.) The one just considered, (4), is a distinction between harming and not-benefiting. It too, alas, does not work.

The above failures suggest (but do not, of course, prove) that *no* simple principle exists which will draw the distinction in question in a philosophically satisfying way. This in turn suggests that either (a) contrary to initial intuitions, no distinction is worth drawing at all or (b) the distinction is going to require a theoretical account of inelegant complexity—i.e., will not be drawable on the basis of some intrinsic distinguishing feature present in blackmail but not in the hard but tolerated cases.

In what follows, I shall begin an exploration of the possibilities offered by (b). I hate abandoning the search for an intrinsic distinguishing feature, because the absence of such a feature makes it much more unlikely that we will be able to rely here on the kind of deontological moral principles of which I am fond. We might instead have to rely here on teleological considerations of social policy—e.g., considerations of *utility* (I am drawing on Ronald Dworkin's distinction between principles and policies—the former representing an individualized concern with right-relevant properties of persons or actions, the latter representing an aggregate concern with the pursuit of desirable social goals.[27]) Most of us believe that we do not need to consider aggregate social utility before we can determine for certain that "Give me your money or I will shoot you" is intolerable whereas "Give me your money (a fair amount) or I will not sell you my automobile" is acceptable. For here there *is* an intrinsic difference of principle—i.e., the former involves a threat to do something I have no right to do, whereas the latter does not.[28] But we have found nothing comparable for our blackmail problem; and so (at least until my imagination comes back in from its wildcat strike) it will be exploring whether reasons of social policy, rather than pure principle, provide plausible grounds for criminalizing blackmail.

Blackmail and Social Policy

As a prelude to an exploration of policy considerations, let me first make clear certain assumptions about the morality of the criminal law. The first is that immorality should be a necessary condition for criminalization but not a sufficient condition.[29] The second is that utilitarian considerations, though unsatisfactory in explicating the concept of immorality, are a reasonable basis on which to answer the question "Which of all immoral action should be criminalized?[30] In brief and oversimplified terms, I am suggesting this: Immorality alone is not a reasonable basis for criminalization. Disutility alone is not a reasonable basis for criminalization. But immorality *plus* disutility *is* a reasonable basis for criminalization.

The application of this pattern of thought to our present problem should be obvious: We could grant that blackmail and hard economic transactions of the kind described are both intrinsically immoral (and immoral for the same reason—e.g., taking an unfair advantage of the victim's vulnerability) and still consistently advocate criminalization for the former but not for the latter. This can be done if we mount an argument that social utility is on balance served by prohibiting blackmail but by allowing transactions of the latter sort. We might, for example, argue that criminalizing blackmail would only deprive people of incentives it would be desirable for them not to have in the first place; whereas criminalizing economic transactions of the baseball kind might deprive people of socially useful incentives.

Let us examine how one such argument (to me a very plausible one[31]) might be developed: Suppose that I am a non-public person—i.e., I have no fame or notoriety (I am not a public figure) and I hold no governmental office (I am not a public official).[32] As it currently stands, *there is no significant economic market in information about my private life*. That this is so is of some disadvantage to me (I can interest no publisher in my memoirs, for example) but it also carries with it considerable benefit—namely, *it is currently in nobody's economic interest to invade my privacy in an attempt to find out secret details of my life*. But what if blackmail were decriminalized? If this happened, then there would suddenly be an economic incentive for such invasions. For now there would be a potential market for secret information about myself: I might be willing to buy it in order to avoid some undesired results of exposure. In short: There is little or no social value in having private information about me or people like me come to light. There is considerable social value in a policy which restrains individuals who might be tempted to invade the privacy of people such as myself.[33] Given this, it would seem to be a reasonable social policy to prohibit blackmail and thus remove any economic incentives for invading the privacy of nonpublic persons. Criminalization would also thwart (if not remove) certain unwholesome but noneconomic incentives for privacy invasion—e.g., spite and jealousy—which can be potent forces in the lives of even non-public persons.

When we move to public persons, however, the problems become much more complex for two reasons: (1) There already is an economic market for information about the private lives of such persons; and thus there already are strong incentives here for privacy invasion. (No sane person would invade my privacy in order to get pictures to sell to *National Enquirer*, because the magazine would not buy them. Jackie Onassis, however, is not so fortunate.) Thus we cannot argue that it is justified to criminalize the blackmail of such persons in order to prevent the development of a market in their privacy. (2) With respect to at least some public persons (public officials especially) it is perhaps socially desirable that individuals (whom we now call "investigative reporters") have some incentive to snoop into their lives. Such snooping sometimes results in citizens learning things that, though embarrassing to the individual involved, are not really relevant to his performance as a public official.[34] But it could be argued that, on balance, the cost may be worth bearing in order that we may derive the relevant information that a policy of snooping reveals. The officials in question may not even, in justice, have too great a complaint here—it not being implausible to argue that this is a burden they take on in return for such benefits as the power that comes from enjoying public trust, immunity from certain lawsuits, etc.[35]

How are we to respond to such complexities? For the present, I shall content myself simply with making a couple of tentative suggestions: (1) With respect to public figures, where there is already an economic market for private inforation about their lives, a person who has that information should be allowed to offer "first refusal" to such a figure and not be charged with blackmail so long as he asks no more than the going market value.[36] To deter this kind of transaction is to protect no one and is to place an unfair burden on the seller of the information should he have some concern for the welfare of the victim—i.e., if he cannot offer the information to the victim for purchase, then the only way for him to protect the victim is to sustain an economic loss in so doing. If one really wants to criminalize even this as blackmail, then it does seem to me that—in consistency—one ought also to seek the prohibition of the wider market (e.g., the ban of such magazines as *National Enquirer*). If one is reluctant to seek such a ban (because, perhaps, of some very real worries about First Amendment matters[37]) then one should, I think, also be willing to tolerate the "market price only blackmailer." (2) Where public officials are concerned (and perhaps in other cases also), it can plausibly be argued that criminalization of blackmail of them is more to protect *our interests as citizens* than it is to protect them as victims. If someone discovers that Senator Jackass is keeping his mistress on the public payroll, then *we* (as citizens) are ill-served if the person who has that information lets the Senator buy his silence concerning it.

We may now summarize the upshot of the foregoing discussion: For reasons of social policy of the kind outlined, there are good reasons for criminalizing blackmail of the private person (we do not want to provide incentives for privacy invasion); good reasons for criminalizing some blackmail of public figures (we do not want to provide incentives for any privacy invasions over and above those we must reluctantly grant to a free press—and thus we will not allow the blackmailer to sell information to the victim for an amount in excess of what the press is willing to pay); and, finally, good reasons for not allowing the blackmail of a public official (we do not wish to provide extra incentives or opportunities for such officials to hide from the public information which the public in some sense has a right to have). These final considerations, by the way, also explain why we will not allow blackmail where the threat is to do something that a person not only has a right to do but *should* do—e.g., report crime to the police. We do not want to provide incentives or opportunities for persons to shield crime from the proper authorities. We do not want to provide a person with an incentive for *not* doing his duty.

None of the above reasons of policy apply to hard economic

transactions of the kind depicted in the earlier baseball example. For consider the following two points: (1) Society has an interest in limiting privacy invasions to those which must be tolerated in order to maintain a free press. We think that there is something intrinsically wrong about turning the details of a person's life into economic commodities, and thus we allow it *reluctantly* as the lesser of two evils (the greater evil would be to chill the press).[38] But nothing comparable is the case with the baseball example— e.g., we do not find turning baseballs into economic commodities something which is in itself objectionable, something to be tolerated only if strong reasons demand it. (2) We could inhibit transactions in privacy without thereby inhibiting economic life and bargaining in general. For we simply take substantive categories (e.g., persons) and rule those categories out of the economic domain in a clear way—e.g., because we have a rule of the form "you cannot sell people," we do not thereby inhibit the rest of economic life. The person who finds that he cannot sell his sister Brünnhilde into slavery is not thereby given so unclear a warning that his incentive to trade in other commodities (e.g., spears and shields) is thereby inhibited. So too with private information. One can imagine ways of taking it (at least partially) out of the economic domain which would not have a general inhibitory effect. For example: There is no reason to suppose that the command "You cannot sell private information about Brünnhilde's sex life" will produce economic paralysis in an eager entrepreneur.[39]

This way of proceeding, however, does not work for our other transaction. For what we are to say here? Do we say "You cannot sell baseballs" or "You cannot ask too much for a baseball" or "You must be generous when pricing baseballs (or anything else?) to a father who wants one for his sick child" or what?[40] The kind of worries which such weird and vague criminal restrictions would introduce into economic life might well inhibit those general incentives which are, for better or worse, the lifeblood of a capitalistic economy.

I am sure that there are many other policy considerations which would be worth mentioning on the blackmail question, but at present I can think of only one more: Blackmail and the privacy invasions it invites tend to lead to harassment that is *unending* in nature. Unlike other economic transactions, blackmail transactions often put the victim in a position where he is never really sure if he has finally bought the commodity or service—i.e., the silence, the freedom from exposure.[41] The blackmailer is like the person who sells you shoes for an agreed price of $20, sneaks them out of your closet every week or so, and then sells them back to you (perhaps for $30 and then $40) again, and again, and again—endlessly.[42] Society might well want to inhibit transactions of this potentially oppressive character. (Of course, if this were the *only* reason for criminalizing blackmail, then we should allow each blackmailer one offer without penalty—criminalizing only repetition.)

Conclusion

What I have said about blackmail has been in many respects extremely tentative—as my subtitle "A Preliminary Inquiry" should suggest. I am still in the midst of thinking about the many issues involved with this topic, and thus I am much more confident in my account of what does *not* work than I am that I have explored all relevant possibilities or that my positive suggestions are worthwhile. In the future I hope to write at much greater length on the topic of *threats* (including threats to reputation) and shall consider, in addition to blackmail, the related topics of bribery, non-reputational extortion, duress, slander and libel.[43] The present essay simply breaks the ground on one aspect of this ongoing concern; and my hope for it is that, at the very least, it will provoke responses from which I (and others interested in the topic) can benefit. Of course, it is possible that someone might want to publish a response which would be a devastating and disrespectful refutation of everything I have to say. I think it is only fair that such persons should be warned that I possess a large collection of incriminating pictures of a great many members of the philosophical and legal professions.[44]

NOTES

1. Formerly Detective-Inspector, Scotland Yard. The quotation is from his *Crooks and Crime: Describing the Methods of Criminals From the Area Sneak to The Professional Card Sharper, Forger or Murderer and The Various*

Ways in which They are Circumvented and Captured (London: Seeley, Service, 1928). This and many other gems are cited in Mike Hepworth's *Blackmail: Publicity and Secrecy in Everyday Life* (London: Routledge and Kegan Paul, 1975). Hepworth's book is an anecdotal and sociological account of the history of blackmail and blackmail legislation (especially in England) which reveals—as the quotation from Ferrier illustrates—that the offense was originally perceived in class terms: the crime of a lower order person against a gentleman. Hepworth also points out how the rise of blackmail and the rise of journalism went hand in hand.

2. *Extortion* (obtaining or attempting to obtain property through threats or menaces) and *blackmail* are legally the same. Frequently in ordinary language, however, the term "blackmail" is reserved for cases where the extortionate threat is the threat to *expose*, to reveal a secret with the intent to impair reputation. In this paper the term will also be so limited—"blackmail" herein being equivalent to "reputational extortion." On extortion generally, see proposed Federal Criminal Code, S.1437, 95th Cong., 2d Sess. (1978).

3. I introduce the qualifications of innocent acquisition and non-obscenity to at this point bracket off pure blackmail from other worries. If your privacy was violated in order for me to obtain the pictures, for example, you have a complaint against me quite independent of the blackmail question. So let us suppose some scenario of this kind: a professional photographer took the pictures at your request, you forgot to pay him before you left the city, he held the pictures for two weeks and then threw them away, they fell out of the garbage truck on the way to the dump, and then I found them and recognized you.

4. See Hepworth *supra*, n. 1, p. 12, for a discussion of the prevalence of this view during the early days of blackmail legislation.

5. Vinit Haksar, "Coercive Proposals," *Political Theory*. (February, 1976): 65–79.

6. For a discussion of the relationships between moral decency and rights (and a clarification of the distinctive between Minimally Decent Samaritans, Good Samaritans, Very Good Samaritans, and Splendid Samaritans), see Judith Thomson's "In Defense of Abortion," *Philosophy and Public Affairs*, vol. 1, no. 1 (1971): pp. 47–66. As Thomson points out, I can be highly morally lacking even in cases where I violate no one's rights. For example: I am sitting in a lounge chair next to a swimming pool. A child (not mine) is drowning in the pool a few inches from where I am sitting. I notice him and realize that all I would have to do to save him is put down my drink, reach down, grab him by the trunks, and pull him out (he is so light I could do it with one hand without even getting out of my seat). If I do not save him I violate no rights (strangers do not have a right to be saved by me) but would still reveal myself as a piece of moral slime properly to be shunned by all decent people.

7. By "tolerated" here I mean "not criminalized." We may well dis-

approve of such transactions and even void, on moral grounds, such contracts. We do not, however, jail a person simply for offering such a contract as we do the person who offers the blackmail contract.

8. Haksar, *supra* n5, argues that an offer is coercive if it involves taking an unfair advantage of the vulnerability of the person to whom the offer is made. My question is this: why criminalize some coercive offers and not others?

9. Glanville Williams, "Blackmail," *The Criminal Law Review* (1954), p. 163.

10. *Ibid*. Should the reasonable belief that what the blackmailer demands is rightfully *owed* to him be a defense? According to the proposed Federal Criminal Code (*supra* note 2) and the Model Penal Code (1962) the answer is *Yes*. I, however, have grave doubts about this "we may take the law into our own hands" defense. See *United States v. Pignatelli*, 125 F.2d 643 (2d Cir.), *cert. denied*, 316 U.S. 680 (1942). In that case Judge Augustus Hand said: "Threats to damage another's reputation are no proper means for determining a controversy. It may be adjusted either by suit or by compromise but settlement must not be affected by using defamation as a club."

11. "Blackmail would not be illegal in the free society. For blackmail is the receipt of money in exchange for the service of not publicizing certain information about the other person. No violence or threat of violence to person or property is involved." Murray N. Rothbard, *Man, Economy, and State*, Vol. I, p. 443, n. 49 (Princeton, D. Van Nostrand 1962).

12. Also Proudhon's famous claim that "All private property is a form of theft" is in part based on the blackmail analogy.

13. Daniel Lyons has spoken of such issues in terms of what he calls a *germaneness* condition. See his "Welcome Threats and Coercive Offers," *Philosophy*, October 1975, pp. 425–36.

14. Robert Nozick, *Anarchy, State and Utopia* (New York: Basic Books, 1974), pp. 84ff.

15. Nozick gives his analysis as a "rough" *definition* of a productive economic exchange, then suggests that he has only given a necessary condition, and finally suggests that getting the matter just right "is not worth the effort it would require" (p. 85 note). I hope I am being fair to him.

16. Let me remind the reader again: the issue here is *criminalizing* blackmail. I am willing to grant, for purposes of this paper, that we may legitimately deplore blackmail and attempt to do *something* to blunt its consequences. My question here is whether we should take the extreme step of criminalization. (All steps including criminalization will, of course, be rather inefficacious because the victim, in order to use the legal process, will have to run a high risk of the very thing he most fears: exposure.)

17. It is, of course, important here that I not be *responsible* for your unhappy situation—e.g., not the one who set you up with the girl,

took the pictures, etc., or—in the other case—intentionally or negligently gave you the disease.

18. For a general discussion of the dangers lurking in economic analysis, see Robert Paul Wolff's "Robert Nozick's Derivation of the Minimal State," *Arizona Law Review*, Vol. 19, No. 1, 1978, pp. 7–30. As Wolff points out, when some things are assigned a price they cease to be the things they were—e.g., if my honor has a price, I simply have no honor.

19. "You are not allowed to make a person buy his reputation. . . . The criminality of blackmail represents a social judgment that one may not manipulate as an income producing asset knowledge about another person's past; you may not sell to that person forbearance to use your knowledge of his guilt." H.V. Ball and L.M. Friedman, "The Use of Criminal Sanctions in the Enforcement of Economic Legislation: A Sociological View," *Stanford Law Review*, vol. 17, 1965. See also Warren and Brandeis, "The Right of Privacy," 4 *Harvard Law Review*, 1890.

20. The law of libel and slander is instructive to pursue in this regard. The classic case, of course, is *New York Times v. Sullivan* 376 U.S. 254. See also: *Curtis Publishing Co. v. Butts* 388 U.S. 130, *Rosenbloom v. Metromedia* 403 U.S. 29, and *Gertz v. Robert Welch* 418 U.S. 323.

21. This is very like *State v. Harrington* (128 Vt. 242, 260 A. 2d 692, 1969) in which an attorney was convicted of attempted extortion. This case and its implications for the legal profession are interestingly discussed in Joseph M. Livermore's "Lawyer Extortion," *Arizona Law Review*, Vol. 20, No. 2, 1979, pp. 403–12.

22. I can *deprive* you of a benefit or *withhold* a benefit from you. The latter expression suggests that the benefit is somehow mine to give. These (and other) complexities will simply be ignored in what follows.

23. "There is worked into our moral system a distinction between what we owe people in the form of aid and what we owe them in the way of noninterference." Philippa Foot, "Abortion and the Doctrine of the Double Effect," *Oxford Review* (1967). But what is aid and what is noninterference?

24. Let it not be thought that I am naive enough to believe that the concept of a "normal baseline" will prove easy to explicate.

25. Remember that blackmail is not libel or slander. What the blackmailer proposes to tell is *true*.

26. There would, of course, be problems in making this precise. Does one lapse into performing a Y act make one permanently or totally a non-X person? Or does it take several or a pattern? This no doubt depends heavily on what Y and X are. One act of obstructing justice no doubt makes someone undeserving of the title of honorable judge, as one act of child murder makes one undeserving of the title of good father. But does one act of impulsive and regretted sexual infidelity make one undeserving of the title of loyal husband? I do not pretend to be sure about any of this.

27. Ronald Dworkin, *Taking Rights Seriously* (Cambridge: Harvard Uni-

versity Press, 1977). Index entries at p. 293 under heading "principles and policies."

28. In general, if it is wrong to do X it is wrong to threaten to do X. But there are exceptions. I may not kill you in order to stop your theft of my stereo equipment, but I may threaten to kill you. And suppose one believes it would be immoral to use atomic weapons. Does it follow that one must then (in consistency) believe that it is immoral to threaten their use? I am not sure. Since there are exceptions to the noted principle, might not some extortion cases be exceptions? This needs to be thought about some more.

29. The *legal moralist* is someone who believes that *all* immortality should be criminalized. This, I believe, would make the criminal law overbearingly intrusive into people's lives and is thus unacceptable. Making immorality merely a necessary condition, however, will not have this consequence.

30. The criminal law is, in part, a *technique* for social control. It is well suited for control of some immorality, but not for other immorality. Thus utilitarian considerations (considerations of good versus bad consequences) are surely highly relevant to a decision concerning its use.

31. In developing the following discussion, I have profited from conversations with Joseph M. Livermore.

32. These public/private distinctions have been held to be relevant in the law of libel and slander. See *supra* note 20.

33. Though some blackmailers (such as the one I initially described) are innocent of privacy invasions, many would not be. And one would hardly want to provide additional temptations here.

34. Sometimes, of course, it is hard to decide what is and what is not relevant. Is the official's sexual conduct relevant? Is his history of psychiatric visits? Is his alcohol use? And who should make the decision of relevance—the official himself or the press?

35. Again, of course, it is difficult to know where to draw the line here. The public official may legitimately be regarded as having given up certain rights to privacy which the nonpublic person enjoys, but surely even the most important of our public officials should enjoy *some* rights of privacy.

36. This concept of "market value" needs more work. In one sense, the market value of a commodity is not set until *all* bids for the commodity are in. But in this case I am suggesting that one bid (the victim's) be discounted in determining the market value of a piece of information. Is this restriction acceptable?

37. Typically, reputation is not regarded as so important a right or value that the state may restrain or "chill" free expression in advance (prior restraint) in order to protect it. Instead, the state allows after-the-fact remedies—e.g., suit for libel or slander.

38. See *supra* notes 20, 32, and 37.

39. The *plausible* argument for allowing a market in private inforation is that a certain amount of this must be tolerated in order to avoid

chilling a free press, *not* that such toleration is required to keep a capitalistic economy healthy.

40. Note the problem: the restrictions which are sufficiently specific (e.g., "Do not sell baseballs") do not get at what bothers us about the case; the restrictions which seem to get at what bothers us (e.g., "Don't overcharge the father of a sick child") are so vague and nebulous— so open to subjective interpretation—that they would surely chill commerce. (Also, as criminal statutes, they would no doubt be voided for being overbroad or vague.) Perhaps with more inventiveness than I have shown, one could draft a rule which would (a) be clear, (b) have no serious inhibiting power over mainstream economic transactions, and (c) focus on what indeed morally repels us about the transaction in question. The issue should be thought about some more.

41. In some cases (e.g., when one is buying negatives) one can *almost* be sure; but even here there are no real guarantees.

42. This, of course, is not *exactly* right. To speak the shoes out of your closet is an act no one has the *right* to perform; but here I am focusing, not on the rights involved, but on the radically *open-ended* nature of the blackmail transaction. The example, though artificial, does illustrate this. Some others: The mechanic, well-known to all of us, who always fouls up something a bit more expensive than the thing he is currently working on—the fouled object usually breaking down about two weeks later and requiring another and even more expensive visit (during which he does something else to continue the series). Also, there is the drug seller who offers cheap prices at first and then charges more and more as your dependency rises.

43. The blackmailer seems to exhibit two failings: he is a *coercer* (in some as yet unclear sense) and he is a threat to *reputation*. He thus cuts across several categories of moral and legal interest.

44. Many persons were kind enough to talk with me about the topic of blackmail, and those who do not see the influence of their conversation in the present preliminary study will surely see it in the longer work to follow. In particular, I want to thank the following: Joseph Cowan, Dan Dobbs, Robert M. Harnish, Ann Kerwin-Yokota, Keith Lehrer, Joseph Livermore, Ronald Milo, Judith Thomson, and David Wexler. I am particularly grateful to Ellen Canacakos for listening to and reading more of my thoughts on this topic than anyone should reasonably be expected to tolerate and for providing me with many hours of valuable discussion and commentary.

Study Questions

1. In a well-written essay, explain why you agree or disagree with Professor Murphy's views about the legitimacy of blackmail of public persons under the circumstances he describes?

2. To what extent do you think questions of social utility (i.e., consequentialist considerations) are relevant to the blackmail question?
   Could one, instead, argue that there are questions of intrinsic rights
   involved—e.g., the right to one's privacy, even *if* one is a "public
   person"?

Objectivity, Epistemics and an Ethic of Journalism

Anthony Serafini

In 1951—the thirteenth year of the Nieman Fellowship program for professional journalists at Harvard—Professsor Edward Walsh of the department of journalism at Fordham University surveyed the Fellows of that year for their views on education for journalists. The results were striking. Many of the finest journalists of the day had grave reservations about the value of any sort of extended formal education in journalism. Of those that did support such education, the majority appeared to believe that, at the very least, the education of a journalist ought to consist of heavy doses of liberal arts courses. Lou Lyons himself, the esteemed Curator of the Nieman program spoke as follows: "In general, I am for providing the maximum chance for studies of a general nature—history, literature, philosophy, economics, sociology, etc., and a minimum of time on techniques of journalism . . . My impression is that journalism programs are tending toward a greater concern for educational background and a lesser time for techniques and that this is, in most instances, good."

Dana Adams Schmidt of the *New York Times* responded by urging that ". . . the best preparation for journalism is a four-year liberal arts course followed by a postgraduate year at a school of journalism such as the one at Columbia. . . . I do not believe in four years, or even two years of undergraduate journalism courses. Journalism is not a body of knowledge like law or medicine; it is primarily a technique. And one year should be plenty of time to master the technique insofar as it can be mastered at school."

Hoke M. Norris of the *Winston-Salem Journal* echoes similar sentiments when he urges that, "I do think the liberal arts education is the best preparation for journalism. . . ."

Schmidt's opinion is perhaps a bit more extreme than most but his sense of the nature of journalism education still exists. Even today, the controversial Accrediting Council for the Association for Education in Journalism and Mass Communications embodies these skeptical philosophies in its stated requirement that no school of journalism or mass communications should devote more than one-quarter of its course work to "technical" training in, e.g., news reporting, editing, advertising and so forth. Failure to follows these guidelines has, in recent history, precipitated the flap at the Boston University program: they lost their accreditation and the controversy over this dramatic turn of fate is still sending shock waves through journalism schools throughout the nation.

Procedural and legal questions aside, the Boston University crisis does raise once again the doubts and fears of the Nieman Fellows of 36 years ago. If, indeed, journalism is not a body of knowledge, but a technique, then serious questions arise as to what, exactly, journalists should know. In the rest of this paper, I wish to analyze the role of philosophy in journalism education. I believe an argument can be made that philosophy has rather a special place in journalistic education.

Why? On the conceptual level, there are certain structural similarities between journalism and philosophy. In a sense, both are "meta" disciplines. While the above critics argue that journalism has no "content" of its own, is this not, in a way, also true of philosophy? Perhaps we all recall our freshman philosophy courses, where we were told that philosophy is "parasitic" on other disciplines—that philosophy takes as its subject matter, *other* fields of knowledge. Ergo, one has philosophy of religion, philosophy of science, philosophy of education, etc., etc.

Is not this much true of journalism? The "subject matter" of the journalists' activity is, precisely that which forms the content and subject matter of other fields of knowledge, as much is the case with philosophy. There are, e.g., science journalists, whose job is to write crisp accurate prose about science—interpreting its results to the world of nonscientists at large. But science—that of which the science journalists write of—is not part of any mythic body of knowledge called "journalism." *Mutatis mutandis*, the same is true of the political journalist, whose livelihood is parasitic upon the subject-content of politics and political goings-on in the real world. Thus there is a natural, ontological fellowship between journalists and philosophers.

But there are other reasons why, in my judgment, a journalist should have more training in philosophy rather than in economics or history (without denying the importance of the latter). If philosophy has a practical, *raison* it is, arguably, critical, reasoned thought, the avoidance of logical fallacies and the construction of sound arguments as well as the drawing of sound inferences and the making of solid inductive leaps. Few, I think, would dispute the general principle—the role and importance of logic in everyday life.

Yet how much more important is it that journalists have sound training in logic, in order to avoid errors in reasoning that could destroy the credibility of a presidency or—in the worst case scenario—the world.[4] Nonetheless, I believe that the Norris position is right in what it asserts, but wrong in what it implies. For the present, let me make the following observations: first, it is quite true that journalism is not a "body of knowledge" in the sense that, say, history or chemistry is a "body of knowledge."[5] Chemistry consists of sets of law-like generalizations from experience, accumulations of observed data, results of empirical experimentation, extrapolations from known to unknown facts and so forth. History also, displays some of these qualities: history consists also of accumulations of data, hypotheses to explain the data, law-like generalizations under which may be subsumed further laws and further data and so forth.

Journalism, by contrast, displays none of this. (Of course, writings of journalists are filled with facts and information taken from *other* fields—the fields that journalists write about—but that information is the property of the other subject matter.)

Put differently, the journalist's activity is also a "meta" activity (though not in precisely the same sense that philsophy is): it, too, takes as its subject matter, the ideas and concepts of *other* fields. True, there is a difference in that philosophy's job is not (or not merely) to act as a conduit for information, but to clarify fundamental assumptions (Does God exist? Is matter real?) about other disciplines.

Even so, daring to press the analogy further, it could be argued that journalism too, in its own way, deals with "fundamentals." The journalist's way of dealing with "fundamental assumption" consists in the probing, interviewing (yes, even intimidating) of politicians, scientists, tyrants and butchers in dogged pursuit of the truth (Who *really* ordered such-and-such a raid, or arms deal, or political ouster: who *really* runs U.S. foreign affairs?).

Thus it seems, that since both fields are interpreters, so to speak, of the work of other people in other fields, it is logical to assume that the sort of understanding and concerns a philosopher must have may well be similar to the sort of understanding and skills a journalist should have. In a word, philosophy, I am arguing, is the best and closest "model" for journalism.

Still, these comments are quite general and, perhaps, "protected" from serious controversy precisely because of this generality. For that reason, I would like to point out three more specific ways in which journalism would benefit from the study of philosophy.

According to most historical critics, as well as virtually all contemporary practioners, the job of journalism is merely to "state facts," to convey information from one arena to another—from, e.g, the most private corridors of governmental bureaucracy, to the most public street corners of every village and town—without the intrusion of any of the journalist's personal biases, whims, caprice or prejudices. This, of course, is the much-discussed problem of "objectivity" in journalism.

Yet, when I had the opportunity of teaching journalistic ethics for the first time at the University of Massachusetts journalism department in 1982, I was staggered by how unaware most academic journalists were of the vast literature on "objectivity" written by philosophers. In all the literature I covered in preparation for a course, there occurred not a single mention, for example, of Israel Scheffler's classic *Science and Subjectivity*.

By contrast, the reams of *journalist-authored* literature on the topic leaned toward the naive and the simplistic. Most articles leaned toward an apparently tempting as well as confessional/self-therapeutic conclusion that journalistic "objectivity" is impossible anyway, so why pretend to it? A natural conclusion of course, especially since it tends to exonerate journalists from responsibility when grossly *un*objective pieces find their way to print.

In fact, had journalists been aware of the vast amount of work already done on objectivity [where the journalistic version of the problem is merely a special case], they might have realized that the tempting above-mentioned conclusion is still very much up in the air from a philosopher's perspective.[2]

My purpose in this paper is not to argue for or against such conclusions: they may, in the long run, even be correct. The point, however, is that this is an instance of the inefficiency of reflecting about philosophical matters in ignorance of the literature. (A special case of the *general* problem of lack of communication between academic disciplines.) What most journalists do not appreciate, regarding this vexing question of "objectivity," is: a) the problem is not peculiar to journalism and b) a vast literature on it, such as Israel Scheffler's writings, exists and stretches back for centuries. How profitable could journalists' investigations of the concept of objectivity (as applied to journalism) be, if he or she has to constantly reinvent the wheel?

What I found were journalists exploring a lot of dead ends, propounding arguments that philosophers had dismissed years earlier, and so forth. I also found that some few journalists had done some innovative and original work. But, again, the enterprise as a whole is riddled with inefficiency. If philosophers have already done considerable spade work on objectivity, why should journalists not take advantage of it?

More specifically, most journalists appeared not to have even heard of, say, the Heisenberg uncertainty principle, with its rather obvious implications for the observer as intruder or interferer with the observation process.[6] Is the uncertainty principle merely a theoretical concern at the level of day-to-day life, important only at the subatomic level? Or does it have a macroscopic counterpart which "infects" the macroscopic observations of the journalist, making it impossible for the journalist to report on a phenomenon without, in some way, also becoming part of it (Can one "merely" broadcast a hostage crisis without *ipso facto* becoming part of it?).

Then too, there are epistemological problems critically important for, but not unique to journalism. Philosophers have long concerned themselves with such classic epistemological questions as the nature, definition and limits of human knowledge. Yet it is difficult to imagine any human activity where this problem is more acute or of greater urgency than journalism. The importance of the issues for journalism can be seen merely by surveying some classic epistemological problems and seeing how they apply to journalism.

In the *Thaetetus*, the question is raised as to what, precisely, are the conditions under which a person can be said to KNOW that a proposition, *p*, is true. As Chisholm recasts this scheme, S can be said to know that p is true if and only if: p is true, S believes p, and S has "adequate evidence"[3] that p is true. As we will see shortly, there is reason to hold that the concept of p is true. As we will see shortly, the concept of "adequate evidence" very likely varies from one communication medium to another (magazines vs. daily papers, e.g.).

Related to this are a number of other epistemological problems, such as the alleged "incorrigibility" of physical object assertions. Can we ever be absolutely certain that any given assertion about the physical universe is true? Austin, e.g., in *Sense and Sensibilia*, argues that incorrigibility is an unattainable chimera, while philosophers like Norman Malcolm argue that incorrigibility is possible with respect to physical object assertions.

Naturally, the examples philosophers typically pick to discuss epistemic problem lack a certain urgency. Austin talks about the concept of evidence where claims are made about the presence or absence of pigs,[7] while Malcolm discusses inkwells on desks in front of him.[8] This, of course, is sound enough, as such philosophers are concerned to establish certain general truths about knowledge, and examples picked from anything but "ordinary" situations could distract readers from the analysis.

Yet very similar questions can be raised as to the nature, definition of, and epistemic criteria of knowledge in the supercharged, critical situations that journalists often must deal with—and how much the more important is it to establish epistemic criteria in such situations? Knowing the alleged fragility of even the most ordinary claims to knowledge, it is just conceivable that journalists would pause a bit when confronted with informants swearing with "absolute certainty" that such and such happened or so-and-so killed someone. As philosophy professor Odell and journalism professor Merrill, suggest, ". . . when one claims, as journalists must constantly do, that some event took place in the past, on the grounds that certain witnesses are willing to attest to it, one's claim is nowhere neatly so well grounded."[9]

Referring again to the Chisholm/Protagoras schemata which has received so much attention over the years from philosophers, I would note that this too has applications to journalistic practice. Under what circumstances does a certain degree of evidence count as "adequate evidence" in journalism? And will this differ among the different media? Arguably, the evidential standards of newspaper journalism have to be lower than magazine journalism. For example: In a daily paper, the reporter has 24 hours to check on his facts, while in a magazine story he or she may have several months, thereby allowing for more time for fact-checking. Epistemic criteria for such issues remain uncharted territory: again, the importance of philosophy in journalistic training—as a vehicle for epistemic consciousness-raising at the very least—is immeasurable.

On still another front, one can note that the main tool of journalism is, after all, *language*. Would not journalism be better prepared to carry out its tasks if it had *some* inkling of how the variety of theoretical views in that branch of philosophy known as the philosophy of language could affect the day-to-day practice of journalism? To pick just one possibility: during my teaching at the University of Massachusetts, I noted that a favorite topic of discussion among academic journalists (usually, by the way, retired newpapermen) was the relative importance of "hard" journalism versus "soft" journalism—the importance of hard news vis.-à-vis. comic strips, crossword puzzles, advice columns and so forth. Most journalists again fall into the initially tempting view that, "of course" hard journalism is "more important" than soft.

But it has to be noted that this view depends on the parallel, yet far more fundamental question of the nature and purpose of language *per se*. As any student of philosophy knows, the early positivists tended to view the "fact-stating" function of language as having far greater value than emotive and other uses of language. Indeed, they viewed it as being virtually the only legitimate use of language. And this ancient prejudice is the mirror and philosophical underpinning for the "hard" journalism bias. In later years, of course, many positivists softened their views. This occurred in the later Wittgenstein. He softened his view and treated such "second-class" uses of language as joke-telling, story-telling, exclamations, etc., as equally valid members of the tree of language uses.

A deeper appreciation of the very nature and function of language itself would, inevitably, assist the journalist in thinking more carefully and deeply about the relative importance of "hard" news (analogue to "fact-stating" use of language) vis-à-vis "soft" news (analogue to emotive, illocutionary, satirical, etc., functions of language).

The ultimate question, of course, is what to do about this. One possible answer is to "inject" philosophy into the curriculum of schools and departments of journalism. On how or even whether to do this, opinion is still divided, and that schism manifests itself very obviously in the curricular structure of the assorted schools of journalism around the country. The Newhouse School at Syracuse University, for example, tends toward a more vocational "nuts & bolts" approach with a heavy emphasis on magazine journalism. The department of Journalistic Studies at the University of Massachusetts does, to its credit, try for a stronger, liberal arts orientation, with courses in Journalistic Ethics, Philosophical Issues in Language, Cultural Issues in Journalism and so forth.

Finally, of course, there are the many vexing problems in journalistic ethics. Since this is, in a way, the most obvious application of philosophy to journalism and journalistic practice, I leave it for last. Despite the rather obvious importance of journalistic ethics, given such scandals as the Myron Farber and Janet Cooke cases in recent years, the situation is even worse than it is with the problem of "objectivity." At least a literature on the latter, by philosophers, existed, though journalism is not tapping it, but philosophers aren't even *writing* all that much about issues in journalistic ethics.

It is surprising, really, how neglected this field is by philosophers and how much philosophizing in a vacuum—theorizing without being informed by history—has gone on by journalists. Outside of censorship, and occasional pieces on the ethics of advertising, there are still relatively few traditional problems in journalistic ethics that academic philosophers discuss. There is little on junketing, propaganda and the news, first versus Sixth Amendment conflicts, etc., etc.

Partly for that reason, partly because of a general lack of communication between the fields, other ethical issues in journalism are tackled by journalists in seat-of-the-pants fashion. Journalists struggle and flounder helplessly in the logico/linguistic/epistemic tangles of a free press vs. a fair trial, reporter conflicts of interest, responsibilities to sources, etc.

Unaware of and thus unable to draw nourishment from such

doctrines as act-and-rule utilitarianism, Nozickian ultraminimal states, deontological ethics, prescriptivism, Rawlsian decision procedures for ethics, etc., etc., academic journalists continue to drown in the intellectual debris of their own creation.

Primitive relativism ("each reporter has to work out this issue for himself") or facile applications of that great friend of the non-philosopher, "situation ethics," is almost a foregone conclusion.

What is to be done? I am arguing that philosophy should join hands with academic journalism, because the two fields are cousins anyway (because of the structural similarities and affinities between the two disciplines that I outlined earlier). At the very least, it would provide for more variety, efficiency and diversity in departments of journalism and, consequently, in the thought processes of the graduates of such schools.

Diversity, of course, is nothing new. This sort of variety is, or ought to be, a good thing. Certainly the power of the American academic tradition is plurality. Academic Philosophy itself, for example, varies enormously and, predictably, a retreat into the safety of some kind of schools now hire philosophers fulltime to handle, say, medical ethics as well as medical epistemology, journalism schools could do likewise. As a further development along these lines, new models of journalism education are possible. One conceivable model might require that those interested in careers in journalism take a normal, four-year liberal arts program, with at least a minor in Philosophy, possibly followed by four years as a working journalist. After that, and where feasible, their respective newspapers, magazines or stations could send them on a year's "sabbatical" to return, Nieman-style, to a major university to sit in on Philosophy courses of their choosing. They could also meet periodically in seminars with distinguished visiting philosophers and journalists to exchange ideas.

In short, there is a philosophic crisis in journalism today. Anyone witnessing such press immoralities as the Myron Farber case, the Janet Cooke fiasco, the serious charges of sensationalism, e.g., hostage crises, which, arguably, endanger lives, etc., etc., knows of the philosophical vacuum in journalism.

Perhaps John C. Merrill of Louisiana State University best sums up the problem in his book, *Philosophy and Journalism*; "Journalists, at least on the level of language, seem to be interested in such subjects as objectivity, truth, credibility, ethical behavior, journalistic quality, meaning, logical discourse, propaganda and the news, persuasion, journalistic ideology, journalistic rights and responsibilities, censorship, social purpose, and the impact of journalism . . . Philosophy should, in our view, be the foundation of modern journalism—an enterprise which, according to most of its practitioners, attempts to get at the truth and provide a reliable and interesting map of the territory of reality, or at least that part of reality that most impinges on our daily lives and needs."[5]

NOTES

1. Hutchins, Robert A., *A Free and Responsible Press*, University of Chicago Press, 1947, p. 11.
2. *Ibid.*, pp. 13–14.
3. *Ibid.*, p. 14.
4. See for example, Howard Kahane, *Logic and Contemporary Rhetoric*, Wadsworth Publishing Co., 1980. Strictly a logic text, this work nonetheless has far more examples of fallacious reasoning taken from the various news media, than from any other source.
5. Norris, not being a philosopher, did not consider the possibility that journalism, while it may not be a body of *empirical* knowledge, could possibly be a body of conceptual, a priori knowledge, much as philosophy or mathematics is.
6. Teachers of Philosophy are, of course, used to bright physics students handling in papers "vindicating" free will on the basis of this famous principle. Even so, the principle is not without some philosophical import. See, for example, Milic Capek's, *The Philosophical Import of Contemporary Physics*, Van Nostrand Company, 1961, especially, pp. 238–240 & 289–294.
7. Chisholm, Roderick, *Theory of Knowledge*, Prentice-Hall, 1970, p. 6.
8. Austin, J. L., *Sense and Sensibilia*, Oxford University Press, 1962, 110, and, generally all of chapter IX.
9. Malcolm, Norman, *Knowledge and Certainty*, Prentice-Hall, 1963, the essay "Direct Perception," ("The Verification Arguments," in the same volume is also relevant).
10. Merrill and Odell, *Philisophy and Journalism*, Longman Publishing Co., p. 55.
11. For a more detailed discussion of this theme, see my article, "Achievements, Illocutions and the Concept of Teaching," *Educational Theory*, spring, 1976.
12. In April of 1981, Janet Cooke of the *Washington Post* received a Pulitzer Prize for a poignant account of an eight-year-old heroin addict named "Jimmie." Days later, it was discovered that the story was a total fabrication. Miss Cooke returned the prize and resigned in disgrace.

13. I recently issued a call to philosophers for papers for an anthology on ethics that I'm under contract to put together: so far, none of the papers I've received has been in the area of communications ethics.
14. Merrill and Odell, PHILOSOPHY AND JOURNALISM, Longman Publishing Co., preface, p. IX.

Study Questions

1. Do you agree with Serafini that philosophy is really essential to the training of journalists?
2. Serafini makes considerable fuss over the similarities between the concept of "objectivity" as it appears in scientific discourse, and as it is used by journalists? Is the similarity really so great? Or could it be argued that scientists and journalists use the notion so differently that the results of research in the two fields would be of little use to one another.

The Press,
the Government,
and the
Ethics Vacuum

John C. Merrill

Immanuel Kant said a mouthful when he proclaimed that nothing can be called good without qualification except a Good Will. By emphasizing the Will-to-be-Ethical he demolished (or thought he did) the doctrine of utilitarianism and other teleological theories of ethics and tied morality inextricably to the agent's motives and dedication to duty. Consideration of consequences and speculation about future results of actions, said Kant, is not a rational way to proceed into the difficult, but supremely important, realm of ethics.

The view of ethics which Kant expressed is a tough one. It assigns an agent moral worth only if he acts from duty—from the recognition that he has incurred an obligation and must fulfill it. The rightness or wrongness of an action has nothing to do with its consequences. Such an ethical philosophy demands faithfulness and consistency to principle and wipes out the concept of consequences and moral determinants; therefore, any consideration of expediency disappears from the moral arena.

Kant's is a rather absolutist and formalistic theory of ethics, and it is understandable that it would not find great favor in any system which enthrones the concept of individualism, competi-

Communication, 1981, Vol. 6, pp. 177–191
0305-4233/81/0602-0177$06.50/0
© 1981 Gordon and Breach, Science Publishers, Inc.
Printed in the United States of America

tion, and a maximum degree of personal autonomy. It is not strange, therefore, that journalists and government officials in the United States find little to their liking in Kantian ethical perspectives.

By and large, people in press and government conceive of ethics as prudential actions in certain circumstances which will achieve some preconceived plan of theirs—whether it is to get information from a source or to get a certain block of votes or keep certain knowledge from the public for one reason or another. What the journalists and the government officials too often do is to engage in trying to attain their ends and justifying or rationalizing the means they use. This, according to Kant, is not ethics at all. I have found, however, in discussions at journalism conferences that, almost without exception, participants shy away from absolutes and the Kantian emphasis on "duty to principle," preferring to wallow relativistic and personal morality where any option they choose can be justified as the ethical one.

Little wonder there is an ethics vacuum in American journalism and government today.

Here is another of Kant's dicta that generally falls on deaf ears in American government and journalism: "So act as to treat humanity, whether in thine own person or in that of any other, in every case as an end withal, never as a means only."

How foreign this ethical principle is to the typical workaday world of the journalist and government official! The name of the game in this pragmatic world is *using people to achieve desired ends.* Whether it is getting news or getting to a source who can guide in the getting of news—or whether it is the achieving of a foreign policy—the average journalist or government official constantly surveys the scene for persons who can help him reach his goals. A kind of Machiavellian pragmatism permeates the entire press and government, causing functionaries in both areas to operate consciously or unconsciously according to the dictum, "The end justifies the means."

So, I am suggesting in this paper that in Press and Government there is an ethics vacuum and the reasons are really twofold. First, the foundations of ethics in Press and Government circles are vague and confusing and are beset by relativism and pragmatism so that no system of ethics ever really coalesces. And, second and probably more importantly, I believe that in neither the press nor in government is there any real desire (or Will) for a coherent and unified system of ethics. Let us look a little deeper into the sad state of ethics today and deduce some reasons why there is the vacuum I have mentioned.

I

Every discussion of press ethics inevitably gets into the area of governmental news coverage. And, when government officials are talking about the ethical dimensions of their activities, it does not take long for them to turn to their relationship to journalism. Today, the press and government are manifesting at least a surface interest in the ethics of their respective institutions—and, what is more interesting, in the ethics of the other.

Perhaps this concern with ethics has arisen because public criticism—even cynicism—has broken forth in society and because people have lost faith in both institutions. The average citizen has begun to suspect that both government and press have abandoned a concern for public service and the public interest and have retired into their own little worlds of arrogant self-interest and power-grabbing.

The observer looking first at government in this country has no trouble understanding the growing public cynicism, and even hostility being generated. He sees his government officials engaged in shady deals of all kinds, with a few of them offered up occasionally as scapegoats for many others. He sees his elected representatives, even those at the very highest levels, surrounding themselves with rude, crude, and haughty advisers and assistants, participating in questionable acts while trying to justify them by maintaining that they are legal.

A concern for legality, not ethics, is evident at every level of government. And polls show that no more than five per cent of the American people have any real faith in their government officials. People in government sense this, of course, even without the polls, but there is really no incentive for them to do anything about it. They have become complacent; they have become impressed with their own importance or with a feeling that whatever they do will make no real difference; they have lost their integrity in the process of winning and staying in office. They are seen, by and large, as self-centered and arrogant, manifesting empathy and public concern only as part of the larger political game that swirls around them. They are secure in the belief that traditional respect for the institutions and trappings of government will protect them and they will survive in spite of the fact that they are operating in an ethics vacuum.

II

Journalists and others who are part of the mammoth institution of the press should not take much satisfaction in the low state of government today. The press itself does not fare much better with the people; it may not fare as well. Increasingly, the American citizen has serious doubts about the press, about its dedication to public welfare, about its concern for truth, accuracy, and good taste; about its courage, its dedication to pluralism and diversity, and its sense of fair play and basic honesty—in short, its integrity and social responsibility.

The public increasingly sees in the press a bid for power and bigness, and insensitivity in dealing with the private—and the public—lives of citizens, a selfish and often harmful use of its considerable freedom, its defensive and often overbearing attitude, and its consistent pandering to low taste and sensationalism.

The press sees itself in a quite different light, of course. It perceives itself as the saviour of American democracy—a sort of watch-dog-on-government and at the same time a kind of "fourth branch" of government. Here is the way a typical American editor might speak:

> I am the conscience of the people; I cause our nation's citizens to look deep into themselves, to see their weaknesses and their strengths, and to desire to rise to higher levels of achievement. I am the guardian of democracy and the supplier of information by which Americans can make intelligent decisions. I am also the watcher of big institutions—especially Government, and I keep these institutions honest and protect the interests of the people. . . .

Such words have a hypnotic ring to them; they get into the psyche of the journalist and he begins to believe them himself.

They lull him into a thoughtless and complacent sleep, from which he seldom stirs. And when he does (as is happening today), this stirring manifests itself in a kind of defensive reaction—a momentary concern with journalism's purposes, objectives, and responsibilities. This thrusts the press, in spite of itself, into the area of ethics.

Journalism seminars, conventions, conferences, and workshops are hammering away at "ethical concerns." But the hammer blows are weak and ineffectual—mainly because each one has a different kind and size hammer and few of them have really studied the basic principles of hammering. At these conferences an ethical question (e.g., Should sources of information be revealed in the stories?) is trotted out so that the convention-goers can console themselves with a little discussion. Since journalists really don't want resolution, conclusions are never reached, and every case ends as an open question to be talked about at the next conference. So, it is "ethics talk time" today for the press—that time which comes and goes in cyclic motion throughout American history. Journalists claim to be searching for some basics to agree upon; they are writing codes of ethics; they are looking, they say, for some moral stability. But, in spite of renewed activity and talk, they are finding little.

Instead, they are faced with a host of fundamental, but puzzling, questions—some of which follow: What should be journalism's basic stance toward government? What are the responsibilities of the press toward government and vice versa? Where is the source of such responsibilities? Why should journalism feel that it represents the people to a greater extent than does government? Why should not government be a watchdog on the press instead of the other way around? Why should the press see itself as an adversary to government instead of a friend and partner? Why should the press more than the government have to defend a "people's right to know"? Why should the press expose the inner workings of government and not those of business enterprises of the country—including the press itself?

Inherent in such questions are several facts about American journalism. For one thing, the country's press has set itself up as a foe of government and as a friend and ally of the people. The implication, of course, is that Government is *not* a friend and ally of the people. The main reason for all this confusion is that there is really no consistent and logical philosophy of journalism or press-government symbiosis in the United States—all the high phrases of Thomas Jefferson and others notwithstanding. The old libertarian mystique about truth winning out in a free encounter with falsehood has lost much of its appeal in today's more skeptical, critical, and even cynical society where increasingly a paternalistic and collectivistic value system is making significant inroads.

The press, because of the traditional strength of the First Amendment, is almost the last bastion of capitalistic power in the intellectual sector of American society. It champions the virtues of individualism, competition, pluralism, etc., even as the press itself retreats into the safe confines of the big corporation where competition and individualism are all but extinguished, and dull, predictable, and conformist journalism spreads its faded colors and jaded voices across the land.

Indicative of the ethical malaise of the press are two notable journalistic shibboleths. Perhaps if we look at them (and there are dozens of others), we can understand why the press is confused every time it tries to deal with ethics and to find some meaningful moral understanding. Briefly the two I want to deal with are these:

- the press and government are adversaries.
- the people have a "right to know".

III

Let us look at the first one—the adversarial relationship of press and government. Many of the ethical problems of the press spring from this assumption: that the press must be a check on government, be a critic of government, keep the government honest, and on and on. This belief causes the press to dig and probe, snipe and snoop; it causes the press to speculate, to deal in gossip and innuendo in its attempt to unearth corruption in high places. This press concept is responsible, I believe, for the press's accentuating the negative in governmental matters—of seldom revealing positive activities. It fosters the idea—or is the creature of the idea—that the government is necessarily and inherently evil and must be checked. And, in this little game which the press sees itself playing, the press has set itself up as the institution which must keep the government honest. Today, as an increasing number of voices are asking who checks the checker, the press falls back on its constitutional freedom guarantee, and when all the rhetoric is done, the answer from the press is essentially this: Nobody checks the checker. The press is free and autonomous. I happen to think that it should be free—but only if significant numbers of journalists are constantly concerned about ethics.

What I'm saying, of course, is that the press is confused about ethics because it is confused about its freedom. It sees its freedom endangered if it puts too much emphasis on its "responsibility." Talk of responsibility leads to obligations and duties, say the journalists, and therefore tends to restrict press freedom. So the journalists always get back to stressing press FREEDOM and de-emphasizing press RESPONSIBILITY. Most journalists, if they think about this deeply, see the escalated talk and concern about press responsibility as a potential danger to press freedom—and, subconsciously at least—they desire to evade it, to push it away from them, and to talk of other matters. So, it is my belief that this constant and deep antipathy to the concept of "social responsibility" keeps the press from giving much continuing and serious thought to ethics.

Of course, what the journalists could do is to recognize that the concept of "press freedom" can just as easily include the freedom to be an ally or apologist for government as to be an adversary or foe of government. In fact, when the press convinces itself that it is an adversary of government, it thereby restricts its own freedom by setting for itself a limiting role. This is really not consistent with libertarian theory, and it would seem that journalists who talk about "press freedom" would cease all this talk about the "adversary role of the press."

Another problem which impinges on ethics in this area is this: If there really is (as most journalists believe) an adversary relationship between press and government, then the press should openly and forthrightly recognize and face it. It takes at least two to be "adversaries." What the press wants of this relationship, it seems to me, is a *one-sided* battle, with the government resisting the urge to fight. In this relationship, if it is to be a truly adversarial one, the government would fight the press—be secretive, sly, devious, blunt, etc.—to the best of its ability. The press would try to get the news it wanted from government and the government would try to keep the news it wanted back from the press. This would be a true adversarial relationship: but it is one, I'm afraid, the press does not really want in spite of its pronouncements to the contrary.

IV

Now, let us turn to the other journalistic concept (that the people have a right to know) mentioned earlier. This one, too, is fraught with semantic and logical problems, and is one which causes many anxious moments for those journalists (and government officials, too) who think seriously about ethics.

The press drags this right-to-know concept out all the time. It is one of the biggest missiles in the press's arsenal, with journalists using it to justify almost any action. I even heard Walter Cronkite recently use it as a synonym for "press freedom," strange as that may seem. Many press people, obviously not comfortable with the right granted them in the First Amendment, feel they must justify their activities vis-à-vis government by appealing to a people's right to know. We're not really getting this information for ourselves, the press people seem to be saying; we're getting it for the people who have a right to know it. Therefore, you people in government are obligated to give it to us because we are representatives of the people. Isn't this strange? I always thought that the government officials were the representatives of the people, and the press people were profit-making collaborators with the capitalistic system and not representatives of anybody, really, except publishers and other media owners and managers who contend in the World of Big Business.

I won't go into a discussion here of the philosophical or legal justification for any "people's right to know." Perhaps one can infer such a "right" from the free press clause of the Bill of Rights; many think they can. Others don't believe such a "right" has a Constitutional basis. At any rate, if there is such a right, then the press had better get its act together, for it is abridging this "right" every single day. And it is abridging it in the name of editorial self-determination or "press freedom." (How then could people like Cronkite use the two concepts synonymously?)

Journalists constantly decide what they will or will not publish; they arbitrarily determine what the public will or will not know. They call this "editing," of course, or making editorial decisions. Certainly they don't call it news management—they reserve that epithet for government officials. But it really is *news* management; this type of activity really is what journalism is all about. And part of that management process in a free and open society is withholding news from the people. The journalists know this, and yet they persist in talking about and advocating a "people's right to know." They had best be careful about their avowed belief in such a right, for the American people one day may ask them to put up or shut up.

However you may feel about this issue—or for that matter, the earlier one on "adversary journalism," I think you can see that such concepts, well-entrenched in the traditional rhetoric of American journalism, evidence a considerable confusion in the minds of journalists about the nature of press freedom. And this leads to difficulty in developing any kind of consistent journalistic ethics. No wonder there is an ethics vacuum in American journalism. The basic philosophical foundation stones are not very solid and the mortar holding them together is rapidly turning to powder.

V

Both government and the press are protective of their perceived "rights" and jealous of the other's transgression into secret areas. In October, 1979, Supreme Court Justice William J. Brennan, who has been a strong defender of press freedom, told off the nation's journalists in a speech in New Jersey. He charged the press with engaging in vehement, unreasonable, and unintelligent attacks on the Supreme Court.

In effect, Justice Brennan was questioning the press's ethics. By being irresponsible, he said, the press is destroying its credibility on issues vital to its future welfare and to the proper functioning of government. Justice Brennan didn't say just what the "proper functioning" of government is, but—like journalists talking about their proper functions—he seemed to assume that *he* knows. At any rate, Justice Brennan cited—by name—newspapers that had indulged in "inaccurate reporting" of Court decisions, and he listed—by name—newspapers and newsmen whose criticism he saw as stemming from their failure to understand what the Court decided in a particular case or why it reached its decision. His main point was that the press still clings to the old concept of the First Amendment that more or less prohibits any interference with freedom of expression. The Court, said Justice Brennan, has moved beyond that concept to use the First Amendment also to protect other things—e.g., the structure of the communicative process through which citizens exercise their right of self-government.

This statement of Justice Brennan is representative of the expanding concept of "press freedom" in this country. And, as the concept changes and expands, it naturally leads to charges and countercharges of "unethical actions." This sniping between government and the press is escalating, and the criticism on both sides is being done, of course, in the name of responsibility to the people. I would say that Justice Brennan, however confusing his rationalization may be, is largely concerned with ethics. Journalists who are appalled by the audacity of his position are concerned mainly—not with ethics—but with *freedom*. Kant had more to say about the Will to be ethical than about the Will to be free, although freedom is an important consideration in ethics. Freedom, however, is not an *ethical* end in itself—rather, it is a means to ethical action or a necessary "given" for ethical (or unethical) action.

Like you, I have heard the press castigated by government for its power, its callousness, its defensiveness, its vulgarity, its bigness, its lack of intelligence, its distance from the people, its sensational and atypical news presentation, its inaccuracies, its lack of professionalism, and its lack of a meaningful code of ethics. I may have missed a few indictments, but you can fill in the blanks.

The press, of course, hurls most or all of these same criticisms back at government. Both press and government look at ethics from a vested-interest and relativistic perspective, shying away from any absolutes and relegating ethics to particular times, circumstances, and problems. Also, it is obvious that each side is more concerned with the other's ethics than with its own; therefore, little real ethical progress is made.

The press, for its part, is so protective of its traditional idea of individualism and pluralism that it resists anything that might result in standardization or conformity—anything, of course, except a growing trend toward "groupism," chain ownership, consolidation, and the like. (But this seemingly contradictory development can be explained, perhaps, by saying that, in spite of its rhetoric of individualism, the press is really just another growth-oriented part of the "capitalistic machine.") At any rate, the press seems to see everything beyond a strictly personal or individualized ethics as endangering diversity and, by extension, journalistic freedom. (The press always gets back to its freedom.) And, as has been said, the press does not deny that it is a business or profit-making enterprise, one that sells a product to customers.

VI

In neither government nor press circles is there a strong effort being made to break through self-serving platitudes and to gain any real insight into the ethical issues that beg to be dealt with. It would seem that journalists and government officials would meet and talk about critical moral problems affecting themselves and the public at large. They do meet together occasionally, but not often. Instead, usually they meet separately and air their own grievances, defend themselves against criticism, and hurl criticisms at the other.

For example, government, according to the journalists, is too much engaged in an elaborate system of obfuscation or "news management," designed to protect itself when threatened. It is interesting, they say, that in 1971, when CBS scratched the surface of the giant governmental information system in "The Selling of the Pentagon," the television program resulted in attacks on the network by the Vice President as well as in a Congressional investigation, not of the Pentagon but of CBS. It is estimated today, point out press spokesmen, that the federal government alone spends more than $400 million a year on programs of "public information," more than twice the combined expenditures for newsgathering by the two major wire services, the three large TV networks and the ten largest newspapers in the country. Nearly 7,000 federal employees are engaged in creating tendentious news, far more than the number of journalists employed in Washington to report and comment on the information spewing from governmental offices.

The government's rationale, of course, for such "news man-agement" is that it must inform the public of government activities, protect national security, and maintain social stability. In addition to the highly structured system of public information, government employees provide the press with much additional information in the form of "leaks." For reasons best known to themselves, gov-ernment officials make a practice of feeding secrets to reporters. This practice is what Max Frankel of *The New York Times* has called "monstrous and hypocritical."

But the press should not feel too smug about its own role in such affairs, for reporters are usually quite willing to cooperate in their own manipulation by government. It is quite common for journalists to report the isolated news of government—leaks and non-leaks—as if they were related to nothing else, to a larger pattern of meaning. The press seldom tries to give the audiences the real story behind the "leaks" and, more often than not, pub-lishes the stories without giving the names of the sources. And this, in spite of the press's avowed belief in the "people's right to know." Furthermore, the press seldom questions the direction which government is taking the country. As a result, most of the real questioning of society is given over to radical voices and groups, most of whom the press treats with scorn and contempt.

Perhaps it is too much to ask that U.S. media people not only to report the American reality but to hold it together. Yet, more and more, as other social institutions default and the power of the mass media grows, that seems to be their assignment. Under the circumstances, the crucial questions they will have to answer—for themselves as well as their critics—are neither political nor professional, but moral. Ethical decisions confront the journalist at every turn. Most often the journalist looks on his decision-making as "professional" or institutionalized and deals with it as such—rather than approaching it from a truly ethical perspective. "It's newsworthy in the traditional sense," says the journalist, "so I'll print it." This is an example of considering journalism from a pragmatic or professional perspective instead of going to the eth-ical level. In fact, many reporters think they are dealing ethically with issues when they are simply reacting habitually like Pavlov's dogs.

This journalistic reflex action is understandable for several rea-sons. Beyond the fact just mentioned, that the journalists in America are highly institutionalized, creatures of habit, they are part of a highly competitive, capitalistic enterprise; as such they are largely concerned with doing what "works" best. Second, they are suspicious of "social ethics" or any group-imposed rules or any system of restraints that might cause them to lose their sense of identity and freedom. And last, and probably most important of all, is the fact that journalists know very little about philosophical ethics and appear not to care deeply about learning. In other words, they appear not to have what might be called the Kantian "Will to be ethical."

What has just been said about journalists can, of course, also be said of government officials. Both groups are engulfed in the daily routine of habit, tradition, and pragmatics, leaving the business of morality—personal and social—to theologians and academics. And, as all of us know full well, there is a vast gulf—and little real communication—between the academic world and the worlds of government and journalism.

VII

Academic conferences, conventions, and workshops have some value in improving ethical understanding, to be sure, but we are so detached from the daily activities of government and journalism that our impact is negligible. We might better help fill the ethics vacuum if we would have more integrated conferences where we could share our ethical concerns not only with our fellow academics, but also with journalists and government officials. At least we could all get a glimpse at how significant the ethics vacuum really is and how very far we have to go in filling it.

It might also be worthwhile if we in the academic world would engage in more criticism of the ethical performance of government and journalism. We need to have more papers, more speeches, more articles and books detailing specific ethical cases, analyzing and questioning their handling—and criticizing the ethics of their final resolution. We need to be forthright and open in this criticism, and bring our best analytical powers to bear on these important questions. For far too long the ethical dimensions of both government and journalism have been pushed over into the corners of scholarly concern.

As academic persons we should and could do more to focus an intellectual spotlight on the problems of ethics in government and press. But I am not really very optimistic about our willingness to confront the powers of government and press with their ethical weaknesses. And also, I have seen too much in the field of journalism and have heard too many rationalizations of journalistic actions to have much hope that the press really wants to act ethically. I have reason to believe, that government officials are likewise fundamentally uncaring. So regardless of how much discourse we academicians may furnish from our detached perspectives about ethics, I am doubtful that much will be done. However, this is not to say that we should not try, even though the realities of the situation appear to militate against any successful solution of the growing ethical problems.

Why am I pessimistic? Because nobody in journalism or in government really wants to be told that he or she is acting unethically. Journalists and government officials as a rule want ethical questions to remain unresolved, up-in-the-air, so to speak. This way they never have to feel guilty or have a definite verdict of unethical practice attached to them. Many persons in the press see themselves as serving as a check on government, and there is the evident belief among large numbers of government people that they must restrain the press from irresponsible and harmful actions. Where do we academics come in? Certainly we don't have the overt power exercised by either of these two institutions, but we do have considerable influence. We do enjoy the luxury of detachment and time and, if we have the will and courage, we can serve as a kind of ethical check on both government and journalism. Certainly they both enjoy watching us and commenting on our activities. Maybe it's our turn for a change.

We have an ethics vacuum in this country, to be sure. And we have one simply because that is what journalists and government officials desire. The ethical person is not really the successful person in journalism or government today; this is a truism, although it is seldom stated so bluntly. Those persons who seriously want to be ethical had best stay out of both fields unless they are satisfied to sit in frustrated silence on the sidelines of the game, unable to attain prominence in the hard-fought, Machiavellian battle for power, prestige, and success.

Immanuel Kant's idea of a Will to do the right thing—to be

ethical—is essentially a dead concept with press and government today. So we have an ethics vacuum. And it is one which will remain with us, I am convinced, as long as the American competitive spirit militates against a strict and formalistic ethics.

Study Questions

1. Merrill argues that the prime cause of the "ethics vacuum" in journalism today is the fact that journalists tend to shy away from the notion of Kantian "absolute" principles, "preferring to wallow in relativistic and personal morality where any option they choose can be justified as the ethical one." Do you agree with this, or could it be argued that other factors are responsible for the lack of ethics in journalism? (Such as fierce competition between networks, in the case of TV journalism.)
2. Merrill suggests at some point that, instead of fostering an adversarial relationship with the government, it could try and act more as ". . . an ally or apologist for government . . ." State why you agree or disagree with this view.

Foundations and Limits of Freedom of the Press

Judith Lichtenberg

I confess that I do not entertain that firm and complete attachment
to the liberty of the press which is wont be excited by things that
are supremely good in their very nature.

Tocqueville, *Democracy in America*

Freedom of the press is guaranteed only to those who own one.

A.J. Liebling, *The Press*

De Tocqueville and Liebling notwithstanding, freedom of the press
in democratic societies is a nearly unchallengeable dogma—essential, it is thought, to individual autonomy and self-expression,
and an indispensable element in democracy and the attainment
of truth. Both its eloquent theoreticians and its contemporary popular adovcates defend freedom of speech and freedom of the press
in the same stroke, with the implication that they are inseparable,
probably equivalent, and equally fundamental.

At the same time we know that the press in its most characteristic modern incarnation—mass media in mass society—works
not only to enhance the flow of ideas and information but also to
inhibit it. Nothing guarantees that all valuable information, ideas,
theories, explanations, proposals, and points of view will find
expression in the public forum.[1] And indeed many factors lead
us to expect that they will not. The most obvious is that "mass

This article was written under a grant from the John and Mary R. Markle Foundation, whose
generous support I gratefully acknowledge. Among the many people who commented on
earlier versions of this article, I especially want to thank Lee Bollinger, Owen Fiss, Robert
Fullinwider, David Luban, Claudia Mills, Richard Mohr, Thomas Scanlon, and Michael
Schudson.

media space-time" is a very scarce commodity: only so much news, analysis, and editorial opinion can be aired in the major channels of mass communication. *Which* views get covered, and in what way, depend mainly on the economic and political structure and context of press institutions and the characteristics of the media themselves.

These are some of the most important factors: (1) More often than not, contemporary news organizations belong to large corporations whose interests influence what gets covered (and, what is probably more central, what does not) and how.[2] (2) News organizations are driven economically to capture the largest possible audience, and thus not to turn it off with whatever does turn it off—coverage that it too controversial, too demanding, too disturbing. (3) The media are easily manipulated by government officials (and others), for whom the press, by simply reporting press releases and official statements, can be a virtually unfiltered mouthpiece. (4) Characteristics of the media themselves constrain or influence coverage; thus, for example, television lends itself to an action-oriented, unanalytic treatment of events that can distort their meaning or importance.

It is not surprising, therefore, that a great range of opinion and analysis outside the narrow mainstream rarely sees the light of the mass media. This lack of diversity manifests itself in two ways. One is simply lack of adequate exposure to information and ideas that are true or interesting or useful, that help us to understand the world better or make life more satisfactory in one way or another. The range of views considered respectable enough to appear regularly in the American mass media is extraordinarily narrow.[3] As a result, we are more ignorant and more provincial than we could be, and we may be worse off in other ways as well.

The other consequence more directly concerns justice: the press, once thought of as an antidote to established power, is more likely to reinforce it, because access to the press—that is, the mass media—is distributed as unequally as are other forms of power. It is not, of course, that the less powerful never speak in the mass media or that their doings are never reported, or never sympathetically. But the deck is stacked against them, because the press itself a formidable power in our society, allied intimately (although not simply) with other formidable powers. Displacing the attention of the media from the usual sources of news—the words and deeds of public officials and public figures—often demands nothing less than the politics of theater, for which those using such tactics may also be blamed.[4]

There are regulations meant to remedy these defects, to counteract the tendencies inhibiting diversity in the press. Current policy includes the Fairness Doctrine, which requires broadcasters to devote a "reasonable percentage" of broadcast time to public issues in a way that presents contrasting viewpoints; rules limiting multiple ownership of media properties; and the designation of public access channels on cable systems. Nothing like the Fairness Doctrine applies to the print media, which, it is commonly thought, are rendered immune to such regulations in the United States by the First Amendment.[5] In any case, regulations mandating coverage of any kind, or enacting even limited rights of access to the press (whether print or electronic), are much in dispute today.[6] In part the dispute centers on the utility of such regulations—whether they produce or can be made to produce the intended effects. But at least as important in the current controversies is a central question of principle. Critics of regulation argue that freedom of the press, like freedom of speech, is at the core of what our society is about, and that commitment to it prohibits the policies in question: regulation of the press is incompatible with freedom of the press.

I believe that we have misunderstood what a modern democratic society's commitment to freedom of the press means and should be. Unlike freedom of speech, to certain aspects of which our commitment must be virtually unconditional, freedom of the press should be contingent on the degree to which it promotes certain values at the core of our interest in freedom of expression generally. Freedom of the press, in other words, is an instrumental good: it is good if it does certain things and not especially good (not good enough to justify special protections, anyway) otherwise. If, for example, the mass media tend to suppress diversity and impoverish public debate, the arguments meant to support freedom of the press now turn against it, and we may rightly consider regulating the media to achieve the ultimate purposes of freedom of the press.

I

The press is often described as having a special "watchdog function" or as being a kind of "fourth branch of government." Some writers, noting the First Amendment's mention of freedom of the press in addition to freedom of speech (the only reference in the Constitution, they emphasize, to a specific commercial enterprise), argue that the press is entitled to special protections, beyond those accorded speech in general. Yet when we examine the most famous arguments for freedom of the press, we find nothing to distinguish them from those for freedom of speech or expression generally. Mill's discussion in *On Liberty* begins by asserting the necessity of "liberty of the press" and proceeds to enumerate arguments for freedom of expression in general. Similarly, in "What Is Enlightenment?" Kant defends freedom of the press with general arguments for the benefits of freedom of thought and discussion.[7] And it is much the same with the other standard sources in the literature of freedom of the press: the press is treated as a voice, albeit a more powerful one, on a par with individual voices, and defending press freedom is then tantamount to a general defense of free speech.

In one way there is nothing wrong with this. The arguments for freedom of the press *are* arguments for a more general freedom of expression. But it does not follow that whatever supports freedom of speech also supports freedom of the press, for at least two related reasons that we shall look at below. First, considerations internal to the theory of free speech itself may provide reasons for limiting freedom of the press. That is what is at issue in the claim that the contemporary mass media may suppress information and stifle ideas instead of promoting them.[8] Second, the modern press consists largely of vast and complex institutions that differ in essential respects both from individuals and from the early press, around which the concept of freedom of the press grew.[9] Arguments that support freedom of expression for individuals or for small publications do not necessarily support similar freedoms for the mass media. But contemporary defenders of freedom of the press commonly assimilate the new forms to the old.

It remains to be seen, then, to what extent the arguments for free speech support freedom of the press.

II

We want free speech for many reasons. Some involve essentially individual interests, others the public interest or the common good. Some have to do with politics, or democratic politics in particular; others concern intellectual values like truth; still others have to do with promoting certain virtues of character, like tolerance.[10] Some involve the interest of speakers, others the interests of listeners or society at large. Some arguments emphasize the disadvantages of suppressing speech rather than the advantages of allowing it. These considerations vary in strength and persuasive power, and not all support free speech in the same way. But one thing is clear: and "monistic" theory of free speech, emphasizing only one of these values, will fail to do justice to the variety and richness of our interests in free speech.

But plurality is not miscellany. It is striking that these considerations do not stand to one another accidentally as distinct arguments for a single conclusion, but are bound to one another in various interesting ways. Each of the main arguments I shall consider shares assumptions with some of the others. (Together they stand as a fine example of Wittgensteinian family resemblances.) In some cases, this is not surprising; in others, the connections are less apparent. I hope to make some of these connections clear in what follows, and so to go some way toward explaining why the existence of a variety of arguments for free speech is not simply fortuitous.

Let me begin by imposing some order on these arguments. We can start by asking what we want when we want free speech. I believe that we have two main goals: the first is that people be able to communicate without interference, and the second is that there be many people communicating, or at least many different ideas and points of view being communicated. These commitments can be described in terms of two basic principles. One we may call the *noninterference* or *no censorship principle*: one should not be prevented from thinking, speaking, reading, writing, or listening as one sees fit. The other I shall call the *multiplicity of voices principle*: the purposes of freedom of speech are realized when expression and diversity of expression flourish. Although, as we shall see, the arguments for free speech demonstrate the importance of both these principles, they seem capable of conflict. Indeed, their conjunction partly explains our dilemma about freedom of the press: government intervention seems to intrude upon the first principle, but it may advance the second.

In theory and often in practice, the principles are compatible: my being free from interference to speak in no way inhibits others from expressing themselves. I can write in my diary and you can write in yours; I can distribute my propaganda in the airport and you can distribute yours. (Even here we can see the beginnings of strain: the airport will support only so many.) To the extent that the principles peacefully coexist, and assuming that communication is a natural human urge, we satisfy the multiplicity of voices principle, a "positive" principle requiring that something (talk, conversation, debate) happen, when we satisfy the "negative" noninterference principle, which requires that something (interference) not happen. Yet in fact the freedom of editors and publishers from outside control can inhibit the multiplication of voices in the public forum. A newspaper may not interfere with a person's right to speak or write, but it may very well prevent her from expressing her views in that newspaper, even if it is the only one in town, and even if she has a legitimate and significant grievance or point of view and no comparable opportunity to publicize it. Such decisions are simply exercises of the newspaper's editorial autonomy, which appears to fall neatly under the noninterference principle. It may seem just as obvious that when this principle clashes with the multiplicity of voices, it is the latter that must give way.

But things are not so simple; what seems obvious may be false. Our interests in free speech make it plausible to speak of a fundamental right or freedom to think and speak and write and listen and read without interference; but there is no "right to publish" or right to editorial autonomy in the same sense. No one—not even network presidents or newspaper publishers—possesses a fundamental right to editorial autonomy that is violated by regulation designed to enhance the multiplicity of voices.

To see why this is so, we must first examine the main arguments for free speech.

III

Among our deepest interests in free speech is a concern about individual autonomy and self-expression that cuts across any particular social or political ideal that is likely to divide us. Basically, we take it to be of overriding importance that a person be able to think for himself, that whatever his "outer" condition he not be intellectually or psychologically subjugated to another's will.[11] Autonomy so understood requires freedom of speech because of the close connection between thought and language. A person cannot think freely if he cannot speak; and he cannot think freely if others cannot speak, for it is in hearing the thoughts of others and being able to communicate with them that we develop our thoughts. Thus autonomy requires freedom to speak as well as freedom to hear. And it implies freedom of speech for others as well as for oneself—not simply on grounds of fairness but in order to attain one's own interests in freedom of speech.

To value autonomy is to value a certain intellectual or psychological condition, distinct from "outer" freedom—the ability to govern our actions. We want the latter as well, of course, but outer freedom is subject to all the limits that the rights and like fredom of others impose. An appeal to freedom-in-general will not, then, carve out special protections for speech. But autonomy, conceived as the ability to think for oneself, differs from this much broader freedom of action. And it is precisely because one person's autonomy does not limit another's that we can value autonomy in an unqualified, nearly absolute way.

Yet the focus on autonomy might seem to signal an exaggerated preoccupation with the inner life. Surely, it will be objected, our interest in freedom of speech does not derive only from our concern with freedom of thought; surely we want also to be able to express our thoughts "in the world." Our fundamental interest in freedom of expression is an interest not only in freedom to think for ourselves but also in communicating our thoughts to others, leaving a mark on the world, making outer what is inner.

As I have already acknowledged, the inner/outer distinction is overstated, because thinking requires language, and language requires communication—because often we do not know what we think or feel until we put our inchoate inner goings-on into words or discuss them with others. Yet there remains a distinction between autonomy, the ability to think for oneself, and self-expression, the communicating of one's thoughts to others. Both are important components of our interest in free speech.

Some critics resist the argument from self-expression, however, because they believe it proves too much. Since anything one might wish to do can be considered a mode of self-expression, the argument easily becomes an argument for liberty-in-general that again fails to make speech special.[12]

So we need a way of preventing self-expression from swallowing up the whole of action. We want to protect a person when she criticizes another but not when she punches him in the nose. I believe a relevant distinction can be drawn based on the notion of essentially symbolic expression. Freedom of speech protects expression that is essentially symbolic. Natural language is the obvious example but not the only one; painting and mathematics, for example, are also essentially symbolic. Punching someone in the nose, however, while expressive, is not essentially symbolic.

What is so special about symbolic expression? It is definitively associated with human beings; it is the primary means by which we communicate beliefs, ideas, even feelings (its importance is not, then, tied exclusively to our rationality); its success requires distinctively human responses—understanding, and not mere reaction. Although some instances of speech (performatives) are rightly considered actions, and although all speech is action in a trivial sense, it is appropriate to distinguish speech from action insofar as speech possesses intentionality, insofar as it means something, insofar as what is expressed is "about" something.

So understood, self-expression is a legitimate and important ground for free speech.

IV

Very different from the arguments from autonomy and self-expression is the argument from democracy, usually credited to Alexander Meiklejohn.[13] Since democracy means popular sovereignty, Meiklejohn argues, the citizens in a democracy, as the ultimate decision makers, need full (or at least a lot of) information to make intelligent political choices. Meiklejohn's argument stresses two functions of freedom of speech and press in a democracy. One is the informative function: free speech permits the flow of information necessary for citizens to make informed decisions and for leaders (public servants) to stay abreast of the interests of their constituents (the sovereign electorate). Second, and not easily separated from the first, is the critical function: the press in particular serves as the people's watchdog, ensuring independent criticism and evaluation of the established power of government and other institutions that may usurp democratic power.

But Meiklejohn's account ignores an essential feature of democracy and an important function of free speech. Democracy means not only that "the people" are collectively self-governing, but also that they are equal in an important sense. The democratic equality of persons bears on free speech in two ways. First, democracy functions as it should only when each person's interests are represented in the political forum; freedom of speech and press enhances opportunities for representation. Second, we show the sort of respect for persons associated with democracy both by acknowledging that anyone (regardless of race or class or lack of company) may have a view worth expressing, and by assuming that people can be openminded or intelligent enough to judge alien views on their merits. Only under these conditions can majority rule become morally respectable and not merely the best of a bad lot of decision procedures.[14]

The second point connects the democratic argument for free speech with the argument that freedom of speech is an indispensable means to the attainment of truth. The belief that anyone might make a valuable contribution to the search for truth or for better ways to do things does not mean that we think "anyone" is likely to. It means: (1) There is no way of telling in advance where a good idea will come from. (2) Valuable contributions to arriving at truth come in many forms, speaking the truth being only one of them. We arrive at truth or the best policy largely by indirection. (3) Thus, much of the value of a person's contribution to the "marketplace of ideas" is its role in stimulating others to defend or reformulate or refute, and that value may be quite independent of the merits of the original view. Even fallacy has its place in the search for truth. These are essentially Mill's points in chapter 2 of *On Liberty*.

As I suggested earlier, the connection between the arguments from democracy and truth is not simply serendipitous. Most of us are democrats not only because we believe in an ultimate moral equality but in part because we believe that *things turn out better* in democracies. If this is not simply crude relativism (truth or goodness is whatever the majority thinks it is), then it must be rooted in the belief that the public exchange of ideas transforms popular decision making into something morally and epistemologically respectable. Moreover, egalitarianism, a linchpin of democracy, and fallibilism, a central assumption in the argument from truth, are mutually supportive: the first bids us to attend to the views of the "lowly" and the second to question those of the expert and the elite.[15]

V

The interconnections among the various grounds for free speech help us understand another of its standard defenses. Both Kant and Mill stressed the role of freedom of expression in human self-realization or self-development. While commentators usually cite chapter 2 of *On Liberty* for the argument from truth, the whole work is an extended defense of the connection between freedom of expression and self-realization. Quoting Wilhelm von Humboldt, Mill proclaims that "the end of man . . . is the highest and most harmonious development of his powers to a complete and consistent whole," and that for this two conditions are requisite, "freedom, and variety of situations."[16] A variety of ideas is obviously both a precondition of and an essential ingredient in the latter. Kant argues that the "public use of man's reason," by which he means a person's ability to communicate ideas to the public at large, is essential to human enlightenment.

On its face the argument from self-realization is vulnerable to the same kind of objection made against the argument from self-expression: all sorts of things (education and travel, for example) may enhance self-development, and nothing in the argument distinguishes speech. Self-development—making the most out of oneself, or making oneself as wise as possible—is surely an admirable goal, but one so broad and open-ended that it fails to mark out speech.

But this objection is not persuasive. One reason is that allowing people to speak and listen costs incomparably less than providing education and travel.[17] But there is another reason too. The foregoing objection conceives of self-realization or self-development as what we might call a "maximizing" concept: more is better, and nothing distinguishes the essential from the rest. Although for many purposes this is perfectly reasonable, I think self-development has a more circumscribed core that serves to bridge the arguments from autonomy and from truth.

For a large area of human interests, the arguments for free speech from truth and from self-realization are so closely related as to be practically inseparable. The reason is that where "morals, religion, politics, social relations, and the business of life"[18] are concerned, truth, if we speak of truth at all, must be something inseparable from the process of arriving at it, and has therefore a great deal to do with the virtues of intellect and character central to self-development.[19] As Mill argues, "Truth, in the great practical concerns of life, is so much a question of the reconciling and combining of opposites that very few have minds sufficiently capacious and impartial to make the adjustment with an approach to correctness, and it has to be made by the rough process of a struggle between combatants fighting under hostile banners."[20] The nature of truth in these matters determines the nature of wisdom: "If the cultivation of the understanding consists in one thing more than in another, it is surely in learning the grounds of one's own opinions . . . on every subject on which difference of opinion is possible, the truth depends on a balance to be struck between two sets of conflicting reasons."[21] This is one essential element in enlightenment and self-development—not being everything you are capable of being, but understanding the bases and limitations of your views. So understood, self-development is very close to autonomy. Nor are the virtues here purely intellectual; the self-awareness Mill describes requires fairness and encourages tolerance. Moving from the individual to the society, an enlightened society is one in which, following public dialogue and debate, a balance has been struck between conflicting interests. Enlightenment is thus inseparable from the democratic process.

All our interests in free speech have an important social and even a public component. To satisfy them, a certain quantity and diversity of speech must exist and be heard—a multiplicity of voices. That there must be a multiplicity of voices if free speech is to advance the causes of democracy and truth is obvious. But the same goes for autonomy and self-development, values that can seem purely private and isolated from the public world, and that may at first sight seem to support only the noninterference principle. This is not only because all thinking involves language, which is public, but because thinking for oneself is a matter not of coming up with wholly original ideas but rather of subjecting one's ideas, which come largely from others, to certain tests.[22] Autonomy is not a matter of believing what you feel like believing, as freedom, on some accounts, is a matter of doing what you feel like doing and therefore tantamount to noninterference. Autonomy and self-development in an intellectual vacuum are impossible. Thus a multiplicity of voices is central to achieving individual autonomy and not only to the more obviously social goods, democracy and truth. And, on the other hand, noninterference— the opportunity to express oneself and to hear others express themselves—is as essential to the attainment of the social values underlying free speech as to the individual.

VI

Taken together, these arguments support a strong free speech principle, one that enables individuals and groups to think, speak, write, listen, read, and publish freely.

Even under a strong free speech principle, however, all such activities take place under constraints. I may read what I like, but not without your permission if the only copy of my favorite book happens to be in your private library. I may orate on the evils of fluoridation, but not (unless she permits) in the dentist's waiting room. I may write what I think is a groundbreaking tract, but nothing guarantees its publication in the journal of my choice (or any, for that matter).

How do we account for these constraints? One way is to say that our commitment to free speech amounts only to prohibitions against restriction by *government*, leaving open restriction by private parties. But this is unsatisfactory, because insofar as we value free speech we will want to remove obstacles to it from whatever source, public or private. That we are morally barred from taking remedies when the obstacle is private must be demonstrated; it cannot simply be assumed.[23]

A related account of the constraints on free speech asserts that a person's freedom of speech is limited by the property rights of others. But this is inadequate because it suggests both that property rights are ultimate, simple, and straightforward, marking a natural line between mine and thine, and that they always take priority, setting a rigid framework within which free speech (and other important moral and political principles) must maneuver a narrow course.

But the system of property relations, and its connection with other interests, is much more complicated than this account allows. Ownership rights over things (including everything from your toothbrush to the corner drugstore to General Motors) evolve in response to a variety of factors. Some are moral values, like privacy and equality. Some are pragmatic considerations: convenience, efficiency, and utility. Property rights are complex sets of relationships: with different kinds of property one can do different things; hardly ever can one do with one's property exactly what one pleases. Zoning laws; eminent domain; regulations concerning environmental protection, public utilities, health and safety—all attest to the qualified nature of property rights even in a system such as ours that accords great respect to private property.

If property relations did not have this character, the idea of a free speech principle (or anything rightly called a principle) would be very frail. However one thinks any specific free speech issue should be settled, a commitment to free speech of the kind embodied in the First Amendment means that when free speech clashes with other interests, the former has a pressing claim that is not automatically defeated by competing claims of property rights.

We can illustrate this point about the flexible and responsive character of property rights with an example from outside the area of free speech. On a simplistic view of property rights, a person who owns a restaurant ought to be able to exclude potential customers at will. But American law prohibits discrimination on the basis of race; one who opens a restaurant must serve anyone, assuming he is not rowdy, drunk, or inappropriately dressed, and that the restaurant is not full. Our law is based on a strong commitment to equality, or the wrongness of racial discrimination. The law applies to "public accommodations," so called although restaurants and hotels are ordinarily considered private property. How do we justify this law?

In several ways. First, we distinguish between a restaurant and a person's dinner table. One is legally free to discriminate on the basis of race in choosing one's dinner guests. Although morally we disapprove of all manifestations of racial discrimination, we may hold that the value of privacy, of a sphere over which the individual is sovereign, is so important that it overrides or excludes the principle of equality. (A person's home is her castle; we do not say that a person's hotel is her castle.) Indeed, the near reverence with which we as a society regard private property derives in good part from thoughts of other people invading our homes or using our toothbrushes—from imagined violations of *personal* property. Such violations encroach on privacy, but not everything we call "private property" is private in this sense. Our acceptance of discrimination "within the home" also reflects the belief that in this sphere state coercion is not only wrong but largely ineffective, perhaps counterproductive: you can't legislate morality in *this* way.

But in opening a restaurant, which has an explicitly commercial purpose, one acknowledges the diminished importance in that realm of privacy; thus the assertion of privacy in defense of discrimination rings hollow. In addition, although a restaurant is privately owned, it depends on a variety of public benefits and privileges, the most obvious being a license to operate.[24] It therefore ceases to be a wholly private institution.

We can apply a similar analysis to the examples I gave above. First, the case of my favorite book found only in your private library. Here my "right to read" does not include the right to enter your library without your permission. Two kinds of reasons support this conclusion. First, as in the case of choosing one's dinner guests, the value of privacy within a limited sphere is too important to sacrifice; and coercion in this sphere would probably be ineffective. At the same time we acknowledge the importance of the ability to read freely through the institution of public libraries. It is rare for the book I want to be available only in one private place.[25] Public libraries are a means of fulfilling free speech values without having to invade other important interests.

The case of speechifying on fluoridation in the dentist's office can be understood in a similar way. Being able to orate on the subject of one's choice does not give one absolute discretion as to "time, place, and manner" (in the language of constitutional discussion), nor does it amount to the right to harangue a captive audience. Public space—streets and parks—is adequate to accommodate the interests at stake here.

We can sharpen our understanding of the relation between free speech and property values by examining a series of free speech cases on the right to speak or distribute literature on private property, and especially in shopping centers. Some of these cases do, and some do not, uphold the free speech claims in dispute. Taken together, they illuminate the subject at issue here.

In *Marsh* v. *Alabama* (1948), the first important case, the Supreme Court upheld the right of a Jehovah's Witness to distribute religious literature on a sidewalk in a company town—a town wholly owned by a shipbuilding company but otherwise indistinguishable from myriad other small southern towns.[26] In *NLRB* v. *Babcock & Wilcox* (1956), the Court ruled that a company could refuse to allow union organizers to distribute literature in the parking lot and on the walkway leading from it to the plant entrance, since alternative channels of communication with the workers existed.[27] Twelve years later, in *Amalgamated Food Employees* v. *Logan Valley Plaza*, the right of those involved in a labor dispute to picket a business within a shopping center complex was upheld.[28] *Central Hardware Co.* v. *NLRB* (1972) also involved union organizers on company property, this time in the parking lot of the store.[29] The Court ruled that reasonable alternative means of reaching the employees were available, and thus that *Babcock* rather than *Logan Valley* controlled. Decided at the same time was *Lloyd* v. *Tanner*, upholding the right of a shopping center to exclude those distributing leaflets against the Vietnam War, on the grounds that the subject matter was unrelated to the purposes of the shopping center and so could be adequately "discussed" elsewhere.[30] Finally, in *PruneYard Shopping Center* v. *Robins* (1980), a case involving the distribution of handbills in opposition to a United Nations resolution against "Zionism," the Court upheld the California Supreme Court's ruling that access to shopping centers is protected by the California Constitution, and that such provisions do not violate the property rights of shopping center owners.[31]

At least two related principles emerge from these decisions. The first, articulated in *Marsh*, is that insofar as a private corporation adopts the functions of a municipality, it assumes the obligations with respect to free speech that fall to public bodies. Gulf Shipbuilding owned the streets and sidewalks in Chickasaw, Alabama; it provided police protection, sewerage, and other services. It was therefore required to permit First Amendment freedoms to be exercised in the usual manner, on streets and sidewalks.

Part of the rationale for this principle leads to the other important principle implicit in these decisions. Chickasaw had no public streets and sidewalks; thus no comparable alternatives existed for the exercise of free speech rights. How heavily free speech weighs against property rights—and is it clear from these decisions that this is a question of degree varying from case to case—depends on the availability of reasonable alternative means of communicating. What constitutes a reasonable alternative, in turn, will depend on physical facts, on the nature of the message to be communicated, and (relatedly) on the intended or appropriate audience. What distinguishes *Logan Valley* from *Babcock* and *Central Hardware* is the physical layout—the existence of a genuine shopping center, and not simply a private business with a parking lot—which made other means of communicating with workers ineffective. What distinguishes *Lloyd* from all three is that the speakers' message—concerning the Vietnam War—bore no special relation to the business of the shopping center, so that leafletting could reasonably take place elsewhere.

This last argument might be disputed on grounds that return us to the first principle. If shopping centers have become our modern Main Streets—if they have replaced downtown business districts as the hub of commercial and social life—then to that extent the principles implicit in *Marsh* ought to apply. The shopping center in *Lloyd* employed a security force with police powers within the center; it had an auditorium used by various groups (most fee-paying), including presidential candidates, and walkways where the Salvation Army and similar charitable groups were permitted to solicit donations. In the suburbs where shopping centers reign, there may be nowhere else to find large numbers of people not locked in their cars. The California Supreme Court's construal of its constitution's free speech provision to permit individuals access to shopping centers, which was upheld in *PruneYard*, rests on precisely this kind of reasoning.[32]

VII

The case of publishing, central to our discussion of freedom of the press, raises further complications. What is obvious is that no one has a right to publish, if that means a right to succeed in publishing where one chooses. I may send off my writings to any number of book or journal publishers—that is to say, I have the right to *try* to publish—but whether I succeed depends, ordinarily, on choices that they are entitled to make.[33]

This is just to acknowledge that the ability to publish is embedded in a system of property relations. But this is the beginning, not the end, of inquiry. For, as I have argued, property rights are not the simple and ultimate given from which all policy choices must begin; they themselves result from the interplay of a variety of considerations moral and pragmatic. And exactly what rights and duties follow upon property ownership in a particular kind of case depends on the interests at stake there.

It does not suffice, then, simply to assert the property rights of publishers and editors against all claims to regulate the press. The publishers may say, "It's my newspaper and I can print what I want," but the question remains why we should accept the absolutist conception of property rights lurking in that statement as defining the publisher's role. The appeal to property rights may explain why it is the publisher—rather than the reporter or the printer or the janitor—in whom editorial authority is invested, but it does not explain why newspapers and other media organizations should be immune from regulation when other businesses are not.

The answer cannot be that editorial autonomy is implicit in the commitment to free speech, for, as we have seen, the free speech principle does not imply a right to publish where one chooses. And that is as true for newspaper owners and network presidents as for anyone else. This point undercuts a great deal of the moral suasion that is supposed to attach to the assertion of editorial autonomy; editorial autonomy—unlike the kind of individual autonomy I discussed earlier—is not a fundamental human right, and defending it requires more than the appeal to the nobility of free speech values.

We can now see that the typical claim of editorial autonomy by publishers and editors is really a disguised property claim—it is the assertion of a property right in the guise of a free speech right. Since, as we have seen, property claims are not always decisive, and since the "right" to free speech does not equal the right to editorial autonomy, the defense of editorial autonomy requires something more. If, even where there are serious costs to diversity and public debate, we grant publishers or editors the right of editorial autonomy, that is because on the whole doing so is the best way to advance free speech values. The question, to which we shall return below, is whether a policy of nonregulation of the press is good for the values underlying free speech.[34]

Let me put these conclusions in terms of the two basic principles I described earlier as characterizing our interests in free speech: *noninterference* and the *multiplicity of voices*. Obviously, our worry about editorial autonomy is that it can inhibit the multiplicity of voices. But does the noninterference principle not support editorial autonomy? And how do we arrive at the judgment (which may seem to conflict with a standard liberal presumption in favor of noninterference as definitive of liberty) that multiplicity of voices takes priority over noninterference?

The answer has two parts. First, while the term "noninterference" covers some crucial free speech values, it is made to carry more weight than it can bear. Its essential core is autonomy: what we fear most when we fear interference with freedom of expression is mind control, Big Brother–style, being thrown into prison for opposing the government, and generally the extreme suppression we find in totalitarian regimes. Everyone can agree that these form the core of our concern with free speech—it is the freedoms at stake here that must be protected first and foremost. As soon as we get beyond these fundamental freedoms, however—as soon as the question is not whether one may speak, but where and in what form—the ability to express oneself becomes entangled with questions of property. It is not that at that point noninterference ceases to matter, but that its value is spread so thin as to make it a useless guide to action: the question is whether to interfere with my freedom to orate in the dentist's office or with her freedom to exclude trespassers from her property. The fact that here the dentist's claim wins hands down shows that noninterference-in-matters-of-speech is not the knockdown argument it sometimes seems. "Time, place, and manner" restrictions—often added as if they were minor qualifications—lie at the heart of the matter.

While the first part of the answer shrinks the scope and power of the noninterference principle, the second enhances the multiplicity of voices. All the arguments for freedom of expression, with the possible exception of the argument from self-expression, demonstrate the centrality not of simply speech but of discussion, debate, diversity of ideas and sources of information. They point to the multiplicity of voices as their central and unifying theme. Noninterference is sovereign in its place—but its place is much smaller.

VIII

Doctrines do not become dogmas for nothing. Considering the press in all its variations over the last several hundred years, we may be satisfied that overall freedom of the press does work to advance the values of free speech. Ever since colonial times, the United States has seen a great abundance of publications of every description: pamphlets, newsletters, magazines, newspapers, and journals spanning the whole spectrum of social and political thought.

What, then, is the complaint? It is that the cornucopia has less and less to do with the spread of information and the formation of public opinion in our society. Most people get the vast majority of their news from the mass media—from the three commercial networks, *Time* and *Newsweek*, the wire services and daily newspapers. The *New York Times* and the *Washington Post* are the essential sources for those who hope to understand economic or political affairs in American society. It is not simply that each person learns mostly from one source but that we all learn from the same few sources. Moreover, the mass media do more than provide the news. They are instrumental in shaping our world view, and so play a role in our society much greater than that of their forerunners.

Several things account for the special role of the mass media. None is individually sufficient to distinguish them or to justify special treatment, but together they add up to a compelling set of reasons. One simple fact is the increasing extent and power of media corporations, which are often part of and interlocked with other large corporations. It would be naive to think that the economic and political interests of these institutions do not get reflected in their informational "products."[35] To the extent that they do get reflected, less powerful interests and perspectives get less than a fair hearing in the political forum.

But this is only the most obvious source of the problem. Partly the mass media are mass in virtue of the size of their audiences and the extent of their penetration within a population. In some cases, a mass medium may function as a monopoly, and this is a powerful argument for ensuring diversity. More and more cities and towns in the United States, for example, are served by only one newspaper. But most mass media institutions are not monopolies: there are, after all, three commercial networks, and they do compete. Yet the economics of the mass media, in which profit is the uppermost consideration, make it virtually impossible for any to provide programming that differs significantly from the others. In this respect the nonmass media are different. Economically, their aim is often more modest: to survive. Their primary purpose often lies in advancing a point of view, or promoting discussion of certain issues.

Out of the differences between the mass media and the ordinary press emerges a difference in role, a role both defined by the mass media themselves and assumed by others. Precisely because the mass media do not present themselves as having a distinctive point of view but rather as describing the world "as it is," and because people take them to be engaged primarily in this descriptive enterprise, they bear a responsibility for presenting many sides of an issue that the nonmass media do not. The small publications (on the order of the *National Review*, the *New Republic*, and the *Nation*) do not in general purport to be engaged in this purely descriptive activity. They would, I think, be more likely to characterize what they do as analysis or interpretation of events— or opinion—rather than pure reportage.[36] As such they function as elements in the public forum. But in a crucial sense the *New York Times* and the *Washington Post* constitute the forum itself.

We should perhaps always view with suspicion proposals to tamper with deeply entrenched practices, and freedom of the press is no exception. But the change in practice, if there is to be one, would reflect not a new attitude toward "the press" but rather the rise of a new institution, the mass media. The concept of freedom of the press developed in the seventeenth and eighteenth centuries. The mass media began to come into being only in the 1830s with the penny press. Prior to this, political newspapers made no pretense of objectivity or neutrality, and were marked by a degree of vitriol and bias unmatched today.[37] They were financed by political parties, candidates for office, or political factions, who were directly responsible for editorial policy.[38] But this was common knowledge, and it is safe to assume that readers did not view these publications as sources of "the truth" about the world, as we regard the mass media today.[39]

IX

Our earlier discussion of speech in shopping centers bears directly on the mass media, and it is appropriate here to draw the lessons from it. There are obvious analogies between the modern American shopping center and the mass media. Both mass media organizations and shopping centers consist of large private organizations that serve (one as an essential part of its role, the other accidentally) as forums for discussion and debate; both have largely driven out smaller competitors. Each has assumed an essentially different function from those of the institutions out of which it has evolved. The shopping center is more than a collection of private stores; it includes the spaces between and around them, and so replicates not just the businesses of Main Street but the municipality as well. Analogously, the mass news organization is not simply a larger version of its predecessor; for all the reasons described in the last section, it has become not only an actor but the stage as well. Alternative channels of communication to the mass media are not comparable to it, and so not satisfactory: they cannot possibly reach the same or equivalent audiences. Thus the principle that emerges from the shopping center cases, that the weight of arguments for access depends on the availability of reasonable alternative channels of communication, suggests the appropriateness of regulating the media.[40]

Some will resist the analogy between shopping centers and mass media, for at least two reasons. In the first place, the shopping center cases produce a mixed bag of results and hardly provide resounding support for the rights of free speech. Second, the analogy ignores an important difference between shopping centers and the mass media: the opposing interests of the latter are themselves free speech interests, while those of the former are merely property interests. Once this difference is taken into account, it will be argued, the interests of those who desire access to the mass media pale to insignificance.

In response to the first objection, we should remember that the

principle in the shopping center cases takes the form of a hypothetical: *if*, or *to the extent that*, reasonable alternative channels of
communication do not exist, to that extent the claims of free speech
weigh more heavily. The Court's view that in many cases reasonable alternatives to the shopping center do exist does not affect
the principle. I believe it is clear that the antecedent is fulfilled in
the case of the mass media: small journals and pamphlets are not
reasonable alternatives to CBS and the *New York Times*.

How important, then, is the fact that the interests not only of
those desiring access but also of their opponents are free speech
interests? (Partly free speech interests, anyway; like shopping centers, mass media organizations are also commercial enterprises.)
Journalists and media executives imagine that granting access
rights must entail censorship of their own views, or, what may
seem worse, coercion to publish something against their will. But
we need to examine these fears more carefully. One concern is
that in being forced to publish an opinion, a person or an organization will be identified with a view it does not hold, and this
is very troubling. But a "contingent" right of access, say, to respond to an attack in a newspaper, does not have this character;
no one wants to prevent the publisher from disowning the view.
The other fear rests on the belief that having to publish one thing
means that one is unable to publish something else, and so in
effect amounts to censorship. In the real world, however, not every
inability to publish due to having to publish something else can
be seriously regarded as censorship. If a network cancels "Wheel
of Fortune" to carry a political debate, censorship is not at issue.
Moreover, publishing is not always a zero-sum game; it is sometimes possible just to publish more.[41]

It does not follow, then, that because news organizations, unlike shopping centers, possess significant free speech interests and
not merely property interests, access claims are stripped of their
legitimacy or their power. What follows is just that we may sometimes have to weigh one free speech interest against another.

X

No one likes to have his freedom curtailed, and so it is not surprising that journalists and media professionals find the foregoing

arguments extremely distasteful. I have been trying to show why some of the most important weapons in journalists' defense of freedom of the press do not find their mark, and in the process to explode some of the rhetoric surrounding the role of the press in our society, by analyzing the idea of a "right" to editorial autonomy and the interconnections and confusions between speech and property interests. Still, it may be argued, I have neglected an argument against government regulation just as fundamental as those I have rejected. This is the simple idea that the press must be free of government interference just because, whatever the defects or corruptions of the press, government can never be trusted to correct them. The prospect of regulators regulating their own potential critics appears to involve a basic conflict of interest. The principle implicit here, that the state should not interfere in the workings of the press, is as fundamental as any.

The appropriate response is not that we can trust government more than opponents of regulation believe, but that we can trust others less. Regulation is needed just because private power poses a grave threat to the independence and integrity of the press. Reasonable people will disagree, of course, about whether the dangers to the press posed by enormous concentrations of private power are so great that we must risk government regulation, or whether the state is so untrustworthy, its motives so compromised by conflict of interest, that we must take our chances and leave the mass media entirely in the hands of corporations.

Against the latter view—that here government cannot be trusted, period—several things can be said. First, anyone who suspects government so unrelentingly needs to justify his (relative) trust of corporations. Both, after all, are made up of human beings with (we may assume) similar psychologies and motivational structures. Second, the state is not a monolithic force but a collection of varied agencies, some of which can be more insulated from partisan politics than others. Third, support of government regulation of the press is compatible with strict opposition to censorship. The point is not to prevent news organizations from expressing their views but to ensure the expression of other views; and, as I argued earlier, the latter does not entail the former. Finally, only some forms of regulation involve the kind of intrusion that is so worrisome. Two broad approaches to regulation of the media are usually distinguished. *Content regulation* makes specific demands of press institutions to cover certain kinds of issues, to cover them in a certain way, or to provide access to certain points of view. (The Fairness Doctrine is the most prominent example.) *Structural regulation* instead builds rules and constraints into the structure and organization of the media taken as a whole. Structural regulation includes a variety of approaches. Certain rules prohibit multiple ownership of news organizations, and others designate a number of cable channels for public access. Economic incentives can be offered to news organizations to promote diversity or provide services that are unlikely to be provided in the unrestricted marketplace. Subsidies can be given to public media institutions. Government currently subsidizes public broadcasting with tax dollars, but other approaches are possible. One attractive proposal is to exact a "spectrum fee" from broadcasters for the privilege (now granted free) of being able to broadcast,[42] and to use the funds to finance public broadcasting or to subsidize groups lacking the resources to penetrate the major avenues of mass communication.

Structural approaches to regulation considerably weaken the objection that in principle government is in no position to regulate the press; they demonstrate that how intrusive regulation is depends on the form it takes, something over which we have a great deal of control. Structural approaches also counter the argument that regulation is counterproductive—that it causes "chilling effects" because news organizations, fearing, for example, that controversial programming will trigger Fairness Doctrine complaints, will simply avoid conflict by airing innocuous or frivolous programs. These objections still hold for content regulation, but even there their validity and force is still very much under debate.

I do not mean by the brevity of this discussion to suggest that these objections have been overcome. On the contrary, they require more discussion than is possible here. My point is rather to relocate the focus of debate about freedom of the press and the justifiability of its regulation, from the realm of rights and principles to that of practical possibility and utility—to questions about what works to produce more diversity, and whether regulation does more harm than good. The debate needs to be relocated not, of course, because rights and principles have no place in the discussion of these issues or in the formation of public policy, but because the press appears to be claiming special rights not possessed by the rest of us, and these require special justification. If press institutions or their agents have special rights, it is because the people as a whole have granted them; if the people have granted them, it is because doing so is to the benefit of us all. It is the unthinking assumption that we are all better off if the mass media are left to their own devices that is challenged by the character of the mass media and their role in the structure of contemporary society.

NOTES

1. This formulation is neat but misleading. Viewed in purely quantitative terms, information is plentiful; indeed the problem is that we are flooded with it and must take measures to stem the tide. When we talk about enhancing or inhibiting the flow of ideas and information, then, we are thinking about quality and diversity, not mere quantity. Our concern is that we find less diversity in the mass media than we could and should, and than we would in the absence of *mass* media altogether.

2. See, e.g., Ben Bagdikian, *The Media Monopoly* (Boston: Beacon Press, 1983), esp. chap. 3; Tom Goldstein, *The News at Any Cost* (New York: Simon and Schuster, 1985), chap. 5; Peter Dreier and Steve Weinberg, "Interlocking Directorates," *Columbia Journalism Review*, November/December 1979.

3. As compared, for example, with the European press, I mean to include here not just pure opinion (in the sense used by journalists)— what is found on the editorial and op-ed pages—but explanatory journalism and news analysis as well as straight news. The narrowness is evident, for example, in the debate about providing military aid to the Nicaraguan Contras—no one argues that we ought to support the Sandinistas ("opinion"); in analysis of the arms race and arms control, where American government allegations that apparent moves by the Soviets toward arms reduction are merely public relations ploys are rarely questioned (news analysis); and in coverage of events—compare, for example, the amount of coverage allocated to the murder of Alex Odeh, Los Angeles regional director of the American-Arab Anti-Discrimination Committee, during the Achille Lauro crisis, with that allocated to the murder of Leon Klinghoffer. For a critical analysis of American media coverage of terrorism and related phenomena, see Edward S. Herman, *The Real Terror Network: Terrorism in Fact and Propaganda* (Boston: South End Press, 1982). Views out of the mainstream do occasionally appear, but not often or prominently enough to engage public debate.

4. Especially for a nonjournalist, specifying what of importance is not

reported is fraught with paradox, since it requires independent access to news sources. How do you know what is news except by following the usual sources? But see, e.g., Jerry Kammer, "The Navajos, the Hopis, and the U.S. Press," *Columbia Journalism Review*, July/August 1986, on the media's neglect of the federal government's largest forcible relocation since the internment of Japanese-Americans in World War II: the relocation of Navajo Indians as part of an attempt to resolve a historic fued between the Navajos and the Hopis. Unlike Wounded Knee, this story has not (yet) become theater.

5. The crucial case is *Miami Herald v. Tornillo*, 418 U.S. 241 (1974), where the Supreme Court held that a newspaper was not required to print a reply by a candidate attacked in editorials. The case contrasts sharply with *Red Lion Broadcasting v. FCC*, 395 U.S. 367 (1969), in which the Court upheld the FCC's requirements that radio and television stations provide free reply time to those attacked in station broadcasts.

6. By limited rights of access I mean so-called "contingent" access rights, those triggered by actions of a news organization—such as editorials attacking a candidate of the kind involved in *Miami Herald*.

7. "The *public* use of man's reason must always be free, and it alone can bring about enlightenment among men . . . by the public use of one's own reason I mean that use which anyone may make of it as *a man of learning* addressing the entire *reading public*" (*Kant's Political Writings*, ed. Hans Reiss [Cambridge: Cambridge University Press, 1970], p. 55).

8. Such "internal" arguments are also made to restrict nonpress speech—to justify not tolerating the intolerant, or silencing the heckler, for example. The success of such arguments rests largely on their internal character, especially since the First Amendment (or, more generally, a serious commitment to free speech) means that a much stronger justification is required to restrict speech than to restrict most other activities. Thus the argument that the values of free speech themselves justify restriction has a persuasive force that most other arguments for restriction lack. See Owen Fiss, "Why the State?" in *Democracy and the Mass Media*, ed. Judith Lichtenberg, forthcoming.

9. For a related argument see Owen Fiss, "Free Speech and Social Structure," *Iowa Law Review* 71 (1986): 1408–10.

10. For the argument from tolerance, see Lee C. Bollinger, *The Tolerant Society: Freedom of Speech and Extremist Speech in America* (Oxford: Clarendon Press, 1986).

11. For a view of autonomy as the preeminent value in freedom of expression, see Thomas Scanlon, "A Theory of Freedom of Expression," *Philosophy & Public Affairs* 1 (1972). The emphasis on inner freedom goes back at least to Epictetus and Socrates.

12. See Frederick Schauer, *Free Speech: A Philosophical Inquiry* (Cambridge: Cambridge University Press, 1982), chap. 4, for this kind of objection.

13. Meiklejohn, *Political Freedom* (New York: Harper, 1960), pp. 8–28.

14. Some democrats (and others) would emphasize another value bearing on free speech that Meiklejohn ignores: political participation. If, as

Aristotle and Hannah Arendt believed, the good life includes public activity and the good society supports a high degree of civic participation, the political value of free speech will not be exhausted by its informational, critical, or even its representational functions. But although participation is a value, I do not believe it is an indispensable precondition of democracy, as equality is. At most, the more participation the better. Even this is not obvious, since political involvement precludes other valuable commitments for which many people would choose to sacrifice it. (Participation might still be better for the society, even if not for all participating members.) In any case, the value of civic participation is a further argument for the worth of freedom of speech.

15. It does not follow that there is a strict deductive relationship (in either direction) between the arguments from truth and democracy. Socrates was certainly a fallibilist and an eloquent defender of the argument from truth but was no democrat, precisely because he doubted that people in general could put aside their passions and prejudices long enough to hear a case on its merits. It is much more difficult to imagine a democrat not committed to the argument from truth, however. (That is partly because of the complex nature of truth in "the great practical concerns of life," in Mill's words. See below, next section.) But it may be possible. My claim is just that these arguments have a natural affinity, and especially that a democrat is almost certain to subscribe to the argument from truth.

16. On Liberty (Indianapolis: Bobbs-Merrill, 1956), pp. 69–70.

17. It does, of course, cost something to protect free speech and to keep order in the face of occasional violent outbreaks. Sometimes, traditions may even die and governments fall partly as a result of free speech. But education also creates these risks (if they are risks), in addition to its enormous monetary costs.

18. Mill, On Liberty, p. 44.

19. For a general view of truth as inseparable from the criteria for settling truth claims—a consensus theory of truth—see Jürgen Habermas, "A Postscript to Knowledge and Human Interests," Philosophy of the Social Sciences 3 (1973): 166–72; and Thomas McCarthy, The Critical Theory of Jürgen Habermas (Cambridge: MIT Press, 1978), pp. 299–307.

20. Mill, On Liberty, p. 58.

21. Ibid., p. 44.

22. See Karl Popper, Conjectures and Refutations: The Growth of Scientific Knowledge (New York: Harper Torchbooks, 1968), esp. p. 352.

23. For a defense of the view that early liberal theorists were just as concerned to prevent concentrations and abuses of private as of state power, see Stephen Holmes, "Order, Fairness, and Intelligent Government," in Democracy and the Mass Media, ed. Judith Lichtenberg; for the idea of the state as a countervailing power to private powers heavily imprinted with "social structure," see Owen Fiss, "Why the State?"

24. It might be argued that this begs the question. Since opponents of

antidiscrimination laws may also object to the entire system of public accommodations licensing as an illegitimate encroachment to their rights. I strongly suspect, however, that few who opposed the civil rights laws took this principled stand. They did not object to health and other regulations governing their restaurants, but insisted only that it was their (God-given) right to exclude blacks.

25. Perhaps I want to read your rare edition, though. Tough luck: the values of free speech support access to the content of books, not their form.

26. 326 U.S. 501.

27. 351 U.S. 105.

28. 391 U.S. 308.

29. 407 U.S. 539.

30. 407 U.S. 551.

31. 447 U.S. 74.

32. *Robins* v. *PruneYard Shopping Center*, 23 Cal. 3d 899, 907.

33. If these attempts fail, I may choose to publish my essay "privately" (as we say): I may engage a printer, or have my essay duplicated, or perhaps find a "vanity" press. Here too I am dependent on others who own things that I need; like the ordinary book or journal publisher, they are at liberty to refuse to handle my work (although they are much less likely to). The argument that follows supports the conclusion that if *everyone* whose cooperation was necessary for me to publish my essay refused to cooperate (i.e., if no one would sell me access to a copy machine, and no one would sell me a copy machine, and no one would sell me paper for it), the state ought to help me get my essay published in some form.

34. For a similar argument concerning the press's "right" to maintain confidentiality of sources, see Ronald Dworkin, "The Farber Case: Reporters and Informers." in *A Matter of Principle* (Cambridge: Harvard University Press, 1985), pp. 373–80.

35. See note 2 above. It does not follow that the news is crassly ideological; indeed, news organizations' need for a mass audience may dictate that news *not* be ideological in the usual sense, for this might turn off large numbers of people. The bias in the news toward official statements as against those of critical outsiders is a built-in advantage for officials that implies no explicit ideological message. See Gaye Tuchman, "Objectivity as Strategic Ritual: An Examination of Newsmen's Notions of Objectivity," *American Journal of Sociology* 77 (1972). The economic and political interests of news organizations manifest themselves most clearly in what does *not* make its way into the news, and in how stories relevant to the organizations' interest are reported.

36. I am opening a large can of worms here. The critique of the mass media rests partly on the claim that no sharp line can be drawn between "news" and "editorial" (and in turn between fact and value), that much of what is presented as news involves judgments of value and other controversial judgments. A better understanding of these

complications by members of the press and the public might help to put the mass media's role in perspective.

37. The alternative was commercial newspapers, which consisted mainly of advertising and shipping news. See Michael Schudson, *Discovering the News: A Social History of American Newspapers* (New York: Basic Books, 1978), pp. 14–15.

38. *Ibid.*

39. See Anthony Smith, *Goodbye Gutenberg: The Newspaper Revolution of the 1980s* (London: Oxford University Press, 1980), chap. 1 (esp. p. 30), for the view that readers now look to newspapers for "facts" rather than for an overall ideological picture of the world, as they did in the seventeenth and eighteenth centuries.

40. We might put this in terms of Habermas's notion of an "ideal speech situation." The aim of regulation would be to approach (although never, realistically, to achieve) an ideal speech situation: to equalize the chances of all participants or points of view to speak—to speak, that is, approximately as often and as loudly as others. Only in such circumstances, according to Habermas, can the quest for truth be free of distorting influences such as explicit or implicit relations of domination. Habermas's concern here is with truth, but the point applies to the other arguments for free speech as well. See Habermas, "Towards a Theory of Communicative Competence," *Inquiry* 13 (1970): 371–74; and McCarthy, *The Critical Theory of Jürgen Habermas*, pp. 307–10.

41. This would be true if newspapers were granted subsidies to cover costs of expanded op-ed pages and the like. Ironically, this argument makes the case for access to print stronger than the case for access to broadcast media, since the latter, as time-based rather than space-based, contains an inherent limit that the former does not. This conflicts with the standard view (rooted in First Amendment tradition) of the print media as more resistant to regulation than broadcasting.

42. For a defense of the spectrum fee idea, see Henry Geller, "Current Government Policy re Mass Communications," in *Democracy and the Mass Media*, ed. Judith Lichtenberg.

Study Questions

1. State why you agree or do not agree with Professor Lichtenberg's contention that ". . . government regulation of the press is compatible with strict opposition to censorship?"

2. Explain why you believe or do not believe that we must trust the government to some extent—if only because the "private power" that controls the media can be trusted even less. In this connection, do you agree with her contention that ". . . the state is not a "monolithic

force but a collection of varied agencies, some of which can be more insulated from partisan politics than others?" (Note that many thinkers have denied this, arguing that, in effect, no government agency can stray very far from the views and wishes of the President, if they are to survive.)

Is Objectivity Possible?

Donald McDonald*

Truth and politics are on rather bad terms with each other. No one, as far as I know, has ever counted truthfulness among the political virtues. . . . Seen from the viewpoint of politics, truth has a despotic character. It is therefore hated by tyrants, who rightly fear the competition of a coercive force they cannot monopolize, and it enjoys a rather precarious status in the eyes of governments that rest on consent and abhor coercion.

—Hannah Arendt

The antidote for political deviousness is journalistic integrity. Since truthfulness is not a political virtue, it has to be a journalistic virtue.

But perhaps integrity and truthfulness are terms that are too morally intense, too loaded with accusatory implications for an analysis aimed at discovering both the enabling and limiting elements in the practice of public-affairs journalism. Journalistic objectivity is a better term. Badly misunderstood and badly applied as it has been in the history of American journalism, objectivity subsumes all the mass-communication virtues—moral, artistic, and intellectual. It covers the individual journalist and the institution that employs him. And while it is a goal it is also a process, a kind of operational guideline, a demanding but not impossibly idealistic criterion of professional competence.

Objectivity (not to be confused with objectivism, a specialized and technical philosophical theory of knowledge) is here used to mean simply an essential correspondence between knowledge of a thing and the thing itself. The best translation of the term into its journalistic application may have been furnished by the Free-

* Mr. McDonald is editor of *The Center Magazine* and former dean of the Marquette University College of Journalism. This article is reprinted from *The Center Magazine* (Center for the Study of Democratic Institutions, Santa Barbara, Calif.), Vol. IV, No. 5, Sept./Oct., 1971.

dom of the Press Commission in 1947. The Commission said that, among other things, the press owes to society "a truthful, comprehensive, and intelligent account of the day's events in a context which gives them meaning."

I suppose that no reporter or editor would take exception to such a definition of the journalist's responsibility. Not many reporters get up in the morning and say to themselves, "Today I am going to file a lying, incomplete, ignorant report of an event taken out of context." But then how account for the quality of public-affairs journalism in this country? Arthur R. Murphy, the former chairman of *McCall's* magazine, has said that in spite of our 10,000 newspapers, 8,000 magazines, and 7,000 radio and television stations, Americans suffer from an "understanding gap" and are "ill-informed and confused about major issues and events."

Objectivity is problematic in public-affairs journalism because elements and practices in the reporting process are taken for granted and perpetuated by journalists when they should be critically examined. The reporter, the reader-viewer, the conventions of American journalism, the forms and processes of the communications institutions, language, the investigative and interpretive functions of the reporter, all affect the objectivity of mass communication. A misunderstanding or malfunctioning of any of them is enough to defeat or at least seriously impair the efforts of even the most nobly motivated journalist.

Let us begin with the reporter. From the myriad of details of an event or situation, the reporter selects those which seem to him most significant, investigates and asks questions to clarify the meaning of what he has perceived, and then organizes his knowledge in a report. What the reporter selects for attention, the weight he puts on the various elements, the kinds of questions he asks, are all influenced by the personal history he brings to his work.

Indeed, even what he initially preceives is conditioned by his history. Some years ago, Dr. Robert Livingston, then with the National Institute of Mental Health, on a visit to the Center, reported that experiments by neurosurgeons and neurophysiologists indicate that man's entire nervous system, in its interpreting, sensing, and transmitting to the brain the information it receives, builds up through the years total-response patterns which, as they stabilize, thenceforth affect in a definite accept-reject manner the perceiving capacity of a person.

We are familiar with the classic psychological and sociological experiments testing the ability of students to perceive, recall, and report staged dramatic incidents they have witnessed. The wildly varying reports of the same incident reflect what Walter Lippmann has called the tricks of memory and the incessant creative quality of the imagination of the witness.

According to Lippmann, experience seems to show that the reporter brings something to the scene which later he takes away from it. A report is the joint product of the knower and the known, in which the role of the observer is always selective and usually creative. The facts we see depend on where we are placed and the habits of our eyes.

A few years ago, when Lillian Ross's book, *Reporting*, appeared, her publisher claimed that one never doubts that what she sees is the truth. But a reviewer in the *Times Literary Supplement* demurred. "One eyewitness," the reviewer said, "tells us what she has seen and heard and put together; it is not the truth about anything, but one person's selection from the chaos of facts, images, words, all the ingredients of experience she has witnessed from her single viewpoint. We might guess more about the truth or at least the heart of the matter, all the omissions and distortions, if we knew more about the reporter, her psychological blocks, and the limits of her experience, but it is a conceit of this school of reporting to pretend to omit the reporter. The reporter, however, is human and therefore limited, and if we have no knowledge of her limitations we are merely being deceived."

The reviewer went on to say that "James Agee was at the opposite extreme as a reporter. He wrote in perhaps the greatest work of reportage of this century, *Let Us Now Praise Famous Men*, about a tenant farmer: 'I know him only so far as I know him: and all of that depends as fully on who I am as on who he is.' Thus Agee accepted, as Miss Ross apparently does not, that any subject is sieved through a reporter's self and, therefore, Agee showed the interplay between himself and the people and places he was trying to describe."

Now, whether Miss Ross rejects what Mr. Agee accepted, and whether or how it would be feasible for every reporter to reveal within every report his "psychological blocks and the limits of his experience," and whether Miss Ross's reporting is "not the truth about anything" are all arguable. What is not deniable is the sieving process through which reality must pass in the reporter's work. The question is, how can reality emerge from this subjective process without being essentially diminished and distorted? I do not think the answer lies simply in the reporter's showing the interplay between himself and the things he is reporting. At best this permits the reader to discount the report for its acknowledged subjective elements, but it leaves him waiting for a more satisfying, more objective, less distorted account of public affairs.

When the reporter moves from relatively uncomplicated, concrete, even physical phenomena into the realm of the abstract and the complex—i.e., studies, conferences, programs, policies on urban affairs, race and ethic relations, foreign and military affairs, economic and fiscal conditions, the administration of criminal justice, cultural ferment, youth unrest, population problems, environmental issues, politics, and government—the value judgments he must make at every critical stage in his investigation and interpretation of the facts must reflect the values he already holds. Again, these values flow from his personal history. They are the products of his education, his religious experience, his childhood, family life, social and economic background, friendships and associations, national ties and culture, as well as his emotional life and experiences, and his reason.

Take just one of the value-influences in the reporter's life: his national ties. Both individual reports of the Vietnam war and overall coverage have differed markedly from nation to nation. This cannot be attributed altogether to external censorship. I.F. Stone once noted that an Associated Press dispatch on American military, political, and diplomatic activity in Vietnam, prepared for publication in the French newspaper, Le Monde, contained material far more critical of the United States than anything filed by the A.P. for consumption in American newspapers.

A book by Jay Epstein raised serious questions about the Warren Commission's investigation of the Kennedy assassination. Richard Rovere has said that Epstein is a scholar who had done what the American press should have done when the Warren Commission report was issued. "It should have cast a very cool eye on the report and sought to learn from those who prepared it how it was prepared, who did the heavy work, and what individual workers thought of the collective product. Mr. Epstein's scholarly tools happen to be those employed day in and day out by journalists. But the press left it to a single scholar to find the news."

Epstein suggested that a kind of national loyalty seems to have got in the way of the journalists and their reporting obligation. They produced a "version of the truth . . . to reassure the nation and protect the national interest."

George Orwell's classic essay, "Politics and the English Language," suggests not only that politics and language can be mutually degrading when in the hands of corrupt persons, but that all of us, including reporters, go along rather uncritically with the degrading process. A paragraph from Orwell's essay, written more than 30 years ago, is an uncomfortable reminder that little has changed in those three decades:

> In our time, political speech and writing are largely the defense of the indefensible. Things like the continuance of British rule in India, the Russian purges and deportations, the dropping of the atom bombs on Japan, can indeed be defended, but only by arguments which are too brutal for most people to face, and which do not square with the professed aims of political parties. Thus political language has to consist largely of euphemism, question-begging, and sheer cloudy vagueness. Defenseless villages are bombarded from the air, the inhabitants driven out into the countryside, the cattle machine-gunned, the huts set on fire with incendiary bullets: this is called *pacification* Millions of peasants are robbed of their farms and sent trudging along the roads with no more than they can carry: this is called *transfer of population* or *rectification of frontiers*. People are imprisoned for years without trial, or shot in the back of the neck, or sent to die of scurvy in Arctic lumber camps: this is called *elimination of unreliable elements*. Such phraseology is needed if one wants to name things without calling up mental pictures of them . . .

No one can, or perhaps ever will, prevent politicians and political organizations from using language this way. The question is whether journalists can rise above natural allegiance to their nation and report the realities obscured by this kind of partisan euphemism.

Another element in the reporting process affecting objectivity is the journalistic conventions, as distinguished from journalistic processes. The latter inhere in the very nature of the medium (newspaper, magazine, radio, television) and are to that extent inescapable, though sometimes they can be modified in the interest of objectivity. Journalistic conventions, however, were established to meet historical conditions. As such they can be sharply modified, or even discarded and new ones substituted when those historical conditions no longer exist, or when, again in the interest of objective reporting, the conventions are no longer useful or even obstructive. But conventions have a way of hanging on.

The most pernicious journalistic convention is the notion that a thing is not newsworthy until it becomes an event; that is, until something happens. Two things follow from this: first, significant phenomena that are not events (e.g., situations, trends, conditions) go largely unreported; second, often the context which can make even an event meaningful, is either not reported or reported inadequately.

It was not until Michael Harrington wrote his book on poverty in America (*The Other America*) that national consciousness was focused on a situation existing in the backyard of every metropolitan newspaper in the United States.

It was not until Richard Harris reported in *The New Yorker* on the unethical conditions in the ethical-drug industry that the American people were alerted to a situation that the wire services or even a metropolitan newspaper could have investigated and reported years before.

At the height of the Watts riots in 1965, a white Protestant churchman in Los Angeles shook his head and said, "I hadn't known such conditions [despair, unemployment, resentment among the blacks] existed in that area."

Even as sophisticated a newspaper as *The New York Times* has not always been able to free itself from the notion that "something has to happen" before you can publish. The May, 1966, issue of *Times Talk*, the house newsletter written by and for staff members of the *Times*, contains an article by Tom Wicker, of the *Times*' Washington bureau, on the circumstances surrounding the paper's publication that year of a series of articles on the Central Intelligence Agency. Six members of the *Times* had spent months interviewing, researching, writing, rewriting the material for those articles. At last they were ready for publication. But it seems they really were not ready.

"Turner Catledge [then executive editor of the *Times*]," Wicker said, "had insisted from the first on having an adequate news peg. Months now had passed since the 'Singapore incident' set the whole thing off. Weeks were to pass before the right time came to publish. Finally *Ramparts* magazine broke the Michigan State case, in which it was discovered that C.I.A. agents had been given cover in a big aid program the university operated for the Diem regime in South Vietnam."

Also in the news at that time was a slander suit in a Baltimore court involving a C.I.A. agent.

"Thus," Wicker continued, "with the C.I.A. in the news again, the time was ripe, public interest was awakened, and our editors thought we had the justification we needed for five articles, twenty-three thousand words in all, trying to answer the questions we had asked ourselves those long months ago. Hastily, over a weekend, we wrote the news-peg material into the pieces and gave the galley proofs a last close check for accuracy and for any updating needed."

Another convention of American journalism is that the reader interest can only be attracted by conflict, novelty, or recency. This leads the reporter to neglect that which can make his report meaningful, the context. The Los Angeles *Times*, ordinarily fastidious in its reporting of public affairs, lapsed a few years ago with some no-context reporting in its coverage of strikes by county social-welfare workers and hospital employees. The paper detailed the conflict elements in the strikes: the accusations and counteraccusations by strikers and county supervisors, the actions by pickets and nonstrikers, the threats and counterthreats. But aside from one vague reference to "working conditions" the reporters did not tell the readers the context of the strikes. The actual pay and working conditions of the workers, the level of their education,, their conpensation related to the nature of their work and cost of living, the history of salary increases, the comparison of pay scales with those of similar workers in other cities—none of this contextual material was furnished until a week or two later after letters had been sent to the editors pointing out the omission.

This convention—that reader interest can only be attracted and held by the bizarre, by conflict, novelty, recency—stemmed in part from the days when newspapers competed with each other for readers within the same community, when the educational level of the average American adult was low, and when the time and energy the American worker could give to informing himself on public affairs was sharply limited. Those conditions no longer exist.

There are other journalistic conventions that need reëxamination, perhaps discarding. James Reston has described, in *Foreign Affairs*, how the press associations invented the headline or all-purpose agency news story which could be published at length in the large city papers or cut in half for the middle towns or reduced to a paragraph for the very small papers. This solution to a technical problem had results nobody in the Associated Press or United Press International intended. "It tended to sharpen and inflate the news," Reston wrote. "It created a tradition of putting the most dramatic fact in the story first and then following it with paragraphs of decreasing importance. Thus it encouraged not a balanced but a startling presentation of the news, based on what one of my irreverent colleagues calls the 'Christ, how the wind blew!' lead. This was fine for the news of wrecks or murders, but was a limiting and distorting device as news of foreign policy became more and more complicated."

Reston is convinced that newspaper journalists must twist themselves around and "see these wider perspectives of the news, the causes as well as the effects. . . . Ideas are news, and are not covering the news of the mind as we should. This is where rebellion, revolution, and war start, but we minimize the conflict of ideas and emphasize the conflict in the streets, without relating the second to the first."

I have often been struck by the way in which serious books—the "news of the mind"—are handled by the American press. When they are not ignored, they pop up in book pages, more often than not as notices rather than reviews. The idea that books such as Lewis Mumford's *The Myth of the Machine*, or Jean Gottmann's study of the metropolitan city, or Ivar Berg's *Education and Jobs: The Great Training Robbery* are important news events, or, better, serious treatments of public affairs worth reporting as such, does not occur in a climate of conventional journalistic values.

A third element in the reporting process is the thing reported. It is a commonplace that complexity is a characteristic of public affairs. Robert Lekachman, the economist, has criticized the mass media for not respecting the complexity of economic issues which, he says, almost always relate to other problems of civil rights, urbanization, transportation, education, space and science research. But with few exceptions these are reported, Lekachman says, as items of interest only to the business and financial community. Thus, a Presidential message on the budget and the economic condition of the nation—a matter of wide-ranging social, cultural, and political ramification—will be explained, if it is explained at all, in narrow terms and invariably in the business section of the newspaper.

Public-affairs issues are complex not only in their horizontal relationships with other issues but also vertically in their own historical antecedents. The meaning of American involvement in Vietnam is largely bound up with an historical sequence of events which started in the late nineteen-forties and which were themselves influenced by our obsession with communism (which had *its* antecedents), as well as with the history of Vietnam itself and that people's two-thousand-year relationship with China and its much briefer relationship with France.

Too, public-affairs issues are usually not neat, beginning-middle-and-end "stories," but continually unfolding realities, and therein lies another dimension of their complexity. The reporter's accounts will be faithful to that fact if they are themselves openended, provisional, constantly revised as the issues play themselves out and as reactions follow actions.

The task of the objective reporter is to discover and communicate the coherence of a complex, unfolding reality. He can do it by his contextual reporting; by plainly showing the unavoidable but significant gaps in his information; by recapitulating and reviewing the reality in print when important new facts become available; by continuous surveying of the current literature which may illuminate shadowy areas; and by interviewing experts and scholars for further illumination.

Einar Ostgaard of the Peace Research Institute in Olso and Jacques Ellul, the French social critic, are not the only ones to have commented on the discontinuities in the mass media's presentation of great public issues. But none have made the point more sharply.

Ostgaard traces the discontinuities to the way the media define newsworthiness. As long as news must have a certain simplicity, easy reader identification, closeness in either a physical or cultural sense, and excitement—as long as this kind of news barrier is in effect, there will be little or no continuity in the presentation of world events.

"Certain news media," Ostgaard writes, "will attempt to present a continuous report of what happens. But as long as a decision on whether or not to publish a story is also based on [the above] considerations, the result must be a certain degree of discontinuity. . . . A report from London may appear on a Monday, drop out of sight on Tuesday and Wednesday for lack of space (although the news agencies are still dutifully reporting), reappear on Thursday, but by now [there is] a mystery since what went on in the interim was never published."

The interim developments were omitted "because these happenings were no longer 'news.' Proximity in time is often a major prerequisite for a news story. Thus, the shorter the time it takes for an event 'to happen' the more likely it is to be reported fully, and conversely, the longer the time it takes, the larger the probabilities that only an incomplete picture of the event will be presented. This time factor is also probably related to the degree to which the event will appear to be exciting and this contributes to the 'sensationalism' factor."

Ostgaard quotes from Bernard Cohen's study of the matter: "In hopping from issue to issue, from crisis to crisis, the correspondent deals in political discontinuities" and gives a "grossly uneven, often misleading picture of the world and its political relationships and problems. . . . So far from reflecting difficult international realities as they confront the statesman [such reporting] has no politically relevant public-opinion uses. . . . If the reporting of developments in terms of conflict exacerbates conflict, then, *mutatis mutandis*, the simplification of foreign-affairs reporting exacerbates the dangers of simplification in the approach to complex issues."

Ellul noted in his book, *The Political Illusion*, that "man has discontinuous consciousness, and the first effect of news on him is not to make him more capable of being a citizen but to disperse his attention, to absorb it, and present to him an excessive amount of information that he will not be able to absorb, information too diverse to serve him in any way whatever. . . .

"As a result, a truly stupefying lack of continuity is created, for if one information item merely effaces the other on the same

subject, it would not be so bad; but a continuous flow of information on a specific question, showing a problem's origin, growth,
crisis, and denouement is very rare. Most frequently my attention,
attracted today by Turkey, will be absorbed tomorrow by a financial crisis in New York and the day after tomorrow by parachutists
in Sumatra. In the midst of all this, how can a man not specially
trained perceive the slightest continuity, experience the slightest
political continuity; how, finally, can he understand? He can literally only react to news."

The processes of the communications media, as distinct from the
conventions adopted by journalists, inhere in the nature of the
media and in their forms—primarily the printed words and photographs of the newspaper and magazine, the broadcast language
of radio, and the words and motion pictures of television. Obviously, inherent processes cannot be discarded and replaced. But
if their distinctive effects are understood and their limitations recognized, they can be used more effectively in the interest of objective reporting; at the minimum, working journalists will be less
likely to deceive themselves as to how "truthful, comprehensive,
and intelligent" are their accounts of public affairs.

When the Army-McCarthy hearings were televised in the 1950s,
it seemed that for the first time the essence of what had come to
be called McCarthyism was communicated to the American people. Television sight and sound revealed something about Joseph
McCarthy which print journalists had labored in vain to reveal in
the preceding four or five years. Professional opinion pollsters say
that McCarthy's decline dates from those hearings.

Similarly, television documentaries on the working and living
conditions of migratory farm workers, on life in the black ghettos,
on the treatment given in homes for the aged and the mentally
ill, on drug addiction, on conditions in prisons, have communicated those realities in a way that print journalists cannot hope
to match through the written word.

And it was not until John F. Kennedy and Richard Nixon were
simultaneously compared and contrasted in their televised Presidential campaign debates in 1960 that many American people
formed a judgment as to the character and capabilities of the
candidates.

We can go back to Cardinal Newman and all the way back to

Aristotle for an explanation of what it is and why it is that televised communication has a more immediately powerful and gripping impact than print and why, at the same time, it is so severely limited in other respects.

Television simulates personal experience. While our understanding of a thing through experience may be far from complete, our assent to the existential judgment of the reality of that thing will be, in Newman's distinction, real as compared to notional. If one is told Britain is an island, Newman said, one makes a notional assent. If one actually sees that Britain is an island, sails all around it, one's assent to the truth becomes real.

But assent is not always equivalent to understanding. Experience, Aristotle said, is of individual things; understanding and wisdom are of causes and universals. "We do not regard any of our senses as wisdom, yet surely these give the most authoritative knowledge of particulars. But they do not tell us the 'why' of anything."

Although television is by its nature sense-oriented, engaging our sight and hearing, and therefore primarily concerned with particulars, it can explore the "why" of things when it also engages our reason. The more probing televised documentary films travel a respectable distance in that direction.

But it is the simulated personal experience, and all the moral and emotional content, the immediacy, and the self-involvement in personal experience that characterize television's effect. Undoubtedly we experience far more than we understand, and it is probably no less true that it is experience rather than understanding that most influences our behavior, even when the televised experience is not only simulated but manipulated, as Joe McGinnis showed us in his report, *The Selling of the President*. Certainly the contrived image of Richard Nixon and the rigorously controlled conditions under which he was presented to the viewers in 1968 resulted in many of them apparently acting on *that* experience of Mr. Nixon rather than on any genuine knowledge of the man.

The power of television to influence behavior is not diminished because politicians, and the television journalists themselves, can falsify the reality they are broadcasting. Indeed, the effectiveness of the deception underscores the power of the television medium as such.

But for an understanding of complex public-affairs issues and a grasp of the "why" of an event, we need more than the sight and the sound provided by television, more than the uncontrived experience of what the camera and microphone in the hands of truthful and competent broadcast journalists can convey to us, more than the moral conviction and emotional involvement aroused by such an experience. We need the opportunity for recurrent study and reflection on these issues. In short we need to make room for the work of reason. And for that, the printed word is indispensable.

It is the special temptation of television newsmen to believe that visibility and meaning are synonymous. But one television journalist, Walter Cronkite, resists the temptation. He has said that electronic journalism will never replace the written word in the communication of the meaning of public affairs. In the interest of objectivity, television reporters can, in the very act of reporting, make clear to their viewers what aspects of an issue or situation their medium must leave either unreported or only partially reported, and the reasons why.

The time and space allotted for reporting significantly affect the objectivity of the journalist's work. It can be argued that speeed is a convention rather than an inherent process of mass communication. I think it is more accurate to say that the daily rhythm and tempo of mass communication correspond to the rhythm and tempo of human life itself. But it must also be said that a mutual, or reciprocating, action occurs: i.e., the rhythm and tempo of human action, the affairs of mankind, can be adjusted to meet the requirements of the communications media. When a President times an outburst of indignation so that it will be seen on the television screen in the evening or be read in the Sunday morning metropolitan papers of the nation, obviously public affairs have been adjusted to the rhythm of the media. (The Presidential display, at its inception, may be what Daniel Boorstin has described as a "pseudo-event," but once it occurs it is an authentic public affair, more or less rich, more or less significant, but a public affair nonetheless.)

Objectivity is affected not so much by mutual adjustments in rhythm and tempo between the media and the actors in the drama of public affairs as it is by the easy—often lazy—assumption adopted by some journalists that their breathless journalism is adequate to the communication of public affairs. It is the indiscriminate application of speed and the forcing of all public affairs, no matter how complex, obscure, and developmental they may be, into the mold of instant journalism that threatens objectivity.

Obviously many human affairs have their regular diurnal aspect. Sporting contests, stock-market activities, educational programs—these have their clocklike patterns, they are predictable, they mesh with the mass media communication timetables. But it is axiomatic that the more serious and consequential the public affairs, the untidier they will be and the more unmanageable they will be by any of the metronomic standards set by the print and electronic media.

Those metronomic imperatives sometimes exert a fascinating effect on editors and a bizarre, distorting effect on their journalism. Douglass Cater in his book, *The Fourth Branch of Government*, tells about one Washington wire-service editor who, in a running story, in order to have "something of interest" for editors of both morning and afternoon papers, "creates" stories by baiting public officials with "conflict queries."

Although language is the indispensable tool of the journalist, one need not read very widely on the subject nor think about it at any great length to realize that language demands the ultimate in craftsmanship, moral sensitivity, and intelligence. How language is used is crucial to the possibility of objective journalism. Herewith, some testimony to the difficulties in making language serve the cause of objectivity:

> Much self-control and great disinterestedness are needed by those who would realize the ideal of never misusing language. A man who habitually speaks and writes correctly is one who has cured himself, not merely of conscious and deliberate lying, but also (and the task is much more difficult and at least as important) of unconscious mendacity.
>
> —Aldous Huxley

> Nothing is more common than for men to think that because they are familiar with words they understand the ideas they stand for.
>
> —Cardinal Newman

> [The Thomists] showed that language and meaning depend on the past experiences of men; that different words can mean different

things to different men; that neither language nor knowledge is identical with reality. The Scholastic maxim—"never deny; rarely affirm; always distinguish"—is a medieval way, if you wish, of warning against the dangers of over-generalization.

—Margaret Gorman

If there is one thing certain, the truth will not be caught once and for all in a net of words alone.

—Weller Embler

The spoken word and the reading of its written equivalent are both of them fundamentally the exercise of choice at every step—choosing not only the right sounds and combinations of sounds but also the right words and combinations of words to fit the continually emerging patterns both of language and of life.

—Joshua Whatmough

The fact remains that, imperfect as words are as symbols of our ideas and as expressions of our thoughts, the journalist cannot dispense with them. Words may not be sufficient, but they are necessary. Even Marshall McLuhan's envisioned electric future in which experience will be communicated visually and configurationally rather than in the sequential, linear form of the printed word is a communication impossibility without the use of language.

Let us stipulate, then, that language alone is an imperfect medium for the expression of truth. Words can be inexact when precision is needed; ambiguous when univocal meaning is required; connotative when definition and denotation are demanded; allusive when identity is sought.

But it would be too easy and certainly misleading to conclude that the infelicities of language are indefeasible. After due allowances are made for the irreducible element of imperfection in words as signs of things and thoughts, it seems obvious that the task of communicating through language is primarily intellectual. Clear expression begins with clear thinking.

The task is also one of artistry. The craftsmanship of putting clear thoughts into clear language is complicated, but not defeated, by the ambiguity of words. Here the emphasis on speed in mass communication can be a crippling condition imposed on the public-affairs journalist. No matter how much the responsible journalist respects words and the intellectual and craft demands which their usage imposes, it is virtually impossible for him to develop the requisite intellectual and artistic habits of his editors enforce their deadlines inflexibly and indiscriminately, no matter how complex, subtle, and historically embedded may be the thing he is reporting.

Ordinarily public affairs do not happen or exist with their explanatory context already built into them. They must be investigated, not simply looked at. And then the materials must be interpreted.

American editors and publishers old enough to remember the era of personal journalism which existed well into the twentieth century are still wary of any effort to interpret the news. They identify interpretation with opinion, prejudice, slanting, distortion, surmise, speculation, and advocacy. And all of these qualities were indeed distinguishing features of old-time personal journalism. It sought to move and persuade rather than enlighten readers.

Reacting against this, publishers developed what they thought was a splendid alternative, an objectivity so narrowly defined that what was eliminated was not only opinionated editorializing in the news columns but also any opportunity for the reporter to put what he was reporting into a context which would make it meaningful. This was thought to be the objectivity of the scientist in his laboratory, meticulously recording what his senses perceived, impersonal, unprejudiced, and, above all, humble before the demonstrable fact. Actually the scientist was doing much more than this: his investigations led him to look for causes and relationships, and his intuitive and creative faculties were never idle.

But this only partly understood scientific model on which journalistic objectivity was patterned is ill-adapted to the work of the public-affairs reporter. The truths of public affairs are not encompassed by their appearances, or by what can be perceived only by the senses. As Eric Sevareid pointed out some years ago, when journalists confined their coverage of the late Senator Joseph McCarthy simply to what the senator said and did, far from producing objective journalism they were producing "the big lie." For the truth, or the meaning, of McCarthy could never be discerned from any particular statement he made or act he performed. It could only be discerned by relating the particular action to previous, possibly contradictory, actions; to the web of current and contemporary history in which the actions took place; and to known realities which the senator had ignored or misstated but which were relevant if readers were to be able to understand the senator and to form a judgment about his responsibility.

Of course, publishers and editors are not so naïve as to think that flat, one-dimensional, surface reporting is adequate to the needs of readers. But the solution some of them propose—a division of labor, with the reporter furnishing the facts in the news columns and editorial writers supplying the interpretation and analysis on the editorial page or in specially designated columns labeled "interpretive report"—is practically ineffectual and, I suspect, even theoretically untenable. It assumes that fact-gathering and interpreting are separable reporting functions. I think a convincing case can be made that fact-gathering, investigation, and interpretation are integral aspects and, for the purpose of the objective report itself, they are indivisible.

Certainly interpretive reporting contains subjective elements. But it will be an essentially objective act to the extent that the interpretation is grounded in the realities of an event or situation and to the extent that these grounds are clearly shown and evaluated by the reporter within his report. There is no reporting— even the "scientifically" objective, bare-facts reporting—which is free from subjective influence; the reporter does have to be subjective in selecting which of the bare facts he will include in his report. But the reporter's subjective judgment cannot be described as manipulative and distorting when it is oriented to the objective realities of the thing he is reporting.

The interpretive reporter and the editorialist both make judgments. The reporter's judgments are aimed at clarifying the meaning of public-affairs issues and problems. The editorial writer's judgments are aimed at persuading the reader about the rightness or wrongness of policies, programs, ideas; and at moving him to take a position on them. The distinction here is between clarification and rhetoric.

The most useful analysis of how the public-affairs reporter must work in investigating and interpreting his materials is in a book that was not written for journalists. In *The Modern Researcher*, Henry Graff and Jacques Barzun, two Columbia University historians, take up the problems of the working historian which happen in most respects to be the problems of the working public-affairs journalist: finding the facts; verifying the facts; handling ideas; truth, and the causation of and conditions surrounding events; discernible patterns in public affairs; and the sources and correctives of bias.

When Douglass Cater wrote his book on journalism in Washington, D.C., in 1959, he noted that there were more than three thousand public-information officers working for the federal government compared to twelve hundred newspaper and broadcast reporters in the capital. I doubt whether that ratio has altered significantly since 1959. And if you add to government public-information officers all the public-relations men working in Washington for private and special-interest lobbies and organizations, one can begin to perceive the magnitude of the journalist's task as he seeks to write objectively about what is happening.

The relationship of the reporter to his source is complicated not only by the sheer numbers of governmental and private public-relations men who stand between their clients and the public as shields and interpreters. It is also complicated by the special power of some of the highest government officials to reward or punish journalists by giving or withholding information according to how "coöperative" the journalists are; by the present Justice Department's unprecedented harrassment of reporters (requests for identification of their sources, attempts to subpoena the notes on which they have based their stories and broadcasts, grand-jury investigations of reporters who publish classified government documents); and often by the journalists' own inability, or unwillingess, to develop investigative techniques to counter the manipulative and intimidating tactics of government officials.

It must also be admitted that laziness and lack of enterprise in the use of alternative sources of information are not unknown vices of journalists. T.R.B., the Washington columnist for *The New Republic*, once attended a hearing by the Senate Judiciary Subcommittee on Anti-Trust and Monopoly. He discovered that "the one hundred largest manufacturing monsters in the United States increased their share of net capital assets of all U.S. manufacturing from 45.8 per cent to 56.9 per cent in the years from 1947 to 1962. . . . Textron has acquired sixty-nine manufacturing enterprises; Martin-Marietta picked up two hundred and forty-six million dollars worth of mergers. . . . Three big oil companies recently— Continental, Socony, and Gulf—each absorbed a fertilizer company; only one major independent fertilizer company remains. . . . Only three reporters were at the hearing when we looked in."

But even the most enterprising and intelligent of the Washington journalists are victims of that peculiar capital infirmity known as the "background briefing," that device by which government officials float trial balloons, attack their critics, and gild their programs on a not-for-attribution basis. The inviolable ground rule is that, while reporters may use anything they wish from these briefings, they must not identify the government official who gives them the information. The reporter who disobeys the rule is banned from background briefings, loses out on stories that his competitors are filing, and may lose his assignment if not his job.

Ben Bradlee, executive editor of the Washington *Post*, has complained bitterly about the background briefing: "We shudder righteously at the thought of withholding the name of a bank robber, a party giver, a campaign contributor. Why do we go along so complacently withholding the identity of public officials? By doing so we shamelessly do other people's bidding. We knowingly let ourselves be used for obvious trial balloons and for personal attacks. In short, we deman our profession."

Bradlee suggests that the more flagrant abuses of the background briefing might be eliminated if the press sharply limited and persuaded government officials to limit the amount of unattributed information; insisted on at least agency attribution ("White House sources," "State Department experts" instead of "high government officials" or "government sources"); and refused to let a background briefer indulge in personal attack without being identified.

Presidents as news sources use the immense authority of their office and have developed over the years a variety of wiles to keep reporters in line and to minimize the possibility of the searching and informed questions ever arising at news conferences. James Reston has recalled how Lyndon Johnson tamed the reporters: "He knew that the Washington press corps was full of specialists, some of whom had devoted most of their careers to the study of foreign affairs, or the federal judiciary, or science or military affairs, and therefore not only knew their subjects, but probably knew more about them than he did. If he announced his news conferences in advance, they would come running with their well-informed and awkward inquiries. So he simply did not announce his news conferences. He called them when only the White House corespondents were around, and then usually on the weekends when only a few of them were on duty. He held them in his own executive office, where he was not on display before the cameras, but talking intimately with the reporters who travel with him all the time and are not only familiar to him but subject to his system of punishments and rewards, which can be embarrassing to a reporter on a highly competitive beat."

The objective public-affairs reporter, whether he is working in the superheated atmosphere of Washington or covering City Hall in Milwaukee, has to walk a narrow line. He must develop a relationship with his source that is intimate enough to generate confidence and yield information but detached enough to enable him to be truthful in his writing even when the truth may not flatter the source of his information. The goal of government officials and the goal of journalists are one—the common good. But it does not follow that the journalist serves the common good by joining hands with and following the bidding of the officials. He serves it by maintaining that amount of distance which is required for cool, detached objectivity.

It is possible for most, if not all, reporters for a newspaper, news service, television station or network to be objective in the performance of their individual tasks, or to aspire to objectivity, but for the institution which employs them to be profoundly nonobjective. How the institution uses its reporters, the working conditions it has set up for them, the news policies it has established, the extent to which the commercial and profit interests influence its communication performance all determine in the end whether the journalism produced will be objective.

Out of the thousands of events, situations, and conditions that might be reported each day, only a relatively few are printed or broadcast. Despite its slogan, *The New York Times* does not really publish all the news that is fit to print. It selects some news and it rejects other, even though both may be fit to print. The *Times* receives two and a half million words a day; it selects 185,000 (less than one percent) for publication.

The question is, what is the basis and what are the principles which guide newspaper editors and television news directors both in their selection and in their handling of news? Historically, the answer to that question has been diverse, as all the foregoing might have suggested by now.

There is a sense in which a communications medium can be said to be objective if all of its individual reports, no matter how trivial the subjects, are true accounts. A newspaper like the *Daily News* in New York, assuming its various sensational items are accurately reported, can be said to be just as objective as *The New York Times*. But in a much deeper sense, the picture of the world as found in the *Times* is far truer, more objective, more bona fide than that in the *News*. This is partly because there is between all newspapers and their readers an implicit contract, a promise that they will furnish readers with the information they need if they are to function as responsible citizens in our society.

I do not think the problem of objectivity—whether in the individual reporter or in the institution—can be separated from the question of the over-all significance of the final product. Just as the objectivity of the individual reporter depends on his perception, selection, and ordering of the essential rather than the accidental elements of the event or situation he is reporting, so the objectivity of the newspaper or television station or network depends on the consistent selection of the most important aspects of contemporary life that will be assigned to the reporters for their investigation and interpretation.

It is not enough for the institution to be occasionally significant in many areas of public affairs, or to be consistently significant in one or two areas. If it falls short of over-all significance it presents a distorted picture of the world to its clientele.

What is required for a journalism of significance in any communications institution is a wise, experienced person with sufficient authority to make and enforce news policy for his paper, wire service, television station or network, and with sufficient resources (able reporters and editors, adequate time and space) to carry out that policy. Each of these elements—wisdom, experience, authority, enforcement, resources—is indispensable. One still hears of newspaper situations, which mut be astounding to laymen, in which the wire editor (the real gatekeeper who selects the non-local stories that will pass through the news barrier and into the paper) is virtually sovereign and, in actual effect, determines news policy which may or may not be the policy the publisher or editor-in-chief would adopt if they were at that gate.

The wise director of news policy knows: (a) what constitutes "the good life," humanly speaking; (b) the present human condition; and (c) the contemporary events, developments, and forces which most directly and profoundly affect the human condition and the prospect for the good life.

Theoretically the commercial profit-making nature of mass communications need not compromise the efforts to produce a journalism of integrity. In practice, the theory often fails to stand up, or, more accurately, it is allowed to collapse.

It is true that newspaper editors no longer suppress stories that offend their advertisers. But I do not recall that the television industry, when it was heavily supported by tobacco advertising, came even remotely close to the newspapers and magazines in the number of news stories it aired about the relationship between cigarette smoking and lung cancer. And I cannot recall any television documentaries on this disease which national health officials say is of epidemic magnitude; if there have been documentaries, they cannot begin to compare in number or depth with those done by the television industry on the problem of, say, drug abuse. The commercial influence is always present in the media. The evidence suggests that the opportunity, desire, and ability to make enormous profits in the communications media sometimes results in shabby reporting of public affairs. Network officials say that they have corporate responsibilities to their stockholders and must show an improved profit picture each year.

When Fred Friendly, then a top news executive with the Columbia Broadcasting System, wanted to broadcast Senate Foreign Relations Committee hearings five years ago, the network overruled him and scheduled a rerun of an "I Love Lucy" show. Friendly resigned and later pointed out that he had not asked C.B.S. to suffer a net loss but only to take a very mild reduction in the gigantic profits they were making.

When Kenneth A. Cox was a member of the Federal Communications Commission, he criticized the F.C.C. and the radio industry for a situation in which the commission could renew, as they did on one occasion, the licenses of 21 stations without bothering to inquire into the adequacy of their service, as required by law, in the areas of public affairs, agriculture, instruction, and religion. The stations had proposed devoting than five percent of their time to those areas.

Mr. Cox noted that radio is now about 50 years old and that

"surely it should strive to be—with due allowance for the admitted need for a viable economic base—something more than a jukebox, a ball park, and a news ticker." He said it was ridiculous to argue that the broadcaster who devotes twenty-three hours of each day to commercially sponsored programming is being subjected to an impairment of his freedom to speak if he is asked by the F.C.C. whether it would not better serve the public interest if more than 25 or 30 minutes of the remaining hour in the day could be devoted to public affairs.

I once took part in a seminar with newspaper, radio, and television news officials on the question of what the media can contribute to intergroup understanding and harmony in the community. One of the radio officials rather proudly reported that his station had often presented public-service programs on community problems, and he stated—also very proudly—that some of these "programs" ran as long as five minutes. It was obvious that, by his standards, five minutes of air time represented a considerable amount of money. But, of course, it bore little relationship to the magnitude and gravity of the problems in his community.

It is common knowledge that salaries paid to business, management, and advertising staff members of newspapers are substantially higher than those paid to reporters. Salary is not the only measurement of the regard which publishers have for the quality of public-affairs reporting, but it is a major measurement and, in the minds of most reporters, the decisive measurement.

Competent, highly motivated public-affairs reporters have been migrating for a generation from the newspapers and wire services to para-journalistic work (e.g., administrative and legislative work for congressmen). In one recent year, only 20 percent of students graduating from journalism colleges chose to go into news reporting.

The reader of the newspaper account or the viewer of a television news broadcast or documentary brings to it his own personal history. And if the reporter is subject to "tricks of memory" and the "incessant creative quality of his imagination," the reader is no less susceptible. If he distorts or misreads a report it may be his fault, the reporter's fault, or just due to the ambiguity of words. Barzun and Graff say:

The reader brings something with him to every act of reading. He brings his own experience of life and a variable amount of knowledge gathered from previous reading. The result is that unless the vocabulary of a new piece of reading matter is visibly technical and strange to him, he will almost always think he understands it. This will happen even when what is said is badly put, repeatedly misleading, or adroitly tendentious. The whole power of propaganda lies in this human propensity to catch the drift, to make out a meaning, to believe what is in print, with no thought of resistance by analysis and criticism.

It may be assumed that if reporters will write with precision, make distinctions not fussily but with an exactness necessary to an understanding of the material, in short, if reporters will display in their work intellectual and critical power, their readers will develop a comparable virtue. The possibility will then be enhanced that what the reporter has understood and put into words (or, for television, into words and motion photography) the reader will understand. In that event, objective communication will have been accomplished.

But is objectivity in the over-all reporting of public affairs generally and consistently possible in American journalism? I think it is, not in the sense of objectivity as the total truth about anything (something which historians have never succeeded in capturing), and not in the sense of objectivity as meaning the absence of all subjective elements. But objectivity as meaning a substantially truthful account of contemporary public affairs is well within the possibility of the mass-communications media despite many practical difficulties.

These are some of the things that must be done to overcome the difficulties (other suggestions have been made in the course of this article):

Recognition of the existence of the reporter's personal history and experience and their effect on his work, with constant effort made to broaden and objectify that experience, and hence his values.

More professional education and training in the art of investigative reporting, both in professionally-oriented journalism schools or university departments (preferably following a liberal arts undergraduate education) and on job with newspapers and television stations.

Insistence that reporters and editors bring to their work a broad educational experience so that they can interrelate the economic, political, social, and cultural elements of public affairs and provide the context which will illuminate what they are reporting.

A proper balance of specialization and rotation of reporters' assignments to avoid superficiality on the one hand and the boredom, laziness, and uncritical, routinized approach often associated with the unvarying assignment on the other.

Vigilance from the editor's desk (spot comparisons, for example, of the reporters' dispatches with those of other American reporters and, in the case of international assignments, with the reports of foreign writers).

Careful fitting of reporters to the kind of assignments on which they could probably be more consistently objective, and a constant review of that fit.

Providing the working conditions (sufficient space, time, and professional understanding) to enable reporters to do careful work.

A continuing communications commission to monitor the performance of the press and television and to make public its evaluations.

Extension and refinement of the ombudsman-like idea initiated by a few newspapers to give readers a critical voice that will be heard in the operation of the papers.

Subordination of the profit-making of a newspaper or broadcasting station to the service of its communication function.

Better use made of the wire services by subscribing papers and, where the wire services are inadequate, more rigorous demands by the individual editors.

It is possible for the citizen with a great deal of time and a considerable expenditure of money to keep himself adequately informed on the public affairs of the day by reading several newspapers and a half-dozen or more journals and magazines, watching the televised documentaries, and picking up the best of the books on contemporary issues.

But it should be equally possible for citizens, without making such an extraordinary investment of their time and money, to subscribe to their hometown newspaper, watch the television news and public-affairs programs, and perhaps subscribe to one magazine or journal and be confident that their opinions and actions on public affairs are based on an understanding of the issues. I do not think this is now the case. But I do think it is possible.

Study Questions

1. Defend McDonald's concept of "objectivity" against some real or hypothetical arguments against it.
2. State why you agree or disagree with the author's contention "news" should be re-defined so that "trends," rather than events, are the essential constituents of its meaning.

On Integrity in Journalism

James A. Michener

It was one of the saddest weeks in the history of American journalism. It was John Peter Zenger in reverse.

A major newspaper was humiliated. One of the most necessary professions in the world was made to look shoddy. A prize treasured by all who enter that profession was made to look laughable. And a woman reporter of extraordinary talent, who could write as well as Ida Tarbell or Maggie Higgins, was disgraced, bringing ridicule upon two minorities who had long battled for good jobs in journalism: Women and blacks.

When blind Samson pulled down the central pillars of the temple at Gaza, the entire structure fell. When Janet Cooke turned in a fake story, she knocked down the central pillar of her profession—integrity—and the reverberations went far.

Every concept in the above paragraphs merits a chapter of philosophical discussion, and in years to come this will be provided in schools of journalism and in the bars where proud newsmen and newswomen meet after work. I should like to stress a few core ideas.

The newspaper. A paper such as the *Los Angeles Times* or the *Chicago Tribune* is a national treasure, kept alive with difficulty, kept vital only because millions trust it and thousands work to preserve its reputation. This nation would perish if its free press were strangled, which is why I am willing to forgive papers,

magazines and television stations the howling errors they sometimes make. We could not live rewarding lives without the media.
And anyone who finds glee in the embarrassment of the *Washington Post* should remember how avidly one reaches for it when
one has been out of the country for a few weeks, missing the
news it brings.

Insofar as the *Post's* carelessness made this debacle possible, it
deserves rebuke, and I suppose it is castigating itself adequately
without my help. But since no media agency can protect itself
fully against downright fabrication, the *Post* deserves our compassion. It will be a better paper after this wrenching experience.

Sources. Miss Cooke's disaster could be titled "Son of Deep
Throat." In the Watergate case, the *Post* got away with launching
a major story without disclosing sources, and a tradition evolved,
there and elsewhere, that a reporter did not have to reveal where
he got his facts. This was a dangerous precedent, and when Miss
Cooke refused to tell even her editors the names of her sources,
she was free to write whatever she wished.

For legal and common-sense reasons, a newspaper may not
wish to reveal its sources to the general public, but the editors
certainly should demand that their writers prove the veracity of
their stories. In this case, Miss Cooke was responsible to no one.

Newspapers cannot long retain their credibility if they accept
unchecked reports. One of the pleasures of my professional life
has been working with *Life* and *Reader's Digest*, whose editors
checked every word I submitted. I mean, until they placed a blue
dot over every word as they verified it, the story could not be
sent to the printers, and the trouble they saved me, and themselves, was remarkable. That kind of checking would have uncovered the fraud in this case.

The prize. Custodians of the Pulitzer Prizes must review their
procedures, for they administer an award which ennobles the
profession. Winning it insures a newsman of a lifetime job, with
honor. It encourages small newspapers to keep plugging, and it
makes cartoonists bolder. In this instance, the controlling advisory
board chose to override the recommendations of its jury of experts
composed of editors and specialists and handed the feature-
writing prize to Miss Cooke, whose article had not even been

submitted to the jury on feature writing. So the advisory board got its fingers badly singed, for it is wrong to seek advice and then ignore it.

The reporter. Two facts are conspicuous. Miss Cooke can write. She would make a fine novelist, because when I first read her story I noticed how well she depicted the setting, the characters, the dialogue. With the intensity of the present experience behind her, I suspect that she can apply her talent in some kind of writing other than newspaper work. She need not be mortally wounded by this disastrous beginning.

The second fact is that Miss Cooke progressed so fast in her profession that she did not learn its great traditions. She may have thought she had, but she had not even begun. The traditional news reporter begins slowly under some cantankerous editor with high professional and grammatical ideals. One hobnobs with policemen and bartenders and mayors and congressional aspirants and learns painfully to distinguish between truth and fiction. One is knocked about by one's equally gifted colleagues and watches what happens when either blind ambition or excessive drinking destroys a promising talent.

Always there is the steady accumulation of standards: "I do not betray confidences." "I refuse to touch that kind of story." "I must have two confirmations of a statement like that."

In my own case, one sentence lives with me still and guides my work: "If that stinker says it's Tuesday, even money says it's Friday."

It takes about a decade to make a good newsman. Miss Cooke graduated from the University of Toledo, not Vassar as she claimed, in 1976. In 1979, at the age of 25, she landed a job with the *Post*. In 1980, at the age of 26, she wrote her famous story about the 8-year-old black boy who shot heroin given him by the man who lived with his mother.

She had used charisma, unquestioned talent and a fierce ambition to attain a position sought after by thousands, but she reached it without two essential attributes: A deep commitment to the historical traditions of her profession and an understanding of what makes a newspaper acceptable to its community.

She had not paid her dues, and in a moment of crisis she was left without self-protection.

The minorities. When she came to Washington, it was not as mere Janet Cooke. Whether she admitted it or not, she came also as a representative of our two most important minorities: Professional women, and blacks. As a black woman with a pleasing personality, she was doubly valuable to the *Post*, which publishes in a city with a large black population, for she was what is known as a twofer. The management could cite her twice in claiming that it did not practice discrimination, and the only person better to hire would have been a black female Puerto Rican. That could be called a hat trick, a phrase borrowed from sports indicating that one person covered three constituencies.

It is possible, although the record shows no evidence of this, that the *Post* grabbed Miss Cooke as the solution to a problem, and that had she been an ordinary white male from the Missouri School of Journalism she might have been investigated much more thoroughly. It is possible that her stories were handled with more tenderness than would otherwise have been the case.

Those whom society nominates as symbols are obligated to perform doubly, because a poor exhibition will do double damage. If Gloria Steinem acts the fool tomorrow, all women will suffer. If Carl Rowan messes up his television program, all blacks are denigrated.

The damage Miss Cooke has done to black and women reporters is incalculable, and she should have anticipated this when she wrote her fake story and allowed it to be nominated for a Pulitzer.

I am a Quaker, a graduate of Swarthmore College, a former naval officer, a former official of the Democratic Party, and a writer, and I am kept in line partly because I would be mortified if my poor behavior brought dishonor to those institutions which served me so generously. I must be watchful that my actions do not diminish them, because in this case we are all members of various minorities.

Credentials. The most curious aspect of this scandal is that the *Post* did not check Miss Cooke's credentials. Her record, with its shifts and contradictions, had to awaken suspicions, and when my wife read it to me as we drove north on the day the Pulitzers were announced and I heard her history, I cried: "Watch that Sorbonne bit! Watch those four foreign languages!"

Why was I so dubious? For two good reasons. In almost every

institution in which I have worked, some misguided person has claimed university degrees he did not have, and I believe you could go to any campus in this country, if checks had been carelessly made, and find some professor using a spurious degree. When someone says she has studied at the Sorbonne, warning whistles should toot.

When I worked with the military police at one point, I found that when young men pose as officers, dressing up in bemedaled uniforms to charm small-town girls, they usually claim to be Marine majors. Colonels or generals would alert suspicions, while mere Army or Navy uniforms would lack glamour.

With military-police impostors it's the Marine major, with academics the Sorbonne.

Apprenticeship. We should insist that young men and women serve proper apprenticeships, because throughout history that is how standards and traditions have been kept high.

The number of attractive-looking young people posing as newsmen on television with never a shred of hard-news experience is shocking. The parade of people reporting to newspaper offices without any knowledge of English or of American history is appalling.

Young people learn their profession, whatever it may be, by studying the best work of their predecessors, and I shall never forget the delight with which I saw a great painting done by Giovanni Bellini which had been copied by his pupil Titian. Rubens had learned by copying Titian to see what his secrets were, and Delacroix had copied Rubens. Van Gogh did a marvelous adaptation of Delacroix, so that we had five of our greatest, most distinctive painters, men of the most intense personal style and integrity, striving to learn what good artists of the past had accomplished.

Recent requirements that a company must have a balanced staff should not be interpreted as meaning that it must have an incompetent one or one ignorant of the great traditions.

The Pulitzers. Suggestions have been made that reporters on a newspaper is important as the *Washington Post* should not degrade themselves by competing for prizes. Nonsense. People with aspirations have always appreciated recognition from their peers, and I respect John Paul Jones who left the American fleet to serve in Russia's because the former would not promote him to admiral while the latter would. There are legitimate milestones in every profession, and it is not ignoble to mark them off.

I feel especially involved in this case because, as a young man, I won a Pulitzer.

I did not aspire to it. I did not campaign for it. But when it arrived it remade my life, enabling me to do those things to which I did aspire. Without the Pulitzer, I might never have made it as a writer. With it, excellent things became possible.

I am worried about this debacle because it has befouled institutions that are important to me. I hope things can be worked out.

Study Questions

1. Michener appears to be guardedly tolerant of journalistic errors, urging that ". . . I am willing to forgive papers, magazines and television stations the howling errors they sometimes make. We could not live rewarding lives without the media." State why you agree or disagree with this view. Specifically, does a greater responsibility fall on, say, magazines than newspapers, given the fact that they have more time to check a story?
2. Michener suggests that "Newspapers cannot long retain their credibility if they accept unchecked reports." The argument has been made (by press critic Edward Jay Epstein and others) that reporters must hide their sources from such checking, lest they lose the sources as a valuable fount of information in the future. State why you agree or disagree with the latter argument against disclosing sources.

Privacy and the Right to Privacy

H.J. McCloskey

The right to privacy is one of the rights most widely demanded today. Privacy has not always so been demanded. The reasons for the present concern for privacy are complex and obscure. They obviously relate both to the possibilities for very considerable enjoyment of privacy by the bulk of people living in affluent societies brought about by twentieth-century affluence, and to the development of very efficient methods of thoroughly and systematically invading this newly found privacy. However, interesting and important as it is as a socio-philosophical inquiry, the concern of this paper is not with why privacy has come to be so highly prized, but rather with whether it is rightly prized, and if so, when and why. This means that my concern will be with what privacy is, what is its domain, whether there is a right to privacy, and, if so, whether it is an ultimate, basic, albeit, a *prima facie* right, or simply a conditional right.

A. What is Privacy? To What is the Right to Privacy a Right?

We demand recognition of our right to privacy, we complain when privacy is invaded, yet we encounter difficulties immediately we seek to explain what we mean by privacy, what is the area, the content of privacy, what is outside that area, what constitutes a

664

loss of privacy, a loss to which we have consented, a justified loss, an unjustified loss. This problem is more acute in respect of privacy than with the rights of life, liberty, equality of opportunity, and the like, even though with each of these there is a problem of conceptual clarification to be solved before the nature and the basis of the right can be determined.

In seeking to clarify the concept of privacy, little help is to be gained from the writings of the great liberals, privacy being a value which has been overlooked and left unexamined by the great philosophers of liberalism. John Locke's writings contain no reference to what we now call privacy. Rousseau was evidently insensitive to the claims of privacy. Kant's importance for liberalism lay in his concern for respect for persons; he seems nowhere to have related this to privacy. Wilhelm von Humboldt was preoccupied with securing and defending the individual's liberty, and seemed unaware of privacy as a value. Although in the area of political thought J.S. Mill is most celebrated for his defence of liberty, he was even more concerned with other values, pleasure and the absence of pain, intellectual goods such as rationality, rational belief, knowledge, and human self-development. He was not insensitive to injustices. Yet, in all his voluminous writings, he nowhere expressed awareness of or concern for privacy, even though the economic and social conditions of his day were such that very few could enjoy privacy, and even though he bitterly resented any intrusions into the privacy of his relationship with Harriet. The same lack of awareness of and concern for privacy is evident in the writings of L.T. Hobhouse, R.H. Tawney, and others. With socialist liberals such as Tawney, there is rather a clear willingness to invade privacy to reduce injustice and to extend liberty. In the U.S., liberal thought has been less affected by utilitarianism and much more deeply inspired by concern for respect for persons, than in Britain, yet the writings of its leading thinkers show the same lack of awareness of privacy as do those of British thinkers.

James Fitzjames Stephen, in his perfunctory discussion in *Liberty, Equality, Fraternity*, provides a notable exception to this tendency of liberal thought.[1] Stephen saw privacy as relating to the more intimate and delicate relations of life, as something that ought to be respected by the individual himself, by other persons, by public opinion, and by the law. Stephen's brief discussion seems to be the sum total of liberal philosophical thought on privacy up to a decade ago, and even so, his contribution no doubt emanated from Stephen as a lawyer as much as from him as a philosopher.

It is the lawyers of the U.S., through criminal and civil law, and through the interpretation of the Constitution, who have contributed most to the development of the political ideal of privacy. Valuable though it is, the legal approach to privacy is of less value to the philosopher than might be expected, partly because the law's concern very reasonably has been with wrongful invasions of privacy, not with the philosophical question of what constitutes an invasion of privacy, partly because the impetus of law-making in the U.S. on privacy sprang from an article by S.D. Warren and L.D. Brandeis in which privacy was explained in terms of one's being let alone, all "not leavings alone" coming to be viewed as invasions of privacy, which they are not.[2]

The past decade has produced a significant amount of thoughtful writing which bears on what privacy is, such that, by looking at suggestions in this writing, we are most likely to gain help in our inquiry. The conclusion to be argued for here, although less negative and relativistic than that of the Younger Committee, will fall short of the hopes of those who seek a clear, well-defined concept of privacy.

The relevant part of that committee's report runs

57 It might seem a prerequisite of our task that we should have agreed what privacy is and be able to say what we mean by it. The "Justice" Committee on Privacy said:

'In the course of our work, we have become increasingly aware of the difficulties which seem to beset any attempt to find a precise or logical formula which could either circumscribe the meaning of the word "privacy" or define it exhaustively. We think that there are two underlying reasons for this. First and foremost, the notion of privacy has a substantial emotive content in that many of the things which we feel the need to preserve from the curiosity of our fellows are feelings, beliefs or matters of conduct which are themselves irrational. Secondly, the scope of privacy is governed to a considerable extent by the standards, fashions and mores of the society of which we form part, and these are subject to constant change, especially at the present time. We have therefore concluded that no purpose would be served by our making yet another attempt at developing an intellectually rigorous analysis. . . . At any given time, there

will be certain things which almost everyone will agree ought
to be part of the "private" area which people should be allowed
to preserve from the intrusion of others, subject only to the
overriding interest of the community as a whole where this
plainly outweighs the private right. Surrounding this central area
there will always be a "grey area" on which opinions will differ,
and the extent of this grey area, as also that of the central one,
is bound to vary from time to time.' (*Privacy and the Law*, p. 5,
para. 18).

58 The majority of us regard the 'Justice' Committee's conclusion
as one more indication, and a highly significant one, that the
concept of privacy cannot be satisfactorily defined. We have
looked at many earlier attempts. . . . Either they go very wide,
equating the right to privacy with the right to be let alone, or
they boil down to a catalogue of assorted values to which the
adjective 'private' or 'personal' can reasonably, but not exclusively, be attached.

A clear, well-defined concept is to be realized only by way of
a stipulative definition. However, it is possible to distinguish concepts distinct from privacy which have been confused with that
of privacy, and thereby to make clearer the core notion of privacy.
To look now at some of the more important attempts to characterize privacy.

1. *Privacy as consisting in being let alone.* There are many versions
of this account, that of Warren and Brandeis, although linked with
and suggestive of other, radically different accounts, being the
most important. They wrote:

> These considerations lead to the conclusion that the protection
> afforded to thoughts, sentiments, and emotions, expressed through
> the medium of writing or of the arts, so far as it consists in pre-
> venting publication, is merely an instance of the enforcement of
> the more general right to be let alone. . . . The principle which
> protects personal writings and all other personal productions, not
> against theft and physical appropriation, but against publication in
> any form, is in reality not the principle of private property, but of
> inviolate personality.[3]

The Nordic Conference wrote in like vein of the "right to be
let alone". A.F. Westin, in his otherwise admirable *Privacy and
Freedom*, offers many different, mutually inconsistent accounts of
privacy, among them being one in terms of privacy as consisting

in solitude, or small group intimacy, these often being equated with being let alone. M.L. Ernst and A.U. Schwartz in *The Right to Be Let Alone*, also write of privacy in the context of seclusion and solitude, observing:

> [Privacy consists in being] protected from intrusion upon himself, his home, his family, his relationships and communications with others, his property and his business affairs, including intrusion by spying, prying, watching and besetting and the unauthorized overhearing . . . of spoken words.[4]

This latter account moves towards the distinct account of privacy and the right to privacy in terms of control over and possession of the right of selective disclosure.

There is initial plausibility in the account of privacy as consisting in being let alone. If one is let alone, one's privacy would seem to be secure. Is this really so? I suggest that it all depends on what is meant by being let alone. If a tourist visiting a new country innocently spies on people from his liner, using binoculars to observe them gardening, entertaining friends in their gardens, getting drunk, he has, in an important sense, let them alone; yet he has invaded their privacy. On the other hand, if a person is shipwrecked on a lonely island, and no one bothers about his fate, it is not clear that it is privacy that he is enjoying. Yet he is being let alone. Vague though this account is, it covers too much and things other than privacy in such a way that it will not do as a guide to what is involved in the right to privacy. To enjoy *seclusion* or *solitude* is usually, although not necessarily, to enjoy privacy. Yet they clearly are distinct things. It would be a mockery to guarantee a person his privacy by ensuring that he enjoys solitude on a remote island. Privacy is something that we can enjoy and wish to enjoy in society. It is not clear that it is meaningful outside of societies.

Some writers construe the intrusion of noise and obnoxious smells into one's home as invasions of privacy. Indeed, all nuisances which invade the home are seen as such. This would be the case if privacy consisted in being let alone. So too, to be assaulted, would be to suffer a loss of privacy. Against this, I suggest that that of which it would be reasonable to complain with the noise, smell, assault would be loss of enjoyment, harm, injury, but not a loss or invasion of privacy. To be hurt, to suffer loss of enjoyment and other goods, is not to suffer loss of privacy, unless one is to construe everything that harmfully affects one as involving a loss of privacy. On such a view, to be affected, either harmfully or beneficially, would be to lose privacy, unwillingly or willingly. Some seek to argue, more moderately, that it is only when such evils enter one's private domain, that one suffers a loss of privacy. It is not any unwanted smell, noise, etc., that invades one's privacy, but unwanted smells, noises and nuisances that enter one's own private dwelling that do so. This is to move towards an account of privacy in part at least in terms of an area of privacy relating to one's person and personal domain. This kind of account will be examined later.

Liberty and being let alone are commonly equated. The negative concept of liberty is commonly explained in terms of being free from interference, in being let alone. Yet privacy, negative liberty, and being let alone, are clearly, evidently distinct. Not to let a person alone may be to deprive him only of his negative liberty, or it may simply be to interfere with him in other ways as by assaulting him or benefiting him in a way that is desired/undesired by him. In a secondary sense of leaving alone, to spy on a person is not to leave him alone; it is to invade his privacy. In a more basic, primary sense, to coerce a person into doing what he does not want to do, is not to leave him alone; it is to invade his liberty, not his privacy. Here it may be replied that all loss of liberty is *ipso facto* a loss of privacy. Against this, it may easily be shown that privacy and liberty are conceptually distinct. Privacy can be totally invaded throughout the whole of a person's life, without his knowledge, without his liberty being in any way restricted, and without the person becoming any less a person *qua* person. By contrast, the greater the interference with a person's liberty, the more inclined we are to think of him as being rendered incapable of being a full person. Complete interference in the form of control of his thoughts, decisions, actions during the whole of his life, is incompatible with his remaining a person in the Kantian sense of person. Secondly, privacy and negative liberty may conflict. Part of the right to liberty is the right to observe, know, report, publish, free of interference. Consider the right to freedom to bird-watch. The ideal society for the lover of negative liberty as the sole political value would be one in which there is as little interference by way of coercion as possible, where the only coercion that is accepted, is coercion against coercive interference. Yet members of such a community could invade the privacy of their fellows without interfering with their liberty, as by eavesdropping, person-watching as a hobby, and the like. These are not forms of interference in the sense relevant to negative liberty. Thirdly, the contrasts with negative liberty are interference and coercion; the contrasts with privacy are many, including some such as publicity, which are not contrasts with negative liberty. Similarly, the protections needed for the one may differ from those needed for the other.

2. *Privacy as the lack of disclosure, and the right to privacy as the right to selective disclosure.* Privacy and the right to privacy have been explained in terms of knowledge of the self and its extensions, and the right to determine what is known about one's self. In this connection, in *Private Rights and the Freedom of the Individual* (Ditchley Foundation Paper 41), it is observed of a seminar conducted about privacy that:

> The word is easily used, but it was soon seen that it had different implications for different people. This made it much harder to define what precise rights should attach to it than to consider the general concept in relation to other factors. It was accepted that it concerned two main elements in the attitudes of the individuals or groups in their outlook on society. These were, first, the claim to be let alone and secondly, the claim by a holder of information to decide for himself what should be disclosed, at what time and to whom.[5]

This would appear to be the account favored by Elizabeth Beardsley in "Privacy: Autonomy and Selective Disclosure":

> The norm of autonomy is, I have argued, what gives our obligation to respect another's right of selective disclosure its moral rationale. But selective disclosure constitutes the conceptual core of the norm of privacy.[6]

A.F. Westin seems at times also to adopt this view:

> Privacy is the claim of individuals, groups or institutions to determine for themselves when, how and to what extent information about them is communicated to others.[7]

This view is espoused by many others including Warren and Brandeis when they write of the right to privacy as the right of an individual to be free from undesired or unwarranted revelation to the public of matters regarding which the public is not concerned, and R.B. Parker who, in "A Definition of Privacy," wrote:

> The definition of privacy defended in this article is that *privacy is control over when and by whom the various parts of us can be sensed by others.*[8]

In terms of this general view that the right to privacy is the right of the individual to determine what is known or communicated about him, privacy, it would seem, would relate to all the facts relating to one's self and to what are parts and extensions of one's self. There are obvious problems here, problems relating to marking off the self and its real extensions from the non-self, and to showing, as against the ordinary, very inclusive claims to privacy that commonly embrace much more than this, that this is all that relates to privacy. These problems constitute no basic objection to the theory. However they do bear on the need for a detailed elaboration of it and of its practical implications.

A basic objection to this account is that it fails to attend to the important points made by Stephen, namely, that we can show lack of respect for our own privacy, that we can improperly forgo our own privacy. A person who bares his soul to all is commonly thought not to have a proper respect for his own privacy, he gives it up too readily, he lacks a decent reticence. This account implies that self-disclosure can involve neither invasions nor loss of privacy that leads to acquiescence and even consent to such invasions, causes them to become neither invasions nor losses of privacy. Yet part of that about which those concerned with privacy are concerned, is this phenomenon of people getting used to their privacy being invaded so that they come freely to accept this and no longer to demand a right to privacy, or to privacy in those areas that are regularly invaded. People today have freely accepted vast inroads into their privacy. They have accepted intelligence and other psychological and medical tests for their children, where the information obtained may now be stored in data banks; they accept questionnaires by schools, universities, employers, banks, creditors, and many others, with little or no protest. They demand that their newspapers report news based on invasions of privacy of those in the public eye, those before the courts, and those who suffer great misfortune or good fortune, and they seek to foster in those whose privacy is invaded the belief that they ought to consent to such invasions of their privacy. Clearly, there are considerable difficulties then in the way of explaining privacy in terms of selective disclosure. The relationships between consent and losses and invasions of privacy are multifarious and complex. Concern for privacy may dictate the protecting of people against their own consent. It may dictate the creating of conditions which free them from having to decide whether they are willing to give up privacy to secure some desired good.

3. *Privacy as the absence of publicity.* This kind of thinking about privacy in terms of selective disclosure has also led to the suggestion that privacy consists in the absence of publicity about one's person, one's affairs, and the like. Certainly, those concerned with privacy are concerned with and about unwanted publicity. Suzanne Uniacke in an unpublished paper argues that this is a view of privacy I espouse in "The Political Ideal of Privacy."[9] This was not my intention, even though I did write to the effect that publicity is the basic contrast with privacy. However this is so only in the very technical sense of publicity as openness to some other person. To lose one's privacy is for some information about one to become public in the sense of becoming known by one or more persons. It need not involve publicity in the sense of the publicizing of the information. The eavesdropper, the Peeping-Tom, and other pryers, deprive persons of privacy, whether or not they publicize what they learn. Indeed, what they may learn may be such as not to be for them communicable knowledge. Nonetheless, clearly, anyone concerned with privacy must be vigilant about publicity, as the more certain kinds of information are publicized, the greater is the loss of privacy.

4. *Privacy and secrecy.* Privacy and secrecy are obviously distinct, so that to respect secrecy is not necessarily to respect privacy, to force the divulging of what is secret, is not necessarily to invade privacy. Indeed, the whole logical grammar of expressions relating to secrecy is different from that of those relating to privacy. More importantly, secrecy may relate to things that have nothing to do

with privacy. Thus, after the sudden deaths of the directors, the chief clerk may be the only one to have the secret knowledge of the combination of the company's safe. Coercively to force him to reveal this knowledge—for example, by threatening dismissal— is not to invade his privacy. Similarly, it may be possible to show respect for all of a man's secret knowledge and yet to show no or scant respect for his privacy, for example, where he is a person who lacks a decent reserve or reticence.

5. *Privacy as exclusive access.* E. van den Haag in "On Privacy" gives a somewhat similar account:

> Privacy is the exclusive access of a person (or other legal entity) to a realm of his own. The right to privacy entitles one to exclude others from (a) watching, (b) utilizing, (c) invading (intruding upon, or in other ways affecting) his private realm.[10]

> Privacy is the exclusive right to dispose of access to one's proper (private) domain.[11]

This leads van den Haag to suggest that privacy is best to be treated as a property right, the right to privacy being like a property right to dispose of access to one's proper (private) domain. This view is distinct from the seemingly similar view put by J.J. Thomson that so-called privacy rights are really a cluster of derivative rights, rights in many cases derivative from or analogous with property rights, but such as not to be *sui generis* privacy rights.[12]

Clearly, claims to exclusive access are claims to privacy only if the access is to something personal, something relating to privacy. This leads on to the problem of determining what is the personal, the private, that underlies this right to exclusive access. In this it shares a common problem with the distinct view that privacy relates to selective disclosure. What is true and important in this account is its stress on access as something distinct from disclosure. Both appear to be involved in privacy. Thus, while it may be the case that a person does not know what are his inner motivations, and hence not be in a position to disclose or not disclose what they are, access to them by a state psychiatrist contrary to his wishes constitutes an invasion of privacy. What privacy dictates is that access to them be exclusively under that person's control. None the less various of the points made in respect of privacy explained in terms of selective disclosure relate also to privacy explained in terms of exclusive access. To respect the right of exclusive access by buying and thereby obtaining the consent of a person to access to his realm of the private is not necessarily to respect his privacy. He may confer on those from whom he is seeking credit the right to full access to all aspects of his life. Yet those who exercise this right show lack of respect for his privacy. Similarly, even though they buy right of access to what is private, scandal newspapers and their readers show scant respect for the privacy of those whose confessions they buy.

6. *Respect for privacy as respect for personal autonomy.* Various of the foregoing accounts seek to relate privacy and liberty, privacy and autonomy. Obviously, privacy and respect for privacy, autonomy and respect for autonomy, are related. Many breaches of the right to privacy will be breaches of the duty to respect autonomy; many will involve lack of regard for the wishes of others. However, the latter need not involve lack of respect for autonomy. Thus secret spying which is never discovered by the victim need involve no lack of respect for autonomy. Consider here the girl who, unknown to herself, has been spied on by a man she knows and whom she may or may not be willing to see her naked. Has her will been forced in either case, if the man never talks and if she never comes to know what he has done? It has been suggested here that such actions of invading privacy, even secret, unknown invasions, involve a forcing of the will, a loss of autonomy. The girl wishes to act free from observation. If spied upon, she is no longer free to opt for the unobserved action. Two replies are sufficient to meet this argument. Even if the girl hoped and desired that the man she loved would secretly observe her beauty, her lover who did so without her permission would be invading her privacy. There would however be no thwarting of her will. Further, many things other people do and do not do, are counter to our wishes. To vote a sitting member out of office is to thwart his wishes. It is not to violate his autonomy, even less is it to invade his privacy. Such a view of autonomy would imply that only one being can enjoy autonomy, and that all others would be at risk of becoming his slaves in order to respect his autonomy.

* * *

7. *Privacy, trust, respect, love, friendship and respect for persons.*
C. Fried, firstly in "Privacy"[13] and more recently in *An Anatomy of Values: Problems of Personal and Social Choice*[14] while not defining privacy and the right to privacy, seeks to bring out the area of privacy, what it involves, and its deep interrelation with other values, the values of respect, love and friendship in particular. He seeks to base the right to privacy on the right to respect, and on the value and possibility of love and friendship, these being based on the morality of respect for persons, the right to privacy being seen as an aspect of the right to respect as a person. Thus he writes:

> To respect, love, trust, feel affection for others and to regard ourselves as the objects of love, trust and affection is at the heart of our notion of ourselves as persons among persons, and privacy is the necessary atmosphere for these attitudes and actions, as oxygen is for combustion.[15]

Many others have sought to explain the nature and value of privacy along similar lines. Thus we find J. Rachels in "Why Privacy is Important"[16] seeking to explain the importance of privacy in terms of its making love and friendship possible, whilst S.I. Benn in "Privacy, Freedom and Respect for Persons"[17] seeks to relate privacy and respect for privacy with respect for persons, he construing all lack of respect for privacy as involving lack of respect for persons as autonomous beings, as choosers, secret invasions involving the additional lack of respect that deceit involves.

If construed as attempts to define privacy, such accounts would encounter various of the difficulties already noted in (5) and (6) above. However they are more plausibly and accurately to be construed as attempts to explain the importance of privacy and of how privacy relates to our basic values. However, as is evident from J.H. Reiman's very damaging critique of Rachels' and Frieds' discussions, and of their implied very strange and debased accounts of love and friendship on the one hand and of the knowledge that is gained through such practical sciences as psychiatry, urology, sexology, on the other, the relationship is a subtle, complex one, one that is extremely difficult to unravel.[18]

*   *   *

8. *Privacy as being lost by the wrongful appropriation or exploitation of one's personality, the publicizing of one's private affairs with which the public has no legitimate concern.* S.H. Hofstadter and G. Horowitz offer an account which links with that given by van den Haag, one which explains the right to privacy as a special kind of property right. They write:

> It (the right to privacy) may be described broadly as the right against unwarranted appropriation or exploitation of one's personality; or the publicizing of one's private affairs with which the public has no legitimate concern; or the wrongful intrusion into one's private activities in such a manner as to outrage a person of ordinary sensibilities or cause him mental suffering, shame or humiliation.[19]

This kind of account of the right to privacy is essentially an attempt to mark off illegitimate invasions of privacy rather than to define and mark out the domain of privacy. It rests on more basic views concerning privacy itself. Greater clarity of thought is to be achieved by separating the questions of what privacy is, what is its domain, and what infringements of privacy are justifiable, what is unjustifiable. Such an account is also exposed to the difficulties to which all attempts to explain privacy rights as kinds of property rights are exposed, namely, that payment in full of the price demanded is still compatible with gross invasion of privacy, that compensation by way of payment of damages, no matter how great the payment, may be no more real compensation for lack of respect for privacy than is financial compensation for loss of sight or limbs.

9. *Privacy defined in terms of feelings such as mental suffering, shame, embarrassment, humiliation.* An attempt may be made to define what is private, and hence what constitutes an invasion of privacy, along the lines suggested in the latter part of the statement in (8) above, namely, in terms of certain human feelings. Thus it is suggested that privacy relates to that which, when known or made public, outrages a person of ordinary sensibilities or causes him mental suffering, shame or humiliation. This approach has the advantage or seeming advantage over others of explaining privacy in a way that takes note of the social relativity in respect of what is considered to be a matter of privacy. Thus, according to one's society and the period of the society, matters relating to sexual conduct,

eating, drinking, ancestry, grief and so on, may or may not be matters of privacy. The Younger Committee declined to attempt to define privacy at least in part because what are regarded as matters of privacy may change even within the one society. In our society, much that 40 years ago was regarded as a matter of privacy—social background, salary, possessions, marital state if divorced, nature of illnesses, various sexual matters, facts about relatives and forebears—are not now so regarded. This is readily explicable if privacy is to be defined in terms of feelings, and the area of privacy in terms of matters which, if known and publicized, cause or would reasonably cause such feelings to be aroused. It has the further seeming advantage of relating offences against privacy with offences against decency, since the latter are socially relative, and this because they are defined in terms of acts which arouse feelings of embarrassment, shame, distress, indignation.

However there are very considerable difficulties in the way of such an account of privacy. Part of our objection to totalitarian regimes is that they render persons of ordinary sensibilities no longer outraged, hurt, shamed or humiliated by invasions of privacy. The invasions become so frequent, so commonplace, the emotional reactions and hurts cease to follow. This is true even of the losses and invasions of privacy experienced in the armed services in war, in institutional life as in a public hospital, etc. Persons of ordinary sensibilities become used to all their affairs becoming known, to the most intimate details of their lives and thoughts becoming common knowledge and handled with insensitivity, so that before long only the hypersensitive are outraged, hurt, shamed, or humiliated. Clearly, any account of privacy and of what constitutes losses and invasions of privacy, must explain life under Nazism, and life in institutions, the armed forces, and the like, as life with little privacy. It is true that any account of privacy, to be satisfactory, must offer a satisfactory explanation of the relativity of beliefs about what is the area of privacy, but it cannot make such relativity basic to privacy.

A further objection is that many things besides loss of privacy may cause the feelings identified with loss of privacy. Offensive and indecent conduct, as well as public imprudent, stupid, cowardly conduct may also cause such feelings. Further, people may have grandiose or obsessive ideas about the area of their privacy and include in it much that does not in fact relate to privacy. Thus they may believe, wrongly, that what relates to their forebears and relatives relates to their privacy, and feel embarrassment if it is discovered that they are murderers, lunatics, prostitutes, or menials. Imprudent, stupid, cowardly conduct of one's self, whether public or private, does relate to privacy, but this is not because of the feelings which publicity about it may arouse. On the other hand, the conduct, roles, etc., of other people, whether or not connected with one by blood or marriage do not relate to one's privacy, whatever publicity about them may cause one to feel, and this because facts about them are not facts about one's self. They are other people. The facts relate to their privacy if they are still alive.

10. *Privacy as relating to the person, to the personal, personality, inviolate personality.* Other accounts of privacy stress the person and the protection of the personal in the person. In one way or another, most of the foregoing accounts involve the relating of privacy to the self, to the person as a unique self, but not as a stressed aspect of the account. Thus P. A. Freund in "Privacy: One Concept or Many" in this context speaks of the protection of the interest of personality.[20] Warren and Brandeis in their influential article stressed that the principle of respect for privacy is that of "inviolate personality." The private is seen to relate not to everything and anything about the individual but to him as a person and as a unique person.

Such an account of privacy in terms of access to, awareness and knowledge of a person's self, readily explains what is true in other accounts. Most people desire that in at least certain areas and respects, they not be known about or intruded upon; they desire to have some control over access to themselves and publicity concerning what relates to themselves as selves. This is the nature and the extent of the connection between privacy and autonomy. Not all losses of privacy are unwanted, and when not unwanted, we usually although not always, decline to call them intrusions, invasions, violations of privacy. The entering into any human relationship involves some loss of privacy, some intrusions of others into what is, or is of, one's self. The closer, the more intimate the relationship, as in being a member of a family, a lover, a friend, the more freely and properly is privacy usually given up; it is given up none the less. Those so yielding up part of their privacy are opting for kinship, love, friendship, ahead of privacy. They may, as in love, marriage, the family, seek to create a larger self which becomes the focus of a new privacy.

Whether the acquisitive, proprietoral desires to control privacy which are so common in our society are natural, innate desires, or simply socially acquired desires, can be determined only by scientific research which, at this point of time, has not reached clear answers. If there are no innate, but only acquired, socially inculcated desires for privacy—or if the innate desires are easily eradicated—this will clearly affect the duties persons and states will have in respect of the privacy of others.

While it is true that people commonly feel indignation, shame, distress and embarrassment when the private is intruded upon or made public, they may experience quite other feelings, pleasant feelings such as those of pride and joy, as when a private, secret act of heroism or altruism is revealed. This is because they see themselves as being inspected, exposed to judgment. Much of the relativity in respect of what causes these feeling responses in different communities and in different ages, is due to different views being taken of the nature and content of the self and of what are extensions of the self. It is also true that different social conditions, moral and religious beliefs, make different things important to a person's person; they may even make him into a different self. Why publicity is seen to be so directly in conflict with privacy, is also evident from this account. Given the Kantian view of the good life, it is easy to see why respect for privacy, respect for persons, and the personal virtues and values noted by Fried, are so intimately linked.

To fill out this account, it would be necessary to say more about what constitutes a person's unique self, as it is through it that we must fill out the content of privacy. This is no easy task, and is one that can simply be noted here. The person's unique self is a thinking, feeling, self-conscious being, typically aware of its self-identity. Its thoughts, feelings, and body are clearly its own, not someone else's. There is no problem at this point about the area of the private. The problem arises in respect of extensions of the self which come to be identified with the self. Persons come to see many products of their labour as extensions of themselves, and as entitled to the same privacy as they themselves—diaries, paintings, books. They come also to see their families as extensions, and with them, their possessions, and even anything they identify with themselves. Clearly, not all that is seen to be an extension of the self is such, and hence, not all that is thought to be in the area of privacy is really so. The test is, is it of the self or not of the self? However our thinking something to be of, or not it is so. To this extent there will be some scope to mould the area of the private. So too, if it is desirable that feelings such as embarrassment, shame, distress are to be associated with invasions of privacy—I do not believe that it is so—to that extent social and legal measures could be used to foster the arousal of these feelings by and only by genuine losses of privacy, or only by illegitimate losses of privacy.

B. Grounds of the Right to Privacy

Very many different types of arguments are advanced in defence of a right to privacy. Many derive the right from some more basic right, seeking to show that some more basic right can be secured only if the right to privacy is respected. More commonly, the right to privacy is construed as one of the basic rights of men. Here it is contended either that there is something intrinsically valuable about privacy and its enjoyment such that persons thereby have a right to it, or that, unless persons enjoy privacy, they cannot be full persons, that in this respect, privacy is like liberty. Against the latter views, I shall argue that such claims lack empirical and metaphysical support, and that, when respect for privacy is morally obligatory, it is because privacy is involved in securing, attaining, enjoying other goods, respecting other, more basic rights, and hence, that in so far as there is a right to privacy, it is a derivative right, derived from concern for other values and rights, a conditional right, one that not simply may be overridden but one that ceases to be any sort of right at all, when respect for privacy is not dictated by concern for these other values and rights. This is to argue that it is not an intrinsic, *prima facie* right like the right to life, one which remains a real right even when it is legitimately overridden, and which may give rise to claims and duties when overridden. The following appear to be among the more important arguments for a right to privacy:

The right to respect for privacy as based on the utility of such respect.

The utility of respect for privacy has been defended by reference to utilitarian goods such as pleasure, happiness, self-development, and to nonutilitarian values including justice, honesty, respect for persons. The arguments in terms of the latter values which represent the enjoyment of privacy as not simply a means to, condition of, such values, but as intertwined with respect for them, may best be considered later. Our problem here is: is there a moral right to privacy? The utilitarian arguments are more typically stated as arguments for the legal protection of privacy, arguments for a legal right to privacy, and not as arguments for there being a moral right. Yet, clearly, it may be useful for the state to confer legal rights even where there are no corresponding moral rights. Is this so with privacy? Or can a moral right to privacy successfully be grounded on utilitarian considerations?

Quite clearly, invasions of privacy may cause great evils, and they may permit and lead on to other evils. One argument here parallels the utilitarian argument against indecent, offensive, conduct, claiming that the hurt caused by invasions of privacy is itself a reason for respecting and protecting privacy, and hence for acknowledging a moral and legal right to privacy. This is a very unsatisfactory argument, as unsatisfactory as is the argument for making indecent, offensive conduct criminal. In each case, the hurt suffered by the "victim" is one which ought to be borne for the sake of the greater good of liberty. Further, until it is clear beyond doubt that the hurt is caused not by socially inculcated feelings which can readily be changed by education and training, but by ineradicable innate feelings, there is no case provided by this argument for acknowledging either a moral or a legal right to privacy.

The more basic utilitarian argument is that invasions of privacy involve or lead on to other evils. The Peeping-Tom (but not the Peeping-Jane) may be a rapist and not simply a voyeur, the spy may be a blackmailer, the industrial spy a thief, the police and security agent may harass us, disrupt our private lives, ruin our careers, and the like. And all may significantly reduce our purely private enjoyment of our own. At best this is an argument for the legal protection of privacy, where there is a danger of such evils resulting from invasions of privacy. As already noted, there may be no ground for the protection of privacy against Peeping-Janes (unless their peeping is related to theft or some other evil). It is not an argument for a moral right to privacy. The legal right towards which this kind of argument is directed is a very limited one, and one derived from non-privacy rights, rights to bodily integrity, to life, to property and to liberty.

In assessing the case for such a legal right to privacy, it is necessary to weigh the goods that are secured against the goods lost and the evils brought into being. Among the goods lost are those lost because the police have been unable to solve crimes, apprehend criminals, obtain evidence necessary for securing convictions; there are also those goods lost in respect of national security as in war, if security agents are prevented from invading the privacy of innocent and suspected persons alike. The price paid here is very high. More serious still are the evils involved in making such acts crimes. Morally innocent persons, voyeurs, and the like, are rendered criminals, and hence to suffer all the evils of punishment and of becoming social misfits for life because ex-criminals. Innocent dependants will suffer. They are not all who are affected. All members of society are constrained in their action. Their liberty is gravely circumscribed. By so constraining people, other evils come into being, other goods are prevented. Such effects are already evident in the operation of the U.S. laws relating to privacy. Liberty too is defended in terms of its utility. Mill's most famous arguments were along these lines. If they have any basis in truth, and I believe that they do have some basis, to that extent the limitation of liberty for the sake of privacy is at risk of the goods of liberty. Whatever be the truth here, it is clear that the calculus is not an easy one to work out, and further, that until it is clear that the calculus is in favour of protection of privacy, in each specific area, things should be left as they now are.

Privacy and justice. An extension of this argument is that from justice, that if there were no protection of privacy, there would be grave injustices, and that respect for justice is vitally involved in respect for persons.

It is obviously true that great injustices are being perpetrated, and will in the future be made possible, by unrestricted invasions of privacy being permitted. This argument most commonly, but not only, arises in respect of data banks, and the use made of the information that is stored in them. Injustices result from misuse of true information, about a person's criminal record, health, employment record, credit-rating and its basis, and such like. Such

information has been unjustly used by those who might be
thought to have a right to it. It has also been passed on without
cost to those who might be thought to have a right to it. It has
also been passed on without cost to those who can have no claim
to have it, newspapers, banks, retail stores. Indeed, whoever will
pay a small fee seems to be able to obtain it. Not relevant to this
particular argument, but relevant to the case for protection of
privacy, is the consideration of the ways and means, often illegal,
used to collect this information. Thus deserving, honourable citizens may be ruined because their files contain the information
that they were convicted for stealing when aged 12, or that they
had treatment for a mental illness when aged 25, or that they
have changed jobs a number of times between the ages of thirty
and forty.

This argument cannot be ignored. If privacy is to be protected
against such evils, it may not be necessary to ban all invasions of
privacy. However, those whose names are on file must have a
right of access to the information so that, even if it is true, they
may know what they have to combat. Secondly only relevant
information should so be collected. Prolems about what is relevant
and what not, are considerable, but guiding principles are possible. Thirdly, where information is obtained from a person under
conditions of confidentiality, as by a bank in respect of a mortgage,
that information should be confidential between those parties, and
not be available for the bank to pass on to other banks, agencies,
newspapers. Breach of such confidentiality should be made a criminal offence, with punitive and/or civil damages where the person
suffers significantly from the breach of confidentiality. This must
hold equally of doctors, hospitals, government agencies such as
social welfare departments, taxation, education.

Probably the greatest concern about data banks is that they
store and propagate false facts about persons. The injury here is
not one of injury to privacy, but that of libel, defamation, slander,
with the consequent injustices. Because the owners of data banks
demand and successfully achieve for themselves complete legal
right to privacy in respect of their information and misinformation,
it is difficult, for the ordinary person well-nigh impossible, to
determine when such injuries are being perpetrated against him,
and by whom. Although no more an offence against privacy than
is defamation as it ordinarily occurs, those concerned with privacy

and the evils that occur as a result of its lack of protection, must take note of this evil. Again, open access to such information by those concerned, is an essential first step; again, rendering such lies and the propagation of lies, crimes with punitive damages attached is an essential second step. The state should leave available also the present rights to damages via the laws relating to slander, defamation and libel. Tough measures are essential to this area to stop on the one hand the high-handed, often irresponsible compilation and distribution of this material, and on the other hand, to prevent the distress, injustices, and even the ruination of lives that now occur.

Privacy as a basic need. Many argue that there is a need for privacy. Westin draws analogies with animals which are claimed to have a similar need for privacy. The need for privacy is variously explained as a need for an area of seclusion, of intimacy, of security from observation by others, an area in which one can let off steam, and the like. It is claimed that the need is one which, if not satisfied, leads to a stunted development as a human being and person, and such that we shall not be able to develop the delicate, sensitive feelings and relationships so vital to our development as persons.

This is an empirical, factual claim—or at least purports to be such—yet only the scantiest empirical support is offered by those who adopt this view. On the other hand, the observation of other societies, of how people have fared in prisons, concentration camps, institutions, does little to support this claim. Typically, if a need is not met, this results in ill-health, and disorders of various kinds. Consider here lack of food, sleep, air, affection. Yet lack of privacy seems not to result either in ill-health or in disorders. Societies have failed to respect privacy, as we understand privacy and in the senses in which privacy is claimed to be a need, without their members suffering from either physical or mental ill-health as a result. Consider here slaves in slave-owning societies, those who serve long sentences in prisons, those confined in concentration camps, those who live in very closely supervised totalitarian societies such as China, and those who live in small villages and whose lives are an open book to all others.

A related, more modest claim that we need privacy to develop the finer human feelings is more interesting. More will be said of this in connection with Fried's argument from respect for persons.

Here it is sufficient to note that Bunyan's *Pilgrim's Progress* is only one of the best known of the very many sensitive creations of human imagination and feeling to be written in prison, and that it is indicative of the deep, delicate, sensitive feelings and relationships that develop in prisons and concentration camps. To this it may perhaps be replied that such feelings are merely carry-overs from personalities and characters which were developed in societies in which privacy has been respected, that Bunyan was a formed Bunyan before he entered prison. Further it is pressed as a fact that in communes in which the members have never known privacy, deeper human feelings do not develop. Communes are very special, ideologically based societies. It is hard to know what could be concluded from such claims if true. I suggest that the examples cited of modern totalitarian states and slave-owning societies tell against such atypical societies.

Privacy and freedom. Arguments for privacy from freedom have been urged, even though to protect privacy is to restrict freedom. What is construed as an argument from freedom is that from the claim that the individual has a right to control of knowledge about himself. This is not an argument from freedom; not to have such exclusive control is not to lack freedom. To be granted such control is to be granted something distinct from and other than freedom. Another argument which relates privacy and liberty is to the effect that to invade privacy is to invade liberty—the person who is spied upon is unfree. He wishes to act under conditions free of observation and is unable to do so. A curious view of freedom is involved in this claim, it being suggested that any one doing what another person desires he not do, is infringing his enjoyment of his liberty. Secret spying and prying need involve no curtailment of liberty, no coercion, no impeding or preventing of individuals realizing their wills, being masters of their destinies. However, it is true that often an invasion of privacy may also be an invasion of liberty as well as of other rights. Unrestricted bugging, phone-tapping, mail-reading, reading of thoughts, may well influence us to curtail our actions, but usually only as a result of our own free choice, and not because of coercion. More basically, others may gain the knowledge and power to manipulate us, to thwart our wishes, to frustrate our efforts, by invading our privacy. Concern is felt about the use of information gained by invasions of privacy via data banks in this connection.

I suggest that this argument points to a real problem. To protect liberty we need to restrict liberty, and this can be true in the area of privacy as it is in other areas. If there is a case for the legal protection of liberty, it extends that far to the legal protection of privacy. However, the issues here are complex and complicated. Each restriction of privacy for the sake of liberty must be weighed against the loss of liberty involved in the legal protection of privacy and in the light of the liberty that is protected. A blanket protection of privacy is not justified by this argument from liberty. Much liberty, more importantly, the liberty to inquire and to gain knowledge, more particularly about man and men, the liberty to engage in psychological, historical, biographical inquiries, and to publish and to share with other scientists, historians, thinkers, the world, what one has discovered, is a basic liberty, one that is the very core of the structure of our liberal society. So to protect privacy that this liberty, and similar kinds of liberties, are curtailed or lost, is to threaten the very life of our society as a liberal society.

Relevant to this, although a distinct point, is the consideration that the liberal society is an open society, the open society, in which truth is knowable, accessible, assessable; a society which gives maximum protection to privacy must of necessity be a closed society. A closed society is exposed to very many evils to which an open society is not exposed.

A lover of privacy may reply to all this, that the areas of privacy which need protection for the sake of liberty can safely be marked off without seriously jeopardizing the freedom to inquire in the ways indicated here. This may be possible; if so, it needs to be shown to be so. I greatly doubt whether it can be done because one never knows in advance what piece of knowledge is going to be important. In any case, those concerned to defend privacy are unlikely to be content to restrict the protection of privacy along these lines.

Privacy as dictated by respect for persons. Many different arguments have been suggested here. That of C. Fried proceeds by relating respect for persons, respect, love, friendship and trust. Fried argues that love, friendship and trust are possible only in societies in which persons enjoy and accord to others a significant amount of privacy. Fried seeks to combine this claim with an acknowledgment of the relativity of matters which are matters of privacy, these being such as may be determined by convention. Whilst it appears to be the case that there is a close connection between privacy and respect for persons, respect, trust, love and friendship, the details of Fried's argument are unconvincing. Trust is still possible in the absence of all privacy—it may not be any longer necessary, it may not be called upon, but it is still possible. Friendship and love involve a voluntary forgoing of privacy and may dictate the invasion of the privacy of the other. Both are possible without trust. Respect for privacy would seem to be dictated by respect for persons only in that persons commonly wish their privacy to be respected, hence in so far as we ignore such wishes, without good reason, to that extent we show lack of respect. If we have good reason to ignore a person's wishes, for example, if we suspect that he is concealing a tumour which is now operable but which will soon become inoperable and fatal, we are showing no lack of respect in intruding on his privacy in this matter. This suggests that it is not respect for privacy as such but respect for the wishes of persons that is dictated by respect for persons. Fried's discussion is much richer and fuller than these brief comments bring out. However, this brief discussion does suggest that not a great deal by way of a case for the legal protection of privacy follows from this kind of argument, the more so as it would be, not privacy, but what persons think to be matters of privacy that should be respected and protected.

Privacy as valuable for its own sake. Basic rights are those which are not derived from more basic rights, but relate to some ultimate value, good or duty which is possessed of intrinsic value, worth, moral binding force. Nothing that emerged from our examination of the concept of privacy suggests that privacy relates to something of intrinsic worth or value. In this respect privacy differs from life of persons, from self-development of persons, from justice, and even from liberty, even though there is room for argument as to the source of the value of liberty, it seemingly not being intrinsic but due to liberty being an essential element and condition of being a person. Privacy relates to the lack of something. Its definition must be essentially negative. How can the absence of something have intrinsic value? Any value it has must relate to the absence of evils or to this absence being a condition of goods, or the like. What is valuable if anything in this area is valuable, is the state of mind or the existence of the person who enjoys privacy, not privacy in and for itself. Perhaps a better comparison here would be with pleasure or happiness. We have discovered nothing about privacy to suggest that it has intrinsic value in the way that pleasure and happiness do. And, in so far as the state of mind or existence of the person who enjoys privacy is valuable, it will be so because it contains goods such as pleasure and happiness.

If this contention that privacy has no intrinsic worth or value is sound—and to rebut it much more than has been done to date will be needed by so elucidating privacy that it is self-evidently of value—then there can be no basic moral right to privacy which parallels the traditionally recognized rights to life, self-development, moral integrity, liberty. Any right to privacy will be a derivative one from other rights and other goods. This means that it will be a conditional right, and not always a right. Whether or not it will be a derivative right, derivative from the rights to life, self-development, justice, moral integrity, and the like, will depend on practical considerations as to whether respect for privacy is necessary for the enjoyment of these rights. Sometimes it will be, and sometimes it will not be so involved. Thus again, any attempt to give blanket legal protection to a right to privacy as favoured in the U.S. will be in danger of protecting what ought not to be protected, and of thereby unjustifiably restricting liberty, inquiry, and equally important, the realization of justice.

Besides being subject to qualifications by reference to its very basis, and to clashes with other rights (and this is where the public interest but not public curiosity may create a right to invade privacy), there are inbuilt limitations. It is evident that we can consent to forgo privacy, properly, as in marriage, friendship, and certain other social relationships, putting certain areas of our lives outside the sphere of privacy for certain other persons. Consent may however be improperly given and improperly accepted—improperly given as when a person betrays himself and his own privacy by selling his sordid confessions, improperly accepted in those cases, and in respect of many credit-worthiness inquiries and compilations of credit data banks with the clients' cooperation. The issues here are complex and do not readily lend themselves to regulation by the state, especially by the use of the criminal law. Civil laws, the setting up of advisory bodies, the stating of guidelines concerning respect for privacy may help, but ultimately, the proper respecting of privacy must depend on the individual person's moral responsiblity and integrity.

To conclude. To be plausible, any account of privacy must explain privacy as something distinct from being let alone, solitude, secrecy, liberty, and such like, and as something *sui generis.* When so explained, privacy of itself does not provide grounds for believing men as men to possess a basic moral right to privacy. Any right to privacy must be based on other rights and goods. For this reason, and for reasons inherent in its nature, such a right must be a qualified, conditional right. Efficient, just protection of it, without injury to the enjoyment of other rights and goods, is fraught with difficulties. The law is a clumsy, insensitive instrument. If used to protect privacy in those areas where concern for other rights and values dictates the protection of privacy, the law must be made sensitive, and be used with the greatest of sensitivity and with an awareness of the values behind privacy which it is seeking to safeguard.

NOTES

1. J.F. Stephen, *Liberty, Equality, Fraternity*, R.J. White (ed.) (Cambridge: C.U.P., 1967), 160. First edition (London: Smith, Elder & Co., 1873).
2. S.D. Warren and L.D. Brandeis, "The Right to Privacy," *Harvard Law Review* **IV**, No. 5 (December 1890–91), 193–220.
3. *Op. cit.*, 206.
4. M.L. Ernst and A.U. Schwartz, *The Right to Be Let Alone* (New York: Macmillan & Co., 1962), 17.
5. C.F.O. Clarke, *Private Rights and the Freedom of the Individual* (Enstone; The Ditchley Foundation, 1972), 8.
6. E. Beardsley, "Privacy: Autonomy and Selective Disclosure," *Nomos* **XIII** 1971 (J.R. Pennock and J.W. Chapman (eds) New York; Atherton), 70.
7. A.F. Westin, *Privacy and Freedom*, 1971 (London; Bodley Head, 1967), 7.
8. R.B. Parker, "A Definition of Privacy," *Rutgers Law Review* **27**, No. 1 (Summer 1974), 275–296.
9. H.J. McCloskey, "The Political Ideal of Privacy," *Philosophical Quarterly* **21**, No. 85 (October 1971), 303–314.
10. E. van den Haag, "On Privacy," *Nomos* **XIII** (1971), 149.
11. *Ibid.*, 151.
12. J.J. Thomson, "The Right to Privacy," *Philosophy and Public Affairs* **4**, No. 4 (Summer 1975), 295–314.
13. C. Fried, "Privacy," *Yale Law Journal*, **77**, No. 3 (January 1967–68), 475–493.
14. C. Fried, *An Anatomy of Values: Problems of Personal and Social Choice* (Cambridge: Harvard, 1970).

15. "Privacy," op. cit., 477–478.
16. J. Rachels, "Why Privacy is Important," *Philosophy and Public Affairs* **4**, No. 4 (Summer 1974), 323–333.
17. S.I. Benn, "Privacy, Freedom and Respect for Persons," *Nomos* **XIII** (1971), 1–26.
18. J.H. Reiman, "Privacy, Intimacy and Personhood," *Philosophy and Public Affairs* **6**, No. 1 (Fall 1976), 26–44, esp. 29–39.
19. S.H. Hofstadter and G. Horowitz, *The Right to Privacy* (New York: Central Book Co., 1964), 7.
20. P.A. Freund, "Privacy: One Concept or Many," *Nomos* **XIII** (1971), 182–198.

Study Questions

1. Do you agree with McCloskey's contention that ". . . the principle which protects personal writings . . . not against theft and physical appropriation, but against publication in any form, is in reality not the principle of private property, but of inviolate personality?" Why or why not?

2. One of McCloskey's most important conclusions is that "privacy," to the extent that it qualifies as a "right," is not a basic right, but ". . . a derivative right, derived from concern for other values and rights." State why you agree or disagree with this, focusing specifically on the authors arguments in defense of this contention.

Myron Farber's Confidential Sources

Christians, Rotzoll
& Facklen

Reporter Myron A. Farber had been with the New York *Times* nearly ten years when he was assigned to follow up a lead provided by Eileen Milling, a public relations consultant and writer who had begun an investigation of unexplained deaths at Riverdell Hospital in Oradell, New Jersey. Several surgical patients had died during postoperative care, allegedly after receiving doses of curare, a muscle-relaxing drug.

Farber faced some formidable obstacles in his investigation. The deaths had occurred in 1965, ten years in the past. Witnesses and relatives had moved away or themselves had died. Laboratory reports were on a technical level beyond a layman's ken, and some hospital files were missing. Nevertheless, after four months of digging, Farber filed his stories. They received frontpage play in the *Times* on 7–8 January 1976.

The stories presented evidence that a "Dr. X" had seen the victims shortly before their deaths, and that the drug curare had been found in his hospital locker by a suspicious medical colleague. Farber's stories led to the indictment of Dr. Mario E. Jascalevich, a 51-year-old Argentine-born surgeon, in May 1976. The case was brought to trial in early 1978.

What began as a routine newspaper investigation soon turned into a major test of reporters' First Amendment privileges. On 19 May 1978, trial judge William J. Arnold permitted defense attorney Raymond Brown to issue a subpoena for the notes held by Farber and the *Times*. Brown contended that the notes were essential to his client's defense. Complicating the proceedings was a book contract between Farber and Doubleday worth $75,000, of which Farber had already received a $37,000 advance. Brown contended that Farber stood to profit should Jascalevich be convicted and that he had concocted the allegations to advance his career.

Both Farber and the *Times* denied Brown's charges and refused to surrender notes, claiming that they contained information on sources who had been promised confidentiality. When Farber and the *Times* again declined to hand over notes for a private inspection by the judge, they were each cited for contempt. Farber was fined $1000 and sentenced to six months in the Bergen County jail, the sentence to begin after he complied with the subpoena; in the meantime he was to be confined to jail. The *Times* was fined $100,000 plus an additional $5000 for each day its editors resisted the court's authority. The *Times* finally turned over its files on August 18, but 10 days later a New Jersey Superior Court judge accused the *Times* of sanitizing its files. The $5000-per-day fine was reinstated.

At the same time, Farber surrendered an incomplete book manuscript which he claimed would not establish the guilt or innocence of the accused. Farber was still not willing to compromise on the matter of his personal notes.

Appeals were filed with the New Jersey Supreme Court. The state shield law guaranteed protection, lawyers argued, but on September 21 the court ruled 5–2 against Farber and the *Times*.

In the meantime, the Jascalevich trial was grinding toward its thirty-fourth week, the longest murder trial ever held in the state. When arguments were finally over, the jury needed only a few hours to decide that the prosecution had not proven its case. Jascalevich was acquitted. Farber was released after spending a total of 40 days in jail. The *Times* made its last payment on the fine, which by now totalled $285,000.

The case against Jascalevich was closed, but the matter of reporter's privilege was still pending appeals to the United States Supreme Court. On November 28 the Court decided not to review the contempt convictions. The decisions left standing the New Jersey Superior Court ruling that reporters do not have absolute privilege to keep sources confidential when defendants in a criminal trial need information for their defense.

* * *

The defense attorney's clever flamboyance, an inept judge, and Farber's unwise book contract prevented this case from being legally definitive or even illuminating. Its moral dimensions are not focused sharply either. However, two questions need to be considered whenever situations similar to this one arise: promise keeping and special privilege. How journalists treat confidential sources is an explosive issue in the law, generating various statutes to shield the press and stirring hot tempers at professional conventions. The moral domain warrants consideration as part of the answer regarding reporters and confidentiality.

We ought to keep our promises, a Kantian would suggest. A direct application of this rule to Myron Farber solves the ethical issue immediately—he made a vow to his sources of information and that pledge must be upheld regardless of circumstances. Farber himself appeals to this notion, at least in part, by telling the Superior Court judge: "If I give up my file I will have undermined my professional integrity and diminished the credibility of my colleagues."

However, that knee-jerk conclusion obscures an important detail—a man is on trial for murder and he stands trial largely because of Farber's investigation. Because certain crucial issues remain unanswered, Judge Arnold wants to determine whether Farber's materials ("all statements, pictures, memoranda, recordings, and notes of interviews") have any relevance to the case. The defense attorney has contended that Farber "collaborated with the State's prosecutor to concoct charges of murder against an innocent citizen for pecuniary gain and to advance their careers." Others speculate that Farber had been hoodwinked in a conspiracy to frame Mario Jascalevich.

Does not the crucial character of Farber's testimony make for an exception to one's fundamental obligation toward promise keeping? Certainly promise keeping needs no justification, and the breaking of promises does. The necessity of a fair hearing for someone accused of murder can qualify as such a rare exception. As Aryeh Neier, Executive Director of ACLU, argued: If Jascalevich can prove Farber's sources are *essential*, then Farber must tell. The sources "enjoy a right to anonymity as against the government, but not against a person placed on trial on criminal charges as a result of their accusations."[21] In this regard, Farber made a rash vow to his sources not to reveal their identity under any circumstances whatsoever. He thereby uncritically pledged too much. Farber should have communicated this possible exception to his sources at the very beginning. Otherwise he allows himself no opportunity to act on his conscience.

Actually Farber's adamant position is not based strongly on a categorical view of promise keeping. He really grounds his claims on a morally problematical appeal to special privilege. Ironically in wishing no exception to his confidentiality pledge, he seeks exception for his profession and the pursuit of its particular interests. Democratic societies depend on judicial fact finding and on the general obligation to testify. Farber remains silent on the grounds of journalistic privilege, contending, in effect, that he belongs to a special class immune from a responsibility born by the populace at large. The New York *Times* put it delicately in an editorial: "Frightened sources daily offer our reporters fact, confession, rumor or accusation on condition that their identity must remain secret. To betray one such source would jeopardize all. We cannot do the work that the community should prize the most if we are forced to reveal our informants and confidential notes."[22] Underneath the polite phrasing, however, the *Times* is contending that its reporter is not an ordinary citizen, but a professional journalist and thus entitled even to ignore subpoenas. Farber's frequent reference to his employer, "the nation's premier newspaper," gave his well-intended exclusivism a touch of arrogance. But few people outside the profession itself have been willing to confer a blanket exemption on the press as an institution. Nearly all Supreme Court justices, for example, interpret the First Amendment as conferring some measure of special status on the news media, yet the majority do not carry newsmen's privilege to the extreme of cavalierly disregarding the Sixth Amendment. Considerations in this case ought to reflect the plight of someone on trial for murder.

In many situations, pledges of confidentiality can be made with integrity and fully honored. However, journalists ought to promise with painstaking care. Sometimes sources seek confidentiality precisely because they fear a trial on serious charges. Promises, therefore, can be made too rashly. Reporters following their conscience in this complex arena may have to suffer occasionally, either by losing a story or two, or by going to jail if honoring a deliberate promise requires it. "For those journalists who insist they must make absolute promises of confidentiality in order to do their jobs, reporting will inevitably be a risky occupation. Let their badge of professionalism be a willingness to take those risks, rather than a willingness to seek special legal privileges."[23]

NOTES

1. Editorial in the *Washington Post*. 12 February 1969. Quoted in John L. Hulteng, *The Messenger's Motives* (Englewood Cliffs, N.J.: Prentice-Hall, 1976), p. 81.
2. Walter Lippmann, *Public Opinion* (New York: The Free Press, [1922] 1949), Part 7, pp. 201–30.
3. Quotations for this case are taken from Robert Woodward and Carl Bernstein, *All the President's Men* (New York: Simon and Schuster, 1974), pp. 205–24.
4. *Ibid.*, p. 210.
5. *Ibid.*, p. 224.
6. This commentary focuses on the contribution of journalists in uncovering Watergate, though measuring the size of that contribution is debatable. Judge Sirica attempts to document that the judiciary (including special prosecutors) were primarily responsible for developing the case and securing the resolution. See John Sirica, *To Set the Record Straight* (New York: W.W. Norton, 1979).
7. Jules Witcover, "Two Weeks That Shook the Press," *Columbia Journalism Review* 10 (September/October 1971):9.
8. *Ibid.*, p. 10.
9. *Ibid.*, p. 11.
10. Cf. Ben H. Bagdikian, "What Did We Learn?" *Columbia Journalism Review* 10 (September/October 1971):47.
11. A.M. Rosenthal, "Why We Published," *Columbia Journalism Review* 10 (September/October 1971):17–18.
12. Edward Jay Epstein, "Journalism and Truth," *Commentary* 57 (April 1974):36–40.
13. Leslie Maitland, "High Officials Are Termed Subjects of a Bribery Investigation by FBI," *New York Times*, 3 February 1980, pp. 1,26.
14. "Abdul's Sting," *New York Times*, 5 February 1980, p. A22.
15. David Rosenbaum, "The Federal Corruption Inquiry: Questions on FBI Techniques," *New York Times*, 8 February 1980, p. B6.
16. Marjorie Margolies, "The Billy Viscidi Story," *The Washingtonian*, vol. 14, no. 8, May 1979, p. 125.
17. *Ibid.*, p. 126.
18. *Ibid.*, p. 127.
19. *Ibid.*, p. 127.
20. *Ibid.*, p. 128.

21. Aryeh Neier, "The Rights of Farber's Sources," *The Nation* 227 (16 September 1978):229.
22. "Our Man in Jail," *New York Times*, 6 August 1978, p. E16.
23. Robert M. Kaus, "The Constitution, the Press, and the Rest of Us," *The Washington Monthly*, November 1978, p. 55.

Study Questions

1. How could one argue that Farber was under no obligation whatsoever to reveal his sources? (State and use a moral philosopher of history—Kant, Mill, Plato, etc.—who would be most relevant to this task.
2. The authors contend that Farber's adamant stance was really based not on promise-keeping, but on *special privilege*. Explain why you agree or disagree with this claim, backing up your answers with clear and strong arguments.

Reflections on the Ethics of Televangelism

Robert C. Good

In recent years television has enabled evangelists to beam their message into the residences of large numbers of Americans. For example, Jimmy Swaggart's television programs reach eight million viewers each Sunday. Jerry Falwell's Gospel Hour airs over 350 stations to 438,000 households and over the Liberty Broadcasting Network to 1.5 million cable television subscribers. In April of 1987, *The PTL Show*, hosted by Jim Bakker, reached 13.5 million households via its own satellite network to 178 stations.[1] What are televangelists trying to accomplish in their television programs? At least two things come to mind. They are surely attempting to convince those who hear them to live a life which is dominated by religious faith. In addition, they are trying to get their listeners to donate money to their ministries. The total receipts of televangelists come close to $2 billion a year. Jimmy Swaggart's 1986 revenues were estimated at $140 million.[2] Oral Roberts has spent 31.0% of his air time on financial appeals, Rex Humbard 42.6%, Jerry Falwell and Jim Bakker 23.0%, and James Robison 36.0%.[3] Are televangelists succeeding in controlling people's behavior? We will discuss this question.

Here is an argument which is designed to show that televangelists do control the behavior of their listeners. Televangelists are skillfully using their listeners as a means to fulfill their own ends. The goal on their television programs is to get their listeners to think that happiness will result from the adoption of religious beliefs. What sort of happiness? Why, eternal life, of course! The basic message that is transmitted to viewers is that accepting the doctrines of the evangelist's religion and contributing money to help the evangelist's ministry going will lead to the viewer's having a tremendous sense of well-being caused by the confidence that eternal life awaits.

What televangelists are doing is morally objectionable. Viewers are not deciding for themselves what they wish to believe. Moreover, they are not making up their own minds about what they will do with their "extra" money. This is because viewers are overpowered by the ever-growing number of televangelists who create and control the interests, wants, and desires of their audiences. The result of this is that people are not determining for themselves what they want to be doing. In other words, televangelists present a threat to personal autonomy, insofar as they dictate the beliefs and actions of their listeners.

The claim that televangelists are controlling the behavior of their viewers might be thought to be patently absurd. Let's take a look at three reasons for thinking that the claim is absurd.

First, it is obvious that the television shows of an evangelist have different impacts on different people. For example, a particular evangelist's television show may cause Viewer A to adopt the beliefs the evangelist proposes and to mail money to support the ministry. However, that same television show may have no effect on Viewer B who watches the show but chooses not to subscribe to the evangelist's beliefs and elects not to make any financial contributions to the ministry. The point is that televangelists are not controlling the behavior of their viewers because viewer responses to their programs differ widely.

This first reason for thinking that it is absurd to maintain that televangelists are controlling viewer behavior is not as strong as it initially appears. It is, of course, undeniable that televangelists are followed by some and not by others, that some contribute to televangelistic ministries and others do not. However, it is plain that the televangelist does prescribe the beliefs and donation habits of his regular viewers. It is these regular viewers, the faithful followers of the televangelist, that are having their needs, wants, and desires shaped and molded by the televangelist. Ignoring the potential they have to think for themselves about what they want and need, and declining to take the opportunity to reflect on where their money should go, they simply believe and give as the televangelist stipulates.

A second reason for thinking it absurd to assert that televangelists control viewer behavior is that today's viewers are fairly sophisticated. Today's viewers realize that televangelists have as their fundamental concern the acquisition of funds to sustain their ministries. That is, today's viewers understand that televangelists are essentially self-interested. This understanding leads viewers to be suspicious about the claims being made by televangelists. The point is that televangelists cannot possibly be controlling the skeptical viewers of television we have in this country.

Like the first, this second reason for thinking it absurd to hold that televangelists control viewer behavior is not a compelling one. Certainly there are those viewers of television who distrust the altruistic posture of evangelists. These viewers believe that the primary motive televangelists have is to collect as much money as possible, and they further believe that televangelists will say anything on the air if it prompts people to mail donations. However, it is crucial to realize that a large number of viewers have a very different view on what motivates televangelists. A substantial number of people seem to believe that televangelists have been specially chosen by God to become ministers and that they are involved in the selfless activity of letting people know that they can be saved by adopting faith in God. Surely lots of people are convinced that televangelists are devoting their lives to a truly noble cause, namely, letting people know how they can develop the proper relationship with the Almighty. Now, a viewer such as this does act as the televangelist says he should act. That is, he believes the things the televangelist tells him to and he contributes money so that the ministry can continue. It looks as if this type of viewer is being controlled by the televangelist.

A third reason for denying the plausibility of the thesis that televangelists control viewer behavior appeals to the idea that televangelists are simply involved in persuasion. Part of what life involves is dealing with attempts at persuasion that are directed your way. When the televangelist asks you to commit yourself to religious faith and to support the ministry financially, he is just one among many persuaders that you encounter everyday. What is the difference between the evangelist's trying to get us to do something and other people, trying to get us to do something?

There is none. Friends and acquaintances continually try to tell us that happiness will result if we do the things they suggest, e.g., buy an excercise bike, eat at the new Vietnamese restaurant, go to see a movie, etc. The same goes for the televangelist. He is attempting to get us to believe that happiness will result if we do what he suggests. The point is that televangelists use the same procedures of persuasion that all persuaders employ. Televangelists, therefore, have no more effects on us than our friends and acquaintances. They are certainly not controlling anyone's behavior.

This third reason for alleging that it makes no sense to say that televangelists control viewer behavior is also not a good one, and it is important to see why. It is preposterous to claim that the persuasion engaged in by televangelists is no different in nature from other acts of persuasion people deal with. Why? Think about the manner in which televangelists present themselves to their viewers. Televangelists assert with tremendous confidence that they have special knowledge regarding what God wants us to do. Are other acts of persuasion directed our way characterized by the persuader's telling us that we ought to do what he suggests because God wants us to do it? Usually not! This shows that the persuasive techniques utilized by televangelists have an extra dimension not normally found in ordinary acts of persuasion. Furthermore, the persuasive strategy employed by televangelists differs in another crucial way from ordinary persuasive strategies. Televangelists imply that eternal life will not be yours if you do not endorse the religious beliefs they proffer. As a matter of fact, eternal damnation could be suffered by you as a consequence of not doing as the evangelist says. When acts of persuasion are directed our way, are they commonly characterized by the threat that you will be damned if you do not do what the persuader suggests? Hardly! The point is that the stakes laid down by televangelists regarding our decision to have faith or not are considerably greater than what is at stake in the vast majority of ordinary persuasive encounters.

I have been claiming that televangelists interfere with the autonomy of their viewers. A popular account of autonomy has been offered by Gerald Dworkin.[4] We will now turn to this account of autonomy, focusing on what Dworkin thinks are factors which interfere with autonomy. I will argue that the factors Dworkin calls attention to clearly apply to the relationship between tele-vangelists and their viewers.

Let me use the terms "first-order desires" and "second-order desires" to explain Dworkin's analysis of autonomy. A person's first-order desires are the desires he has to do things. For example, among my first-order desires may be the desire to buy a candy bar, the desire to visit Cape Cod, and be glad that I have this desire, given that I have always wanted to go there and can afford it at the moment. When we reflect on our first-order desires, we are at the level of second-order desires.

For Dworkin, a person must be both authentic and independent to be truly autonomous. When is a person authentic? This occurs when the first and second-order desires of the person are in harmony. That is, if a person desires that his first-order desires be as they are, if his second-order desires re-affirm his first-order desires, then the person is authentic. It is clear that the faithful followers of a televangelist are authentic. They have the first-order desire to subscribe to the evangelist's beliefs as well as the first-order desire to give money to the ministry. Besides, they approve of these first-order desires. Their second-order desires are in harmony with their first-order desires.

A person must pass a second test before he can be judged to be autonomous, let us recall. A person can be authentic and yet not be independent. If this is the case, the person lacks autonomy. How can a person be authentic and not independent? This happens when the person is the victim of manipulation, deception, or the withholding of relevant information. Even though a person's first and second-oder desires are in harmony, this harmony would disappear if the person discovered that he was being manipulated, deceived, or having relevant information withheld from him. Furthermore, upon realizing the existence of manipulation, deception, or information withholding, the person may no longer have the first-order desires he had previously.

I maintain that the faithful followers of televangelists are not independent. They are the victims of manipulation, deception, and the withholding of relevant information on the part of tele-vangelists. Therefore, the followers of televangelists are not autonomous beings, and, as such, are having their behavior controlled. Let me spell out the nature of this manipulation, deception, and withholding of relevant information.

Manipulation, whatever else it may involve, is characterized by the manipulator's taking advantage of the vulnerabilities of the one he is seeking to manipulate. Televangelists inform their viewers that eternal life will not be theirs without their endorsement of certain religious beliefs. Televangelists are aware of the anxiety and uncertainty that their viewers have about what will happen to them when they die. Viewers want a psychologically satisfactory answer to what their fate will be. Taking advantage of these vulnerabilities of the members of their audience, televangelists proclaim that they have a plan of action people can follow which will guarantee them eternal life.

An evangelist would clearly be deceiving his contributors if he told them that the money they sent in was going to support the ministry when, in reality, much of it was going directly into the personal funds of the evangelist. Recently, Jim Bakker, the former head of the *PTL* ministry, was indicted on charges that he diverted more than $4 million in church funds for his personal use.[5] One would presume that the first and second-order desires of contributors to an evangelist's cause would not continue to be in harmony if they learned that the evangelist himself was pocketing a healthy share of the money collected. One would also presume that awareness of such corruption should also cause contributors to televangelism not to continue to have the first-order desire to contribute.

Evangelists withhold relevant information from their viewers. The evangelist presents himself to his viewers as having knowledge of God's will. The evangelist tells his viewers that he knows the one right way to lead one's life so as to ensure eternal life. What relevant information is being withheld here? The evangelist certainly realizes that his answer to what constitutes the proper religious life is just one answer among many other competing answers. Why doesn't the evangelist inform people of this? Then, he could put forth arguments to show why his formula for achieving eternal life is superior to formulas being offered by competing religions and competing evangelists. Viewers would then be able to compare these dueling world views and perhaps decide with which religion, if any, they wish to cast their lot.

A poignant recent example of an evangelist's withholding relevant information from his viewers is Jimmy Swaggart's reported (and apparently acknowledged) involvement with a prostitute. From his pulpit Mr. Swaggart regularly and vehemently denounced the very sort of behavior he practiced himself. What should a follower of Mr. Swaggart make of all this? It might dawn on such a follower that Mr. Swaggart has made a mockery of his own religious messages. Perhaps it should also occur to such a follower that Mr. Swaggart's hypocritical ways demonstrate that his ministry does not merit regular financial contributions.

When all is said and done, what I'm attempting to urge upon my readers here is that televangelists interfere with viewers' developing certain habits of mind that are intrinsically valuable, namely, developing one's powers of reasoning, asking for evidence and justification, and understanding the variety of alternative lifestyles they could pursue, and so forth. Simply doing and believing exactly what televangelists tell one to do and believe is not leading an examined life. To the extent that televangelists are aware that many people can be influenced by their television programs to lead such an unexamined life, they are seeking to control people's behavior.

NOTES

1. These figures were reported in *Time* Magazine's cover story article of April 6, 1987, entitled "TV's Unholy Row."
2. See *Time* (April 6, 1987).
3. These figures were reported in Razelle Frankl, *Televangelism: The Marketing of Popular Religion* (Carbondale: Southern Illinois University Press, 1987), p. 134.
4. Gerald Dworkin, "Autonomy and Behavior Control," © 1976 Institute of Society, Ethics, and the Life Sciences. It is reprinted in Joseph DesJardins and John McCall, *Contemporary Issues in Business Ethics* (Belmont, California: Wadsworth, 1985), pp. 159–166.
5. *New York Times*, (December 11, 1988). Reported here also was that the indictment said that Mr. Bakker defrauded as many as 150,000 viewers of "The PTL Club" by soliciting contributions that were not used for their intended purpose.

Study Questions

1. Explain why you agree or disagree with the author's contention that televangelists control viewer behavior. Be specific about where you agree and disagree about points the author makes to support his contention.

2. Many people admire a successful advertising campaign that gets people to buy a certain product. Why shouldn't we admire an evangelist who stages a successful campaign to get people to contribute to his ministry?
3. What reasons might someone give to show that televangelism has had a *beneficial* impact on American society?

The Strange Tilted World of TV Network News

*Edward Jay Epstein**

Early each weekday evening, 50 million Americans settle down before a television screen to get their main dose of events of the day. It's network news time, time for Walter Cronkite, John Chancellor or Howard K. Smith and Harry Reasoner to tell us what's going on in the world. But is it the straight word we get? Unfortunately, no. The report is loaded with bias.

This bias is not a product of the newsmen's personal dishonesty or connivance. Rather, it is the product of a reporting system with a decided tilt built into its basic structure. To understand it, let's look at what happens backstage and off-camera at network-news headquarters. Consider a typical day at ABC last year.

It begins not at the scene of some plane crash or other noteworthy event, but at 9:30 a.m. in the network's offices on New York's West 66th Street. There executive producer Av Westin and his staff—all New Yorkers—have assembled to plan the evening news broadcast, to decide in essence what the "news" will be. The three national wire services list hundreds of possible stories—truce infractions in Vietnam, record-breaking commodity prices, revelations on Watergate, etc. But, in the 22 minutes of news time on a half-hour program, only six to eight film stories can be presented.

---

* Edward Jay Epstein, a political scientist and journalist, has taught at Harvard and at M.I.T. He is the author of *Inquest*, a study of the Warren Commission. In 1973, after five years of close study, he published *News From Nowhere*, the first in-depth look at television network news.

This morning, as every morning, before he even arrives at the office, Westin has started his search for the "significant" news by reading the New York *Times*. And he has already concluded that the housewives' boycott of beef will likely be "the story of the day." A check of other sources turns up nothing stronger, so he begins the meeting by order a "whip-around"—correspondents in different parts of the country all giving individual reports on the same subject, the boycott. His senior producer immediately telephone's ABC's six major bureaus—in New York, Chicago, Miami—plus affiliates in Philadelphia and San Francisco, and spells out in considerable detail the stories which correspondents are to seek out. All involve interviews of protesting housewives at supermarkets, to depict a "spontaneous" nationwide movement to roll back meat prices.

Just after 11 a.m., ABC's Washington producer calls in with word of the Washington stories being covered that day. Westin "orders" one on government cutbacks of poverty programs, which he believes fits "the broad trends of the newsday." For the rest of the program, he decides to use material from the "bank"— stories filmed and edited a few weeks before, but still relevant.

By midafternoon, correspondents are telephoning in their scripts for "final approval." News editors scan late wire-service copy to see what stories should be included in the "pad'—news items read by the anchormen with no special "graphics"—that can be dropped if the program runs long. By 4 p.m., all the "boycott" stories are completed and being edited in New York to heighten the action, the elements of confrontation and protest. Finally, at exactly seven o'clock eastern time, Reasoner introduces himself and begins the program.

Study the scene, and four major tilts stand out: 1) Virtually all our national news is filtered through and controlled by a group of men in one city, New York. 2) Most national-news footage is drawn from just four metropolitan centers—New York, Washington, Chicago, Los Angeles. 3) National "news" is, in fact, routinely *created*, by starting with general hypotheses rather than with actual happenings. 4) Events that are visually exciting are more likely to get air time than others which may be equally or more significant. Let's focus on these tilts in detail:

1. New York Fulcrum. At all three networks, the events to be covered, the story line, the correspondent and the editing are all tightly supervised from New York. And correspondents usually must accept the New York view in formulating their story. In 1971, NBC's White House correspondent Herbert Kaplow objected to asking President Nixon at a televised news conference a question forwarded by the New York producer because he felt his questions were more germane. So the producer simply assigned an additional correspondent to the conference to ask the question. Several months later Kaplow was removed from the White House beat (and eventually he left NBC for ABC).

Because of their common base in New York City, news executives and editors tend to receive very similar information. Most notably, all the network decision-makers I have interviewed rely on a single newspaper each morning—the New York *Times*. "Like it or not," one executive explains, "the *Times* is our bible: it tells us what is likely to be considered important by others."

When Westin took charge of the ABC Evening News in 1969, he was given a mandate to alter the tilt, to create a news product "radically different" in outlook, "more evenly balanced" politically than the NBC and CBS newscasts. (The strategy was dicated by management for commercial and competitive, rather than political, reasons.) As general policy, Westin ordered that if one side of a controversial issue is presented, the other side must be given equal time within seven days. "But in practice," he told me, "the outlook was hard to change. Producers always gave the liberal side first stab, and the most dramatic piece of film," while the more conservative side "was made to react and answer." The "eastern-liberal syndrome," as he calls it, tends to favor sweeping reform over maintaining the status quo, so newsmen operating out of New York, sharing this perspective, quite naturally favor criticism rather than defense of social institutions.

To achieve a measure of balance, Westin then tried to "reverse the perspective," giving the defense (of abortion laws, for example) "first stab." This succeeded in specific instances, but it could not be applied generally. The outlook of news correspondents and field producers was too ingrained and deep-rooted; they resisted organizing the news counter to it.

2. Limited Geography. Most of the news footage used to illustrate national stories is drawn from only four metropolitan centers— New York, Washington, D.C., Chicago and Los Angeles. Over 80 percent of the networks' domestic camera crews and correspondents are stationed in these cities. Permanent hookups are maintained there, so film stories can be electronically "fed" to the broadcast center in New York with (usually) no extra charge against the program's budget. In most other cities, special microwave channels have to be leased, at heavy expense. In other words, network news is set up in such a way that stories from a few cities are much more convenient and less expensive than stories from the rest of America.

To be sure, network-news crews do venture out into the hinterland in the case of a major news happening, such as the Indian uprising at Wounded Knee, S.D. But on more routine coverage, the path of least resistance is followed. For instance, CBS illustrated a report on President Nixon's transportation policy with footage of cars traveling on the freeway in Los Angeles and subway cars in New York City. The suggestion was that reliance on the automobile, and the failure of mass transportation, were leading to "self-destruction" of the cities. But while the problems of Los Angeles and New York are impressive, and complex, they are not necessarily representative. And the same holds for such other national problems as urban violence, ecology, civil rights and inflation.

3. Created News Affiliated stations buy network news programs to get a truly national news service, which will help them fulfill the public-service requirements of their broadcasting license. Network producers must therefore transform local happenings into national stories. This is accomplished daily and routinely at all three networks by acts of creation—concentrating on themes, or general hypotheses about America, rather than simply responding to events. After a national theme is chosen—meat boycotting, or all-out guerrilla "war" by the Black Panthers—appropriate event are sought to illustrate it.

In this modern form of alchemy, the news undergoes a significant change. The closing of a single gas station is abstracted from the complex surrounding circumstances that tie the event to a single locality, so it can illustrate "the energy crisis." Or a drug arrest in a single high school is simplified, its ramifications magnified, so it can illustrate a national "drug epidemic." This process tends to escale incidents to crisis proportions.

4. Necessary Conflict. Local news programs report on happenings that are of immediate interest to local residents—even if they are merely ball scores, fires or weather forecasts. But network news programs report on more diffuse matters, and to give them more universal appeal, news executives try for gripping, concentrated visual action, including violence. As an NBC cameraman said, "We're paid to get head-busting stuff, not scenic beauty."

But "action" must be instantly comprehensible—there's little time for explanation. So what works best, the networks have found, is a violent confrontation between two sides clearly defined, whether by race, sex, uniforms or physical appearance. The sit-in phase of the civil-rights movement is commonly cited as the prime example of "television at its best." The cause was universally known, and the sides—black demonstrators, white uniformed policemen—were immediately recognizable on the screen.

In contrast, producers shun "demos" (demonstrations) in which the antagonists are not easily distinguished. For example, networks rarely show film of blacks arguing with blacks, on the ground that it would only confuse the audience. In other words, it fails to stereotype opponents.

Network crews require many hours to reach the scene and set up their equipment. Thus, a carefully organized demonstration such as the media-oriented (Wounded Knee "uprising" (which informed the networks almost a week in advance of planned activities) is more likely to receive coverage. The "moratoriums" protesting the Vietnam war were more easily covered because they were brilliantly organized. Camera locations were pinpointed for the networks well in advanced.

How Inevitable? If national television news leans in certain directions because of the way it is organized, then organizational change should reduce built-in biases. For example, there is no law requiring that network news be centrally selected, and edited in New York. Just as the wire services have regional wires, the networks *could* offer four or five separate "Evening News" programs, originating in different geographic centers. While more costly, they might provide more relevant news service.

Similarly, if the networks revised their policy of charging news-program budgets for using stories from the more distant sections of America, "national stories" might be more reflective of the whole. Again, this would increase operating costs.

Networks could attempt to locate trends of true national significance by employing polls, sampling, and ganglia of local reporters stationed throughout America—as the Associated Press does. But investing in such behind-the-scenes resources would again add to the networks' expenses.

Finally, the need for showing conflict may be rooted in the requisite for a national audience. Only at the risk of losing viewers could a network lessen the demand for conflict in its news

In short, the networks could level the "tilt" in their news by accepting, at least temporarily, a decrease in their profits. Since citizens are becoming increasingly dependent on the networks for an accurate picture of the society they live in, there is a compelling argument for the situation to be rectified.

Study Questions

1. Epstein suggests that organizational change in the major networks might be accomplished to avoid the problems he discusses. One such sugestion is his idea of having evening news programs originating in different geographic centers—not just New York City as is presently done. Do you think this is a workable policy? Why or why not?

2. Epstein's general argument is that, news is often distorted because networks often "create" theories about America, rather than merely responding to events. Often, this is done by taking events out of context: a theme is selected and then stories are selectively sought to "confirm" it. Thus, a closing of a single gas station, according to Epstein, may be ". . . abstracted from the complex surrounding circumstances that tie the event to a single locality, so it can illustrate the 'energy crisis'."

   From your watching of TV news, do you agree with Epstein's description of it? Defend your answer.

BIBLIOGRAPHY

Part I. Some Classical/Contemporary Ethical Theories

ARISTOTLE AND VIRTUE THEORIES

Williams, B.A.O., "Aristotle on the Good," PHILOSOPHICAL QUARTERLY, 12, 1962: 289–296.

Hardie, W.F.R., "The Final Good in Aristotle's Ethics," PHILOSOPHY, 40, 1965, 277–295.

Cooper, John M., REASON AND THE HUMAN GOOD IN ARISTOTLE, Harvard University Press, Cambridge, Mass. 1975.

KANT

Kant, Immanuel, CRITIQUE OF PRACTICAL REASON, Lewis White Beck, translator, Bobbs-Merril Co., 1956.

Kant, Immanuel, FOUNDATIONS OF THE METAPHYSICS OF MORALS, Lewis White Beck, translator, Bobbs-Merrill Company, Inc. 1959.

Wolff, Robert P., ed., KANT; A COLLECTION OF CRITICAL ESSAYS, Anchor Books, Garden City, N.Y. 1967, especially Haezrahi, Pepita, "The Concept of Man as End-in-Himself."

MacIntyre, Alasdair, "What Morality Is Not," PHILOSOPHY, 32, 1957: 325–335.

Darwall, Stephen, "Two Kinds of Respect," ETHICS, 88, 1977, 36–49.

Downie, Robert S., and Elizabeth Telfer, RESPECT FOR PERSONS, Allen & Unwin Ltd., London, 1969.

Dworkin, Gerald, "Moral Autonomy," in H. T. Engelhardt, Jr and Daniel Callahan, eds., MORALS, SCIENCE AND SOCIALITY, The Hastings Center, Hastings-on-Hudson, 1978.

MILL AND LIBERTY

Mill, John Stuart, ON LIBERTY, London, Parker, 1859.

Bayles, Michael D., "Legislating Morality," Wayne Law Review, 22, 1976: 759–780.

Gorovitz, Samuel, ed., MILL; UTILITARIANISM, WITH CRITICAL ESSAYS, Bobbs-Merril Co., New York. 1971.

Berlin, Isaiah: *Four Essays on Liberty* (New York: Oxford University Press, 1969).

Dworkin, Gerald, "Marx and Mill: A Dialogue," PHILOSOPHY AND PHENOMENOLOGICAL RESEARCH, 76, 1967, 368–381.

Golding, Martin P., PHILOSOPHY OF LAW (Englewood Cliffs, N.J., Prentice-Hall, Inc. 1975.

Hart, Herbert L.A., LAW, LIBERTY AND MORALITY (Stanford, California, Stanford University Press, 1963).

McCloskey, H.J., "Mill's Liberalism," PHILOSOPHICAL QUARTERLY, 13 143–54: 1963.

Radcliff, Peter, ed., LIMITS OF LIBERTY; STUDIES OF MILL'S ON LIBERTY, (Belmont, California, Wadsworth Publishing Company, Inc., 1966).

Rees, J.C., MILL AND HIS EARLY CRITICS (Leicester, England: University College, 1956).

Bayles, Michael D., "Criminal Paternalism," in J. Roland Pennock and John W. Chapman, eds., THE LIMITS OF LAW, NOMOS, 15 (New York: Lieber-Atherton Press, 1974) 174–188.

Dworkin, Gerald, "Paternalism," MONIST, 56 (1972) 64–84.

Feinberg, Joel, "Legal Paternalism," CANADIAN JOURNAL OF PHILOSOPHY, 1, 1971, 105–124.

Murpy, Jeffrie G., "Incompetence and Paternalism," ARCHIVES FOR PHILOSOPHY OF LAW AND SOCIAL PHILOSOPHY, 40, 1974, 465–486.

Wikler, Daniel, "Paternalism and the Mildly Retarded," PHILOSOPHY AND PUBLIC AFFAIRS, 8, 1979, 377–392.

METAETHICAL WRITINGS

Held, Virginia, "Justification: Legal and Political," ETHICS, 86, 1975, 1–16.

Serafini, Anthony, "Achievements, Illocutions and the Concept of Teaching," EDUCATIONAL THEORY, spring, 1976.

Rawls, John "Outline of a Decision Procedure for Ethics," PHILOSOPHICAL REVIEW, 66, 1957, 177–197.

Baier, Kurt, THE MORAL POINT OF VIEW; A RATIONAL BASIS OF ETHICS, Cornell University Press, Ithaca, NY, 1958, especially chapter 12.

Prichard, H.A., "Does Moral Philosophy Rest on a Mistake?" MIND, 21 1912, 21–37.

Rawls, John, A THEORY OF JUSTICE, Harvard University Press, Cambridge, Mass, 1971, especially chapter nine.

Wellman, Carl, "The Ethical Implications of Cultural Relativity," JOURNAL OF PHILOSOPHY, 60, 1963, 169–184.

Ladd, John, ed., ETHICAL RELATIVISM, Wadsworth Publishing Company, Inc. Belmont, California, 1973.

Glover, Jonathan, CAUSING DEATH AND SAVING LIVES, Penguin Books, Inc. New York, N.Y., 1977, chapter two.

Rachels, James, "Can Ethics Provide Answers?" HASTINGS CENTER REPORT, 10, June, 1980: 32–40.

Stevenson, Charles, L., FACTS AND VALUES, Yale University Press, New Haven, Conn., 1963.

Part II. Medical Ethics

Kumar, Dharma, "Should One be Free To Choose the Sex of One's Child?", Journal of Applied Philosophy, 2, October, 1985, pp. 197–204.

MacIntyre, Alasdair, "How Virtues Become Vices: Values, Medicine and Social Context, in H.T. Engelhardet Jr. and S.F. Spicker, eds. EVALUATION AND EXPLANATION IN THE BIOMEDICAL SCIENCES, D. Reidel Publishing Company, Dordrecht, Holland, 1975, pp. 97–111

Beauchamp, Tom L., "Paternalism and Bio-Behavioral Control," MONIST, 60 (1977) 62–80.

Brahams, Diana, "The Hasty British Ban on Commercial Surrogacy," Hastings Center Report, F17, February 17, 24–33 "Paternalism," in Warren T. Reich, ed., ENCYCLOPEDIA OF BIOETHICS (New York, Free Press, 1978) vol. 3, pp. 1194–1200.

Schaffner, Kenneth F., "Ethical Problems in Clinical Trials," Journal of Medicine and Philosophy, 11, November 1986, pp. 297–315.

Kottow, Michael H., "Medical Confidentiality: An Intransigent and Absolute Obligation," Journal of Medical Ethics, 12, September, 1986, 117–122.

Self, Donnie J., "The Relationship of Personhood to Medical-Ethical Decision Making," Personalist Forum, 1, Fall, 1985, pp. 76–98 (A particularly acute critique of the common way of looking at "personhood" in terms of consciousness and value creation).

McConnell, Terrence, "Permissive Abortion Laws, Religion, and Moral Compromise," Public Affairs Quarterly, vol 1, number 1, January, 1987.

Capron, Alexander Morgan, "Anenchephalic Donors: Separate the Dead from the Dying," 17, February, 1987, 5–9.

Buchanan, Allen, "Medical Paternalism," PHILOSOPHY AND PUBLIC AFFAIRS, 7 (1978): 370–390.

Wilkinson, Greg, "Psychoanalysis and Analytical Psychotherapy in the NHS—A Problem for Medical Ethics," Journal of Medical Ethics, 12, 87–90, June, 1986.

Feldman, Eric, "Medical Ethics The Japanese Way," Hastings Center Report, 15, 21–24, October, 1985.

Mahowald, Mary Silver, Jerry Ratcheson, Robert A., "The Ethical Options in Transplanting Fetal Tissue," Hastings Center Report, 17, February, 1987, 9–15.

"Gillon, Raanan, "Do Doctors Owe A Special Duty of Beneficience to their Patients?", Journal of Medical Ethics, 12, December, 1986, 171–173.

Howe, Kenneth, "A Required Pre-Clinical Medical Ethics Course: Three Years Experience," Teaching Philosophy, 9, March 1986, 35–44.

Norman Frost (co-author names missing here), "Passive Euthanasia of Defective Newborn Infants: Legal Considerations," JOURNAL OF PEDIATRICS, vol. 88, 1976, pp. 883–889.

Grisez, Germain and Boyle, Joseph, LIFE AND DEATH WITH LIBERTY AND JUSTICE, University of Notre Dame Press, Notre Dame, Indiana, 1979.

Self, Jonnie J., Skeel, Joy D., "Potential Roles of the Medical Ethicist in the Clinical Setting," Theoretical Medicine, 7, February, 1986, 13–32.

Downing A.B., ed., EUTHANASIA AND THE RIGHT TO DEATH; THE CASE FOR VOLUNTARY EUTHANASIA, Humanities Press, New York, 1969.

Singer, Peter, "Making Laws on Making Babies," Hastings Center Report, 15, August, 1985, 5–6.

Veatch, Robert M., DEATH, DYING AND THE BIOLOGICAL REVOLUTION; OUR LAST QUEST FOR RESPONSIBILITY, Yale University Press, New Haven, Conn., 1976.

Mishra, P., "Euthanasia: A Moral Necessity," Indian Philosophical Quarterly, 13, March, 1986.

Price, A.W., "Moral Theories; Aristotle's Ethics," Journal of Medical Ethics, 11, September, 1985, 150–152.

Brody, Baruch, "On the Humanity of the Foetus," in Robert L. Perkins, ed., ABORTION; PRO AND CON, Schenkman, Cambridge, Mass., 1974, pp 69–90.

Law, Susan A.T., "The Teaching of Medical Ethics from a Junior Doctor's Viewpoint," Journal of Medical Ethics, 11, March, 1985, 37–38.

Moon, Joseph B.; Graber, Glenn C., "When Danny Said No: Refusal of Treatment By a Patient of Questionable Competence," Journal of Medial and Human Bioethics, 6, Spr/sum, 1985, 12–27.

English, Jane, "Abortion and the Concept of a Person," CANADIAN JOURNAL OF PHILOSOPHY, vol. 5, no. 2, October, 1975, pp. 233–243.

Thomson, Judith Jarvis, "A Defense of Abortion," PHILOSOPHY AND PUBLIC AFFAIRS, vol. 1, Fall, 1971, pp. 47–66.

Armstrong, Robert, "The Rights to Life," JOURNAL OF SOCIAL PHILOSOPHY, vol. 8, Jan., 1977, pp. 13–19.

Rachels, James, "More Impatient Distinctions and a Defense of Active Euthanasia," Mappes and Zembaty, eds, BIOMEDICAL ETHICS, McGraw-Hill, NY, NY, 1981, pp. 355–359.

Engelhardt, H. Tristam, "Euthanasia and Children: The Injury of Continued Existence," THE JOURNAL OF PEDIATRICS, 83, July, 1973, pp. 170–171.

Part III. Business Ethics

Thomson, Judith Jarvis, "Preferential Hiring," PHILOSOPHY AND PUBLIC AFFAIRS, 2, no. 4, Summer, 1973.

Simon, Robert, "Preferential Hiring: A Reply to Judith Marvis Thomson, PHILOSOPHY AND PUBLIC AFFAIRS 3, no. 3, spring, 1974.

Hensel, Paul J., "Ethical Dilemmas in Marketing: A Rationale," Journal of Business Ethics, 5, February, 1986, pp. 63–67.

Held, Virginia, "Reasonable Progress and Self-Respect," THE MONIST, vol 57, January 1973, pp. 12–27.

Everett, William Johnson, "Oikos: Convergence in Business Ethics," Journal of Business Ethics, 5, August, 1986, 313–325.

French, Peter A., "The Hester Prynne Sanction," Journal of Business Ethics.

Roberts, David, "Moral Managers and Business Sanctuaries," Journal of Business Ethics, 5, January 1986, pp. 203–208.

Business and Professional Ethics, 4, Winter, 1985, 19–32.

Duran, Jane, "Rights in the Workplace: Access to Personnel Files," Public Affairs Quarterly, vol. 1, number 1, January, 1987.

De George, Richard T., "Theological Ethics and Business Ethics," Journal of Business Ethics, 5, December, 1986, 421–432.

Emmalizadeh, Hossein, "The Informative and Persuasive Functions of Advertising: A Moral Appraisal—A Comment," Journal of Business Ethics, 4, April, 1985, pp. 151–153.

Gibson, Roger F., "Corporations, Persons and Moral Responsibility," Thought, 21, summer, 1986, 17–26.

McMahon, Thomas F., "Models of the Relationship of the Firm to Society," Journal of Business Ethics, 5, January 1986, pp. 181–191 (A particularly good analysis, in terms of "rights" and "power" models, of the relationship of a firm to society).

Williams, Oliver F., "Can Business Ethics be Theological: What Athens Can Learn from Jerusalem," Journal of Business Ethics, 5, December, 1986, 473–484.

De George, Richard, ed., and Pichler, J. A., editor, ETHICS, FREE ENTERPRISE, AND PUBLIC POLICY, Oxford University Press, N.Y., N.Y., 1978.

Johnson, Harold L., "Bribery in International Markets: Diagnosis, Clarification and Remedy," Journal of Business Ethics, 4, December, 1985, pp. 447–456.

Hosmer, Larue T., "The Other 338: Why a Majority of Our Schools of Business Administration Do Not Offer a Course in Business Ethics," Journal of Business Ethics, 4, February, 1985, pp. 17–22.

"Ethical Issues in Advertising," in JUST BUSINESS, Tom Regan, editor, pp. 235–270.

Moser, Martin R., "A Framework for Analyzing Corporate Social Responsibility," Journal of Business Ethics, 5, February, 1986, pp. 69–72.

Des Jardins, Joseph R., McCall, John J., "A Defense of Employee Rights," Journal of Business Ethics, 4, October, 1985, pp. 367–376 (This paper

argues convincingly that despite the importance of such rights, the notion of employee rights has not been analyzed and defended in previous literature. This, the authors accomplish very nicely).
De George, Richard T., "Turing Machines, Expert Systems, and Human Knowledge," Logos, 7, 1986, 99–112.
Schmidt, David P., "Patterns of Argument in Business Ethics," Journal of Business Ethics, 5, December, 1986, 501–509.

Part IV. Journalistic/Ethics

Devlin, Patrick, "Law, Democracy and Morality," UNIVERSITY OF PENNSYLVANIA LAW REVIEW, 110, 1962: 635–649.
Feinberg, Joel, RIGHTS, JUSTICE AND THE BOUNDS OF LIBERTY, Princeton University Press, Princeton, N.J., 1980.
Jenkins, Iredell, SOCIAL ORDER AND THE LIMITS OF LAW< Princeton University Press, Princeton, N.J., 1980.
Berger, Fred R., ed., FREEDOM OF EXPRESSION, Wadsworth Publishing Company, Inc. Belmont, California, 1980.
Leiser, Burton, LIBERTY, JUSTICE AND MORALS, Macmillan Company, New York, 1973.
THE REPORT OF THE COMMISSION ON OBSCENITY AND PORNOG-RAPHY, Government Printing Office, Washington, D.C., 1970.
Scanlon, Thomas, "A Theory of Freedom of Expression," PHILOSOPHY AND PUBLIC AFFAIRS, 1, 1972: 204–226.
Feinberg, Joel, SOCIAL PHILOSOPHY, Prentice-Hall, Inc. Englewood Cliffs, N.J., 1973.
Devlin, Patrick, THE ENFORCEMENT OF MORALS; Oxford University Press, New York, 1965.
Leiser, Burton M., LIBERTY, JUSTICE AND MORALS, 2nd edition, Macmillan, New York, 1979.
Berger, Fred R., ed., FREEDOM OF EXPRESSION, Wadsworth, Belmont, California, 1980.
Cockburn, Alexander, "Wanted: An Irresponsible Press," Harpers, April, 1981.
Merrill, John C., & Odell, Jack S., PHILOSOPHY AND JOURNALISM, Longman, Inc, New York, N.Y. (especially chapters 4, 5 & 7).
Merrill, John C., Barney, Ralph, ETHICS AND THE PRESS, Hastings House, 1975.
Report by the Hastings Center, "The Teaching of Ethics in Higher Education," New York, The Hastings Center, 1980.
C.J. Bontempo and S.J. Odell eds., "Philosophy and Public Policy," in THE OWL OF MINERVA, McGraw-Hill, New York, NY.
Lapham, Lewis H., "Gilding the News," Harper's, July, 1981.
Merrill, John C., and Fisher, Harold, THE WORLD'S GREAT DAILIES, New York, Hastings House, 1980.
"A Review of Teaching Ethics in Journalism Education," by Christians and Covert, in Teaching Philosophy, vol. 4, April, 1981.
Griffin, Emory, THE MIND CHANGERS; THE ART OF CHRISTIAN PER-SUASION, Tyndale House, Wheaton, Ill., 1976.

Phelan, John M., DISENCHANTMENT; MEANING AND MORALITY IN THE MEDIA, Hastings House, New York, N.Y. 1980.

COMMISSION ON FREEDOM OF THE PRESS, A FREE AND RESPONSIBLE PRESS, University of Chicago Press, Chicago, 1947.

Merrill, John C., THE IMPERATIVE OF FREEDOM, Hastings House, New York, 1974.

Barron, Jerome A., FREEDOM OF THE PRESS FOR WHOM?, Indiana University Press, Bloomington, 1971.

Johannesen, Richard L., ed., ETHICS AND PERSUASION; SELECTED READINGS, Random House, New York, 1967.

Hulteng, John L., THE MESSENGER'S MOTIVES: ETHICAL PROBLEMS OF.

Berns, Walter, FREEDOM, VIRTUE AND THE FIRST AMENDMENT, Louisiana State University Press, Baton Rouge, 1957.

Hook, Sidney, THE PARADOXES OF FREEDOM, University of California Press, Berkeley, 1967.

THE NEWS MEDIA, Prentice-Hall, Englewood Cliffs, N.J., 1976.

Stonecipher, Harry W., EDITORIAL AND PERSUASIVE WRITING; OPINION FUNCTIONS OF THE NEWS MEDIA, Hastings House, New York, 1979.

Merrill, John C., THE IMPERATIVE OF FREEDOM; A PHILOSOPHY OF JOURNALISTIC AUTONOMY, Hastings House, New York, 1974.

Griffith, Thomas, HOW TRUE; A SKEPTIC'S GUIDE TO BELIEVING THE NEWS, Little, Brown & Co, Inc. 1974.

Johannesen, Richard L., ETHICS IN HUMAN COMMUNICATION, Waveland Press, Prospect Heights, 1981.

Holbrook, David, ed., THE CASE AGAINST PORNOGRAPHY, Library Press, New York, 1973 (This book includes articles attacking pornography from a number of differing philosophical orientations).

Whalen, Charles, YOUR RIGHT TO KNOW, Random House, New York, 1973.

Kahane, Howard, LOGIC AND CONTEMPORARY RHETORIC, Wadsworth, Belmont, Ca., 1967.

Dyal, Robert, "Is Pornography Good for You?", Southwestern Journal of Philosophy, vol. 7, Fall, 1976, pp. 95–118.

Merrill, John C., EXISTENTIAL JOURNALISM, Hastings House, New York, 1977.

Harris, S.J., THE AUTHENTIC PERSON, Argus Communications, Miles, Ill., 1972.

Rivers, William L., Schramm, Wilbur and Christians, Clifford, *Responsibility in Mass Communications*, NY, Harper & Row, 1980.

Berger, Fred, FREEDOM OF EXPRESSION, Wadsworth, Belmont, Ca., 1980 ("The Moral Theory of Free Speech and Obscenity Law, pp. 99–127 & "Women Fight Back," (pp. 128–133, excerpted from Susan Brownmiller's book, AGAINST OUR WILL; MEN, WOMEN AND RAPE, 1975) RESPONSIBILITY IN MASS COMMUNICATION, Harper & Row, 1980.

Stein, Robert, MEDIA POWER; WHO IS SHAPING YOUR PICTURE OF THE WORLD?, Houghton-Mifflin, Boston, 1972.

Poper, Karl R., THE OPEN SOCIETY AND ITS ENEMIES, Princeton University Press, Princeton, 1930 (especially chapters 7).

Berger, Fred R., "Pornography, Sex and Censorship," in Social Theory and Practice, vol 4, spring, 1977, pp. 183–209.

Thayer, Lee, ed., ETHICS, MORALITY AND THE MEDIA, Hastings House, New York, 1980.

Righter, Rosemary, WHOSE NEWS? POLITICS, THE PRESS, AND THE THIRD WORLD, Burnett, London, 1978.

Rubin, Bernard, ed., QUESTIONING MEDIA ETHICS, Praeger, New York, 1978.

INDEX